SOCIAL WORK PRACTICE
WITH SURVIVORS OF
SEX TRAFFICKING AND
COMMERCIAL SEXUAL
EXPLOITATION

SOCIAL WORK PRACTICE WITH SURVIVORS OF SEX TRAFFICKING AND COMMERCIAL SEXUAL EXPLOITATION

EDITED BY
ANDREA J. NICHOLS,
TONYA EDMOND, AND
ERIN C. HEIL

Columbia University Press
New York

Columbia University Press
Publishers Since 1893
New York   Chichester, West Sussex
cup.columbia.edu

Library of Congress Cataloging-in-Publication Data
Names: Nichols, Andrea J., editor. | Edmond, Tonya, editor. | Heil, Erin C., editor.
Title: Social work practice with survivors of sex trafficking and commercial sexual
    exploitation / edited by Andrea J. Nichols, Tonya Edmond, and Erin C. Heil.
Description: New York : Columbia University Press, [2018] | Includes bibliographical
    references and index.
Identifiers: LCCN 2017041358 (print) | LCCN 2017048897 (ebook) |
    ISBN 9780231543361 | ISBN 9780231180924 (hardback : alk. paper) |
    ISBN 9780231180931 (pbk.)
Subjects: LCSH: Human trafficking victims—Services for. | Prostitutes—
    Services for. | Social work with prostitutes.
Classification: LCC HQ281 (ebook) | LCC HQ281 .S745 2018 (print) |
    DDC 306.74—dc23
LC record available at https://lccn.loc.gov/2017041358

Columbia University Press books are printed on permanent
and durable acid-free paper.
Printed in the United States of America

Cover design: Jordan Wannemacher

CONTENTS

PROLOGUE

ANDREA J. NICHOLS, PhD, WASHINGTON UNIVERSITY
IN ST. LOUIS

ERIN C. HEIL, PhD, SOUTHERN ILLINOIS UNIVERSITY,
EDWARDSVILLE

Sex trafficking has increasingly become an area of public concern and activism. Despite this heightened attention, sex trafficking and commercial sexual exploitation (CSE) are not well understood in the public and political spheres, even within the antitrafficking movement and among social workers. In particular, there is a gap in the collective knowledge related to social work practice with survivors of sex trafficking and CSE. For this reason, it becomes more important than ever to disseminate knowledge from survivors, practitioners, and researchers in order to advance such knowledge and practice techniques in this field. With heightened public and political attention, our understandings of sex trafficking have shifted, but our practice knowledge lags behind.

Society's changing perceptions of sex trafficking are rooted in a history of grassroots activism and the resulting legislative shifts (Boxill & Richardson, 2007; Kalergis, 2009; Nichols, 2016). While sex trafficking has always existed, albeit under different labels (such as "commercial sexual exploitation" or, in the justice system, "juvenile prostitution"), redefining sex trafficking through key legislation and activism created a shift in the justice system, in practice, and in academia. According to federal law, sex trafficking is "the recruitment, harboring, transportation, provision, obtaining, patronizing, or soliciting of a person for the purposes of a commercial sex act, in which the commercial sex act is induced by force, fraud, or coercion, or in which the person induced to perform such act has not attained 18 years of age" (22 U.S.C. § 7102). Simply put, under U.S. federal law, any commercial sex act involving a minor equates to sex trafficking; for adults, commercial sex under conditions of force, fraud, or coercion is considered sex trafficking.

Yet researchers and practitioners report limitations to this definition, in that the service population involved in commercial sex extends beyond the legal criteria for sex trafficking. This population includes adults involved in commercial sex who do not experience force, fraud, or coercion (or are unable or unwilling to report it), who experience difficulty in accessing services, and who often face criminalization instead of assistance (Egyes, 2016; Gerassi, Nichols, & Michelson, 2017; Heil & Nichols, 2015; Oselin, 2014). Some researchers refer to CSE as commercial sex involvement as a constrained choice, or as a situation in which some vulnerability is being exploited, such as age (e.g., minors), intellectual disability, poverty, or homelessness (Nichols, 2016; Reid, 2011). Legally, CSE is inherently sex trafficking if a minor is involved (Lloyd, 2012). For adults, it is not sex trafficking unless force, fraud, or coercion is present. Other researchers refer to this "grey area" population as sex workers, some of whom are involved as a free choice but others are involved as a constrained choice (Egyes, 2016). This book focuses on sex trafficking but also on the wider service population involved in commercial sex.

The authors of this book have different experiences and ideologies. Some prefer the legal language of "sex trafficking," and others prefer "commercial sexual exploitation," "sex work," or some combination of terms. The editors believe that it is important that various knowledge bases "speak for themselves" and reflect the reality of the various ideologies present within the field at large. Service providers can analyze their own approaches to understand how their biases might impact their work with survivors. As will be seen in various parts of this book, mirroring the language that survivors use is extremely important, and it is also important to create a nonjudgmental environment respecting how they view and interpret their situations. People accessing various types of services may not identify with the terms *sex trafficking, commercial sexual exploitation,* and *modern-day slavery,* the language that is commonly used in the antitrafficking movement, or *sex work* (Nichols & Heil, 2015).

Every individual's experience in sex trafficking and sex trade more broadly is complex and nuanced, and social workers should recognize survivors' diverse narratives. There are multiple types of sex trafficking, including but not limited to familial trafficking, pimp-controlled trafficking, and survival sex. These "categories" are fluid and not mutually exclusive. Categorization is useful as a teaching tool to those unfamiliar with the dynamics of trafficking/CSE, but these are not rigid categories.

Familial trafficking (in legal terms) involves family members, such as a parent or other relative, who facilitate children's involvement in commercial sex or involve adult family members through force, fraud, or coercion. Intergenerational dynamics of sex-trading are well documented as well (Oselin, 2014;

Raphael & Myers-Powell, 2010). *Survival sex* describes situations in which individuals sell or trade sex to meet basic needs like food, shelter, water, and clothes. Survival sex is incredibly common among homeless youth, and multiple studies show this to be one of the most common forms of sex trafficking. Because of legal age designations, anyone who is a minor involved in survival sex legally meets the criteria for trafficking. Yet adults will not meet the criteria if force, fraud, and coercion are not present. The legal definitions and age designations are relatively arbitrary, but they can impact the work that social workers do when collaborating with or assisting survivors. For example, any legal benefits (see chapter 7) are bound by legal definitions, and social services may also be impacted by legal definitions. Importantly, adults involved in commercial sex who cannot or do not want to prove force, fraud, or coercion are criminalized in U.S. legal systems. This fact also impacts advocacy, macro practice, community collaboration, and service provision.

Pimp-controlled trafficking can take many forms. Not all pimps are traffickers; those who involve minors or who engage adults through force, fraud, or coercion are legally labeled as traffickers (Marcus, Horning, Curtis, Sanson, & Thompson, 2014). Pimps can be male or female, and many of those who are female first sold sex themselves (Raphael & Myers-Powell, 2010). Raphael and Myers-Powell (2010) found in interviews with ex-pimps in Chicago that all of the women in their sample and half the men had sold sex themselves prior to becoming pimps. Some relationships with pimps are characterized by extreme violence, while others are not (Marcus et al., 2014; Raphael, Reichert, & Powers, 2010). Cases of trafficking involving abduction, kidnapping, and overt force are relatively rare, but they do occur (Polaris Project, 2014). Sometimes pimps are friends, same-age peers, family members, or people who work informally as a manager or facilitator (Curtis, Terry, Dank, Dombrowski, & Khan, 2008; Dank, Yahner, et al., 2015; Lutnick, 2016; Raphael & Myers-Powell, 2010). In other instances, pimps-as-traffickers are boyfriends, husbands, or partners who become romantically involved and then emotionally manipulate, force, or coerce their partners into commercial sex. While this dynamic, often referred to as the "boyfriend pimp," is often discussed in the context of cisgender heterosexual girls, cisgender gay boys, transgender girls, and others, including adults, are also known to have experienced this type of trafficking or CSE (Dank, Yahner, et al., 2015; Egyes, 2016; Heil & Nichols, 2015).

The work examining sex trafficking more broadly traditionally focused on cisgender heterosexual girls. Early work drawing from the criminal justice system and social service organizations found sex trafficking to almost exclusively involve women and girls. Anywhere between 90 and 100 percent of victims were found to be female (Banks & Kycklehahn, 2011; Polaris Project, 2014). This research was limited, however, because for individuals to access services and to be "counted" as trafficked, those in social services and in the justice system had to identify and acknowledge them as such. In contemporary times, it remains the case that boys and men, as well as transgender people, are often disregarded by law enforcement and criminalized instead (Dank, Yu, et al., 2015; Egyes, 2017; Lutnick, 2016). Thus, statistics coming from these data sources are not likely to provide an adequate depiction of sex and gender dynamics.

This problem may be due to the fact that survival sex, without the presence of a third-party trafficker, is the more common form of trafficking experienced by men, boys, and transgender people and is consequently overlooked because survival sex is not often understood as a form of trafficking (Curtis et al., 2008; Dank, Yahner, et al., 2015). The emphasis on women and girls is also likely due to traditional ideas about gender, which lead people to view CSE-involved (white) cisgender women and girls as victims and cisgender men and boys, and transgender people, as free agents and criminals (Dank, Yu, et al., 2015; Lutnick, 2016). Research also finds that anti-LGBTQ+ (lesbian, gay, bisexual transgender, queer) bias plays a role in the stigma and unequal treatment of LGBTQ+ people in the justice system (Dank, Yu, et al., 2015), as well as in related gaps in services (Heil & Nichols, 2015). This stigma is heightened for racially marginalized groups (Dank, Yu, et al., 2015; Egyes, 2017).

As research began to examine the experiences of other populations in addition to cisgender women and girls, our knowledge base expanded. For example, studies on homeless or transient youth populations engaged in largely street-level sex work found nearly equal representation of male and female trafficked/ exploited youth and a higher representation of transgender youth (Curtis et al., 2008; Dank et al., 2014). LGBTQ+ identities have also been found to heighten risk. One study found that of 641 youth in 10 cities, 24 percent of LGBTQ+ youth were trafficked for sex, compared to 20 percent of non- LGBTQ+ female youth and 12 percent of non- LGBTQ+ male youth (Loyola University New Orleans's Modern Slavery Research Project, 2017).

The work examining sex trafficking among homeless or transient youth has limitations as well. Curtis et al. (2008) indicated that their study was limited in that cisgender young women and girls were more likely to have an exploiter and were less likely to be included in the sample given the research methodology used—a referral, in which the individual would meet in person for an interview. A survivor involved with an exploiter could perceive this situation as dangerous and consequently avoid it. This work also tends to be drawn from homeless youth populations involved in street-level sex work, or survival sex, and may not reflect populations working in other sectors of the commercial sex industry or through pimp/trafficker-controlled sex trade. Thus the editors recommend looking at these various data sources as pieces of a puzzle that provide knowledge and information about the nuances of sex trafficking and exploitation, including the roles of racism, transphobia, homophobia, and traditional sexism rather than establishing prevalence in sex trafficking regarding sex, gender, or sexual orientation.

Until very recently, the bulk of the academic research and literature examining sex trafficking and CSE centered on ideological debates (Farley, 2004, 2005; Madden-Dempsey, 2010; Outshoorn, 2005; Weitzer, 2010). This dynamic is rooted in the history of "the sex wars" between various feminist and political groups, which continue into the present day. In sum, liberal feminists highlight choice in commercial sex involvement, viewing freedom of choice and body autonomy as supporting women's rights, while radical feminists view commercial sex as reflecting sexual objectification and widespread oppression of women. Politically, neoliberals advocate freedom from the constraints of the state in regard to sex work (while criminalizing sex trafficking), whereas abolitionists view sexual commerce as regimented domination of women's bodies and as a form of modern-day slavery that should be eradicated. Radical feminists tend to support abolitionist ideologies and polices, whereas liberal feminists tend to support neoliberal ideologies and policies. Such work overlaps with critiques and perspectives of justice system involvement, the role of law enforcement, the impact of criminalization, and prostitution policy (see Nichols, 2016, for an overview). These debates impact coalition work, funding agendas, and community collaboration, and they may also color individual practice (Gerassi et al., 2017). In direct practice, social workers must be careful to provide a nonjudgmental space and not let adherence to any particular perspective impact their work by delegitimizing the ways clients define their experiences. Academic research from 2000 to 2010 overwhelmingly emphasized these ideological debates while virtually ignoring social service practice with survivors of trafficking and exploitation.

While more recently the body of work examining social work practice with survivors of sex trafficking and CSE has been growing, there remains a gap in the field (Busch-Armendariz, Nsonwu, & Cook Heffron, 2014; Macy & Graham, 2012; Macy & Johns, 2011; Valandra, 2007). This is problematic, as research shows that social workers are interacting with trafficked and exploited people and either may not know it or may work directly with this population but lack practice knowledge. Social service providers "encounter trafficking victims among clients of agencies that provide services related to child advocacy, child protection and welfare, criminal justice, domestic violence, health care, homelessness outreach and shelter, juvenile justice, and victim advocacy" (Macy & Graham, 2012, p. 60). Additionally, social service providers may encounter trafficked or exploited people in foster care, youth-serving agencies, and drop-in centers, or in collaboration with the criminal justice system (Curtis et al., 2008; Heil & Nichols, 2015; Reid, 2011).

This edited volume intends to fill a gap in the literature by specifically emphasizing the practices of social service providers with identified survivors of sex trafficking/CSE or those otherwise involved in commercial sex in need of social services. Researchers, students, and practitioners will find that this volume illustrates key practice techniques with sex-trafficking/CSE survivors through vignettes and an accessible "how-to" format for social workers. Sex trafficking/ CSE is viewed as an emerging practice area; as such, this is a contribution that will likely have some level of demand from practitioners and schools of social work. The book is intended to be used as a handbook for practitioners, as a key teaching text in courses for students, or as a reference for training workshops or continuing education for practitioners.

The editors developed this volume to meet a recognized need for it. They drew from their own expertise as well as the expertise of the contributors to provide a useful tool for practitioners and students of social work and related fields. Andrea J. Nichols, who holds a background in sex trafficking/CSE and related practices as a community-action researcher and professor, regularly teaches the course Sex Trafficking to graduate-level social work students. Coeditor Tonya Edmond brings distinct expertise to this volume, with her extensive background in social work as a practitioner, professor, and researcher working in the areas of interventions with women, evidence-based trauma treatments, and trauma-informed care. Coeditor Erin Heil offers expertise on various aspects of the criminal justice system and researches and teaches in the areas of human trafficking and human rights.

However, it is the expertise of the contributors that is the cornerstone of this book. The authors were specifically selected and invited to contribute to this edited volume because of their recognized and distinct contributions to the field of sex trafficking and CSE. They offer various areas of expertise and diverse experiences. They are survivors, practitioners, researchers, professors, graduate students, and directors of nationally renowned programs serving trafficked and exploited people, including Girls Education and Mentoring Services (GEMS), My Life My Choice, and the Sex Workers Project. More detailed biographical statements can be found at the end of this book. The editors were thrilled with the authors' generosity and willingness to contribute.

The book is organized into four parts—Practice Techniques, Practice with Specific Populations, Programmatic Design, and Prevention and Outreach. Part I begins with a chapter that describes the importance of survivor-centered practice and highlights the diverse experiences of survivors. The next two chapters focus on identifying trafficked and exploited people and on safety planning. The following chapter describes the Stages of Change, or transtheoretical, model that is used by GEMS, and this is followed by a chapter examining evidence-based trauma treatments. The next chapter examines harm-reduction programming and the rights-based perspective of social work practice. The last chapter in this section discusses the legal framework for sex trafficking and exploitation in order to guide social workers' practices in collaboration with legal services, and it also highlights barriers to accessing services due to the criminalization of adults who sell sex.

Part II focuses on practice with distinct populations, beginning with a chapter examining practices with trafficked immigrant women, who often experience multiple forms of exploitation and trauma. This is followed by a chapter describing the disproportionate victimization of African American people in sex trafficking and exploitation, as well as Afrocentric perspectives and practices. Following this is a chapter describing the distinct risk factors experienced by LGBTQ+ individuals, related practices, and structural-level activism of social workers to counter such risk factors. The last chapter in this section examines the unique risks and needs experienced by sex-trafficked girls with intellectual disabilities.

Part III investigates programmatic design, emphasizing the Sanctuary Model as a trauma-informed organizational model. Two chapters then examine problematic policies, including a chapter examining exclusionary policies within a broad array of organizations, and another detailing problematic policies in the Department of Children's and Family Services; both chapters offer recommendations for shifts in programmatic design. The last chapter in Part III describes the single-point-of-contact social worker model and discusses the importance of this model to improving outcomes for people who have experienced trafficking/exploitation, as well as the relevant application of social work perspectives within practice.

Part IV discusses prevention and outreach efforts, beginning with the My Life My Choice prevention curriculum; the next chapter presents a macro-structural analysis of risk factors and implications for prevention and outreach. The last chapter critically examines the imagery often used in antitrafficking efforts and offers recommendations for images and wording for outreach and prevention materials, as well as community education and awareness materials, to avoid mischaracterization and reexploitation and to include diverse populations.

References

Banks, D., & Kyckelhahn, T. (2011). Characteristics of suspected human trafficking incidents-2005-2008. Bureau of Justice Statistics. Retrieved from www.bjs.gov

Boxill, N. A., & Richardson, D. J. (2007). Ending sex trafficking of children in Atlanta. *Affilia, 22*(2), 138–149. doi:10.1177/0886109907299054

Busch-Armendariz, N., Nsonwu, M., & Cook Heffron, L. (2014). A kaleidoscope: The role of the social work practitioner and the strength of social work theories and practice in meeting the complex needs of people trafficked and the professionals that work with them. *International Social Work, 57*(1), 7–18.

Curtis, R., Terry, K., Dank, M., Dombrowski, K., & Khan, B. (2008). *Commercial sexual exploitation of children in New York City, volume one: The CSEC population in New York City: Size, characteristics, and needs.* U.S. Department of Justice. Retrieved from https://www.ncjrs.gov/pdffiles1/nij/grants/225083.pdf

Dank, M., Bilal Khan, P., Downey, M., Kotonias, C., Mayer, D., Owens, C., . . . Yu, L. (2014). *Estimating the size and structure of the underground commercial sex economy in eight major US cities.* The Urban Institute. Retrieved from http://www.urban.org/sites/default /files/alfresco/publication-pdfs/413047-Estimating-the-Size-and-Structure-of-the -Underground-Commercial-Sex-Economy-in-Eight-Major-US-Cities.PDF

Dank, M., Yahner, J., Madden, K., Banuelos, I., Yu, L., Ritchie, A., . . . Conner, B. (2015). *Surviving the streets of New York: Experiences of LGBTQ youth, YMSM, and YWSW engaged in survival sex.* Urban Institute. Retrieved from http://www.urban.org/research/publication/surviving -streets-new-york-experiences-lgbtq-youth-ymsm-and-ywsw-engaged-survival-sex /view/full_report

Dank, M., Yu, L., Yahner, J., Mora, M., Pelletier, E., & Conner, B. (2015). *Locked in: Interactions with the criminal justice and child welfare systems for LGBTQ youth, YMSM, and YWSW who engage in survival sex.* Urban Institute. Retrieved from http://www.urban.org/sites /default/files/publication/71446/2000424-Locked-In-Interactions-with-the-Criminal -Justice-and-Child-Welfare-Systems-for-LGBTQ-Youth-YMSM-and-YWSW-Who -Engage-in-Survival-Sex.pdf

Egyes, L. (2016). Borders and intersections: The unique vulnerabilities of LGBTQ immigrants to trafficking. In E. Heil & A. Nichols (Eds.), *Broadening the scope of human trafficking* (pp. 107–123). Durham, NC: Carolina Academic Press.

Farley, M. (2004). "Bad for the body, bad for the heart": Prostitution harms women even if legalized or decriminalized. *Violence Against Women, 10*(10), 1087–1125.

——. (2005). Prostitution harms women even if indoors: Reply to Weitzer. *Violence Against Women, 11*(7), 950–964.

Gerassi, L., Nichols, A., & Michelson, E. (2017). Lessons learned: Benefits and challenges in community based responses to sex trafficking and commercial sexual exploitation. *Journal of Human Trafficking, 3*(4), 1–18.

Heil, E., & Nichols, A. (2015). *Human trafficking in the Midwest: A case study of St. Louis and the bi-state area.* Durham, NC: Carolina Academic Press.

Kalergis, K. I. (2009). A passionate practice addressing the needs of commercially sexually exploited teenagers. *Affilia, 24*(3), 315–324. doi:10.1177/0886109909337706

Lloyd, R. (2012). *Girls like us: Fighting for a world where girls are not for sale.* New York, NY: Harper Perennial.

Loyola University New Orleans's Modern Slavery Research Project. (2017). Labor and sex trafficking among homeless youth. Retrieved from https://covenanthousestudy.org/landing /trafficking/docs/Loyola-Research-Results.pdf

Lutnick, A. (2016). *Domestic minor sex trafficking: Beyond victims and villains.* New York, NY: Columbia University Press.

Macy, R. J., & Graham, L.M. (2012). Identifying domestic and international sex-trafficking victims during human service provision. *Trauma, Violence, & Abuse, 13*(2), 59–76.

Macy, R. J., & Johns, N. (2011). Aftercare services for international sex trafficking survivors: Informing U.S. service and program development in an emerging practice area. *Trauma, Violence, & Abuse, 12*(2), 87–98.

Madden-Dempsey, M. (2010). Sex trafficking and criminalization: In defense of feminist abolitionism. *University of Pennsylvania Law Review, 158*(6), 1729–1778.

Marcus, A., Horning, A., Curtis, R., Sanson, J., & Thompson, E. (2014). Conflict and agency among sex workers and pimps: A closer look at domestic minor sex trafficking. *The ANNALS of the American Academy of Political and Social Science, 653*(1), 225–246. doi:10.1177/0002716214521993

Nichols, A. J. (2016). *Sex trafficking in the United States: Theory, research, policy, and practice.* New York, NY: Columbia University Press.

Nichols, A. J., & Heil, E. C. (2015). Challenges to identifying and prosecuting sex trafficking cases in the Midwest United States. *Feminist Criminology, 10*(1), 7–35. doi:10.1177 /1557085113519490

Oselin, S. (2014). *Leaving prostitution: Getting out and staying out of sex work.* New York, NY: New York University Press.

Outshoorn, J. (2005). The political debates on prostitution and trafficking of women. *Social Politics: International Studies in Gender, State and Society, 12*(1), 141–155. Retrieved from http://muse.jhu.edu/journals/social_politics/vo12/12.1outshoorn.html

Polaris Project. (2014). *Sex trafficking in the U.S.* Retrieved from http://www.polarisproject .org/human-trafficking/sex-trafficking-in-the-us

Raphael, J., & Myers-Powell, B. (2010). From victims to victimizers: Interviews with 25 ex-pimps in Chicago. DePaul College of Law. Retrieved from http://media.virbcdn.com/files/cc /FileItem-149884-depaul25_Pimp_Research_Final_Aug2010.pdf

Raphael, J., Reichert, J., & Powers, M. (2010). Pimp control and violence: Domestic sex trafficking of Chicago women and girls. *Women & Criminal Justice, 20*, 89–104.

Reid, J. A. (2011). An exploratory model of girls' vulnerability to commercial sexual exploitation in prostitution. *Child Maltreatment, 16*(2), 146–157.

Valandra. (2007). Reclaiming their lives and breaking free: An Afrocentric approach to recovery from prostitution. *Affilia, 22*, 195–208.

Weitzer, R. (2010). The movement to criminalize sex work in the United States. *Journal of Law and Society, 37*(1), 61–84. Retrieved from http://papers.ssrn.com/abstract=1558068

SOCIAL WORK PRACTICE WITH SURVIVORS OF SEX TRAFFICKING AND COMMERCIAL SEXUAL EXPLOITATION

PART I

PRACTICE TECHNIQUES

P art I includes chapters that examine practice techniques with survivors of sex trafficking and commercial sexual exploitation (CSE). Chapter 1 discusses information that is typically absent or misunderstood in conversations about survivors of sex trafficking/CSE. It introduces the multifaceted, extensive, and expansive nature of the commercial sex industry in the United States and shows how this industry impacts survivors' varied lived experiences. It also explains how external and internal factors combine to create diversity among the experiences of survivors. Understandings of such factors can guide individualized services that are sensitive to the particular needs and strengths of each survivor. By giving an overview of survivors' common body of knowledge while simultaneously acknowledging diverse experiences, the chapter clarifies the vital importance of involving survivors in service provision and utilization. It also shows that the length of time since exiting the condition of exploitation affects survivors' understanding of healing, a topic that is absent in current research. The chapter further presents some of the implications of acknowledging and respecting the contributions of long-term survivors. It is an important introduction to the book, showing that the wide variety of experiences in CSE makes it impossible to apply a one-size-fits-all approach to practice.

Given the diverse backgrounds and experiences of survivors, it is unsurprising that there are challenges to identifying sex-trafficked and exploited people. Chapter 2 notes that a serious challenge for the antitrafficking field is identifying sex-trafficked and commercially sexually exploited people and connecting them with services. Professionals who work in service sectors with vulnerable groups of people who may be trafficked, such as those who work in child welfare, healthcare, juvenile justice, intimate partner violence, rape and sexual assault, housing, and immigration, are critically important first-responders who can identify trafficked persons, respond with compassion, and connect them to information, resources, and support. Because of a lack of training and expertise, however, social workers may encounter people who are experiencing trafficking but are unable to identify these persons as such, resulting in missed opportunities to assess needs and provide appropriate services. To help address such urgent knowledge gaps, chapter 2 presents recommendations for screening, assessing, and identifying CSE and people who have experienced trafficking across various social work settings.

Once an individual is connected to services, safety planning is key to reducing further victimization. Chapter 3 details such safety planning techniques. Survivors of sex trafficking/CSE commonly experience high rates of exploitation and abuse, making safety planning a crucial factor in practice. Further, it is generally well known that many trafficked and exploited people will return to exploitive situations several times before successfully leaving, and thus it is imperative for social workers to acknowledge that safety plans are not just for those trying to leave but also for individuals choosing to stay. As evidence-based practices specific to survivors of sex trafficking are being developed, practitioners can learn from the practice field of intimate partner violence/domestic violence, as well as from protocols designed by organizations working with trafficked and exploited people, to tailor and individualize their responses to the safety needs of survivors. The chapter describes the relationship between intimate partner violence/domestic violence and sex trafficking/commercial sexual exploitation; explains the history and purpose of safety plans; illustrates key principles of survivor-centered advocacy as a foundation for safety planning; offers recommendations for assessing risks and safety planning with survivors; and covers important considerations for safety planning, including working with law enforcement, dealing with technology concerns, and working with those experiencing co-occurring disorders.

Once an individual is in a place of safety, specific practices become important. Chapter 4 describes the transtheoretical model, "stages of change," and motivational interviewing in the context of working with young women and girls who are experiencing domestic trafficking and commercial sexual exploitation. Girls Educational and Mentoring Services (GEMS), a survivor-led organization and the nation's largest service provider to exploited and trafficked girls and young women, details the techniques of using practice-based evidence. Practice-based evidence is uncovered when practitioners and organizations identify successful practices in the course of their work. Rachel Lloyd, president, survivor, and founder of GEMS, explains why such practice techniques are so effective with survivors of commercial sexual exploitation and trafficking, both for the survivors themselves and for the service providers, law enforcement personnel, and legal and healthcare professionals who encounter them.

While practice-based evidence is important, so is evidence-based practice. Chapter 5 discusses evidence-based trauma treatments and their applicability to trafficked and exploited people. The chapter reviews eye movement desensitization and reprocessing, cognitive processing therapy, skills training in affective and interpersonal regulation, narrative storytelling, and their applicability as trauma treatments to survivors of sex trafficking/CSE. The chapter also examines best practices for choosing a trauma treatment, and relates social work practice to the practice competencies established by the Council on Social Work Education. Chapter 6 focuses on the theory and practice of harm reduction in working with sex workers and individuals experiencing sex trafficking. It briefly explores prior efforts to address the harms associated with sex work and trafficking and then examines evaluations of sex worker programs centered on harm reduction. Such evaluations suggest that these programs preserve clients' basic human rights and their dignity and worth, providing nonjudgmental and flexible services to clients without requiring that they abstain from sex work. By focusing on the clients' narratives to secure safety in their work, practitioners are able to highlight and empower clients' natural strengths as well as encourage clients to more consistently engage in social services. Concluding this chapter are recommendations for harm reduction in social work practice.

Chapter 7 maintains that while it is important for social workers to identify and provide services to victims of human trafficking, it is also important to understand the legal implications of identifying a victim or survivor of trafficking. This chapter breaks down federal and state laws connected to human trafficking and also describes the legal resources available to victims of trafficking, including vacating convictions, immigration applications, and criminal prosecutions. The chapter focuses on how social workers and attorneys can work together to provide the best resources and legal services to survivors. Chapter 7 also shows how social service providers can best help victims walk through the criminal justice and immigration processes, as well as access other legal benefits. Such practices are an important part of social workers' "toolkit" in any organization serving trafficked and exploited people.

CHAPTER 1

SURVIVORS

A Diverse Community with a Common Body of Knowledge

MELANIE WEAVER, MFA, ARTIST, ACTIVIST, 38+ YEAR
SURVIVOR, PhD STUDENT, ARIZONA STATE UNIVERSITY

The most pervasive misconception about survivors is that they are a homogenous group. This oversimplification results in several erroneous beliefs: that survivors' lived experiences of the commercial sex industry are similar, that their responses to being sold are predictable (Alcoff, 1991), and that their healing journeys are identical. The reality is far more complex. Survivors make up a diverse community, and their individual stories of both trauma and healing are varied and complex (American Psychological Association, 2014; Cojocaru, 2015). The one definitive factor uniting this community is the experiential knowledge and understanding of the commercial sex industry and of the oppression, dominance, and subjugation inherent in the sale of human beings who have been dehumanized as sex objects.

Commercial Sexual Exploitation in the United States

The commercial sex industry in the United States encompasses myriad expanding circumstances in which something of value is exchanged for sexual acts (Farley, 2006; Reid, 2010). In this chapter, commercial sexual exploitation of children (CSEC) refers to the involvement of any person under the age of eighteen in any area of the commercial sex industry. Commercial sexual exploitation (CSE) refers to involvement of any person over the age of eighteen who participates without full freedom of choice.

Sex trafficking includes all situations in which the persons used do not have freedom of choice. It is not a new phenomenon in the United States. Over the past four decades, it has had many names, which have changed as awareness has grown. The sale of children has been called child prostitution, child pornography, juvenile prostitution, teen prostitution, sexual exploitation of youth, domestic minor sex trafficking (DMST), and, as used in this chapter, commercial sexual exploitation of children (CSEC) (Reid, 2010). The sale of adults has been called prostitution, pornography, forced trafficking, domestic sex trafficking (DST), adult forced prostitution (AFP), and in this chapter, commercial sexual exploitation (CSE).

Persons currently involved in the commercial sex industry may also self-identify as "sex workers." They typically work independently of a facilitator or trafficker and describe sex work as a job, separate and distinct from who they are as individuals. Their self-perception is that they are free agents who are able to choose involvement, decline engagements, benefit financially, and exit sex work at any time (Carter, 1987). Sex workers have the freedom to take precautions and protect themselves, and this sense of agency mitigates the sense of vulnerability that contributes to psychological damage (Delacoste & Alexander, 1987). None of those factors are true of persons used in sex trafficking. Trafficked persons do not have freedom to choose, do not benefit fully financially, and are not able to exit at any time. To survive, their identities are often subsumed beneath the contempt directed at them. They become what they are forced to do, and this identity contributes greatly to the psychological destruction they experience (Farley et al., 2004).

The commercial sex industry thrives on the sale of persons, from infancy through adulthood. Survivors' involvement in CSE can be limited to one form, for a short period, or can extend to multiple forms over a long span of time (Dalla, 2000). Distinctions made between minors and adults have a direct impact on criminalization, prosecution, and access to services. However, these distinctions are problematic because they obscure the reality that one group directly feeds into the other. Children who experience sexual exploitation are more vulnerable to CSEC as teenagers. Teenagers sold on the streets age into adults sold on the streets (Farley et al., 2004). Adults involved in the commercial sex industry often entered as minors. The average age of entry has been debated, with early studies focusing only on youth populations (Lutnick, 2016). Those who enter as adults may have different experiences than those who enter as children (Oselin, 2014; Reid, 2012; Reid & Piquero, 2014). Simplistic categories, even regarding issues that might seem very clear, deny the complexity of factors that contribute to survivors' lived experiences.

There are multiple forms of trafficking, as well as multiple mediums and venues in which trafficking takes place. For example, the development of the Internet has contributed to the expansion of the commercial sex industry.

The Internet facilitates distribution (pornography, child pornography), expedites connections (escort prostitution, pimp-controlled prostitution, sex tourism, delivery services, pedophile rings, forced marriage/mail-order brides), and presents the opportunity for the emergence of new forms (Internet prostitution via live video chat is the online version of phone sex, and virtual realities are contemporary versions of peep shows) (Sher, 2013).

Brothels operate from interior spaces. Commercial properties may front as legitimate businesses (spas, saunas, nail parlors, massage parlors) or openly participate in the commercial sex industry (bars, strip clubs, dance clubs, "gentlemen's" clubs, topless clubs, adult video arcades) (Murphy & Venkatesh, 2006). Residential brothels cross all class lines: they include private parties in mansions, sexual servitude in middle-class homes, roving brothels of boys in rental homes, and children sold for the price of drugs in apartments. Multiple forms of exploitation can occur simultaneously within one residence (children used in pornography, sold in prostitution, and abused in ritualized practices).

Street prostitution, hustling, survival sex, and gang prostitution occur in a combination of interior and exterior spaces. Interior venues include hotels, motels, malls, abandoned buildings, restrooms, public transit, personal vehicles (cars, trucks, vans, RVs), and commercial vehicles. Exterior venues include streets, alleyways, doorways, parks, truck stops, and rest stops. Geographic locations vary according to "wherever pimps and traffickers can make the most money, for example near military bases, near political or business conventions" (Farley, 2006).

The circumstances of CSE inform survivors' knowledge of the commercial sex industry. CSE spans all classes and cultures, and both class and culture impact survivors' lived experiences. A twenty-year-old college student working at a high-end escort service has different experiences of CSE than a fifty-year-old homeless woman working skid row to support a meth addiction (Burnes, Long, & Schept, 2012).

The knowledge base acquired by very young children sold in underground networks would not include solicitation because traffickers control arrangements and transactions. Sometimes children and teens continue to live at home, attending school and participating in sports while being trafficked (Flores, 2013). Some survivors experience multiple types of exploitation. Strip clubs can be an entry point leading to street prostitution (Lloyd, 2012) or part of an exit process after pimp-controlled prostitution (Sher, 2013). Male escort experiences differ from those of gay men involved in hustling, and the experiences of transgender people are also distinctly nuanced (Dank, Yahner, et al., 2015; Dank, Yu, et al., 2015; Lutnick, 2016). Persons exiting the commercial sex industry may or may not self-identify as survivors. Historically, men have been less likely to identify as survivors. The common understanding shared among the community of survivors is that the commercial sex industry is exploitive in all its forms, regardless of independence or agency, and that survival and recovery take incredible strength (Dalla, 2000; Farley et al., 2004). Survivors' individual experiences and resulting knowledge base are specific to the circumstances of their involvement in the commercial sex industry and reflect the breadth of the CSE continuum.

Survivors' Varied Lived Experiences of CSE: External Contributing Factors

Two sets of interrelated factors contribute to a survivor's lived experience of being trafficked. The first set is *external* and the second set is *internal*. Six external factors that significantly affect a survivor's lived experience include the relationship to traffickers, the age of entry, the setting, the buyers, the frequency and level of physical violence, and the length of time sold.

The survivor's *relationship to the trafficker(s)* has a direct effect on the level of betrayal involved in entry into CSE. The value that the relationship has to the person sold affects the level of betrayal experienced. Peers (schoolmates, neighborhood friends, same-age boyfriends, same-age girlfriends, gang members) sell friends for status, allegiance, belonging, power, and greed. A boyfriend who sells a girlfriend to classmates not only earns status but also gains income. If the meaning of the victim's relationship with this boy was a "first love," then the angst of adolescence will magnify the sense of betrayal (Lloyd, 2012).

Homeless youth often use survival sex as a means to obtain food, clothing, and shelter without the involvement of a third party or trafficker. Some runaways form friendships that take on the importance of families and share their income with the group. If decisions are made collaboratively, then the level of felt betrayal will be low to nonexistent (Dank, Yahner, et al., 2015). The true betrayal in these cases is betrayal by the society that ignored the survival needs of these teenagers.

The type of trafficker determines the *age of entry* into CSEC/CSE. Parents, stepparents, and close relatives have unquestioned access to children and are able to initiate involvement in CSEC from infancy onward. Pedophile networks fixate on children of specific genders and ages. "New friend" strangers target young teenagers. Peer teens sell teens, and gangs sell teenagers and young adults. Pimps manage stables of young teens, teens, and adults. Brothels sell children, teens, and adults. Organized crime networks specialize in efficiently selling victims of all ages.

The type of trafficking determines the *physical context* in which it occurs. The location can be urban, suburban, or rural. The setting can be interior or exterior, commercial or domestic, public or private. The type and context often relate to the number of times a person is sold within a twenty-four-hour period.

Forced marriage, "domestic" work, and sexual servitude may involve only one sale, to one person or family, in one residence, whereas traveling pimps who are trafficking teens at truck stops may sell to dozens of men per night.

The men who are *buyers* come from every socioeconomic class, race, and ethnicity. They span the continuum, from "average Joes" to sociopaths. Their motivations range from sexual control to engagement in torturous perversions (Malarek, 2011). The buyers, location, and type of exploitation are interconnected. The men who buy children from residential houses include pedophiles, serial rapists, psychopaths, sociopaths, and organized crime members. Migrant workers buy girls in the fields. Men in the military buy sex from women in establishments set up near military bases (brothels, clubs, and bars).

The *frequency and level of physical violence* survivors experience vary according to several factors. Pimps who use physical dominance to maintain control are frequently violent toward their victims. Buyers perpetrate more violence on girls, women, and transgender women than on men (Farley & Barkan, 1998). Sadistic buyers are extremely violent, to the point of torture. As the experiences of violence increase (both in types and severity), the symptoms of PTSD (numbing, flashbacks, and hyperarousal) accumulate (Farley & Barkan, 1998).

The *length of time sold* varies from one day to an entire lifetime. Parents, stepparents, boyfriends, or close relatives sell their children for many different reasons (drug money, sexual perversions, pedophilic desires, sociopathic or psychopathic urges, or simply greed). Control by parental figures or relatives can easily extend through the teen years. For many, as the time lengthens, trauma multiplies (Farley, 2003). (See chapter 17 for macrostructural external factors.)

Survivors' Varied Lived Experiences of CSE: Internal Contributing Factors

In addition to the *external* factors that affect a survivor's experience of trafficking, there are *internal* factors that combine to create vastly different experiences of trauma. Five significant internal factors that affect a survivor's lived experience are developmental age, socialization, enculturation, identity formation, and temperament (Wessells, 2006).

The survivor's *developmental age* is distinct from his or her chronological age. A survivor's problem-solving abilities expand with each developmental milestone. As children develop, they gain the ability to generalize, to think more abstractly and reason more clearly. Multiple forms of abuse can negatively affect this developmental progression (Garbarino & Kostelny, 1996). Children at earlier stages of development are easier to manipulate and control than older children. Children and teens with delayed development are vulnerable because they do not have the perception necessary to defend themselves or to know when someone who acts kind is being deceptive (Elman, 1997). (See chapter 11 on girls with intellectual disabilities.)

Familial *socialization* prior to trafficking can either provide a shield or leave a void. Children who are socialized within a supportive family and learn to form close relationships are less vulnerable to being lured into situations of CSE. In contrast, children who grow up with abuse or neglect are more vulnerable because of their desire for belonging and love. Pimps target these children by offering an illusion of family (Lloyd, 2012).

Socialization also occurs through media and pop culture. The sexualization and objectification of women and girls, the sensationalized dream of fame, and the glorification of pimping are rooted in portrayals by the media (Lloyd, 2012). Pimps can lure vulnerable teens by promising romance and glamorizing "the life" (Campbell, 2006). They exploit the human need for love and belonging and the media-induced dream of fame. These "new boyfriends" first lavish the teen with affirmation and attention, expensive clothing, dates at restaurants, promises of fame, and an upscale place to live (Hotaling, Miller, & Trudeau, 2006). Later, these teens often describe feeling that this was the first person in their life who ever understood them. When the relationship turns exploitive and the teens are forced into CSE to "pay back" the money spent on them, the strength of that initial bond remains.

Enculturation affects a person's experience of CSE in a variety of ways. Children raised in communities where prostitution is normalized are more likely to accept it as an alternative to poverty (Oselin, 2014), whereas children who live in a culture that condemns prostitution have an increased burden of shame and stigma (Sallmann, 2010). In CSE, the enculturation process transitions a person from "this is what I do" to "this is who I am."

An *identity* defined by CSE is based on subjugation and violation. Accepting this identity can be a means of survival. Identity formation is a fluid process, "constructed through dynamic interaction between the individual and members of society" (Wessells, 2006). There are potentially three significant stages of identity formation: prior to entering, during CSE, and after exiting. A sense of identity prior to CSE, with personalized beliefs, values, and morality, facilitates the process of identity re-formation after exiting. Children sold by their parents, or children who grew up in abusive homes and lost their teen years to CSE, never had the opportunity to form a personal sense of identity. Thus, they have fewer resources from which to draw after leaving. Creating or re-creating an identity afterward is just as much a social process as taking on an identity to survive CSE.

A survivor's *temperament* can buffer or magnify the impact of CSE. Survivors who are novelty seeking, adventurous, and impervious may adapt more easily. One such survivor described being "addicted to the danger, to the risk, the excitement . . . it was like a high to get home alive a lot of times" (Dalla, 2000).

While everyone has the capacity to enjoy adventure, some temperaments are, by nature, more "drawn to the danger, the excitement, and the 'glamour' of street prostitution" (Dalla, Xia, & Kennedy, 2003). Safety and life without abuse can feel boring (White & Lloyd, 2014).

Survivors' Years of Experience After CSE

The final, and perhaps the most dynamic, distinction to make between survivors is the length of time that has passed since survivors successfully exited the commercial sex industry. Chronological age tells only a fraction of the story. Two seventeen-year-old survivors can have vastly different recovery chronologies. One can be a seven-*day* survivor, just beginning the second week out of trafficking, while another can already be a seven-*year* survivor, who began counseling when trafficking ended at ten years old. As awareness and personal healing progress, survivors gain experience, expertise, knowledge, insight, and understanding about dealing with and healing the aftereffects of CSE. The amount of distance, measured in both psychological and physical time and space, creates enormous differences in perspectives and healing experiences.

The wealth of knowledge that long-term survivors have is an undervalued resource in the antitrafficking movement. In 2014, the American Psychological Association, recognizing the extensive knowledge and expertise of long-term survivors, recommended that conversations in the antitrafficking movement include long-term survivors because their voices are essential to finding solutions (American Psychological Association, 2014). Many older survivors both exited and healed prior to the current antitrafficking movement (Limoncelli, 2010), often without the assistance of any intervention programs. They have lived for decades with the physical, mental, and emotional ramifications of CSE. In the years after exiting CSE, they have pursued education and careers and attained professional standing in their fields.

These people have a unique understanding of the long-term outlook for survivors, and their perspectives are vital to any attempt to understand the survivors' ongoing needs. Indeed, they are the only people who can provide insight into the needs of survivors as they age. Yet their strength, ability to overcome the effects of CSE, and decades of experience remain undocumented in research.

Survivors who exited during the 1970s or 1980s have lived with the heaviest social burden of stigma related to the commercial sex industry. During that time, the concept of exploitation did not exist, and virtually no distinction was made regarding factors that contribute to exploitation. Prostitutes were openly condemned in almost every setting. For many survivors, the only viable option after exiting CSE was to "pass" as a nonsurvivor.

Survivors who exited during the 1990s also experienced the social denial that children and teens were being sold in the United States. Understanding of survivors' lives and experiences was extremely limited, and resources were almost nonexistent. It is unlikely that these survivors worked with mental health practitioners who had prior experience working with survivors of CSE. As one survivor recounted, "I wonder why I keep going to therapists and telling them I can't sleep, and I have nightmares. They pass right over the fact that I was a prostitute and I was beaten" (Hotaling, Miller, & Trudeau, 2006).

Survivors who exited during the evolution of the current antitrafficking movement may have received assistance during the early stages of their exiting process. They grew up under the influence of media-based sexualization and objectification of women and girls, where pimps are glorified and prostitution is normalized as glamorous (Farley, 2006). These survivors experienced the emergence of new terminology while they were exiting CSE. They witnessed the beginnings of a transition from "prostitute" and "hooker" to "victim of commercial sexual exploitation" and "survivor of the commercial sex industry." They may have even worked with mental health practitioners who had prior experience with survivors of CSE.

Far from being irrelevant, ten- to thirty-plus-year survivors bring a long-range perspective to conversations about healing. Shared laughter and hope are gifts that survivors give each other. The sense of belonging found in laughing together is like a phrase that has no accurate translation in other languages. Laughter is the manifestation of human resilience. It enables acceptance of uncomfortable realities (Lloyd, 2012). It affirms humanity. It empowers, allowing years of rejection and stigmatization to fall away. While laughter disappears for a time, when it emerges again, it renews life and strengthens the bonds of community between survivors.

As the antitrafficking movement progresses into the future, the lived experiences of long-term survivors can provide the expertise and knowledge to support survivors in a comprehensive and individualized manner. Organizations that have traditionally excluded survivor involvement in their policy making and program design "sideline expertise and silence essential voices" (American Psychological Association, 2014). In fact, maintaining a damage-centered, deficit perspective of survivors (as lacking, irreparably broken, damaged, and ruined) perpetuates the very ethos of CSE (Tuck, 2009). When nonsurvivors speak for victims, they unknowingly maintain the very domination they seek to redress (Alcoff, 1991).

Survivor-Defined and Survivor-Centered Services

The five internal factors influencing each survivor's lived experiences of CSE offer some keys to providing survivor-centered services. The challenges facing each individual are connected to their *socialization, development, encultura-tion, identity formation*, and *temperament*. Survivor-centered service means that "mission and program services are developed through a survivor's lens rather than what might be best for professionals or the structures in which they work" (Busch-Armendariz, Nsonwu, & Heffron, 2014). Diverse, flexible programs, extensive networks, and comprehensive care are vital to meeting the specific needs of each survivor (Hotaling, Burris, Johnson, Bird, & Melbye, 2004). A one-size-fits-all approach cannot succeed (Valandra, 2007) because it is not possible for one solution to address the needs of every type of survivor (Sher, 2013).

While survivors' lived experiences of CSE are incredibly varied, every experience of CSE is based on domination, dehumanization, objectification, and commodification (Farley et al., 2004). The *socialization* process of CSE also instills values that are the opposite of mainstream culture's values, in that the victimization "changes one's perceptions of and beliefs about others in society . . . by indicating others as sources of threat or harm rather than sources of support" (Macmillan, 2001). Survivors' voices are vital to providing services that are sensitive to the ramifications of this socialization process. Because of their common knowledge and shared understanding of the dynamics of CSE, survivors often find it easier to trust other survivors (Valandra, 2007). There is less to explain, and there is an intuitive sense that someone "gets it" (White & Lloyd, 2014). Behaviors that are incomprehensible to nonsurvivors make sense to survivors. Without survivors' voices, frustration often leads to blaming the victim.

Service providers facilitate healing by providing resources that allow sur-vivors to grow *developmentally* (American Psychological Association, 2014). A survivor may simultaneously have a preadolescent understanding of bound-aries in healthy relationships and an ancient understanding of victimizing human behaviors. CSE distorts "an individual's sense of agency, self-efficacy, and perceptions of others in the social world" (Macmillan, 2001). Restorative support builds self-confidence and fosters healthy coping mechanisms.

Cultural competence is a vital component of survivor-centered services. Survivors' *enculturation* directly affects their definitions of healing. "To be effective, specialized intervention strategies need to be culturally grounded" (Busch-Armendariz et al., 2014), taking into account both the expectations of survivors and the expectations their cultures place on them. One survivor explained: "African American women need to work with African American professionals who can provide both tough love and gentle guidance. We aren't white, and we aren't going to learn to be white. . . . We need each other" (Valan-dra, 2007). (See chapter 9 on Afrocentric approaches.)

Likewise, Native American youth express the importance of "having a chance to talk about this issue with other Native youth" and "having Native adults you can talk with who will not blame or judge" (Pierce, 2012). LGBTQ+

(lesbian, gay, bisexual, transgender, queer) youth, who have often experienced both familial and societal rejection, benefit greatly from the opportunity to talk to both mentors and peers in the queer community (Schwarz & Britton, 2015). (See chapter 10 on social work with LGBTQ+ people.) As with LGBTQ+ youth who have been disowned by their families, if a survivor's culture equates virginity with familial honor, reintegration may not be possible. Survivors who are cut off from their communities will need additional support. (See chapter 8 on practice with immigrant populations.)

As previously stated, the formation of *identity* is a social process (Wessells, 2006). Society condemns people involved in CSE and refers to them as "whores" (Sallmann, 2010), erasing the value of the entire person. The restoration of humanity occurs through interactions with people, in the same way that dehumanization in commercial sex occurred through interactions with people. Creating a new identity after CSE is a central part of the healing process (Oselin, 2014). Since survivors have intimate knowledge about this process, their involvement facilitates healing (Lloyd, 2012; Oselin, 2014).

Antitrafficking organizations are a part of the society in which they operate. As such, they have an unconscious tendency to view survivors through the same lens as society, to think of them as irreparably damaged or "less than human" (Sallmann, 2010). This deficit approach increases the burdens of individuals who are already traumatized and carrying heavy burdens. Survivors are uniquely positioned to provide support that does not simply replicate these "patterns of domination," shame, and stigma (Schwarz & Britton, 2015). There is less temptation to criticize a survivor who, for example, chooses not to utilize all of the programs offered (Schwarz & Britton, 2015). Respecting survivors as capable human beings who can make choices about their lives lays the foundation for different choices in the future (Hotaling et al., 2006; Lloyd, 2012). (See chapter 4, which details the Stages of Change model.)

Empowerment happens through a strengths-based approach, through listening, accepting, and supporting each person's priorities and right to choose. Meaning-making is an individual process. Some survivors only find meaning in helping other survivors (Blac, 2012). Others find meaning in dedicating themselves to becoming loving parents (McDonald, 2013). Understanding how a person defines meaning and "healing" is a key to coordinating and providing individualized resources. Even if survivors have similar needs, they may not prioritize them in the same way. The only way to know how best to support a survivor is to take the time to listen to how he, she, or they defines support.

The last key provided by internal factors is *temperament*. Survivors with novelty-seeking or sensation-seeking temperaments are more prone to drug addiction (Milivojevic et al., 2012). They are also more prone to feeling addicted to the danger inherent in the commercial sex industry. For some survivors, success in leaving the life includes meeting their innate need for novelty and adventure in alternate, less destructive ways. Survivors with more contemplative temperaments feel a need to understand their experiences (Moran, 2015).

Survivors have had different experiences in the commercial sex industry. They have various reasons for leaving and various motivations for recovery. Some survivors have access to multiple resources, and some have virtually none (Lee, 2010). Priorities and goals differ for each survivor. Providing adequate assistance requires a willingness to listen and an individualized approach tailored to the specific needs of each survivor.

References

Alcoff, L. (1991). The problem of speaking for others. *Cultural Critique, 20*, 5–32.

American Psychological Association. (2014). *Report of the Task Force on Trafficking of Women and Girls*. Retrieved from http://www.apa.org/pi/women/programs/trafficking/report.aspx

Blac, S. (2012). *The rebirth of Suzzan Blac*. San Diego, CA: Bettie Youngs Books.

Burnes, T. R., Long, S. L., & Schept, R. A. (2012). A resilience-based lens of sex work: Implications for professional psychologists. *Professional Psychology: Research and Practice, 43*, 137–144.

Busch-Armendariz, N., Nsonwu, M. B., & Heffron, L. C. (2014). A kaleidoscope: The role of the social work practitioner and the strength of social work theories and practice in meeting the complex needs of people trafficked and the professionals that work with them. *International Social Work, 57*(1), 7–18.

Campbell, R. (2006). *Marked women: Prostitutes and prostitution in the cinema*. Madison, WI: University of Wisconsin Press.

Carter, S. (1987). A most useful tool. In F. Delacoste & P. Alexander (Eds.), *Sex work: Writings by women in the sex industry* (pp. 159–165). Pittsburg, PA: Cleis Press.

Cojocaru, C. (2015). Sex trafficking, captivity, and narrative: Constructing victimhood with the goal of salvation. *Dialectical Anthropology, 39*(2), 183.

Dalla, R. L. (2000). Exposing the "pretty woman" myth: A qualitative examination of the lives of female streetwalking prostitutes. *Journal of Sex Research, 37*(4), 344–353.

Dalla, R. L., Xia, Y., & Kennedy, H. (2003). "You just give them what they want and pray they don't kill you": Street-level sex workers' reports of victimization, personal resources, and coping strategies. *Violence Against Women, 9*(11), 1367–1394.

Dank, M., Yahner, J., Madden, K., Banuelos, I., Yu, L., Ritchie, A., Mora, M., & Conner, B. (2015, February 25). *Surviving the streets of New York: Experiences of LGBTQ youth, YMSM, and YWSW engaged in survival sex*. Urban Institute. Retrieved from http://www.urban.org/research/publication/surviving-streets-new-york-experiences-lgbtq-youth-ymsm-and-ywsw-engaged-survival-sex/view/full_report

Dank, M., Yu, L., Yahner, J., Mora, M., Pelletier, E., & Conner, B. (2015, September). *Locked in: Interactions with the criminal justice and child welfare systems for LGBTQ youth, YMSM, and YWSW who engage in survival sex*. Urban Institute. Retrieved from http://www.urban.org/sites/default/files/publication/71446/2000424-Locked-In-Interactions-with-the-Criminal-Justice-and-Child-Welfare-Systems-for-LGBTQ-Youth-YMSM-and-YWSW-Who-Engage-in-Survival-Sex.pdf

Delacoste, F., & Alexander, P. (Eds.). (1987). *Sex work: Writings by women in the sex industry*. Pittsburg, PA: Cleis Press.

Elman, R. A. (1997). Disability pornography: The fetishization of women's vulnerabilities. *Violence Against Women, 3*, 257–270.

Farley, M. (2003). Prostitution and the invisibility of harm. In M. E. Banks and E. Kaschak (Eds.), *Women with visible and invisible disabilities: Multiple intersections, multiple issues, multiple therapies* (pp. 247–269). Binghamton, NY: Hayworth Press.

———. (2006). Prostitution, trafficking, and cultural amnesia: What we must not know in order to keep the business of sexual exploitation running smoothly. *Yale Journal of Law and Feminism, 18*, 101–136.

Farley, M., & Barkan, H. (1998). Prostitution, violence, and posttraumatic stress disorder. *Women and Health, 27*(3), 37–49.

Farley, M., Cotton, A., Lynne, J., Zumbeck, S., Spiwak, F., Reyes, M. E., . . . & Sezgin, U. (2004). Prostitution and trafficking in nine countries: An update on violence and posttraumatic stress disorder. *Journal of Trauma Practice, 2*(3–4), 33–74.

Flores, T. (2013). *The slave across the street: The harrowing true story of how a 15-year-old girl became a sex slave.* New York, NY: Random House.

Garbarino, J., & Kostelny, K. (1996). What do we need to know to understand children in war and community violence? In R. J. Apfel & B. Simon (Eds.), *Minefields in their hearts: The mental health of children in war and communal violence* (pp. 33–51). New Haven, CT: Yale University Press..

Hotaling, N., Burris, A., Johnson, B. J., Bird, Y. M., & Melbye, K. A. (2004). Been there done that: SAGE, a peer leadership model among prostitution survivors. *Journal of Trauma Practice, 2*(3–4), 255–265.

Hotaling, N., Miller, K., & Trudeau, E. (2006). Commercial sexual exploitation of women and girls: A survivor service provider's perspective. *Yale Journal and Feminism, 18*, 181.

Lee, Taylor. (2010). In and out: A survivor's memoir of stripping. In C. Stark and R. Whisnant (Eds.), *Not for sale: Feminists resisting prostitution and pornography* (pp. 56–63). Victoria, Australia: Spinifex Press.

Limoncelli, S. A. (2010). *The politics of trafficking: The first international movement to combat the sexual exploitation of women.* Redwood City, CA: Stanford University Press.

Lloyd, R. (2012). *Girls like us: Fighting for a world where girls are not for sale: A memoir.* New York, NY: Harper Perennial.

Lutnick, A. (2016). *Domestic minor sex trafficking: Beyond victims and villains.* New York, NY: Columbia University Press.

Macmillan, R. (2001). Violence and the life course: The consequences of victimization for personal and social development. *Annual Review of Sociology, 27*, 1–22.

Malarek, V. (2011). *The Johns: Sex for sale and the men who buy it.* New York, NY: Skyhorse Publishing.

McDonald, C. (2013). *Cry purple: One woman's journey through homelessness, crack addiction and prison to blindness, motherhood and happiness.* San Bernardino, CA: CreateSpace Independent Publishing.

Milivojevic, D., Milovanovic, S. D., Jovanovic, M., Svrakic, D. M., Svrakic, N. M., Svrakic, S. M., & Cloninger, C. R. (2012). Temperament and character modify risk of drug addiction and influence choice of drugs. *The American Journal on Addictions, 21*(5), 462–467. doi: 10.1111/j.1521-0391.2012.00251.x.-467

Moran, R. (2015). *Paid for: My journey through prostitution.* New York, NY: W. W. Norton.

Murphy, A. K., & Venkatesh, S. A. (2006). Vice careers: The changing contours of sex work in New York City. *Qualitative Sociology, 29*(2), 129–154. doi: 10.1007/s11133-006-9012-2

Oselin, S. S. (2014). *Leaving prostitution: Getting out and staying out of sex work.* New York, NY: New York University Press.

Reid, J. A. (2010). Doors wide shut: Barriers to the successful delivery of victim services for domestically trafficked minors in a southern US metropolitan area. *Women and Criminal Justice, 20*(1–2), 147–166.

——. (2012). Exploratory review of route-specific, gendered, and age-graded dynamics of exploitation: Applying life course theory to victimization in sex trafficking in North America. *Aggression and Violent Behavior: A Review Journal, 7*(3). Retrieved from http://works.bepress.com/joan_reid/17/

Reid, J. A., & Piquero, A. (2014). Age-graded risks for commercial sexual exploitation of male and female youth. *Journal of Interpersonal Violence*. Retrieved from http://works.bepress.com/joan_reid/24/

Sallmann, J. (2010). Living with stigma: Women's experiences of prostitution and substance use. *Affilia, 25*(2), 146–159.

Schwarz, C., & Britton, H. E. (2015). Queering the support for trafficked persons: LGBTQ communities and human trafficking in the Heartland. *Social Inclusion, 3*(1).

Sher, J. (2013). *Somebody's daughter: The hidden story of America's prostituted children and the battle to save them.* Chicago, IL: Chicago Review Press.

Tuck, E. (2009). Suspending damage: A letter to communities. *Harvard Educational Review, 79*(3), 409–428.

Valandra. (2007). Reclaiming their lives and breaking free: An Afrocentric approach to recovery from prostitution. *Affilia—Journal of Women and Social Work, 22*(2), 195–208.

Wessells, M. G. (2006). *Child soldiers: From violence to protection.* Cambridge, MA: Harvard University Press.

White, S., & Lloyd, R. (2014). *The survivor's guide to leaving.* New York, NY: Girls Educational and Mentoring Services.

CHAPTER 2

IDENTIFICATION, ASSESSMENT, AND OUTREACH

REBECCA J. MACY, MSW, PhD, UNIVERSITY
OF NORTH CAROLINA AT CHAPEL HILL

A serious challenge for the antitrafficking field is identifying and connecting sex-trafficked and commercially sexually exploited (CSE) people with services and remedies (Andretta, Woodland, Watkins, & Barnes, 2016; Baldwin, Eisenman, Sayles, Ryan, & Chuang, 2011; Okech, Morreau, & Benson, 2011). The perpetrators and networks that promote sex trafficking and CSE seek to keep their activities and the people involved concealed. Likewise, people who have experienced trafficking may not self-identify as such and seek help for their situations because of real or perceived fears of the consequences of disclosure, as well as negative experiences with authorities and service providers in the past (Ahn et al., 2013; Andretta et al., 2016; Baldwin et al., 2011; Gallagher & Holmes, 2008). Furthermore, people who have experienced trafficking may not even realize that they can access antitrafficking remedies, services, and supports because of cultural and language barriers for foreign-born individuals and because of lack of knowledge about antitrafficking resources generally (Andretta et al., 2016; Baldwin et al., 2011; Gallagher & Holmes, 2008). For all these reasons, identification of and outreach to people who have experienced trafficking remain serious challenges in antitrafficking work.

Despite traffickers' best efforts to hide their activities, CSE and sex-trafficked persons do come into contact with health and human services sectors for a variety of reasons, such as child protection investigations, homelessness services, and routine healthcare, as a few examples (Baldwin et al., 2011). Professionals who work in service sectors with vulnerable groups of people who may be trafficked or who are at risk of trafficking, such as child welfare, healthcare, juvenile justice, gender-based violence, and housing and immigration, are critically important first-responders who can identify trafficked persons, respond with compassion, and connect trafficked persons with information, resources, and support.

Given the profession's emphasis on social justice and working with marginalized groups of people, social workers are especially well positioned to identify and connect CSE and sex-trafficked persons to services (Hodge, 2014; Kotrla, 2010; Okech et al., 2011). Unfortunately, although there are exceptions, many social workers are not trained in identifying trafficking. Further, social workers are often situated in organizations and systems that do not emphasize the issue of sex trafficking in regular service delivery (Fong & Cardoso, 2010; Goździak, 2010). Thus, social workers may encounter people who have experienced trafficking without identifying these persons as such, resulting in missed opportunities as well as inadvertent complicity with the systems that perpetuate trafficking (Okech et al., 2011). To help address these urgent practice knowledge gaps, this chapter presents recommendations for screening, assessing, and identifying CSE and trafficking across various social work settings.

Research on Identification, Assessment, and Outreach

As with any area of professional practice, recommendations for enhancing social workers' capacities for identifying and intervening in sex trafficking should be based on the best available evidence. Nevertheless, there is very little research of any kind that evaluates human-trafficking identification and intervention practices (Andretta et al., 2016; Bespalova, Morgan, & Coverdale, 2016; Cannon, Arcara, Graham, & Macy, 2016), and few studies use the most rigorous research methods (e.g., study designs with comparison groups or randomization; Dell et al., 2017; van der Laan, Smit, Busschers, & Aarten, 2011). Thus, the currently available evidence to guide social workers in identifying and intervening in human trafficking is minimal and incomplete.

To date, most screening instruments and assessment protocols have been developed by advocacy and nonprofit organizations in which systematic evaluations of recommended practices are not promoted and may not be easily conducted. With only a few exceptions (e.g., Andretta et al., 2016; Simich, Goyen, Powell, & Mallozzi, 2014), most of the resources and guidelines for practice have not been rigorously investigated or evaluated. However, such resources are nonetheless a form of practice-based evidence and can be useful to social workers in this developing area.

For all these reasons, the practice guidelines presented in this chapter draw heavily from relevant systematic reviews concerned with checklists and procedures for identifying people who are being trafficked (Ahn et al., 2013; Bespalova et al., 2016; Macy & Graham, 2012; Stoklosa, Dawson, Williams-Oni, & Rothman, 2016). After methodically gathering and analyzing materials developed by advocacy, nonprofit, and service provider organizations, the reviews determined that recommended identification tools and practices varied in their content, length, and format. Nonetheless, this practice-based knowledge represents some of the best, currently available evidence that can be used to inform trafficking identification and responses. Rigorous research on the value and efficacy of such practice-based identification protocols and tools is critically important and urgently needed. Until such evidence is produced, however, findings from these systematic reviews can help guide social work practice.

Social workers should also be concerned with the professional training and education necessary to ensure that they can successfully carry out screenings and assessments in their everyday, professional practice. Using a quasi-experimental, pre- and post-data collection design, a study of trafficking identification training determined that simply increasing the numbers of trained professionals in one community did not affect the number of telephone calls to a trafficking hotline or the number of new victim identifications (Potocky, 2011). The training interventions evaluated in this study were delivered in group settings, were one to three hours long, and addressed the following topics: definitions of human trafficking, indicators that may suggest trafficking, and recommended communication and follow-up strategies with persons who may be trafficked (e.g., contacting the local trafficking hotline number). Although preliminary, such findings suggest that, in addition to training, social workers need identification checklists, as well as standardized guidelines and procedures, to promote and ensure the successful identification of trafficked persons (Gallagher & Holmes, 2008; Stoklosa, Showalter, Melnick, & Rothman, 2016).

Much of the literature concerned with human-trafficking identification has either focused on both labor and sex trafficking or focused on human trafficking generally (e.g., Ahn et al., 2013; Bespalova et al., 2016; Simich et al., 2014). Even when researchers aimed to develop practice guidelines specifically for sex trafficking, their work drew on sources concerned with both labor and sex trafficking (e.g., Macy & Graham, 2012). Undoubtedly, there are considerable commonalities in risk factors, identification signs, and effective intervention strategies for people who have experienced labor trafficking as well as people who have experienced CSE and sex trafficking. Likewise, trafficked persons may have experienced both labor and sex trafficking. Nonetheless, there are also likely unique risk factors, identification signs, and effective intervention strategies for people who have experienced CSE and sex trafficking. These aspects of CSE and sex trafficking are not yet well known. Nonetheless, persons who have experienced CSE and sex trafficking may have specific needs that demand tailored identification and outreach strategies.

CSE and sex trafficking also intersect with many highly politicized issues, including child protection, immigration, and sex work (Decker, 2013; Sapiro, Johnson, Postmus, & Simmel, 2016). Those who work with CSE and sex trafficking must cooperate with other professions (such as child welfare, criminal justice, healthcare, housing, legal aid, and victims' advocacy) that often have very different definitions of human trafficking and outcome goals for trafficking survivors (Sapiro et al., 2016; Schwarz et al., 2016; Simich et al., 2014). At this time, federal, state, and community policies concerning the status of CSE and sex-trafficked persons are evolving toward identifying these persons as victims and survivors, emphasizing their safety and well-being, and discouraging prosecuting people for any criminal activities that are associated with their trafficking victimizations. Nonetheless, the content, interpretation, and application of such policies and laws vary across states and communities (Gallagher & Holmes, 2008). In other words, human trafficking is a complex and dynamic area of social work practice. Given the developing and shifting nature of the anti–human trafficking field, social workers are encouraged to keep abreast of policy changes at the federal, state, and especially community level.

Given all these complexities, there are no guarantees that even when trafficked persons are identified that local communities will have the systems and policies in place to ameliorate their situations (Schwarz et al., 2016). Accordingly, social workers who identify CSE and sex-trafficked persons may find that they need to be strong, persistent advocates for empowerment and protection to ensure trafficked persons' safety and well-being. They need to be well prepared to identify and respond to trafficked persons wherever they appear in the service system.

Screening, Assessment, and Identification

Given that trafficked persons can appear in various service sectors and are not likely to self-identify, all professional social workers should be (a) on the lookout for trafficking indicators among their clientele; (b) prepared to conduct brief human-trafficking screenings; and (c) prepared to sensitively and appropriately respond to survivors' immediate needs, including helping survivors with safety planning.

First and foremost, social workers must consider their professional practice approaches. The National Human Trafficking Resource Center (https://traffickingresourcecenter.org/) offers a practice tool and flow chart for medical professionals (available here: https://traffickingresourcecenter.org/resources/human-trafficking-assessment-medical-professionals) that can also be useful in screening, identifying, and responding to human trafficking. Readers are encouraged to access, review, and keep a copy of this resource available for use in their professional practice.

Trauma-Informed and Survivor-Centered Approaches

Although social workers may not be familiar with CSE and sex trafficking, many are familiar with and have training in the trauma-informed service approaches that are increasingly being used across many human service sectors (e.g., Elliott, Bjelajac, Fallot, Markoff, & Reed, 2005). Trauma-informed principles urge human service professionals and organizations to (a) recognize the effects of violence on human development and survivors' coping; (b) ensure that services are accessible and readily available for survivors; (c) address co-occurring problems concurrently and comprehensively; (d) ensure that services are culturally and linguistically relevant; (e) minimize any possibility of retraumatizing survivors; and (f) emphasize survivors' education and choice and resilience (Elliott et al., 2005). By ensuring that their practices and organizations follow such trauma-informed principles, social workers can provide a context in which CSE and sex-trafficked persons can be identified while also ensuring sensitivity and support when responding to their concerns and needs (Macy & Johns, 2011; Sapiro et al., 2016; Stoklosa, Showalter, et al., 2016).

In addition to using trauma-informed service philosophies to guide their practice, social workers should take practical steps to enhance their capacities to identify and respond to sex-trafficked persons. For example, they should post signs and literature highlighting human-trafficking information in their service settings (e.g., bathrooms, private offices, waiting rooms) to signal that their service organization is aware of trafficking and is well prepared to respond to disclosures by trafficked persons (Williamson, Dutch, & Clawson, 2010). Such signs and literature should be provided in multiple languages, along with information and text that help trafficked persons who might not yet self-identify as such to begin to recognize their situation and to realize that help is available.

Identification and Screening Strategies

Trafficking Indicators

As a first step in identifying CSE and sex-trafficked persons, social workers should be on the lookout for indicators, or "red flags," of human trafficking among their clientele. See the box at the end of this chapter for a brief checklist of these indicators. Although the presence of such indicators does not mean a client is a sex-trafficked person, it does indicate the need for further screening and investigation.

Specifically, a social worker should be aware when a client (a) is escorted by another person who will not allow the client to be alone with the social worker or speak on her or his own behalf; (b) presents as anxious, depressed, and/or fearful; (c) if foreign-born, presents with a lack of identification and/or official documents or cannot access these documents; (d) does not appear to be able to leave her or his employment or to move or pursue work and educational goals; (e) if a child or adolescent, is not attending school at all or not attending regularly; (f) if a child or adolescent, presents with belongings that are not typical (e.g., hotel keys, designer clothing, new cell phones that are appear regularly); (g) appears to be branded and/or has odd tattoos with special meanings, shows signs of physical abuse or medical neglect, and/or has untreated sexually transmitted infections; and (h) presents with answers that seem scripted and/or presents with confused information about her or his personal history and current life circumstances (Andretta et al., 2016; Bespalova et al., 2016; Macy & Graham, 2012; Schwarz et al., 2016; Stoklosa, Dawson, et al., 2016). When working with clients, all these indicators should prompt social workers to screen for CSE and sex trafficking.

In addition to these indicators, social workers are encouraged to be mindful of the known risk factors for trafficking. People appear to be at increased risk for CSE and sex trafficking when they struggle with a lack of education, family instability, housing insecurity or homelessness, poverty, and/or substance abuse; have a history of abuse, family violence, and/or trauma; have a history of involvement with systems such as child protection and foster care, as well as the criminal justice system, including juvenile justice; identify as LGBTQ+ (lesbian, gay, bisexual, transgender, queer); and have a disability, particularly an intellectual disability (Andretta et al., 2016; Macy & Graham, 2012; Reid, 2016; Sapiro et al., 2016; Schwarz et al., 2016; Stoklosa, Dawson, et al., 2016). Of course, people can experience any one or more of these life circumstances or situations without being involved with sex trafficking. Nonetheless, social workers are encouraged to be mindful of these risk factors in their work with clients. When clients present with both the risks and indicators noted here, social workers should plan to sensitively inquire and screen these clients for experiences with trafficking.

Screening Questions

Once social workers note trafficking indicators, they should screen the client using specific questions. Reviews and syntheses of practice-based guidelines suggest that social workers should ask clients about their life and situations in five areas (Andretta et al., 2016; Bespalova et al., 2016; Macy & Graham, 2012): (a) employment (How did you first hear about your job? Has anything been said or done to make you afraid to leave your job?); (b) living environments (Where do you eat and sleep? Can you come and go as you please?); (c) safety

(Is anyone forcing you to do anything that you do not want to do? Do you have to ask permission to eat, sleep, or use the bathroom?); (d) travel and immigration (for those who are foreign-born, Has your identification or documentation been taken from you? During your trip to this country, how did the people with you treat you?); and (e) relationships (Who is your boyfriend/partner? How old is he? Does he have other girlfriends/partners?). In addition to questions concerning employment, social workers should query child and adolescent clients regarding whether they can and do attend school. See the box at the end of the chapter for a brief checklist of these questions. Based on client responses from these various areas, social workers should then determine whether the client is someone who is experiencing CSE or sex trafficking. Even if the client's status is not certain or clear, social workers should err on the side of caution and offer clients support and services to address trafficking.

Not Just What Is Asked, but How It Is Asked

Practice guidelines and the research literature show that to accurately identify CSE and sex-trafficked persons, social workers must be sensitive and strive to build positive working relationships with their clients (e.g., Macy & Graham, 2012; Schwarz et al., 2016; Simich et al., 2014). Research particularly underscores the need for social workers to build trusting relationships with trafficked persons to enable them to feel comfortable responding to direct questions about sensitive human-trafficking topics (e.g., receiving money for sex; Macy & Graham, 2012; Simich et al., 2014; Williamson et al., 2010).

To develop such positive working relationships, social workers should meet with survivors alone in confidential settings, such as a private room or office in which discussions cannot be overheard. In light of one of the indicators already noted—that traffickers may escort trafficked persons to all meetings with professional helpers—social workers may need to use creativity and ingenuity to find acceptable reasons to meet with a client in private that do not raise the alarm of escorts who may be traffickers. Social workers should also ensure that screening interviews are conducted with the client's culture and language foremost in mind. To this end, social workers will need to seek out interpreters and/or cultural experts who are knowledgeable about the client's background, culture, and heritage. In seeking such consultants and interpreters, they should ensure that these persons are (a) well trained in interpretation; (b) safe members of the community who are in no way involved in human trafficking; and (c) individuals who can also interpret and assist the client in a nonjudgmental, supportive, and confidential manner.

Importantly, when considering how best to implement screening questions and discussions with clients, social workers should explain their role as service

providers and the confidentiality policies under which they are bound, especially any limits to confidentiality (e.g., Macy & Graham, 2012). Social workers
are bound by their professional codes, their organizational policies, and their
jurisdiction's laws and policies concerning the confidentiality of the information that clients disclose. Such laws and policies mean, for example, that they
may be required to contact child protection and/or law enforcement authorities
if they learn that clients or others are in danger, particularly if the client(s) or
others are minors (under the age of eighteen).

Although such policy requirements exist, little practice or research literature has studied how social workers should report to child protection and/
or law enforcement in such a way that also ensures survivors' confidentiality,
safety, self-determination, and well-being. Given that anti-trafficking policies
and services vary considerably from community to community, reports to child
protection and/or law enforcement authorities may not lead to enhanced safety
and/or beneficial services for survivors (English, 2017). Thus, before reaching
out to child protection and/or law enforcement in response to human trafficking, social workers are urged to develop collaborative relationships with child
protection workers and law enforcement officers who are knowledgeable and
prepared to respond to human-trafficking crimes and survivors. By establishing positive working relationships with well-informed child protection and law
enforcement professionals in their local community, social workers may be able
to ensure positive outcomes for survivors when such reports are made.

In addition, social workers should help clients understand the consequences
of social workers' professional reporting requirements so that clients can disclose only as much information as they are comfortable disclosing. Thus, social
workers should alert clients to any limits to confidentiality as early as possible
in the screening interview. These discussions may initially discourage survivors from disclosing their circumstances and experiences. Nevertheless, this
transparency may help build trusting relationships with trafficked persons over
time, as well as help inform and prepare trafficked persons for disclosures to
other social workers in the future.

Initial Response and Safety Planning

Nearly all recommended guidelines direct professionals who encounter
human-trafficking survivors to contact the National Human Trafficking Resource
Center (1-888-373-7888; https://polarisproject.org/national-human-trafficking
-resource-center). This nationwide, toll-free phone line provides responses
in over two hundred languages and guidance on local resources (Ahn et al.,
2013; Bespalova et al., 2016). Some practice-based guidelines recommend
that providers contact law enforcement, especially when survivors' situations

pose immediate danger (Macy & Graham, 2012). Before contacting local law enforcement, social workers should seek and obtain survivors' consent and permission to do so (Stoklosa, Showalter, et al., 2016). As mentioned earlier, before reaching out to law enforcement, social workers should also have established relationships with officers who are knowledgeable and prepared to respond to human trafficking.

Unfortunately, there is little guidance in the literature concerning recommended practices for developing effective and robust safety plans for persons who are currently experiencing CSE and sex trafficking, including what strategies should be used and what resources could be most helpful for trafficked persons (Macy & Graham, 2012; Schwarz et al., 2016). Nonetheless, recommendations do strongly encourage social workers to work with trafficked persons to develop safety plans that are individualized and tailored to their needs (see chapter 3). Furthermore, growing numbers of communities are developing aftercare services for survivors, as well as community protocols for responding to CSE and sex trafficking. If social workers are fortunate enough to work in communities and settings where such protocols and services exist, they are urged to use these resources when working with trafficked persons to develop safety plans.

Screening: Successful Outcomes

In the best possible scenario, social work professionals will execute the recommended screening and response guidelines just presented in ways that lead to trafficking identification, tailored safety plans, and connections to helpful services that enable survivors to exit their trafficking situations. In turn, these initial interventions will lead people who have experienced trafficking into long-term, safe, confidential services that promote their resilience and recovery. It is more likely, however, that such identification will take time, repeated contacts, and the development of a trusting relationship between the trafficked person and the social worker. Further complicating this reality is the likelihood that people who have experienced trafficking may not be able or allowed to interact with the same social worker repeatedly. For example, they may be relocated and thus not able to build relationships with social workers.

Accordingly, all social workers should be well prepared to (a) screen and ask about human trafficking; (b) listen and respond in ways that affirm the trafficked person and do not blame that person; (c) offer helpful resources and referrals; and (d) offer themselves as a nonjudgmental resource for the future. One contact between a social worker and a trafficked person might not lead to a safety plan. However, that one contact—if positive and helpful—may lead the trafficked person to seek help from another social worker in the future.

Practical Assessment Questions and Strategies

For most social workers who are situated in typical social service settings, guidance on brief screening tools (as already described), identification, and immediate response may be sufficient. However, for social workers who are working directly with human-trafficking survivors and/or working in settings where they need to conduct in-depth assessments of clients' situations, the Vera Institute of Justice Trafficking Victim Identification Tool (https://storage. googleapis.com/vera-web-assets/downloads/Publications/out-of-the-shadows-identification-of-victims-of-human-trafficking/legacy_downloads/ human-trafficking-identification-tool-and-user-guidelines.pdf) will be helpful.

The Institute of Justice in-depth identification tool assesses key dimensions of human trafficking by asking questions in three domains: migration, work, and working and living conditions (Simich et al., 2014). See the box at the end of the chapter for a brief checklist summary of these domains. In the domain of migration, which is relevant for clients who are foreign-born, the instrument addresses topics such as how the client came to be in the United States, how the client's travel to the United States was arranged, and who was involved with the client's travel and migration. In the domain of work, the instrument queries clients for details concerning unpaid and unofficial work, work for which the client believes he or she was not paid adequately, and whether the client feels unsafe in his, her, or their living and working environments. In the domain of living and working conditions, the instrument queries clients concerning living at the same place where they are also working, being able to leave the living or work situation freely, being monitored in their living or work situations, being tricked or pressured into work, and being threatened with being reported to authorities (e.g., child protection, criminal justice, immigration).

The tool is available at no cost (see the website just listed) in both a comprehensive and shorter version. Both versions are available in English and Spanish. Readers are urged to download and review the full instrument before using these questions with clients and trafficked persons. In rigorous pilot testing, the tool was determined to be reliable in distinguishing both sex and labor trafficking across diverse clients, including by age, gender, and country of origin (Simich et al., 2014).

The guidelines accompanying the instrument underscore the points already discussed regarding how such questions are asked, such as building a trusting relationship, asking direct questions in a sensitive manner, and emphasizing the survivor's safety, support, and well-being. Likewise, the administration guidelines recommend that social workers administer the instrument with clients who are known to the social worker and the service organization in which the assessment is being conducted. In other words, social workers should not administer this assessment to trafficked persons at a first meeting or in a brief interview. Ideally, this detailed instrument will be administered over more than one meeting to give the trafficked person the opportunity to tell her, his, or their story and to help manage any feelings of trauma that may arise from such discussions.

Implications for Practice

As readers can tell from the recommendations for screening, assessment, identification, and response just presented, the identification of CSE and sex-trafficked persons is not likely to happen if left to self-disclosure or happenstance. Social workers—as well as readers from other professions and disciples—should be mindful that screening tools, guidelines, and protocols, as well as sensitivity, care, and concern, are all necessary to create an environment in which sex-trafficked persons can disclose their experience and be connected with the appropriate resources and supports. Thus, social work practitioners are urged to seek out training and education in trafficking identification and response. Ideally such training will not only inform social workers of indicators and recommendations for responses, but also enable them to practice and hone their skills for asking questions appropriately and sensitively. Such training should also help prepare social workers to develop safety plans for sex-trafficked persons that are contextualized to the resources, supports, and realities that exist in the communities in which they practice.

To ensure that the issue of CSE and sex trafficking is regularly addressed in all aspects of client services, leaders of social work organizations should seek to develop systematic organizational protocols and policies for screening and identifying sex-trafficked persons. Such protocols and practices should include regular trainings for social workers and include refresher trainings once staff have completed initial trainings.

Social workers are also encouraged to engage in community outreach efforts. They can help identify CSE and sex-trafficked persons by seeking to inform and educate their communities about trafficking, including its prevalence, its types, its warning signs, and trafficking survivors' rights and remedies, as well as available resources (Kotrla, 2010; Okech et al., 2011). With growing public interest in CSE and sex trafficking, social workers may find that they are readily invited to network with community groups, neighborhood watches, nonprofit organizations, religious organizations, schools, and youth groups. By educating their wider communities about the problems of CSE and sex trafficking, social workers can help facilitate identification of trafficked persons, as well as potentially increase resources and supports to help sustain their organizations' antitrafficking efforts.

In a related vein, social workers are encouraged to build and strengthen interagency collaborations among the various professional sectors that are working to address and ameliorate human trafficking, including child welfare, the court system, juvenile justice, law enforcement, emergency shelters, and victim advocates (Boxill & Richardson, 2005; Okech et al., 2011; Schwarz et al., 2016). Such interagency connections can help ensure that social workers can provide all necessary services to trafficked persons once they are identified.

Last but not least, social workers are encouraged to document and evaluate promising practices for trafficking identification and response, including promising approaches for training and educating social work professionals. As discussed earlier, the limited evidence and lack of research on trafficking identification represent a serious gap in the practice knowledge for social work professionals who seek to ameliorate trafficking and help survivors. Likewise, effective interventions for addressing CSE and sex trafficking will undoubtedly evolve given that this is a complex and dynamic area of professional practice. As Simich and colleagues (2014) stated: "translating this knowledge [about human trafficking] into practice is just beginning" (p. 238). As professionals who are concerned with social justice and human rights, social workers can and should take the lead in developing practice knowledge into evidence regarding how best to identify and connect people who are sex-trafficked with services, remedies, and hope. Practitioners learn effective practices from experience, developing practice-based evidence. Practice knowledge, or "practice-based evidence" can provide a basis for future research to then develop "evidence-based practice."

Indicators, Topics, and Questions for Identifying, Assessing, and Assisting Sex-Trafficked and Commercially Sexually Exploited People

Indicators of Trafficking (Andretta et al., 2016; Bespalova et al., 2016; Macy & Graham, 2012; Schwarz et al., 2016; Stoklosa, Dawson, et al., 2016)

- **Accompanied:** Is escorted by another person who will not allow the client to be alone with the social worker or speak on her or his own behalf
- **Distressed Affect:** Presents as anxious, depressed, and/or fearful
- **Lack of Identification (for those who are foreign-born):** Presents with a lack of identification and/or official documents or cannot access these documents
- **Lack of Freedom:** Does not appear to be able to leave their employment or to move or pursue their work and educational goals

- **Not Attending School:** If child or adolescent, is not attending school at all or not attending regularly
- **Unlikely Belongings:** If child or adolescent, presents with belongings that are not typical (e.g., hotel keys, designer clothing, new cell phones that are appear regularly)
- **Physical Signs:** Branding and/or odd tattoos, evidence of physical abuse or medical neglect, or untreated sexually transmitted infections
- **Rehearsed and/or Confused:** Presents with answers that seem scripted and/or presents with confused information about personal history and current life circumstances

Screening Topics and Example Questions (Andretta et al., 2016; Bespalova et al., 2016; Macy & Graham, 2012)

- **Employment:** How did you first hear about your job? Has anything been said or done to make you afraid to leave your job? Can you attend school, and do you attend school?
- **Living environments:** Where do you eat and sleep? Can you come and go as you please?
- **Safety:** Is anyone forcing you to do anything that you do not want to do? Do you have to ask permission to eat, sleep, or use the bathroom?
- **Travel and immigration (for those who are foreign-born):** Has your identification or documentation been taken from you? During your trip to this country, how did the people with you treat you?
- **Relationships:** Who is your boyfriend/partner? How old is he? Does he have other girlfriends/partners?

Assessment Topics and Example Questions (Simich et al., 2014; see the full instrument for details and before using these questions with clients and trafficked persons)

- **Migration (for those who are foreign-born):** How did you come to the United States? How was your travel to the United States arranged? Who was involved with your migration?
- **Work:** Do you do unpaid and unofficial work? Do you do work for which you believe you have not been paid adequately? Do you feel unsafe in your living and working environments?
- **Living and Working Conditions:** Are you living at the same place where you're working? Are you able to leave the living or work situation freely? Are you monitored in your living or work situation? Are you tricked or pressured into work? Are you threatened with being reported to authorities (e.g., child protection, criminal justice, immigration) by anyone in your living or work situation?

References

Ahn, R., Alpert, E. J., Purcell, G., Konstantopoulos, W. M., McGahan, A., Cafferty, E., et al. (2013). Human trafficking: Review of educational resources for health professionals. *American Journal of Preventive Medicine, 44*(3), 283–289. doi:10.1016/j.amepre.2012.10.025

Andretta, J. R., Woodland, M. H., Watkins, K. M., & Barnes, M. E. (2016). Towards the discreet identification of commercial sexual exploitation of children (CSEC) victims and individualized interventions: Science to practice. *Psychology, Public Policy, and Law.* Advance online publication. doi: 10.1037/law0000087

Baldwin, S. B., Eisenman, D. P., Sayles, J. N., Ryan, G., & Chuang, K. S. (2011). Identification of human trafficking victims in health care settings. *Health and Human Rights: Natural Disasters and Humanitarian Emergencies, 13*(1), 36–49. Retrieved from http://www.jstor.org/stable/healhumarigh.13.1.36

Bespalova, N., Morgan, J., & Coverdale, J. (2016). A pathway to freedom: An evaluation of screening tools for the identification of trafficking victims. *Academic Psychiatry, 40*(1), 124–128. doi:10.1007/s40596-014-0245-1

Boxill, N. A., & Richardson, D. J. (2005). A community's response to the sex trafficking of children. *The Link: Connecting Juvenile Justice and Child Welfare, 3*(1), 3. Retrieved from http://66.227.70.18/programs/juvenilejustice/thelink2005winter.pdf

Cannon, A. C., Arcara, J., Graham, L. M., & Macy, R. J. (2016). Trafficking and health: A systematic review of research methods. *Trauma, Violence, & Abuse.* doi:10.1177/1524838016650187

Decker, M. R. (2013). Sex trafficking, sex work, and violence: Evidence for a new era. *International Journal of Gynecology and Obstetrics, 120*(2), 113–114. doi:10.1016/j.ijgo.2012.11.001

Dell, N. A., Maynard, B. R., Born, K. R., Wagner, E., Atkins, B., & House, W. (2017). Helping survivors of human trafficking: A systematic review of exit and post exit interventions. *Trauma, Violence, & Abuse.* doi:10.1177/1524838017692553

Elliott, D. E., Bjelajac, P., Fallot, R. D., Markoff, L. S., & Reed, B. G. (2005). Trauma-informed or trauma-denied: Principles and implementation of trauma-informed services for women. *Journal of Community Psychology, 33*(4), 461–477. doi:10.1002/jcop.20063

English, A. (2017). Mandatory reporting of human trafficking: Potential benefits and risks of harm. *AMA Journal of Ethics, 19*(1), 54–62. Retrieved from http://journalofethics.ama-assn.org/2017/01/pfor1-1701.html

Fong, R., & Cardoso, J. B. (2010). Child human trafficking victims: Challenges for the child welfare system. *Evaluation and Program Planning, 33*(3), 311–316. doi:10.1016/j.evalprogplan.2009.06.018

Gallagher, A., & Holmes, P. (2008). Developing an effective criminal justice response to human trafficking lessons from the front line. *International Criminal Justice Review, 18*(3), 318–343. doi:10.1177/1057567708320746

Goździak, E. M. (2010). Identifying child victims of trafficking. *Criminology & Public Policy, 9*(2), 245–255. doi:10.1111/j.1745-9133.2010.00623.x

Hodge, D. R. (2014). Assisting victims of human trafficking: Strategies to facilitate identification, exit from trafficking, and the restoration of wellness. *Social Work, 59*(2), 111–118. doi:10.1093/sw/swu002

Kotrla, K. (2010). Domestic minor sex trafficking in the United States. *Social Work, 55*(2), 181–187. doi:10.1093/sw/55.2.181

Macy, R. J., & Graham, L. (2012). Identifying domestic and international sex-trafficking victims during human service provision. *Trauma, Violence, & Abuse, 13*(2), 59–76. doi:10.1177/1524838012440340

Macy, R. J., & Johns, N. (2011). Aftercare services for international sex trafficking survivors: Informing U.S. service and program development in an emerging practice area. *Trauma, Violence, & Abuse, 12*(2), 87–98. doi:10.1177/1524838010390709

Okech, D., Morreau, W., & Benson, K. (2011).Human trafficking: Improving victim identification and service provision. *International Social Work, 55*(4), 488–503. doi:10.1177/0020872811425805

Potocky, M. (2011). Human trafficking training and identification of international victims in the United States. *Journal of Immigrant & Refugee Studies, 9*(2), 196–199. doi:10.1080/15562948.2011.567159

Reid, J. A. (2016). Sex trafficking of girls with intellectual disabilities: An exploratory mixed methods study. *Sexual Abuse: A Journal of Research and Treatment.* doi:10.1177/1079063216630981

Sapiro, B., Johnson, L., Postmus, J. L., & Simmel, C. (2016). Supporting youth involved in domestic minor sex trafficking: Divergent perspectives on youth agency. *Child Abuse & Neglect, 58*, 99–110. doi:10.1016/j.chiabu.2016.06.019

Schwarz, C., Unruh, E., Cronin, K., Evans-Simpson, S., Britton, H., & Ramaswamy, M. (2016). Human trafficking identification and service provision in the medical and social service sectors. *Health & Human Rights: An International Journal, 18*(1), 181–191.

Simich, L., Goyen, L., Powell, A., & Mallozzi, K. (2014). *Improving human trafficking victim identification: Validation and dissemination of a screening tool.* New York, NY. Vera Institute of Justice. Retrieved from https://www.ncjrs.gov/pdffiles1/nij/grants/246712.pdf

Stoklosa, H., Dawson, M. B., Williams-Oni, F., & Rothman, E. F. (2016): A review of U.S. health care institution protocols for the identification and treatment of victims of human trafficking. *Journal of Human Trafficking, 3*(2), 116–124. doi:10.1080/23322705.2016.1187965

Stoklosa, H., Showalter, E., Melnick, A., & Rothman, E. F. (2016): Health care providers' experience with a protocol for the identification, treatment, and referral of human-trafficking victims. *Journal of Human Trafficking.* doi:10.1080/23322705.2016.1194668

Van Der Laan, P., Smit, M., Busschers, I., & Aarten, P. (2011). Cross-border trafficking in human beings: Prevention and intervention strategies for reducing sexual exploitation: A systematic review. *Campbell Systematic Reviews, 7*(9). doi:10.4073/csr.2011.9

Williamson, E., Dutch, N. M., & Clawson, H. J. (2010). *Medical treatment of victims of sexual assault and domestic violence and its applicability to victims of human trafficking.* U.S. Department of Health and Human Services, Office of the Assistant Secretary for Planning and Evaluation, Washington, DC. Retrieved from https://aspe.hhs.gov/report/medical-treatment-victims-sexual-assault-and-domestic-violence-and-its-applicability-victims-human-trafficking

SAFETY PLANNING WITH SURVIVORS OF SEX TRAFFICKING AND COMMERCIAL SEXUAL EXPLOITATION

ABBY HOWARD, MSW, LCSW, UNIVERSITY OF DENVER

AMBER SUTTON, MSW, LMSW SAFEHOUSE OF SHELBY COUNTY

S urvivors of sex trafficking commonly experience high rates of exploitation and abuse, both of which increase their risk of revictimization and the likelihood that they will experience trauma symptoms or trauma bonding (Barasch & Kryszko, 2013; Herman, 1997). Safety planning with survivors is a crucial intervention for both reducing harm and preventing victimization, as trafficking usually involves prolonged and repeated exposure to trauma and the resulting serious or persistent mental health conditions such as depression, anxiety, or personality disorders (Clawson, Salomon, & Grace, 2007). Practitioners working with this population must be aware that survivors may return to the trafficking situation several times before successfully leaving; therefore, safety plans are not just for those trying to leave but also for individuals choosing to stay.

While research on best practices for working with survivors of sex trafficking is still a relatively new and growing field, it is imperative that safety planning and other intervention measures are established in evidence-based frameworks. As evidence-based practices specific to survivors of sex trafficking are being developed, practitioners can look to models drawn from the practice field of intimate partner violence/domestic violence, as well as protocols designed by organizations working with trafficked and exploited people, to tailor and individualize their responses to the safety needs of survivors of sex trafficking. This chapter seeks to do the following: (1) discuss the correlation between intimate partner violence/domestic violence situations and sex trafficking/commercial sexual exploitation; (2) describe the history and purpose of safety plans; (3) outline the key principles of survivor-centered advocacy, a foundation for safety planning; (4) offer recommendations for assessing risks and safety planning with trafficking survivors; and (5) discuss important considerations for safety planning, including working with law enforcement, dealing with technology concerns, and helping those experiencing co-occurring physical or mental health issues.

There are some limitations and important considerations to note in this chapter as well. First, this chapter focuses primarily on safety planning within the United States and does not discuss the various cultural contexts that must be considered when working with survivors of sex trafficking in different countries. Second, this chapter addresses safety planning with adults, not minors, as a minor in a sex-trafficking case would require mandated reporting and involvement of children's services, and the ability to help children staying in a trafficking situation would be limited.

Parallels of Sex Trafficking and Commercial Sexual Exploitation with IPV

Sex trafficking shares many common denominators with intimate partner violence/domestic violence (IPV/DV). Both are forms of gender-based violence that are marked by patterns of control and that are able to distort survivors' ability to trust others, increase levels of posttraumatic stress and depression, and inflict other extensive emotional damage (Interface Children Family Services, n.d.). *Gender-based violence* is a term used to describe violence that occurs because of the patriarchal societal expectations associated with gender and the greater power of cismales compared to ciswomen and transgender men and women (Shakil, 2016, p. 121). While there is no question that trafficking can be perpetrated by females and that males can be victims, it is important to note that individuals identifying as female, including cisgender and transgender females, experience many more forms of sexual violence and exploitation than cisgender males.

When the traffickers are parents, family members, or, in many cases, the boyfriends/girlfriends or partners of the survivor, domestic violence and sex trafficking often co-occur. According to research on survivors of domestic minor sex trafficking, over 44 percent report that the person who is exploiting or pimping them out is also their boyfriend (Barasch & Kryszko, 2013). A study of social service providers working with survivors of sex trafficking compounded these findings, stating that "the majority of social service providers who worked with sex trafficking survivors maintained that pimps posing as boyfriends represented one of the most common forms of sex trafficking" (Heil & Nichols, 2015, p. 58). Yet traffickers/exploiters are not always intimate partners, and sometimes a third party is not present—as in cases of survival sex, where someone trades or sells sex to have basic needs met.

Survivors of sex trafficking and commercial sexual exploitation, like those of IPV/DV, encounter and endure emotional, physical, sexual, and psychological abuse at the hands of their traffickers. Traffickers use similar techniques to those who abuse and batter; the goal is to create barriers for survivors, making it incredibly difficult to leave. These techniques include coercion and control, isolation, loss of autonomy, and traumatic bonding. But while there are several similarities and even co-occurring cases of IPV/DV and sex trafficking, practitioners should be aware that trafficked and sexually exploited people may have distinct safety planning needs that cannot be gleaned from the wealth of research on IPV/DV. For example, in some trafficking situations, survivors may experience abuse at the hands of several different perpetrators, including traffickers, buyers of commercial sex, and "wife-in-laws."[1] However, because of the large overlap in dynamics between the two fields, it is useful for practitioners working with sex trafficking and sexual exploitation survivors to build on the work from the IPV/DV field.

What Is Safety Planning?

It is suggested that safety planning originated around the 1970s as the battered women's movement identified research on best practices for increasing safety and reducing risk among survivors of domestic violence. Advocates found that empowering survivors in regards to their specific safety risks, both life- and partner-generated, could not only reduce their risk of harm but potentially help them leave a violent situation (Davies & Lyon, 2014). Davies and Lyon (2014) define life-generated risks as "risks associated with circumstances over which a person has little or no control, whereas partner-generated risks are dangers that result directly from what the partners do" (p. 19). For the purpose of this chapter, partner-generated risks will be referred to as "trafficker-generated risks." The following box provides examples of both life- and trafficker-generated risks.

The National Domestic Violence Hotline defines a safety plan as a "personalized and practical plan that includes ways to remain safe while in the relationship, planning to leave, or after a survivor has left" (National Domestic Violence Hotline, 2015). A safety plan is intended to comprehensively address the realistic situation of a survivor, including the physical, psychological, children-related, relational, financial, familial, and legal risks of both staying and leaving (Davies & Lyon, 2014). Focusing solely on physical violence does not take into account the other risks a survivor is considering when deciding to stay or leave a violent situation. Safety plans are most effective when they are

Life- and Trafficker-Generated Risks

Life-Generated Risks

- Economic Distress/Poverty
- Lack of Employment
- Physical Health Conditions
- Stigma/Discrimination
- Home Location/Access to Transportation
- Mental or Emotional Health Conditions
- Lack of Support

Trafficker-Generated Risks

- Physical Injury, Death, STD/STI
- Psychological Harm/Abuse, Suicidality
- Abuse of Children, Risk of Losing Children to Partner
- Loss of Income/Job, Loss of Housing, Damaged Possessions
- Threats to Friends/Family, Loss of Support from Friends/Family
- Loss of Relationship with Partner
- Loss of Residency Status, Arrests/Legal Repercussion

Source: Adapted from *Domestic Violence Advocacy* (Davies & Lyon, 2014).

individualized, client-centered, continuous, and not solely focused on the survivor leaving the trafficking situation (Siniscalchi & Morris, 2014).

Survivor-Centered Advocacy Approaches to Safety Planning

The most well-researched and documented form of safety planning to date is victim-defined or victim-centered advocacy, which was established by Jill Davies and Eleanor Lyon from their research and work in communities in the late 1990s through the Model Court Response Project (Davies & Lyon, 2014). Victim-centered advocacy, which today is more commonly called as survivor-centered advocacy (SCA), respects the autonomy and self-determination of each survivor and understands that safety planning is not simply a single act, but rather a dynamic process that involves continual relationship building and risk analysis with the survivor to establish "a partnership for safety" (Davies & Lyon, 2014, p. 89).

Forming a rapport with a survivor increases the effectiveness of the safety plan; however, some practitioners may have difficulty honoring the survivor's right to self-determination if they disagree with the survivor's choices or fear that those choices could put the survivor at greater risk. My Sister's Place (MSP), which was founded in New York in 1976 and provides services to both IPV/DV and human-trafficking survivors, reminds practitioners that both IPV/DV and human-trafficking survivors are "natural safety planners," and yet some of the safety measures taken by survivors may appear to be risky to those outside the situation, including service providers (Siniscalchi & Morris, 2014, p. 4). Practitioners should also be aware of the potential of setting up a power dynamic and hierarchical relationship between themselves and the survivor, which would limit their ability to collaborate and see survivors as the experts on their situation. To foster this rapport and effectively begin assessing for risk, practitioners should consider the seven key principles of SCA (Davies & Lyon, 2014), discussed in the following sections.

Start with a Survivor's Concerns

A service provider may consider sex trafficking or commercial exploitation to be the highest concern; however, it is important to meet survivors where they are and determine what they want to discuss first. A service provider might start a session by saying, "I'm glad you came in to see me today. Where would you like to start?" to honor the survivor's right to self-determination and to first seek to understand the survivor's current perspective.

Listen Effectively

Practitioners need to utilize paraphrasing and summarizing skills to ensure that they understand the survivor's perspective and goals. An example of summarizing with a survivor would be "It sounds like you are feeling scared to leave for the following reasons . . ."

Invite Conversation with Open-Ended Questions

Open-ended questions create a space for survivors to share openly and freely about their situation, whereas closed-ended questions can often lead to simple "Yes" or "No" answers that could limit the exploration process, thus reducing the ability to form a comprehensive safety plan. A practitioner trying to assess what the survivor has tried in the past could ask, "What have you tried in the past to leave? How effective was it?"[2]

Use Common Language as Opposed to Professional Jargon

Many common terms and phrases in the antitrafficking advocacy world, such as *human trafficking, exploitation, abuser, batterer,* and *enslavement,* will rarely be used by the survivor, and if used by the practitioner, could build resistance or weaken the rapport. Seeking first to understand the language the survivor uses and mirroring that language, such as by using *boyfriend* instead of *trafficker,* will build trust. Furthermore, when introducing a safety plan, using common terminology rather than clinical terms will increase willingness and engagement on the part of the survivor. An example of lay terminology for describing safety planning could sound like "I'd like to talk about ways to help you stay as safe as possible today."

Speak in a Survivor's Primary Language and Use Interpreter Services When Needed

It is best practice to always use a neutral, third-party interpreter to reduce the risk of a trafficker or someone connected to the trafficker falsely interpreting on the survivor's behalf and returning the survivor to the trafficking situation. A presentation by the St. Louis Rescue & Restore Coalition (STLRRC) described a case of a non-English-speaking woman from Bosnia being trafficked in St. Louis (Howard, 2012). When law enforcement agents came in contact with the survivor, they did not use a third-party neutral interpreter and instead someone the woman knew. Unbeknownst to the law enforcement agents at the time, the "interpreter" was also connected to the trafficker, and the woman continued to be trafficked for another few years before she was able to escape and become connected with a local survivors' group.

Validate the Survivor

Validation is a strength-based skill that not only builds rapport but also helps increase the survivor's sense of self-efficacy. If practitioners focus on survivors' strengths and what they have done that was effective in the past, survivors may have more confidence in their ability to make change. One example of a validation for a survivor who is trying to protect her children is "It sounds like you have been through a lot and managed to the best of your ability. You obviously care very deeply for your children."

Create a Safe Space to Talk and Explain Confidentiality Policies and Legal Protections

Consider meeting in private locations where the survivor can freely disclose, but also consider external variables that could contribute to how safe survivors feel, such as whether the door is blocked and whether they have easy access to leave if they feel triggered or unsafe for any reason.

Assessing Risks of Trafficking and Sexual Exploitation and Making Safety Plans

In order to form an effective safety plan, a practitioner must first be aware of the red flags and signs of a trafficking or sexually exploitive situation. Depending on whether a survivor is currently living with a trafficker, attempting to leave, or has recently left, different red flags and risk factors may be present. The following box outlines some of the key assessment questions to ask when a person is

Trafficker-Generated Risks: Staying and Leaving

Assessing the Risk of Physical Harm

Staying with the Trafficker

- Does your partner [trafficker] hit you?
- How many times a week?
- Does your partner [trafficker] force you to have sex?
- How many times a week?
- Does your partner [trafficker] refuse to practice safe sex?

Attempting to Leave the Trafficker

- Does your partner [trafficker] threaten to harm you physically?
- Does your partner [trafficker] threaten to kill you or hurt or kill someone you love or care about?
- Does your partner [trafficker] threaten to sexually assault you?

Assessing the Risk of Psychological Harm

Staying with the Trafficker

- Does your partner [trafficker] use verbal or emotionally abusive tactics?
- What are they?
- How do they impact you?
- Does your partner [trafficker] force you to take drugs or use alcohol?
- Do you think about suicide?
- Do you think about homicide?

Attempting to Leave the Trafficker

- Does your partner [trafficker] continue to use emotionally abusive tactics with you?
- Does your partner have contact with you?
- What type of contact is it and how frequent?
- Do you use substances to cope with the stress?
- Do you think about suicide?
- Do you think about homicide?

Assessing Financial Risk

Staying with the Trafficker

- Does your partner [trafficker] control your money or make decisions on what you can buy?
- Does your partner [trafficker] limit how much you can work or take the money you make?
- Does your partner [trafficker] keep your identification documents such as ID, Social Security card, etc.?
- Does your partner [trafficker] destroy or damage your personal items?

Attempting to Leave the Trafficker

- Does your partner [trafficker] have access to your bank accounts or places you keep your money?
- Do you have access to your driver's license or Social Security card?
- Does your trafficker have these items in his or her possession?

Source: Adapted from *Safety Planning with Battered Women: Complex Lives/Difficult Choices* (Davies, Lyon, & Monti-Catania, 1998, pp. 50–52).

staying with a trafficker and when a person is attempting to leave or has recently left a trafficker. The questions can be used for several purposes besides assessment; for example, they can help practitioners expand their own understanding of the individual's trafficking experience. Furthermore, these questions allow the practitioner to hear from survivors what they have already tried, how they perceive their situation, and the types of risk they experience. It can be tempting to encourage leaving as the only solution, but without a thorough assessment a practitioner could unknowingly increase the risk to a survivor if the survivor fears the trafficker would become more lethal when she or he attempts to leave. The authors assume that the agencies and individuals asking these questions have already received or will be receiving training in providing resources to the survivor regarding the responses to these questions (e.g., harm reduction, substance use, safer sex practices, suicide assessment, and financial literacy).

Phone-Based Safety Planning

Depending on the type of service an agency provides, safety plans could be administered over the phone or in person. For practitioners facilitating a safety plan over the phone, the protocol presented in table 3.1 can be followed to ensure the safety of not only the survivor but also of the practitioner and anyone else involved in the survivor's life who could be impacted by the trafficker. After these initial phone safety assessment questions have been completed, the practitioner can begin completing the safety plan with the survivor based on the skills and assessment questions described in the previous sections of this chapter.

Lethality Assessments

Another tool that advocates and survivors can make part of a safety plan is a lethality assessment. A lethality assessment is a series of questions and statements to help advocates identify survivors who are at highest risk of serious injury or death due to violence by their intimate partner or trafficker. There are certain factors that increase risk for lethality, including a trafficker's access to weapons, forced sex, drug and alcohol history, jealousy, and employment status (unemployed/underemployed). By conducting a lethality assessment with victims, the advocate is able to communicate concerns to the victims and connect them with appropriate resources. There are several lethality assessments available, including the Maryland Model, created by the Maryland Network Against Domestic Violence; the Mosaic Method created by Gavin de Becker; and the Danger Assessment created by Dr. Jacquelyn Campbell. The following box provides an example of the Campbell Danger Assessment. The questions can be modified depending on the gender of the trafficker/survivor.

TABLE 3.1 Protocol for Over-the-Phone Safety Plan

Assessment Question	Resource Provided and Additional Steps
1. Are you in a safe location to talk with me? If YES proceed to Question 8 If NO proceed to Question 2	
2. Is it safe to leave the location where you currently are?	
3. Where can you go?	• Provide recommendations such as "Safe Places," gas stations, restaurants, etc. • Document the location and phone number
4. Is there anyone you trust who can meet you there (police, friend, neighbor, etc.)?	• If survivors cannot call a person to meet them there, offer to get the number and contact the person on their behalf.
5. Do you have a safe place to sleep?	• Provide referrals for shelters, hotlines, and possible resources, depending on survivors' needs.
6. Do you have transportation, and do you know how to get there?	• Provide referrals and assistance with directions.
7. If survivors can't leave on their own, ask the following questions: Why isn't it safe to leave on your own? Would it be safe to leave at a different time and call me back? Would it be safe to have someone come pick you up (police, friend, service provider)?	
8. If YES, ask the following questions: How long is it safe for me to stay on the phone with you?	
9. If you feel unsafe at any time and want to hang up, is there a safe word we can use?	• Clarify and confirm a safe word.
10. Is it okay for us to call you back?	• If, YES, get the phone number for calling back. • Document plan for contacting the survivor back if that is an option.
11. Can you call us back? What would you like us to do if we don't hear from you by a certain time?	• Document plan for the survivor to call back, or what the survivor would like you to do if not heard from.

Source: Adapted from *Polaris Project National Human Trafficking Crisis Response Protocol*, pp. 94–97. https://polarisproject.org/sites/default/files/Polaris-Global-Toolkit.pdf

Lethality Assessment for Trafficking Survivors

Using a calendar, mark the approximate dates during the past year when you were beaten by your trafficker or partner. Write on that date how bad the incident was according to the following scale:

1. Slapping, pushing; no injuries and/or lasting pain
2. Punching, kicking; bruises, cuts, and/or lasting pain
3. "Beating up"; severe contusions, burns, broken bones
4. Threat to use weapons; head injury, internal injury, permanent injury
5. Use of weapons; wounds from weapon

   (If ANY of the descriptions for the higher number apply, use the higher number.)

Mark YES or NO for each of the following. ("He" refers to your trafficker, partner, husband/wife, ex, or whoever is currently physically hurting you.)

___1. Has the physical violence increased in severity or frequency over the past year?

___2. Has he ever used a weapon against you or threatened you with a weapon?

___3. Does he ever try to choke you?

___4. Does he own a gun?

___5. Has he ever forced you to have sex when you did not wish to do so?

___6. Does he use drugs? By drugs, I mean "uppers," amphetamines, speed, angel dust, cocaine, "crack," street drugs, or mixtures.

___7. Does he threaten to kill you and/or do you believe he is capable of killing you?

___8. Is he drunk every day or almost every day (in terms of quantity of alcohol)?

___9. Does he control most or all of your daily activities? For instance: does he tell you who you can be friends with, when you can see your family, how much money you can use, or when you can take the car? (If he tries, but you do not let him, check here:____)

___10. Have you ever been beaten by him while you were pregnant? (If you have ever been pregnant by him, check here:___)

___11. Is he violently or constantly jealous of you? (For instance, does he say, "If I can't have you, no one can"?)

___12. Have you ever threatened or tried to commit suicide?

___13. Has he ever threatened or tried to commit suicide?

___14. Does he threaten to harm your children?

___15. Do you have a child that is not his?

___16. Is he unemployed?

___17. Have you left him during the past year? (If you *never* lived with him, check here: ____)

___18. Do you currently have another (different) intimate partner?

___19. Does he follow or spy on you, leave threatening notes, destroy your property, or call you when you don't want him to?

___ Total "Yes" Answers

The following questions may also be used to assess not only the level of risk but also how clients perceive their current situation; the purpose is to further build rapport, understanding, and trust with the survivor:

- How does this person define her experience?
- What are the trafficker-generated risks and life-generated risks facing a survivor?
- What are the potential barriers, such as those relating to safety, housing, the law, mental health, medicine, community supports, culture, religion, language, and education? Taking into account the context of the relationship with the survivor and trafficker is important as well.
- What are the safety needs if the trafficker is a romantic partner or a parent or family member?
- What has the survivor already tried, and how did it work or not work?
- How does the survivor anticipate the trafficker will respond to his, her, or their actions?
- What safety risks are associated with individuals engaging in survival sex—how can an advocate use a harm-reduction model, or what resources are necessary?

Source: Adapted from Jacquelyn Campbell's *Danger Assessment* (2001).

Additional Safety Plan Considerations—Technology

When safety plans were first conducted in the early 1970s, technology played a very different role than it does today. Many people, even those who may be experiencing life-threatening situations such as homelessness or trafficking, have access to a cell phone or may also have access to the Internet. While technology can serve as a resource, it can also be a means for the trafficker to track or invade the survivor's privacy. Cases have been reported of traffickers who tracked their victims' cell phones and IP addresses on the computers they used in addition to hacking their e-mail and bank accounts electronically (Howard, 2012). Therefore, assisting survivors with safety planning while considering technology could be lifesaving. This could include helping survivors change passwords and usernames, limit personal information, and use a different computer. Since traffickers are present online and could use social media to communicate with the survivor, it is important to provide recommendations about social media settings and how to prevent the trafficker from locating the survivor through Facebook or other social media platforms. It is also important to consider and talk through with the survivor any private messages, e-mails, texts, voicemails, and the like that could be used if the survivor is looking to build a case against the trafficker, as all of these mediums could serve as documentation that harassment, stalking, abuse, trafficking, and other forms of violence likely occurred. Resources such as free government phones can be given out, and resources such as crisis lines and other support services can be saved in the phone under code names so that the trafficker cannot easily identify that the survivor is working with social services and deduce that he or she is potentially trying to leave.

Collaboration with Law Enforcement and Legal Services

If clients are adults, it is up to their discretion if they would like to report their situation to law enforcement. Depending on certain variables and what survivors think the act of reporting might do to their level of safety, they may choose not to disclose. It is important to honor survivors' choices and support them in their decisions, even if the practitioner feels there is a sound case that could potentially result in the arrest of a trafficker. Survivors of sex trafficking may fear the potential legal consequences attached to reporting the crime to law enforcement or social service agencies. First, since prostitution is illegal in most states and there is a great stigma against people engaged in sex work, they may fear arrest, fines, or prosecution, which could intensify the secrecy of the situation, adding yet another barrier to accessing resources. In addition, for those who are not U.S. citizens, concerns about deportation may impede safety and access to resources. Practitioners working with survivors of sex trafficking and sexual exploitation need to be aware of the resources available for legal services, including protective orders, legal permanent residency, T and U Visas, and legal programs that work to prevent the risk of criminalization of this vulnerable population (Clawson & Dutch, 2008).

As with domestic violence survivors, the advocate can survey the sex-trafficking survivor's experiences and perceptions regarding law enforcement. There is a push to involve the U.S. government and U.S. attorneys in work with trafficking survivors, even though survivors may distrust the system based on past interactions. Involvement with the criminal justice system can be dangerous for survivors, especially if the trafficker has connections to or relationships with individuals involved in law enforcement. If legal precautions such as obtaining an order of protection are a part of the plan, knowing the laws and protections of each state will benefit survivors greatly. The sole focus of a safety plan cannot be to catch the trafficker, but rather to promote survivors' agency and input by focusing on strategies they have used in the past to keep themselves safe. The key is to help survivors regain a sense of control over their lives, and this begins with making decisions; "the direction of advocacy must be kept in the victims' hands" (Davies & Lyon, 2014, p. 16). Safety plans should allow for brainstorming other options when the criminal justice system isn't one of them.

Substance Abuse

It is common knowledge that there is a significant overlap between individuals who have experienced extensive, untreated trauma and those who are addicted or abusing substances. People who have experienced trafficking and sexual exploitation hold a heightened risk for substance abuse issues, particularly women who began trading sex in adulthood as a way to support an addiction (Oselin, 2014). It is also important to remember than many traffickers use substances to coerce and control their victims. Advocates working with survivors will need to take into account survivors' current substance use and how this could jeopardize their ability to enact a safety plan. If there is substance use, whether through self-medication or through force and coercion, harm-reduction techniques and access to appropriate mental health referrals and crisis intervention services need to be part of the conversation when designing a safety plan (Miller, 1999).

Vignette of Safety Planning

The following vignette is an example of a real-life safety planning session that occurred in person with a twenty-year-old female survivor who had experienced both domestic violence and commercial sexual exploitation. The interviewer in this vignette has a strong rapport with the client, and they have met several times over the past four months. At this point in their work together, the survivor is considering returning to the men who have abused and exploited her. The name of the survivor and other minor details have been changed to protect her identity.

Interviewer: Hi, Monique. Thanks for meeting with me today. It is good to see you.

Monique: Thanks. It is good to see you, too.

Interviewer: How are things going?

Monique: They're okay. I'm staying over at the [Hotel Name] with Joe. He said I can stay as long as I want.

Interviewer: I know last time we talked you mentioned Joe is letting you stay for free and that you feel safe with him. What has it been like this past week with him?

Monique: Yes, he's cool. He doesn't lay a finger on me and is helping me find work.

Interviewer: What type of work are you looking for?

Monique: I want to work at the Dollar Store. I had an interview yesterday.

Interviewer: Congratulations! How did you feel like it went?

Monique: Really well I think. I was nervous though.

Interviewer: That's so normal. I get nervous in interviews, too.

The interviewer and Monique continue to talk about what is on Monique's mind and build rapport by first discussing topics that are not directly related to the safety plan.

Interviewer: How are things with Collin? (Collin is Monique's ex-boyfriend who has physically and sexually abused her. Collin's father forces her to have sex with him in exchange for a place to stay and to have sex with his friends in exchange for weed.)

Monique: Well, I'm still talking to him over the phone and we text. He really wants me to come back and promises things will be different this time. I still love him, but I also hate him at the same time.

Interviewer: What do you think would make you go back to be with Collin?

Monique: Probably if he could promise me his Dad wouldn't fuck me. I just want to be with Collin and would rather be there than staying in a hotel with Joe.

Interviewer: It sounds like you miss Collin and want to see what it would be like to try things with him again.

Monique: Yeah, but do you think that's stupid?

Interviewer: No, I don't think that is stupid, Monique. And, I want you to be as safe as possible and am concerned that if nothing has changed then you are at risk for being physically and sexually abused again.

Monique: I know. I don't know what hold he has over me.

Interviewer: Remember when we talked about the "cycle of violence"?

Monique: Yes, he's trying to win me back in the honeymoon stage.

Interviewer: Yes, I think so. But, I support you and want you to be as safe as you can, so can we talk about some ways to keep you safe no matter what you choose to do?

Monique: That sounds good.

Interviewer: What's your main concern?

Monique: I'm scared his Dad is going to force me to have sex with him again.

Interviewer: When would his Dad normally force you to have sex with him? Were there any trends?

Monique: Yep. He would get drunk or high and then when Collin would leave he'd force me to suck his dick or more.

Interviewer: What have you already tried and how did those things work?

Monique: Well, I try to not be there alone with him and once I even locked the door to my room, but he knocked it down and threatened to cut me with his knife.

Interviewer: How safe do you feel when Collin is home?

Monique: It depends. When he is in a good mood he is great and his Dad won't pull any tricks when he's around. But, if Collin gets pissed he usually takes it out on me.

Interviewer: What typically sets Collin off?

Monique: Honestly, it can be anything. Sometimes just hearing one of his sports teams lost can be enough to make him have a total tantrum. But, usually it is if he gets jealous and thinks other guys are hitting on me.

Interviewer: What have you tried when Collin gets upset?

Monique: Well, I'm a fighter so usually I just fight back, which makes him even more angry. He's stronger than me so he wins.

Interviewer: I wonder what would happen if you didn't fight back.

Monique: He might just leave me alone or not hit me as bad. I could also try to go for a walk and not be around. He doesn't like me to leave, but I've left before to go for a walk and he doesn't care too much. And, if I bring back McDonald's or something it can sort of ease things over.

Interviewer: It sounds like you have a good technique up your sleeve for deescalating Collin, at least some of the time.

Monique: (Laughs) McDonald's solves a lot in this world.

Interviewer: (Laughs) Who knew? (Pauses) So, you're good at knowing when Collin is getting upset; you know the signs?

Monique: Totally. I can read him like a book.

Interviewer: And, for you, it can be safer to not fight back, but to leave if you can and maybe bring back some food.

Monique: (Nods) Yes, I need to try that more often.

Interviewer: What makes it challenging for you to not fight back?

The interviewer continues to assess Monique's triggers for fighting back as well as possible coping skills she could use to reduce the impulse. The interviewer also discusses options with Monique that she can use to stay as safe as possible if she does fight back and/or if she can't leave for some reason. Often survivors' "safety measures" appear to the practitioner as high risk. As seen in the case of Monique, she continually returned to her abuser's house even though she knew she would experience physical abuse and sexual exploitation. However, as the practitioner utilized survivor-centered advocacy, it became clear that this action, while subjecting the client to abuse, ultimately kept her safer in the long term because her boyfriend would often become increasingly violent to the point of being lethal when she was not living with him. Actions that clients take for safety are not always free of risk or harm; however, clients are experts on their situations, and when they are treated as such and empowered through survivor-centered safety planning, there is a greater chance of safety.

Conclusion

Sex trafficking and sexual exploitation are not new crimes; however, social service providers are still learning the best ways to identify survivors and conduct safety planning to keep them as safe as possible. By utilizing the best practices from the field of domestic violence/intimate partner violence, such as survivor-centered advocacy and generalized safety planning, social workers and survivors of trafficking can collaboratively create safety plans that address their risks and needs. Service providers need to be aware of the challenges survivors of trafficking face and continue to work within a client-centered framework to keep both survivors and themselves safe.

References

Barasch, A., & Kryszko, B. (2013). The nexus between domestic violence and trafficking for commercial sexual exploitation. In J. L. Goodman & D. A. Leidholdt (Eds.), *Lawyer's manual on human trafficking: Pursuing justice for victims* (pp. 83–94). New York, NY: Supreme Court of the State of New York. Retrieved from http://www.nycourts.gov/ip/womeninthecourts/pdfs/LMHT.pdf

Campbell, J. (2001) *Danger assessment*. Retrieved from http://www.ncdsv.org/images/dangerassessment.pdf

Clawson, H., & Dutch, N. (2008). *Addressing the needs of victims of human trafficking: Challenges, barriers and promising practices*. Washington, DC: U.S. Department of Health and Human Services, Office of the Assistant Secretary for Planning and Evaluation. Retrieved from https://aspe.hhs.gov/system/files/pdf/75471/ib.pdf

Clawson, H. J., Salomon, A., & Grace, L. G. (2007). *Treating the hidden wounds: Trauma treatment and mental health recovery for victims of human trafficking*. Washington, DC: U.S. Department of Health and Human Services, Office of the Assistant Secretary for Planning and Evaluation. Retrieved from https://aspe.hhs.gov/system/files/pdf/75356/ib.pdf

Davies, J., & Lyon, E. (2014). *Domestic violence advocacy* (2nd ed.). Thousand Oaks, CA: Sage.

Davies, J., Lyon, E., & Monti-Catania, D. (1998). *Safety planning with battered women: Complex lives/difficult choices*. Thousand Oaks, CA: Sage.

Heil, E., & Nichols, A. (2015). *Human trafficking in the Midwest*. Durham, NC: Carolina Academic Press.

Herman, J. (1997). *Trauma and recovery*. New York, NY: Basic Books.

Howard, A. (2012). *Human trafficking 101*. St. Louis, MO: St. Louis Rescue & Restore Coalition.

Interface Children Family Services. (n.d.). *Domestic violence & human trafficking*. Retrieved from http://www.icfs.org/assets/pdf/DVandHumanTraffickingFactSheet.pdf

Miller, W. R. (1999). *Enhancing motivation for change in substance abuse treatment*. Rockville, MD: Center for Substance Abuse Treatment.

Missouri Coalition Against Domestic and Sexual Violence. (2012). Understanding the *Nature and Dynamics of Domestic Violence*. Jefferson City, MO: Author.

The National Domestic Violence Hotline. (2015). *Path to safety*. Retrieved from http://www.thehotline.org/help/path-to-safety/

Oselin, S. (2014). *Leaving prostitution: Getting out and staying out of sex work*. New York, NY: New York University Press.

Polaris Project. (n.d.). *Client services*. Retrieved from http://www.polarisproject.org/what-wedo/client-services

——. (n.d.). *Building the global safety net for victims of human trafficking: A toolkit for hotlines*. Retrieved from https://polarisproject.org/sites/default/files/Polaris-Global-Toolkit.pdf

Shakil, M. (2016). Gender based violence: A paradoxical analysis. *Journal of Humanities and Social Science, 21*(3), 118–125. Retrieved from http://www.iosrjournals.org/iosr-jhss/papers/Vol.%2021%20Issue3/Version-1/P210301118125.pdf

Siniscalchi, A., & Morris, K. (2014). *Safety planning for trafficking clients and staff*. Retrieved from http://www.slideserve.com/rich/safety-planning-for-trafficking-clients-and-staff

CHAPTER 4

CHANGE IS A PROCESS

Using the Transtheoretical Model with Commercially Sexually
Exploited and Trafficked Youth and Adults

RACHEL LLOYD, MA, SURVIVOR; FOUNDER
AND PRESIDENT, GEMS

Since its inception eighteen years ago, Girls Educational and
Mentoring Services (GEMS), a survivor-led organization and the
nation's largest service provider to commercially sexually exploited
and domestically trafficked girls and young women, has been using the Transtheoretical Model (TTM) of Change (Prochaska & DiClemente, 1983) and
Motivational Interviewing (MI) (Miller & Rollnick, 1991) to support victims
and survivors in every area of their lives. While the TTM has been criticized for
lacking validated outcomes, this chapter will explain why its use is so effective
with commercial sexual exploitation and trafficking, both for the survivors
themselves and critically for the service providers, law enforcement personnel,
and legal and healthcare professionals who encounter them.

GEMS uses the TTM (more commonly called the Stages of Change model)
to help survivors undergo clinical counseling, move into supportive housing,
address substance abuse, and, critically, reengage with education. Because the
most common challenge for social service professionals is helping trafficked
individuals move from victimization to safety, this chapter will focus on using
the TTM to support and empower survivors to leave their traffickers and exit
the commercial sex industry.

In this chapter, the terms *trafficker*, *exploiter*, and *pimp* are used interchangeably. *Trafficker* is the legal definition, *exploiter* is a more encompassing term
that denotes a variety of exploitive relationships that may or may not meet the
legal definition of trafficking, and *pimp* is the term that victims and survivors
are more likely to use themselves. The terms *victim* and *survivor* are used to

define separate stages of an individual's experience. *Victim* denotes an individual who is still in an exploitive and abusive situation, and *survivor* denotes someone who is moving out of the trafficking and exploitation. This is in keeping with the GEMS Victim, Survivor, Leader model (Lloyd, 2008), which identifies those three specific stages that individuals move through on their road to healing and safety. Individuals who experience relapse, as defined by the TTM, are still referred to as survivors because they have had the initial experience of coming into contact with services and support and can recognize the exploitive nature of their situation, often for the first time. This chapter explores the use of the TTM with commercially sexually exploited and trafficked victims and survivors and discusses how this work is similar to and different from current work that uses the model with domestic violence victims.

Background of GEMS

GEMS was founded in 1998 by Rachel Lloyd, a survivor of commercial sexual exploitation (CSE), to address the unique needs of CSE and domestic trafficking (DT). As a survivor-led and survivor-informed organization, GEMS provides comprehensive, holistic services through its innovative Victim, Survivor, Leader model, which supports girls and young women at all stages of involvement in the commercial sex industry (Lloyd, 2008). GEMS services include a multipurpose drop-in center, individual and group counseling, two transitional housing programs, an alternative to incarceration program through the criminal court system, a family court advocacy and intervention program, an education-focused program, youth leadership, youth employment, and a wide variety of therapeutic, artistic, psychoeducational, and recreational groups and activities. In addition, GEMS provides preventive education and early intervention to high-risk girls and young women through outreach programs in schools, detention facilities, group homes, and residential treatment centers.

GEMS also has a national training program that provides intensive professional education on the issue of CSE and DT and on the GEMS Victim, Survivor, Leader model; the program trains youth service providers, residential program staff, law enforcement personnel, and healthcare and legal professionals. In 2015, GEMS served 437 girls and young women who had experienced CSE and DT, provided outreach and preventive education to 607 youth considered at high risk, and trained over 2,000 professionals who interact with CSE youth. GEMS is the largest provider of services to commercially sexually exploited and domestically trafficked girls and young women in the country.

Since its inception, GEMS has used the Stages of Change model (Prochaska & DiClemente, 1983; Prochaska, DiClemente, & Norcross, 1992) to help thousands of girls and young women ages twelve to twenty-four in exiting or escaping the commercial sex industry and to support them in various other behavior changes in their lives, including returning to school and moving into a residential program. All staff members at GEMS, including those in a fiscal or administrative capacity, are trained in the Stages of Change model, and all GEMS training sessions for professionals include specific training in using the Stages of Change with survivors of CSE and DT. The Stages of Change framework is integral to GEMS's work and is a critical component of its Victim, Survivor, Leader program model.

The Transtheoretical Model of Change

"I had to learn that change is okay. Change can be better than before, and it may be hard but it's okay."—

GEMS member (Guthrie, 2011)

Use of the TTM has been documented with myriad populations who are working to change behavior patterns, primarily those related to health, such as smoking, substance abuse, and eating disorders. The overarching concept of the model is that individuals progress through defined stages; they can cycle back and forth or stay stuck in a stage for an undetermined period of time. Going through the stages is critical to lasting and authentic change. Prochaska and DiClemente (1983) recognized that individuals' struggles with changing behavior patterns could not be defined by a simple dichotomous paradigm—namely, ready versus not ready—because this did not take into account the complexities of individuals' thought processes and the natural human resistance to change. The model has been frequently used with populations who need to change their behavior to live healthier, safer lives, partly because of its simplicity, and partly because it captures the nonlinear, frequently long-term, one-step-forward-and-two-steps-back nature of every human change process.

The model has six main components: precontemplation (outside the change process), contemplation, preparation, action, maintenance, and relapse. *Precontemplation* is outside the change process because in that stage the individual is not considering change and does not believe change is necessary. At *contemplation*, the individual has begun to consider the basic idea of change and is often struggling with its pros and cons. *Preparation* occurs when the

"I would enter and get out, enter and get out."—GEMS member (Guthrie, 2011)

individual begins to think even more seriously about change and starts to take some small steps toward an eventual goal of change. *Action* is when the change process actually occurs. *Maintenance* is new behavior that is sustained over for six months or more. *Relapse*, one of the most critical components of the model, is when the individual returns to the old behavior. As *relapse* is part of the model's cycle, it promotes the understanding that individuals frequently struggle with sustained change, or *maintenance*, and may often return to familiar behaviors. Contrary to popular belief, however, they are still within the change process (unlike those in *precontemplation*) and can return to any of the stages at any time. The model promotes the idea that *relapse* is not the end of a change process but rather just one more stage within a dynamic, fluid, and cyclic process that is completely normal for any individual attempting life changes.

As is evidenced by this explanation and the language used, initially the Stages of Change model was used as a tool for addressing unhealthy or "problem" behaviors; however, in the mid-1990s, healthcare providers struggling for ways to provide supportive intervention to victims of domestic violence (DV) or intimate partner violence (IPV) began to use the Stages of Change model in their work (Frasier, Slatt, Kowlowitz, & Glowa, 2001). The critical difference in using this model with victims of IPV or trafficking versus with individuals struggling with addiction is that it is of course not the individual engaging in the "problem" behavior but rather the abuser. Some domestic violence advocates encourage using the term *returning* instead of *relapse* to remove any sense of stigma or shame that *relapse* can conjure up (Frasier et al., 2001). For victims of CSE and trafficking, this distinction is even more critical, given that their behavior is centered on an activity, sex for money, that is illegal and is frequently seen as immoral, whereas for domestic violence victims the act of staying with or returning to their abuser is not against the law. In both cases, however, there is real judgment directed at victims who don't "act like victims" and who struggle with the change process (Annitto, 2011; Burman, 2003; Frasier et al., 2001; Lloyd, 2005, 2011).

As with domestic violence victims, using the Stages of Change model with this population should not in any way be construed as some indication that victims are to blame for their own abuse, that change is solely on them, or that they are somehow addicted to money or sex (a common fallacy among the general public). Victims of trafficking are not addicted to their exploitation. One of the complexities that emerges when working with trafficking victims who have had a relationship with their trafficker is that there may be behavior that looks and operates very similarly to substance addiction and the subsequent withdrawal. There are myriad reasons for this, and emerging research on brain functioning in romantic love and its potential to become a "love addiction" shows that similar pathways in the brain are activated in both love addiction, particularly when the individual experiences rejection, and cocaine addiction (Fisher et al., 2010).

While a provider who is familiar with the pimp's abuse of the victim, and who perhaps even observes the effects of physical violence, may struggle with the concept of "love" toward this individual who has used, exploited, and violated the victim, it is critical to remember that the feelings of love—emotionally, chemically, and neurologically—are very real. As with working with domestic violence victims, it can be difficult for providers and law enforcement to understand how a victim can still have love for an individual who appears to be "bad," especially when, unlike most batterers, traffickers are actually using this relationship as their employment and source of income and have methodically and intentionally created a scenario in which the victim feels a strong attachment to them just for the purpose of economic gain.

Some providers believe that immediately tearing down what seems to be a delusional belief helps victims realize that the exploiter does not love them and is simply using them; however, this approach does significant damage to any potential trust and relationship building between the victim and the provider. It also negates any interactions outside of the violence and exploitation that the victim has had with her pimp—such as eating dinner together, watching TV, and talking—that can and frequently do happen in a trafficker-victim relationship that is framed in a romantic context. It is important for the provider to recognize that, as with domestic violence victims, there are often moments of calm or affection, particularly if a grooming stage occurred, and those moments can be incredibly powerful in a volatile and unpredictable bonding process. Telling the victim that it isn't a "real" relationship negates her reality, and she will frequently shut down and become protective of the relationship and the exploiter. This reaction is in keeping with victims who have experienced *trauma bonding* (Carnes, 1997) or, in extreme cases, the more commonly known term in popular culture, *Stockholm Syndrome* (Graham, 1994).

While these terms are not recognized in the DSM, trauma bonding and to a lesser extent Stockholm Syndrome describe behaviors and patterns seen in victims of child abuse or domestic violence, individuals who have been in hostage situations or cults, and prisoners of war. These behaviors seem illogical to others, including resistance to the rescuer, support of the abuser (exploiter), and an "inability to engage in behaviors that may assist in their release or detachment" (Carver, 2016). These behaviors have nothing to do with addiction and everything to do with trauma and the control, or even simply the perception of the control, used by the exploiter. This is a critical distinction and one that is frequently misunderstood by law enforcement and service providers, who may view victims' unwillingness to seek help or their returning to their exploiter as proof that they somehow "like it." However, the very real biological attachments that can be formed in romantic relationships and that function in a similar fashion to drug addiction, when combined with the psychological impacts of trauma bonding, particularly for a child or young person whose life has been marked with insecure attachments, prior child abuse, and often trauma bonding to an abuser, make for an incredibly potent cocktail of attachment to the trafficker that can seem very hard to break.

Some providers may feel that using the Stages of Change model places too much responsibility or onus on the victims and holds them responsible for things that they can't control, like the lack of available resources and most importantly their trafficker's actions. In using this model with this population, it is vital to note that there are very real outside forces that do not exist within the Stages of Change framework as it is applied to health behaviors. Using the model for smoking cessation makes sense in that a cigarette cannot force itself to be smoked by the individual. In trafficking and domestic violence situations, the abuser/exploiter is a random actor whose behavior cannot be accounted for within each stage, and therefore the use of the model and the support and services given must take that into consideration at each stage.

Resources are also a critical priority, particularly in the active (action, maintenance, and relapse) stages. Supporting a victim in reaching the action stage is destined to fail if there are no shelter beds for her when she decides to make that move. When basic needs such as food, shelter, and clothing are not met for a survivor, and often for her children too, or her prior arrests for prostitution impede her ability to find employment, she may feel that she has no other choice than to enter the relapse or returning stage. The model therefore must be used in a larger context that includes the very real threat of violence and repercussions and that takes into account the very real lack of services for survivors of CSE and DT. Finally, the impact of sexism, classism, racism, poverty, lack of affordable childcare, lack of affordable housing, lack of living wage employment, and the social and legal stigma faced by survivors of the commercial sex industry must be understood and accounted for when using this model and when working with victims and survivors in any context.

Despite those caveats, GEMS has found the Stages of Change model to be extremely effective in working with this population, in training staff, and in altering perceptions. While the efficacy of a stage-based intervention approach in working with health behaviors has been critiqued (Brug et al., 2005), it can be posited that given the significant difference between smoking cessation and leaving a trafficker, there is also a significant difference in how and why this model can be so effective with victimized populations. The primary difference is that the attachment is not, in most cases, to a physical substance. There may be coexisting substance abuse, but for victims under the control of a trafficker, the primary issue is normally the separation from the trafficker and the love, family, and stability he seems to represent, along with the fear and psychological control that the victim experiences. Although the brain is impacted by feelings of romantic love or longing, the research does not show that the brain is permanently changed by those experiences, in contrast to the way that substances can permanently alter neural pathways and brain chemistry to create potentially lifelong cravings.

Even those individuals who experience severe love addiction and limerence can and generally do get over the object of their affection. And trauma-informed approaches and evidence-based models, such as prolonged exposure (PE), cognitive processing therapy (CPT), eye movement desensitization and reprocessing (EMDR), and stress inoculation training (SIT), have been found to be effective in working with victims and survivors of trauma (Chard & Gilman, 2005). While not independently evaluated, GEMS's own work shows five years of annual success rates of over 70 percent of girls and young women leaving and remaining free from trafficking and CSE when they are engaged in intensive services. This success cannot be directly linked to the sole use of the Stages of Change model, as there are myriad services and supports that individuals receive and engage with at GEMS, but it can be theorized that using the Stages of Change model, as part of the specialized Victim, Survivor, Leader model, as the foundation of all engagement and treatment approaches has a real impact on the efficacy of services.

Perhaps the most critical component of the Stages of Change model and the reason for its success at GEMS, as well as the reported success of other programs that have received training from GEMS, is how it impacts the staff themselves and the way they see and treat the girls and young women. This shift in attitude and approach has been documented with law students trained on the Stages of Change model at a domestic violence clinic: "It is simply one of the most important things to understand as a DV attorney. Understanding this model helped reduce my personal stress level. I came to understand that some decisions made by the client weren't the result of my own personal failures. Even if I explained the law perfectly and my client understood that she had a strong case, it was ultimately up to the client what she wanted to do" (Stoever, 2013). Without the Stages of Change model, service providers tend to group clients (known as "members" at GEMS) into two categories—"ready/ not ready"—and believe that their role is to somehow transform someone as quickly as possible from "not ready" to "ready," or they commonly feel that they should focus on the "ready" individuals and dismiss the "not ready" group until of course they are somehow "ready" by themselves.

This black-and-white approach is exactly what the Stages of Change model was designed to address, as it is prevalent in every discipline, including social work, given a natural human instinct to simplify and categorize others. This sets the stage for a judgmental (even if unintentionally) approach, often leaves entire groups of victims outside of services, and places extreme pressure on the staff member. This pressure is then put on the victim, who feels that she is disappointing the staff member, or in some cases failing at an actual court mandate, when she does not become automatically ready to quickly make a huge life change and then remain in a permanently changed state. As one law student in the DV clinic explains, "I remember very clearly how angry I was with her. I felt like I was working so hard to help her and she wasn't helping herself. I remember thinking that I couldn't fight *for* her if I also had to fight *with* her. . . . I now realize that she had gone from the preparation and action stages back to contemplation. But at the time I felt disappointed and frustrated with her" (Stoever, 2013).

Expecting quick or easily sustained change and being disappointed or even angry when it doesn't occur places an unfair and unrealistic burden on the victim. Life changes do not work in that immediate, linear, and permanent way for any individual, especially for victims of sustained violence and childhood trauma who have frequently confused abuse with love and seen sexual interaction as shameful, secret, and often transactional. And change for victims of trafficking, for whom resources are often scarce and services often unintentionally reinforce their stigma and victimization, feels like an incredibly frightening, hopeless, and often impossible task. Expectations from service providers or law enforcement that change is just a decision based on apparently clear evidence (to the individual on the outside) that their situation is harmful, that their trafficker is simply using them and they would be foolish to go back, simply increase the feelings of shame, defensiveness, protection of the abuser, and disconnection from the external world.

Survivors of CSE and DT know firsthand that change is an extremely complicated process that frequently sees them returning multiple times to either the trafficker or the commercial sex industry even if they don't have the theoretical framework to explain it.

Victims often believe that change is uniquely hard for them alone. It is important to provide a framework through the Stages of Change model and normalize how challenging change is for everyone, especially for victims of CSE. Understanding that they are not alone in their struggles is key for victims who have felt perpetually isolated and abnormal. The statement "it's a normal

"I was scared, nervous, not knowing and it's just being scared of the unknown. The square life was like another planet to me so it was like how am I gonna do this, this is what I'm used to and overall it was just a bunch of mixed emotions. I left more than once. I would leave and something would seem to pull me back or it seemed like one step forward, four steps back and that would lead me back to the thought of going back but every time I went back, it would get worse, mentally and physically."—Kristina (Lloyd & White, 2014) response to an abnormal situation" is frequently repeated for and by GEMS members and helps ensure that they see their feelings and actions, whatever they are, as normal responses to abuse and exploitation. Therefore, for staff trained in TTM, a girl being unsure about whether to leave a clearly abusive pimp who makes her consistently sad is neither viewed nor treated as abnormal or illogical but simply as part of the contemplation stage, in which she is beginning to weigh the good versus bad in her life without yet reaching a conclusion or taking action. For victims, being able to talk these feelings through with a trusted support person instead of trying to hide whatever positive feelings they still have for their exploiter is an important part of their change process, removes the sense of secrecy or shame they may have, and makes it far more likely that they will move forward to the preparation stage. Within this "change is a process" framework, it is critical that victims and survivors know that their actions are neither shocking nor disappointing to the providers engaging with them and that they have unconditional support at every stage of their journey.

Sometimes staff can confuse unconditional support, however, with an implicit or explicit acceptance of the situation and the victim's exploitation. The provider's role is not to simply accept the status quo but actively, albeit gently and carefully, engage in the questions and conversations that will empower a victim to confront the situation and move forward, stage by stage. The most effective tool for this process is Motivational Interviewing (MI) (Miller & Rollnick, 2002), a goal-oriented, client-centered counseling style that complements the TTM, although it must be used judiciously in the *precontemplation* stage so as not to come across as judgmental, particularly when victims are already feeling defensive and are worried about stigma. Initial conversations should simply be centered on support, resources, and building a sense of trust and safety. Motivational Interviewing's true effectiveness with this population comes as the relationship between provider and victim grows and victims are in the *contemplation* stage, as it can be used to tease out cognitive dissonance and create ambivalence about their current situation. This delicate balance requires an intuitive and skilled provider. Without a support person to help them engage in the process, victims struggle with leaving in both an emotional and practical sense.

"From the ages of fourteen to sixteen I was in the life and the whole time I wanted to leave. I just honestly did not want to open up to anybody about what I was going through. I kinda just felt like I wanted to handle everything on my own and I kept going back and forth even though I didn't really want to. I tried to stop."—GEMS member (Guthrie, 2011)

Having a support person, someone who can effectively and nonconfrontationally challenge some of the unhealthy beliefs that have been taught to victims by their families of origin, their pimps, the men who bought them, and the society at large begins the cognitive shift component of the initial stages, *precontemplation*, *contemplation*, and *preparation*. These often deeply ingrained beliefs, which are reinforced on a daily basis while victims are in the commercial sex industry or even still dealing with family members or living in the foster care system, include beliefs about themselves, others, and the world outside of "the life," their inherent worth and value, what love is, what healthy love is, their own strength and resilience, what they deserve, what they can achieve, and what a potential future could look like. Unless these belief systems and thought processes are addressed, the provision of resources—another key role for the provider—has little to no impact. This is why the offer of, for example, a shelter bed to a victim in the *precontemplation* and *contemplation* stages will often be refused or accepted only to pacify the provider or law enforcement and then abandoned at the earliest opportunity. Ideally the role of the provider in slowly challenging these beliefs is continuously supplemented and reinforced by other staff within the organization or institution, by the presence and leadership of survivors who have long ago made that shift and can model the positive impacts of long-term maintenance, by groups and activities that give victims a sense of their interests and talents, by the availability of resources that they could one day utilize, by other members/clients who are at varying stages of their own change process, by books, films, and art that share survivors' journeys in their own voices, and even by the posters on the wall that tell victims that they are not alone, that change is possible, that survivors are strong and resilient leaders.

Unfortunately, many providers work in a vacuum where they are the victim's only advocate or clinician or within systems or institutions that often unintentionally reinforce the negative beliefs that victims already hold. In those situations, providers should advocate for everyone engaging with the victim to be trained in both TTM and MI and must work creatively to try to supplement the conversations that they are having by utilizing survivor-created, survivor-informed resources so that victims can receive these healthy messages in multiple ways over a long period of time. Survivors report that these alternate messages stick with them, even when they are still in "the life" or have returned after a period out. One GEMS member participating in a study on resiliency factors among commercially sexually exploited and trafficked youth said "It was kind of crazy because once I had GEMS installed in me it was kind of hard, because I started thinking about [staff]." Another said "I like programs like GEMS cause you know how you said even when you left [speaking to another focus group participant], you still have that GEMS stuff in your head, [you think] 'Oh my God, I don't have to do this.' That's stuff for life" (Guthrie, 2011).

Focus group participants were able to list specific messages that had stuck with them, about themselves, about what they deserved, that the pain wouldn't last forever, and temporary coping strategies:

> "You are beautiful," "You are intelligent," "You are strong," "You can do this, like you don't have to be with him," "It may be hard, but we're gonna get through this," "The cravings are not gonna be there forever," "Right now just try like relax and smoke a cigarette" (Guthrie, 2011).

Members also reported being told that they could always come back, that the door would be open to them no matter what, or that they could call a staff person's cell phone at any time and someone would come help them. These messages, both big and small, gave victims and survivors something to hold on to even when they weren't actively engaged in services and were facing their own internal struggles and negative external messaging. Memories of unconditional support and the encouragement that things could change actively contradicted what they were being told by their exploiters. While they may have relapsed or returned to their exploiter, or never actually left, the messaging took hold and the change process was still active, even though outwardly it may have seemed dormant.

Providers may think that if they don't see active change right away then it is not going to happen or that by returning to their exploiters, survivors show that they were not really "ready" or have not truly changed. But every thoughtful, intentional conversation is planting the seeds for future change, and change often requires multiple attempts for it to be lasting. When providers are effectively using the TTM in conjunction with Motivational Interviewing and tangible resources, their efforts are having an impact, whether it is visible or not. It is also important for providers to realize that frequently the move from preparation to action takes place, not because of some final "breakthrough" conversation, but because external factors and stressors in the victim's life have pushed her, in addiction and recovery parlance, to "hit bottom." Whether it is an experience of violence, getting arrested, another betrayal or disappointment from the trafficker, or often the discovery that the victim is pregnant, there is frequently a precipitating event that moves a victim from preparation to action.

The effective provider's role in this process has been twofold: (1) engaging the victim in intentional conversations that challenge current belief systems to help her move from *precontemplation* or *contemplation* to *preparation* (the "why" she should leave) and (2) ensuring that the victim knows that there is a clear exit route and resources for the *action* stage (the "how" she can leave). Being available and also ensuring that appropriate resources are available to take advantage of this window of opportunity is the critical next step. The next task is to offer consistency, close engagement, and continued resources that support the survivor in moving forward with education, employment, and stable housing once the survivor is in the *action* stage; providers must also be prepared for the potential, but not inevitable, *relapse* stage. They must have patience with the process and with the victim's actions if she continues to cycle back and forth through the stages.

Supportive providers are critical to the process, but not the sole factor, in the change cycle. Providers who see the victim as solely responsible for cognitive and behavioral change will be judgmental in their attitudes and behaviors when dealing with the victim. Likewise, providers who see themselves as the sole force for change in a victim's life and responsible for "saving" or "rescuing" her will express disappointment and frustration when addressing the victim. The Stages of Change model, combined with Motivational Interviewing, provides a balance for trained providers and ensures that the victim's interactions with the provider are healthy, empowering, intentional, and supportive.

For these reasons, perhaps the most important impact of the Stages of Change model is on the service providers and professionals themselves who engage with trafficked and exploited individuals. The shift in perception and expectations that comes with the Stages of Change model allows providers to understand where an individual might be on the change continuum and to address their needs and behaviors at that stage. The model encourages providers to simply support an individual in moving from one stage to the next, however long that takes, rather than expect that they can somehow move an individual from "not ready" to "ready" or from a place of not believing that there is a problem with the exploitation they are experiencing to immediately leaving their trafficker. This shift can decrease the feelings of frustration and burnout that providers often experience in working with victims of trafficking, especially those who are in the *precontemplation* and *relapse* stages, and allows providers to see change as a complex, individual process that they are not personally responsible for but rather serve as a support in empowering victims and survivors to move from stage to stage.

The actions and attitude of the provider, while not responsible for the change process, can and do make a significant difference in how an individual engages and responds to the provider, builds trust and rapport with the provider, and is able to receive intentional and directive support in moving to the next stage. If providers understand that change is a long and nonlinear process and that patience is a critical component of using the stages of change, they begin to be more patient in their work. A patient, nonjudgmental, and supportive provider who understands the Stages of Change process can utilize the model intentionally and thoughtfully through Motivational Interviewing and through key conversations and actions at each stage. A frustrated or judgmental provider will, of course, shut down this process and reinforce negative beliefs that the survivor already has about herself.

The Stages of Change model can sometimes feel counterintuitive because it is based on decision making by the victims themselves, who are frequently traumatized and struggling to make healthy decisions. When providers question survivors' ability to make good decisions or engage in the change process, program policies and public policies reinforce the idea that trafficked or exploited individuals are incapable of making decisions and must be protected from their own decisions (which often looks a lot like being penalized). The lack of personal agency and control and the idea that they are incapable of decision making can unfortunately be reminiscent of a pimp's control. Whether that doubt in a survivor's ability to make choices comes from a well-intentioned, protective place or a place of scorn or dismissal ultimately makes little difference to the victims themselves, who continue to believe that they cannot trust themselves to make healthy decisions: "If I am allowed access to my phone I will definitely call my pimp," and "If I'm allowed outside alone for a few minutes I will certainly take that opportunity to run away."

While obviously programs can and should make thoughtful protective policies, particularly when serving children, they should be made in the context of the Stages of Change model and an understanding that while immediate change can be enforced in the short term, the likelihood of that change being permanent is minimal, and real authentic change has to come from within the individual. Programs and providers should implement approaches that come from a place of victim/survivor empowerment, not fear or control. While there must be a foundational understanding, that being exploited or trafficked was never a victim's "choice," providers should believe that with authentic support and legitimate resources, ultimately survivors have the ability to make healthy choices for their lives. If providers engaging with individuals don't start their work from this belief, it becomes difficult for a victim, whose judgment and decision making have been consistently controlled and stripped away, to believe it for themselves. And if they can't believe in their own ability to make healthy decisions independently, it becomes even harder for them to see a future for themselves that is free of their exploiter and the commercial sex industry.

The Locus of Control model has been used effectively with victims and survivors of sexual assault to help victims move from an internal to external to balanced locus of control (Porter & Long, 1999). It starts from an unequivocal place of "it wasn't your fault" (internal), for as long as that takes to be internalized, and supports the victim in recognizing that while bad things happen in the world (external), she can make choices to try to protect herself in the future (balanced). This approach is critical with victims of CSE and trafficking, who frequently see their involvement in the commercial sex industry as their "choice" despite the circumstances, their lack of choices, their age at the time of recruitment, and the trafficker's intent to recruit and control them. Choice therefore becomes a critical issue to address, and the Stages of Change model, while based on individual future choices, must be used in the context that no individual ever chooses to be a victim of violence, exploitation, trafficking, and abuse.

Although the idea that no one chooses to be a victim of violence and that individuals don't return to violent situations because they somehow "miss" the violence should be a universally accepted one, it's clear from the decades-long work of the domestic violence movement that it isn't. The perennial frustration for advocates of domestic violence victims is the explicit and implicit questioning of victims' rationale and choice, namely, "Why doesn't she just leave?" Despite huge strides forward in the fight against domestic violence and real progress in understanding the process of victimization and all the psychological and practical reasons why victims don't "just leave," that question and all its variations remain. Variations include minimizing the violence ("well, it can't be that bad if she hasn't left yet"), being deep frustrated with victims returning ("how could she go back to that?"), misunderstanding the process of leaving ("she keeps going back; she must like it"), and ultimately being apathetic, especially when people can actually intervene in some way ("there's no point in taking this report/getting this shelter bed/requesting an order of protection. She'll go back anyway; they always do").

The same questions, the same frustration, and the same victim blaming are frequently seen toward victims of CSE and trafficking, despite the progress that has been made in raising awareness and despite the fact that the victims are frequently youth and/or people with extensive prior histories of trauma and a scarcity of options and resources. While there has been a demonstrably higher level of awareness over the last five years in both the general public and in professionals and providers interacting with youth, this awareness is not the same as understanding the specific needs and challenges that this population faces or having the corresponding skills to address them. Within the public health framework of "knowledge, skills, attitude" (Centers for Disease Control, 2012), the awareness that domestic trafficking is happening in the United States has significantly increased over the last five years; however, attitudes toward victims and survivors still need to shift, and the skills to support them, engage them, and provide effective services to them are still lacking.

Unfortunately, awareness materials and media often depict young (overwhelmingly white) children in chains, with duct-taped mouths, kept in boxes or basements, looking tearful and frightened, just waiting for someone to rescue them. Social workers or other professionals who have learned about trafficking through this kind of sensationalized imagery, and through training that focuses on rescuing little girls from bad men, struggle when confronted with the realities of actual victims and survivors. The victims they had pictured who would be grateful to be rescued from such horror don't line up with the complex individuals in front of them who deny that there's even a problem, proclaim love and loyalty to their exploiter, and have no desire to leave, let alone be rescued. Victims are then labeled as resistant and difficult. In an article for Reuters titled,

"Sex Trafficking Victims May Push Rescue Away, U.S. Experts Say," this perspective is captured clearly: "Survivors of sex trafficking can be among the most difficult crime victims to assist, often resisting help, refusing to see themselves as victims and returning to their traffickers, experts say. Added to that, they can be smart, manipulative and deceptive, using the same behaviors they learned to survive on anyone who tries to help them" (Wulfhorst, 2016).

The idea that this is the hardest population to work with, that victims are manipulative, deceptive, and are so perpetually damaged that they will always return to their exploiter, is prevalent in the antitrafficking movement. This gloomy perception fails to account for victims' strength, resiliency, and very real, if not immediately apparent, desire to be happy, safe, and free from abuse; nevertheless, it impacts public policy (detention and incarceration for victims) and organizational approaches to this work.

The Stages of Change framework has the capacity to impact both the attitudes and skills of providers working with this population. After GEMS national training sessions that utilized the Stages of Change model, participants in evaluations were able to note both a change in attitude toward the victims and even a change in their feelings about their own role in supporting victims: "I feel less hopeless when I'm trying to help CSEC clients by understanding stages of change." They understood how the model could be used to support the victims through the new skills they'd gained: "Understanding the stages of change has helped me have a realistic view of success/failure with these clients and see how me and my coworkers can be helpful" (Agencies Plus Consulting, 2010).

Being able to view success as helping a victim move from precontemplation ("I'm fine, everything's great, I love him, this is the way my life is") to contemplation ("Maybe things aren't that great, I don't like it when he hits me") is a critical step for providers. Not seeing relapse as failure but recognizing that it's part of the change process and knowing how to effectively support a survivor in that stage ("you have nothing to be ashamed of, you're not starting from square one, look how much progress you've already made, leaving is hard— sometimes you have to practice leaving") makes a real difference for survivors in those moments. Having knowledge of commercial sexual exploitation and trafficking and the impact of this type of violence and coercion on a victim is an important first step, but until that knowledge is matched with an attitude shift toward victims' behaviors and the skills to engage and empower victims, victims won't receive the support necessary to move through the stages of change and reach a maintenance stage of the safe and healthy life they deserve. People connect to people, not programs, and so it is critical that the people who are engaging with victims and survivors of trafficking understand the complex and often convoluted path to change so that they can recognize that their role is to serve as a guide, a support, a coach, along the way and that ultimately survivors, of all ages and backgrounds, have the resilience and tools within themselves to create change.

Using the Transtheoretical/Stages of Change Model with Victims and Survivors of Commercial Sexual Exploitation and Trafficking

Precontemplation (outside the actual "cycle" of change)

- Validate feelings but offer resources. Identify at least one thing that the victim views as a need that can be met, whether getting an ID, going to a doctor, or buying a winter coat.
- Work quickly to engage and build trust.
- Deliver on resources. Work to identify another need that can be met.
- Validate feelings and gently query the victim's sense of safety and support.
- Suggest that there are options. Provide examples of options. Begin MI approach and work to tease out one area of concern or discontent with the situation.
- Affirm the decision to be engaged in services even if there is a mandated component.
- Affirm strength and survival skills.

Contemplation

- Follow up on area of concern.
- Validate feelings of hesitation to explore. Refrain from pushing too hard.
- Use pros and cons list for victim to complete herself. Discuss pros and cons list with victim.
- Address the cognitive dissonance and work to gently challenge belief systems as dictated by the pros and cons list.
- Keep pros and cons list to bring back out at next conversation.
- Remind victim of her concerns and fears.
- Remind her that she doesn't have to make any decisions and that it's just a discussion of a possible alternative.
- Affirm the strength of the victim and her willingness to address the situation.

Preparation

- Have tangible resources to help you describe to the victim what leaving would look like and where she would go.
- Create a safety plan with the victim.

- Remind the victim of her desire for an alternate future if she goes back to the contemplation stage.
- Discuss new pros and cons of actually leaving.
- Affirm the victim's strength and courage to have the conversation and to begin thinking through leaving.

Action

- Have resources available for when the victim is able to leave.
- Affirm the victim's courage and decision to leave.
- Provide intensive support for initial stages.
- Prepare the victim for potential feelings of deep loss and/or wanting to return.
- Discuss a plan if feelings of returning emerge.

Maintenance

- Continue to provide resources and support.
- Provide ongoing counseling to discuss feelings about leaving and the new life.
- Work to help the survivor build a broader support system. Engage the survivor in activities, services, and supportive relationships.
- Look out for signs of boredom that can lead to depression.
- Affirm the survivor's strength and courage in getting free from exploitation.
- Recognize that while the survivor may have left the trafficker, she may continue to engage in some aspects of the commercial sex industry.
- Affirm the survivor's courage, strength, and perseverance.

Relapse/Return

- Maintain contact.
- Affirm the survivor's value.
- Reject the sense of shame or feelings of disappointing others.
- Talk through triggers that precipitated relapse.
- Remind survivor of success and positive feelings and accomplishments during action or maintenance period.
- Remind survivor that change is a process and that returning is normal.
- Affirm the survivor's strength and courage.

References

Agencies Plus Consulting. (2010). *CSEC Community Intervention Project Training Evaluation Report*.

Annitto, M. (2011). Consent, coercion, and compassion: Emerging legal responses to the commercial sexual exploitation of minors. *Yale Law & Policy Review, 30*(1), 1–71.

Brug, J., Connor, M., Harre, N., Kremers, S., McKeller, S., & Whitelaw, S. (2005). The Transtheoretical Model and stages of change: A critique: Observations by five commentators on the paper by Adams, J. and White, M. (2004) Why don't stage-based activity promotion interventions work? *Health Education Research, 20*(2), 244–258.

Burman, S. (2003). Battered women: Stages of change and other treatment models that instigate and sustain leaving. *Brief Treatment and Crisis Intervention, 3*(1), 83–98. doi:10.1093/brief-treatment/mhg004

Carnes, P. J. (1997). *The betrayal bond: Breaking free of exploitive relationships*. Deerfield Beach, FL: Health Communications.

Carver, J. (2016). *Love and Stockholm syndrome: The mystery of loving an abuser*. Retrieved from: https://counsellingresource.com/therapy/self-help/stockholm/

Centers for Disease Control and Prevention. (2012). *Knowledge, skills, and attitudes (KSAs) for the public health preparedness and response core competency model*. Retrieved from http://www.midamericacphp.com/wp-content/uploads/2009/12/KSA.pdf

Chard, K., & Gilman, R. (2005). Counseling trauma victims: 4 brief therapies meet the test. *Current Psychiatry, 4*(8), 50–63.

Fisher, H. E., Brown, L. L., Aron, A., Strong, G., & Mashek, D. (2010). Reward, addiction, and emotion regulation systems associated with rejection in love. *Journal of Neurophysiology, 104*(1), 51–60. doi:10.1152/jn.00784.2009

Frasier, P. Y., Slatt, L., Kowlowitz, V., & Glowa, P. T. (2001). Using the stages of change model to counsel victims of intimate partner violence. *Patient Education and Counseling, 43*(2), 211–217. doi:10.1016/S0738-3991(00)00152-X

Graham, D. (1994). *Loving to survive: Sexual terror, men's violence and women's lives*. New York, NY: New York University Press.

Guthrie, P. (2011). *Identifying resiliency factors in commercially sexually exploited and trafficked youth: A qualitative study* (Doctoral dissertation). Retrieved from ProQuest Digital Dissertations. http://www.proquest.com/products-services/dissertations/order-dissertation.html

Lloyd, R. (2005). Acceptable victims? Sexually exploited youth in the U.S. *Encounter: Education for Meaning and Social Justice, 18*(3), 6–18.

——. (2008). *From victim to survivor, from survivor to leader*. New York, NY: Girls Educational and Mentoring Services.

——. (2011). *Girls like us: Fighting for a world where girls are not for sale*. New York, NY: Harper.

Lloyd, R., & White, S. (2014). *The survivor's guide to leaving*. Girls Education and Mentoring Services.

Miller, W. R. and Rollnick, S. (1991) *Motivational interviewing: Preparing people to change addictive behavior*. New York: Guilford Press.

Miller, W., & Rollnick, S. (2002). *Motivational interviewing: Preparing people to change*. New York, NY: Guilford Press.

Porter, C., & Long, P. (1999). Locus of control and adjustment on female adult survivors of childhood sexual abuse. *Journal of Child Sexual Abuse, 8*(1), 3–25.

Prochaska, J. O., & DiClemente, C. C. (1983). Stages and processes of self-change in smoking: Toward an integrative model of change. *Journal of Counseling and Clinical Psychology, 51,* 390–395.

Prochaska, J. O., DiClemente, C. C., & Norcross, J. C. (1992). In search of how people change: Applications to addictive behavior. *American Psychology, 47*(9), 1102–1114.

Stoever, J. K. (2013). Transforming domestic violence representation: Freedom from violence, using the Stages of Change Model to realize the promise of civil protection orders. In D. Kiesel (Ed.), *Domestic violence: Law, policy, and practice* (3rd ed.). Dayton, OH: LexisNexis.

Wulfhorst, E. (2016, June 22). Sex trafficking victims may push rescue away, U.S. experts say. *Reuters.* Retrieved from http://www.reuters.com/article/trafficking-victims-usa -idUSL1N1972LK

CHAPTER 5

EVIDENCE-BASED TRAUMA TREATMENTS FOR SURVIVORS OF SEX TRAFFICKING AND COMMERCIAL SEXUAL EXPLOITATION

TONYA EDMOND, MSW, PhD,
WASHINGTON UNIVERSITY IN ST. LOUIS

Sex trafficking (ST) and commercial sexual exploitation (CSE) are complex experiences that usually include exposure to a wide array of traumatic events that often begin in childhood and continue throughout adulthood. The stories that survivors have shared with practitioners and researchers reveal high prevalence rates of child sexual abuse (33–84 percent; Ahrens, Katon, McCarty, Richardson, & Courtney, 2012; Clawson, Dutch, Solomon, & Grace, 2009; Fong & Berger Cardoso, 2010; Simons & Whitbeck, 1991; Vranceanu, Hobfoll, & Johnson, 2007), physical abuse (51 percent; Roe-Sepowitz, 2012), emotional abuse (65 percent; Roe-Sepowitz, 2012), neglect (28.9 percent; Cole, Sprang, Lee, & Cohen, 2014), witnessing of intimate partner violence (IPV) (51 percent; Cole et al., 2014), witnessing of community violence (28.6 percent; Cole et al., 2014), and child welfare involvement (53.5 percent; Cole et al., 2014). The Adverse Childhood Experiences (ACE) Study (Felitti et al., 1998) has indicated that experiencing six or more adverse events in childhood can shorten one's lifespan by twenty years; one sample of ten- to twenty-year-olds who had experienced commercial sexual exploitation reported an average of five different trauma types (Cole et al., 2014).

For survivors of child maltreatment, with or without child CSE, the journey into adulthood brings with it increased risks for numerous forms of revictimization that include emotional, psychological, physical, and sexual abuse by intimate partners and/or sexual assault by dates, partners, acquaintances, and strangers (Arata, 2000; Messman & Long, 1996; Noll, Horowitz, Bonanno, Trickett, & Putnam, 2003; Schaaf & McCanne, 1998).

These traumatic experiences are pervasive in our culture, but even more common for survivors of CSE/ST, who endure additional forms of psychological (100 percent), physical (88.9 percent), and sexual violence (83.3 percent) while being exploited or trafficked (Muftić & Finn, 2013). A social worker at a St. Louis area nonprofit that specializes in serving adult survivors of ST/CSE recently shared that the average ACE (adverse childhood experiences) score for its clients is ten traumatic events. Not every survivor of ST/CSE has a history of childhood trauma or has experienced all of these types of adult interpersonal violence, but social workers serving this population need to recognize that in all likelihood these clients' overall trauma exposure will be high and the mental health consequences substantial.

Mental Health Consequences

The magnitude and relentless nature of the trauma experienced by survivors of CSE/ST cause complex forms of psychological distress that manifest in significant interpersonal, behavioral, and mental health difficulties. Survivors' sense of self can be damaged (Curtis, Terry, Dank, Dombrowski, & Khan, 2008; Smith, Vardaman, & Snow, 2009), and they often have attachment issues that impact affect regulation, relational skills, trust, boundaries, and intimacy (Banovic & Bjelajac, 2012; Clawson & Goldblatt Grace, 2007; Cole et al., 2014; Curtis et al., 2008; Smith et al., 2009). Many engage in self-injurious behaviors and struggle with suicidal tendencies (Cole et al., 2014; Greene, Ennett, & Ringwalt, 1999; Van Brunschot & Brannigan, 2002). The most frequently identified mental health symptoms are PTSD, anxiety, depression, dissociation, and substance abuse (Banovic & Bjelajac, 2012; Cecchet & Thoburn, 2014; Cole et al., 2014; Farley, Baral, Kiremire, & Sezgin, 1998; Hardy, Compton, & McPhatter, 2013; Nadon, Koverola, & Schludermann, 1998; Oram, Stockl, Busza, Howard, & Zimmerman, 2012; Roe-Sepowitz, 2012; Tsutsumi, Izutsu, Poudyal, Kato, & Marui, 2008). The prevalence estimates of these primary trauma symptoms reflect substantial clinical distress—PTSD (69 percent; Muftić & Finn, 2013), depression (60 percent; Muftić & Finn, 2013), anxiety (48–97.7 percent; Oram et al., 2012), and drug and alcohol abuse (75 percent [drug] and 27 percent [alcohol]; Farley et al., 2004).

These mental health conditions often co-occur with PTSD, increasing the likelihood of a substance abuse disorder (Chilcoat & Breslau, 1998; Kessler et al., 1997); both PTSD and these mental health conditions already increase risks for revictimization (Lalor & McElvaney, 2010; Steel & Herlitz, 2005). An adult survivor of child sexual abuse/assault who has PTSD and depression is 13.7 times more likely to experience some form of revictimization (Lalor & McElvaney, 2010).

The chronic exposure to multiple types of trauma, including the prolonged nature of CSE/ST and the multifaceted constellation of trauma symptoms that we see in these survivors, constitutes complex trauma (Hardy et al., 2013). Consequently, for many survivors it is more accurate and useful to conceptualize their symptoms as complex PTSD, to reflect the presence of both PTSD and these additional trauma-generated symptoms (Herman, 1997; Roth, Newman, Pelcovitz, van der Kolk, & Mandel, 1997). It is precisely because of the complexity and unique dynamics of the trauma experienced during ST/CSE that social workers, survivors, and activists in the antitrafficking field have advocated for comprehensive service models and specialized trauma-focused interventions (Cole et al., 2014; Edmond, 2016; Hardy et al., 2013; Heffernan & Blythe, 2014; Heil & Nichols, 2015; Lloyd, 2012; Macy & Johns, 2011; Reid, 2010).

To date, there is no specialized, trauma-focused, evidence-based treatment for ST/CSE, and there is an absence of data on the effectiveness of using existing evidence-based trauma treatments with ST/CSE survivors. Although reasonable comparisons have been made to the experiences of child sexual abuse (Cole et al., 2014) and domestic violence (Roe-Sepowitz et al., 2014), which are also common experiences for survivors of CSE/ST, differences in the severity of impact have been noted. Cole and colleagues (2014) compared a sample of sexually abused/assaulted youth to commercially sexually exploited youth between ten and twenty years old and found that "involvement in commercial sex, over and above the effects of sexual abuse and assault, is associated with emotional, developmental, psychological, and behavioral dysregulation in those involved" (p. 14). Despite comparable numbers and types of traumatic events (an average of five), the CSE survivors had significantly higher scores on PTSD, substance abuse, and sexualized behaviors. Overall they displayed more functional impairment, risk behaviors, clinical problems, and trauma symptoms, suggesting that our existing evidence-based trauma treatment approaches may need to be modified to address the unique effects of CSE/ST.

Defining Evidence-Based Practice

For some social workers, the notion of evidence-based practice engenders concerns about a loss of autonomy and flexibility and the imposition of a rigid, manualized approach that negates the importance of the therapeutic relationship. Understandable concerns have been raised about the applicability of evidence-based models in studies that lack diversity and exclude participants with the complex trauma histories and co-occurring mental health disorders that many of our clients experience. Furthermore, the absence of models developed specifically for ST/CSE survivors or the lack of evidence of the effectiveness of existing models with ST/CSE survivors might lead some practitioners to conclude that there are no evidence-based models worth considering. When making clinical decisions about how best to meet your client's needs, a critical analysis of these issues is warranted.

It can be helpful to distinguish between evidence-based practice as a process and evidence-based treatments. The *process* of engaging in evidence-based practice involves formulating a practice question, locating the best available evidence to answer that question, assessing the quality of the evidence, integrating that evidence with your professional judgment and client preferences, and reviewing the outcome (Sackett et al., 1996; Howard, McMillen & Pollio, 2003). The *best available evidence* in newly emerging fields like sex trafficking is sometimes practice-based evidence until research-based evidence is available. Too often when we talk about evidence-based practice, practitioner expertise and client preferences get left out of the discussion, but these are critical aspects of the process.

Evidence-based treatments are specific interventions that have been demonstrated to be effective in achieving a specific set of outcomes. When engaging in the evidence-based practice process, we should carefully examine each evidence-based treatment to assess with whom it has worked, under what conditions, to achieve what specific outcomes. We should consider how applicable and feasible the intervention is within our practice context, with our knowledge and skill set, and with consideration of our client's preferences. This is as important in our assessment of the evidence as the quality of the research design.

Recommended Evidence-Based Trauma Treatments

In selecting the interventions to recommend for treating the psychological effects of ST/CSE, I considered those factors that demonstrated effectiveness (1) in reducing PTSD, depression, and anxiety (primary mental health outcomes); (2) with adult survivors of child sexual abuse and intimate partner violence (chronic and complex traumas that have similarities to CSE/ST); (3) across a wide range of trauma types (high ACE scores); and (4) with diverse samples of participants (identities similar to those of ST/CSE survivors). In addition, consideration was given to the feasibility of implementing the interventions within the service structures of both ST/CSE-specific programs and the allied agencies that provide mental health services.

Eye Movement Desensitization and Reprocessing (EMDR)

EMDR therapy is an evidence-based trauma treatment that uses a three-pronged approach to identify and address past distressing or traumatic events, current triggers, and possible future concerns across eight phases of treatment. The first phase involves obtaining a thorough trauma history and an understanding of the client's presenting problem or concerns. Phase two involves preparing the client for treatment by developing treatment goals, providing psychoeducation about trauma and the EMDR treatment approach, and practicing relaxation techniques, which is particularly important for survivors with complex trauma histories. Phase three moves the client through an assessment process that follows an established protocol: (a) identify the presenting issue to be addressed; (b) identify the memory associated with the presenting issue; (c) ask the client to hold an image of the memory that best captures that experience; (d) identify a primary negative self-belief connected to the memory; (e) identify a desired positive belief to replace the negative cognition; (f) identify the negative emotions associated with the memory; and (g) identify any physical sensations in the body connected to the memory. During this assessment phase, information is also gathered from the client to assess the strength of the desired positive cognition (scale of 1–7) and the intensity of the negative emotions (scale of 0–10).

Phase four is called desensitization and marks the beginning of the trauma-processing work. The trauma memory is activated by asking the client to bring up the image associated with the trauma, negative self-beliefs, emotions, and body sensations, while alternating bilateral stimulation is induced through either eye movements (visual), hand taps/vibrations (tactile), or sounds delivered through head phones (auditory). The trauma processing with bilateral stimulation is done in short sets that last for approximately twenty to thirty seconds, during which the client is instructed to just notice what happens. After a set of bilateral stimulation, clients are asked to share what they noticed, which could be a thought, feeling, image, or body sensation. Whatever emerges becomes the focus during the next round of bilateral stimulation. This process continues throughout the session with periodic assessments of the emotional distress connected to the original target memory, which typically decreases during the session. Resolution of the emotional distress is signaled by a rating of 0–1 on the subjective units of distress scale. It is in this phase that processing occurs across the three prongs of past traumatic experiences, current trauma-related triggers, and anticipated future challenges. The number of sessions needed in phase four to facilitate sufficient processing to reach adaptive resolution varies across clients, with complex trauma typically requiring more time than single-incident traumas.

Although this phase has been compared to gradual or prolonged exposure, it differs in a few important ways. The exposure time occurs in short bursts of twenty to thirty seconds without the repeated, detailed, out-loud recitation of the trauma narrative required in prolonged exposure. This has potential advantages in reducing distress for both the client and the counselor. Prolonged exposure also includes homework that involves listening to the tape-recorded trauma narrative every day and engaging in in vivo (in real life) exposure. In contrast, minimal homework is needed in EMDR during this process, which could reduce potential barriers to treatment engagement.

In the fifth phase, bilateral stimulation is used to install the desired positive cognition, with successful installation being achieved when the client indicates that the positive cognition feels true, rating it a 6 or 7 on a 7-point scale. Phase six involves a body scan, during which the client retrieves the target memory to assess whether it generates any unprocessed residual physical sensations. If any physical sensations are noticed in the body, those sensations become the target for additional processing through bilateral stimulation as described in phase four. Phase seven is closure, and this occurs at the end of each session even if additional trauma processing will be needed in the next session. Clients are encouraged to use relaxation skills between sessions and to keep a log of any distressing thoughts, feelings, imaginings, or physical sensations that may occur. Phase eight is reevaluation, which involves reevaluating the target memory; reviewing the client's log for any new material that may have emerged between sessions; assessing for any remaining distress related to past traumatic experiences, current traumatic triggers, and future potential challenges; and processing anything that needs to be addressed to reach a state of adaptive resolution.

EMDR therapy has been rigorously tested through more than thirty randomized controlled trials and several meta-analyses; these studies have generated a substantial body of evidence that EMDR is an effective treatment for PTSD for both single-incident and complex trauma (Bisson et al., 2007; Bradley, Greene, Russ, Dutra, & Westen, 2005; Davidson & Parker, 2001; Seidler & Wagner, 2006; van Etten & Taylor, 1998). These studies have shown that in addition to PTSD, EMDR significantly reduces other co-occurring trauma symptoms such as depression and anxiety. Although studies have demonstrated meaningful clinical outcomes within one to three sessions, this has usually been demonstrated with clients who were only addressing a single traumatic incident, such as a natural disaster or motor vehicle accident. Clients who have experienced complex trauma generally require a longer course of treatment (Edmond & Lawrence, 2015; Edmond & Rubin, 2004). The typical length of an individual session is ninety minutes; however, the pace, length, and number of sessions needed are tailored to the needs of the client.

Most EMDR studies have involved survivors who have experienced a broad array of trauma types (sexual assault, witnessing homicide, traumatic loss, or life-threatening injury), including complex traumas: child sexual abuse, child physical abuse, and intimate partner violence (Edmond & Lawrence, 2015). Over 100,000 practitioners around the world, on six continents and across fifty-four countries, have been trained to use EMDR (Maxfield, 2009).

The knowledge base that has been developed has come from EMDR studies conducted with children and adults (six to seventy-nine years old), men and women from numerous countries, and multiple ethnic groups, and consistently positive outcomes have been found (e.g., Capezzani et al., 2013; de Roos et al., 2011; Diehle, Opmeer, Boer, Mannarino, & Lindauer, 2014; Högberg et al., 2007; Jaberghaderi, Greenwald, Rubin, Zand, & Dolatabadi, 2004; Nijdam, Gersons, Reitsma, de Jongh, & Olff, 2012; Wanders, Serra, & de Jongh, 2008). In the United States, studies have included people who identified as white, African American, Hispanic, Native American, Alaskan Native, and Asian Pacific Islander.

EMDR is considered one of the most effective treatments for PTSD in adults and children, and it has been endorsed as such in several national and international guidelines, including those of the International Society for Traumatic Stress Studies, the Cochrane Database, the Evidence Based Clearinghouse for Child Welfare, the Department of Veteran's Affairs, the National Registry of Evidence Based Programs and Practices of the Substance Abuse and Mental Health Services Administration, and the World Health Organization (Edmond & Lawrence, 2015). EMDR has been found to be as effective as other evidence-based trauma treatments (prolonged exposure, cognitive processing therapy, cognitive-behavioral therapy), with some indications that it achieves results in a shorter amount of time, with fewer sessions, and with less homework (Ironson et al., 2002; Lee, Gavriel, Drummond, Richards, & Greenwald, 2002; Power et al., 2002) and lower dropout rates (Ironson et al., 2002; Rothbaum, Astin, & Marsteller, 2005; Taylor et al., 2003; van Etten & Taylor, 1998).

Applicability of EMDR to ST/CSE

Although survivors of ST/CSE have not explicitly been identified in any EMDR studies, there is an abundance of evidence that EMDR is effective in reducing or eliminating clinically significant levels of trauma symptoms, including PTSD, depression, and anxiety in children, adolescents, and adult survivors who have experienced complex trauma that included sexual violence. The fact that EMDR is effective with people from many different cultural backgrounds is particularly salient given the need to serve both domestic and international survivors of CSE/ST. EMDR has also been used to address a number of other clinical issues that may be affecting survivors of ST/CSE, including substance abuse, eating disorders, borderline personality disorder, psychosis, pain management, and somatic disorders (de Roos et al., 2010; Mosquera & Gonzalez-Vazquez, 2012; Schneider, Hofmann, Rost, & Shapiro, 2008; van den Berg & van der Gaag, 2012). However, the evidence base for effectiveness on these issues is only beginning to emerge.

Another strength of EMDR that could be helpful across service sectors addressing ST/CSE is that it can be flexibly integrated with a variety of theoretical orientations and clinical approaches, including cognitive-behavioral, psychodynamic, body-centered, and systems perspectives (Shapiro & Laliotis, 2011). Within the ST/CSE field there is recognition of the importance of empowering survivors and using a strengths-based approach. This aligns well with EMDR in that there is recognition of client's ability to facilitate their own healing and an expectation that there be minimal therapist interference during the trauma-processing phase of the work. All of these factors illustrate the potential viability of EMDR as an effective trauma treatment with this population; this has been recognized in the ST/CSE literature, both practitioners and scholars have recommended the use of EMDR (Clawson & Goldblatt, 2007; Edmond, 2016; Kotrla, 2010; Wilson & Butler, 2014).

Cognitive Processing Therapy (CPT)

CPT is a short-term, manualized form of psychotherapy for the treatment of PTSD that is based on social cognitive theory and information processing theory. It was originally developed specifically to treat PTSD in rape survivors through individual psychotherapy (Resick & Schnicke, 1992 & 1993), but evolved in its application to treat PTSD in survivors of several different types of trauma. It is considered a short-term treatment in part because it is designed specifically to treat PTSD, which it can do relatively quickly, but is not designed to address all trauma-related issues such as attachment and relationship difficulties or personality disorders, which some survivors also need to work on in their healing process. Survivors with those issues can benefit from CPT if they have PTSD, but it is important to be clear about what the intervention is able to effectively treat.

The treatment can be used in individual and group formats or a combination of both. The course of treatment is typically twelve weekly individual sessions; although variable treatment length options exist, the actual number of sessions needed is determined by symptom measures and client readiness (generally four to eighteen sessions) (Galovski, Blain, Mott, Elwood, & Houle, 2012; Resick, Monson, & Chard, 2014). It is possible to conduct two sessions per week if the client wants and is able to do so, but it is not recommended to do CPT less than once per week. The group version is generally conducted across sixteen sessions. The primary focus is on helping the client recognize the connections between thoughts and feelings and to develop skills to challenge negative or unhelpful thoughts and beliefs (i.e., stuck points). Particular attention is given to addressing unhelpful beliefs related to safety, trust, power/control, self-esteem, and intimacy that are negatively affecting functioning, especially within social relationships.

CPT includes the following phases: (1) pretreatment assessment; (2) psycho-education about trauma, PTSD, and cognitive-behavioral theory; (3) trauma processing; (4) skill development for challenging cognitions; (5) trauma themes; and (6) planning for the future. In the assessment phase it is recommended that a trauma history be completed, along with measures of PTSD and depression. If the group format is being used, survivors need to be assessed to ensure that they are appropriate for a group (can be present, engaged, and not disruptive). Phase two occurs across sessions 1 to 3, with sequential homework that includes a trauma impact statement, ABC (activating event–beliefs–consequences) worksheets, and a written trauma account.

Phase three, processing the trauma, occurs during sessions 4 and 5. This involves having the client read the trauma accounts with the therapist, who will gently challenge the stuck points, particularly those related to self-blame. It is important to note that CPT can be equally effective with or without the inclusion of a written trauma narrative; CPT-Cognitive (CPT-C) is an effective variation of CPT that does not require a written narrative (Resick et al., 2008). Clients can be offered a choice between models. Both CPT and CPT-C start with education about PTSD and the cognitive model. The trauma is addressed through either a written narrative or cognitive worksheets. The client is given out-of-session work after each session to practice skills for challenging stuck points (unhelpful beliefs that disrupt healing—"It was my fault") and creating alternative thoughts/meaning (Resick et al., 2014). When CPT is done in a group, the written narrative is either conducted in an individual session or is omitted.

Phase four (sessions 6 and 7) emphasizes learning how to challenge your thoughts and reflects a progression of skill development. In this phase clients use challenging questions and challenging belief worksheets and learn to identify problematic thinking patterns. Phase five addresses the core trauma themes (safety, trust, power/control, esteem, and intimacy) using challenging belief worksheets throughout sessions 8 to 12. Phase six (facing the future) occurs during termination (session 12) and involves reviewing the work that has been done, comparing a final impact statement with the initial impact statement, and identifying new goals or additional work that needs to be addressed.

CPT has been shown to effectively treat a number of co-occurring disorders and trauma symptoms (PTSD, depression, anxiety, guilt, shame, and anger) with survivors of child maltreatment (physical and sexual), intimate partner violence, rape, military sexual assault, and military combat in both individual and group formats (Bass et al., 2013; Chard, 2005; Galovski et al., 2012; Iverson, Resick, Suvak, Walling, & Taft, 2011; Monson et al., 2006; Resick et al., 2008; Resick, Nishith, Weaver, Astin, & Feuer, 2002; Schulz, Resick, Huber, & Griffin, 2006; Surís, Link-Malcolm, Chard, Ahn, & North, 2013). Impressively, a five-year follow-up study found that survivors treated with CPT maintained their treatment gains and did not "relapse" (Resick, 2010).

In these studies CPT has been shown to be effective with adolescents and adults, and with males and females from diverse ethnic backgrounds, including white, African American, and Hispanic survivors. CPT has been found to be similarly effective for immigrants and refugees from Bosnia-Herzegovina and Afghanistan, even with the use of interpreters (Schulz et al., 2006). In addition, it has been shown to be effective with sexual trauma survivors from the Democratic Republic of Congo (Bass et al., 2013). Very few studies on CPT reported information about socioeconomic status, but one indicated that half the sample was very low income.

Extensive literature reviews reflected in guidelines for the treatment of PTSD reveal that the strongest evidence of effectiveness is with cognitive-behavioral approaches, including cognitive processing therapy (Hamblen, Schnurr, Rosenberg, & Eftekhari, 2016). CPT has been found to be as effective as prolonged exposure and better than other cognitive-behavioral approaches (Bisson et al., 2007; Powers, Halpern, Ferenschak, Gillihan, & Foa, 2010; Rizvi, Vogt, & Resick, 2009; Seidler & Wagner, 2006). PTSD treatment guidelines that have endorsed CPT include those of the International Society for Traumatic Stress Studies (Foa, Keane, Friedman, & Cohen (2008) and the VA/DoD Clinical Practice Guideline for Management of Post-Traumatic Stress (Management of Post-Traumatic Stress Working Group, 2010). CPT has also been recognized by the Institute of Medicine as an effective treatment for PTSD (Institute of Medicine, 2007), and it was chosen by the Veteran's Administration for national dissemination for the treatment of PTSD caused by combat or military sexual assault (U.S. Department of Veterans Affairs, National Center for PTSD, March 30, 2017)

Applicability of CPT to ST/CSE

No survivors of ST/CSE were explicitly identified in any of the CPT studies. However, the demonstration of its effectiveness in treating an array of trauma symptoms, particularly PTSD, depression, guilt, and shame in adolescents and adult survivors who have experienced complex trauma, including child sexual abuse and intimate partner violence, suggests that CPT could be a viable treatment option for male and female survivors of ST/CSE. Further support for CPT with survivors of ST/CSE is found in its successful application with survivors of sexual violence perpetrated in war and conflict zones in Bosnia, Afghanistan, and the Democratic Republic of Congo. The effectiveness of CPT with culturally and ethnically diverse survivors from the United States and other countries makes it potentially helpful for both domestic and international survivors of CSE/ST.

One exciting aspect of the Democratic Republic of Congo study (Bass et al., 2013) was that trauma symptoms were significantly reduced with the use of psychosocial assistants as group facilitators. Although they only had the equivalent of a high school education, the psychosocial assistants had one to nine years of experience working with survivors of sexual trauma. They received two weeks of training and effectively implemented a CPT group protocol without the inclusion of a trauma narrative. This has potential implications for ST/CSE programs that use survivors as peer leaders and paraprofessionals. If this could be done in the Congo, it would seem possible to achieve similar outcomes with paraprofessionals in the United States.

This model in either individual or group formats could be particularly helpful across different service settings that address ST/CSE. For example, individual CPT might be most helpful when referrals to community mental health agencies are made, while groups could be more applicable in residential treatment and transitional housing settings. Another element of flexibility is the inclusion or omission of the written narrative, which serves as an exposure component in facilitating trauma processing. For some survivors, having the option to bypass the written narrative might reduce barriers to engaging in treatment. This is a good example of when client preferences need to be recognized as an essential element of evidence-based practice.

Skills Training in Affective and Interpersonal Regulation/Narrative Story Telling (STAIR/NST)

STAIR/NST (Cloitre, Cohen, & Koenen, 2006) is a cognitive-behavioral, two-stage trauma treatment that was initially developed for adult survivors of childhood abuse with complex trauma histories that included adult traumatic events. A stage-based approach to trauma treatment is considered especially useful in developing a strong therapeutic alliance and in facilitating engagement and reducing dropouts by focusing on functional issues that affect daily living. Originally, STAIR/NST was delivered in an individual format across 16 sessions. In stage one (STAIR), the first 8 sessions focus on emotion regulation and relationship skills training. In stage two (NST), the remaining 8 sessions employ a modified version of prolonged exposure called narrative storytelling therapy. STAIR has also been adapted by Cloitre (2015) to be delivered in a 12-session group format.

The primary goal of the first stage of STAIR is to improve functioning in daily life for people who have significantly impaired functioning as a result of chronic trauma, PTSD, and comorbid mental health problems (Cloitre et al., 2014). This goal is addressed by skills training in emotion regulation and interpersonal relationships. The focus on these core areas was based on data obtained from adult survivors of childhood abuse that demonstrated that 42 percent of functional impairment could be explained by PTSD, interpersonal problems, and emotion regulation problems (Cloitre, Miranda, Stovall-McClough, & Han, 2005). The second phase, narrative storytelling, focuses on talking about one's traumatic experiences, connecting the trauma to feelings and beliefs about one's self and others, and employing the knowledge and coping skills developed in phase one.

The STAIR manual (Cloitre et al., 2006) recommends that a comprehensive assessment be made before treatment begins. Trauma history, PTSD, emotion regulation difficulties, interpersonal problems, risky or harmful behaviors, resilience and coping strategies, and readiness for treatment should be assessed. The first session consists of an overview of the treatment approach with an explanation of why it can be helpful, a review of the survivor's trauma history and goals for treatment, training in focused breathing, and an assignment to practice the breathing technique between sessions as a coping strategy. The next three sessions focus on the connections between trauma and emotions by providing psychoeducation and opportunities to develop skills in regulating emotions. Attention is given to emotional awareness, being able to recognize and name emotions, learning how emotions influence actions (emotion regulation), and beginning to act and relate to people in a way that is consistent with one's own values (emotionally engaged living). Emotion regulation includes deepening recognition of the body sensations and thoughts that are connected to emotional reactions and how those connect to behaviors. Throughout this process, survivors are learning about and expanding their emotion regulation skills and capacity for tolerating distress. They do this by practicing new strategies that connect to their bodies, thoughts, and/or behaviors, such as focused breathing, progressive muscle relaxation, thought stopping, positive imagery and self-talk, emotion surfing, slowing down, taking a time out, doing something pleasurable, and asking for support.

Sessions 5 to 8 take the insights learned about emotions into the realm of relationships. Survivors learn about how trauma impacts their relationships, and they begin to identify and change their relationship patterns. They learn to pay attention to their thoughts and feelings in interpersonal situations, to recognize the expectations they are holding of the other person, and to see how they behave as a result. They learn to recognize power dynamics in relationships and the difference between aggressive and assertive behaviors. They practice saying no, asking for what they want and need, and allowing themselves and others to make mistakes and forgive. They allow themselves and others to ask for and receive support and to feel pleasure, joy, uncertainty, and pride in their accomplishments and growth. This learning cultivates a sense of agency, assertiveness, flexibility, intimacy, and compassion (for self and others) in relationships. Throughout STAIR sessions, survivors are given in-session activities and outside-of-session assignments that include the use of tools and worksheets to help them practice with real-world experiences. The STAIR group protocol includes the same content but allows for a greater number of sessions for emotion and relationship skill development. It can be a stand-alone intervention or can be followed with the individual treatment, narrative storytelling, that occurs in phase two.

Narrative storytelling (NST), which is a modified version of prolonged exposure, takes place across 8 sessions of individual therapy. It begins with providing a rationale for telling the trauma narrative (which effectively treats PTSD) and continues by reviewing current PTSD symptoms, treatment goals, emotion regulation skills, and difficulties in the past week in implementing emotion regulation and relationship skills. The modifications developed by Cloitre and her associates (2002, 2014), include elimination of the in vivo exposure component, the addition of grounding exercises after exposure-based trauma processing, and the integration of cognitive reappraisal of the meaning of the traumatic experiences with particular attention given to interpersonal schemas. The first session of NST also includes identifying a core set of traumatic memories that will be addressed in this phase of the trauma processing work and assessing the subjective levels of distress (0–100 scale). Between sessions, homework includes reviewing the rationale for NST, practicing emotion regulation and relationship skills, practicing daily positive imagery or self-statements, and practicing focused breathing twice a day. Throughout NST, the therapist provides survivors with support and encouragement, reminds them of the rationale and their goals for the work, and helps them feel safe and stay focused on the specific memory being processed. In the final session of NST, the survivor and therapist review progress toward established goals, identify what has been accomplished, determine what next steps are needed to continue healing, and develop strategies to prevent relapse, including referral to additional resources.

From the beginning, STAIR/NST was developed to address the trauma treatment needs of survivors of chronic, complex trauma who were struggling with coexisting mental health disorders. The first study to evaluate the effectiveness of STAIR/NST (Cloitre, Koenen, Cohen, & Han, 2002) included adult female survivors of childhood abuse who met criteria for PTSD. Their levels of comorbidity were high, with 45 percent having major depression, 79 percent an anxiety disorder, 25 percent past substance abuse disorder, 16 percent past eating disorder, and nearly half reporting histories of self-harming behaviors or suicide attempts. The women were ethnically diverse (white 46 percent; African American 20 percent; Hispanic 15 percent; Asian, Caribbean, and American Indian 19 percent), had a range of education levels, and were predominately low income: in other words, a sample in a research study that looks like the clients we serve in the real world. The survivors experienced clinically significant reductions in PTSD, depression, anxiety, dissociation, anger, affect regulation difficulties, and interpersonal skills deficits. Another important finding was that the positive therapeutic alliance developed in phase one, in conjunction with increased emotion regulation skills, had a significant impact on the reductions of PTSD achieved in phase two (Cloitreet al., 2002; Cloitre, Stovall-McClough, Miranda, & Chemtob, 2004). In a subsequent study, Cloitre and colleagues (2010) found very similar outcomes in a sample of ethnically diverse adult women survivors of childhood abuse who also had significant trauma exposure in adulthood (domestic violence, sexual assault, physical assault), averaging 6.57 lifetime traumas. In addition to PTSD, this group of complex trauma survivors had high rates of both axis I and axis II mental health disorders. STAIR/NST achieved higher rates of full PTSD remission, greater improvements in affect regulation and interpersonal problems, and lower dropout rates than a support/exposure comparison treatment. Three- and nine-month follow-up assessments revealed that the therapeutic gains were maintained over time.

Although STAIR/NST was originally developed to respond to the treatment needs of adult women survivors, an adolescent school-based group version (STAIR-A) has been developed, and an initial evaluation found significant improvements in resilience, along with reductions in depression and anxiety, in an ethnically diverse sample of girls between eleven and sixteen years old (Gudiño, Leonard, & Cloitre, 2016). The narrative storytelling was not included, but a written trauma narrative was added as an outside-of-group exposure homework activity, which did not appear to be sufficient to significantly reduce PTSD in a group with a high level of trauma exposure. However, in a recent pilot study testing a brief adolescent inpatient group model of STAIR without NST (Brief STAIR-A), significant reductions in PTSD and depression symptoms and increases in coping self-efficacy were found (Gudiño et al., 2014). The ethnically diverse sample of adolescents (ages twelve to seventeen) had experienced multiple types of trauma and had an array of comorbid mental health diagnoses; they included males, females, and a male-to-female transgender person.

The volume of publications for STAIR/NST is much smaller at this stage of its development than is true of EMDR or CPT. Nonetheless, the emerging evidence is compelling and has led to its inclusion on SAMHSA's National Registry of Evidenced-Based Programs and Practices. Additionally, the National Child Traumatic Stress Network lists STAIR/NST among the mental health interventions and trauma-informed treatment approaches that it and its related centers have used to raise the standard of care for traumatized youth and families, and the Evidence Based Clearinghouse for Child Welfare has rated it as a promising practice.

Applicability of STAIR/NST to CSE/ST

The effectiveness of STAIR/NST has been demonstrated with survivors who share many characteristics of ST/CSE survivors: ethnically diverse (white,

African American, Hispanic, Asian, and American Indian); male, female, and transgender; ages eleven to mid-forties; predominately low income; and varying levels of education. Furthermore, every study of STAIR/NST and its modified versions has intentionally included survivors of chronic, complex trauma that started in childhood who are struggling with serious mental health difficulties as a consequence of the pervasive trauma exposure they have endured. The fact that STAIR/NST was designed not only to treat PTSD, but also to address broader areas of daily life functioning (affective and interpersonal regulation) that are developmentally disrupted by childhood trauma exposure, makes it a conceptually strong fit with adolescent and adult survivors of ST/CSE. The demonstrated ability to meaningfully improve affect regulation and relationship skills in survivors with complex trauma histories and comorbid mental health conditions suggests that STAIR/NST could be a useful option for addressing some of those same areas of impaired functioning that negatively impact ST/CSE survivors and increase their vulnerabilities to exploitation and revictimization.

One example of this applicability is in the area of substance abuse. Research indicates that there is a significant relationship between emotion regulation difficulties and use of drugs and alcohol as coping mechanisms (Caetano, Nelson, & Field, 2003). Use of drugs and alcohol has been linked to increased risks of revictimization, particularly sexual assault and intimate partner violence (Lalor & McElvaney, 2010; Steel & Herlitz, 2005), which ST/CSE survivors are already at increased risk for experiencing. By improving emotion regulation skills, STAIR/NST may be helpful in reducing both substance use and revictimization. This possibility is supported by data from a STAIR/NST study of 911 survivors that, in addition to reductions in PTSD, found a significant reduction in reliance on use of drugs and alcohol as a coping strategy and a significant increase in the use of social support (Levitt, Malta, Martin, Davis, & Cloitre, 2007). Providing survivors of ST/CSE with enhanced emotion regulation and interpersonal skills could significantly increase their coping self-efficacy and decrease the risk of engaging in negative coping strategies (e.g., substance use).

The stage-based approach, with an initial emphasis on skill development to build resilience through strengthening emotion regulation and interpersonal effectiveness, could help ST/CSE survivors navigate the challenges of engaging in treatment and developing a therapeutic relationship. Additionally, with their newly acquired coping strategies and expanded distress tolerance, ST/CSE survivors would be better equipped to actively engage in the trauma processing work in NST, something they may not otherwise be willing to do. That said, it is also useful to have an evidence-based treatment that has the flexibility to have the STAIR phase as a stand-alone option that can be delivered either in an individual or group format. Even though the full STAIR/NST model appears to produce the strongest outcomes, particularly for PTSD, this flexibility could be helpful for an individual client who does not want to participate in the narrative storytelling phase (client preferences) or for an agency that has the capacity to provide group, but not individual, treatment.

Choosing Between Treatment Options

This chapter has discussed EMDR, CPT, and STAIR/NST in depth to provide social work practitioners an opportunity to consider the potential application of these trauma treatments with ST/CSE survivors, given the degree of evidence available, the intervention characteristics, the unique mental health needs of this population, and the service setting where they practice. In the absence of specific trauma-focused treatment approaches designed specifically for ST/CSE, social workers will need to use their judgement, in conjunction with client preferences, to assess the quality of the evidence, the generalizability of the findings, the appropriateness of the interventions, and the feasibility of implementation, in order to select the treatment that best fits their practice context. EMDR, CPT, and STAIR/NST are all good clinical options that, once implemented with survivors of ST/CSE, will need to be evaluated in practice and research to determine if similar levels of effectiveness can be obtained or if there will be a need for modifications. This would be an excellent opportunity for a community-university partnership to help advance trauma-focused mental health treatment for ST/CSE survivors.

It is important to acknowledge that the three interventions selected for this chapter are not an exhaustive list. They each have unique qualities that make them good candidates for consideration with this population. However, there are a number of other evidence-based trauma treatments that could also be useful under the right circumstances. Prolonged exposure is one of the most extensively researched, well-established, evidence-based treatments for PTSD that exists. It has been shown to be as effective as EMDR and CPT (Bisson et al., 2007; Powers et al., 2010; Rizvi et al., 2009; Seidler & Wagner, 2006), but not better than either. It is, in a modified form, the main component of narrative storytelling, phase two of STAIR, which appears to be driving the biggest reductions in PTSD in that intervention (Cloitre et al., 2012). However, despite its effectiveness, clients and practitioners are reluctant to use it, and given the challenges of treatment engagement with ST/CSE survivors, adding potential barriers seems unwise. It also offers less flexibility than CPT or STAIR/NST, which can be implemented in both individual and group formats.

Dialectical behavior therapy (DBT) is an evidence-based treatment for people with a diagnosis of borderline personality disorder (BPD) who engage in self-harming behaviors, struggle with intense affect regulation difficulties, and often need psychiatric hospitalization. This may be the treatment of choice for some survivors of ST/CSE, but it also reflects a severity of distress that most complex trauma survivors do not express. It was not included in this chapter because it requires substantial resources in training, number of staff, and time, which makes it less feasible for many programs serving ST/CSE survivors. In addition, EMDR, CPT, and STAIR/NST have all generated significant trauma symptom reductions with survivors diagnosed with BPD, and STAIR/NST increases affect regulation skills.

It has been suggested that trauma-focused cognitive-behavioral therapy (TFCBT), an evidence-based trauma treatment for children and adolescents, could be a viable treatment option for CSE child survivors (Cole et al., 2014). A recent study testing the effectiveness of TFCBT with CSE child survivors and war exposure in the Democratic Republic of Congo found improvements in PTSD, depression, anxiety, and conduct and prosocial behaviors (O'Callaghan, McMullen, Shannon, Rafferty, & Black, 2013). This finding further strengthens support for TFCBT with CSE child survivors. The only reason TFCBT was not a focal point of this chapter is that its application is only with children, whereas EMDR, CPT, and STAIR/NST offer treatment options across a wider age group.

Competency-Based Social Work Practice

As social workers grapple with the complexities of responding to the trauma treatment needs of survivors of ST/CSE, they should be able to demonstrate the practice competencies that the Council on Social Work Education (CSWE) has established, in the educational policy and accreditation standards (EPAS). The nine competencies include (1) Demonstrate Ethical and Professional Behavior; (2) Engage Diversity and Difference in Practice; (3) Advance Human Rights and Social, Economic, and Environmental Justice; (4) Engage in Practice-informed Research and Research-informed Practice; (5) Engage in Policy Practice; (6) Engage with Individuals, Families, Groups, Organizations, and Communities; (7) Assess Individuals, Families, Groups, Organizations, and Communities; (8) Intervene with Individuals, Families, Groups, Organizations, and Communities; and (9) Evaluate Practice with Individuals, Families, Groups, Organizations, and Communities. "EPAS recognizes a holistic view of competence; that is, the demonstration of competence is informed by knowledge, values, skills, and cognitive and affective processes that include the social worker's critical thinking, affective reactions, and exercise of judgment in regard to unique practice situations" (EPAS, 2015, p. 6). Such competencies are key to developing professional social work curriculum and standards.

To help guide specialized practice within social work, CSWE is working with various national task forces to adapt the nine generalist competencies to reflect the competencies needed for specialty areas like trauma. The Task Force on Specialized Trauma Competencies developed a curricular guide, which includes descriptions of each competency, a core set of practice behaviors, and a set of curricular resources (readings, exercises, assignments, and multimedia) for social work programs to use in their Masters of Social Work (MSW) courses. It is anticipated that the Specialized Practice Curricular Guide for Trauma Social Work Practice will be disseminated in 2017. The description for Competency 8: Intervene with Individuals, Families, Groups, Organizations and Communities, is particularly salient for this chapter and provides critically important guidance that social workers working with ST/CSE survivors should implement to reflect competent trauma-informed practice (see the following box).

Trauma Curricular Guide

Competency 8: Intervene with Individuals, Families, Groups, Organizations and Communities

Specialized Practice Competency Description

Social workers addressing trauma strive to create trauma-informed systems of care that recognize and respond effectively to signs of traumatic distress in human beings across their lifespan and throughout the various service settings that clients access. This requires intervening across micro, mezzo and macro systems. Trauma social workers understand that human relationships are essential to the healing process, bring a compassionate and non-judgmental stance to their work, and build relationships with clients based on safety, support, respect, and trust. They work to enhance psychological, emotional, physical, and spiritual safety in individuals, families, communities, or organizations. They are mindful of the effect they can have on their clients and of the impact their clients' trauma histories can have on them. Social workers are knowledgeable about the theoretical and empirical foundations of trauma-informed evidence-based practice and apply that knowledge to identify and implement developmentally and culturally appropriate, trauma-focused interventions. Trauma social workers facilitate healing with client systems by processing trauma experiences within somatic, affective, cognitive and spiritual domains in a phase-based approach that attends to safety and meaning making. Trauma social workers value strengths-based and empowerment-oriented approaches to practice that recognize promotive and protective factors, resiliency, and opportunities for post-traumatic growth in individuals, families, organizations, and communities. Trauma social workers build practice-based evidence to determine how to intervene in the absence of research-based evidence, when new interventions are emerging, or modifications and adaptations are needed for cultural or contextual reasons. Trauma-informed organizations proactively promote self-care, supervision, and training in evidence-based interventions to support professional development and to address risks of vicarious traumatization. Trauma social workers advocate for social justice because they understand that systemic and structural inequality and oppression increase risk factors for and exacerbate the adverse consequences of exposure to trauma, including historical trauma. They advocate for expanding access to trauma-informed care and culturally appropriate evidence-based trauma treatments, particularly for those most vulnerable and marginalized in our society

Competency Behaviors

- Apply knowledge of the theoretical and empirical foundations of trauma-informed evidence-based practice.
- Critically select and implement developmentally and culturally appropriate trauma-informed evidence-based interventions in conjunction with practitioner expertise and client preferences to address the adverse consequences of trauma.
- Modify and adapt interventions if needed to effectively address cultural differences or contextual/environmental challenges with awareness of the need for continual evaluation.
- Advocate for the advancement of trauma-informed systems of care, expanded access to effective trauma-focused interventions, and social justice for marginalized and oppressed people who are most at risk for experiencing trauma.
- Mobilize the strengths of clients and systems to enhance individual, group, family and community resilience.
- Develop and employ self-care strategies that support resiliency and well-being, to address the impact of compassion fatigue and vicarious traumatization.

Conclusion

Social workers have been at the forefront of activists' efforts to address child sexual abuse, sexual assault, intimate partner violence, and now sex trafficking and commercial sexual exploitation. We come to these issues with a sociopolitical analysis of the layers of structural oppression that facilitate the sexual commodification of human beings. We bring an intersectional lens to this work,

Resources

VA/DoD Clinical Practice Guideline for Management of Post-Traumatic Stress (2010): *http://www.healthquality.va.gov/guidelines/MH/ptsd/cpg_PTSD-FULL-201011612.pdf*

Trauma Assessment Measures—National PTSD Center: *https://www.ptsd.va.gov/*

Adverse Childhood Experiences Resources: *https://www.cdc.gov/violence prevention/acestudy/resources.html*

"The Past Is Present: Understanding the Effects of Unprocessed Memories and Using EMDR Therapy in Treatment," by Francine Shapiro, Ph.D.: *https://www.goodtherapy.org/emdr-therapy-web-conference.html*

Cognitive Processing Therapy [online training]: *https://cpt.musc.edu/*

Skills Training in Affect and Interpersonal Regulation (STAIR) [online training]: *https://www.ptsd.va.gov/professional/continuing_ed/STAIR_online_training.asp*

National Child Traumatic Stress Network (NCTSN): *http://www.nctsn.org/*

understanding that the experiences of survivors are deeply impacted by race-, class-, and gender-based oppression. The use of evidence-based treatments does not preclude bringing this analysis into our clinical work. Social workers are advocates for social and economic justice, ever mindful that, regardless of our role, we work to facilitate change across micro-, mezzo-, and macrosystems, including the ones in which we work. Advancing the development of trauma-informed systems of care and the use of evidence-based treatments is a social justice issue. We must work to expand ST/CSE survivors' access to effective trauma treatments.

References

Ahrens, K. R., Katon, W., McCarty, C., Richardson, L. P., & Courtney, M. E. (2012, January). Association between childhood sexual abuse and transactional sex in youth aging out of foster care. *Child Abuse & Neglect, 36*(1), 75–80. doi:10.1016/j.chiabu.2011.07.009

Arata, C. M. (2000). From child victim to adult victim: A model for predicting sexual revictimization. *Child Maltreatment, 5*(1), 28–38. doi:https://doi.org/10.1177/1077559500005001004

Banovic, B., & Bjelajac, Z. (2012). Traumatic experiences, psychophysical consequences and needs of human trafficking victims. *Vojnosanitetski Prgled, 69*(1), 94–97. doi:10.2298/VSP1201094B

Bass, J. K., Annan, J., Murray, S. M., Kaysen, D., Griffiths, S., Cetinoglu, T., Wachter, K., Murray, L. K., & Bolton, P. A. (2013). Controlled trial of psychotherapy for Congolese survivors of sexual violence. *New England Journal of Medicine, 368*(23), 2182–2191. doi:10.1056/NEJMoa1211853

Bisson, J., Ehlers, A., Matthews, R., Pilling, S., Richards, D. & Turner, S. (2007). Psychological treatments for chronic post-traumatic stress disorder: Systematic review and meta-analysis. *British Journal of Psychiatry, 190*(2), 97–104. doi:10.1192/ bjp.bp.106.021402

Bradley, R., Greene, J., Russ, E., Dutra, L., & Westen, D. (2005). A multidimensional meta-analysis of psychotherapy for PTSD. *American Journal of Psychiatry, 162*, 214–227.

Caetano, R., Nelson, S., & Field, C. (2003). Association between childhood physical abuse, exposure to parental violence, and alcohol problems in adulthood. *Journal of Interpersonal Violence, 18*, 240–257. doi:10.1177/0886260502250074

Capezzani, L., Ostacoli, L., Cavallo, M., Carletto, S., Fernandez, I., Solomon, R., . . . Cantelmi, T. (2013). EMDR and CBT for cancer patients: Comparative study of effects on PTSD, anxiety, and depression. *Journal of EMDR Practice and Research, 7*(3), 134–143. doi:https:// doi.org/10.1891/1933-3196.7.3.134

Cecchet, S., & Thoburn, J. (2014). The psychological experience of child and adolescent sex trafficking in the United States: Trauma and resilience in survivors. *Journal of Psychological Trauma, 6*(5), 482–493. doi:10.1037/a0035763

Chard, K. M. (2005). An evaluation of cognitive processing therapy for the treatment of posttraumatic stress disorder related to childhood sexual abuse. *Journal of Consulting and Clinical Psychology, 73*(5), 965–971. doi:10.1037/0022-006x.73.5.965

Chilcoat, H. D., & Breslau, N. (1998). Posttraumatic stress disorder and drug disorders: Testing causal pathways. *Archives of General Psychiatry, 55*(10), 913–917. doi:10.1001 /archpsyc.55.10.913

Clawson, H. J., Dutch, N., Solomon, A., & Grace, L. G. (2009). *Human trafficking into and within the United States: A review of the literature*. Washington, DC: U.S. Department of Human and Health Services, Office of the Assistant Secretary for Planning and Evaluation. Retrieved from https://aspe.hhs.gov/report/human-trafficking-and-within-united-states-review-literature

Clawson, H. J., & Goldblatt Grace, L. (2007). *Finding a path to recovery: Residential facilities for minor victims of domestic sex trafficking* (Human Trafficking: Data and Documents, Paper 10). Washington, DC: U.S. Department of Human and Health Services, Office of the Assistant Secretary for Planning and Evaluation. Retrieved from https://aspe.hhs.gov/report /finding-path-recovery-residential-facilities-minor-victims-domestic-sex-trafficking

Cloitre, M., Cohen, L., & Koenen, K. C. (2006). *Treating survivors of childhood abuse: Psychotherapy for the interrupted life*. New York, NY: Guilford Press.

Cloitre, M., Koenen, K. C., Cohen, L. R., & Han, H. (2002). Skills training in affective and interpersonal regulation followed by exposure: A phase-based treatment for PTSD related to childhood abuse. *Journal of Consulting and Clinical Psychology, 70*(5), 1067–1074. doi:10.1037/0022-006X.70.5.1067

Cloitre, M., Stovall-McClough, C. K., Miranda, R., & Chemtob, C. M. (2004). Therapeutic alliance, negative mood regulation, and treatment outcome in child abuse-related posttraumatic stress disorder. *Journal of Consulting and Clinical Psychology, 72*, 411–416. doi:10.1037/0022-006X.72.3.411

Cloitre, M., Miranda, R., Stovall-McClough, K. C., & Han, H. (2005). Beyond PTSD: Emotion regulation and interpersonal problems as predictors of functional impairment in chronic PTSD related to childhood abuse. *Behavior Therapy, 36*, 119–124.

Cloitre, M., Stovall-McClough, K. C., Nooner, K., Zorbas, P., Cherry, S., Jackson, C. L., et al. (2010). Treatment for PTSD related to childhood abuse: A randomized controlled trial. *American Journal of Psychiatry, 167*(8), 915–924. doi:http://dx.doi.org/10.1176/appi .ajp.2010.09081247

Cloitre, M., Petkova, E., & Wang, J. (2012). An examination of the influence of a sequential treatment on the course and impact of dissociation among women with PTSD related to childhood abuse. *Depression and Anxiety, 29*(8), 709–717.

Cloitre, M., Henn-Haase, C., Herman, J. L., Jackson, C., Kaslow, N., Klein, C., Mendelsohn, M. Petkova, E. (2014). A multi-site single-blind clinical study to compare the effects of STAIR Narrative Therapy to treatment as usual among women with PTSD in public sector mental health settings: Study protocol for a randomized controlled trial. *Trials, 15*, 197. doi. org/10.1186/1745-6215-15-197

Cloitre, M., Kulkarni, M., Jackson, C., Weiss, B., & Gupta1, C. (2015). Skills training in affective & interpersonal regulation, STAIR group essentials. Unpublished training manual.

Cole, J., Sprang, G., Lee, R., & Cohen, J. (2014). The trauma of commercial sexual exploitation of youth: A comparison of CSE victims to sexual abuse victims in a clinical sample. *Journal of Interpersonal Violence, 31*(1), 122–146. doi:10.1177/0886260514555133

Curtis, R., Terry, K., Dank, M., Dombrowski, K., & Khan, B. (2008). *Commercial sexual exploitation of children in New York City, volume one: The CSEC population in New York City: Size, characteristics, and needs* (Center for Court Innovation, 56). Retrieved from http://www.ncjrs.gov/App/publications/abstract.aspx?ID=247061

Davidson, P. R., & Parker, K. C. H. (2001). Eye movement desensitization and reprocessing (EMDR): A meta-analysis. *Journal of Consulting and Clinical Psychology, 69*(2), 305–316. doi: 10.1037/0022-006X.69.2.305

de Roos, C., Greenwald, R., den Hollander-Gijsman, M., Noorthoorn, E., van Buuren, S., & De Jongh, A. (2011). A randomised comparison of cognitive behavioural therapy (CBT) and eye movement desensitisation and reprocessing (EMDR) in disaster-exposed children. *European Journal of Psychotraumatology, 2*(1), 5694. doi:http://dx.doi.org/10.3402 /ejpt.v2io.5694.

de Roos, C., Veenstra, A. C., De Jongh, A., den Hollander-Gijsman, M. E., van der Wee, N. J. A., Zitman, F. G., et al. (2010). Treatment of chronic phantom limb pain using a trauma-focused psychological approach. *Pain Research and Management, 15*(2), 65–71. doi:http:// dx.doi.org/10.1155/2010/981634

Diehle, J., Opmeer, B. C., Boer, F., Mannarino, A. P., & Lindauer, R. J. (2014). Trauma-focused cognitive behavioral therapy or eye movement desensitization and reprocessing: What works in children with posttraumatic stress symptoms? A randomized controlled trial. *European Child & Adolescent Psychiatry, 24*(2), 227–236. doi:10.1007/s00787-014-0572-5

Edmond, T. (2016). EMDR. In A. Nichols, (Au)., *Sex trafficking in the United States: Theory, research, policy, and practice.* New York, NY: Columbia University Press.

Edmond, T., & Lawrence, K. (2015). Eye movement desensitization and reprocessing (EMDR). In *Encyclopedia of social work.* Washington, DC: National Association of Social Workers Press and Oxford University Press.

Edmond, T., & Rubin, A. (2004). Assessing the long-term effects of EMDR: Results from an 18-month follow-up study with adult female survivors of CSA. *Journal of Child Sexual Abuse, 13*(1), 69–86. doi:http://dx.doi.org/10.1300/J070v13n01_04

EPAS. (2015). Council on Social Work Education. Accreditation process. Retrieved from https://www.cswe.org/getattachment/Accreditation/Accreditation-Process/2015 -EPAS/2015EPAS_Web_FINAL.pdf.aspx

Farley, M., Baral, I., Kiremire, M., & Sezgin, U. (1998). Prostitution in five countries: Violence and post-traumatic stress disorder. *Feminism & Psychology, 8*(4), 415–426. doi:10.1177/0959353598084002

Farley, M., Cotton, A., Lynne, J., Zumbeck, S., Spiwak, F., Reyes, M. E., . . . Sezgin, U. (2004). Prostitution and trafficking in nine countries: An update on violence and posttraumatic stress disorder. *Journal of Trauma Practice, 2*(3–4), 33–74. doi:10.1300/J189v02n03_03

Felitti, V. J., Anda, R. F., Nordenberg, D., Williamson, D. F., Spitz, A. M., Edwards, V., . . . Marks, J. S. (1998, May). Relationship of childhood abuse and household dysfunction to many of the leading causes of death in adults: The Adverse Childhood Experiences (ACE) Study. *AJPM: American Journal of Preventive Medicine, 14*(4), 245–258. doi:http://doi.org/10.1016/S0749-3797(98)00017-8

Foa, E. B., Keane, T. M., Friedman, M. J., & Cohen, J. A. (2008). *Effective treatments for PTSD: Practice guidelines from the International Society for Traumatic Stress Studies* (2nd ed.). New York, NY: Guilford Press.

Fong, R., & Berger Cardoso, J. (2010). Child human trafficking victims: Challenges for the child welfare system. *Evaluation and Program Planning, 33*(3), 311–316. doi:10.1016/j.evalprogplan.2009.06.018

Galovski, T., Blain, L., Mott, J. M., Elwood, L., & Houle, T. (2012). Manualized therapy for PTSD: Flexing the structure of cognitive processing therapy. *Journal of Consulting and Clinical Psychology, 80*(6), 968. doi:10.1037/a0030600

Greene, J. M., Ennett, S. T., & Ringwalt, C. L. (1999). Prevalence and correlates of survival sex among runaway homeless youth. *American Journal of Public Health, 89*(9), 1406–1409. doi:10.2105/AJPH.89.9.1406

Gudiño, O. G., Leonard, S., & Cloitre, M. (2016). STAIR for girls: A pilot study of a skills-based group for traumatized youth in an urban school setting. *Journal of Child and Adolescent Trauma, 9*(1), 67–79.

Gudiño, O. G., Weis, R., Havens, J. F., Biggs, E. A., Diamond, U. N., Marr, M., . . . Cloitre, M. (2014). Group trauma-informed treatment for adolescent psychiatric inpatients: A preliminary uncontrolled trial. *Journal of Traumatic Stress, 27*(4), 496–500. doi:10.1002/jts.21928

Hamblen, J. L., Schnurr, P. P., Rosenberg, A., & Eftekhari, A. (2016). Overview of psychotherapy for PTSD. Washington, DC, National Center for PTSD, US Department of Veterans Affairs. Retrieved from https://www.ptsd.va.gov/professional/treatment/overview/overview-treatment-research.asp.

Hardy, V., Compton, K., & McPhatter, V. (2013). Domestic minor sex trafficking: Practice implications for mental health professionals. *Affilia: Journal of Women and Social Work, 28*(1), 8–18. doi:10.1177/0886109912475172

Heffernan, K., & Blythe, B. (2014). Evidence-based practice: Developing a trauma-informed lens to case management for victims of human trafficking. *Global Social Welfare, 1*(4), 169–177. doi:10.1007/s40609-014-0007-8

Heil, E. C., & Nichols, A. (2015). *Human trafficking in the Midwest: A case study of St. Louis and the bi-state area.* Durham, NC: Carolina Academic Press.

Herman, J. (1997). *Trauma and recovery: The aftermath of violence—from domestic abuse to political terror.* New York, NY: Basic Books.

Högberg, G., Pagani, M., Sundin, Ö., Soares, J., Åberg-Wistedt, A., Tärnell, B., et al. (2007). On treatment with eye movement desensitization and reprocessing of chronic post-traumatic stress disorder in public transportation workers—A randomized controlled trial. *Nordic Journal of Psychiatry, 61*(1), 54–61. doi:http://dx.doi.org/10.1080/08039480601129408

Howard, M. O., McMillen, C. J., & Pollio, D. E. (2003). Teaching evidence-based practice: Toward a new paradigm for social work education. *Research on Social Work Practice, 13*(2), 234–259.

Institute of Medicine. (2007). *Treatment of PTSD: An assessment of the evidence.* Washington, DC: National Academies Press.

Ironson, G., Freund, B., Strauss, J., & Williams, J. (2002). Comparison of two treatments for traumatic stress: A community-based study of EMDR and prolonged exposure. *Journal of Clinical Psychology, 58*(1), 113–128. doi:10.1002/jclp.1132

Iverson, K. M., Resick, P. A., Suvak, M. K., Walling, S., & Taft, C. T. (2011). Intimate partner violence exposure predicts PTSD treatment engagement and outcome in cognitive processing therapy. *Behavior Therapy, 42*(2), 236–248. doi:http://doi.org/10.1016/j.beth.2010.06.003

Jaberghaderi, N., Greenwald, R., Rubin, A., Zand, S., & Dolatabadi, S. (2004). A comparison of CBT and EMDR for sexually-abused Iranian girls. *Clinical Psychology & Psychotherapy, 11*(5), 358–368. doi:10.1002/cpp.395

Kessler, R. C., Crum, R. M., Warner, L. A., Nelson, C. B., Schulenberg, J., & Anthony J. C. (1997). Lifetime co-occurrence of DSM-III-R alcohol abuse and dependence with other psychiatric disorders in the national comorbidity survey. *Archives of General Psychiatry, 54*(4), 313–321. doi:10.1001/archpsyc.1997.01830160031005

Kotrla, K. (2010). Domestic minor sex trafficking in the United States. *Social Work, 55*(2), 181–187. doi:https://doi.org/10.1093/sw/55.2.181

Lalor, K., & McElvaney, R. (2010). Child sexual abuse, links to later sexual exploitation/high-risk sexual behavior, and prevention/treatment programs. *Trauma, Violence, & Abuse, 11*(4), 159–177. doi:10.1177/1524838010378299

Lee, C., Gavriel, H., Drummond, P., Richards, J., & Greenwald, R. (2002). Treatment of PTSD: Stress inoculation training with prolonged exposure compared to EMDR. *Journal of Clinical Psychology, 58*(9), 1071–1089. doi:10.1002/jclp.10039

Levitt, J. T., Malta, L. S., Martin, A., Davis, L., & Cloitre, M. (2007). The flexible application of a manualized treatment for PTSD symptoms and functional impairment related to the 9/11 World Trade Center attack. *Behaviour Research & Therapy, 45*(7), 1419–1433. Retrieved from http://www.sciencedirect.com/science/article/pii/S0005796707000083?via%3Dihub

Lloyd, R., (2012). *Girls like us: Fighting for a world where girls are not for sale, an activist finds her calling and heals herself.* New York, NY: HarperCollins.

Macy, R. J., & Johns, N. (2011). Aftercare services for international sex trafficking survivors: Informing U.S. service and program development in an emerging practice area. *Trauma, Violence, & Abuse, 12*(2), 87–98. doi:10.1177/1524838010390709

The Management of Post-Traumatic Stress Working Group. (2010). *VA/DoD clinical practice guideline for management of post-traumatic stress.* Washington, DC: Department of Veterans Affairs, Department of Defense.

Maxfield, L. (2009). EMDR milestones: The first 20 years. *Journal of EMDR Practice and Research, 3*(4), 211–216. doi:https://doi.org/10.1891/1933-3196.3.4.211

Messman, T. L., & Long, P. J. (1996). Child sexual abuse and its relationship to revictimization in adult women: A review. *Clinical Psychology Review, 16*(5), 397–420. doi:https://doi.org/10.1016/0272-7358(96)00019-0

Monson, C., Schnurr, P., Resick, P., Friedman, M., Young-Xu, Y., & Stevens, S. (2006). Cognitive processing therapy for veterans with military-related posttraumatic stress disorder. *Journal of Consult Clinical Psychology, 74*(5), 898–907.

Mosquera, D., & Gonzalez-Vazquez, A. (2012). Disturbo borderline di personalità, trauma e EMDR. *Rivista di Psichiatria, 47*(2 Suppl.), 26–32. doi:10.1708/1071.11736

Muftić, L. R., & Finn, M. A. (2013). Health outcomes among women trafficked for sex in the United States: A closer look. *Journal of Interpersonal Violence, 28*(9), 1859–1885. doi:10.1177/0886260512469102

Nadon, S. M., Koverola, C., & Schludermann, E. H. (1998). Antecedents to prostitution: Childhood victimization. *Journal of Interpersonal Violence, 13*(2), 206–221. doi:10.1177/088626098013002003

Nijdam, M. J., Gersons, B. P., Reitsma, J. B., de Jongh, A., & Olff, M. (2012). Brief eclectic psychotherapy v. eye movement desensitisation and reprocessing therapy for post-traumatic stress disorder: Randomised controlled trial. *British Journal of Psychiatry, 200*(3), 224–231. doi:10.1192/bjp.bp.111.099234

Noll, J., Horowitz, L., Bonanno, G., Trickett, P., & Putnam, F. (2003). Revictimization and self-harm in females who experienced childhood sexual abuse: Results from a prospective study. *Journal of Interpersonal Violence, 18*(12), 1452–1471. doi:https://doi.org/10.1177/0886260503258035

O'Callaghan, P., McMullen, J., Shannon, C., Rafferty, H., & Black, A. (2013). A randomized controlled trial of trauma-focused cognitive behavioral therapy for sexually exploited, war-affected Congolese girls. *Journal of the American Academy of Child & Adolescent Psychiatry, 52*(4), 359–369. doi:10.1016/j.jaac.2013.01.013

Oram, S., Stockl, H., Busza, J., Howard, L. M., & Zimmerman, C. (2012). Prevalence and risk of violence and the physical, mental, and sexual health problems associated with human trafficking: Systematic review. *PLoS Medicine, 9*(5), e1001224. doi:10.1371/journal.pmed.1001224

Power, K. G., McGoldrick, T., Brown, K., Buchanan, R., Sharp, D., Swanson, V., & Karatzias, A. (2002). A controlled comparison of eye movement desensitization and reprocessing versus exposure plus cognitive restructuring versus waiting list in the treatment of post-traumatic stress disorder. *Journal of Clinical Psychology and Psychotherapy, 9*, 299–318. doi:10.1002/cpp.341

Powers, M., Halpern, J., Ferenschak, M., Gillihan, S., & Foa, E. (2010). A meta-analytic review of prolonged exposure for posttraumatic stress disorder. *Clinical Psychology Review, 30*(6), 635–641. doi:http://doi.org/10.1016/j.cpr.2010.04.007

Reid, J. A. (2010). Doors wide shut: Barriers to the successful delivery of victim services for domestically trafficked minors in a southern U.S. metropolitan area. *Women & Criminal Justice, 20*(1–2), 147–166. doi:http://doi.org/10.1080/08974451003641206

Resick, P. (2010). *Long term follow-up of a clinical trial of cognitive processing therapy and prolonged exposure therapy.* Paper presented at the Sixteenth Annual Trauma Symposium at the 2010 National Trauma Institute, San Antonio, TX.

Resick, P. A., Galovski, T. E., Uhlmansiek, M., Scher, C. D., Clum, G., & Young-Xu, Y. (2008). A randomized clinical trial to dismantle components of cognitive processing therapy for posttraumatic stress disorder in female victims of interpersonal violence. *Journal of Consulting and Clinical Psychology, 76*(2), 243–258. doi:10.1037/0022-006X.76.2.243

Resick, P. A., Monson, C. M., & Chard, K. M. (2014). *Cognitive processing therapy: Veteran/military version: Therapist's manual.* Washington, DC: Department of Veterans Affairs.

Resick, P. A., Nishith, P., Weaver, T. L., Astin, M. C., & Feuer, C. A. (2002). A comparison of cognitive-processing therapy with prolonged exposure and a waiting condition for the treatment of chronic posttraumatic stress disorder in female rape victims. *Journal of Consulting and Clinical Psychology, 70*(4), 867–879. doi:10.1037//0022-006x.70.4.867

Resick, P. A., & Schnicke, M. K. (1992). Cognitive processing therapy for sexual assault victims. *Journal of Consulting and Clinical Psychology, 60*(5), 748–756. doi:10.1037//0022-006x.60.5.748

——. (1993). *Cognitive processing therapy for rape victims: A treatment manual.* Newbury Park, CA: Sage.

Rizvi, S., Vogt, D., & Resick, P. (2009). Cognitive and affective predictors of treatment outcomes in cognitive processing therapy and prolonged exposure for posttraumatic stress disorder. *Behaviour Research and Therapy, 47*(9), 737–743. doi:http://doi.org/10.1016/j.brat.2009.06.003

Roe-Sepowitz, D. E. (2012). Juvenile entry into prostitution: The role of emotional abuse. *Violence Against Women, 18*(5), 562–579. doi:10.1177/1077801212453140

Roe-Sepowitz, D. E., Hickle, K., Dahlstedt, J., & Gallagher, J. (2014). Victim or whore: The similarities and differences between victim's experiences of domestic violence and sex trafficking. *Journal of Human Behaviorin the Social Environment, 24*(8), 883–898. doi. org/10.1080/10911359.2013.840552

Roth, S., Newman, E., Pelcovitz, D., van der Kolk, B., & Mandel, F. S. (1997). Complex PTSD in victims exposed to sexual and physical abuse: Results from the DSM-IV field trial for posttraumatic stress disorder. *Journal of Traumatic Stress, 10*(4), 539–555. doi:10.1002/ jts.2490100403

Rothbaum, B. O., Astin, M. C., & Marsteller, F. (2005). Prolonged exposure versus eye movement desensitization and reprocessing (EMDR) for PTSD rape victims. *Journal of Traumatic Stress, 18*(6), 607–616. doi:10.1002/jts.20069

Sackett D. L, Rosenberg, W., Gray, J., Haynes, R., & Richardson, S. (1996). Evidence based medicine: what it is and what it isn't. *British Medical Journal, 312*, 71–72.

Schaaf, K. K., & McCanne, T. R. (1998). Relationship of childhood sexual, physical, and combined sexual and physical abuse to adult victimization and posttraumatic stress disorder. *Child Abuse & Neglect, 22*(11), 1119–1133. doi:10.1016/S0145-2134(98)00090-8

Schneider, J., Hofmann, A., Rost, C., & Shapiro, F. (2008). EMDR in the treatment of chronic phantom limb pain. *Pain Medicine, 9*(1), 76–82. doi:10.1111/j.1526-4637.2007.00299.x

Schulz, P. M., Resick, P. A., Huber, L. C., & Griffin, M. G. (2006). The effectiveness of cognitive processing therapy for PTSD with refugees in a community setting. *Cognitive and Behavioral Practice, 13*(4), 322–331. doi:10.1016/j.cbpra.2006.04.011

Seidler, G. H., & Wagner, F. E. (2006). Comparing the efficacy of EMDR and trauma-focused cognitive-behavioral therapy in the treatment of PTSD: A meta-analytic study. *Psychological Medicine, 36*(11), 1515–1522. doi:https://doi.org/10.1017/S0033291706007963

Shapiro, F., & Laliotis, D. (2011). EMDR and the adaptive information processing model: Integrative treatment and case conceptualization. *Clinical Social Work Journal, 39*(2), 191–200. doi:10.1007/s10615-010-0300-7

Simons, R. L., & Whitbeck, L. B. (1991). Sexual abuse as a precursor to prostitution and victimization among adolescent and adult homeless women. *Journal of Family Issues, 12*(3), 361–379. Retrieved from http://journals.sagepub.com/doi/abs/10.1177 /019251391012003007

Smith, L., Vardaman, S. H., & Snow, M. (2009). *The national report on domestic minor sex trafficking: America's prostituted children.* Arlington, VA: Shared Hope International.

Steel, J., & Herlitz, C. (2005). The association between childhood and adolescent sexual abuse and proxies for sexual risk behavior: A random sample of the general population of Sweden. *Child Abuse & Neglect, 29*(10), 1141–1153. doi:10.1016/j.chiabu.2004.10.015

Surís, A., Link-Malcolm, J., Chard, K., Ahn, C., & North, C. (2013). A randomized clinical trial of cognitive processing therapy for veterans with PTSD related to military sexual trauma. *Journal of Traumatic Stress, 26*(1), 28–37. doi:10.1002/jts.21765

Taylor, S., Thordarson, D. S., Maxfield, L., Fedoroff, I. C., Lovell, K., & Ogrodniczuk, J. (2003). Comparative efficacy, speed, and adverse effects of three PTSD treatments: Exposure therapy, EMDR, and relaxation training. *Journal of Consulting and Clinical Psychology, 71*(2), 330. doi:http://dx.doi.org/10.1037/0022-006X.71.2.330

Tsutsumi, A., Izutsu, T., Poudyal, A. K., Kato, S., & Marui, E. (2008). Mental health of female survivors of human trafficking in Nepal. *Social Science & Medicine, 66*, 1841–1847. doi:10.1016/j.socscimed.2007.12.025

VA/DoD (Department of Veterans Affairs/Department of Defense) (2010). VA/DoD Clinical practice guideline for the management of posttraumatic stress, version 2.0. Washington, DC: Veterans Health Administration, Department of Defense. Retrieved from http:// www.healthquality.va.gov/Post_Traumatic_Stress_Disorder_PTSD.asp

Van Brunschot, E. G., & Brannigan, A. (2002). Childhood maltreatment and subsequent conduct disorders: The case of female street prostitution. *International Journal of Law and Psychiatry, 25*(3), 219–234.

van den Berg, D. P., & van der Gaag, M. (2012). Treating trauma in psychosis with EMDR: A pilot study. *Journal of Behavior Therapy and Experimental Psychiatry, 43*(1), 664–671. doi:10.1016/j.jbtep.2011.09.011

van Etten, M., & Taylor, S. (1998). Comparative efficacy of treatments for posttraumatic stress disorder: A meta-analysis. *Clinical Psychology and Psychotherapy, 5*, 126–145.

U.S. Department of Veterans Affairs, National Center for PTSD (March 30, 2017). Dissemination of evidence-based psychotherapy for PTSD in Veterans Affairs. https://www.ptsd.va.gov/professional/treatment/overview/dissemination-ebp-ptsd-va.asp

Vranceanu, A. M., Hobfoll, S. E., & Johnson, R. J. (2007). Child multi-type maltreatment and associated depression and PTSD symptoms: The role of social support and stress. *Child Abuse & Neglect, 31*(1), 71–84. doi:10.1016/j.chiabu.2006.04.010

Wanders, F., Serra, M., & de Jongh, A. (2008). EMDR versus CBT for children with self-esteem and behavioral problems: A randomized controlled trial. *Journal of EMDR Practice and Research, 2*(3), 180–189. doi:https://doi.org/10.1891/1933-3196.2.3.180

Wilson, B., & Butler, L. D. (2014). Running a gauntlet: A review of victimization and violence in the pre-entry, post-entry, and peri-/post-exit periods of commercial sexual exploitation. *Psychological Trauma: Theory, Research, Practice, and Policy, 6*(5), 494–504.

CHAPTER 6

CLIENT-CENTERED HARM REDUCTION, COMMERCIAL SEX, AND TRAFFICKING

Implications for Rights-Based Social Work Practice

KATHLEEN M. PREBLE, PhD, MSW, UNIVERSITY OF MISSOURI-COLUMBIA

C ommercial sex work, both exploitive and voluntary, has been an enduring part of human history. Ancient texts, including the Code of Hammurabi (ca. 1772 BCE), the Arthasastra of Kautilya (ca. third century BCE), and religious texts such as the Bible, Torah, and Quran, have documented the procurement as well as humane treatment of slaves, including the sexual slavery of women. Female slaves had special value in Indian (Shabbir, 2008) and Egyptian societies until the eighteenth century CE, serving various purposes ranging from nursing to prostitution (Rodriguez, 1997; Sharma, 1978). Historical research has also revealed that former female slaves and prostitutes would often return to concubinage after emancipation to earn an income (Rodriguez, 1997). Recent studies have suggested that the similar patterns of behavior that occur today (Cimino, 2012; Davidson, 2013) can be attributed to the sex-trafficking victim's sense of shame, indebtedness to her traffickers, and perceived lack of viable alternatives (support services, employment) (Davidson, 2013).

Today many emancipation efforts are based on the perception that sex workers and trafficked people lack autonomy and that it is the responsibility of the "rescuer" to liberate these victims by forcibly placing them in shelters or formal exiting programs where their freedom can be limited for their safety (Ahmed & Seshu, 2012; Soderlund, 2005; Wahab & Panichelli, 2013). These responses, although based on good intentions, may actually lead to future harm when sex workers and trafficking survivors return to the sex trade from which they were "rescued" (Cimino, 2012; Sen & Nair, 2004; Soderlund, 2005) or develop other negative coping strategies to deal with previous traumas (Mayhew & Moss-man, 2007). As a result, responses to commercial sex and trafficking, ancient and modern, have questioned this violation of the client's human rights and self-determination (Wahab & Panichelli, 2013). More and more, scholars are calling for serious exploration of harm-reduction strategies with sex worker populations (Bromfield, 2016; Cusick, 2006; Hickle, Luckock, & Lodge, 2015; Preble, Praetorius, & Cimino, 2016; Rekart, 2006; Todres, 2011) and for an end to abolitionist and law enforcement–based initiatives, which are increasingly being seen as violations of basic rights (Bromfield, 2016; Jackson, 2016; Soder-lund, 2005; Wahab & Panichelli, 2013).

This chapter seeks to explore client-centered, harm-reduction intervention and practice strategies that social workers can consider when working with women involved in the commercial sex trade, whether by force or by will. The chapter begins by briefly exploring the harm-reduction paradigm (HRP) and how it can help lead to ethical social work intervention practices by focus-ing on the resiliency and strengths of the client. Following this discussion is a brief overview and critique of U.S. approaches to commercial sex worker and sex-trafficking interventions, including the role of the social worker, during various periods of time. The chapter concludes by examining empirical eval-uations of harm-reduction programs as well as recommendations for social workers in the field. It should be noted, however, that few empirical evaluations of sex worker interventions are available (Benoit & Millar, 2001; Cimino, 2017; Mayhew & Mossman, 2007; Rabinovitch & Strega, 2004; Simpson, 2009).

Harm-Reduction Paradigm

Harm reduction aims to reduce the risk of harms associated with risk-taking behav-iors through behavioral, environmental, and, in some instances, pharmaceutical means while not requiring a complete elimination of the risky behavior (Blume & Logan, 2013; Brocato & Wagner, 2003; Preble et al., 2016). The idea of harm reduction originated in response to several scientific challenges to abstinence-only paradigms combating substance addiction (Blume & Logan, 2013). Advocates also sought to empower grassroots efforts to control the spread of HIV and other com-municable blood pathogens among intravenous drug users (Blume & Logan, 2013). Early on, addiction scientists established that the use of substances was highly influenced by beliefs about substance use: that addicts could recover "naturally" and that addiction could be predicted by certain consequences and beliefs about addiction (Blume & Logan, 2013).

Guided by five principles (italicized in following text), HRPs are inherently client-centric and are "sensitive to the importance of cultural relevance in help-ing clients" (Blume & Logan, 2013, p. 637). They are *humanistic* in that they acknowledge that humans make risky choices and that this human behavior ought not be judged. Educating clients about their risk-taking behavior and offering ongoing support to people engaged in risky behaviors are ways of humanizing, rather than demonizing, the people engaged in the negative behavior (Hickle & Hallett, 2015). The paradigms also include the *pragmatic* idea that interventions should be realistic and focused on incrementally reducing the harms associated with risk-taking behavior. This is accomplished through *goals* established with clients to reduce harmful behavior. Efforts to help clients should be based on ideas of *empowerment* to allow clients to be the experts in what will ultimately enable them to successfully reduce or eliminate the risky behavior, while the practitioner assists the client in reaching these goals by focusing on small, achievable objectives. Hickle and Hallett (2015) describe this as "providing a means to change behaviors" (p. 303). Finally, harm-reduction paradigms engage in *community collaboration* to reinforce, within informal settings, the commitment to and support for minimizing individuals' risk-taking behavior (Brocato & Wagner, 2003; Hickle & Hallett, 2015; Thompson, 2014).

It is often not highlighted that sex workers and trafficking survivors have a variety of coping mechanisms that are based on their life experiences, culture, and future plans (Rekart, 2006). Therefore, "harm reduction initiatives for sex workers should build on their strategies, value their distinctive differences, not conflict with their culture and traditions, and increase their options for self-determination, autonomy, and control" (Rekart, 2006, p. 2125). In other words, service provision for women involved in sex work or sex trafficking ought to recognize clients' resiliency and build upon the strengths developed by clients over their lifetime. Service providers, quite simply, should recognize that sex workers and trafficked persons have strengths. Recent studies have shown that social and community support systems are critical to mitigating risks associated with trafficking and providing support associated with having been trafficked; therefore, it is also critical to collaborate with similar populations, such as voluntary sex workers (Decker et al., 2015; Preble, 2016).

Rather than ostracizing these populations by shunning them or assuming they need to change, service providers using HRP programming ought to understand the resiliency inherent in surviving the experiences of sex work. HRP applications appear to be ideal in reducing the need to impose highly restrictive, paternalistic visions of "recovery" or "rehabilitation" onto clients, as is typically seen in abolitionist and abstinence-only programs that presume to know what's best for the client (Ahmed & Seshu, 2012; Cusick, 2006; Soderlund, 2005). Harm-reduction applications also encourage practitioners to work with clients on an ongoing basis to reduce the harms associated with the sex trade while working toward the goals that clients establish for themselves (Rekart, 2006). These goals may include a total removal from the sex trade (Cusick, 2006; Rekart, 2006), but HRPs also encourage practitioners to understand and be sympathetic to the nuances found within the population (e.g., indoor vs. outdoor prostitution, cisgender vs. transgender) and the risks associated with these differences (Cimino, in press).

Harms Related to Commercial Sex Work and Sex Trafficking

Aside from the vulnerabilities associated with becoming involved in the sex trade in the first place (whether by force or not), there are several harms associated with actually being involved in the sex trade. Scholars identify these harms as debt, mental health instability, exposure to drug use, sexually transmitted infections (STIs), prior abuse history, violence, discrimination, exploitation (such as trafficking), criminalization, and stigma (Cimino, 2012; Cusick, 2006; Hickle & Hallett, 2015; Lutnick & Cohan, 2009; Preble, 2015; Preble et al., 2016; Rekart, 2006). Indeed, criminalization can exacerbate harms to sex workers and trafficking populations by restricting access to safety and police, preventing sex workers from reporting violence and crimes committed against them, preventing sex workers from being able to exit sex work due to restrictions in employment after obtaining a criminal record related to prostitution activities, and perpetuating stigma about the population (Cimino, in press; Lutnick & Cohan, 2009).

Moreover, it is important to recognize that this population holds a variety of views related to the legality of the trade, which underscores notions of choice and coercion (Lutnick & Cohen, 2009). In a study asking current sex workers about their thoughts on the legalization, decriminalization, or criminalization of sex work, Lutnick and Cohan (2009) found that of all the participants (N = 247), most advocated for the decriminalization of sex work (71 percent, n = 175) because they believed decriminalization would protect them from harm and allow them greater freedom to interact with police and to access safety and support networks, as well as "give them more freedom to choose non-sex work related employment in the future" because they would not have a criminal record (p. 41). Over a third (39 percent, n = 95) of the participants wanted to see the legalization of sex work, with the industry being regulated by public health departments (Lutnick & Cohan, 2009). Though the majority of Lutnick and Cohan's (2009) participants identified with decriminalization and legalization, a few preferred criminalization (7 percent, n = 18). For these sex workers, being regularly forced to have screenings for STIs and to provide documents of work to regulatory bodies seemed like a violation of privacy; moreover, because criminalization restricts the supply of workers, those remaining could earn higher wages (Lutnick & Cohan, 2009). The idea of allowing sex workers to define themselves and their experiences within the world of sex work reflects the principles of harm reduction.

Cusick (2006) points out that the harms associated with sex work and trafficking may be exacerbated by the setting in which the sex work takes place;

these findings were echoed by Cohan et al. (2006). "Low-status" street prostitutes and sexual minorities in sex work (i.e., transgender), for example, may experience greater harm or combination of harms than sex workers (i.e., erotic dancers, escorts) who may be perceived as less problematic than street-based sex workers (Cimino, 2012; Preble, 2015). Further, sex work may coexist with other illicit markets where drug dealing, child abuse, and sexual exploitation exist (Cusick, 2006).

Cohan and colleagues (2006) found that certain types of sex work and categories of sex workers (cisgender, transgender) carry unique risk factors for experiencing violence, STI transition, and other experiences. For example, of the 783 participants in their study, 53 percent ($n = 418$) had a history of family or intimate partner violence, and transgender participants (57.9 percent; $n = 73$) experienced significantly higher risk of work-related violence (by customers, police; 53 percent; $n = 67$) than cisgender sex workers (female, 36 percent, $n = 152$; male, 27 percent, $n = 50$). Street-based sex workers reported the highest rates of violence in the study (62 percent). For these reasons, interventions should be informed by the setting in which the target population is engaged. One such example of this kind of interaction is the St. James Infirmary program in San Francisco, which was established in 1999 by leaders from the sex worker community in collaboration with the San Francisco Department of Public Health (Cohan et al., 2006). It was the first such program in the United States and has been successful in encouraging relationships and community building among sex workers and the larger community (Cohan et al., 2006).

Many of the harms noted by scholars who study sex trafficking and sex work appear to be linked to exacerbated deficiencies in structural supports within society prior to and during sex work, which are further intensified by the isolation and stigma associated with the involvement in the sex industry even after exiting (Preble, 2015; Wahab & Panichelli, 2013). The Cohan et al. (2006) findings show that sex workers do form supportive communities and that these communities serve as protective factors. For this reason, perhaps a powerful tool to reduce the individual and public harms associated with the sex trade may be a harm-reduction model that engages sex workers and sex-trafficked individuals in support services for ongoing care ranging from risk reduction (condom distribution and STI testing) to more comprehensive social service interventions (safety planning and exiting services).

Brief Overview of U.S. Approach to Sex Work and Trafficking Interventions

Before discussing the evaluations of harm-reduction programs for sex workers and trafficking survivors, let us first briefly review how we have approached the needs of this population in the past and more recently. This review will perhaps shed light on ethical, empowering, and justice-promoting services for our clients. It may also shed light on why service providers have been slow in adopting harm-reduction models to address the needs of this population.

Progressive Era Social Work with Sex Workers

Christian leaders and progressive era reformers, including social work pioneers such as Jane Addams and Josephine Butler, viewed social vices as problems to overcome through a process of elimination and moral advising (Smolak, 2013). During this time, immigration, public health, corruption, and working conditions for women "were factors linked to prostitution [and] overshadowed by moral concerns" (Smolak, 2013, p. 3). For example, Addams "argued that the low wages paid to women were a leading *cause* of women turning to prostitution . . . [and] would cease to exist if the social conditions that caused it were corrected" (Smolak, 2013, p. 5). Driven by a coalition of feminists, Christians, and doctors, each seeking a different goal, various attempts were made to rescue "fallen" women through efforts such as safe houses, crusades, and advocacy, all in the effort to rescue helpless women from being forced into prostitution (Bergquist, 2015; Smolak, 2013). Such legal reforms as the Mann Act, established to respond to the threats of "white slavery," as well as more local responses such as the Committee of Fifteen in New York City, regulated moral behavior and monitored public health threats such as venereal disease (Smolak, 2013). Physicians, in addition, wanted to educate the public about sex, the changing public views on the male need for sex, and other issues related to public health. However, they appeared to be "overshadowed by the louder voices of the strictly moral approach" (Smolak, 2013, p. 8).

Religious Context in Social Service Provision

As described in the prologue to this volume, the sex wars heavily influenced U.S. policy and service responses to sex work and trafficking. Historically, U.S. policy and religion have intersected in their approach to a variety of issues, including sex work (Zimmerman, 2010). Contemporary definitions of sex work typically focus on sexual exploitation and only secondarily on nonsexual forms of slavery, thereby encouraging ideological and moral discussions of prostitution, labor market protection, and immigration laws (Weitzer, 2011). As a consequence, the dialogue is often extremely political and highly influenced by policymakers and other "key actors" who have their own "political agendas that may influence how they choose to use the information they have at their disposal" (Tyldum & Brunovskis, 2005, p. 18). For example, one subgoal of the

Trafficking Victims Protection Act (TVPA) is simply to eradicate prostitution, which, as a goal, is not only far too broad to actualize but also clearly promotes an abolitionist agenda. While faith-based organizations have good intensions, many do not have prior experience working with sex workers or trafficked individuals, yet they receive federal funds to service this population because of the emphasis on faith-based agencies and policies such as the Prostitution Loyalty Oath, discussed in the next section (Chuang, 2010; Zimmerman, 2010).

Moreover, the evidence that faith-based organizations provide "better" services than their secular counterparts is scant. For example, there are few studies examining the outcomes of faith-based organizations to determine if they effectively reduce risk among their target populations (Dodson, Cabage, & Klenowski, 2011; Monsma & Smidt, 2013). The findings in these studies suggest that faith-based social service agencies are no more effective in reducing risk than their secular counterparts (Dodson et al., 2011; Monsma & Smidt, 2013).

The Trafficking Victims Protection Act and the Prostitution Loyalty Oath

As just mentioned, the United States formally outlined its policy against the trafficking in humans through the TVPA, which was initially established in 2000. Originally detailing the "three Ps" (prevention, protection, and prosecution), this law enforcement act has been central to the U.S. response both domestically and internationally. The TVPA has been reauthorized four times since its inception, under three different presidents (Clinton, G. W. Bush, and Obama), each of whom added his agenda to the law. For example, the 2003 TVPA reauthorization (signed by President G. W. Bush) included a little-known policy called the "Prostitution Loyalty Oath" (PLO), to which any agency applying for federal dollars to fund antitrafficking initiatives had to agree (Decker et al., 2015; Zimmerman, 2010). This oath mandated that agencies formalize a statement disavowing the "[promotion], support, or [advocacy of] the legalization or practice of prostitution" (TVPRA, 2003).

The consequences of the PLO reverberated throughout the nation as agencies that refused to create such policies lost federal funding to support clients that they had served prior to the policy's implementation (Chuang, 2010; Decker et al., 2015; Zimmerman, 2010). The result has been that agencies with little or no expertise in assisting sexually exploited populations have received funding, and other agencies have modified their missions to continue receiving funding. Concern has grown over the quality of care available to victims of sexual exploitation (Zimmerman, 2010). Furthermore, agencies providing harm-reduction services (such as HIV testing and provision of condoms) to the general public, as well as to sex workers, lost funding if they did not accede to this policy, regardless of whether they had any connection to trafficking support services or not (Decker et al., 2015; Zimmerman, 2010). In the summer of 2013, the Supreme Court struck down the Prostitution Loyalty Oath as unconstitutional (Decker et al., 2015); however, the policy implemented in the previous ten years is still dominant and is only now being examined in terms of its effect on STI risk reduction (Decker et al., 2015).

In a quick examination of the language used by progressive era advocates and today's antitrafficking responders, one can begin to see striking similarities between these responses. Today, as in the progressive era, sex work and trafficking are often framed in moralistic terms. Trafficking in persons, especially women and children, is popularly discussed as a "scourge" with campaigns such as "Not for Sale," the U.S. government's "Rescue and Restore" program, and blockbuster films such as *Taken* and other mainstream media representations that suggest a paternalistic, moral duty to rescue women and girls from this obvious abuse.

As the sex wars continue, so does the lack of clarity of who is, and who is not, included in these efforts—who is, and who is not, a "worthy" victim. Abolitionist work has been critiqued for focusing on worst-case scenarios and trafficking involving kidnapping, abduction, and confinement, and using the language of slavery. Researchers have noted that a majority of sex trafficking survivors in the U.S., as well as others within the sex industry, do not have this experience. Legal definitions of sex trafficking have also been critiqued for being too narrow, thereby marginalizing or criminalizing those who do not fall within this narrow scope. Social workers often discuss issues regarding the worthiness of those needing assistance (Bergquist, 2015), but as Wahab and Panichelli (2013) state, "it is time to seriously grapple with the ethical considerations involved with social work practice focused on people in the sex industry" (p. 344). For over a decade, social work scholars such as Wahab have been calling for social workers to take a more ethical and less moralistic role in working with sex workers. Wahab and others advocate for destigmatizing sex workers, supporting sex workers who want to leave the industry even while they continue to work, and validating sex workers' experiences in the sex trade, whether they are being sexually exploited or are working consensually (Sloan & Wahab, 2000).

As noted in Hynes (2015), social workers in Sweden, where the solicitation of sex work is illegal and few HRPs exist for sex workers, have lamented that the criminalization of sex work has reduced their ability to assist sex workers. Perhaps more troubling, they have seen funds be diverted to prosecutorial actions in lieu of preventive outreach, resulting in "deteriorating conditions" for sex workers and the denial of sex workers' right to self-determination by forcing them to accept a "victim" status to receive services (Hynes, 2015). The schism between the realities that frontline social workers see and the policies directed toward this population appears to create a paradox to which real solutions are difficult to find when practitioners are focused on ideals and not actual practice solutions. Perhaps one way to change directions in the sex wars debate—ultimately getting away from who is, and who is not, a "worthy victim"—is to explore harm-reduction paradigms that involve the needs of the public, sex workers engaged in the sex trade, and ethical social work practice.

Human Rights and Ethical Approaches to Sex Worker and Sex-Trafficking Interventions

Examinations of the efficacy of sex worker and trafficking interventions have been increasing but are still few in number (Decker et al., 2015; Wahab & Panichelli, 2013). However, there is a growing body of literature examining the use of social work values, ethics, and principles to evaluate intervention programming (Alvarez & Alessi, 2012; Sloan & Wahab, 2000; Wahab & Panichelli, 2013). In considering interventions with sex workers and sex-trafficked individuals, several scholars have begun a dialogue about the need to preserve the dignity and worth of the client, as well as to promote clients' basic human rights while engaging them in services (Alvarez & Alessi, 2012; Brocato & Wagner, 2003; Decker et al., 2015; Hodge, 2014; Wahab & Panichelli, 2013).

Decker and colleagues (2015), in a review of eight hundred studies examining the impact of HIV on human rights abuses against sex workers, found that across policy responses and various nations the human rights abuses against sex workers *facilitated* HIV vulnerability and undermined the efficacy of prevention programs. The human rights abuses identified by Decker and colleagues (2015) included increased risk of homicide, state repression, exposure to physical and sexual violence, confiscation of condoms and syringes as proof of sex work, limited access to the justice and health systems, forced rehabilitation and STI screenings, and lack of labor protection. To address the effects of these abuses, Decker and colleagues (2015) recommend implementing policies and practices that "enable sex workers to exercise their rights to nondiscrimination" (p. 8) by promoting community engagement with sex workers and empowering them to utilize their rights, reforming legal frameworks to be more focused on the human rights of sex workers, and ensuring that the harmful effects of having experienced human rights abuses are ameliorated. "[Simply] providing HIV prevention and treatment services [without addressing prior abuses] will remain an insufficient and misguided response" (Decker et al., 2015, p. 9). Rather, in order to make rights-based HIV response programs more effective, efforts should be made to increase evidence-based interventions with sex workers (such as the St. James Infirmary, PEERS, and PAR, discussed later in this chapter), decriminalize sex work, and hold accountable the perpetrators (governmental and individual) who violate the body and rights of sex workers (Decker et al., 2015).

HRP Programs Versus Diversion and Abstinence-Only Programs

It appears, particularly since the Prostitution Loyalty Oath was struck down in 2013, that there ought to be an emergence of interest in harm-reduction programming in the United States (Decker et al., 2015). There are typically three strategies for assisting exiting sex workers: holistic supportive services, diversion programs, and harm-reduction programs. There are few program evaluations that distinguish between these strategies (Mayhew & Mossman, 2007). Holistic supportive services, such as Veronica's Voice and the STOP-IT program, are designed to prevent sex workers from ever returning to the industry (Cimino, 2012; Preble et al., 2016; Simpson, 2009). Diversion programs, such as the RISE program in Tarrant County, Texas, and Project ROSE in Phoenix, Arizona, offer court-supervised intervention for individuals arrested on prostitution-related offenses (Cimino, 2012). Central to the success of diversion programs is the client's willingness to adhere to a "prostitution-free" lifestyle upon completing the diversion programming, which could include case management, housing assistance, and mental and physical health treatments (Cimino, 2012). However, these programs have been criticized because of their ability to coercively engage clients in the programs to avoid formal charges (Roe-Sepowitz, Gallagher, Hickle, Pérez Loubert, & Tutelman, 2014) and to engage clients when they are not ready to exit the industry (Cimino, 2012; Wahab & Panichelli, 2013).

These criticisms have ignited debates about the violation of basic human rights and dignity and the right of sex workers to autonomously make choices regarding their bodies and lives free from externally coercive influences. In a particularly poignant public debate, Wahab and Panichelli (2013) argued that some sex worker intervention programs, like Project Rose, have done more harm than good "under the cover of kindness" in that they ignore the rational decision-making capabilities of sex workers and trafficked women "for their own good" by arresting sex workers and then offering diversion programming as an alternative to criminal charges (Wahab & Panichelli, 2013). Wahab and Panichelli (2013) maintain that this form of assistance violates several ethical standards by targeting an oppressed group, encouraging structural violence against this population, and coercing participants to accept services they may not actually want because of the threat of criminal arrest. Moreover, this strategy runs the risk of overlooking sex trafficking because the power to determine victim status is in the hands of the service provider—not the sex worker. Thus, a trafficked person is not able to define their own experience; rather, subjective determinations of service providers determine who is criminal and who is victimized.

Harm-reduction programs are designed to mitigate sex workers' exposure to harm (e.g., violence, sexually transmitted diseases, and substance use) but do not emphasize that sex workers completely exit the sex industry (Cimino, 2012; Mayhew & Mossman, 2007; Wilson, Critelli, & Rittner, 2015). Programs for sex workers that focus only on harm reduction, such as the Red Umbrella Project in New York City, focus on increasing safety and providing safe drop-in locations, with the aim of "early intervention" (Simpson, 2009). However, harm-reduction programs typically focus on substance abuse treatment, which can alienate non-substance-using sex workers (Cusick, 2006). Rekart (2006) suggests that effective harm-reduction programs ought to be rights-based and include aspects of education, empowerment, prevention, care (including sexually transmitted disease detection), occupational health and safety, and decriminalization of sex workers.

Harm-Reduction Program Evaluations and Recommendations

As has been suggested, HRPs for sex workers have primarily focused on the intersection of substance use or STI prevention and sex workers (Cimino, 2012; Cusick, 2006; Wilson et al., 2015). Historically, there have been very few evaluations of harm-reduction models (Cimino, 2012; Cusick, 2006; Wilson et al., 2015). However, especially since the striking down of the Prostitution Loyalty Oath, there has been increased interest in using harm-reduction techniques and in examining the outcomes of harm-reduction programs around the world (Bungay et al., 2013; Carrière, 2008; Decker et al., 2015; Hickle & Hallett, 2015, Lim et al., 2015, Nguyen, 2015; Open Society Institute, 2015; Preble et al., 2016; Wilson et al., 2015; World Health Organization, 2013), as evidenced, at least anecdotally, by the increase in literature pertaining to harm reduction and sex work and trafficking since 2013. Furthermore, harm-reduction models, of late, have begun broadening their services to include those who are not substance users and not victims of intimate partner violence and a more diverse population of sex workers such as males, transgendered persons (World Health Organization, 2013), and Native Americans (Pierce, 2012).

Wilson and colleagues (2015) indicate in their comprehensive review of intervention services for sex workers that HRP programs have demonstrated a significant decrease in exposure to substance use, incarceration, risky sexual behaviors, violence, and time engaged in sex work. Rabinovitch and Strega (2004) state that the success of the PEERS program (a harm-reduction program in Victoria, British Columbia, founded and informed by sex workers) derives from its emphasis on building clients' strengths, recognizing that sex work often parallels other forms of dehumanizing and dangerous work that women perform, understanding the need for mutual respect between sex workers and the agencies wanting to assist them, and recognizing that sex workers are indeed the experts on which the success of PEERS depends. Over time, PEERS has identified four guiding principles: choice, capacity building, harm reduction, and trust.

Another program, the Persons at Risk Program (PAR) located in Ontario, Canada, was evaluated by Bodkin, Delahunty-Pike, and O'Shea (2015). In this qualitative study ($N = 14$), participants stated that PAR's HRP approach helped them stay engaged in the program and ultimately helped them access nonjudgmental healthcare and law enforcement services. Participants also indicated that flexibility in the hours to receive services, accessible locations, ease of access to mental health services, and the guarantee that the healthcare and law enforcement providers are female also were important aspects of the PAR program. In another recent study, Preble and colleagues (2016) found that participants ($N = 13$), using a faith-based service provider who only worked with those actively exiting the sex trade in the American Southwest, articulated the need for HRP services that included having individualized plans to meet their particular service goals, not requiring complete abstinence from sex work to receive services, and addressing barriers to service engagement such as childcare, transportation, and other basic services. These recommendations, in turn, also reduce harms related to participating in and exiting from the sex industry, while also helping to imagine one's life beyond the sex trade.

The International Harm Reduction Development program (IHRD) and the Open Society Institute (OSI) partnered to provide comprehensive HRP programming to sex workers in several European nations, including HRP information, education, counseling, referrals (e.g., medical, legal), follow-up services for clients, and organizational capacity building for the agencies involved. After six months of implementation, they evaluated the outcomes of the programming begun among the 6,500 sex workers contacted and initiated in these services (Open Society Institute, 2015). Findings of this report indicate that 95 percent ($n = 6,200$) of the sex workers contacted through HRP outreach returned for follow-up services, and 78 percent ($n = 5,100$) participated in the syringe exchange program (Open Society Institute, 2015). This result appears to demonstrate that HRP-informed programs succeed in reaching out to traditionally marginalized and distrustful populations. Organizations that had previously been working with sex workers but had not been using HRPs reported a 25 percent increase in sex worker engagement once they did implement HRPs (Open Society Institute, 2015). Organizations engaged in needle exchange programs with sex workers also reported an increase in sex worker engagement once HRP programming was expanded within these agencies. They recommend increased funding for agencies to include or improve HRPs, as well as extensive community building, not only between agencies and the target population, but also among policymakers to cultivate support for these projects (Open Society Institute, 2015).

Hynes (2015) completed a comparative policy analysis of three countries with different policies regarding sex work: South Africa, Sweden, and New Zealand. Though in all three nations stigma against sex workers limits access to legal, health, and economic resources, New Zealand's policy approach, in which sex workers are legally recognized and harm-reduction programming is more frequently utilized, increased health and safety practices among sex workers and helped to reduce the social stigma surrounding the population (Hynes, 2015). Even so, Hynes (2015) argues that "until sex workers have more state-sanctioned support, efforts to enhance their health and wellbeing will be inhibited" (p. 16). Benoit and Millar (2001) found that sex workers (N = 201) are more often than not forced to accept a victim status to receive services, which counters their lived experience narrative. This disconnect further exacerbates the invisibility they feel in society and is reflected in the lack of coherent support services that meet their physical and mental needs. Moreover, criminalizing sex work in general appears to do more harm than good because it marginalizes sex workers and forces them to exist in the shadows of our communities, thus increasing the dangers to which they are exposed (violence, STIs, and little economic, legal, and social power with which to advocate for themselves) (Benoit & Millar, 2001). Hence, there is a strong need for more outreach to advocate for sex worker rights, more continuity in physical and mental health services and in services for basic needs such as housing and job training, and more sex worker–friendly training for service professionals who may engage with sex workers in their environments to reduce the potential stigma and resulting bias that prevent sex workers from receiving the social and legal protections they need.

Mayhew and Mossman (2007), in evaluating five service agencies for sex workers to determine "best practices," identified service areas that ought to be included in response programs to help sex workers successfully exit the industry. These service areas include holistic services, outreach, facilitation of free choice, education, and flexibility in service locations and hours, all of which appear to mimic the ideals of HRP programming. Indeed, agencies with more HRP programming tended to see more sex workers exiting the trade than those agencies that employed non-HRP programming (e.g., abstinence-only or diversion programs) (Mayhew & Mossman, 2007).

Another recommendation comes from Lazarus, Chettiar, Deering, Nabess, and Shannon (2011), who examined perceptions of comfort and self-efficacy among 73 female sex workers. Though they were not examining the effects of HRPs with their study population, they found that when women lived in environments in which they felt that the power structures surrounding them were relatively equal, they began to develop peer support groups and work together in groups. Similar findings were reported in Campbell and Mzaidume (2001) ($N = 15$), who studied safe sex practices among a community of sex workers; however, to ensure that the other sex workers in their community regularly used condoms and other safe sex practices, these women felt the need to engage in surveillance and punishment. Here it is important to recognize the need for sex worker engagement in an organized community with other sex workers to empower their sense of self-efficacy, both individually and as a collective whole.

Recommendations and a Call for Social Work Action

Through this examination of literature surrounding the effects of HRPs and sex worker populations, several recommendations can be made. As social workers, our code of ethics calls upon us to adhere to several principles when working with our clients, client communities, and fellow colleagues. The principle of social justice calls upon us to "pursue social change, particularly with and on behalf of vulnerable and oppressed individuals and groups of people" (National Association of Social Workers, 2008). Sex workers, because they are involved in a criminalized occupation, are relegated to the shadows of our society, where they lack open and honest interaction with the social, legal, and economic resources that are afforded other disenfranchised groups; this condition makes their ability to mitigate risk-taking behaviors precarious, at best. Valuing the dignity and worth of the person and the importance of human relationships is the heart of the harm-reduction paradigm. Social workers respect the dignity and worth of the individual by treating each client respectfully, being "mindful of individual differences and cultural and ethnic diversity, [seeking] to enhance clients' capacity and opportunity to change and to address their own needs, and [resolving] conflicts between clients' interests and the broader society's interests in a socially responsible manner" (National Association of Social Workers, 2008). Hence, at our core is the desire to empower our clients by building their strengths so that they may address their needs within society—on their own. To do this, we must engage in human connection; "relationships between and among people are an important vehicle for change" (National Association of Social Workers, 2008).

To this end, see the following box, which indicates the principles of the harm-reduction paradigm; cites recommendations found in the literature pertaining to sex work, sex trafficking, and the use of HRPs; and outlines what social workers can do to apply these recommendations in practice.

HRP Principles, Recommendations, and a Call for Social Work Action

Humanistic

Honor human behavior and the "right" to take risks in behavior free from judgment.

Recommendations

- Recognize the human rights of sex workers.
- Refrain from requiring implicit victim status from sex workers.

Social Work Actions

1. Recognize the self-determination and dignity and worth of the sex worker (Decker et al., 2015).
2. Recognize sex workers' agency in the sex trade (Benoit & Millar, 2001) and their need to exercise free will (Mayhew & Mossman, 2007; Rabinovitch & Strega, 2004).
3. Recognize that acknowledging agency does not imply there are "worthy" and "unworthy" clients; all clients are worthy of services (Hynes, 2015; Wahab & Panechelli, 2013).
4. Provide services regardless of clients' intent to leave sex trade.

Pragmatic

Strive for realistic interventions focused on incrementally reducing risk-taking behaviors.

Recommendations

- Ensure ease of access to needed services: mental health, physical health, legal, educational, and social services.
- Recognize that exiting sex workers return to the sex trade on average five times before ultimately leaving.

Social Work Actions

1. Create an advisory board of clients who can help agencies and policymakers understand gaps and needed improvements to existing services.

2. Ensure that clients and potential clients have access to services anytime they might need them (by having flexible hours and multiple locations) (Bodkin et al., 2015).
3. Ensure that clients have necessary support structures to effectively engage in the services being provided (childcare, transportation, education) (Preble, 2015; Rabinovitch & Strega, 2004).
4. Exercise patience, without requiring sex workers to abstain from their main source of income (Cimino, 2012; Mayhew & Mossman, 2007).
5. Create programming keeping in mind that some clients will still be actively involved in the sex trade. Address the needs of the client by working on small achievable goals.
6. Focus on strength-building principles in practice (Preble, 2016; Rabinovitch & Strega, 2004).

Goal Establishment and Empowerment

Strive to reduce risky behavior and recognize that clients are the experts in knowing what will work for them in reducing these behaviors.

Recommendations

- Recognize that sex workers are the experts of their lived experience and so know how best to achieve the goals they establish for themselves.
- Recognize that sex workers potentially have access to and knowledge about sexually trafficked individuals.

Social Work Actions

1. Focus treatment goals on the individual needs and desires of the client—not funder- or program-originated goals (Preble, 2016; Rabinovitch & Strega, 2004).
2. Allow clients to receive services without an abstinence requirement or promise to leave the sex trade (Preble, 2016).
3. Create partnerships between sex workers and antitrafficking groups to assist each other in identifying and responding to individuals being trafficked in the sex trade (Preble, 2016).

Community Collaboration

Reinforce commitment and support to minimize risk-taking behavior.

Recommendations

- Recognize the need for sex workers to create a community.
- Recognize the need for improved public and service professional education surrounding the realities of sex work to reduce the stigma associated with sex work.

Social Work Actions

1. Create a sex worker–informed public awareness effort (Mayhew & Mossman, 2007; Rabinovitch & Strega, 2004).
2. Create a sex worker–informed training to offer service professionals (social, legal, and health) (Benoit & Millar, 2001; Open Society Institute, 2015).

References

Ahmed, A., & Seshu, M. (2012). "We have the right not to be 'rescued' . . .": When anti-trafficking programmes undermine the health and well-being of sex workers. *Anti-Trafficking Review, 1*(103), 149–168.

Alvarez, M. B., & Alessi, E. J. (2012). Human trafficking is more than sex trafficking and prostitution: Implications for social work. *Affilia, 27*(2), 142–152.

Benoit, C., & Millar, A. (2001). *Dispelling myths and understanding realities: Working conditions, health status, and exiting experiences of sex workers: Short report.* Victoria, BC: Department of Sociology, University of Victoria.

Bergquist, K. J. S. (2015). Criminal, victim, or ally? Examining the role of sex workers in addressing minor sex trafficking. *Affilia, 30*(3), 314–327. doi: https://doi.org /10.1177/0886109915572844

Blume, A. W., & Logan, D. (2013). Harm reduction approaches. In P. M. Miller (Ed.), *Interventions for addiction* (pp. 633–641). San Diego, CA: Academic Press.

Bodkin, K., Delahunty-Pike, A., & O'Shea, T. (2015). Reducing stigma in healthcare and law enforcement: A novel approach to service provision for street level sex workers. *International Journal for Equity in Health, 14*(35), 1–18.

Brocato, J., & Wagner, E. F. (2003). Harm reduction: A social work practice model and social justice agenda. *Health and Social Work, 28*(2), 117–125.

Bromfield, N. F. (2016). Sex slavery and sex trafficking of women in the United States: Historical and contemporary parallels, policies, and perspectives in social work. *Affilia, 31*(1), 129–139.

Bungay, V., Kolar, K., Thindal, S., Remple, V. P., Johnston, C. L., & Ogilvie, G. (2013). Community-based HIV and STI prevention in women working in indoor sex markets. *Health Promotion Practice, 14*(2), 247–255.

Campbell, C., & Mzaidume, Z. (2001). Grassroots participation, peer education, and HIV prevention by sex workers in South Africa. *American Journal of Public Health, 91*(12), 1978–1986.

Carrière, G. L. (2008). Linking women to health and wellness: Street Outreach takes a population health approach. *International Journal of Drug Policy, 19*(3), 205–210.

Chuang, J. A. (2010). Rescuing trafficking from ideological capture: Prostitution reform and anti-trafficking law and policy. *University of Pennsylvania Law Review, 158*(6), 1655–1728.

Cimino, A. N. (2012). A predictive theory of intentions to exit street-level prostitution. *Violence Against Women, 18*(10), 1235–1252.

——. (2017). Sex work and adult prostitution: From entry to exit. In M. Bourke and V. Van Hasselt (Eds.), *Handbook of behavioral criminology: Contemporary strategies and issues.* New York, NY: Springer.

Cohan, D., Lutnick, A., Davidson, P., Clongier, C., Herlyn, A., Breyer, J. . . . Klausner, J. (2006). Sex worker health: San Francisco style. *Sexually Transmitted Infections, 82*(5), 418–422.

Cusick, L. (2006). Widening the harm reduction agenda: From drug use to sex work. *International Journal of Drug Policy, 17*(1), 3–11.

Davidson, J. O. C. (2013). Troubling freedom: Migration, debt, and modern slavery. *Migration Studies, 1*(2), 176–195.

Decker, M. R., Crago, A. L., Chu, S. K., Sherman, S. G., Seshu, M. S., Buthelezi, K., . . . Beyrer, C. (2015). Human rights violations against sex workers: Burden and effect on HIV. *The Lancet, 385*(9963), 186–199.

Dodson, K. D., Cabage, L. N., & Klenowski, P. M. (2011). An evidence-based assessment of faith-based programs: Do faith-based programs "work" to reduce recidivism? *Journal of Offender Rehabilitation, 50*, 367–383. doi:10.1080/10509674.2011.582932

Hickle, K., & Hallett, S. (2015). Mitigating harm: Considering harm reduction principles in work with sexually exploited young people. *Children & Society.* doi:10.1111/chso.12145

Hickle, K., Luckock, B., & Lodge, C. (2015). Exploring the conceptual and ethical challenges of a child's rights based approach to addressing child sexual exploitation. University of Sussex, Center for Social Work Innovation and Research. Retrieved from https://www.beds.ac.uk/__data/assets/pdf_file/0003/487101/Kristi-Hickle.pdf

Hodge, D. R. (2014). Assisting victims of human trafficking: Strategies to facilitate identification, exit from trafficking, and the restoration of wellness. *Social Work, 59*(2), 111–118.

Hynes, M. (2015). Sex work and the law in South Africa, Sweden and New Zealand: An evidence based argument for decriminalization. *The Journal of Global Health.*

Jackson, C. A. (2016). Framing sex worker rights: How US sex worker rights activists perceive and respond to mainstream anti–sex trafficking advocacy. *Sociological Perspectives, 59*(1), 27–45.

Lazarus, L., Chettiar, J., Deering, K., Nabess, R., & Shannon, K. (2011). Risky health environments: Women sex workers' struggles to find safe, secure and non-exploitative housing in Canada's poorest postal code. *Social Science and Medicine, 73*(11), 1600–1607.

Lim, S., Peitzmeier, S., Cange, C., Papworth, E., LeBreton, M., Tamoufe, U., . . . Decker, M. R. (2015). Violence against female sex workers in Cameroon: Accounts of violence, harm reduction, and potential solutions. *JAIDS: Journal of Acquired Immune Deficiency Syndromes, 68*, S241–S247.

Lutnick, A., & Cohan, D. (2009). Criminalization, legalization, or decriminalization of sex workers: What female sex workers say in San Francisco, USA. *Reproductive Health Matters, 17*(34), 38–46.

Mayhew, P., & Mossman, E. (2007). *Exiting prostitution: Models of best practice.* Wellington, New Zealand: Ministry of Justice. Retrieved from https://www.viceversadundee.org.uk/files/exiting_prostitution.pdf

Monsma, S., & Smidt, C. (2013). Faith-based interventions for at-risk Latino youths: A study of outcomes. *Politics and Religion, 6*, 317–341. doi:10.1017/S1755048312000727

National Association of Social Workers (NASW). (2008). *Code of Ethics of the National Association of Social Workers*. Washington, DC: NASW Press. Retrieved from https://www.socialworkers.org/pubs/code/code.asp

Nguyen, A. (2015). *Incorporating harm-reduction provisions in legislation to improve the well-being of sex workers* (CSW Policy Brief 17). Oakland, CA: eScholarship, University of California.

Open Society Institute (OSI) and International Harm Reduction Development (IHRD). (2015). *Sex worker harm reduction initiative mid-year report: A guide to contacts and services in Central and Eastern Europe and the former Soviet Union*. Retrieved from http://www.who.int/hiv/topics/vct/sw_toolkit/sex_work_harm_reduction_initiative.pdf?ua=1

Pierce, A. (2012). American Indian adolescent girls: Vulnerability to sex trafficking, intervention strategies. *American Indian and Alaska Native Mental Health Research: The Journal of the National Center, 19*(1), 37–56.

Preble, K. M. (2015). Creating trust among the distrustful: A phenomenological examination of supportive services for former sex workers. *Journal of Aggression, Maltreatment and Trauma, 24*(4), 433–453.

——. (2016). *Victims' perceptions of power and identity intersections: A human trafficking experience* (Doctoral dissertation). University of Texas at Arlington.

Preble, K. M., Praetorius, R. T., & Cimino, A. (2016). Supportive exits: A best practices report for a sex worker intervention. *Journal of Human Behavior in the Social Environment, 26*(2), 162–178.

Rabinovitch, J., & Strega, S. (2004). The PEERS story: Effective services sidestep the controversies. *Violence Against Women, 10*(2), 140–159.

Rekart, M. L. (2006). Sex-work harm reduction. *The Lancet, 366*(9503), 2123–2134.

Rodriguez, J. P. (1997). *The historical encyclopedia of world slavery* (Vol. 1). Santa Barbara, CA: ABC-CLIO.

Roe-Sepowitz, D. E., Gallagher, J., Hickle, K. E., Pérez Loubert, M., & Tutelman, J. (2014). Project ROSE: An arrest alternative for victims of sex trafficking and prostitution. *Journal of Offender Rehabilitation, 53*(1), 57–74.

Sen, S., & Nair, P. M. (2004). A report on trafficking in women and children in India 2002–2003. New Delhi: NHRC, UNIFEM, ISS Project. Retrieved from http://nhrc.nic.in/Documents/ReportonTrafficking.pdf

Shabbir, M. (Ed.). (2008). *Human rights in the 21st century: Challenges ahead*. New Delhi: Rawat Publications.

Sharma, R. R. (1978). Slavery in the Mauryan period (c. 300 BC–c. 200 BC). *Journal of the Economic and Social History of the Orient, 21*(2), 185–194.

Simpson, B. (2009). *Changing perspectives: Calgary Network on Prostitution: Environmental scan final report*. Retrieved from http://bsimpson.ca/reports/prostitution/environmental_scan_2009.pdf

Sloan, L., & Wahab, S. (2000). Feminist voices on sex work: Implications for social work. *Affilia, 15*(4), 457–479.

Smolak, A. (2013). White slavery, whorehouse riots, venereal disease, and saving women: Historical context of prostitution interventions and harm reduction in New York City during the Progressive Era. *Social Work in Public Health, 28*(5), 496–508.

Soderlund, G. (2005). Running from the rescuers: New U.S. crusades against sex trafficking and the rhetoric of abolition. *nwsa Journal, 17*(3), 64–87.

Thompson, T. L. (Ed.). (2014). *Encyclopedia of health communication*. Los Angeles, CA: Sage Publications.

Todres, J. (2011). Moving upstream: The merits of a public health law approach to human trafficking. *North Carolina Law Review, 89*(2), 447.

Tyldum, G., & Brunovskis, A. (2005). Describing the unobserved: Methodological challenges in empirical studies on human trafficking. *International Migration, 43*(1–2), 17–34.

TVPRA. (2003). US Department of State. Retrieved from: https://www.state.gov/j/tip/laws/61130.htm

Wahab, S., & Panichelli, M. (2013). Ethical and human rights issues in coercive interventions with sex workers. *Affilia, 28*(4), 344–349.

Weitzer, R. (2011). Sex trafficking and the sex industry: The need for evidence-based theory and legislation. *The Journal of Criminal Law and Criminology, 101*(4), 1337–1369.

Wilson, B., Critelli, F. M., & Rittner, B. A. (2015). Transnational responses to commercial sexual exploitation: A comprehensive review of interventions. *Women's Studies International Forum, 48*, 71–80.

World Health Organization (WHO). (2013). *Implementing comprehensive HIVSTI programmes with sex workers: Practical approaches from collaborative interventions.* Retrieved from http://www.who.int/hiv/pub/sti/sex_worker_implementation/en/

Zimmerman, Y. C. (2010). From Bush to Obama: Rethinking sex and religion in the United States' initiative to combat human trafficking. *Journal of Feminist Studies in Religion, 26*(1), 79–99.

CHAPTER 7

THE HIDDEN TRUTH

How Our Policies and Practices Can Both Help
and Harm Victims of Human Trafficking

LYNLY S. EGYES, ESQ., THE SEX WORKERS PROJECT

I walked into the waiting room and saw Danielle, a young cisgender woman referred to me by the District Attorney's Office. I smiled at her and made a hand gesture to follow me. As we walked to the room, I told her my name was Lynly and that I was a lawyer. The minute we entered the room and the door closed, Danielle blurted out, "I was told you would be nice to me and that you wouldn't care that I have done prostitution." I smiled and said, "The name of the program I work with is the Sex Workers Project. We provide legal and social services to anyone who works in the sex industry, regardless of whether they are doing it by choice, circumstance, or coercion. I have worked with hundreds of victims of trafficking as well as people who have engaged in prostitution by choice. So no, I don't care that you have done prostitution. I only care what brought you to my office today."

I watched as she began to relax and her story came tumbling out. She was in an abusive relationship and she began stripping to make money and keep her husband happy. Slowly stripping turned into prostitution and emotional abuse turned into physical. She told me the District Attorney's Office referred her because she wanted support cooperating with law enforcement, needed immigration help, and needed to get connected to a social worker.

Over the next year, Danielle, her social worker Amy, and I worked together as a team to fully unravel her story. I learned why Danielle didn't reach out to law enforcement sooner and when she did, she was turned away by other trafficking organizations and law enforcement because she had a master's degree and spoke five languages, so she couldn't be trafficked. She was also shamed by a social worker when she disclosed that she had engaged in prostitution, and the word *trafficking* to her meant that someone was kidnapped off the street and sold to a brothel. Amy taught her breathing exercises to deal with the anxiety caused by talking about her trauma. She also gave Danielle a grounding object to hold on to during the really tough meetings, and she gave me some helpful tips on how to best ask Danielle questions. Our team approach worked well because Danielle's goals, to have her trafficker prosecuted and put in jail and to obtain a green card, were met. And even when her legal case was closed, she continued to come to our office for therapy with Amy.

This chapter first outlines the legal framework of human trafficking in the United States and then discusses how certain policies and practices undermine the goal of assisting victims of trafficking. It then offers suggestions for improving current law and policy, as well as practical tips for social work professionals working with victims of human trafficking in legal contexts.

What Is Human Trafficking?

Before we can address these policies and practices, we must first understand and define human trafficking. Human trafficking was not defined by federal statute until the Trafficking Victims Protection Act (TVPA) was created in 2000.[1] This means that before 2000 the crime of "human trafficking" did not exist. Human trafficking, legally speaking, is a fairly new concept. Because this is a "new" label of crime and victimization, social workers should not expect individuals to come in and reveal that they are victims of trafficking in need of assistance. Most survivors do not know that they have experiences that fit within the definition of human trafficking.

Human trafficking is a crime under federal and international law.[2] Each individual state within the United States also criminalizes some trafficking activity.[3] Prior to the passage of the TVPA in 2000, there was no comprehensive federal law to prosecute traffickers or to protect victims of trafficking. The TVPA defines labor trafficking and sex trafficking separately, but both fall under the umbrella of "a severe form of trafficking" (see Prologue).

The TVPA does more than just define and criminalize human trafficking. It also provides protections to trafficking victims, including immigration options for survivors of trafficking. It created the T visa, which allows victims of trafficking to apply for a nonimmigrant visa to remain in the United States, and provides mandatory restitution for trafficking victims. This is a potentially important benefit for people who have experienced trafficking and are undocumented or whose citizenship is in another country (discussed in more depth later in this chapter).

One of the interesting things that the TVPA did *not* do was include a physical transport or movement requirement within its definition of trafficking. This is important because many people mistakenly believe that a person has to be moved from country to country or from state to state to be considered a victim of human trafficking. This is not the case. If a person was born in Queens, New York, and lived in the same house his whole life, and at age twelve his mother forced him into prostitution within his home, he would be considered a trafficking victim under federal law, even though his mother never transported him anywhere.

Understanding How People Are Trafficked

Human trafficking looks different in every situation; however, almost all trafficking experiences have aspects of force, fraud, or coercion or a combination of two or three of those elements.[4] It's easy to understand what force looks like: physical violence, which can include rape, beatings, food and sleep deprivation, or physical confinement that induces a person to provide some form of labor, including sexual labor. For example, Allison[5] was forced into street-based sex work by an abusive romantic partner. When Allison refused her partner's demand, he whipped her with television wires until she finally agreed.

However, traffickers also use fraud to induce victims into labor. Fraud may involve false promises regarding employment, wages, working conditions, or other situations. One example of fraud is when traffickers subject victims to debt bondage or peonage.[6] In this situation, the trafficker demands labor as a means to repay a real or alleged debt, yet the trafficker does not apply the victim's wages accurately against the debt and may charge high levels of interest. Traffickers also charge victims money for transportation, housing, food, and other items. Interest may be added if a person cannot fully pay back the amount. Victims may be charged more money if the trafficker believes they have behaved badly. This behavior traps victims in a cycle of debt that they may never be able to pay back.

For example, Tina agreed to pay $10,000 for a visa to come to the United States. Once she arrived, she was told she needed to pay interest on the $10,000 and was assigned an apartment to live in. She was charged rent for the apartment but was not allowed to look for anything cheaper, and she was charged for food, electricity, and the blanket she used at night. The debt was recorded in a black book. Every night Tina was taken to a strip club and was told she had to work to pay the debt. She had to dance and take her clothing off and go in the backroom with customers and provide sexual encounters for money. Tina was told that there was someone always watching her. After three months, Tina paid back the original $10,000 but was actually in more debt because of the interest that had accrued and all of the money she was charged. She owed $20,000 before she could escape her trafficker.

Coercion can be tricky to understand because it can look different for different people. It is really important for the social worker to look at the experience through the eyes of the person who has experienced the coercion. In a brothel, sex workers might enter the situation voluntarily agreeing to engage in sex work, but circumstances and treatment of the workers might make them want to leave. Coercion, to keep victims engaged in prostitution and prevent them from leaving, will look different for each worker based on their own past experiences. One worker might only need to witness the madam physically harming or threatening to harm another worker when that worker tries to leave. That might be enough coercion to keep the worker there. However, others might not feel coerced into staying and engaging in prostitution unless they are directly threatened. Yet others might need to try to escape, get beaten, and be brought back to the brothel to feel coerced and forced to work there.

Coercion might not necessarily be a direct threat to the individual but rather a threat to someone's family or loved ones. In Rachel's case, she met a man in Mexico. He told her that he really liked her and they started dating. He then brought her home to meet his family. Once they were there he wouldn't let her leave. She was forced to spend the night, and in her culture, spending the night when you're not married can be considered a loss of reputation. After she spent the night with him in his house, he told her that he loved her and wanted to marry her. They married and had a baby together. He convinced her to leave the baby in Mexico and come with him to the United States so that they could make money and build a house for their family. Once in the United States, Rachel's husband took her passport from her and then told her that if she didn't engage in prostitution, she would never see her child again and he would harm Rachel's parents.

Julie met her boyfriend in Queens, New York. Julie is from Central America and fled her home country because of persecution based on her gender identity. After they met, her boyfriend learned that she was undocumented. He also learned that she was terrified of returning to her home country because she believed she would be beaten, raped, and killed. Julie's boyfriend then began to threaten to call immigration on her if she didn't engage in sex work. Therefore, to ensure her own safety from having immigration called on her, Julie started working and giving her money to her boyfriend. He also made her pose for naked photos and threatened to send the photos home to her family members, outing her as a sex worker and as a transgender woman. One day, the threats escalated to actual violence and she called the police. When the police arrived, because Julie did not speak English, her boyfriend was able to control the narrative, and Julie was arrested. She went to criminal court, and the court issued an order of protection *in favor of her boyfriend.* Julie, having nowhere to go, went back to living with him. Anytime she did not follow his rules, work on the street, or obey him, he would say, "I will call the police and tell them that you violated the order of protection."

In both of these cases we see many different forms of coercion. Rachel's passport was held. Holding another person's identity documents can be viewed as coercive. Rachel's husband said that she would never see her children again if she didn't work. He also threatened physical violence against Rachel's parents. Threats to a child or a family member are considered coercive behavior. In their initial relationship, he created a situation where Rachel would suffer a loss of reputation if she didn't marry him because they spent the night together in his house. Although this might not be coercive in certain cultures, this is considered a coercive tactic in Rachel's culture.

In Julie's case, the coercion was initially the threat to call immigration. Julie's boyfriend also coerced her through threats of outing her to her family as a sex worker and a transgender woman. Lastly, he used law enforcement to help him coerce her into prostitution. He had her arrested, had an order of protection issued, and then used that order of protection to ensure that she worked by threatening to call the cops if she didn't.

Coercion can be explained this way: when individuals feel that something bad will happen to them if they do not engage in the form of labor they are being asked to engage in, there is most likely a coercive aspect to the situation.

The Force, Fraud, and Coercion Exception: Young People Who Trade Sex

The TVPA's definition of a severe form of trafficking includes inducing anyone who is not yet eighteen years old into commercial sex. Commercial sex is defined as any sex act in which anything of value is given or received. This means that any person under the age of eighteen who has voluntarily traded sex for money, food, clothing, drugs, shelter, and so on is considered a victim of trafficking under the law. However, because it is still a criminal act for a young person to engage in prostitution, a person younger than eighteen who is considered a trafficking victim can at the same time be convicted of prostitution and put in jail. Taking this one step further, persons in New York who are younger than seventeen (the age of consent) and engaging in sex work can be arrested *for their own attempted statutory rape.*[7]

The Invisible Victims

Social workers should not assume that they know what a trafficking victim looks like or make judgments about how a victim should act. Many survivors of trafficking do not meet media portrayals of victimization.

If the words *human trafficking* are entered into Google Image, what comes up is quite horrifying, exploitative, and often not an accurate depiction of human trafficking (see also chapter 18). Most of the images are of young girls, some with barcodes on their heads. There is one image in particular of girls being forced into bottles and put on a conveyor belt. These are the popular images most people think of when they hear the term *human trafficking*: young, cisgender girls or cisgender women with tattoos, being forced into prostitution or pornography. The other image that often comes to mind is a situation like that depicted in the movie *Taken,*[8] which involves abduction (see Chuang, 2010; Heil & Nichols, 2015; Hoyle, Bosworth, & Dempsey, 2011; Nichols, 2016 for critiques).

These images and stories make up a very small part of what trafficking actually looks like, but these stereotypes and preconceived notions present huge barriers to identifying victims, helping victims escape trafficking situations, and helping victims receive the help and support they need once they do escape. Globally, most people who are trafficked are not trafficked into prostitution or commercial sex.[9] The majority of people are trafficked into other forms of labor. The real risk is that all these other victims then become invisible. Social workers must be aware that young people trade sex for a variety of different reasons, and not all of them feel that they are being victimized. Social workers should not assume that trading sex is the worst part of their life. Many young people trade sex because it is safer to live on their own than to go back to an abusive birth or foster home.

When these people go looking for services or immigration help or to report their victimization to law enforcement, they do not look like a "trafficking victim" and therefore are turned away. Police reports are not taken, immigration help is not provided, and distrust in systems that were created to help is instead reinforced. Our stereotypes and preconceived notions are particularly harmful when victims are asking for help.

When I was at the Family Detention Center in Artesia, New Mexico, I identified multiple women who were survivors of trafficking and had been ordered deported. I approached the detention and removal officer from Homeland

Security and told him that there are trafficking victims here in this room. I said, "I'm concerned that their claims were not heard correctly because people didn't recognize that they were victims. I'm asking you to stay the deportation of the following individuals until their cases can be fully evaluated." He looked at me, laughed, and said, "No." He told me that none of them were victims of trafficking and in fact none of them had told him they were victims of human trafficking. I responded to him, "Why would you expect them to know what that word means?" (I would be more concerned if victims actually said they were victims of human trafficking.) He ignored me and went back to his work.

This is a perfect example of women and children being held in detention who do not fit someone's idea of human trafficking. He not only thought that trafficking victims looked a specific way, but he also expected the victims to know the words *human trafficking* in order to be able to receive help and support. This expectation that victims should be able to articulate fully what has happened to them and fit it within the legal definition is unrealistic. Many people do not know that what has been happening to them is illegal, and very few people, including lawyers, understand the legal definition of human trafficking in the United States. It is a social worker's job to educate and debunk the myths that trafficking victims look and act a certain way. Social workers can often be helpful in legal cases by providing supportive letters or evaluations documenting a client's experience. Often survivors have a hard time fully telling their story in one meeting with an attorney, but if the survivor has a social worker, the social worker can provide concise and easily understood evidence of a client's victimization through these letters and evaluations.

Another stereotype I regularly hear is that victims of trafficking are somehow broken and need to be fixed or saved. Trafficking victims are not broken people. Most of my clients find me after they have escaped the trafficking situation either on their own or with help from other people. Often law enforcement is not involved in their escape.

To truly be client centered, it is important for social workers to understand that they are not saving their clients or patients. Having a savior complex, when working with survivors of trafficking, is dangerous and harmful to the survivors (Hoyle et al., 2011). People come to my office for a variety of different reasons, and I have had only two clients walk in who have said, "I am a trafficking victim."[10] What's good about working at a place called "Sex Workers Project" is that we will provide services to anyone who has worked in the sex industry or has been profiled as a sex worker. No client has to self-identify as a trafficking victim. Clients come to my office often for help with criminal issues or immigration or other legal issues. Often it is only after a screening that I discover they are a victim of human trafficking. My job is not to focus on their victimization; my job is to provide the legal help they desire. If I only saw my clients as victims, I would miss the fact that they need help with custody issues, housing issues, or something else that has nothing to do with trafficking. Social workers must not turn trafficking victims into one-dimensional people whose only issue is their victimization. Individuals might come in who are victims of trafficking but need services for another aspect of their lives; maybe they are overwhelmed by a new child or are experiencing anxiety related to a job. The social workers I work with tell me regularly that clients don't always want to talk about their victimization, and they might not even consider their victimization the worst experience in their lives.

How Our Immigration System Contributes to Trafficking

It is not uncommon for trafficking victims to enter the United States on valid work visas. However, the conditions of some of these visas can create the perfect storm for people to be trafficked. Many of these visas are for agricultural workers, nannies, and domestic workers. One problem with these visas is that people often pay a recruitment fee that can be anywhere from $100 to $5,000. Some victims pay this up front, but other victims are expected to pay it back once they come into the United States. As discussed earlier, creating a debt that someone has to work off can make it very easy for trafficking to occur. Sometimes workers are given contracts prior to coming into the United States that explain how much they will make. However, the contract is often changed once they enter; the amount of money is often lowered, and new conditions are added later into the contract. The person might be required to live in housing that is provided by the employer and might have to pay for food and other necessities. There is no oversight to these contracts and no ban on recruitment fees.

One glaring misstep for immigration, when trying to curb human trafficking, is tying a work visa to one employer. This policy means that if workers are in a harmful working environment, they cannot leave the situation and work for someone else without breaking the terms of their visa. If they do choose to leave, they risk losing their legal status to work and could be deported. Once this happens, it is almost impossible for a person to reenter the United States. That means that for a worker who is being coerced or forced into work—that is, trafficked—the ramifications of leaving the job are high. It also means that employers are given no incentive to treat a worker well because they know the worker cannot leave. Employers and traffickers take advantage of this fact and regularly threaten to call immigration or the police on their workers if they try to leave. Traffickers also exploit these fears to ensure that workers do not call the police to report unsafe and dangerous working conditions (Hopper, 2004).

Domestic workers are often brought into the country on work visas. Some of these situations can turn into trafficking. In these instances, workers are often isolated and possibly never permitted to leave the house or only permitted to leave the house with their boss, creating a situation where the worker has little or no access to the outside world to ask for help. Sleep and food deprivation is another way that domestic workers are coerced into working. Working eighteen- or twenty-hour days is typical. Money is often withheld, and in some cases people are never paid. Victims are told that if they escape, the police will come and harm them. Some traffickers will threaten to call the police and tell the police the victim stole something from them.

Jayla came into the United States on a temporary worker's visa. She was brought in by a wealthy family to take care of the children. She signed a contract stating that she would be making minimum wage, and she gave a copy of the contract to the consular officer during her visa interview. When she arrived, she was told there was a change in her employment. She was told she had to sign a new contract that was not translated into her language, and her passport was confiscated from her. She was given a dirty mattress and told to sleep in the basement. For the next three years, Jayla slept only four to six hours a night and had nothing to eat but the scraps of food that remained on the family's plates once they were done eating. The children she was charged with taking care of were encouraged by their father to hit Jayla. Some nights, the father would come to the basement and rape her. She had to cook and clean every day, and often the wife would come home and make an area dirty again just so she would have to clean it. Jayla was terrified of leaving because she thought her parents in her home country would be harmed. She also felt there was no way out because she didn't know anything about the country. She was fearful of law enforcement in the United States because she was constantly told that the family had friends who were police officers.

Jayla's case is an example of the overlap of labor trafficking and sexual exploitation. Many trafficking cases that may just be considered trafficking into labor include horrific sexual abuses as part of a way to coerce and control victims (Kim & Hreshchyshn, 2004). Social workers should know that victims may have been told that if they try to receive medical attention, report to the police, or even tell anyone what has happened to them, they will either be deported or returned to the place they escaped from. For these reasons, it is important for social workers to make it clear that what clients are telling them is completely confidential.

If the United States wanted to decrease trafficking in these situations, there are a number of things the government could do. It could prohibit charging recruitment fees to anyone who applies for a temporary visa. It could require labor recruiters to register with the U.S. government. The United States could change the policy of temporary visas to allow workers to leave a bad work situation and find work somewhere else in the country. Also, the United States could require employers to give workers contracts in the workers' language and be forced to follow through on those contracts. Inspections or home visits could be put in place for highly vulnerable workers, and the U.S. government could stop issuing worker visas to employers and families where trafficking has already been identified. Keeping these immigration-related policy recommendations in mind, social workers can become politically involved and advocate at a policy level on behalf of their clients and those in similar situations.

Why Decriminalizing Prostitution Can Help Trafficking Victims

Currently, prostitution is criminalized in every state in the United States, with the exception of certain counties in Nevada. It is illegal for a person to have sex with another person in exchange for something of value, and both parties can be arrested and placed in jail for doing so. This policy of criminalization affects trafficking victims in many negative ways. First of all, if individuals are being trafficked into commercial sex, they can be arrested and convicted of prostitution. Many of my clients have been arrested and convicted of prostitution multiple times. One of my clients had almost one hundred convictions for prostitution and related charges. When arrested, many victims have negative experiences with the police or the court system, making it harder to ask for help.

Haley, a young transgender woman, was arrested with her trafficker right next to her. She tried to explain that she didn't want to do prostitution, but she didn't have a choice. The police officer made an offensive transphobic comment and then told her to shut up. My clients have shared with me that these bad experiences are one of the reasons they do not report their traffickers.

If we want to end trafficking in commercial sex, we need to make it as easy and as safe as possible for victims to go to the police. The negative and sometimes violent interactions that occur during arrests for prostitution only hinder a victim's ability to come forward. Another issue is that victims of trafficking may not realize that what is happening to them is illegal. However, their traffickers repeatedly remind them that *prostitution* is illegal and that they will get arrested if they try to go to the police.

One of my clients was being trafficked into commercial sex in a brothel and a bar. One night at the bar, a patron was attacked and the police were called. My client cooperated with information about the patron and received a police report. I asked why she didn't report that she was violently being forced into prostitution and she told me, "Prostitution is illegal. I would have had to admit that I was doing something that was illegal and I was scared."

Police profiling of people as sex workers can create negative experiences with the police because people can be arrested even when they are not engaging in sex work. In New York, the crime of "loitering for the purposes of prostitution" is essentially a law that allows the police to profile people.[11] Profiling of transgender women is particularly common; the phenomenon has been dubbed "walking while trans."[12] I have reviewed criminal complaints that justify these arrests with statements that include "a man wearing a wig in a tight sweater," and "walking up and down the street for ten minutes." The criminalization of transpeople and the resulting false arrests create a feeling in victims that they cannot report anything to the police (Dank et al., 2015).

To help trafficking victims escape, one goal should be to make it easy and safe for people to help victims leave and report the victimization. Let's think about who has access to people who are being trafficked into sex work: the trafficker, other victims, sex workers who are doing sex work by choice, and clients of sex workers. Many of my clients have escaped a trafficking situation because another sex worker or one of their clients helped them leave (see also Jana, Dey, Reza-Paul, & Steen, 2013). Laura was able to escape from her trafficker when she met a client who recognized that she needed help. He asked her if she needed anything, and she broke down and shared with him what she was going through and that she was being forced into prostitution. She said that she didn't feel safe leaving yet. A week later, the client made another request to see Laura. During that second meeting, Laura told him that she felt ready to go. The client arranged for a car to pick her up, and he allowed her to stay with him until she got back on her feet. He provided her with shelter, food, and clothing. When I asked why he never went to the police, he told me that he was scared of getting arrested himself because he had hired a sex worker. Jenny had a similar situation, but it was a sex worker who was doing sex work by choice who helped her escape. They came up with a plan and a distraction so that Jenny could safely leave her trafficker. The sex worker who was helping her then hid Jenny in her basement for three weeks until it was finally safe for her to leave.[13]

If we want victims to be able to escape, why aren't we removing the barriers for people who have access to victims of human trafficking and want to help them escape? It is important to be nonjudgmental when clients come in and share that they have engaged in sex work. Many of our clients have reported that social workers, doctors, and lawyers are judgmental and paternalistic, telling clients they need to stop engaging in sex work in order to receive services. Clients may be forced to decide, "Do I work and feed myself or should I receive the legal and social services I need?" Social workers should be careful to not place their own ideas, beliefs, or judgments about what a person's experience was like working in the sex industry onto their clients. Engaging in sex work might not have been the worst part of the trafficking situation for a survivor.

Criminalization can also turn consensual sex workers into victims of human trafficking. To understand this, it is important to review some of the policies that are put in place when people are arrested and convicted of prostitution. In New York, if people are arrested and convicted of prostitution, that conviction never leaves their records. They cannot get it sealed, and it will never be expunged. So what does this mean when a person is trying to apply for a job? One of the questions that can legally be asked is "Have you ever been convicted of a crime?" A person who has been convicted of prostitution has to answer yes. Further, if a criminal background check is made, it will show that this person has been convicted of prostitution. So how are individuals supposed to find employment besides sex work if they have convictions for prostitution on their record and are unable to get any other job (see also Heil & Nichols, 2015)? This leaves people vulnerable to trafficking and limits their choice and ability to exit prostitution.

Social workers must not assume that just because people are engaged in sex work by choice at one point that they cannot be trafficked at another time. Many people are trafficked multiple times in their lives but also have engaged in sex work by choice. There are circumstances that impact vulnerability and consent in sex work. Constant targeting by the police can make sex workers more reliant on third parties to survive. There is nothing inherently problematic about third parties. Some third parties help a person find work, may drive them to appointments, and provide protection when needed. However, dependence on another person for basic necessities opens up sex workers to exploitation.

For example, Jesse was engaging in sex work to put herself through school and to provide for her child. She had been arrested multiple times on the street, and after a while the police knew her and profiled her as a sex worker, so it was difficult for her to even walk down the street without being arrested. She looked for other jobs but had convictions for prostitution on her record. Because she was constantly being targeted, she had to rely on someone who offered to help her get clients. At first this person was nice, but after working together for a few months, the person became more aggressive and more demanding of her time. The person started creating quotas, and she could no longer say no to clients she did not want to see. To coerce her to continue engaging in prostitution, this person started threatening to call the police and telling her that family court would take her child away. Jesse felt like she had no way out.

Public outing and shaming of people arrested for prostitution can make them ostracized and vulnerable. In some counties in the United States, the police put up photos of people who have been arrested for prostitution on websites, including Facebook. People all over the country are allowed to comment on these people's mug shots and learn that they were arrested for prostitution. If a trafficker is thinking, "How am I going to find a vulnerable person to exploit so I can put this person to work?" all he has to do is check out Facebook or other websites that provide photos of people who have been arrested for prostitution. A trafficker might think that, with an arrest for prostitution in a small town, this person might be shunned by community members and therefore already isolated. A trafficker might think that, with a conviction for prostitution on the individual's record and the whole community knowing this person was arrested, it probably will be difficult to find another job, not to mention that the photos provide the trafficker with the person's name, so that with a simple Google search the trafficker can gather even more information.

Court costs, fines, and diversion programs also work to keep victims in coercive situations by creating a debt that sex workers and trafficking victims must work to pay off. These costs can be thousands of dollars. How does the court think that someone arrested for working as a sex worker is going to be able to pay for this? What type of work does the court think that a defendant must do to be able to pay the court cost?

Further, if this person is trafficked, these court costs are a great way for traffickers to increase the debt a victim owes. A recent article in the *Fayetteville Observer* reported that traffickers were targeting people who were being held in jail and actually paying their bond for them. Once their bond was paid, they were released into the care of this person and then forced into prostitution (Vendituoli, 2016). The criminalization of prostitution does nothing but create more vulnerability to human trafficking and make it difficult for people to leave trafficking situations.

Decriminalization has been an effective policy in creating a safer working environment for sex workers and a better relationship with law enforcement.[14] In 2003, the New Zealand prostitution reform act decriminalized sex work in New Zealand for anyone who was over the age of eighteen. Street-based sex work, as well as working in a brothel, was decriminalized. Although opponents of the act expressed fear that the sex industry and human trafficking would increase as a result, those fears have been unfounded. Five years after the introduction of this law, a committee sanctioned by the New Zealand government found that the sex industry had not increased in size at all (Lutnick & Cohan, 2009; New Zealand Government, 2008). Further, the committee asked the Christchurch School of Medicine to carry out an independent review of decriminalization. This review found that 90 percent of sex workers believed that the Prostitution Reform Act gave them employment, legal, and health and safety rights; 64 percent found it easier to refuse a client when they did not want to see that person, and 57 percent said police attitudes toward sex workers had changed for the better.[15] Previously, the police were the people who enforced criminalization laws, but now they are considered by many to be allies of sex workers in the prevention of violence.

The police in New Zealand have worked hard to build relationships with sex workers to ensure that they can come forward when violence occurs. How does this impact trafficking victims? As discussed earlier in this chapter, the people who have most access to people being forced or coerced into prostitution are sex workers and clients. In New Zealand, neither sex workers nor clients of sex workers are criminalized, which allows for safe reporting of violence and trafficking situations. It is important for social workers to know what tactics have been successful to end or decrease trafficking into commercial sex. Social workers in the trafficking field are often part of stakeholder groups with other social workers, law enforcement, and attorneys. In those situations they might be called on to come up with new ideas to end trafficking, and the New Zealand model, in particular the partnership with law enforcement, could be brought to the table as a successful tactic to decease trafficking into commercial sex.

Questioning the Bifurcation of Labor and Sex

From a victimization perspective, there are not practical differences between sex and labor trafficking. As already discussed, labor trafficking often involves sexual violations, but even when it doesn't, victims lose control of their freedom. The tactics traffickers use to induce a person to engage in prostitution are virtually the same tactics traffickers use against labor-trafficking victims. Traffickers use combinations of emotional or physical abuse, isolation, threats of abuse of the legal process, and sexual violence to ensure that victims engage in whatever form of labor the traffickers desire (Office of Trafficking in Persons, n.d.). One might think that sex trafficking is more inherently harmful because it violates a person's body, but people trafficked into other forms of labor also have their bodies and minds violated through forced labor. The psychological traumas that sex-trafficking victims experience are also present in victims of labor trafficking because both groups are forced to engage in humiliating and degrading behavior against their wills through the use of the same coercive tactics (Community Health Planning and Policy Development, 2008). All victims of trafficking experience different levels of trauma, but these differences are based on individual experiences, not on the type of exploitation. Therefore, arguing that violation of one's body makes trauma worse is inaccurate.

Bifurcation often is based on moral attitudes toward prostitution rather than the actual differences in harm. When morality about prostitution comes into play, common sense often goes out the window. This has huge impacts on victims of trafficking for multiple reasons. First, separating sex and labor for moral reasons minimizes the harms that labor-trafficking victims experience. Second, funding and resources focus mainly on sex-trafficking victims, and labor-trafficking victims are left out of the equation. Third, by focusing on moral issues around prostitution, one might miss opportunities to help and identify sex workers. Social workers must put morality aside and take off any blinders and preconceived notions when working with trafficking survivors. By believing one form of trafficking is worse than the other, a social worker could alienate and harm survivors who are seeking services.

Why Is It Important to Identify Victims of Human Trafficking?

As a lawyer, I have very specific reasons for why I need to identify people as victims of human trafficking. However, I know that for social workers it is different. At the Sex Workers Project, we provide both legal and social services to our clients. In some cases, I partner with social workers so that we can provide holistic services to our clients.

The following sections discuss examples of situations in which it is important to determine whether a person is a victim of trafficking:

The Client Is Not a U.S. Citizen

The TVPA created a visa/nonimmigrant status for people who are victims of human trafficking. Our immigration system in the United States is very complicated, and there are not many immigration options available for people who would like immigration status. If you come across clients who are undocumented or have overstayed a visa, and they are victims of trafficking or have had experiences with trafficking, an attorney should evaluate them for T visa eligibility.[16] In general, it is an attorney's job to prepare immigration applications for clients and represent clients in immigration proceedings. If a social worker thinks a person is eligible, the client should be referred to an attorney who is familiar with T visa applications. Many immigration attorneys are unfamiliar with T visas and will actually apply for a U visa instead; however, T visas have more benefits than U visas. With a T visa, a victim is eligible for public benefits like food stamps and health insurance. There are only 10,000 U visas available every year, so there are never enough to meet the needs of all the applicants. There is now a waiting list of about two to three years. There is no waiting list for a T visa. If a social worker has a client who is believed to be eligible for a T visa, the social worker should bring this up to the lawyer if the lawyer only plans on applying for a U visa.

The Client Has a Criminal Record Connected to an Experience of Trafficking

Victims of trafficking are often forced or coerced into work that is criminalized. My clients have been arrested for prostitution, possession of a weapon, possession of drugs, and myriad other criminal acts. These arrests often lead to criminal convictions on their record. In 2010, New York State passed the first law ever to allow survivors of trafficking to vacate their criminal convictions. Since that time, other states have passed similar laws. If your client has criminal convictions, a lawyer should evaluate the case to determine if the convictions can be vacated.[17]

The Client Is Unsafe and Needs Help and Support from Law Enforcement

After escape, some victims of trafficking are still terrified of their traffickers and would like to report to law enforcement. However, because of bad experiences with law enforcement in the past or misinformation that was given them by their traffickers, they may be afraid to report on their own. If a person is identified as a victim of trafficking and would like help reporting the crime to law enforcement, a lawyer might be helpful in arranging a meeting and protecting the victim's rights moving forward. There are law enforcement agencies that can create a safe environment for a person to go and report a crime. In my practice, attorneys and sometimes social workers will accompany a person to Homeland Security investigations or the FBI to help report the crime. With this information, an investigation might begin against the trafficker(s). Victims in these situations have rights, and it is important to have an attorney present to support clients and assert their rights.[18]

There Are Specific Therapeutic Techniques That Could Be Helpful to Victims of Trafficking

In some cases, victims of trafficking have blocked out their trauma or are unable to explain the trafficking situation in a cohesive timeline. This is quite normal for victims of trauma. In my office, I partner with a social worker who has experience helping people put timelines back together as well as providing lawyers with interviewing techniques and clients with coping mechanisms during the legal process. For example, if a client of mine is seeing a social worker in my office, with the client's permission, I might ask for advice on what language or techniques to use with my client, such as whether to say "victim" or "survivor" or to ask only yes-no questions. Also, with the client's permission I might tell the social worker what I am planning to talk about in the meeting. The social worker will then prep the person on the topic and may give the person some grounding tools. Also, I have arranged meetings so that my client meets with the social worker first, then with me, and then with the social worker again.

The Client Needs Access to Benefits or Services
Available to Victims of Trafficking

There are certain public benefits that are available to survivors of trafficking. These benefits and services include housing assistance, food assistance, income assistance, employment assistance, mental health services, and healthcare.[19] This is not an exhaustive list; there are also different options based on what state the person is located in, and these benefits are often changing. It is important to know what benefits individuals are eligible for based on their status as victims of trafficking. There are resources available that provide this information along with how to access these benefits; see https://www.acf.hhs.gov/sites/default /files/orr/traffickingservices_0.pdf (Department of Health and Human Services, 2012). One difficulty for those who are not U.S. citizens is that benefits offices are often unfamiliar with clients with T visa or continued presence (CP) status.[20] If clients have T status or CP status, it is often helpful for a social worker to accompany them to a public benefits office and help educate the workers about the different statuses.

The Client Might Have a Civil Case Against the
Trafficker and Therefore May Be Entitled to Back Pay

In most trafficking situations, victims are paid little or no money. However, each state has its own minimum wage, and workers may be entitled to the

Danielle has kept in touch with Amy and me over the years. She reaches out during big life events like when she got married and when she had a baby. In our last meeting together, she hugged me and cried. She said, "This [trafficking] could happen to anyone. Even me." Her words have stayed with me over the years. I still have clients come to my office who have been shamed by other organizations telling them they are bad because they engaged in prostitution or are not a victim because they are transgender. Sometimes I see policy shifts for the better, and sometimes I see the creation of more obstacles for trafficking victims to escape and lawmakers ignoring some easy fixes that direct service providers recommend. However, change is possible, and it begins with fully understanding the definition of human trafficking, learning to identify all victims of trafficking, and spotting opportunities to change policies or practices relating to human trafficking for the better.

difference between minimum wage and how much they were paid. Attorneys can file lawsuits to try to get this money back. It is important for social workers to know whether clients were ever in a situation where they made less than minimum wage so that they can be referred to an attorney.

Ways Social Workers Can Change Policy and Practices Relating to Human Trafficking

Invisibility

- Acknowledge that victims may not identify as victims. Use a client-centered approach to mirror the language of your client and to collaboratively work to meet individual goals and needs.
- Know that victims do not typically look like those depicted in media images. Do not make assumptions based on this imagery. Challenge and debunk these myths for law enforcement, friends, and colleagues.
- Victims may not know that their experiences reflect human trafficking. Screen and work collaboratively with clients to meet their needs.
- Use the term *human trafficking* to refer to both sex and labor trafficking so that all victims can be seen.

Immigration

- On a policy level, advocate removal of recruitment fees on temporary visa applications.
- On a policy level, advocate for improved oversight of contracts; contracts must be in the individuals' native language.
- On a policy level, advocate to ban the tie of a visa to one employer.
- Know that traffickers work to create distrust in legal and social services and to promote fear of deportation. Make sure clients know they are speaking confidentially to you.

Criminalizing Victims

- On a policy level, advocate for decriminalizing victims. It will make it easier for them to get a job and to be less vulnerable to police and traffickers, without the court costs, fines, and criminal records.
- On a policy level, advocate to end public shaming programs of sex workers. This increases vulnerability to traffickers.

Benefits for Human-Trafficking Victims

- If you have a client who is a human-trafficking victim, refer to a legal services attorney with experience in T visas.
- If you have a client who is a human-trafficking victim, refer to legal services to vacate criminal convictions. This option will vary by state, as some states do not yet have this provision.
- Determine collaboratively with your clients whether or not to report the trafficking; if they would like to report it, refer them to an attorney. Work with the attorney to see if it would be helpful to help prep the clients for the meeting.
- Social workers versed in trauma care can help victims piece together fragmented memories and thus help them prosecute their trafficker.
- Accompany victims to the public benefits office. To find what benefits are available for people who have experienced trafficking in your state, go to https://www.acf.hhs.gov/sites/default/files/orr/traffickingservices_0.pdf
- Find an attorney referral for any wage-an-hour case if your client was not receiving minimum wage while working; this can include working in prostitution.

Notes

1. The Victims of Trafficking and Violence Protection Act of 2000 (P.L. 106–386), the Trafficking Victims Protection Reauthorization Act of 2003 (H.R. 2620), the Trafficking Victims Protection Reauthorization Act of 2005 (H.R. 972), and the Trafficking Victims Protection Reauthorization Act of 2008 (H.R. 7311) "provide the tools to combat trafficking in persons both worldwide and domestically. The Acts authorized the establishment of the State Department's Office to Monitor and Combat Trafficking in Persons and the President's Interagency Task Force to Monitor and Combat Trafficking in Persons to assist in the coordination of anti-trafficking efforts." http://www.state.gov/j/tip/laws/
2. The Palermo protocols, adopted by the United Nations General Assembly in 2000, created the following international definition for human trafficking (UN General Assembly, 2000):(a) "Trafficking in persons" shall mean the recruitment, transportation, transfer, harbouring or receipt of persons, by means of the threat or use of force or other forms of coercion, of abduction, of fraud, of deception, of the abuse of power or of a position of vulnerability or of the giving or receiving of payments or benefits to achieve the consent of a person having control over another person, for the purpose of exploitation. Exploitation shall include, at a minimum, the exploitation of the prostitution of others or other forms of sexual exploitation, forced labour or services, slavery or practices similar to slavery, servitude or the removal of organs . . . (b) The consent of a victim of trafficking in persons to the intended exploitation set forth [above]

shall be irrelevant where any of the means set forth [above] have been used. (c) The recruitment, transportation, transfer, harbouring or receipt of a child for the purpose of exploitation shall be considered "trafficking in persons" even if this does not involve any of the means set forth in subparagraph (a) of this article; (d) "Child" shall mean any person under eighteen years of age.

Over 150 countries have ratified this protocol.

3. Each state has the power to create its own criminal laws. Through this power, each state decides what aspects of human trafficking to criminalize and what aspects not to criminalize.

4. There is an exception to this rule for people engaging in commercial sex who are younger than eighteen years of age. "The person induced to perform such an act has not attained 18 years of age." 22 U.S. Code § 7102 (9).

5. All of the names in this chapter have been changed, but examples are based on real client experiences.

6. "The term 'debt bondage' means the status or condition of a debtor arising from a pledge by the debtor of his or her personal services or of those of a person under his or her control as a security for debt, if the value of those services as reasonably assessed is not applied toward the liquidation of the debt or the length and nature of those services are not respectively limited and defined." 22 U.S.C. § 7102 (5).

7. Age of consent laws refer to the age a person has to reach before that person is legally able to consent to sex. Age of consent laws differ, but in most states the age is between sixteen and eighteen (in some states there exceptions for two people having sex who are close in age). However, if an adult engages in a sex act with a person under the age of consent, in most states this is a strict liability crime, and the adult can be arrested and convicted of statutory rape whether or not the adult was aware of the age of the young person.

8. *Taken* is a movie about a young, white, cisgender virgin girl who, while on a vacation in another country, is kidnapped and sold to the highest bidder.

9. The International Labour Organization (2016) reports that "18.7 million (90 per cent) are exploited in the private economy, by individuals or enterprises. Of these, 4.5 million (22 per cent) are victims of forced sexual exploitation and 14.2 million (68 per cent) are victims of forced labour exploitation in economic activities, such as agriculture, construction, domestic work or manufacturing."

10. I already know the victim status of some clients who come into my office because they are referred from law enforcement. I work closely with helpful agents at the FBI and at Homeland Security Investigations who will contact me and other lawyers to provide legal representation to victims they encounter.

11. New York Penal Law § 240.37(2), Loitering for the purpose of engaging in a prostitution offense: "Any person who remains or wanders about in a public place and repeatedly beckons to, or repeatedly stops, or repeatedly attempts to stop, or repeatedly attempts to engage passers-by in conversation, or repeatedly stops or attempts to stop motor vehicles, or repeatedly interferes with the free passage of other persons, for the purpose of prostitution, or of patronizing a prostitute as those terms are defined in article two hundred thirty of the penal law, shall be guilty of a violation and is guilty of a class B misdemeanor if such person has previously been convicted of a violation of this section or of sections 230.00 or 230.05 of the penal law."

12. For more information, see Ford (2014).

13. The information about how victims leave trafficking situations comes from my own experience of interviewing and representing hundreds of human-trafficking victims as well as conversations with other attorneys and social workers who also work with trafficking victims.

14. Other countries, such as Germany, Denmark, and the Netherlands, have used other models, such as legalizing sex work or criminalizing clients of sex workers. Research has shown that these models are not effective in ending trafficking (Global Network of Sex Work Projects, 2015).
15. For more information, see New Zealand Government (2008).
16. For more information on T nonimmigrant status, see U.S. Citizenship and Immigration Services (n.d.).
17. For more information, see Sex Workers Project (2012).
18. The Crime Victims' Rights Act (CVRA) became law on October 30, 2004: 18 U.S.C. § 3771 (2004). The CVRA establishes the rights of victims and mechanisms to enforce those rights in federal proceedings: https://www.justice.gov/usao/resources/crime-victims-rights-ombudsman/victims-rights-act
19. https://www.acf.hhs.gov/sites/default/files/orr/traffickingservices_0.pdf
20. Continued Presence (CP) is a temporary immigration status provided to individuals identified by law enforcement as victims of human trafficking. CP is authorized under provisions of section 107(c)(3) of the TVPA, which has since been reauthorized, and is codified at 22 U.S.C. § 7105(c)(3).

References

Chuang, J. (2010). Rescuing trafficking from ideological capture: Prostitution reform and anti-trafficking law and policy. *University of Pennsylvania Law Review, 158*(6), 1655–1728.

Community Health Planning and Policy Development. (2008). *News, health care and human trafficking.* American Public Health Association.

Dank, M., Yu, L., Yahner, J., Pelletier, E., Mora, M., & Connor, B. (2015). *Locked in: Interactions with the criminal justice and child welfare systems for LGBTQ youth, YMSM, and YWSW who engage in survival sex* (Research report). Retrieved from http://www.urban.org/sites/default/files/alfresco/publication-pdfs/2000424-Locked-In-Interactions-with-the-Criminal-Justice-and-Child-Welfare-Systems-for-LGBTQ-Youth-YMSM-and-YWSW-Who-Engage-in-Survival-Sex.pdf

Department of Health and Human Services. (2012). *Services available to victims of human trafficking: A resource guide for social service providers.* Retrieved from https://www.acf.hhs.gov/sites/default/files/orr/traffickingservices_0.pdf

Ford, Z. (2014). How Phoenix convicted a transgender woman for walking down the street. *Think Progress.* Retrieved from https://thinkprogress.org/how-phoenix-convicted-a-transgender-woman-for-walking-down-the-street-1d8d8b15ea19#.do9uk6850

Global Network of Sex Work Projects. (2015). *The real impact of the Swedish model on sex workers: Advocacy toolkit.* Retrieved from http://www.nswp.org/sites/nswp.org/files/The%20Real%20Impact%20of%20the%20Swedish%20Model%20on%20Sex%20Workers%20Advocacy%20Toolkit%2C%20NSWP%20-%20November%202015.pdf

Heil, E., & Nichols, A. (2015). *Human trafficking in the Midwest: A case study of St. Louis and the bi-state area.* Durham, NC: Carolina Academic Press.

Hopper, E. (2004). Underidentification of human trafficking victims in the United States. *Journal of Social Work Research and Evaluation, 5*(2), 125–36.

Hoyle, C., Bosworth, M., & Dempsey, M. (2011). Labeling the victims of sex trafficking: Exploring the borderland between rhetoric and reality. *Social & Legal Studies, 20*(3), 313–329. doi:10.1177/0964663911405394

International Labour Organization. (2016). *21 million people are now victims of forced labour, ILO says.* Retrieved from http://www.ilo.org/global/about-the-ilo/newsroom/news/WCMS _181961/lang--en/index.htm

Jana, S., Dey, B., Reza-Paul, S., & Steen, R. (2013). Combating human trafficking in the sex trade: Can sex workers do it better? *Journal of Public Health, 36* (4), 622–628.

Kim, K., & Hreshchyshn, K. (2004). Human trafficking private right of action: Civil rights for trafficked persons in the United States. *Hastings Women's Law Journal, 16,* 6–7.

Lutnick, A., & Cohan, D. (2009). Criminalization, legalization or decriminalization of sex work: What female sex workers say in San Francisco, USA. *Reproductive Health Matters, 17*(34), 38–46. doi:10.1016/S0968-8080(09)34469-9

New Zealand Government. (2008). *Report of the prostitution law review committee on the operation of the Prostitution Reform Act of 2003.* Retrieved from http://www.justice.govt .nz/policy/commercial-property-and-regulatory/prostitution/prostitution-law-review -committee/publications/plrc-report/documents/report.pdf

Nichols, A. (2016). *Sex trafficking in the United States: Theory, research, policy, and practice.* New York, NY: Columbia University Press.

Office of Trafficking in Persons. (n.d.). *Fact sheet: Human trafficking.* Retrieved from http:// www.acf.hhs.gov/endtrafficking/resource/fact-sheet-human-trafficking

Sex Workers Project. (2012). *Vacating criminal convictions for trafficked persons: A legal memorandum for advocates and legislators.* Retrieved from http://sexworkersproject.org /downloads/2012/20120422-memo-vacating-convictions.pdf

UN General Assembly. (2000, November 15). *Protocol to prevent, suppress and punish trafficking in persons, especially women and children, supplementing the United Nations Convention against Transnational Organized Crime.* Retrieved from http://www.refworld .org/docid/4720706c0.html

U.S. Citizenship and Immigration Services (n.d.). *Victims of human trafficking: T nonimmigrant status.* Retrieved from https://www.uscis.gov/humanitarian/victims-human -trafficking-other-crimes/victims-human-trafficking-t-nonimmigrant-status

Vendituoli, M. (2016, August 12). Sheriff's office investigating human trafficking of inmates. *The Fayetteville Observer.* Retrieved from http://www.fayobserver.com/773eb1f9-e836 -540d-a27b-d3f756d03741.html

PART II

PRACTICE WITH SPECIFIC POPULATIONS

P art II examines social work practice with distinct populations. As
noted in Part I, survivors are not a monolithic group and have
varied experiences and backgrounds. The authors in this section
emphasize unique experiences, heightened risks, and specific needs. Such factors are important to consider when providing survivor-centered services to
meet the distinct needs of various populations and to counter risk factors. The
aim of Part II is to highlight unique and diverse experiences, including those
of immigrant women, Black/African American women and girls, LGBTQ+
(lesbian, gay, bisexual, transgender, queer) people, and girls with intellectual
disabilities.

While sex trafficking and exploitation are not limited to these groups,
this set of chapters highlights varied risks and experiences, working to draw
attention to groups that are often marginalized in the mainstream antitrafficking movement and research literature. Further research is needed to better
respond to the needs of additional groups who may also need specific services,
such as trafficked and exploited people living on Indian reservations (see Heil,
2016; Pierce, 2012) and cisgender heterosexual men and boys (see Bastedo,
2015). There is a paucity of data regarding practice with these populations in
the context of sex trafficking. Heil (2016) emphasizes ways that conflicting laws
and jurisdictional issues negatively impact legal responses to Native people
living on reservations who experience sex trafficking. The U.S. Department
of State (2015, 2016) reported that Native people are at heightened risk for
trafficking and exploitation, yet little work emphasizes social work practice

with Native people (Pierce, 2012). Similarly, much of the work examining sex trafficking of men and boys finds they are disproportionately gay or bisexual (Curtis et al., 2008; Dank et al., 2015; Lutnick, 2016). Little work focuses on men and boys who are heterosexual and cisgender, and the work that is done finds lack of shelter and barriers to services for this population (Bastedo, 2015; Heil & Nichols, 2015). More research is needed to guide practice techniques with these populations.

Chapter 8 focuses on social work practice with immigrant women who have experienced violence in the form of sex trafficking, specifically Central American and Mexican immigrant women in the United States. High rates of various forms of violence in their home countries serve as push factors. Throughout the chapter, the author highlights the interconnected elements that contribute to violence. Immigrant women's narratives include cumulative exposures to and experiences of violence and trauma in which exploitation in the commercial sex industry may be one in a series of traumatic or violent experiences. These women also have many strengths and may use strategies to cope with or resist exploitation. The chapter explains exposure to sex trafficking among immigrant women and then discusses the impacts of sex trafficking on immigrant women's health and well-being. A composite sketch of an immigrant's experience is given to highlight implications for social work practice with immigrant communities impacted by sex trafficking.

Chapter 9 illustrates that sex trafficking and commercial sexual exploitation are recognized as a form of violence involving a disproportionate number of African American adults and children living in poverty-stricken urban areas in the United States. In this chapter, the Afrocentric intergenerational perspective, a strength-based, oppression-sensitive framework, is used to examine the historical, structural, and individual dynamics that influence the lives of African American victims/survivors. The core assumptions and values of the framework are outlined as an assessment tool to help social workers address trauma-specific risks and community supports experienced by African American families at risk for involvement in the sex trafficking industry, as well as to promote culturally responsive practice and policy at all levels of intervention and prevention. Recommendations are included for social work practice, policy, and social change affecting the lives of at-risk African American families.

Chapter 10 delineates the increased risk of sex trafficking and commercial sexual exploitation among LGBTQ+ youth and adults, which is interrelated with heightened runaway risk, family conflict, school bullying, and various forms of structural discrimination. The author details the research examining these heightened risks and barriers to accessing services. The chapter then discusses how social workers can respond to identity-based oppression in barriers to service access and engagement, practice cultural competency, and be active in prevention efforts targeting known LGBTQ+ specific risk factors and their resulting pathways.

Chapter 11 highlights the emerging evidence exposing a heightened risk for commercial sexual exploitation (CSE) currently impacting individuals with intellectual disabilities (ID). The chapter examines the most common presentation of trauma symptoms among individuals with ID, as well as the treatment options for clinicians working with CSE survivors with ID. A review of prior clinical research indicates that the treatment of sexually exploited girls with ID frequently focuses on emotion regulation and challenging behaviors, especially self-injurious and aggressive behaviors. Adapted versions of empirically supported therapy modalities, such as cognitive-behavioral therapy (CBT), dialectical behavioral therapy (DBT), and eye movement desensitization and reprocessing (EMDR), are most commonly recommended for treating trauma symptoms in those with ID. Two case studies demonstrate the use of trauma-focused CBT and EMDR with girls with ID who have experienced CSE. Further research is needed on the efficacy of specific treatment modalities with these individuals.

References

Bastedo, T. (2015). The commercial sexual exploitation of male minors in the United States: A snapshot with strategic implications for prevention education. *Love 146: End Child Trafficking and Exploitation*. Retrieved from https://1at4ct3uffpw1uzzmu191368-wpengine .netdna-ssl.com/wp-content/uploads/2015/01/CSEMMFinalReport_print.pdf

Curtis, R., Terry, K., Dank, M., Dombrowski, K., & Khan, B. (2008). *Commercial sexual exploitation of children in New York City, volume one: The CSEC population in New York City: Size, characteristics, and needs.* New York, NY: Center for Court Innovation. Retrieved from Family & Youth Services Bureau website: https://ncfy.acf.hhs.gov /library/2008/commercial-sexual-exploitation-children-new-york-city-volume-one-csec -population-new

Dank, M., Yahner, J., Madden, K., Banuelos, I., Yu, L., Ritchie, A., Mora, M., &Conner, B. (2015).*Surviving the streets of New York: Experiences of LGBTQ youth, YMSM, and YWSW engaged in survival sex.* Urban Institute. Retrieved from http://www.urban.org/research/publication/surviving -streets-new-york-experiences-lgbtq-youth-ymsm-and-ywsw-engaged-survival-sex/view /full_report

Heil, E. (2016). Sex trafficking in Indian Country: An analysis of anti-trafficking tribal codes, multi-jurisdiction, and unprotected communities. In E. Heil & A. J. Nichols (Eds.), *Broadening the scope of human trafficking research: A reader.* Durham, NC: Carolina Academic Press.

Heil, E., & Nichols, A. (2015). *Human trafficking in the Midwest.* Durham, NC: Carolina Academic Press.

Lutnick, A. (2016). *Domestic minor sex trafficking: Beyond victims and villains.* New York, NY: Columbia University Press.

Pierce, A. (2012). American Indian adolescent girls: Vulnerability to sex trafficking, intervention strategies. *American Indian and Alaska Native Mental Health Research: The Journal of the National Center, 19*(1), 37–56.

U.S. Department of State. (2015). *Trafficking in persons report: 2015.* Retrieved from http://www.state.gov/j/tip/rls/tiprpt/2015/

——. *Trafficking in Persons Report.* (2016). Retrieved from: https://www.state.gov/j/tip/rls/tiprpt/2016/

CHAPTER 8

SEX TRAFFICKING AMONG IMMIGRANT WOMEN IN THE UNITED STATES

Exploring Social Work Response Within a Landscape of
Violence Against Immigrant Women

LAURIE COOK HEFFRON, PhD, LMSW,
ST. EDWARD'S UNIVERSITY

Early U.S. efforts to curb human trafficking were directed toward immigrant women, specifically from Eastern Europe, who were exploited in the commercial sex industry in what has sometimes been called the Natasha trade (Hughes, 2000). In a sense, the U.S. human-trafficking initiative "cut its teeth" on immigrant sex trafficking. Since then, the focus of social services, advocacy, and law enforcement, as well as media attention, has widened to include the commercial sexual exploitation of nonimmigrants and to a lesser degree labor trafficking. While no longer the central focus of the U.S. antitrafficking movement, immigrant women from various countries of origin continue to suffer exploitation in the United States in the form of sex trafficking.

Unfortunately, we still do not have an accurate, comprehensive understanding of the number of immigrant women in the United States impacted by sex trafficking (Bromfield, 2016; Fedina, 2015). Challenges to the identification of trafficked persons, low rates of formal reporting, and traffickers' techniques to prevent detection are in part responsible for the difficulties in defining the scope and prevalence of this problem (Nichols & Heil, 2015). Nonetheless, the U.S. government reported that nonprofit organizations provided services for more than 2,700 human-trafficking victims during fiscal year 2014. Of those, 55 percent were immigrant cases (U.S. Department of State, 2015).

While immigrants from across the globe continue to be exposed to sex trafficking, this chapter will examine social work practice with immigrant women who have experienced violence in the form of sex trafficking, focusing specifically on Central American and Mexican immigrant women's experiences with sex trafficking in the United States.[1] Migration from the "northern triangle" of Central America (El Salvador, Guatemala, and Honduras) to the United States is a recent and growing phenomenon (Rosenblum & Brick, 2011). The high rates of violence experienced by Central American and Mexican women and children migrating to the United States have garnered recent attention in governmental reports, international human rights organizations, research institutes, and private foundations (United Nations High Commissioner for Refugees [UNHCR], 2015). Ban Ki-Moon, secretary general of the United Nations, commented on the high rate of homicide in the region and its connection to other types of violence: "This is more than a spate of killings, it is a crisis—bringing with it great fear and instability to societies. Beyond these appalling numbers, other crimes have emerged—kidnappings, migrant smuggling and human trafficking" (Ki-Moon, 2012).

The notion of an interconnected web of violence—the idea that experiences with one type of violence impact experiences with other types of violence—is an important backdrop to this discussion. These are often stories of cumulative exposures to and experiences of violence and trauma. In other words, exploitation in the commercial sex industry may be one in a series of traumatic or violent experiences encountered by immigrant women. At the same time, immigrant women have shown multiple strengths, strategies, and attempts to cope with or resist exploitation.

The chapter begins with a review of the literature that describes exposure to sex trafficking among immigrant women, as well as the impacts of sex trafficking on immigrant women's health and well-being. Following this foundation, a composite case sketch sets the stage for a discussion of social work practice with immigrant communities impacted by sex trafficking.

Sex Trafficking in the Context of Migration

Multiple risk factors are thought to be associated with international sex trafficking, including high rates of poverty, crime, police corruption, gender inequality, and war or conflict in survivors' countries of origin (Clawson, Dutch, Solomon, & Grace, 2009). Those who recruit immigrants from their home countries for the purposes of exploitation often use false promises of a better life in the United States as an escape from the factors just listed. More specifically, many traffickers promise women legitimate paid work in a bar, restaurant, or other industry. Traffickers also sometimes deceive women under the guise of romance or marriage in order to bring them to the United States and then force or coerce them into the commercial sex industry. The Department of State's *Trafficking in Persons Report* (2015) indicates that immigrant laborers and individuals with limited English proficiency in the United States are at increased risk for being trafficked (U.S. Department of State, 2015). Traffickers often use various strategies of control and coercion, including physical and sexual abuse, threats to harm the victim's family in the home country, threats of deportation, social isolation, and the confiscation of identification and travel documents.

The commercial sexual exploitation of immigrant women in the United States ultimately takes place in a variety of settings, including old-fashioned brothels, massage parlors, spas, karaoke bars, and cantinas (Busch-Armendariz, Nsonwu, Heffron, Garza, & Hernandez, 2009; U.S. Department of Justice, 2015). Recently prosecuted cases provide some examples of common forms of sex trafficking of immigrant women from Mexico and Central America; a particularly common form is taking advantage of vulnerabilities related to immigrant status. For example, in the *Mendez-Hernandez* case, Central American women were coerced into prostitution in Georgia and surrounding states through force, threats, and control of the women's children (U.S. Department of Justice, 2015). The *Lopez-Perez* case is another example of immigrant sex trafficking. Using combinations of physical and sexual assault and psychological coercion, three brothers brought women from Mexico to New York City and surrounding areas, forcing them to meet with up to forty clients a day for as long as five years (U.S. Department of Justice, 2015). In the *Medrano* case in New Jersey and the *Mondragon* case in Texas, women from Mexico and Central America were enticed to the United States with promises of legitimate work and then made to pay off their smuggling debt in cantinas, or bars. They were made to dance with male customers and encourage customers to buy alcoholic beverages. This exploitation sometimes also involved forced prostitution (U.S. Department of Justice, 2007).

Despite the fact that exploitation need not require movement across international borders in order to be considered human trafficking, migration poses distinct exposure to risk. Those who voluntarily migrate to the United States for economic reasons and/or to escape other types of violence are vulnerable to being trafficked during or after transit to the United States. In other words, in addition to being recruited from their home countries and brought to the United States for the predetermined purpose of exploitation, immigrant women may also come to the United States of their own volition and become trafficked during or after crossing into the United States.

It is important to note that the terms *human trafficking* and *smuggling* have different meanings, and yet there is often confusion or conflation of the two. For the purposes of this chapter, I use *human trafficking* to describe the use of force, fraud, or coercion to make someone perform work or commercial sex acts. It does not necessitate movement across or within borders. Smuggling, on the other hand, involves illegal transportation of people across international borders and does not necessarily imply coercion or exploitation. Transnational immigrants may be willingly smuggled into the United States but later become trafficking victims through forced labor or commercial sexual exploitation.

While still largely unexplored in the empirical literature, immigrant women report being exploited in "drop houses" or "safe houses" used by smugglers (Cook Heffron, 2015; Simmons, Menjívar, & Téllez, 2015). During the process of migration north, Mexican and Central American women are often held hostage or detained multiple times on either side of the border between Guatemala and Mexico, near the border between Mexico and the United States, and/or in U.S. destination cities (Cook Heffron, 2015). Smugglers, criminal gang networks, and hostage takers use isolated and remote locations, covered windows, and locked doors as a way to protect immigrants from being discovered and apprehended by immigration officials. In the process, immigrants are often extorted for money before being allowed to continue toward their destinations. During this time of being detained, women's experiences may go beyond extortion to also include sexual violence and/or exploitation. Women may be forced to cook and clean for other immigrants smuggled in and out of the house and/ or for the other extorted hostages waiting for money to ensure their release. Others are specifically held back for the ultimate purpose of forced or coerced sex and/or labor.

For some, the experience of being held hostage and forced to work is repeated multiple times throughout the process of migration, creating a harmful trail of captivity, extortion, rape, and exploitation for sex and labor. However, while many of the drop house experiences described by immigrant women could potentially meet the legal definition of human trafficking, they are rarely viewed as such by law enforcement (Cook Heffron, 2015; Simmons et al., 2015). Regardless, these dynamics can be understood under a broad definition of human trafficking and may be connected to subsequent experiences of violence and exploitation.

Multiple aspects of many immigrant women's experience (little language proficiency, social isolation, gender and economic inequality, little access to employment, no legal immigration status, and lack of knowledge of rights, laws, and services) may exacerbate exposure to violence or exploitation (Alcalde, 2009; Bhuyan & Senturia, 2005; Crandall, Senturia, Sullivan, & Shiu-Thornton, 2005; Menjívar & Salcido, 2002; Vidales, 2010). Exploiting the contemporary climate of restrictive immigration policies, perpetrators often take advantage of immigrant women's undocumented status and socially constructed "illegality" as a tool to gain and maintain power and control. Traffickers often use similar tactics to those of other abusers. These include threats about reporting women to immigration officials (causing legitimate fears of deportation), separation from children, and loss of financial support, which serves as powerful and effective tactics to control and isolate victims (Erez, Adelman, & Gregory, 2009; Raj & Silverman, 2002).

Various legal remedies are available to undocumented victims of exploitation, violence, and abuse. The primary tool is the T visa, created specifically for victims of trafficking (www.uscis.gov). The U visa represents another remedy, providing immigration relief to individuals who have suffered substantial physical or mental abuse as a result of having been a victim of a qualifying criminal activity, including sexual assault, domestic violence, and human trafficking (USCIS, 2013). Trafficked persons may be eligible for other options (such as VAWA self-petition, battered spouse waiver, cancellation of removal, asylum, and continued presence) depending on multiple factors, such as the elements of exploitation or abuse, the location of the violence, or the perpetrator's status.

Virtually all legal immigration relief strategies necessitate the assistance of immigration legal services and require that women engage formally with large systems such as the U.S. Citizenship and Immigration Services. Given that undocumented women experiencing violence or exploitation may not have access to affordable legal services and may be unlikely to seek help from formal systems, immigration relief is often out of reach (Mowder, 2010; Raj and Silverman, 2002; Salcido & Adelman, 2004). Survivors with unresolved immigration cases are often negatively impacted and may have difficulty finding stable and well-paid employment, lack the freedom to visit family in the home country or to bring children to the United States, face deportation, and/or remain vulnerable to further exploitation (Cook Heffron, 2015).

Polyvictimization

It is important that we explore the commercial sexual exploitation of immigrant women within the context of polyvictimization. It is difficult and possibly harmful to consider sex trafficking without also recognizing the intersecting and compounding forms of violence experienced by immigrant women. In other words, it is important to note that those who endure sex trafficking may have also survived other episodes of violence prior to or concurrent with the trafficking situation, such as early childhood sexual abuse, intimate partner violence, sexual assault, or gang violence, in addition to structural violence. Structural violence refers to "violence exerted systematically—that is, indirectly" from social inequalities and oppression (Farmer, 2004, p. 307).

Likewise, while this book focuses on sex trafficking, it is important to remain cognizant of the wider lens of exploitation and the ways that sex trafficking and labor trafficking may overlap. Those who experience sex trafficking may also experience labor trafficking. Along with being forced or coerced into the commercial sex industry through a system of debt bondage, for example, women may also be expected to serve as a waitress or to cook or clean. In addition, sexual violence is frequently a component of both labor trafficking and sex trafficking. Regardless of the type of industry someone is exploited in (be it the commercial sex industry, an escort service, or the agricultural industry), sexual violence may be used as a strategy of control and coercion by traffickers.

These multiple experiences of human-trafficking victimization are often compounded by previous encounters with childhood sexual abuse, physical and sexual violence, and exploitation in immigrants' home countries and during their journeys (Hossain, Zimmerman, Abas, Light, & Watts, 2010). Central American women often migrate because of previous exposure to violence, including intimate partner violence and gang violence (Cook Heffron, 2015; UNHCR, 2015). Furthermore, Mexican and Central American immigrants are vulnerable to a wide range of violence during migration, including verbal and physical abuse, social exclusion, robbery, extortion, assault, torture, kidnapping, rape, and homicide (Infante, Idrovo, Sánchez-Domínguez, Vinhas, & González-Vázquez, 2012; INCIDE Social, 2012). As many as 60 percent of immigrant women may be raped during the journey north through Mexico, and sexual violence is used as a price of passage for those traveling through Mexico and into the United States (Amnesty International, 2010). More than 70 percent of women interviewed at immigrant shelters in Arizona, for example, reported having had an experience with violence before or after migrating to the United States (Conrad, 2013).

Health and Well-Being of Immigrant Trafficking Survivors

Immigrant sex-trafficking survivors endure tremendous physical, psychological, and social consequences of their victimization. Negative health and mental health consequences associated with sex trafficking include severe physical injuries, sexually transmitted infections, shame, and long-term psychological consequences such as self-harming behaviors, substance abuse, anxiety, depression, and PTSD (Hom & Woods, 2013; Hossain et al., 2010; Macy & Johns, 2011). Many tactics of control used by traffickers are comparable to those used in torture and domestic violence—such as assaults, threats, coercion, restriction of freedom, and withholding of information. The inability to control or predict circumstances of trafficking may lead to more intense or prolonged negative mental health outcomes (Hossain et al., 2010).

As previously mentioned, sex trafficking also often co-occurs with other types of violence, such as labor trafficking, intimate partner violence, and sexual assault (Hossain et al., 2010; Nichols and Heil, 2015). Furthermore, those who experience sex trafficking may have experienced multiple types of violence earlier in their lives. Prior experiences of violence may be related to increased risk for negative mental health outcomes (Hossain et al., 2010). Studies of poly-victimization among trafficked immigrant children and adolescents suggest that multiple and compounding experiences of violence may incur additional or heightened trauma symptoms (Turner, Finkelhor, & Ormrod, 2010).

In addition to impacting women's physical and mental health, these experiences have multiple other repercussions. Survivors are often faced with the stress related to being involved in a criminal investigation, the stigma associated with having been involved in the commercial sex industry, lack of social support, challenging reunification with family, and unemployment or underemployment (Hossain et al., 2010). These factors may place survivors in a precarious position of being vulnerable to additional exploitation.

Given the wide-ranging impact of sex trafficking on immigrant survivors, their physical health, mental health, and social needs are immense and multifaceted (Busch-Armendariz, Nsonwu, & Heffron, 2011; Macy & Johns, 2011). These include immediate and long-term needs such as food, housing, medical care, mental health care, legal representation, and employment assistance. Many immigrant survivors are parents and are also in need of services related to transnational parenting and separation from their children or needs related to reunifying with their children and navigating new parent-child relationships and complex legal, health, and educational systems for their children. Finally, survivors often need support or opportunities to create and re-create trusting networks of social support.

While much of the literature focuses on the violence and suffering associated with immigrant sex trafficking, it is undeniable that women draw from and use multiple strategies to resist their exploitation and to cope with the resulting pain and trauma. Despite the circumstances and negative impacts of exploitation, women strategically employ everyday acts to resist violence, to maintain safety, and to survive (Cook Heffron, 2015). In addition, despite often being isolated and having previous supports ruptured through migration, women constantly create and re-create new supports along the way and engage in cosurvival and solidarity with other immigrants enduring similar exploitation. Women also often report drawing strength and motivation from their spiritual faith and from their efforts to seek better opportunities for their families.

Sofia's Case

Sofia's story is a useful starting point in laying a foundation from which to consider practice implications. This story is a composite developed from multiple research and practice interviews with immigrant survivors of domestic violence and human trafficking, in addition to human-trafficking cases covered in the media. Survivors' experiences of and responses to sex trafficking are varied, and Sofia's story illustrates several common elements and patterns and begins to give a sense of the complexity and multiplicity of violence that many immigrant trafficking survivors experience. While we are so often apt to categorize violence against women in distinct and unrelated categories—sexual assault, domestic violence, human trafficking, and femicide—this example begins to unravel and/or collapse the tidy categories of victimization that often direct responses by policymakers and service providers.

Originally from Guatemala, Sofia now lives in the United States with her two children. I met Sofia for an interview on a sunny weekend afternoon on the campus of a large state university. She described her current life as stable and hopeful, and in the quiet setting of privileged academia, it could have been convenient to imagine that this had always been the case. However, as she talked about why she left Guatemala and what happened to her during her journey to the United States, it became palpably clear that her experiences before, during, and following migration to the United States were filled with violence and struggle. At one point during our conversation, she said, "salía de uno ye me metí en otro." In other words, in leaving or fleeing one set of violent circumstances, Sofia found herself in yet another. Her migration story can appear like a series of attempts to escape danger only to land in another dangerous situation.

Sofia grew up in a small town among the indigenous K'iche' community of Guatemala and met her first husband when she was thirteen years old. She had two children with him, and they lived happily for several years. Unfortunately, he passed away, and as a single mother in Guatemala, she found limited work opportunities and had difficulty making ends meet and providing for her children.

In time, Sofia became involved with another man. Things were fine early in this second relationship, and Sofia had another child. However, the relationship shifted, and her partner began beating her frequently and severely. Isolated from family and friends and with inadequate legal or social support, Sofia felt she had nowhere to turn for help or protection in Guatemala. With fear for her life and a strong desire to provide her children with a better future and a good education, Sofia traveled to the United States. She left her children with family in Guatemala, with the intention of bringing them to the United States soon after getting settled.

Sofia spent two months walking and running the more than 1,000 miles to the United States, eventually arriving in San Antonio, Texas, in a house where many other immigrants were being held. Shortly after arriving, police raided the house, and she was turned in to immigration. She was held in a dark, cold room for three days and ultimately detained in another facility for a month before being told she had to sign her deportation papers. While Sofia spoke Spanish fluently, she was not provided language interpretation in her preferred language, K'iche'. She signed the papers in distress and in confusion about what was happening to her, recalling, "estaba cerrada mi mente" (*my mind was closed*). Immigration dropped Sofia on the Mexico side of the Rio Grande River. Without money or resources to find her way, she depended on strangers to help her pay for transit back to Guatemala.

After arriving back home, she tried to find safety for herself and her children by staying with her mother. However, economic conditions were tough as a single mother of three, particularly given her efforts to stay away from her abusive husband, who was stalking and threatening her. On one occasion, he came to her mother's house and asked her to return with the children. When she refused, he severely beat her and threatened to "make her pay." She decided to travel to the United States a second time in search of safety and a future for her children.

The trip was physically grueling and dangerous the second time as well. She traveled in a group guided by a coyote,[2] on foot and by train. They went without food or sleep and hid in the mountains to avoid gunfire from the gangs that control the migration route and train travel. In order to cross the Rio Grande into the United States, they inflated trash bags and held one under each arm to stay afloat. The river swept away two immigrant companions from the group, and one lost his life.

After crossing, the remaining travelers continued walking until they were picked up and taken to an apartment in Houston that was crowded with dozens of other immigrants. Sofia was robbed of her money and made to cook and clean in the apartment for other immigrants shuttled in and out by the coyotes. During this time, Sofia was raped and threatened by one of the coyotes. She also learned that gang members had murdered her oldest daughter on the street in Guatemala, while her youngest daughter watched. Anguished and desperate, she was able to escape the apartment and met a woman who promised to help her. Instead, the woman exploited her in a neighborhood cantina. The woman dropped her off to work at the cantina each night and then picked her up again in the early hours of the morning, demanding Sofia turn over any money she earned. Sofia refused the cantina work, which included commercial sex, and lied to the woman each night, telling her she had lost any money she earned.

Waiting outside the cantina one night at a taco truck, refusing to engage in the work expected of her, she met two men who tried to pick her up, assuming she was a prostitute. When she repeatedly declined their requests, they offered to help. The woman she was staying with had been dropping her off for more than a week and was becoming frustrated that Sofia was not bringing home money. Sofia was nervous about the situation with the woman. Given the offer for help from strangers on the street, she wondered, "¿me arriesgo o no me arriesgo?" (*Do I risk it or not?*). Sofia decided to take the risk and go with the two men, and with their help she began to find shelter and stable work and to make friends. With the support of a local nonprofit, she received a T Visa, which ultimately made her eligible for a work permit, later legal permanent residency (a "green card"), and eventually citizenship. Sofia later brought her children to live with her in the United States.

While this story may read as an impossible litany of violent episodes, it does indeed reflect the multiplicity, complexity, and severity of abuse and exploitation faced by many immigrant women. These episodes go beyond trafficking to include intimate partner and sexual violence, as well as structural violence and oppression. Unfortunately, these experiences are also compounded by historical traumas connected, for example, with sexual violence and genocide perpetrated during colonization and later armed conflict in Central America.

Implications for Social Work Practice

Sofia's story suggests that social workers involved with immigrant survivors of sex trafficking should take the following actions:

1. Improve mechanisms to identify immigrant survivors of sex trafficking
2. Comprehensively assess survivors' strengths and their safety and service needs
3. Apply trauma-informed, survivor-centered practices
4. Strengthen interorganizational capacity, resilience, and discourse
5. Advocate for policy change

Improving Mechanisms to Identify Immigrant Survivors of Sex Trafficking

An important first step in providing services to immigrant survivors of sex trafficking is to develop the individual and organizational capacity to identify survivors. Given their trauma, fear of authorities, and ignorance of rights, immigrants may not make an outcry about the kinds of trauma, violence, or exploitation they have experienced. Furthermore, the recent and troubling displays of hatred, fear, and anti-immigrant sentiment keep immigrants from feeling safe and prevent them from seeking help. Implementing effective screening mechanisms often requires considerable staff training (in particular for first responders, those working in reception areas or answering hotline calls, frontline staff, outreach staff) and the development of appropriate follow-up protocols and procedures for responding to those who are identified as possibly having been trafficked.

Multiple efforts are under way across the country to better screen for and identify immigrant survivors of sex trafficking (Macy & Graham, 2012). These efforts are driven by a growing frustration with limited and/or flawed data and the demand for a better understanding of the scope of trafficking (Bromfield, 2016; Fedina, 2015). In addition, social service providers are looking for ways to better recognize survivors among their current and incoming client communities. One example of a validated and evaluated screening tool (see chapter 2) is the Vera Institute of Justice's Trafficking Victim Identification Tool (or TVIT, available at vera.org), although the sample used for evaluation purposes was 94 percent foreign-born and may need adaptation for domestic populations (Simich, Goyen, Powell, & Mallozzi, 2014).

In addition to screening for sex trafficking or exploitation in the commercial sex industry, social workers interacting with immigrant communities must also be prepared to recognize and assess for the full breadth of victimization experienced by many trafficking survivors and the degree to which survivors are often marginalized in multiple ways. That is, they must screen for previous experiences with violence in addition to any co-occurring violence, which may include early childhood abuse, intimate partner violence, sexual assault, and/or labor trafficking.

Comprehensively Assessing Survivors' Strengths and Their Safety and Service Needs

A comprehensive needs assessment is an important component of any work with immigrant sex-trafficking survivors, regardless of distance in time or geography from the trafficking situation itself (Macy & Johns, 2011). While assessing immediate physical and emotional safety may be primary, the short-term and ongoing bio-psycho-social needs of survivors are also paramount. These include shelter or housing, food, medical and mental health care, legal representation, legal immigration services, employment services, and English-language learning. Social and family functioning are other important areas for assessment (Busch-Armendariz et al., 2011; Macy & Johns, 2011). It is also important to broadly understand the severity and duration of the trafficking situation (Hossain et al., 2010), as well as survivors' individual and familial strategies for resilience, resistance, and coping.

Needs related to separation from and reunification with children and other family members often come later in a survivor's relationship with social service providers. This can be a time of anticipation and relief, in addition to stress and family upheaval (Busch-Armendariz et al., 2011). New service needs often emerge during this time, although survivors may be disconnected from the procedures and services needed following reunification with their children. Survivors often need support in obtaining travel documents and managing immigration processes for their children, making logistical and housing arrangements related to their children's arrival, preparing for the changing dynamics of the parent-child relationship, and navigating children's health and education needs.

In addition, social workers may be asked to participate in survivors' interactions with legal immigration procedures or immigration court. This may involve conducting and documenting psychosocial assessments for the purposes of T or U visas on behalf of sex-trafficking survivors and/or providing oral testimony in immigration court. Social workers unfamiliar with these activities should seek out training and mentorship and carefully consider their own capacity, skills, and expertise in determining how they may engage in this type of practice (see training resources at the National Immigrant Women's Advocacy Project at www.niwap.org and Physicians for Human Rights at physiciansforhumanrights.org).

Finally, social workers must be prepared to recognize, assess for, and address the complexity of survivors' immigration experience (Dewan, 2014). This includes exploration of their pre-, peri-, and postmigration strengths, stressors, and trauma (Perreira & Ornelas, 2013), in addition to their transnational parenting experiences. The term *transnational* implies the flexible sense of belonging, identity, and responsibility that many individuals and families feel. Economic responsibilities, parenting roles, and communication continue to exist across boundaries after an individual has migrated (Furman, Negi, Schatz, & Jones, 2008). Transnational mothers, in particular, often struggle with the basic question of "how to be socially and emotionally present while physically absent" (Carling, Menjívar, & Schmalzbauer, 2012, p. 203). Furthermore, it is critical that social workers increase their awareness of the sociopolitical context within which immigrants operate—a context that is peppered with the criminalization of immigrants facilitated by immigration raids, immigrant detention, and deportation (Cook Heffron, 2015). Despite survivors' immigration status (for example, if they have received the relative stability of a T visa), women are often embedded within mixed-status families and/or live in immigrant communities and are confronted with numerous elements of oppression and social exclusion.

Overall, the assessment of and response to survivors' needs invariably require a wide range of case management tools and the blending of multiple health, legal, and human services. Furthermore, ongoing comprehensive assessment and reassessment are important in order to address the dynamic and transnational long-term needs of survivors and their families (Macy & Johns, 2011).

Applying Trauma-Informed, Survivor-Centered Practices

Much like providing services for other trafficking survivors, responding to immigrant sex trafficking requires careful attention to trauma-informed and survivor-centered practices. In addition to ensuring safety and confidentiality and utilizing nonjudgmental attitudes and words, for example, these approaches also call for providing linguistically and culturally responsive services (Hom & Woods, 2013; Macy & Johns, 2011). Services should be delivered in a survivor's preferred language when possible. An alternative is to ensure that language interpretation and translation services are available in person. A third, though less desirable, strategy is to utilize language lines for telephonic interpretation. Adequate language access may become even more important (and also more logistically challenging) when survivors like Sofia speak a language that is not widely spoken and/or when survivors have a preferred language that is also intricately tied to other sources of marginalization and oppression (such as being part of an indigenous community).

In recognition of the trauma-informed principle of recognizing and strengthening survivors' choices and decision making, information sharing, trust, and transparency are also important. In their work with intimate partner violence services, Kulkarni, Bell, and Rhodes (2012) argue that maintaining mutual and collaborative relationships with survivors may be more important than the resources or services ultimately delivered. A similar approach can be applied to working with immigrant survivors of sex trafficking. Equipping survivors with accurate information is key to fostering trust and choice. For many sex trafficking survivors, the withholding of information has been a tactic used against them by traffickers, who can more easily control and exploit those without full or accurate information about their rights or available resources. It is useful to provide information with patience and to offer the information in a survivor's preferred language. Important information should be shared on more than one occasion, using multiple ways of delivering it (for example, with words, with writing, or with pictures).

Of critical importance to many immigrant sex trafficking survivors is information about their rights as crime victims, in addition to opportunities and possibilities for legal immigration relief. This requires that social workers maintain close working relationships with immigration attorneys, immigrant rights advocates, and others who will be able to appropriately inform survivors of their eligibility for immigration relief and any risks or dangers they may face.

Social workers often struggle against the tendency to view immigrant sex trafficking survivors as a monolithic group. Unfortunately, well-intentioned attempts to be linguistically and culturally responsive to immigrant survivors often run the risk of doing just that. It is critical that social workers recognize the heterogeneity of those who are trafficked, of immigrant women and of immigrants in general. Not all trafficking survivors are the same in terms of their gender identities, roles as mothers, race/ethnic/indigenous identities, or class. Similarly, in supporting a survivor-centered approach, it is important that social workers explore and understand the role the exploitation plays in a survivor's narrative and identity. A trafficking experience may or may not be seen as the defining element of survivors' experience or a priority or primary concern in relation to support or services. Moreover, survivors may not identify what happened to them as trafficking or exploitation (Bromfield, 2016).

Strengthening Interorganizational Capacity, Resilience, and Discourse

Social workers can serve critical roles in helping organizations and communities serve immigrant survivors of sex trafficking, promote organizational resilience, and increase discussions of sensitive debates in the field. Collaborations, partnerships, and interdisciplinary approaches are key to working with immigrant survivors of sex trafficking, because the complexity and multiplicity of their needs demand that social workers work closely with a host of other providers and advocates (Dewan, 2014). Given the multiple types of violence experienced by survivors and their wide-ranging and ongoing needs, social workers often operate in close coordination with a host of partners, including domestic and sexual violence services, immigrant rights groups, law enforcement, refugee resettlement agencies, mental health and healthcare providers, and various governmental agencies. These working collaborative relationships are ultimately more useful to survivors when those involved have patience and listen carefully to the backgrounds, agendas, and motivations of partners and collaborators.

Social workers may be well positioned to train the workforces in their own organizations and beyond. For example, domestic violence and sexual assault service organizations, immigrant rights groups, and healthcare providers may benefit from cross-training opportunities to address the risk for co-occurrence of sexual assault, domestic violence, and/or labor trafficking with sex trafficking, in addition to immigrant women's exposure to violence and exploitation in the pre-, peri-, and postphases of migration. Cross-training may also be necessary in identifying immigrant survivors of sex trafficking and in developing comprehensive assessment and community response plans.

Consistent with a trauma-centered approach, it is also important that social workers develop organizational and community supports to promote resilience and well-being among staff and other responders. Making available clinical supervision, reducing isolation, and offering training and professional development opportunities are useful steps in preventing or addressing the secondary trauma that may accompany work with immigrant survivors of sex trafficking.

Finally, social workers and their colleagues would benefit from increased awareness of and discussions about organizational values and sensitivities to contemporary conversations about immigration reform and debates related to the commercial sex industry (Bromfield, 2016; Wahab & Panichelli, 2013). They could become familiar with current controversies on the distinctions between sex trafficking and prostitution and the varying opinions about the degrees of coercion and self-determination possible in the commercial sex industry, sometimes referred to as the feminist sex wars (Wahab & Panichelli, 2013). While some argue that the commercial sex industry is inherently coercive, violent, and exploitative, others view prostitution or sex work as legitimate, consensual, voluntary work and not equivalent to exploitation or sex trafficking (Sloan & Wahab, 2000).

Advocating for Policy Change

By participating in local and statewide coalitions and survivor-led movements, social workers must also pressure state and federal legislatures to change policies relating to trafficking. They can advocate for policies that ensure that immigrant survivors are adequately informed of their rights and are comprehensively screened for the range of potential immigration relief options; require governmental personnel and contractors working for the U.S. immigration system to undergo in-depth training in human trafficking, trauma, and the rights of trafficking survivors; and promote comprehensive support services for survivors, including adequate funding for such services. Throughout, social workers can ensure that advocacy efforts remain survivor-centered and that survivors occupy leadership roles in policy change efforts.

Conclusion

In sum, social workers working with immigrant survivors of sex trafficking must remain nimble and foster a wide gaze in their efforts to work alongside survivors. Given immigrant survivors' broad exposure to violence and exploitation, the multiplicity of survivors' strengths and needs, and necessary interactions with a host of other providers, the work can easily feel overwhelming. In addition, the agendas of survivors, providers, or other collaborating organizations do not always align. Furthermore, the entire scenario plays out in what can feel like a debilitating larger context of anti-immigrant sentiment, marginalization, and oppression. Nonetheless, as social workers, and as communities, we have an opportunity to step boldly into the fray and to call upon existing resources and build new networks of advocates. We must make central immigrant women's voices, needs, and rights and collectively begin to transform these migration-related crises and trauma into journeys that are neither constrained nor determined by violence and exploitation.

Notes

1. It is important to note that although this chapter focuses on the commercial sexual exploitation of immigrant women, specifically Central American and Mexican women, this type of violence also impacts women from other regions of the world, in addition to youth, men, and the LGBTQ community. It is my hope that some of the concepts highlighted as important in working with this community can also be applied to or stimulate dialogue about work with additional communities of survivors.
2. *Coyote* is a term that is generally used to describe someone who smuggles people across an international border or helps others cross an international border in exchange for a fee.

References

Alcalde, M. C. (2009). Empowering mothering among poor Latina women in abusive relationships. *Journal of the Association for Research on Mothering, 11*(2), 134–142.

Amnesty International. (2010). *Invisible victims: Migrants on the move in Mexico.* London, Amnesty International Publications.

Bhuyan, R., & Senturia, K. (2005). Understanding domestic violence resource utilization and survivor solutions among immigrant and refugee women: Introduction to the special issue. *Journal of Interpersonal Violence, 20*(8), 895–901.

Bromfield, N. F. (2016). Sex slavery and sex trafficking of women in the United States: Historical and contemporary parallels, policies, and perspectives in social work. *Affilia, 31*(1), 129–139. doi:10.1177/0886109915616437

Busch-Armendariz, N. B., Nsonwu, M., & Heffron, L. C. (2011). Human trafficking victims and their children: Assessing needs and vulnerabilities and strengths and survivorship. *The Journal of Applied Research on Children, 2*(1), 1–19.

Busch-Armendariz, N. B., Nsonwu, M. B., Heffron, L. C., Garza, J., & Hernandez, M. (2009). *Understanding human trafficking: Development of typologies of human trafficking.* Austin, TX: The University of Texas at Austin.

Carling, J., Menjívar, C., & Schmalzbauer, L. (2012). Central themes in the study of transnational parenthood. *Journal of Ethnic and Migration Studies, 38*(2), 191–217. doi:10.1080/13 69183X.2012.646417

Clawson, H. J., Dutch, N., Solomon, A., & Grace, L. G. (2009). *Human trafficking into and within the United States: A review of the literature.* Washington, DC: Office of the Assistant Secretary for Planning and Evaluation, U.S. Department of Human and Health Services.

Conrad, M. (2013). *Women's testimonios of life and migration in el Cruce.* Master's thesis, Arizona State University. Retrieved from https://repository.asu.edu/attachments/110603/content /Conrad_asu_0010N_12875.pdf

Cook Heffron, L. (2015). "Salía de uno y me metí en otro:" A grounded theory approach to understanding the violence-migration nexus among Central American women in the United States. Unpublished doctoral dissertation. University of Texas, Austin, TX.

Crandall, M., Senturia, K., Sullivan, M., & Shiu-Thornton, S. (2005). Latina survivors of domestic violence: Understanding through qualitative analysis. *Hispanic Health Care International, 3*(3), 179–187.

Dewan, S. E. (2014). Patterns of service utilization among pre-certified victims of human trafficking. *International Social Work, 57*(1), 64–74.

Erez, E., Adelman, M., & Gregory, C. (2009). Intersections of immigration and domestic violence: Voices of battered immigrant women. *Feminist Criminology, 4*(1), 32–56.

Farmer, P. (2004). An anthropology of structural violence. *Current Anthropology, 45*(3), 305–325. doi:10.1086/382250

Fedina, L. (2015). Use and misuse of research in books on sex trafficking: Implications for interdisciplinary researchers, practitioners, and advocates. *Trauma, Violence, & Abuse, 16*(2), 188–198. doi:10.1177/1524838014523337

Furman, R., Negi, N., Schatz, M. C. S., & Jones, S. (2008). Transnational social work: Using a wraparound model. *Global Networks, 8*(4), 496–503. doi:10.1111/j.1471-0374.2008.00236.x

Hom, K. A., & Woods, S. J. (2013). Trauma and its aftermath for commercially sexually exploited women as told by front-line service providers. *Issues in Mental Health Nursing, 34*(2), 75–81.

Hossain, M., Zimmerman, C., Abas, M., Light, M., & Watts, C. (2010). The relationship of trauma to mental disorders among trafficked and sexually exploited girls and women. *American Journal of Public Health, 100*(12), 2442–2449. doi:10.2105/AJPH.2009.173229

Hughes, D. M. (2000). The "Natasha" trade: The transnational shadow market of trafficking in women. *Journal of International Affairs, 53*(2), 625–651.

INCIDE Social. (2012). *Construyendo un model de atención para mujeres migrantes víctimas de violencia sexual en México* [Care model for migrant women victims of sexual violence in Mexico]. Mexico City: INCIDE Social.

Infante, C., Idrovo, A. J., Sánchez-Dominguez, M. S., Vinhas, S., & González-Vázquez, T. (2012). Violence committed against migrants in transit: Experiences on the northern Mexican border. *Journal of Immigrant and Minority Health, 14*(3), 449–459. doi:10.1007/s10903-011-9489-y

Ki-moon, B. (2012). Secretary-general's remarks to the thematic debate on security in Central America as a regional and global challenge. Retrieved from http://www.un.org/sg/STATEMENTS/index.asp?nid=6054

Kulkarni, S. J., Bell, H., & Rhodes, D. M. (2012). Back to basics: Essential qualities of services for survivors of intimate partner violence. *Violence Against Women, 18*(1), 85–101. doi:10.1177/1077801212437137

Macy, R. J., & Graham, L. M. (2012). Identifying domestic and international sex-trafficking victims during human service provision. *Trauma, Violence, & Abuse, 13*(2), 59–76. doi:10.1177/1524838012440340

Macy, R. J., & Johns, N. (2011). Aftercare services for international sex trafficking survivors: Informing U.S. service and program development in an emerging practice area. *Trauma, Violence, & Abuse, 12*(2), 87–98. doi:10.1177/1524838010390709

Menjívar, C., & Salcido, O. (2002). Immigrant women and domestic violence: Common experiences in different countries. *Gender & Society, 16*(6), 898–920.

Mowder, D. L. (2010). *The relationship between the undocumented immigrant battered Latina and U.S. immigration policy* (Doctoral dissertation). Washington State University, Pullman, WA. Retrieved from http://www.dissertations.wsu.edu/Dissertations/Spring2010/d_mowder_050310.pdf

Nichols, A. J., & Heil, E. C. (2015). Challenges to identifying and prosecuting sex trafficking cases in the Midwest United States. *Feminist Criminology, 10*(1), 7–35. doi:10.1177/1557085113519490

Perreira, K. M. & Ornelas, I. (2013). Painful passages: Traumatic experiences and post-traumatic stress among US immigrant Latino adolescents and their primary caregivers. *International Migration Review, 47*(4), 976–1005.

Raj, A., & Silverman, J. (2002). Violence against immigrant women: The roles of culture, context, and legal immigrant status on intimate partner violence. *Violence Against Women*, *8*(3), 367–398. doi:10.1177/10778010222183107

Rosenblum, M., & Brick, K. (2011). *U.S. immigration policy and Mexican/Central American migration flows: Then and now*. Regional Migration Study Group. Retrieved from http://www.migrationpolicy.org/research/RMSG-us-immigration-policy-mexican-central-american-migration-flows

Salcido, O., & Adelman, M. (2004). "He has me tied with the blessed and damned papers": Undocumented-immigrant battered women in Phoenix, Arizona. *Human Organization*, *63*(2), 162–172.

Simich, L., Goyen, L., Powell, A., & Mallozzi, K. (2014). *Improving human trafficking victim identification: Validation and dissemination of a screening tool*. Washington, DC: U.S. Department of Justice.

Simmons, W. P., Menjívar, C., & Téllez, M. (2015). Violence and vulnerability of female migrants in drop houses in Arizona: The predictable outcome of a chain reaction of violence. *Violence Against Women*, *21*(5), 551–570. doi:10.1177/1077801215573331

Sloan, L., & Wahab, S. (2000). Feminist voices on sex work: Implications for social work. *Affilia*, *15*(4), 457–479.

Turner, H. A., Finkelhor, D., & Ormrod, R. (2010). Poly-victimization in a national sample of children and youth. *American Journal of Preventive Medicine*, *38*(3), 323–330.

United Nations High Commissioner for Refugees [UNHCR]. (2015). *Women on the run*. Washington, DC. Retrieved from http://www.unhcr.org/5630f24c6.html

USCIS. (2013). *I-918: Petition for U non-immigrant status*. Retrieved from https://www.uscis.gov/i-918

U.S. Department of Justice. (2007). *Attorney general's annual report to Congress and assessment of U.S. government activities to combat trafficking in persons: Fiscal year 2006*. Retrieved from http://digitalcommons.unl.edu/humtraffdata/2/

——. (2015). *Attorney general's annual report to Congress and assessment of U.S. government activities to combat trafficking in persons: Fiscal year 2014*. Retrieved from https://www.justice.gov/humantrafficking/file/797606/download

U.S. Department of State. (2015). *Trafficking in persons report: 2015*. Retrieved from http://www.state.gov/j/tip/rls/tiprpt/2015/

——. *Trafficking in Persons Report*. (2016). Retrieved from: https://www.state.gov/j/tip/rls/tiprpt/2016/

Vidales, G. T. (2010). Arrested justice: The multifaceted plight of immigrant Latinas who faced domestic violence. *Journal of Family Violence*, *25*(6), 533–544.

Wahab, S., & Panichelli, M. (2013). Ethical and human rights issues in coercive interventions with sex workers. *Affilia*, *28*(4), 344–349.

CHAPTER 9

AFROCENTRIC INTERGENERATIONAL ASSESSMENT AND RECOVERY FROM SEX TRAFFICKING AND COMMERCIAL SEXUAL EXPLOITATION

VALANDRA, PhD, MSW, LCSW, UNIVERSITY OF ARKANSAS

This chapter begins by reviewing the relevant research in the field regarding the disproportionate representation of African American adults and children among sex-trafficking, commercial sexual exploitation (CSE)/prostitution victim/survivors. An Afrocentric intergenerational perspective is used to analyze structural and individual risk factors affecting the lives of African American victim/survivors. This integrative critical approach is essential for social workers to enable them to recognize how sociocultural and sociopolitical factors differentially impact the lives of African American children, youth, men, and women sex-trafficking victim/survivors. Additionally, it promotes the importance and use of culturally responsive, oppression-sensitive social work interventions across all levels (macro, mezzo, micro) of practice and policy as the best practice strategy with this population.

The Afrocentric (Schiele, 1996) intergenerational perspective (Waites, 2009) is advanced for consideration by social work practitioners as a strength-based intervention tool to assess environmental, cultural, and individual assets and risks and to support resilience, recovery, and healing related to the lived experiences of male and female African American victims/survivors across generations. The chapter highlights the core assumptions and values of Afrocentric and intergenerational assessment tools. Their usefulness is illustrated with sample questions for conducting an intergenerational family assessment. Intergenerational trauma-specific risks and protective sources are highlighted, and relevant macro-, mezzo-, and micropractice and policy implications are discussed and illustrated.

The terms *African American* and *Black* are used interchangeably to mean individuals of the African diaspora with ancestral origins in Black Africa and with a direct family lineage in the United States through the transatlantic slave trade, or any person who self-identifies ethnically as African American and/ or Black. *Sex trafficking, sex trading, survival sex*, and *CSE/prostitution* are used interchangeably to reflect a system of coercion and sexual exploitation of individuals. *Victim* and *survivor* are used together (*victim/survivor*) to reflect a resilience that includes both suffering through and surviving individual, familial, community, and societal violence (Tummala-Narra, 2007). Race-, class-, and gender-based structural oppression is recognized as a significant form of violence and is inextricably linked with sex trafficking/trading and CSE/prostitution in this chapter.

Relevant Research

Scope and Prevalence

To study the experiences of victims/survivors of CSE/prostitution, researchers often rely heavily on sampling pools that come to the attention of the criminal justice system or of mandated social services associated with arrests, diversion programs, and mandated drug and mental health treatment (Martin, Hearst, & Widome, 2010; Martin, Pierce, Peyton, Gabilondo, & Tulpule, 2014). Different practices in policing, arresting, and prosecution, as well as disparities in sentencing, diversion, and social structure, contribute to the overrepresentation of African Americans in those sampling pools (Mears, Cochran, & Lindsey, 2016). These structural realities and their impact make it difficult to provide an accurate and reliable picture of the magnitude of CSE/ prostitution within the African American population. In addition, populations involved in sex trafficking are often hidden and difficult to recruit for research, further skewing statistics. Despite these realities, African Americans living in high-poverty and crime-related communities are particularly at high risk for involvement in the sex-trafficking industry. In a comprehensive examination of the sex-trafficking industry in the United States, Nichols (2016) reported that research indicates that buyers of commercial sex are disproportionately white men; however, sex-trafficking victims are disproportionately Black or Latina women and girls in poverty who are involved with pimps, or are LGBTQ+ and involved in survival sex (Dank et al., 2015; Martin et al., 2014). Sex-trafficking dynamics affecting the lives of African Americans require that social workers be attuned to culturally responsive, oppression-sensitive Afrocentric practices to address the needs of African American sex -trafficking victim/survivors.

National Outlook

Nationally, African Americans are disproportionately victimized in the sex -trafficking industry. Despite making up only 13.3 percent of the U.S. population (Rastogi, Johnson, Hoeffel, & Drewery, 2011), African Americans are 1.5 to 10 times more likely than other races to be confirmed sex-trafficking victims (Banks & Kyckelhahn, 2011). For example, in a U.S. Department of Justice federal human-trafficking task force report of characteristics of suspected and confirmed human-trafficking incidents in 2008–2010, confirmed sex-trafficking victims were more likely to identify as Black (40 percent), than White (26 percent), Hispanic (24 percent), two or more races non-Hispanic (6 percent), or Asian (4 percent). The same report indicated that the majority of confirmed sex -trafficking victims were female (94 percent) and seventeen years of age or younger (54 percent), while the majority (62 percent) of sex-trafficking suspects were Black (Banks & Kyckelhahn, 2011). African American children are also disproportionately victimized in the criminal justice system and the sex-trafficking industry. Nationally, 52 percent of all juvenile arrests for prostitution are African American children (Federal Bureau of Investigation, 2014). African American male and female youth constitute 15.4 percent of the national youth population but are almost 1.5 times more likely to be arrested for prostitution than their White peers (Synder & Mulako-Wangota, 2015). In 2012, nationwide, law enforcement agencies reported that 40 percent of juveniles (under eighteen years old) arrested for prostitution were White, 58 percent were Black, and 1.2 percent were Asian or Pacific Islander (Synder & Mulako-Wangota, 2015). African American youth also experience more severe treatment in the juvenile justice system than their White peers, as empirical evidence strongly suggests that race is a strong predictor of differential treatment at every stage of juvenile justice processing, adding to the risk of victimization of Black sex-trafficking victim/survivors *within* the juvenile justice system (Andersen, 2015).

Statewide Outlook

Statewide, disparities can be even starker. In a study of domestic sex trafficking of girls in Minneapolis, Minnesota, based, in part, on data from Minneapolis police case files and Hennepin County district court records, Martin et al. (2014) found that the majority of "facilitators" (individuals who recruit, promote, and benefit from sex trafficking) and victims (commercially sexually exploited youth) were African American. The authors note that the racial representation of their study is indicative of the role of race and class biases in the criminal justice system as well as race-based stereotypes.

In California, African American girls are disproportionately represented in county statistics of sex-trafficking victims in the juvenile justice system; 92 percent of girls in the Los Angeles County juvenile system for sex trafficking identified as African American, 62 percent were from the child welfare system, and 84 percent were from poor communities within Los Angeles County ("Campaign to Halt Sex Trafficking," 2012). These statistics highlight the significance of how intersecting identities associated with race and over-representation in poverty and the child welfare system place African American children at greater risk for CSE. In Alameda County, 66 percent of children referred for trafficking-specific services were African American (Walker, 2013).

In a study of case files of 389 women in a Phoenix, Arizona, CSE/prostitution diversion program, Clarke, Clarke, Roe-Sepowitz, and Fey (2012) examined the relationship between race, educational level, childhood abuse, drug use, and age of entry into CSE/prostitution among adolescents. They found that African American women were more likely to be engaged in CSE/prostitution as juveniles. Clarke and her colleagues also reported that women who experienced CSE/prostitution as juveniles were more likely to have dropped out of middle school or high school, were more likely to report familial drug problems during their childhood, and first used drugs at a significantly lower age than women who experienced CSE/prostitution as adults.

In an age-graded study of the relationship between African American ethnicity and CSE/prostitution involvement among 1,354 youth found guilty of a serious offense in Philadelphia, Pennsylvania, and Phoenix, Arizona, Reid and Piquero (2014) found that African American males and females were significantly more likely to have experienced CSE/prostitution early in life. The authors reported that among all males experiencing CSE between the ages of eleven and sixteen, 67 percent were African American; and among males between the ages of seventeen and twenty-five, 64 percent were African American. Among all females between the ages of eleven and sixteen, 50 percent were African American; and of females between the ages of seventeen and twenty-five, 40 percent were African American. The risk of early initiation in the CSE/prostitution industry was greater for African American male youth than it was for female African Americans (67 percent and 40 percent, respectively). It is also important to note that in the Reid and Piquero study 40 percent of African American males and 36 percent of females reported no involvement in CSE/prostitution.

These statewide findings show the urgent need for culturally responsive, oppression-sensitive social work practices with African Americans that simultaneously address structural and individual dynamics regarding sex trafficking. In understanding the risks of sex-trafficking victimization among African Americans, it is critically important for social workers to recognize the heterogeneity of African American lived experiences while simultaneously recognizing the pervasiveness of structural barriers, including institutional oppression and discrimination, and race-, class-, and gender-based stereotypes and biases that affect people of color generally and African Americans specifically. These macro-level risks suggest that social workers and organizations must be capable of and comfortable with fluidly moving across macro-, mezzo-, and micro-level systems of practice and policy advocacy.

Major Risk Factors

The vulnerability of African Americans to involvement in sex trading is inextricably linked to structural systems and networks of poverty and crime embedded within a capitalist, patriarchal social and political system of inequity (Boxill & Richardson, 2007; Farley, 2004). Race, class, and gender disparities figure prominently in the economic marginalization of African Americans, resulting in fewer employment and educational opportunities and placing them disproportionately at risk for early involvement in sex trading as a survival mechanism (Dalla, 2006; Monroe, 2005). The literature has firmly established the connection between poverty; homelessness (Hood-Brown, 1998); limited education, job skills, and resources (Rothenberg, 2013); and involvement in the street-level sex-trafficking industry among African Americans living in poverty (Martin et al., 2010; Rosen & Venkatesh, 2008; Valandra, 2007, 2015). More specifically, as Monroe (2005) contends, poverty fosters the development of many undesirable and stigmatizing behaviors, including prostitution. The author draws a direct correlation between the pervasiveness of structural inequalities, poverty, and CSE/prostitution among African American women living in poverty.

One of the outcomes of these circumstances is that African Americans become trapped in generational poverty in a low-wage or underground economy and climate in which sex trading becomes a constrained choice to make ends meet (Benson & Matthews, 1995; Silbert & Pines, 1982). Rosen and Venkatesh (2008, p. 425) state that African Americans make decisions using "bounded rationality" when choices are limited and not ideal or desirable; African Americans trapped in poor urban communities "turn to sex work as a means of *satisficing*[1] the problems and challenges posed by their position in the labor market." Once they are involved in the sex-trafficking industry, substantial barriers can keep African Americans enslaved in a cycle of violence, substance abuse, control, and exploitation by pimps, intimate partners, and traffickers (Baker, Dalla, & Williamson, 2010; Dalla, 2006). Thus the term *modern-day slavery* is appropriate for describing these conditions, in which persons are forced, coerced, or otherwise entrapped in conditions of bondage and servitude that involve the exploitation and abuse of their bodies for labor, sex, or both (*Trafficking in Persons Report*, 2015).

Legacy of Oppression

Regarding African Americans in the United States, modern-day slavery can be seen as an indelible lingering legacy of the chattel slavery that existed during the formation of the capitalist sociopolitical economy of the nation. This legacy continues to generate social and economic conditions that force many African Americans, particularly in urban and low-income communities, into *satisficing* in the underground economy of the sex trade to survive in deplorable living circumstances (Venkatesh, 2006). As Collins frames it:

> The buying and selling of human beings of African descent formed a template for the economic and racial, [and sexual] oppression of Black Americans. . . . their bodies and all that was contained in those bodies (labor, sexuality, and reproduction) were objectified and turned into commodities that were traded in the marketplace. (2005, p. 55)

The context of slavery in America offers a culturally relevant historical lens to deconstruct and examine the structural conditions and life circumstances that create risks associated with the objectification, commodification, and trafficking/trading of Black bodies in America. A historical understanding offers a glimpse into individual, familial, and communal approaches that African Americans have used as part of "the Black helping tradition" (Martin & Martin, 2002, p. 1) to cope with the detrimental consequences associated with internalizing and surviving individual trauma, violence, and abuse and structural forms of oppression. Equally important, the intergenerational transmission of recovery, resilience, and healing can be illuminated. Thus, the legacy of resilience offers social workers a signpost to culturally relevant assessments and intervention options for addressing the unique needs that African Americans at risk for CSE/prostitution have. Individual and interpersonal risk factors, including intrafamilial child sexual and physical abuse, running away, intimate partner violence, drug addiction, and intergenerational exposure to CSE/prostitution in households and neighborhoods, intersect and often increase vulnerability *prior* to any involvement in the CSE/prostitution industry (Kennedy, Bybee, Kulkarni, & Archer, 2012; Kramer & Berg, 2003; Raphael & Shapiro, 2002; Reid, 2011).

The structural and individual risk factors that render African Americans vulnerable to sex trafficking require social work practice and policy approaches and strategies that are contoured to the unique historical, cultural, political, and economic realities that African Americans face. The prevention and intervention efforts social workers engage in to address CSE/prostitution in the lives of African Americans must be about more than raising awareness. Social workers need to address significant structural changes, particularly related to economic and racial inequality. Social workers are better equipped to intervene effectively using a culturally relevant, oppression-sensitive conceptual perspective and a culturally specific assessment and intervention approach. The core assumptions and values of the Afrocentric intergenerational conceptual framework are described next; the framework is used to illustrate culturally specific methods of assessment and intervention across all system levels (macro, mezzo, micro) in practice with African American sex-trafficking survivors.

Afrocentric Intergenerational Perspective

The use of an Afrocentric intergenerational perspective is necessary for understanding and addressing the complexity of African Americans' experiences with the structural oppression that is endemic to the culture of the United States and the subculture of the sex-trafficking industry. The Afrocentric intergenerational lens focuses on the cultural values of African Americans in order to understand and address the intricacies and nuances experienced by victims/survivors. Previous scholarship has examined the industry of sex trafficking primarily through the perspective of various feminist theories and Black-/Africana-Womanist standpoint. These theories propose that structural race, class, and gender inequalities, the feminization of poverty, patriarchy, and capitalism result in the disproportionate representation of women and women of color in the sex-trafficking industry (Holmstrom, 2003; Monroe, 2005; Ntiri, 2001; Saulnier, 1996).

Research examining the intersectionality of race, class, and gender and the Black feminist standpoint through the lived, shared experiences of Black men and women suggests that while gender is ever-present and significant, "seldom do black women experience the world in isolation from black men and seldom do black men experience the world in isolation from black women" (Harnois, 2010, p. 84). Historically, it can be argued that the buying, selling, and trading of male and female Black bodies have affected how African American individuals, families, and communities collectively and intergenerationally respond to, cope with, and recover from structural forms of oppression, including sex trafficking/ trading and CSE/prostitution. The Afrocentric (Schiele, 1996) and intergenerational (Waites, 2009) perspective is a culturally relevant conceptual framework that social workers can use to guide prevention/intervention services grounded in the cultural values and lived experiences of African American victims/survivors.

Afrocentricity and Social Work Practice

The social work profession continually promotes the use of culturally appropriate theoretical perspectives and paradigms to guide its practice with African Americans. Several social work scholars and practitioners have advanced the use of African-centered, Afrocentric, or Africentric theory, practice, and research frameworks and interventions for understanding and assessing the various needs and life conditions experienced by African American families. Schiele contends that

> failure to use the cultural values of people of color in developing new models can be viewed as an implicit expression of Western ethnocentrism, or the belief that Eurocentric values are the only values that can explain behavior and should be the basis for solving people's problems. (Schiele, 1996, p. 284)

African Americans have endured centuries of cultural and racial oppression in the United States as a result of Eurocentric domination, competition, and subjugation (Bell, Bouie, & Baldwin, 1990; Schiele, 1996). A goal of Afrocentrists is to offer a counternarrative of African American humanity anchored in the cultural values and beliefs of African ancestors to challenge and dispel the negative stereotypes, myths, and oppressive ideology about African Americans perpetuated by the dominant white culture and internalized by some African Americans (Schiele, 1994a, 1996). Another goal in promoting the use of an Afrocentric paradigm is to offer social work practitioners a culturally grounded practice framework that highlights the strengths of African Americans and illuminates the detrimental impact of structural oppression in their lives (Manning, Cornelius, & Okundaye, 2004).

Afrocentric Core Assumptions and Values

One of the core assumptions of the Afrocentric paradigm is that individual identity is constructed as a collective identity that is critical to survival and the promotion of harmonious interpersonal relationships. Another core assumption is that the spiritual and nonspiritual realms are equally important in offering a holistic and interdependent understanding of the world. Lastly, valid sources of knowledge are assumed to include both rational/logical and emotional/affective experiences (Asante, 1988; Baldwin & Hopkins, 1990; Schiele, 1994b). Core cultural values and principles associated with an Afrocentric worldview include "interdependence, cooperation, unity, mutual responsibility and reconciliation," according to Africanist scholars Baldwin and Hopkins (1990, p. 170). Historical strengths of African American families include a strong focus on achievement and the work ethic, flexible family roles and strong kinship bonds, a spiritual orientation, and mutual support (Logan, 2001; McAdoo, 2007; Waites, 2009).

Within the context of the helping process, Schiele (1996) asserts that personalization, or establishing a personal connection, between client and worker is an essential element of the professional working relationship and that authenticity and transparency between client and worker are more helpful in achieving personalization than distance and indifference. Reciprocity is another critical element of the professional helping relationship, according to Schiele. The essence of reciprocity, Schiele states, is recognizing and affirming that both client and practitioner have valuable wisdom, knowledge, and expertise and that the process of helping can help the helper as well. These core assumptions, values, and principles provide the foundation needed by social workers using Afrocentric assessment and intervention approaches in their work with African Americans.

Practitioner's Cultural Self-Awareness

A critical step in using an Afrocentric approach with African American victim/survivors of sex trafficking is for the social worker, regardless of background, to judiciously explore African Americans' own worldview and cultural self-awareness. Social work practitioners and researchers are strongly encouraged to employ reflexive practice (self-evaluation of one's own thoughts and feelings often to uncover latent bias), *prior* to engaging African American victim/survivors of CSE/prostitution in treatment and research and on an ongoing basis throughout the intervention or research process (Valandra, 2012). The box titled Practitioner Critical Reflection and Self Awareness Questions offers social work practitioners a list of critical questions for reflection regarding social work with African American survivors of CSE/prostitution.

Self-awareness and critical reflection are consistent with the core values of the social work profession, which require social workers to commit to professional growth and enhancement, cultural competence, and social diversity in understanding how their knowledge base, biases, and world-views shape professional practice (Council on Social Work Education, 2015; National Association of Social Workers [NASW], 2008). The cultural genogram (Hardy & Laszloffy, 1995) can be used by social workers as an effective training tool for self-awareness and reflection. Hardy and Laszloffy assert that too often the client's cultural background is overemphasized to the exclusion of the practitioners' "perceptions of their respective cultural backgrounds. As a result, [practitioners] are rarely challenged to examine how their own cultural identities influence understanding and acceptance of those who are both culturally similar and dissimilar" (Hardy & Laszloffy, 2008, p. 227). The cultural genogram is designed to help practitioners explore how their unique cultural identities may influence their practice approach and effectiveness (Hardy & Laszloffy, 2008).

Culturally Relevant Practice Considerations

Afrocentrists offer practitioners several salient culturally relevant factors for consideration when developing and implementing treatment interventions in working with African American families. Stewart (2004) notes the importance of recognizing that peoples of African descent are not a homogenous monolithic group but may share some commonalities with respect to their overall worldview. This perspective is recognized in the Common Heritage Framework proposed by Freeman and Logan (2004), which has at its core the common ancestral past and cultural factors and traditions that can help explain some of the ways in which Black families have responded to the traumatic conditions of enslavement, colonization, resettlement, and contemporary challenges. Schiele (1996) explains that an Afrocentric explanation of social problems may not be applicable in all situations or social conditions because it is not a universal panacea for all issues affecting the lives of African Americans.

Afrocentrists emphasize understanding the historical roots of Black helping networks and traditions and the cultural values of Black family life, including the value of oral traditions, eldership, Black spirituality, and collectivism (Logan, Freeman, & McRoy, 1990). Importance is also placed on the historical oppression and trauma of slavery, the continued economic, social, and political marginalization experienced by Blacks, and the persistence of this marginalization through pervasive racial disparities and poverty (Gilbert, Harvey, & Belgrave, 2009). It is critical to understand how ongoing exclusionary and discriminatory policies and practices have affected the well-being of family life across generations and have led to the physical and mental health disparities in African American communities today (DeGruy, 2005; Logan, Denby, & Gibson, 2007; Manning et al., 2004).

Summary

The core assumptions and values of the Afrocentric perspective are grounded in African cultural values that have survived the African diaspora and have been adapted to navigate the harsh realities of a legacy of continued oppression and discrimination across major sectors of life in America. The Afrocentric perspective offers social workers a culturally responsive, oppression-sensitive conceptual framework for understanding the challenges facing African American survivors of sex trafficking but also for identifying the resilience and protective factors that have enabled African Americans to persevere across time and generations.

The Afrocentric perspective is consistent with the mission and values of social work and requires social workers to thinking critically and comprehensively to act across all systems of practice and policy advocacy to meet the needs of sex-trafficking survivors. The core assumptions and values are summarized in table 9.1, including key implications for practitioners' consideration when engaging with African American survivors of sex trafficking. The following box identifies critical self-reflection questions that all practitioners can consider when working with African American survivors of sex trafficking. The questions are intended to help social workers gain a better understanding of their own cultural identity and worldview and of how that worldview influences their practice approach and shapes their understanding of other people. Social work

TABLE 9.1 Afrocentric Core Values and Assumptions

Core Assumptions and Values	Key Considerations	Best Practice Implications
• Collectivism • Interdependence • Cooperation • Unity	• Interpersonal relationships • Mutual responsibility • Collaboration • Cooperation • Reconciliation • Reciprocity	• Authentic, transparent, personalized professional working relationships with clients • Practitioner *and* client expertise, wisdom, and knowledge are affirmed and valued • Reciprocity and balance are valued in the interpersonal exchange of knowledge
• Spirituality is recognized in all elements of humanity as a connecting force • Spirituality and morality are inseparable	• Human and nonhuman attributes are valued • Belief in a supreme being does not imply powerlessness • No one religious tradition is valued over others	• Recognize, affirm, and validate client resilience, cultural traditions, cross-generational strengths, and legacies • Historical and current contexts are meaningful
• All sources of knowledge are equally valid, including affect/emotion and feelings	• Embrace feelings as a critically important source of knowledge • Rational, logical reasoning is not the only way of knowing	• Validate and affirm client understanding gained through affective knowledge • Invite emotional sources of knowledge as a means to balance the use of rationality

Sources: Based on Schiele (1994b) and Stewart (2004).

Practitioner Critical Reflection and Self-Awareness Questions

Examination and Understanding of Self

- What do I know about my own worldview and culture?
- What do I already know about the issue or population?
- What are the sources of my knowledge (formal education, practice experience, third party, upbringing, etc.)?
- What questions do I have about what I know?
- How have my personal and professional experiences shaped what I know?
- How does this issue influence my worldview, knowledge, and background?
- How does my worldview influence the way I experience and/or construct this issue, population, and topic?
- What assumptions, presuppositions, biases, attitudes, and beliefs shape my construction of this issue, population, and topic?

Examination and Understanding of Intervention Process

- How does my involvement with this issue, population, and topic benefit or hinder clients?
- How does my involvement with this issue, population, and topic benefit or hinder me personally and professionally?
- How do my agency's policies and practices hinder or help the client's access to culturally responsive, oppression-sensitive services?
- How do the individual, family, and community experience my presence in their lives?
- How do I experience myself in relation to the individual, family, and community involved in this intervention?
- What role has the individual, family, and community played in shaping this intervention?
- What sources of knowledge have I relied on in understanding and intervening to address this issue?
- What sources of knowledge do the individual, family, and community value as credible?
- How do the individual, family, and community define the issue?
- What potential power dynamics are relevant to reflect upon and address?
- Who are the cultural brokers of the family and community and my access to them?
- Are the location and space in which the intervention process occurs accessible and culturally safe for clients?

- What are culturally responsive, oppression-sensitive ways to validate and affirm the client's worldview, cultural traditions, and lived experiences?
- How does the past and present social, economic, and political context shape this intervention process?
- What is the client's perception, understanding, and belief about the goal or outcome of this intervention process?

Source: Based on Valandra (2012).

practitioners are encouraged to consider these questions as an ongoing practice of culturally responsive oppression sensitive social work.

Examination

Afrocentric Intergenerational Assessment and Intervention Approach

The Afrocentric intergenerational practice framework offers social work practitioners a theoretically grounded, culturally responsive, oppression-sensitive assessment and intervention approach to help all system levels address issues affecting the lives of African American survivors of sex trafficking. It illuminates the complex historical, social, economic, and political dynamics that place African Americans disproportionately at risk for involvement in sex trafficking, as well as interlocking community, organization, group, family, and individual factors. In essence, the Afrocentric intergenerational practice framework offers social workers an ecological systems or person-in-environment approach to assessment and intervention. It is also an approach that affirms and restores cultural strengths and intergenerational kinship ties that have contributed to the resilience of families and communities across multiple generations for centuries (Waites, 2009).

Relevant macro-, mezzo-, and micro-level intervention strategies are identified in the following sections and illustrated in the Policy Practice Intervention Strategies grid in table 9.2 to provide social workers with a perspective of policy practice and its links and interconnections across systems and with direct practice interventions. Policy practice encompasses formal federal, state, municipal, and agency/organizational policies as well as informal policies or de facto policies. Policy-sensitive practice involves understanding how policies impact people's lives and intervening accordingly (Fauri, Netting, & O'Connor, 2005). For purposes of the forthcoming discussion, macro-level systems include historical and current societal norms and values, as well as economic, political, and religious ideologies, laws, customs, and practices. Mezzo-level systems include groups, agencies, organizations, communities, and associations and the policies and communal relationships that govern them. Micro-level systems are those that characterize relationships with individuals, family, and friends.

Macro-Level Intervention Strategies

Societal oppression helps make African American youth and adults vulnerable for involvement in the sex-trafficking industry. An Afrocentric analysis of these factors entails an examination of the impact of race and class marginalization on low-income African American communities. The structural racism and classism that result in economic deprivation can push African Americans into selling their bodies in exchange for necessities, as well as into other criminal behaviors (Benson & Matthews, 1995; Rosen & Venkatesh, 2008; Silbert & Pines, 1982). Social work practitioners working with this population must be willing to acknowledge this reality and affirm and validate survivors' perceptions of inequality and associated feelings of injustice as part of the process of building trust and establishing an authentic professional working relationship. Interventions that address and challenge discriminatory housing-, education-, and job-related policies and stressors associated with racial profiling, policing, and incarceration must be considered a natural part of policy practice with this population. The political, economic, and social institutions that oppress people must be targeted if change is to occur in the lives of African Americans at risk for CSE/prostitution. The illustrative policy practice grid in table 9.2 identifies examples of policy issues affecting African Americans and survivors of trafficking, as well as intervention strategies for social workers' consideration.

Mezzo-Level Intervention Strategies

Community issues are also a contributing risk factor for CSE/prostitution in poor Black neighborhoods. An Afrocentric analysis of high-crime, drug-infested, poverty-stricken neighborhoods requires a collectivist approach by social workers and a partnering with key community stakeholders to hold slum landlords, redlining financial institutions, discriminatory employers, and corrupt law enforcement personnel accountable and to ensure equitable and unbiased distribution of housing, financial, and employment opportunities and law enforcement services (Monroe, 2005; Morgen & Maskovsky, 2003). Social workers committed to advocacy and justice can join coalitions and collaborate with organizers at the local level from groups like the #Black Lives Matter movement (http://blacklivesmatter.com), the African American Policy Forum (www.aapf. org), and the National Black Justice Coalition (http://nbjc.org), to name a few organizations dedicated to addressing inequality and injustice. Long-standing national organizations that address structural economic and racial inequalities affecting the lives of African Americans also include the National Association for the Advancement of Colored People (NAACP), the Urban League, the Children's Defense Fund, the National Congress of Negro Women, and the National Council of African American Men (NCAAM). These organizations have a cohesive and comprehensive vision of the value of African Americans' lives. They develop and organize strategies to address the effects of policies that negatively impact educational opportunities and outcomes for Black children, the police brutality inflicted on Black males and females, the need for prison reform, and substance abuse and HIV/AIDs healthcare challenges affecting African Americans communities. These issues contribute to risk factors in economically disadvantaged neighborhoods and place African American children at risk for exposure to and involvement in CSE/prostitution at an early age (Clarke et al., 2012; Cobbina & Oselin, 2011; Martin et al., 2010).

Mezzo-level intervention strategies also need to include the systemic review of organizational policies, practices, and processes within agencies that offer sex trafficking–specific services to identify potentially racist and oppressive practices that might act as a barrier for African Americans in accessing and engaging services. For example, in a study examining the needs of African American women survivors of domestic sex trafficking in the twin cities of St. Paul and Minneapolis, African American women receiving agency services identified unrealistic program expectations and disrespectful service providers as barriers to healing and recovery (Valandra, 2007). As one study participant astutely observed, "They don't understand that it's taken me 30 years to get this way, and it's unrealistic to think that a 96-day treatment program is going to help me just start feeling and sharing emotions, especially in front of strangers" (Valandra, 2007, p. 202). In the same study, women reported that the housing resources offered by agencies were sometimes not much different in quality than the crack houses they experienced when surviving on the streets. It is imperative that social workers hold the organizations with which they work to a standard of professional, accessible, and culturally responsive care in the delivery of services to African American survivors of sex trafficking.

Additionally, social workers must target discriminatory prostitution laws and enforcement practices that are focused more heavily on fines, penalties, and prosecution of Black victim/survivors than of those who coerce, buy, entrap, and sell human beings—modern-day slave traffickers (Edlund & Korn, 2002; Miller, 1993; O'Leary & Howard, 2001). Law-sanctioned discrimination and biased enforcement can be traced directly back to slave codes, black codes, and Jim Crow laws of the South and race-based prejudice in the North in an

TABLE 9.2 Policy Practice Intervention Strategies

Issue	Relevant Policies	Macro Level	Mezzo Level	Micro Level
Discriminatory Housing Practices • Redlining • Credit rationing	• Fair Housing Act of 1968 • Home Mortgage Disclosure Act of 1975 • Community Reinvestment Act of 1977	• Advocate for the enforcement of antidiscrimination housing policies • Join federal and state coalitions and associations to end housing discrimination • Work with public housing associations to lobby for quality, accessible, and affordable housing in low-income communities	• Collaborate with the Urban League and community-development banks to fight racist lending practices • Organize town hall meetings with community stakeholders to develop cooperative loan programs in neighborhoods • Work with civic organizations and faith-based programs to build affordable and accessible housing	• Educate individuals and families about tenants' rights • Facilitate meetings between families and slumlords • Encourage citizens to report slumlords to the housing authorities • Recognize and respect intergenerational living arrangements within households
Educational Disparities • School suspensions and expulsions • Low graduation rates • Dropouts • Pushouts	• Civil Rights Act of 1964, Title IV	• Lobby for reforms in school disciplining policies, such as "zero tolerance" • Advocate for the enforcement of the Education Department Equity and Excellence Commission recommendations • Support restorative methods of school discipline • Join and collaborate with the African American Policy Forum in supporting and empowering Black girls and communities • Support President Obama's My Brother's Keeper initiative • Work with the Children's Defense Fund to improve the educational climate for Black children	• Advocate for culturally responsive, experienced, and fully licensed teachers and administrators in the public school system • Support the involvement of families and students in the development of discipline policies • Use evidence-based research from the National Center for Education Statistics • Support training and professional development for all school personnel • Advocate for the appropriate use of law enforcement in schools • Recognize the criminalization and victimization of Black girls in the educational system	• Facilitate meetings between parents, students, and educators • Help caregivers understand the links between early childhood trauma (sexual, physical, etc.) and school issues • Encourage parents to file complaints of discrimination with the Office for Civil Rights • Support and promote adult literacy and GED programs • Advocate for the development of adult educational programming in low-income communities with flexible evening hours and daycare services • Recognize that barriers to accessing quality education do NOT equate with valuing education less • Inform clients of scholarship opportunities with the United Negro College Fund (UNCF)

TABLE 9.2 *(Continued)*

Issue	Relevant Policies	Macro Level	Mezzo Level	Micro Level
Employment Discrimination • Minimum wage laws • Accessible jobs • Equal pay	• Fair Labor Standards Act (FLSA) • Fair Chance Act • Ledbetter Fair Pay Restoration Act of 2009	• Advocate for an increase in the minimum wage and benefits • Support the Fair Chance Business Pledge and Fair Chance Act • Support gender equity and equal pay for equal work • Collaborate with the National Urban League's job programs' urban youth empowerment program	• Advocate for quality job creation in low-income neighborhoods • Support union organizing • Collaborate with civic organizations, faith-based communities, and other stakeholders in creating job training and preparation programs in urban settings • Understand how the intersections of race, gender, and class employment bias place Black females at risk	• Encourage the formation of unions • Facilitate the filing of employment discrimination complaints • Help individuals understand their legal rights regarding employment discrimination • Help families secure affordable legal representation • Help individuals understand unemployment benefits, policies, and procedures • Encourage youth job development, skill building, and youth mentoring
Law Enforcement Disparities • Criminalization of domestic sex-trafficking victims • Mass incarceration • Racial profiling • Police brutality	• Preventing Sex Trafficking and Strengthening Families Act of 2014 • Trafficking Victims Protection Reauthorization Act of 2013 • Prosecutorial Remedies and Other Tools to End the Exploitation of Children Today Act of 2003	• Advocate for laws that treat survivors of sex trafficking as victims, not criminals, offenders, or delinquents • Campaign for Ban the Box • Lobby for stringent accountability of law enforcement • Lobby for gun control laws • Lobby to reform the Three Strikes Law and fair enforcement of drug laws • Collaborate with and support the Black Lives Matter campaign • Collaborate with the National Black Justice Coalition, the National Women's Justice Institute • Join the NACCP's campaign to end racial profiling	• Advocate for agencies to use protocols that accurately document and assess child victims of domestic child sex trafficking • Promote a collaborative and multidisciplinary approach across systems (law enforcement, child welfare, juvenile justice, healthcare providers, etc.) • Develop effective interagency policies to support sex-trafficking victims • Promote specialized training for professionals • Support community-led initiatives to empower and support positive youth development and leadership • Collaborate with Black fraternities and sororities doing outreach work to address community violence	• Help families recognize warning signs (behavior and language) used to indicate risk of commercial sexual exploitation • Help families living in poverty know their legal and Miranda rights • Help families access affordable, accessible legal services • Support kinship and intergenerational family norms that promote positive self-identity among Black children and youth • Facilitate family efforts to keep children safe from community violence • Promote the development of public safety protocols and plans within families and among individuals to ameliorate potentially fatal interactions with law enforcement and violence in communities and neighborhoods • Promote nonviolence in the home

(continued)

TABLE 9.2 (*Continued*)

Issue	Relevant Policies	Macro Level	Mezzo Level	Micro Level
Health Disparities • Mental health • Physical health • Substance misuse	• Mental Health Parity and Addiction Equity Act of 2008 • Health Revitalization Act of 1993 • Minority Health and Health Disparities Research and Education Act of 2000	• Support the efforts of the National Institute on Minority Health and Health Disparities (NIMHD); the National Association of Black Social Workers; the Association of Black Psychologists; and the National Alliance on Mental Illness • Collaborate with the Racial and Ethnic Mental Health Disparities Coalition to reduce mental health disparities through advocacy for racial and ethnic communities	• Work with the Chamber of Commerce to restrict the licensing of liquor stores in poor neighborhoods • Organize community stakeholders to hold public forums about mental health and substance abuse prevention • Work with community stakeholders to develop comprehensive, culturally appropriate strategies to improve access to healthcare and behavioral healthcare	• Normalize mental health and substance abuse treatment • Encourage the use of culturally sensitive treatment • Identify and promote proactive mental health and substance use allies within intergenerational family networks • Explore and promote non–substance use traditions within intergenerational family networks • Support the use of family group conferencing in addressing mental and behavioral health within intergenerational family networks • Prevent family/domestic violence

attempt to suppress, subjugate, and humiliate the lives and labor of economically trapped African Americans.

Social workers will also need to partner with community stakeholders interested in self-empowered, proactive engagement in traditional collective helping traditions to restore the health of the community. Drawing on the strengths and traditions of Black helping networks, including the local-level NAACP, the Urban League, and Black churches, fraternities, sororities, and civic organizations, can facilitate effective interventions at the community level. Public policies and zoning laws regarding the distribution of liquor stores in poor Black neighborhoods must also be challenged and scrutinized by social workers collaborating with community members.

Micro-Level Intervention Strategies

An Afrocentric analysis of familial and individual risk factors entails a critical look at the intergenerational kinship networks and extended family structures prevalent in African American family life. The Afrocentric core value of collective identity and survival is reflected in African American families' extended family and kinship networks and structures, which have endured the transatlantic slave trade and persisted through the atrocities of slavery, Jim Crow, and segregation (Sudarkasa, 2007; Waites, 2009). Kinship networks provide a lifeline of intergenerational care in addressing family and community social problems and structural oppression in contemporary society (Billingsley, 1992; Logan, 2000; McAdoo, 2007). Waites (2008, p. 5) asserts that "kin keeping is a tradition in the African-American community where families are often multigenerational networks, and blood relatives and fictive kin interact across the life span to provide assistance and care." This intergenerational system of family life and care, deemed as dysfunctional in Eurocentric narratives of African American family life, is considered an asset, strength, and protective factor within the Afrocentric intergenerational perspective (Logan, 2000; McAdoo, 2007; Waites, 2009).

The Afrocentric Intergenerational Assessment Tool

The basic principles of the Afrocentric intergenerational practice model acknowledge generational strengths, roles, conflicts, collaborations, and supports while nurturing intergenerational family connectedness, responsibility, and public policy that addresses generational family needs (Waites, 2009). A significant practice goal of the model is to help family networks develop or maintain intergenerational social cohesion or solidarity across six domains to support healthy family functioning. According to Waites (2009), the six domains of solidarity for assessment of Afrocentric values by social workers are the following:

1. Associational solidarity—traditional patterns of connection; frequency and type of contact; family gatherings, traditions, and customs across generations
2. Affectional solidarity—expressed sentiments and reciprocity of positive regard, emotional ties and conflicts toward the extended family and community
3. Consensual solidarity—shared Afrocentric values and beliefs; collective identity, spirituality, generational respect and value of elders and children, cooperation
4. Functional solidarity—help-seeking and -receiving patterns and expectations, including within and outside the extended family network, Black spiritual resources and helping traditions
5. Normative solidarity—intergenerational roles, responsibilities, and obligations within the family and community collectively
6. Structural solidarity—strengths and barriers related to migration patterns, transportation, travel, and intergenerational access to family and kin networks across geographical regions

The six domains of the assessment model are identified in the box below with questions in each domain that social workers can use in conducting an assessment. The assessment tool is expanded to include specific questions related to African American sex-trafficking victims.

The use of the Afrocentric intergenerational assessment tool with specific attention to the lives of victim/survivors of structural oppression and sex trafficking expands existing social work scholarship specifically in relation to street-level CSE/prostitution among African American males and females (Monroe, 2005; Valandra, 2007). Previous research has examined mothering among African American prostituted women using the Afrocentric intergenerational framework (Valandra, 2015). Protective and risk factors within intergenerational family networks are relevant for assessment and intervention by social workers using an Afrocentric intergenerational approach.

There is little discussion in the literature of the specific protective factors that reduce the risks associated with involvement in, exiting from, and recovery from CSE/prostitution for African Americans. Extended family has been identified as a protective factor that facilitates the exiting and recovery processes (Valandra, 2007) and that provides basic economic and housing support for the children of mothers in the CSE/prostitution industry (Valandra, 2015). Spirituality is also identified as a protective measure that promotes prevention and recovery for some African American victims/survivors of sex trafficking (Valandra, 2007). Intergenerational family networks are identified as a risk factor for CSE/prostitution when there is a history of or active intergenerational family sex trading, intrafamilial child sexual abuse, and/or physical abuse and drug use (Kennedy et al., 2012; Martin et al., 2010; Rosen & Venkatesh, 2008; Valandra, 2007).

Disproportionately high numbers of urban African American boys and girls living in poverty are sexually abused, sexually exploited, physically abused, and exposed to drugs and interpersonal violence *within* their extended family and kinship networks, all of which makes them more susceptible to CSE/prostitution (Clarke et al., 2012; Kennedy et al., 2012; Reid & Piquero, 2014). Given the stigmatizing, victim-blaming responses to child abuse, many children never disclose experiences of intrafamilial child sexual victimization voluntarily or may delay disclosure until well into adulthood (Alaggia, 2004). Some studies have also found that victim blaming and negative race and gender stereotyping are prevalent within African American communities (Neville, Heppner, Oh, Spanierman, & Clark, 2004; Robinson, 2002; West & Johnson, 2013). African American children and adults face additional barriers to disclosing experiences of sexual victimization and family violence (Jacques-Tiura, Tkatch, Abbey, & Wegner, 2010; Kennedy et al., 2012; Valandra, 2005). The history of slavery and stereotypes of African American males and females as hypersexual, promiscuous, and sexually aggressive act as barriers to disclosing experiences of child sexual abuse and sexual assault in adulthood, particularly to authorities (Donovan & Williams, 2002; McNair & Neville, 1996; West, 2006; West & Johnson, 2013; Wyatt, 1992).

Other cultural considerations that complicate disclosure for African Americans include the strong Black woman stereotype (Singleton, 2003; Wilson, 1994) and cultural mandates of racial loyalty in identifying African American men as sex offenders or drug addicts in a race- and class-biased legal and judicial system (Bryant-Davis & Ocampo, 2005; Roberson, 2003; Tillman, Bryant-Davis, Smith, & Marks, 2010). Historical and ongoing mistrust and fear of a criminal justice system characterized by police perpetration of deadly violence against unarmed Black men, women, and children, as well as disproportionate incarceration of Blacks, present additional barriers to formal reporting of abuse that occurs within the home (Jacques-Tiura et al., 2010; Tolliver, Hadden, Snowden, & Brown-Manning, 2016; Wolf, Ly, Hobart, & Kernic, 2003). Alienating and antagonistic relationships between African American communities and the child welfare system related to decades of systematic removal of African American children from their homes make it less likely that abused children will voluntarily disclose experiences of victimization to child welfare and other mandated authorities (Fontes & Plummer, 2010; Jacques-Tiura et al., 2010; Valandra, 2007; Washington, 2001).

Given these cultural barriers to disclosure, social workers using the Afrocentric intergenerational model of assessment can adapt the practice strategies outlined by Waites (2008, 2009) to specifically address the intergenerational family contexts that place African American children and adults at risk for exposure to and involvement in CSE/prostitution (see the box below). This can be achieved to some extent by using the Afrocentric intergenerational social cohesion and solidarity assessment tool to promote Afrocentric intergenerational strengths that can mitigate risk exposure. Social workers can ask questions about family traditions and how they promote culture and family cohesion, as well as how they minimize sexual and physical abuse of members of the family network (associational solidarity). Promoting associational cohesion and solidarity also entails helping families develop explicit plans for pooling resources and communicating to keep children safe from sexual and physical harm at family gatherings, regardless of the setting and purposes of such gatherings.

Culturally grounded dialogues with caregivers about healthy sexual development and intergenerational boundaries that support child and youth safety while maintaining respect for elders can be achieved through questions regarding connections, closeness, and conflicts within the family (affectional solidarity). Exploring how respect and honor are expressed among family members, and what topics are considered taboo within the culture of the family system, can open the door for further dialogue and understanding. Supporting families in discussing topics identified as taboo can be framed as culturally consistent with the oral traditions used to transmit important information across generations within African American culture. Additionally, assessing the families' shared history and important values, beliefs, and traditions (consensual solidarity) can help social workers structure discussions about child safety from sexual and physical victimization *within* the family network that are consistent with existing Afrocentric cultural values regarding the special care for children. Framing family efforts as historically rooted in surviving the traumas of slavery and the routinized sexual violation of African American children can also help family members embrace their collective responsibility to protect current and future generations of African American children and youth from sexual and physical exploitation, regardless of its source within or outside the family system. The practice strategies just identified are summarized in the following box, along with questions social workers can consider that are consistent with Afrocentric cultural values and dynamics and that can be used to assess children's risk of abuse and sex trafficking.

Understanding which family members are recognized as providing support (physical, emotional, financial) can help minimize or counter the behaviors of those family members who place children and youth at risk for sexual and physical abuse and exposure to CSE/exploitation (functional solidarity). As part of the exploration of family allies and protectors, social workers will want to affirm, support, and strengthen the family members' roles as actively engaged protectors of children and youth. Understanding the roles and responsibilities of extended family members (normative solidarity) can help facilitate this process. This requires the social worker to ask questions regarding the roles of parents, grandparents, children, adult siblings, uncles, and aunts and about the expectations, obligations, and responsibilities of each of these family members regarding the physical, sexual, and emotional safety of the children and youth within the family network. Social workers can also assist the family network in protecting children from sexual exploitation within the family system by identifying the proximity and accessibility of protectors to children (structural solidarity) and those family members that create risks for children. Helping families structure transportation and travel needs strategically to create barriers that support child and youth safety and promote accessibility when it facilitates protection is consistent with the Afrocentric intergenerational model of social work practice.

The spiritually conservative values and morality demonstrated in African American communities make it critically necessary that practitioners frame discussions about sexual behavior within the context of promoting child and youth safety and protection to avoid any misinterpretation of "sex talk" as promoting or encouraging sex among minors. Helping family members recognize warning signs of intrafamilial sexual abuse and using culturally sensitive ways of confronting and holding adults within the extended family network accountable (functional and normative solidarity) for abusive behaviors can facilitate the cultivation of healthy intergenerational family functioning and the Afrocentric cultural values of interdependence, cooperation, mutual responsibility, and reconciliation. Another critical component of an Afrocentric intergenerational assessment includes exploring the ways in which members of the family network may have internalized negative views, myths, and stereotypes about African Americans (consensual solidarity) as a coping strategy. The social worker will want to support the development of a positive racial identity and the cultivation of culturally affirming knowledge and prosocial cultural behaviors within the family network that draw on the Afrocentric core assumptions and values identified previously.

Afrocentric Intergenerational Solidarity Model—Questions and Practice

Strategies with African American Victims/Survivors of Sex Trafficking

Associational Solidarity Questions

- Tell me about your family's traditions (holiday celebrations, Sunday dinners, family reunions, etc.).
- How do you participate?
- How does your family keep in touch? How do you keep in touch?
- How does your family traditionally ensure the safety of children at family traditions?

Practice Strategies

- Encourage cross-generation communication, and contact.
- Help family consider methods to communicate and to support each other.
- Encourage family members to participate in family events.
- Encourage families to develop explicit plans for pooling resources and communicating to keep children safe from sexual, physical, and emotional harm.

Affectional Solidarity Questions

- Tell me about the family members you feel close to.
- What makes you feel particularly close to this person?

- Tell me about your extended family and others who are like family. Do you feel close to them?
- Are there certain relationships or duties that you must honor and respect?
- What are the specific ways in which your family demonstrates closeness, honor, and respect for each other? For children?
- What are forbidden or taboo ways of communicating or demonstrating closeness and conflict?

Practice Strategies

- Nurture relationships building, intergenerational kinship, and equable care.
- Encourage supportive family and extended family closeness.
- Encourage family communication regarding closeness and conflicts.
- Help family maintain or develop healthy, safe emotional, physical, and sexual boundaries for all members.
- Encourage discussion and development of strategies for addressing and resolving conflicts and minimizing harm to family members.

Consensual Solidarity Questions

- Tell me about your family's history—grandparents, great grandparents, etc.
- What were/are important values, beliefs, and traditions in your family?
- Do you and your family members share similar beliefs regarding _____ (sex, sex trading/prostitution, drugs, religion, education, violence, sexual or physical abuse of children)?
- Do you feel a connection and pride with the African American community?
- What types of cultural activities do you and your family participate in?
- How does your family demonstrate cultural pride in your children?
- How do your family members deal with conflicting values and beliefs in general? Regarding child safety from abuse in the home?

Practice Strategies

- Engage family in history, reminding them to facilitate an understanding of cultural and family strengths.
- Facilitate healing by engaging family in activities that will enhance cultural pride and self-esteem.
- Encourage intergenerational respect and help family members acknowledge their shared and conflicting visions.

- Help family recognize intergenerational resources and strengths.
- Encourage explicit dialogue regarding child safety in the home.

Functional Solidarity Questions

- How does your family respond when one of its members needs assistance?
- Who are the family members with resources (good, steady job, a home, savings, etc.) in your family? Are they obligated to help in the family?
- Is there an exchange of resources?
- Is sex exchanged for resources?
- Do older family members feel obligated to help younger family members, and is this help reciprocal?
- Are family members expected to support the family through sex trading?

Practice Strategies

- Support flexible family roles and intergenerational kinship.
- Encourage reciprocal intergenerational support and care.
- Assist family in using informal (extended family, church, or faith-based) and formal support systems and legal resources.

Normative Solidarity Questions

- What roles do parents, grandparents, children, adult daughters and sons, aunts, uncles, and others play in your family?
- In your family, what happens when someone is not able to function in his or her role as parent, son, daughter, caregiver, or other?
- What responsibilities, obligations, and expectations do each of your adult family members have regarding the emotional, physical, and sexual safety of the children in your family?

Practice Strategies

- Encourage and support caregiving and other family commitments.
- Develop multigenerational family support programs for grandparents and other kin in raising children and for children caring for dependent elders.
- Encourage the development of an extended family support system.
- Encourage explicit support for the safety of children within the extended family system.

Structural Solidarity Questions

- Where do your family members live?
- What led them to move to_____? Do you visit?
- How do family members travel when they visit one another?
- Are there any barriers to visiting?
- Does your family have a "home place," a residence where family members gather for special occasions?
- How is the emotional, physical, and sexual safety of your children supported during family trips and visits?
- Who helps keep the children in your family safe from sexual exploitation when they are visiting relatives?

Practice Strategies

- Help family overcome travel—and visiting-related barriers.
- Help family members identify a plan for staying connected.
- Develop community intergenerational programs.
- Help family members keep children safe during family trips and visits.
- Help family members explicitly identify allies within the family system who are expected to actively support the safety of children from sexual exploitation within the intergenerational network.

Source: Adapted from Waites, 2009.
Note: Italicized questions are specific to assessing intrafamilial victimization and sex trafficking.

Conclusion

Social workers are in a unique profession that promotes social justice and social change as an integral part of its overall mission, as well as culturally responsive practice that respects the dignity and worth of all human beings and relationships (NASW, 2008). The Afrocentric intergenerational practice approach gives social workers an opportunity to practice what the mission professes. Social work practice regarding sex trafficking must address structural oppression as well as the contextual variables that place African Americans at risk for sex trading. A multisystem approach is necessary to address multiple facets of the problem. To be effective within the family network, social workers are encouraged to explore each intergenerational domain of solidarity and social cohesion with family members and to use the Afrocentric intergenerational assessment tool in conjunction with other empowerment-based, strengths-based strategies and models. For example, Manning and his colleagues (2004) propose an integrated social work practice approach that includes an Afrocentric perspective, ego psychology, spirituality, and empowerment based on African American history and cultural values. Schiele (1996) recognized the goodness-of-fit between the Afrocentric paradigm and the person-in-environment perspective, noting that both help social workers examine human behavior and societal issues across multiple systems, from macro to micro, and their interactions. Most scholarship promotes the use of an integrated collaborative approach to prevention and intervention with victims/survivors of CSE/prostitution (Baker, Dalla, & Williamson, 2010; Martin et al., 2010; Raphael & Shapiro, 2002).

Note

1. *Satisficing*, a combination of *satisfy* and *suffice*, is a concept developed by Herbert Simon (1976).

References

Alaggia, R. (2004). Many ways of telling: Expanding conceptualizations of child sexual abuse disclosure. *Child Abuse & Neglect, 28*, 1213–1227.

Andersen, T. (2015). Race, ethnicity, and structural variations in youth risk of arrest: Evidence from a national longitudinal sample. *Criminal Justice and Behavior, 42*(9), 900–916.

Asante, M. K. (1988). *Afrocentricity*. Trenton, NJ: African World Press.

Baker, L. M., Dalla, R., & Williamson, C. (2010). Exiting prostitution: An integrated model. *Violence Against Women, 16*(5), 579–600.

Baldwin, J. A., & Hopkins, R. (1990). African-American and European-American cultural differences as assessed by the worldview paradigm: An empirical analysis. *Western Journal of Black Studies, 14*, 38–52.

Banks, D., & Kyckelhahn, T. (2011). *Characteristics of suspected human trafficking incidents, 2008–2010: Special report*. Washington, DC: Bureau of Justice Statistics, Office of Justice Programs, U.S. Department of Justice.

Bell, Y. R., Bouie, C., & Baldwin, J. (1990). Afrocentric cultural consciousness and African-American male-female relationships. *Journal of Black Studies, 21*(2), 162–189.

Benson, C., & Matthews, R. (1995). Street prostitution: Ten facts in search of a policy. *International Journal of the Sociology of Law, 23*, 395–415.

Billingsley, A. (1992). *Climbing Jacob's ladder: The enduring legacy of African-American families*. New York, NY: Simon & Schuster.

Boxill, N. A., & Richardson, D. (2007). Ending sex trafficking of children in Atlanta. *Affilia: Journal of Women and Social Work, 22*(2), 138–149.

Bryant-Davis, T., & Ocampo, C. (2005). Racist incident-based trauma. *Counseling Psychologist, 33*(4), 479–500.

Campaign to halt sex trafficking launched in L.A. County. (2012, May 13). *Los Angeles Times*. Retrieved from http://latimesblogs.latimes.com/lanow/2012/sex-trafficking.html.

Clarke, R. J., Clarke, E., Roe-Sepowitz, D., & Fey, R. (2012). Age at entry into prostitution: Relationship to drug use, race, suicide, education level, childhood abuse, and family experiences. *Journal of Human Behavior in the Social Environment, 22,* 270–289.

Cobbina, J., & Oselin, S. (2011). It's not only for the money: An analysis of adolescent versus adult entry into street prostitution. *Sociological Inquiry, 81*(3), 310–332.

Collins, P. H. (2005). *Black sexual politics: African Americans, gender, and the new racism.* New York, NY: Routledge.

Council on Social Work Education. (2015). *Educational policy and accreditation standards.* Retrieved from https://www.cswe.org/getattachment/Accreditation/Accreditation-Process /2015-EPAS/2015EPAS_Web_FINAL.pdf.aspx Dalla, R. L. (2006). "You can't hustle all your life": An exploratory investigation of the exit process among street-level prostituted women. *Psychology of Women Quarterly, 30,* 276–290.

Dank, M., Bilal Khan, P., Downey, M., Kotonias, C., Mayer, D., Owens, . . . Yu, L. (2015). *Estimating the size and structure of the underground commercial sex economy in eight major US cities.* The Urban Institute. Retrieved from http://www.urban.org/sites /default/files/alfresco/publication-pdfs/413047-Estimating-the-Size-and-Structure-of-the -Underground-Commercial-Sex-Economy-in-Eight-Major-US-Cities.PDF

DeGruy, J. (2005). *Post traumatic slave syndrome: America's legacy of enduring injury and healing.* Milwaukie, OR: Upton Press.

Donovan, R., & Williams, M. (2002). Living at the intersection: The effects of racism and sexism on Black rape survivors. *Women & Therapy, 25,* 95–105.

Edlund, L., & Korn, E. (2002). A theory of prostitution. *Journal of Political Economy, 110*(1), 181–206.

Farley, M. (2004). *Prostitution, trafficking, and traumatic stress.* Binghamton, NY: Haworth Press.

Fauri, D. P., Netting, F. E., & O'Connor, M. K. (2005). *Social work macro practice workbook: Exercises and activities for policy, community, and organization interventions.* Belmont, CA: Thomson Brooks/Cole.

Federal Bureau of Investigation. (2014). *Crime in the United States 2014, Uniform Crime Reporting,* Table 43B. Retrieved from http://www.fbi.gov/about-us/cjis/ucr/crime-in-the -u.s/2014/crime-in-the-u.s.-2014/tables/table-43

Fontes, L., & Plummer, C. (2010). Cultural issues in disclosures of child sexual abuse. *Journal of Child Sexual Abuse, 19,* 491–518.

Freeman, E. & Logan, S. (2004). *Reconceptualizing the strengths and common heritage of Black families.* Springfield, Il: Charles C Thomas.

Gilbert, D., Harvey, A., & Belgrave, F. (2009). Advancing the Africentric paradigm shift discourse: Building toward evidence-based Africentric interventions in social work practice with African Americans. *Social Work, 54*(3), 23–252.

Hardy, K. V., & Laszloffy, T. (1995). The cultural genogram: Key to training culturally competent family therapists. *Journal of Marital and Family Therapy, 21*(3), 227–237.

Hardy, K.C., & Laszloffy, T. (2008). Teens who hurt: Clinical interventions to break the cycle of adolescent violence. *Child and Adolescent Social Work Journal, 25*(5), 447–450.

Harnois, C. (2010). Race, gender, and the Black women's standpoint. *Sociological Forum, 25*(1), 68–85.

Holmstrom, N. (2003). The Socialist Feminist Project: An independent socialist magazine. *Monthly Review, 54*(10), 38–48.

Hood-Brown, M. (1998). Trading for a place: Poor women and prostitution. *Journal of Poverty, 2,* 13–33.

Jacques-Tiura, A. J., Tkatch, R., Abbey, A., & Wegner, R. (2010). Disclosure of sexual assault: Characteristics and implications for posttraumatic stress symptoms among African American and Caucasian survivors. *Journal of Trauma & Dissociation, 11*(2), 174–192.

Kennedy, A. C., Bybee, D., Kulkarni, S., & Archer, G. (2012). Sexual victimization and family violence among urban African American adolescent women: Do violence cluster profiles predict partner violence victimization and sex trade exposure? *Violence Against Women, 18*(11), 1319–1338.

Kramer, L., & Berg, E. (2003). A survival analysis of timing of entry into prostitution: The differential impact of race, educational level, and childhood/adolescent risk factors. *Sociological Inquiry, 73*(4), 511–528.

Logan, S. M. (2000). *The Black family: Strengths, self-help, and positive change.* Boulder, CO: Westview Press.

Logan, S. M., Denby, R., & Gibson, P. (2007). *Mental health in the African-American community.* New York, NY: Haworth Press.

Logan, S. M., Freeman, E., & McRoy, E. (1990). *Social work practice with Black families: A culturally specific perspective.* New York, NY: Longman.

Manning, M. C., Cornelius, L., & Okundaye, J. (2004). Empowering African Americans through social work practice: Integrating an Afrocentric perspective, ego psychology, and spirituality. *Families in Society: The Journal of Contemporary Social Services, 85*(2), 229–235.

Martin, E. P., & Martin, J. (2002). *Spirituality and the Black helping tradition in social work.* Washington, DC: NASW Press.

Martin, L., Hearst, M., & Widome, R. (2010). Meaningful differences: Comparison of adult women who first traded sex as a juvenile versus as an adult. *Violence Against Women, 16*(11), 1252–1269.

Martin, L., Pierce, A., Peyton, S., Gabilondo, A., & Tulpule, G. (2014). *Mapping the market for sex with trafficked minor girls in Minneapolis: Structures, functions, and patterns.* Retrieved from http://uroc.umn.edu/sites/default/files/MTM_SexTraf_Summ.pdf

McAdoo, H. P. (2007). *Black families* (4th ed.). Thousand Oaks, CA: Sage.

McNair, L. D., & Neville, H. (1996). African American women survivors of sexual assault: The intersection of race and class. *Women & Therapy, 18*(3), 107–113.

Mears, D. P., Cochran, J., &. Lindsey, A. (2016). Offending and racial and ethnic disparities in criminal justice: A conceptual framework for guiding theory and research and informing policy. *Journal of Contemporary Criminal Justice, 32*(1), 1–26.

Miller, J. (1993). "Your life is on the line every night you're on the streets": Victimization and resistance among street prostitutes. *Humanity & Society, 17*(4), 422–446.

Monroe, J. (2005). Women in street prostitution: The result of poverty and the brunt of inequity. *Journal of Poverty, 9*(3), 69–88.

Morgen, S., & Maskovsky, J. (2003). The anthropology of welfare "reform": New perspectives on U.S. urban poverty in the post-welfare era. *Annual Review of Anthropology, 32*(1): 315–338.

National Association of Social Workers [NASW]. (2008). *Code of Ethics of the National Association of Social Workers.* Washington, DC: Author.

Neville, H. A., Heppner, M., Oh, E., Spanierman, L., & Clark, M. (2004). General and culturally specific factors influencing Black and White rape survivors' self-esteem. *Psychology of Women Quarterly, 28*, 83–94.

Nichols, A. J. (2016). *Sex trafficking in the United States: Theory, research, policy, and practice.* New York, NY: Columbia University Press.

Ntiri, D. W. (2001). Reassessing Africana womanism: Continuity and change. *The Western Journal of Black Studies, 25*(3), 163–167.

O'Leary, C., & Howard, O. (2001). *The prostitution of women and girls in Metropolitan Chicago: A preliminary prevalence report*. Chicago: Center for Impact Research.

Raphael, J., & Shapiro, D. (2002). *Sisters speak out: The lives and needs of prostituted women in Chicago: A research study*. Chicago, IL: Center for Impact Research.

Rastogi, S., Johnson, T., Johnson, D., Hoeffel, E., & Drewery, M. (2011). The Black population: 2010. *2010 Census Briefs*. Washington, DC: U.S. Census Bureau, Department of Commerce Economics and Statistics Administration.

Reid, J. A. (2011). An exploratory model of girl's vulnerability to commercial sexual exploitation in prostitution. *Child Maltreatment, 16*(2), 146–157.

Reid, J. A., & Piquero, A. (2014). Age-graded risks for commercial sexual exploitation of male and female youth. *Journal of Interpersonal Violence, 29*(9), 1747–1777.

Roberson, A. N. (2003). NOW conference workshop: The silence around Black women and rape. *Off Our Backs: a Woman's Newsjournal, 33*(9/10), 45–46.

Robinson, L. S. (2002). *I will survive: The African-American guide to healing from sexual assault and abuse*. New York, NY: Seal Press.

Rosen, E., & Venkatesh, S. (2008). A "perversion" of choice: Sex work offers just enough in Chicago's urban ghetto. *Journal of Contemporary Ethnography, 37*(4), 417–441.

Rothenberg, P. S. (2013). *Race, class, and gender in the United States: An integrated study*. New York, NY: Worth Publishers.

Saulnier, C. F. (1996). *Feminist theories and social work: Approaches and applications*. Binghamton, NY: The Haworth Press.

Schiele, J. H. (1994a). Afrocentricity as an alternative worldview for equality. *Journal of Progressive Human Services, 5*(1), 5–25.

——. (1994b). Afrocentricity: Implications for higher education. *Journal of Black Studies, 25*(2), 150–159.

——. (1996). Afrocentricity: An emerging paradigm in social work practice. *Social Work, 41*(3), 284–294.

Silbert, M. H., & Pines, A. (1982). Entrance into prostitution. *Youth & Society, 13*(4), 471–500.

Simon, H. (1976). *Administrative behavior* (3rd ed.). New York, NY: The Free Press.

Singleton, D. K. (2003). *Broken silence: Opening your heart and mind to therapy—A Black woman's recovery guide*. New York, NY: The Random House Ballantine.

Stewart, P. E. (2004). Afrocentric approaches to working with African American families. *Families in Society: The Journal of Contemporary Social Services, 85*(2), 221–228.

Sudarkasa, N. (2007). Interpreting the African heritage in African American family organization. In H. P. McAdoo (Ed.), *Black families* (4th ed., pp. 29–47). Thousand Oaks, CA: Sage.

Synder, H., & Mulako-Wangota, J. (2015). *Arrest data analysis tool*. Washington, DC: Bureau of Justice Statistics.

Tillman, S., Bryant-Davis, T., Smith, K., & Marks, A. (2010). Shattering silence: Exploring barriers to disclosure for African American sexual assault survivors. *Trauma, Violence, & Abuse, 11*(2), 59–70.

Tolliver, W. F., Hadden, B., Snowden, F., & Brown-Manning, R. (2016). Police killings of unarmed Black people: Centering race and racism in human behavior and the social environment content. *Journal of Human Behavior in the Social Environment, 26*, 279–286.

Trafficking in persons report. (2015). Washington, DC: Office of the Under Secretary for Civilian Security, Democracy, and Human Rights, U.S. Department of State.

Tummala-Narra, P. (2007). Conceptualizing trauma and resilience across diverse contexts: A multicultural perspective. *Journal of Aggression, Maltreatment & Trauma, 14*(12), 33–53.

Valandra. (2005). Hearing the voices of African American children healing from child sexual abuse. *NASW—Specialty Practice Sections—Child Welfare Section Connection*. Washington, DC: National Association of Social Workers.

——. (2007). Reclaiming their lives and breaking free: An Afrocentric approach to recovery from prostitution. *Afflia: Journal of Women and Social Work, 22*(2), 195–2008.

——. (2012). Reflexivity and professional use of self in research: A doctoral student's journey. *Journal of Ethnographic & Qualitative Research, 6*, 204–220.

——. (2015). Protective and proactive mothering: Prostituted African American mothers' use of intergenerational family networks. In R. J. Bromwich & M. M. DeJong (Eds.), *Mothering, mothers, and sex work* (pp. 213–233). Ontario: Demeter Press.

Venkatesh, S. A. (2006). *Off the books: The underground economy of the urban poor*. Cambridge, MA: Harvard University Press.

Waites, C. (2009). *Social work practice with African-American families: An intergenerational perspective*. New York, NY: Routledge.

Walker, K. (2013). *Ending the commercial sexual exploitation of children: A call for multi-system collaboration in California*. California Child Welfare Council. Retrieved from http://www .chhs.ca.gov/Child%20Welfare/Ending%20CSEC%20-%20A%20Call%20for%20Multi -System%20Collaboration%20in%20CA%20-%20February%202013.pdf

Washington, P. A. (2001). Disclosure patterns of Black female sexual assault survivors. *Violence Against Women, 7*(11), 1254–1283.

West, C. (2006). *Sexual violence in the lives of African American women: Risk, response, and resilience*. VAWnet. Retrieved from http://www.vawnet.org

West, C., & Johnson, K. (2013). *Sexual violence in the lives of African American women*. VAWnet. Retrieved from http://www.vawnet.org

Wilson, M. (1994). *Crossing the boundary: Black women survive incest*. Seattle, WA: Seal Press.

Wolf, M. E., Ly, U., Hobart, M., & Kernic, M. (2003). Barriers to seeking police help in intimate partner violence. *Journal of Family Violence, 18*(2), 121–129.

Wyatt, G. E. (1992). The sociocultural context of African American and white American women's rape. *Journal of Social Issues, 48*, 77–91.

CHAPTER 10

SEX TRAFFICKING AND EXPLOITATION OF LGBTQ+ PEOPLE

Implications for Practice

ANDREA J. NICHOLS, PhD, WASHINGTON UNIVERSITY
IN ST. LOUIS

S ocial workers working in youth-serving agencies or homeless shelters, conducting street outreach, or otherwise working with at-risk youth are likely to come into contact with sexually trafficked or exploited LGBTQ+ (lesbian, gay, bisexual, transgender, queer)[1] people. This group is at increased risk of sex trafficking (ST) and commercial sexual exploitation (CSE) because of heightened runaway risk, family conflict, school bullying, and various forms of structural discrimination. Despite the increased risk associated with identity-based oppression on a structural and interpersonal level, LGBTQ+ individuals are strangely absent from a majority of anti-trafficking awareness campaigns and trainings, as well as the bulk of the research examining sex trafficking. In fact, only a handful of sex trafficking–related research studies discuss LGBTQ+ victims. This omission is problematic for a number of reasons, not only because the limited research that does examine this population finds heightened risk, but also because such work documents pathways into sex trafficking/ exploitation, as well as barriers to accessing legal and social services, that hold important implications for prevention and outreach that are not adequately disseminated and used by the anti-trafficking community. Such research implies that social workers should address barriers to legal and social services and engage in prevention that targets risk factors and their resulting pathways.

LGBTQ+-Specific Risk Factors

The extant research suggests that survival sex is the most common form of sex trafficking/ commercial sexual exploitation experienced by LGBTQ+ people, although other forms are not unknown (such as boyfriend pimp-related trafficking and familial trafficking).[2] Survival sex is a term used to describe trading sex for basic needs such as food, shelter, and clothing. Survival sex can be facilitated by peers who are also engaged in survival sex, by buyers who approach youth for sex, or by pimps/traffickers/exploiters, or youth may become involved on their own (Curtis et al., 2008; Dank, Yahner, et al., 2015; Heil & Nichols, 2015; Lutnick, 2016). In a study of LGBTQ+ youth in New York, one respondent (twenty-one years old, black, gay, male) described his entry into commercial sex markets: "I don't remember it that vividly, all I know is just that I was starving. . . . My friend was like, 'Come to the stroll trust me, you'll get somebody.' I was hungry, I was cold, so I did it" (quoted in Dank, Yahner, et al., 2015, p. 19).

When minors engage in survival sex, this legally equates with sex trafficking under federal and many state laws. Some researchers describe adult survival sex as a constrained choice and consequently use the label of *commercial sexual exploitation (CSE)* (e.g., the exploitation of one's economic disenfranchisement), while simultaneously acknowledging the agency and resiliency of people who make this socially conditioned choice (Curtis et al., 2008; Heil & Nichols, 2015; Nichols, 2016). Because commercial sex involvement in the form of survival sex can be viewed as a socially conditioned choice, examining such social conditions is important in prevention and practice. For example, among LGBTQ+ youth involved in ST/CSE, family conflict and parental rejection, as well as school bullying or discrimination, result in runaway/throwaway status, and homelessness, all of which provide pathways into commercial sex involvement primarily in the form of survival sex. For LGBTQ+ adults, discrimination in healthcare, employment, and housing impacts commercial sex involvement. Such factors are described in depth in the following subsections.

Runaway and Homeless Youth

Runaway status and homelessness are correlated with LGBTQ+ youths' commercial sex involvement. Research indicates that among runaway and homeless youth, between 10 and 50 percent become involved in survival sex (Nichols, 2016; Ray, 2006). Research makes it clear that LGBTQ+ youth are overrepresented in the homeless youth population. The True Colors Fund reported (n.d.) that while LGBTQ+ youth make up 7 percent of the general youth population, they constitute 40 percent of the homeless youth population. Similarly, the National Network for Youth indicated that while constituting roughly 10 percent of the youth population, LGBTQ+ youth constitute 20 to 40 percent of homeless youth (Ferguson-Colvin & Maccio, 2012).

Because LGBTQ+ people constitute a much larger percentage of the homeless youth population, there is heighted risk of becoming involved in

ST/CSE in the form of survival sex. Freeman and Hamilton (2008) found in New York that homeless youth often traded sex for a place to stay because shelter space was limited. The same study indicated that of trafficked youth, a considerable proportion (27 percent) identified as lesbian, gay, bisexual, or transgender (LGBT). Freeman and Hamilton also found that LGB youth were seven times more likely than heterosexual youth to engage in survival sex, typically in exchange for shelter, and transgender youth were eight times more likely than cisgender youth. Curtis and colleagues (2008) found a higher proportion of transgender youth in their study of largely homeless or transient youth involved in commercial sex in New York, constituting 4 percent of their sample. Yet the proportion of the population in the United States identifying as transgender is 0.3 percent, indicating that transgender youth are overrepresented in commercial sex (Gates, 2011). Of the research examining LGBTQ+ people involved in the commercial sex trade, lesbians, bisexual women, and transgender men are virtually ignored, under the assumption that these groups do not experience trafficking and exploitation (Dank, Yahner, et al., 2015). However, Dank, Yahner, and colleagues (2015) found that one in six LGBTQ+ youth experiencing ST/CSE in New York was lesbian.

Although New York is pioneering this important research, work in other regions shows strikingly similar dynamics. The Covenant House (2017) found in a study of three cities with a sample of nearly 300 homeless youth— in Philadelphia, Phoenix, and Washington, D.C.—that 39 percent of those who experienced trafficking were LGBTQ+, and 60 percent of transgender youth in their sample experienced trafficking. In a sample of 641 youth in ten cities, one study found that 24 percent of LGBTQ+ youth were trafficked for sex, compared to 20 percent of non- LGBTQ+ females and 12 percent of non- LGBTQ+ male youth (Covenant House, 2017). A study examining five cities in a midwestern state found that of 283 youth involved in commercial sex, 27 percent were LGBT (Fedina et al., 2015). The authors of this study concluded (p. 15) that "targeted prevention and intervention approaches are necessary to reduce runaway episodes and also to prevent runaway behaviors among particularly at-risk youth (e.g., sexual and emotional abuse victims, LGBT youth)."

In sum, there is overrepresentation of LGBTQ+ people in the runaway youth population, increasing the risk of sex trafficking/CSE. So what accounts for this heightened runaway status and homelessness among LGBTQ+ youth? The following subsections examine family and school- based risks that provide pathways to runaway status, resulting homelessness or transient living, and commercial sex involvement. The subsections also examine structural discrimination impacting the workplace, housing, and healthcare, all of which facilitate LGBTQ+ adult involvement in CSE.

Family Risk Factors

The increased risk of trafficking and exploitation experienced by LGBTQ+ youth in part stems from a problematic home life. While this is characteristic of non- LGBTQ+ youth as well, the context is different. Research indicates that problematic home lives largely revolve around parents' nonacceptance of their children's sexual orientation or gender identity (Dank, Yu, et al., 2015; Heil & Nichols, 2015; Koyama, 2011; Nichols, 2016; Schwarz & Britton, 2015).

At times, parents abandon their children by asking them or forcing them to leave the family home. In other instances, the constant conflict resulting from parents' reactions to their children's LGBTQ+ identities makes their home life so unbearable that children run away from home. Regardless of whether children are runaways or throwaways, such dynamics are largely responsible for the disproportionate representation of LGBTQ+ youth in the homeless youth population.

Dank, Yahner, and colleagues (2015, p. 16) found in their qualitative work in New York City that children were forced by parents to leave their homes because of their parents' reactions to their gender identity or sexual orientation, which were based on lack of acceptance, rejection, and homophobic/transphobic fear of influencing siblings:

> My father didn't respect me for who I am because he don't like bisexual people or gay people so from there I came out to him and I told him and then he just kicked me out, because he couldn't take it. (Nineteen years old, Latino, bisexual, male; quoted in Dank, Yahner, et al., 2015, p. 16)
>
> My mom kicked me out . . . she didn't want me being gay, she wanted grandchildren, she didn't like my lifestyle, she didn't pretty much accept it. She still loved me but she just didn't want me being there. And plus I have a little brother so she didn't want me pretty much influencing him in any form or fashion. (Nineteen years old, black, gay, male; quoted in Dank, Yahner, et al., 2015, p. 16)

Similarly, in Heil and Nichols's (2015) case study of the St. Louis bistate area, gay male youth and transgender girls were rejected by their families, and the consequent homelessness made them vulnerable to exploitation:

> So, I was like, pretty much kicked out of my house at like, fourteen. I mean, technically, I left, but, like, they wanted to send me back to Gay camp, where they try to "get the gay out of you." Like, I knew that wasn't possible, and I was like, I just don't belong here. I tried to go to Chicago, hitched [hitchhiking], and ended up in a homeless shelter, and the situation up there just wasn't good, so I came back to Missouri, this time to St. Louis. And there are men, I can tell

you, much older men who are looking for kids just like [I was], who don't know what to do or where to go, living in doorways, abandoned houses, homeless shelters, hotel lobbies, even people's cars if the doors are unlocked, and they offer you things. Like a meal, or "hey come back to my place for awhile, you can stay with me" but it's not for nothing. They want sex for it. And I did that, because I had nothing else. I had nothing. I got picked up outside a homeless shelter, and in a doorway, just sitting outside. That was it, like, was my intro-duction to like sex and also sex work. And I thought he loved me, because he protected me, gave me things, was nice to me, but then, looking back, he was out looking for me, I could have been anyone.

(Gay, male survivor; quoted in Heil & Nichols, 2015, p. 51)

In particular, problematic home lives led to runaway status and home-lessness, which made LGBTQ+ youth susceptible to peer-facilitated and buyer-facilitated entry into survival sex. Furthermore, youth may sell sex on their own, without a peer, buyer, or trafficker/pimp facilitating commer-cial sex involvement (Lutnick, 2016). Youth who are too young to be legally employed, or youth who are minors who do not want to be found, have reduced options for employment (Nichols, 2016). When youth have nothing else, they have their bodies, and survival sex may seem like the only option, or at least the best available option.

To address problematic home lives, social workers can work to provide community education to parents to reduce their rejection of LGBTQ+ youth. Green Chimneys is engaged in a pilot project offering therapy to parents, and shows promise in changing the mindsets of parents, and fostering love and acceptance of their LGBTQ+ children (Gares, n.d.). Social workers in children's services working with trafficked runaway LGBTQ+ children can attempt to reunify them with parents, but depending on the situation, placing children in a foster home may be better than exposing them to continued rejection and conflict in the home. However, "LGBTQ youth in out-of-home care are particularly vulnerable to failed placements, resulting in multiple rejections and frequent changes" (Dank, Yu, et al., 2015). Research finds that children are at times rejected from foster homes as well because of their foster parents' reactions to their LGBTQ+ identity. Because exploitation and marginalization of LGBTQ+ youth occur in foster homes as well as in the homes of biologi-cal family members, it is also important that foster care training be LGBTQ+ inclusive, and any foster homes considered for LGBTQ+ children should be screened as Safe Zone homes. The Safe Zone designation indicates that mem-bers of the household have undergone Safe Zone training, which provides edu-cation in cultural competency/humility.[3] A free two-hour curriculum can be accessed at http://thesafezoneproject.com/. Dank, Yu, and colleagues (2015) further recommend that child welfare systems recruit LGBTQ+ families and ask LGBTQ+ community organizations and groups to consider foster care for LGBTQ+ youth experiencing abuse, neglect, or rejection in their homes.

School Bullying

Another factor that may contribute to the heightened runaway risk of LGBTQ+ children is school bullying. The Gay, Lesbian & Straight Education Network (GLSEN) reported, in the 2014 release of their National School Climate Survey, that LGBT[4] students experienced verbal harassment due to other students' reactions to their sexual orientation (74 percent) and to their gender expression (55 percent). One-third reported experiencing physical harassment from peers at school, such as pushing and shoving, that was directed toward their sexual orientation, and 23 percent was directed toward their gender expression. Moreover, students reported physical assault, such as kicking, punching, and injury with a weapon, directed toward their sexual orientation (17 percent) and toward their gender expression (11 percent). Furthermore, 55 percent reported frequently or often hearing homophobic language, 33 percent reported transphobic language, and 56 percent reported school policies or practices that were discriminatory.

While GLSEN reports that such incidents and experiences are declining, they still affect large numbers of LGBTQ+ children. Importantly, 30 percent reported missing at least one day of school because they felt uncomfortable or unsafe in school, ostensibly as a result of negative school experiences. In addition to negative behaviors from other students, lack of cultural humility may also come from policies and practices exhibited by school administrators and staff, creating a problematic school climate for LGBTQ+ youth (Lutnick, 2016). Qualitative research finds that truancy is a significant risk factor for sex trafficking among LGBTQ+ youth (Heil & Nichols, 2015). When children are not in school, they increase their likelihood of exposure to a pimp or buyer. Negative school experiences may lead to both truancy and runaway behaviors, thereby increasing risk.

Social workers can use the strategies provided by GLSEN and the Williams Institute to decrease negative experiences in schools and thus prevent truancy and runaway risk. GLSEN reported that LGBT students attending schools with an LGBT-inclusive curriculum were 25 percent more likely to feel safe (GLSEN, 2014). An increased sense of safety may improve school experiences, potentially reducing truancy and runaway behaviors. The Williams Institute (Biegel & Kuehl, 2010) provided a list of action steps that educators can use to address concerns in schools related to oppression of LGBTQ+ children and to create an affirming, inclusive environment. This resource includes guidelines for addressing multiple forms of bullying and harassment in school, creating inclusive nondiscriminatory policies, and providing support for and acceptance of gender-affirming behaviors, such as wearing clothes a student feels comfortable in, taking a date of any gender to the prom, developing clubs like Gay Straight Alliances, and providing access to gender-inclusive restrooms. Similarly, GLSEN offers campaigns to improve school climates, including the ThinkB4YouSpeak campaign, Ally Week, Day of Silence, and No Name Calling Week. In addition GLSEN developed a Safe Space Kit, which provides educational tools to address anti- LGBTQ+ bias in schools. GLSEN reports that it sent 60,000 of these kits to middle and high schools across the nation.

School social workers can be leaders in implementing these action steps, campaigns, and strategies recommended by the Williams Institute and GLSEN. Moreover, social workers working in organizations outside of schools who offer Safe Zone trainings in schools, or who do other community work related to nondiscrimination, can partner with schools to facilitate LGBTQ-friendly climates in schools using these resources. Such action is a form of prevention, to prevent initial runaway or truancy behaviors caused by school bullying or discrimination, thereby cutting off a pathway into sex trafficking.

Structural Factors

Thus far, this chapter has largely focused on family- and school-based risk factors for LGBTQ+ youth. However, structural issues also impact LGBTQ+ adults, such as inaccessibility of healthcare as well as workplace and housing discrimination. The Center for Transgender Equality (NCTE) and the National Gay and Lesbian Task Force conducted a national survey of 6,500 transgender people in 2011 and found reports of rampant workplace discrimination and resulting unemployment (Grant et al., 2011). For example, transgender people reported unemployment at twice the rate of the general population, 97 percent reported harassment or mistreatment at work, and 47 percent reported discrimination in hiring, firing, and promotions. The same national survey found that 61 percent of transgender people who were involved in the commercial sex industry reported experiences with employment discrimination (Grant et al., 2011). Given these workplace-based forms of oppression, perhaps it is not surprising that the same study found that transgender people reported higher rates of poverty and lower socioeconomic status (SES) than the general population.

In twenty-nine states, various forms of workplace discrimination directed toward people based on sexual orientation or gender identity are legal (Hunt, 2012), including discrimination in hiring and firing practices, promotion, and wages. Rees (2010) found that among transgender youth, few were able to get an interview for a job, and those who did reported discrimination directed toward their gender identity and expression. Wilson and colleagues (2009) found that commercial sex involvement of transgender youth in Chicago and Los Angeles was directly related to their inability to gain employment because of gender-based discrimination. Such discrimination limits economic opportunities, limits access to healthcare, and contributes to heightened risk of commercial sex involvement to pay for basic needs.

Discrimination in healthcare, such as lack of coverage for hormone therapy or transition-related surgery, also leaves individuals with few options to obtain such gender-affirming healthcare (Hunt, 2012). This dynamic is characteristic of Medicare, many state Medicaid programs, and also Federal Employees Health Benefits Programs. Rees (2010) found that transgender people engaged in the sex trade to access transition-related healthcare. Similarly, Dank, Yahner, and colleagues (2015) found in their New York study that some transgender youth became involved in the sex trade to pay for transitioning-related healthcare. One respondent in their study (twenty-six years old, white and Latina, heterosexual, transfemale) stated, "Sex work just became the next step to helping having the resources, the disposable income to transition" (p. 20).

Another structural factor disproportionately impacting LGBTQ+ people is housing discrimination. A report by Quintana et. al (2010) for the Center for American Progress indicated that 56 percent of gay and 70 percent of transgender people reported housing discrimination. The NCTE found transgender people were denied a home (19 percent) or were evicted (11 percent) because of their gender identity (Grant et al., 2011). Lack of stable housing impacts opportunities and choices. For example, Grant and colleagues (2011) found in a national study that of transgender people who were involved in commercial sex, nearly half simultaneously experienced homelessness. Multiple studies show housing instability as a catalyst to survival sex among LGBTQ+ people. In fact, housing is frequently listed as a salient need among trafficked and exploited people more broadly, and this factor is heightened for people who experience housing discrimination (Curtis et al., 2008; Dank, Yahner, et al., 2015; Heil & Nichols, 2015; Lutnick, 2016).

Discrimination in the criminal justice system may further exacerbate risks to LGBTQ+ youth. For example, Lutnick (2016) highlighted what has become known as "walking while trans": "Young transgender women often experience significant harassment from police officers. Even when they are not trading sex, they are arrested simply because they are transgender and in a certain area— what is referred to as 'walking while trans'" (p. 39). In addition, Dank, Yu, et al. (2015) noted harassment by police reported by LGBTQ+ youth involved in commercial sex. This harassment included arrests for carrying condoms, as a justification for suspicion of prostitution, as well as genital checks, in which transgender people were forced to lift their skirts in an attempt to show their biological sex. This behavior creates distrust of police and authority figures, serving as a barrier to seeking help. Even when they do seek help, LGBTQ+

people may find that their reports of sex trafficking may not be taken seriously by law enforcement (Egyes, 2016).

Social workers can engage in social justice–oriented action on a legislative scale to address structural risk factors, thereby reducing risk of trafficking and exploitation among LGBTQ+ people. Hunt recommends advocating on a legislative level to support the Employment Non-Discrimination Act, which creates federal protections against LGBTQ+ discrimination in all federal, state, and local government agencies, unions, and private employers with more than 15 employees (Hunt, 2012). Amending the Fair Housing Act with the Housing Opportunities Made Equal Act would prohibit housing discrimination related to LGBTQ+ status. Importantly, the Health Equity and Accountability Act works to increase access to healthcare and discrimination in healthcare systems, as well as LGBTQ+ data collection in federally supported health surveys and programs (Hunt, 2012). It may also be useful to create coalitions or task forces that educate law enforcement about trafficking of LGBTQ+ youth. Egyes (2016) reported that such action had some level of success in New York in reducing law enforcement's discriminatory attitudes. Thus, social workers can engage in macro practice, to advocate for social justice to reduce the likelihood of youth and adults engaging in commercial sex markets.

Intersections

It is also important to note that LGBTQ+ identities do not exist in a vacuum. Multiple studies show that LGBTQ+ youth of color are particularly at heightened risk. Such identities may also intersect to produce unique barriers to services. In a sample of 249 youth involved in commercial sex in New York City, Curtis and colleagues (2008) found that 119 were female, 111 were male, and 19 were transgender. Of the transgender youth, a majority were people of color— particularly African American, multiracial, and Hispanic (Curtis et al., 2008). Dank, Yahner, and colleagues (2015) found in interviews with 283 individuals experiencing CSE who were LGBTQ+, YMSM (used to describe heterosexual young men who have sex with men), or YWSW (used to describe heterosexual young women who have sex with women) that "virtually all the youth in our study were of racial minorities, with 37 percent identifying as African American or black, 22 percent as Latino or Latina, and 30 percent with more than one race or ethnicity. Other respondents identified as white (5 percent), Native American (1 percent), or another race (4 percent)" (p. 15). Immigrants are also at risk. Egyes (2016) indicated that LGBTQ+ immigrants face heightened oppression because they simultaneously experience anti-immigrant policies and anti-LGBTQ+ attitudes and behaviors from police officers. For example, undocumented immigrants faced deportation, with law enforcement not willing to view their cases as potential trafficking cases, and LGBTQ+ clients' trafficking cases were similarly dismissed by law enforcement without further investigation. Similarly, Dank, Yu, and colleagues (2015) noted that transgender youth experienced harassment from police, both for their gender identity, race, or ethnicity and for their involvement in commercial sex.

In sum, individuals within the service population may experience multiple threads of inequality simultaneously. Thus, cultural shifts to address racism, transphobia, xenophobia, sexism, homophobia, and heterosexism are needed. This process should start in schools, as indicated in the GLSEN and Williams Institute recommendations discussed previously, but also within communities (such as in faith-based organizations, community centers, and youth-serving agencies, among others), and should address intersecting forms of oppression. However, cultural efforts must be combined with structural shifts and legislative protections. Thus, macro practice is an important area of focus for social justice endeavors.

Likely Spots for Identification and Outreach

The available research indicates that 24-hour coffee shops, libraries, youth-serving agencies, health clinics/vans, hotels, online venues, and homeless shelters are promising spots for identification and outreach of LGBTQ+ trafficked or exploited youth. Heil and Nichols (2015) found that traffickers and buyers trolled "safe spaces" that runaway and homeless LGBTQ+ youth (as well as non-LGBTQ+ youth) were likely to use to get out of the cold or to clean up in the bathroom, such as public libraries and 24-hour coffee shops. Street outreach workers or anti-trafficking organizations engaging in outreach could strategically place outreach posters, or directly engage in outreach, in these same locations. Curtis and colleagues (2008) found that of commercially sexually exploited youth more broadly, 45 percent used hotels in the sex trade. Similarly, in a study explicitly examining LGBTQ+ youth in the sex trade, Dank, Yahner, et al. (2015) found that 57 percent used hotels to meet with their customers. Thus, providing outreach posters at hotels that indicate available resources for exiting the sex trade may be a promising practice for outreach. Researchers report that a majority of those involved in commercial sex also use the Internet to post ads to solicit, which indicates that the Internet could be used in outreach efforts. Some organizations are buying ad space to post outreach materials on websites commonly known to solicit prostitution or adult entertainment (Nichols, 2016).

Curtis et al. (2008) found that the transgender population within their sample of those experiencing CSE were more likely to be living in a shelter than in another living arrangement (the streets, at a friend's house, etc.). While this sample only included nineteen transgender people, this finding indicates that homeless shelters may be another place for outreach efforts. More recently, Dank, Yahner, and colleagues (2015, p.16) found that of LGBTQ+ youth involved in commercial sex, "nearly half the youth we interviewed (48 percent) reported living in a shelter, and another 10 percent said they lived on the street." Heil & Nichols (2015) indicated in their case study that homeless LGBTQ+ youth were picked up by traffickers and buyers in front of homeless shelters.

Healthcare is another avenue for outreach, as youth involved in commercial sex appear to be engaging with healthcare services relatively frequently. Curtis and colleagues found that of transgender youth involved in commercial sex, 37 percent had accessed healthcare systems within the last week, 21 percent in the last month, and another 21 percent in the last six months. They found that youth engaged in commercial sex markets were interacting often with youth agencies' medical vans and clinics, for STI/STD testing, estrogen, minor illnesses, or a general checkup (Curtis et al., 2008).

Youth-serving agencies are another promising avenue for outreach. Heil and Nichols (2015) indicated that LGBTQ+ youth experiencing exploitation or trafficking were interacting with youth-serving agencies, typically in order to access a safe space or to access healthcare. Similarly, over two-thirds of the sample in the study by Curtis and colleagues (2008) had visited a youth-serving agency. Ironically, sometimes youth-serving agencies are where pimps recruit youths or where friends get youth involved in CSE. Basically, pimps and recruiters know the youth are vulnerable and troll these places, or peers simply provide avenues of survival for their friends. Thus, prevention and outreach become doubly important in this setting.

In addition, child protective services, foster care, and juvenile justice systems are important areas for identification and outreach (Dank, Yahner, et al., 2015; Freeman & Hamilton, 2008; Wilson et al., 2009). Research indicates that many LGBTQ+ youth involved in commercial sex have a background of child welfare involvement. In Gragg and colleagues' study (2007), 69 percent experienced child abuse or neglect, and 75 percent had been in foster care. Dank, Yu, et al. (2015) found that more than half their sample of LGBTQ+ youth involved in commercial sex had backgrounds of juvenile justice system involvement.

While sites for identification and outreach are clearly implicated by the research, there are some important considerations for social workers. Importantly, outreach materials must be relatable to this population. Accordingly, it is important for organizations to prioritize images and wording that highlight inclusivity to get LGBTQ+ youth and adults to the door (see chapter 18). In addition, survivor-centered practices are important, as exiting commercial sex may not be the first priority of clients. Safe housing and access to employment and education might be the first priority that will allow individuals to move on to safer means of survival (Dank, Yahner, et al., 2015; Dank, Yu, et al., 2015; Lutnick, 2016). Meeting clients where they are, providing referrals to meet individuals' needs and goals, and working to create safety plans are also priorities (Nichols, 2016).

In sum, organizations that social workers frequently work in—youth-serving agencies, healthcare services, shelters, child protective services, and the juvenile justice system—show opportunities for identification and outreach to LGBTQ+ people. In these places social workers can provide social services to allow exit from a trafficking or exploitive situation for those who would like assistance in leaving the sex trade. At the same time, there has to be "somewhere to go." As indicated in the following section, this has been identified as a serious challenge to service provision for LGTBQ+ people involved in commercial sex (see also chapter 13).

Barriers to Accessing Services

Shelter

Research indicates that a serious barrier to exiting a trafficking/CSE situation is lack of safe housing—shelter or residential housing that is specifically for sex-trafficking/CSE victims, as well as shelter more broadly. Multiple studies show that LGBTQ+ people involved in survival sex would rather do something else and wouldn't engage in survival sex if they had better options. Such studies identify lack of shelter and stable housing as an impediment to exiting situations of trafficking and exploitation, as well as the time limits typically imposed by shelters (Curtis et al., 2008; Dank, Yahner, et al., 2015). Time limits for shelters typically range from two weeks to three months. In that short time span, individuals accessing shelter are expected to make other arrangements for housing and cannot stay indefinitely. Curtis and colleagues (2008) reported that transgender youth indicated that steady employment, education, and stable housing were the main changes needed to exit trafficking/CSE, and rules regarding thirty- and ninety-day shelters made them return to the commercial sex industry because they had nowhere to go and no other options.

While lack of shelter is a challenge for all people experiencing homelessness, there are LGBTQ-specific barriers as well. Rees (2010) indicated that transgender youth did not feel safe in sex-segregated shelters. Transgender people may be forced to access shelters that do not align with their gender identity, problematizing feelings of safety, belonging, and inclusion and thereby increasing the likelihood of living on the streets or accepting solicitations of buyers offering shelter in exchange for sex. In addition, shelter for men and boys more broadly is limited, including those accessed by gay and bisexual men and boys (Bastedo, 2015; Heil & Nichols, 2015). Bastedo found in a survey of thirty-five agencies responding to men and boys involved in commercial sexual exploitation that lack of residential services was cited most frequently as a gap in services that impacted service accessibility for gay men and boys.

Accordingly, there is a need to advocate for increased resources to expand shelter and housing and to create inclusivity for trafficked and exploited LGBTQ+ people. In addition, offering a Sexual Orientation, Gender Identity, and Expression (SOGIE) screening (see the following box) to provide an appropriate shelter setting would uphold principles of cultural humility and increase gender affirmation and safety. SOGIE screening works to identify an individual's sexual orientation and gender identity in a safe and affirming way.

The Center for the Study of Social Policy (n.d.) notes that ensuring confidentiality is important when conducting a SOGIE screening. While most states require child welfare organizations to report a child's biological sex, they do not typically require data collection and sharing related to gender identity, expression, or sexual orientation. The same group maintains that questions about sexual orientation and gender identity should be embedded within a broader framework that emphasizes any related healthcare needs, such as access to hormone therapy. Social workers and practitioners should also be aware that identity, embodiment, and sexuality can be fluid, and youth may or may not consistently adhere to any identity. SOGIE screenings can be informal and conversational or can be conducted as a brief five-question survey. The author recommends an informal conversation after rapport building has already taken place.

Conducting a SOGIE screening allows social workers to refer clients to safe spaces, which is an important part of practice in working with LGBTQ+ youth. As Dank, Yu, et al. (2015, p. 73) stated, "The needs of transgender youth should be considered during the development of LGBTQ-sensitive programming. Transgender youth in our study frequently shared anecdotes about being forced into spaces that were incongruent with their gender identity." Dank, Yu, and colleagues (2015, pp.73–74) recommended that

---

SOGIE Screening[5]

1. Are you a boy, girl, or another identity?
2. Do you feel like a boy, girl, or another identity?
3. Do you usually prefer to wear clothes that usually boys wear, clothes that usually girls wear, or something else?
4. Do you like and/or date girls, boys, both, or neither?
5. Are you gay, lesbian, bisexual, queer, questioning, straight, or another identity? . . .

staff must appropriately address LGBTQ identity during the intake process and ensure LGBTQ youth are not treated differently from heterosexual youth in such determinations. . . . In making housing or classification decisions, personnel must not isolate or segregate LGBTQ youth from other participants, and should not automatically place youth based on their assigned sex at birth but rather in accordance with an individualized assessment that takes into account their safety, gender identity, and preference.

Heil and Nichols (2015) found that service providers were aware of sex -trafficking residential services that were not culturally competent and were consequently viewed as unsafe and inappropriate referrals for their LGBTQ+ clients. Social workers must know where safe spaces for LGBTQ+ people exist. Providing education and training to shelters about sex trafficking of LGBTQ+ people could be an important part of prevention and outreach efforts. Importantly, awareness, inclusion, and cultural humility are key shifts required in organizations serving LGBTQ+ people to better identify, prevent, and respond to the trafficking and exploitation experienced by these groups.

Lack of Awareness and Inclusion in Antitrafficking Efforts

In a survey of thirty-five organizations, lack of awareness of sex trafficking/ CSE of males who are disproportionately gay or bisexual was indicated as the biggest barrier to related prevention education and curriculum (Bastedo, 2015). Moreover, in a review of prevention education programs in schools K-12, only one included LGBTQ+ identities and related risk factors in its curriculum. Government documents, media reports, and community awareness initiatives are similarly exclusionary (Nichols, 2016). Egyes (2016) indicated that police did not take the reports of transgender people experiencing trafficking seriously, as they did not see this as an affected population. Similarly, Bastedo (2015, pp.11–12) reported that "young males [who are disproportionately gay or bisexual] frequently pass unrecognized by service agencies that lack the knowledge and training necessary to identify commercially sexually exploited males/ young men (grade schools, doctor's offices and law enforcement agencies were specifically named by respondents as being in need of identification training)." While education, awareness, and training of individuals in a variety of different social service, community, and law enforcement sectors have expanded, such training does not tend to be LGBTQ+ inclusive. In fact, it emphasizes twelve- to fourteen-year-old white cisgender girls, while ignoring groups of various races, ethnicities, genders, and sexual orientations. "In particular, the ostensibly straight young women who must be rescued by (male) law enforcement through the prosecution process serves as a foil to the numerous queer bodies who are vulnerable, exploited, and trafficked and require culturally competent resources" (Schwarz & Britton, 2015).

To address this invisibility caused by lack of awareness and to promote inclusion, social workers working in antitrafficking organizations should incorporate risk factors of trafficking of LGBTQ+ people in their education and awareness materials and in the prevention curriculum. Similarly, trainings in social service and law enforcement agencies should incorporate curriculum that is LGBTQ+ inclusive and that explains sex trafficking in the form of survival sex and the related risk factors. In this way, a shift in perspective is more likely to occur; social workers working in such organizations will be better able to identify and provide resources to sex-trafficked or exploited LGBTQ+ people.

Imagery in antitrafficking efforts should also reflect diverse images combined with wording that is LGBTQ+ inclusive (see chapter 18). For organizations directly serving trafficked and exploited people, clearly creating a statement indicating that LGBTQ+ people are welcome is important (see chapter 18). Moreover, cultural humility is key, not just in outreach materials, but also in direct practice.

Cultural Competency/Humility

Cultural competence, increasingly referred to as cultural humility, refers to the ability of organizations and their staff to address distinct needs across cultures, and for attitudes, actions, behaviors, policies and practices to guide effective and respectful service provision for all people (Ferguson-Colvin & Maccio, 2012). Cultural humility may be lacking in service provision to sex -trafficked LGBTQ+ youth and adults. Bastedo (2015) indicated that training in cultural humility was needed for those working with LGBTQ+ youth experiencing CSE. The same study found that "LGBTQ youth are at high risk, and may not feel comfortable reaching out to traditional HT service providers, particularly if the provider is faith based, and if there is a perception of discrimination. Relationships with providers and others in this community are critical to breaking down these barriers" (p. 26).

Bastedo (2015, p. 5) also found "the need for relational engagement, most frequently named as 'mentorship,'" as a promising prevention intervention. Similarly, Dank, Yahner, et al. (2015) found that LGBTQ+ youth reported feeling that social services did not help them and thought that follow-up and expression of concern would have been important in assisting them to make changes in their lives. Thus relational engagement with the social worker/practitioner or through peer mentorship models is a promising mode of practice. There is a large body of work supporting the utility of relational engagement, as well as a growing body of work supporting peer mentorship models with sex-trafficked and exploited people more broadly. Organizations should also recruit LGBTQ+ staff.

The Coalition Addressing Youth Sexual Exploitation (CAYSE) provides tips for advocacy when working with LGBTQ+ youth (2013). Some of these principles apply to adults as well. The group documents six principles:

1. Don't impose your own values or opinions on youth.
2. Give referrals and/or suggest service providers that will effectively and respectfully serve LGBTQ+ youth.
3. Don't ask, "Why are you LGBTQ+?" or "How/when did you know you were LGBTQ+?" or other similar questions that are unrelated to the services or situation.
4. Use gender-neutral language. Ask young persons about their preferred gender pronouns. Don't make assumptions about the sexual orientation or gender identity of any party involved.
5. Know that identifying as LGBTQ+ is not just about sex. Moreover, many youth on the streets who engage in sex with the same gender will not identify as LGBTQ+.
6. Listen . . . Let youth educate you. Don't just go with stereotypes you've heard about LGBTQ+ people.

Similarly, the Broadway Youth Center (Brooks, 2014) recommends addressing potential service barriers in an organization. Ways to promote organizational cultural humility in this respect involve providing ongoing LGBTQ+ Safe Zone trainings, as well as offering ongoing professional development. Awareness of organizational structure, practices, policies, and programming is also key, as well as willingness to make changes to promote inclusivity. It is important to hire social workers who specialize in working with LGBTQ+ clients and to create LGBTQ+ support groups to build trust and transformational relationships. In addition, the Broadway Youth Center recommends creating peer-based education programs and addressing all LGBTQ+ homeless youth as if they were trauma and oppression survivors. Other ways of practicing inclusivity and cultural humility involve emphasizing sex-, gender-, and sexual identity–positive messages, keeping program titles general for those who are not "out," providing regular intentional strategic planning around LGBTQ+ inclusivity at all levels of the organization and in programming, streamlining all forms to be inclusive, and providing gender-neutral restrooms (Brooks, 2014).

Cultural humility also involves the use of appropriate and affirming language. For example, the following box[6] provides a list of culturally competent terms related to LGBTQ+ identities. Social workers should familiarize themselves with this language so they can speak competently with LGBTQ+ survivors of trafficking and exploitation.

Androgyny/ous—(adj; pronounced "an-jrah-jun-ee") (1) a gender expression that has elements of both masculinity and femininity; (2) occasionally used in place of *intersex* to describe a person with both female and male anatomy.

Bicurious—(adj) having a curiosity about being attracted to people of the same gender/sex (similar to *Questioning*).

Bigender—(adj) describes a person who fluctuates between traditionally "woman" and "man" gender-based behavior and identities, identifying with both genders (and sometimes a third gender).

Biological Sex—(noun) a medical term for the chromosomal, hormonal, and anatomical characteristics that are used to classify an individual as female or male or intersex. Often referred to as simply "sex," "physical sex," "anatomical sex," or specifically as "sex assigned [or designated] at birth."

Biphobia—(noun) a range of negative attitudes (e.g., fear, anger, intolerance, resentment, erasure, or discomfort) that one may have or express toward bisexual individuals. Biphobia can come from and be seen within the queer community as well as straight society. Biphobic—(adj) a word used to describe an individual who harbors some elements of this range of negative attitudes toward bisexual people.

Bisexual—(adj) describes a person who is emotionally, physically, and/or sexually attracted to males/men and females/women. Other individuals may use this to indicate an attraction to individuals who identify outside of the gender binary as well and may use *bisexual* as a way to indicate an interest in more than one gender or sex (i.e., men and genderqueer people). This attraction does not have to be equally split or indicate a level of interest that is the same across the genders or sexes an individual may be attracted to.

Butch—(noun & adj) a person who identifies as masculine, whether it be physically, mentally, or emotionally. *Butch* is sometimes used as a derogatory term for lesbians, but it is also claimed as an affirmative identity label.

Cisgender—(adj; pronounced "siss-jendur") describes a person whose gender identity aligns with the biological sex assigned at birth (e.g., man and male-assigned). If a person is not transgender, they are cisgender.

Cisnormativity—(noun) the assumption, in individuals or in institutions, that everyone is cisgender and that cisgender identities are superior to trans identities or people. Leads to invisibility of non-cisgender identities.

Closeted—(adj) describes individuals who are not open to themselves or others about their (queer) sexuality or gender identity. This may be by choice and/or for other reasons, such as fear for one's safety, peer or family rejection or disapproval, and/or loss of housing, job, and so on. Also known as being "in the closet." Those who choose to break this silence "come out" of the closet (see *Coming Out*).

Coming Out—(noun) (1) the process by which one accepts and/or comes to identify one's own sexuality or gender identity (to "come out" to oneself). (2) The process by which one shares one's sexuality or gender identity with others (to "come out" to friends, etc.).

Cross-dresser—(noun) someone who wears clothes of another gender/sex.

Feminine of Center; Masculine of Center—(adj) a phrase that indicates a range of terms of gender identity and gender presentation for those who present, understand themselves, and relate to others in a more feminine/masculine way. Feminine of center individuals may also identify as femme, submissive, transfeminine, or more; masculine of center individuals may also often identity as butch, stud, aggressive, boi, transmasculine, or more.

Feminine Presenting; Masculine Presenting—(adj) a way to describe those who express gender in a more feminine or masculine way, for example, in their hairstyle, demeanor, clothing choice, or style. Not to be confused with *Feminine of Center* and *Masculine of Center*, which often include a focus on identity as well as expression.

Femme—(noun & adj) someone who identifies as feminine, whether it be physically, mentally, or emotionally. Often used to refer to a feminine-presenting queer woman.

Fluid(ity)—(adj) generally with another term attached, as in gender-fluid or fluid-sexuality, fluid(ity) describes an identity that may change or shift over time between or within the mix of the options available (e.g., man and woman, bi and straight).

FtM/F2M; MtF/M2F—(adj) abbreviation for female-to-male transgender or transsexual person; abbreviation for male-to-female transgender or transsexual person.

Gay—(adj) (1) a term used to describe individuals who are primarily emotionally, physically, and/or sexually attracted to members of the same sex and/or gender. More commonly used when referring to males/men-identified people who are attracted to males/men-identified people, but can be applied to females/women-identified people as well. (2) An umbrella term used to refer to the queer community as a whole, or as an individual identity label for anyone who does not identify as heterosexual.

Gender Binary—(noun) the idea that there are only two genders—male/female or man/woman—and that a person must be strictly gendered as either/or.

Gender Expression—(noun) the external display of one's gender, through a combination of dress, demeanor, social behavior, and other factors, generally measured on scales of masculinity and femininity. Also referred to as "gender presentation."

Gender Fluid—(adj) describes a gender identity best described as a dynamic mix of boy and girl or man and woman. A person who is gender fluid may always feel like a mix of the two traditional genders but may feel more man some days and more woman other days.

Gender Identity—(noun) individuals' internal perceptions of their gender, and how they label themselves, based on how much they align or don't align with what they understand their options for gender to be. Common identity labels include man, woman, genderqueer, trans, and more.

Gender Non-Conforming (GNC)—(adj) describes someone whose gender presentation, whether by nature or by choice, does not align in a predicted fashion with gender-based expectations.

Gender Normative/Gender Straight—(adj) describes someone whose gender presentation, whether by nature or by choice, aligns with society's gender-based expectations.

Genderqueer—(adj) a gender identity label often used by people who do not identify with the binary of man/woman, or as an umbrella term for many gender non-conforming or non-binary identities (e.g., agender, bigender, genderfluid). Genderqueer people may think of themselves as one or more of the following, and they may define these terms differently: may combine aspects of man and woman and other identities (bigender, pangender); may not have a gender or identify with a gender (genderless, agender); may move between genders (genderfluid); may be a third gender or other-gendered. Includes those who do not place a name to their gender because they have an overlap of, or blurred lines between, gender identity and sexual and romantic orientation.

Gender Variant—(adj) describes someone who either by nature or by choice does not conform to gender-based expectations of society (e.g., transgender, transsexual, intersex, genderqueer, cross-dresser, etc.).

Heteronormativity—(noun) the assumption, in individuals or in institutions, that everyone is heterosexual and that heterosexuality is superior to all other sexualities. Leads to invisibility and stigmatizing of other sexualities. Often included in this concept is a level of gender normativity and gender roles, the assumption that individuals should identify as men and women, be masculine men and feminine women, and finally that men and women are a complementary pair.

Heterosexism—(noun) behavior that grants preferential treatment to heterosexual people, reinforces the idea that heterosexuality is somehow better or more "right" than queerness, or makes other sexualities invisible.

Heterosexual—(adj) describes a person primarily emotionally, physically, and/or sexually attracted to members of the opposite sex. Also known as straight.

Homophobia—(noun) an umbrella term for a range of negative attitudes (e.g., fear, anger, intolerance, resentment, erasure, or discomfort) that one may have toward members of the LGBTQ+ community. The term can also connote a fear, disgust, or dislike of being perceived as LGBTQ+. The term is extended to bisexual and transgender people as well; however, the terms *biphobia* and *transphobia* are used to emphasize the specific biases against individuals of bisexual and transgender communities.

Homosexual—(adj) a [medical] term used to describe a person primarily emotionally, physically, and/or sexually attracted to members of the same sex/gender. This term is considered stigmatizing because of its history as a category of mental illness, and it is discouraged for common use (use *gay* or *lesbian* instead).

Intersex—(noun) someone whose combination of chromosomes, gonads, hormones, internal sex organs, and genitals differs from the two expected patterns of male or female. In the medical care of infants, the initialism DSD ("Differing/Disorders of Sex Development") is used. Formerly known as hermaphrodite (or hermaphroditic), but these terms are now considered outdated and derogatory.

Lesbian—(noun) a term used to describe women attracted romantically, erotically, and/or emotionally to other women.

LGBTQ/GSM/DSG/+ – (noun) initialisms used as shorthand or umbrella terms for all those who have a non-normative (or queer) gender or sexuality; there are many different preferred initialisms. LGBTQ is Lesbian Gay Bisexual Transgender and Queer (sometimes people add a + at the end in an effort to be more inclusive); GSM is Gender and Sexual Minorities; DSG is Diverse Genders and Sexualities. Other popular options include the initialism GLBT and the acronym QUILTBAG (Queer [or Questioning] Undecided Intersex Lesbian Trans Bisexual Asexual [or Allied] and Gay [or Genderqueer]).

Masculine of Center—(adj) a word that indicates a range of personal understandings, in terms of both gender identity and gender presentation of lesbian/queer women who present, understand themselves, and relate to others in a more masculine way. These individuals may also often identity as butch, stud, aggressive, boi, or transmasculine, among other identities.

MSM/WSW—(noun) initialisms for "men who have sex with men" and "women who have sex with women," to distinguish sexual behaviors from sexual identities (e.g., just because a man is straight doesn't mean he's not having sex with men). Often used in the field of HIV/AIDs education, prevention, and treatment.

Outing—(verb) participating in the involuntary or unwanted disclosure of another person's sexual orientation, gender identity, or intersex status.

Pansexual—(adj) describes a person who experiences sexual, romantic, physical, and/or spiritual attraction for members of all gender identities/ expressions.

Passing—(verb) (1) a term for trans people being accepted as, or able to "pass for," a member of their self-identified gender/sex identity (regardless of birth sex). (2) An LGB/queer individual who is believed to be or perceived as straight.

Questioning—(verb & adj) describes individuals who are unsure about or are exploring their own sexual orientation or gender identity.

Same Gender Loving/SGL—(adj) a term sometimes used by members of the African American/Black community to express an alternative sexual orientation without relying on terms and symbols of European descent.

Sexual Orientation—(noun) the type of sexual, romantic, emotional/spiritual attraction one feels for others, often labeled based on the gender relationship between individuals and the people they are attracted to (often mistakenly referred to as sexual preference).

Sex Reassignment Surgery/SRS—(noun) a term used by some medical professionals to refer to a group of surgical options that alter a person's biological sex. *Gender confirmation surgery* is considered by many to be a more affirming term. In most cases, one or multiple surgeries are required to achieve legal recognition of gender variance. Some refer to different surgical procedures as "top" surgery and "bottom" surgery to discuss what type of surgery they are having without having to be more explicit.

Sexual Preference—(noun) (1) the types of sexual intercourse, stimulation, and gratification one likes to receive and participate in. (2) Generally when this term is used, it is being mistakenly interchanged with *sexual orientation*, creating an illusion that one has a choice (or "preference") in whom one is attracted to.

Skoliosexual—(adj) attracted to genderqueer and transsexual people and expressions (people who don't identify as cisgender).

Third Gender—(noun) a term for a person who does not identify with either man or woman, but identifies with another gender. This gender category is used by societies that recognize three or more genders, both contemporary and historic, and is also a conceptual term meaning different things to different people who use it, as a way to move beyond the gender binary.

Top Surgery—(noun) refers to surgery for the construction of a male-type chest or breast augmentation for a female-type chest.

Trans*/Transgender—(adj) (1) an umbrella term covering a range of identities that transgress socially defined gender norms. Trans with an asterisk (*) is often used to indicate that you are referring to the larger group of gender-nonconforming people. (2) A person who lives as a member of a gender other than that expected based on sex assigned at birth.

Transition(ing)—(noun & verb) primarily used to refer to the process trans people undergo when changing their bodily appearance either to be more congruent with the gender/sex they feel themselves to be and/or to be in harmony with their preferred gender expression.

Transman; Transwoman—(noun) an identity label sometimes adopted by female-to-male transgender people or transsexuals to signify that they are men while still affirming their history as assigned female sex at birth (sometimes referred to as transguy). (2) Identity label sometimes adopted by male-to-female transsexuals or transgender people to signify that they are women while still affirming their history as assigned male sex at birth.

Transphobia—(noun) the fear of, discrimination against, or hatred of trans* people, the trans* community, or gender ambiguity. Transphobia can be seen within the queer community as well as in general society.

Transsexual—(noun & adj) individuals who identify psychologically as a gender/sex other than the one to which they were assigned at birth. Transsexuals often wish to transform their bodies hormonally and surgically to match their inner sense of gender/sex.

Transvestite—(noun) a person who dresses as the binary opposite gender expression ("cross-dresses") for any one of many reasons, including relaxation, fun, and sexual gratification (often called a "cross-dresser," and should not be confused with transsexual).

Two-Spirit—(noun) an umbrella term traditionally used by Native American people to recognize individuals who possess qualities or fulfill roles of both genders

Summary of Recommendations

Risk Factors

School Bullying and Discrimination (leading to runaway and homeless youth)

What Social Workers Can Do

- Develop partnerships with schools to implement GLSEN and the Williams Institute recommendations.
- Provide training in cultural humility.

Family-Based Rejection (leading to runaway and homeless youth)

What Social Workers Can Do

- Provide community education and/or therapy to parents to address their rejection of LGBTQ+ youth, and foster positive family relationships.
- Attempt reunification with parents.
- Foster care training that is LGBTQ+ inclusive/screening for Safe Zone home.

Structural Discrimination

What Social Workers Can Do

- Practice gender-affirming healthcare. Engage in macro-practice to advocate for inclusion of gender affirming healthcare in various insurance policies, including Medicaid.
- Engage in political activism to legislatively address identity-based oppression in hiring and wage discrimination.

Barriers

Criminal Justice System–Based (failure to identify, revictimization of LGBTQ+ people)

What Social Workers Can Do

- Partner with your local police departments to provide education about sex trafficking of LGBTQ+ people.
- Challenge practices targeting LGBTQ+ people involved in CSEC.

- Provide training conducted by LGBTQ+ survivors. Build trust by eradicating the practices that build distrust.
- Provide training in cultural humility.

Shelter

What Social Workers Can Do

- Provide SOGIE screening to determine appropriate shelter settings.
- Refer to safe spaces.
- Provide education and training to shelters in your area.
- Practice cultural humility.

Notes

1. The typically appearing acronym LGBTQIA* is not used here, as there is no research supporting that asexual, aromantic, or intersex people are at heightened risk of sex trafficking/CSE. To avoid homogenization and inappropriate use of this acronym, IA identities are not included.
2. As with non-LGBTQ* youth, other factors serving as a catalyst to running away and consequently trading sex for survival involve violence, neglect, or abuse in the home. Intergenerational transmission of prostitution, or getting involved in commercial sex through family members, is a less common factor among LGBTQ youth than other factors. Dank, Yahner, and colleagues (2015) found that only 4 percent of LGBTQ youth in commercial sex markets in New York became involved through family members, and few had pimps or exploiters. Curtis, Terry, Dank, Dombrowski, and Khan (2008) found that only one boy and no transgender youth were recruited into commercial sex markets by boyfriends or pimps. Overall, familial trafficking and boyfriend pimps are implicated to a lesser degree in LGBTQ involvement in commercial sex markets; survival sex is thought to be most common. The chapter consequently focuses on survival sex and the pathways that lead to it among LGBTQ people.
3. *Cultural humility* is language currently replacing the long-used term *cultural competency*, which according to the National Center for Cultural Competence, "is a set of congruent behaviors, attitudes, and policies that come together in a system, agency or among professionals and enable that system, agency or those professions to work effectively in cross-cultural situations." *Cultural humility* will be used throughout the rest of the chapter.
4. The acronym used by the organization is used here to reflect the methodology used by GLSEN.
5. Adapted from Alameda County Social Services Agency (n.d.).
6. Adapted from Killerman (2016).

References

Alameda County Social Services Agency. (n.d.). Information on SOGIE. Retrieved from https://www.prearesourcecenter.org/sites/default/files/content/sogie_information _gathering.pdf

Bastedo, T. (2015). *The commercial sexual exploitation of male minors in the United States: A snapshot with strategic implications for prevention education. Love 146: End Child Trafficking and Exploitation.* Retrieved from https://1at4ct3uffpw1uzzmu191368-wpengine.netdna -ssl.com/wp-content/uploads/2015/01/CSEMMFinalReport_print.pdf

Biegel, S., & Kuehl, S. J. (2010). *Safe at school: Addressing the school environment and LGBT safety through policy and legislation.* Williams Institute and National Education Policy Center. Retrieved from http://nepc.colorado.edu/files/Biegel_LGBT.pdf

Brooks, L. (2014). *Addressing potential service barriers to LGBTQ youth: Concrete intervention strategies* (LGBTQ youth advocate handout). Chicago, IL: Broadway Youth Center.

Center for the Study of Social Policy (n.d.). *Out of the shadows: Supporting LGBTQ youth in child welfare through cross-system collaboration.* Retrieved from http://www.cssp.org /pages/body/Out-of-the-shadows-current-landscape.pdf

Coalition Addressing Youth Sexual Exploitation. (2013). *Working with LGBTQ at-risk youth* (resource sheet).

Covenant House, Loyola University (New Orleans), and University of Pennsylvania. (2017). *Labor and sex trafficking among homeless youth.* Retrieved from http://covenanthousestudy .org/docs/Loyola-Research-Results.pdf

Curtis, R., Terry, K., Dank, M., Dombrowski, K., & Khan, B. (2008). *The commercial sexual exploitation of children in New York City, volume one: The CSEC population in New York City: Size, characteristics and needs. Center for Court Innovation.* Retrieved from Family & Youth Services Bureau website: https://ncfy.acf.hhs.gov/library/2008/commercial-sexual -exploitation-children-new-york-city-volume-one-csec-population-new

Dank, M., Yahner, J., Madden, K., Banuelos, I., Yu, L., Ritchie, A., ... Conner, B. (2015). *Surviving the streets of New York: Experiences of LGBTQ youth, YMSM, and YWSW engaged in survival sex.* Urban Institute. Retrieved from http://www.urban.org/research/publication/surviving -streets-new-york-experiences-lgbtq-youth-ymsm-and-ywsw-engaged-survival-sex /view/full_report

Dank, M., Yu, L., Yahner, J., Mora, M., Pelletier, E., & Conner, B. (2015). *Locked in: Interactions with the criminal justice and child welfare systems for LGBTQ youth, YMSM, and YWSW who engage in survival sex.* Urban Institute. Retrieved from http://www.urban.org/sites /default/files/publication/71446/2000424-Locked-In-Interactions-with-the-Criminal -Justice-and-Child-Welfare-Systems-for-LGBTQ-Youth-YMSM-and-YWSW-Who -Engage-in-Survival-Sex.pdf

Egyes, L. (2016). Borders and intersections: The unique vulnerabilities of LGBTQ immigrants to trafficking. In E. Heil & A. Nichols (Eds.), *Broadening the scope of human trafficking research: A reader* (pp. 107–123). Durham, NC: Carolina Academic Press.

Fedina, L. (2015). Use and misuse of research in books on sex trafficking: Implications for interdisciplinary researchers, practitioners, and advocates. *Trauma, Violence, & Abuse, 16*(2), 188–198. doi:10.1177/1524838014523337

Ferguson-Colvin, K., & Maccio, E.M. (2012). Toolkit for practitioners/researchers working with lesbian, gay, bisexual, transgender, and queer/questioning (LGBTQ) runaway and homeless youth (RHY). National Resource Center for Permanency and Family Connections.

Freeman, L., & Hamilton, D. (2008). *A count of homeless youth in New York City: 2007*. New York: Empire State Coalition of Youth and Family Services.

Gares, J. (n.d.) *Kicked out: LGBTQ youth experience homelessness*. Retrieved from https://www.youtube.com/watch?v=TUhqodigPFk. Finding Home Series. ILT Media.

Gates, G. (2011). *How many people are lesbian, gay, bisexual, and transgender?* Williams Institute. Retrieved from http://williamsinstitute.law.ucla.edu/wp-content/uploads/Gates-How-Many-People-LGBT-Apr-2011.pdf

Gay, Lesbian & Straight Education Network. (n.d.). *GLSEN releases school climate survey*. Retrieved from http://www.glsen.org/article/glsen-releases-new-national-school-climate-survey

Gragg, F., Petta, I., Bernstein, H., Eisen, K., Quinn, L. (2007). New York prevalence study of commercially sexually exploited children. New York State Office of Children and Family Services. Retrieved from: http://www.ocfs. state.ny.us/main/reports/csec-2007.pdf

Grant, J. M., Mottet, L., Tanis, J., Harrison, J., Herman, J., & Keisling, M. (2011). *Injustice at every turn: A report of the National Transgender Discrimination Survey*. Washington, DC: National Center for Transgender Equality and National Gay and Lesbian Task Force. Heil, E., & Nichols, A. (2015). *Human trafficking in the Midwest: A case study of St. Louis and the bi-state area*. Durham, NC: Carolina Academic Press.

Hunt, J. (2012). *Why the gay and transgender population experiences higher rates of substance use*. Center for American Progress. Retrieved from https://www.americanprogress.org/issues/lgbt/report/2012/03/09/11228/why-the-gay-and-transgender-population-experiences-higher-rates-of-substance-use/

Killerman, S. (2016). *Comprehensive list of LGBTQ vocabulary definitions*. Retrieved from http://itspronouncedmetrosexual.com/2013/01/a-comprehensive-list-of-lgbtq-term-definitions/#sthash.r4MUnUWO.dpuf

Koyama, E. (2011, October 8). *Understanding the complexities of sex trafficking and sex work/trade: Ten observations from a sex worker activist/survivor/feminist*. Retrieved from http://eminism.org/blog/entry/268

Lutnick, A. (2016). *Domestic minor sex trafficking: Beyond victims and villains*. New York, NY: Columbia University Press.

Nichols, A.J. (2016). *Sex trafficking in the U.S.: Theory, research, policy, and practice*. New York, NY: Columbia University Press.

Quintana, N. S., Rosenthal, J., & Krehely, J. (2010). *On the streets: The federal response to gay and transgender homeless youth*. Center for American Progress. Retrieved from https://cdn.americanprogress.org/wp-content/uploads/issues/2010/06/pdf/lgbtyouthhomelessness.pdf

Ray, N. (2006). *Lesbian, gay, bisexual and transgender youth: An epidemic of homelessness*. Washington, DC: National Gay and Lesbian Task Force Policy Institute and National Coalition for the Homeless. Retrieved from http://www.thetaskforce.org/static_html/downloads/HomelessYouth.pdf

Rees, J. (2010). *Trans youth involved in sex work in New York City: A qualitative study* (Doctoral dissertation, New York University, New York).

Schwarz, C., & Britton, H. E. (2015). Queering the support for trafficked persons: LGBTQ communities and human trafficking in the Heartland. *Social Inclusion, 3*(1).

True Colors Fund (n.d.). *Runaway and homeless youth act reauthorization*. Retrieved from https://truecolorsfund.org/portfolio/runaway-and-homeless-youth-act-reauthorization/

Wilson, E.C., Garofalo, R., Harris, R.D., Herrick, A., Martinez, M., Martinez, J., & Belzer, M. (2009). Transgender female youth and sex work: HIV risk and a comparison of life factors related to engagement in sex work. *AIDS and Behavior, 13*, 902–913. doi: 10.1007/s10461-008-9508-8.

CHAPTER 11

CLINICAL PRACTICE WITH COMMERCIALLY SEXUALLY EXPLOITED GIRLS WITH INTELLECTUAL DISABILITIES

JOAN A. REID, PhD, LMHC,
UNIVERSITY OF SOUTH FLORIDA ST. PETERSBURG

JULIA STRAUSS, GRADUATE STUDENT, VANDERBILT
UNIVERSITY, REGISTERED BEHAVIOR TECHNICIAN

RACHAEL A. HASKELL, PhD, LCSW, UNIVERSITY
OF SOUTH FLORIDA ST. PETERSBURG

Girls with intellectual disability[1] (ID) experience disproportionately high rates of sexual victimization (Wissink, van Vugt, Moonen, Stams, & Hendriks, 2015) and are at increased risk for commercial sexual exploitation (CSE) or exploitation in sex trafficking (Clawson, Dutch, Solomon, & Grace, 2009; Estes & Wiener, 2005; U.S. Department of State [DOS], 2012). The limited intellectual functionality commonly experienced by those with ID heightens their vulnerability to sexual victimization because they do not understand what is happening during sexual abuse, assault, or CSE (Reid, 2016b; Wissink et al., 2015). Some girls with ID possess very limited understanding of sexual or romantic relationships and may not be able to distinguish a boyfriend from a sex trafficker or buyer of sex (Reid, 2016b). Others girls with less severe disabilities may understand to some degree that they are being exploited but are not able to escape the exploitive situation or grasp their right to say no (Reid, 2016b). Additionally, communicating or disclosing sexual exploitation or sexual assault can be extremely difficult for youth with severe ID. Youth with less severe limitations may not disclose victimization because the trafficker or abuser makes threats against them or their loved ones (Keilty & Connelly, 2001; Reid, 2016b; Wissink et al., 2015). Unfortunately, even when they do report sexual victimization or CSE, youth with ID may be viewed as less credible by law enforcement because of their disability (DOS, 2012; Keilty & Connelly, 2001; Wissink et al., 2015).

A meta-analysis of eight studies of 6,522 children found that the prevalence of sexual violence toward children with intellectual disabilities was 15 percent (Wissink et al., 2015). Overall, Wissink and colleagues (2015) also found the risk of sexual violence to be 4.6 times higher in children with ID than in children without disabilities. Currently, there is insufficient research to estimate the prevalence of CSE among girls with ID; however, the research that has been completed indicates that risk of CSE may be 10 times higher for girls with ID than for those without disabilities (Reid, 2016b).

Additional vulnerabilities to CSE arise because youth with ID are typically viewed as not being sexually active. Consequently, they are not educated about romantic or sexual relationships. In a survey conducted by Isler and colleagues (2009), researchers found that more than half of students over the age of fifteen with ID had received no formal sexual education and 46.7 percent had never had a conversation with their parents regarding sexuality. As a result of this lack of sexual education both at home and at school, youth with ID not only lack basic information about safe sex but, even more dangerously, do not have the knowledge necessary or do not develop the safety skills needed to protect themselves from sexual exploitation (DOS, 2012; Groce 2004; Gust, Wang, Grot, Ransom, & Levine, 2003; Wissink et al., 2015). Sexual education teaches core concepts such as the idea that all people have the right to tell others not to touch their body when they do not want to be touched, with students learning skills such as how to clearly say no, how to leave an uncomfortable situation, and how to identify and talk with a trusted adult if someone is touching them in a way that makes them feel uncomfortable (Future of Sex Education Initiative, 2012). Because of their lack of understanding of sexual relationships, youth with ID are unfamiliar with sexual behaviors and may be confused about which behaviors are legal or illegal, such as whether sexual relationships involving individuals under the age of consent are legal (Keilty & Connelly, 2001; Wissink et al., 2015). In addition, they may fail to realize that they have a right to say no to sexual advances and exploitation because their greater dependence on others may diminish their ability to resist the authority or power of an abuser (Reid, 2016b; Wissink et al., 2015). The perception that youth with ID are not sexually active also elevates their susceptibility to CSE because they may be targeted by sex traffickers who are pursuing greater profits from selling sex with a virgin (Groce, 2004; Phasha & Myaka, 2014; Reid, Huard, & Haskell, 2015).

Lack of awareness of exploitation and limited ability to self-identify combine to create perilous vulnerability, which makes it relatively easy for sex traffickers to manipulate and exploit youth with ID. In response to the emerging evidence of the heightened risk for CSE faced by youth with ID, it becomes imperative to recognize symptoms of post-traumatic stress resulting from CSE and to develop and assess specialized mental health treatment specifically designed for sexually exploited youth with ID. Addressing this need, the current chapter investigates (1) trauma symptoms most commonly observed in girls with ID who have experienced sexual victimization or CSE as described in previous research, and (2) treatment options that should be considered by clinicians working with CSE survivors with ID; these options are drawn from results of clinical research and clinical practice guidelines provided by health organizations. The chapter also includes two case studies.

Comparison of Symptoms of Trauma Survivors with and Without ID

CSE puts youth at high risk for depression, suicidality, post-traumatic stress disorder (PTSD), substance abuse, anxiety, attachment issues, anger problems, and self-harming behaviors (Ijadi-Maghsoodi, Cook, Barnert, Gaboian, & Bath, 2016). Although clinical research into the unique symptomatology of victims of CSE with ID has not yet been completed, extensive research has been conducted on the symptomatology of child and adult victims of sexual abuse with ID. Research is inconclusive as to whether the prevalence of PTSD is higher in trauma victims with ID than in those without ID. Some studies indicate that there is a negative correlation between risk of PTSD and developmental age (Mevissen & de Jongh, 2010). Other study results show no difference in prevalence rates or a higher incidence of PTSD in individuals with ID, which may be solely due to the fact that individuals with ID are at increased risk of experiencing trauma (Mevissen & de Jongh, 2010; Soylu, Alpaslan, Ayaz, Esenyel, & Oruç, 2013). Taken together, these studies indicate that individuals with ID are at risk of developing PTSD at similar rates to the general population.

This body of research also indicates that girls with ID who are victims of sexual abuse or sexual assault suffer similar consequences to the consequences experienced by victims without ID (Sobsey, 1992; Soylu et al., 2013). However, this research, in addition to research on the presentation of diverse psychiatric disorders in those with ID (Fletcher, Loschen, Stavrakaki, & First, 2007), suggests that the *presentation* of trauma symptoms by victims of CSE with ID may differ from that by victims without such disabilities in a few key ways. Importantly, studies indicate that the most common presenting symptoms of PTSD in individuals with ID are behavioral acting out of traumatic experiences, self-injurious behavior, frightening dreams without recognizable content, disorganized or agitated behavior at the time of the trauma, trauma-specific enactments that may appear to be psychotic symptoms, noncompliance in daily activities, and isolation from others (Mevissen & de

Jongh, 2010; Wissink et al., 2015). When considering agitated and aggressive behaviors, it is important to note that "practitioners often overlook psychopathology by attributing severe behavioral disturbances as part of the intellectual disability itself, a phenomenon termed 'diagnostic overshadowing'" (Mevissen & de Jongh, 2010, p. 309). Symptoms such as aggression, risky behavior, or noncompliance may be inaccurately attributed to girls' intellectual disability rather than to traumatic experiences (Mevissen & de Jongh, 2010, p. 311). To help mental health professionals more accurately diagnose individuals with ID, and in collaboration with the American Psychiatric Association, the National Association for the Dually Diagnosed (NADD) published a manual titled the *Diagnostic Manual—Intellectual Disability* (DM-ID), which documents differences in symptomology between individuals with and without ID (Fletcher et al., 2007).

In addition to PTSD, common psychological consequences resulting from sexual victimization observed in girls with ID include depression, anxiety, panic attacks, low self-esteem, shame and guilt, irrational fear, and loss of trust (Sobsey, 1992; Soylu et al., 2013). Soylu and colleagues (2013) found that the rates of major depression were the same in child victims of sexual abuse with or without ID; however, conduct disorder was more frequently diagnosed in child victims with ID. Mansell, Sobsey, and Calder (1992) reported that 19 percent of sexual abuse victims with mild to moderate ID and 31 percent of sexual abuse victims with severe to profound ID developed aggressive behaviors and other behavior problems. These aggressive behaviors and other behavior problems may vary widely but include verbal protests or aggressions such as yelling, aggressive acts toward others, self-injurious behaviors, and refusing to comply with the requests of caregivers (Mansell et al., 1992; Reid, 2016b). Mansell et al. (1992) also found that 57 percent of those with mild to moderate ID and 36 percent of those with severe to profound ID suffered emotional distress after their victimization. These study findings indicate that symptomology may differ among girls with ID based on the severity of their disability. Aligning with this empirical evidence of symptom differentiation, the DM-ID contains a table comparing the PTSD symptoms of those with mild to moderate ID and those with severe to profound ID (Tomasulo & Razza, 2007). The authors emphasize that behavioral acting out of traumatic experiences is more common with individuals assessed at lower developmental ages (Tomasulo & Razza, 2007).

Comparison of clinical reports from fifty-four case files of girls with histories of CSE mirrored the results of the clinical studies just reported (Reid, 2016b). The case files included results from clinical assessments of the core symptoms of PTSD as well as areas of impaired functioning related to trauma (see figure 11.1). The study findings indicated that, based on clinical evaluations or psychological assessments, sexually exploited girls with ID reported higher

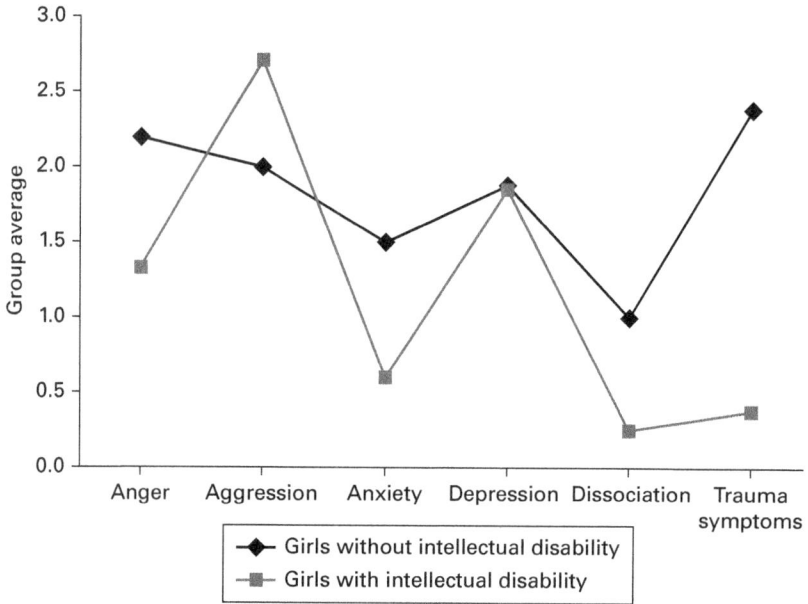

FIGURE 11.1 Clinical Symptom Profiles Comparing CSE Girls with and Without Intellectual Disability ($N = 54$)

(*Note*: Ordinal scale of symptom level: 0 = no symptoms reported; 1 = report of minor symptoms; 2 = clinical concern; 3 = mild to moderate clinical symptoms with diagnosis; 4 = severe clinical symptoms with diagnosis)

levels of aggression, on average, than sexually exploited girls without a disability. Much like the agitation or aggression of those with ID was misidentified as noncompliance rather than trauma symptomatology, the agitated behavior of trafficked girls with ID was frequently interpreted as aggression, risky behavior, or noncompliance and was attributed to the girls' intellectual disability rather than traumatic experiences. Furthermore, the clinical evaluations and results of psychological assessments in the case files indicated that girls with and without ID experienced similar levels of depression. However, girls with ID were clinically assessed with lower levels of other subcategories of symptomology, such as anxiety and dissociation (see figure 11.1) linked to trauma, when compared with assessments of girls without ID. In summary, these study results indicate that the most severe psychological symptoms among sexually exploited girls with ID were aggression and depression. These findings align with the previously mentioned studies regarding the presentation of trauma symptoms among individuals with ID who have experienced sexual abuse or sexual assault.

Previous Clinical Research on Treatment Options for Clients with ID

Just as there is limited research on the trauma symptomotology of victims with ID, the current literature on treatment of victims with ID is also limited specifically to the treatment of victims identified as having PTSD. The present discussion on treatment options will focus on those treatments that are empirically proven to benefit victims of sexual violence with ID. While not all victims of CSE meet the criteria for PTSD, the treatments for PTSD address all of the trauma symptoms that victims of CSE may exhibit. Therefore, while more studies need to be conducted on the treatment of all victims with ID irrespective of a PTSD diagnosis, the present treatments discussed can be applied to the treatment of all victims of CSE with ID that exhibit trauma symptoms. According to Ijadi-Maghsoodi and colleagues (2016), treatment of victims of CSE should focus on addressing the mental health needs of victims with current evidence-based treatment modalities that implement trauma-informed care. They recommend cognitive-behavioral therapy (CBT) for youth with PTSD, as well as multisystemic therapy in which the family, school, and other significant community members are involved in the treatment. For youth with self-harming and maladaptive behaviors, as is the case for many victims with ID, these authors recommend using dialectical behavioral therapy (DBT) to teach distress tolerance, mindfulness, and emotion regulation.

While traditional therapy practices may not be as appropriate or effective when used with victims with ID, Mansell and colleagues (1992) suggest using adapted versions of empirically supported therapy modalities. For example, CBT can successfully treat individuals with PTSD who have ID, especially when imagery rehearsal therapy is used (Mevissen & de Jongh, 2010). One such CBT treatment option that has been specifically adapted for trauma treatment is trauma-focused CBT (TF-CBT). TF-CBT is an evidence-based psychotherapy that utilizes an eight-phase treatment protocol aimed at addressing the needs of children and adolescents with difficulties related to traumatic events (Cohen, Mannarino, Berliner, & Deblinger, 2000). TF-CBT has been found to be effective in reducing post-traumatic symptoms, depression, and aggressive and disruptive behavior problems in child victims of sexual trauma (de Arellano et al., 2014). No TF-CBT studies have yet been identified that include children or adolescents with ID. Another treatment option that can be adapted for use with individuals with ID is DBT, which was developed by Marsha Linehan in 1987 for individuals with emotion dysregulation who are at high risk of suicide (Linehan & Wilks, 2015). This therapy approach focuses on creating a relationship of acceptance and warmth between the therapist and client and using that atmosphere of acceptance to teach and encourage the development of skills that will replace harmful behaviors and help individuals regulate their emotions and cognitions (Linehan & Wilks, 2015). Adapted DBT has also been partially supported as a treatment option for youth with ID. More specifically, research findings indicate that individualized DBT that is adapted to treat individuals with cognitive impairments can significantly reduce emotion dysregulation and challenging behaviors such as aggression, self-injury, and sexual offense; however, adapted DBT has not been effective as a group therapy modality (Brown, Brown, & Dibiasio, 2013; Charlton & Dykstra, 2011; Gilroy, 2015).

Eye movement desensitization and reprocessing (EMDR), developed by Francine Shapiro (2001), has been shown to have a high efficacy rate when treating children with PTSD who have ID (Barol & Seubert, 2010; Mevissen & de Jongh, 2010; Mevissen, Lievegoed, & de Jongh, 2011; Rodenburg, Benjamin, de Roos, Meijer, & Stams, 2009). Trauma symptoms that EMDR has been shown to reduce in individuals with ID who have PTSD include aggressive and disruptive behaviors, negative emotionality, including distress around associated trauma triggers, compulsive behaviors, and psychotic symptoms such as disturbing thoughts and auditory hallucinations (Mevissen, Lievegoed, & de Jongh, 2011). EMDR has been successfully used in many empirical and case studies to treat PTSD in victims with ID, including those with limited verbal capacities (Mevissen, Lievegoed, Seubert, & de Jongh, 2011; Rodenburg, Benjamin, Meijer, & Jongeneel, 2009; Tharner, 2006). The researchers employed the standard EMDR protocol, adapting it when necessary to accommodate the needs of each participant.

Importantly, EMDR is considered effective in treating complex trauma or complex PTSD (Brown & Shapiro, 2006; Korn, 2009; Solomon & Heide, 2005). Complex PTSD, sometimes referred to as disorders of extreme stress not otherwise specified (DESNOS), has been proposed as a mental health diagnosis that incorporates symptomology frequently observed in certain survivors of prolonged trauma such as child sexual abuse, intimate partner violence, and sex trafficking (Choi, Klein, Shin, & Lee, 2009; Farley et al., 2004; Herman, 1992; van der Kolk, McFarlane, & Weisaeth, 2007). Complex PTSD is thought to develop if an individual was in a state of captivity, unable to escape, and under the control of the perpetrator (Cantor & Price, 2007; Herman, 1992). These conditions have been observed in some cases of CSE or sex trafficking, particularly when economic and psychological bonds to a trafficker make it challenging to leave the situation (Farley et al., 2004; Frank & Terwilliger, 2015; Kennedy, Klein, Bristowe, Cooper, & Yuille, 2007; Reid, 2016a, 2016b; Reid, Haskell, Dillahunt-Aspillaga, & Thor, 2013). In addition to the previously mentioned symptoms of PTSD, complex PTSD presents with more pervasive and diffuse symptoms such as personality changes and heightened susceptibility to repetitive harm, both to self-inflicted harm and to harm perpetrated by others (Cantor & Price, 2007; Herman, 1992).

Clinical Cases

While other empirically supported therapy options for PTSD exist (SAMHSA, 2016), EMDR and TF-CBT are the only psychotherapies recommended by the World Health Organization for the treatment of PTSD (World Health Organization [WHO], 2013). The two clinical cases detailed in this chapter involved girls with ID presenting with symptoms associated with CSE-related trauma exposure; the cases feature the use of EMDR and TF-CBT.

CASE #1: Using EMDR to Address CSE-Linked Trauma to Resolve Symptoms of Aggression and Depression

Case #1 Presentation

Gabrielle[2] was an adolescent who had been adjudicated on criminal charges including assault. She was residing in a juvenile justice program designed for delinquent girls with mental health diagnoses. Gabrielle was diagnosed with ID based on results from the administration of the Wechsler Intelligence Scale for Children (WICS-IV) (Wechsler, 2003). Her scores on composite scores (e.g., Full Scale IQ, Verbal Comprehension, Perceptual Reasoning, Working Memory, Processing Speed) on the WICS-IV ranged from 70 to 83, being interpreted as Borderline or Low Average. Gabrielle was placed in the Exceptional Student Education (ESE) program managed at the juvenile justice facility designed for students with ID. The psychiatrist employed by the juvenile justice facility diagnosed Gabrielle with comorbid diagnoses of conduct disorder, intermittent explosive disorder, and depression. Gabrielle was experiencing severe impairment in her interpersonal relationships and was not successfully progressing in her treatment. Her emotional functioning was unstable, leading to outbursts and aggression toward facility staff and other residents. Gabrielle's frequent outbursts resulted in numerous daily takedowns[3] by staff and temporary placement in isolation, known as controlled observation, in a confinement room.[4] Primary treatment goals for Gabrielle included reducing emotional outbursts and daily conflicts with staff and other residents. Gabrielle's outburst and takedowns occurred so frequently that the normal milieu for all girls at the facility was continually interrupted. Her behavior in the confinement room resulted in her remaining in the confinement room for the maximum allowable period.

Gabrielle had previously participated in six months of mental health treatment to address her frequent and increasing aggression. This treatment, which consisted primarily of cognitive-behavioral therapy (CBT) as well as antipsychotic medication, utilized weekly individual sessions, daily group sessions, and monthly family therapy sessions. After six months of therapy, treatment goals had not been reached. During this period, limited success with self-soothing skills had been obtained; Gabrielle remained calm and focused when working on simple word searches—an activity that she found particularly calming. However, Gabrielle's outbursts and takedowns continued to occur on a daily basis or even several times during a 24-hour period.

Case #1 EMDR Treatment and Assessment of Progress

After six months in the juvenile justice facility, Gabrielle was transferred to a new therapist—one of the authors of this chapter. Despite Gabrielle's frequent outburst with staff at the facility, she presented as cooperative during therapy and eager to interact with the therapist. The therapist also observed that Gabrielle had limited verbal abilities and had little to no insight into or explanation for her aggressive behavior. Although Gabrielle had not been diagnosed with PTSD by the facility psychiatrist, her therapist postulated that Gabrielle's aggressive behavior may be linked to previous trauma and utilized EMDR with Gabrielle during two individual sessions. Important to this case, EMDR does not require that clients have insight into their trauma experience and its link to aggression (Worthington, 2012). EMDR is an integrated psychotherapy (Shapiro, 2001) that utilizes an eight-phase treatment protocol to access disturbing life events and present triggers in order to process them to adaptive resolution. The therapist had completed EMDR Therapy Basic Training (Part 1 and 2) presented by EMDR senior trainers selected and trained by Francine Shapiro (EMDR Institute, 2016). In sessions with Gabrielle, the therapist strictly followed the empirically supported EMDR treatment protocol.

Gabrielle's trauma history was vaguely described as sexual assault in her case file. When asked for details regarding her past trauma in order to determine the focus of EMDR treatment, Gabrielle revealed that she and another girl had been gang raped in an incident that involved a firearm. Gabrielle had been raped at gun point and was also forced to watch the rape of another girl at gun point. According to Gabrielle's reconstruction of the assault, the violent assault was part of an initiation into CSE or sex trafficking.[5] Rape and witnessing of rape may be used to create victim fear and submission by strong-arm pimps operating within gang-related sex-trafficking rings (Frank & Terwilliger, 2015; Kennedy et al., 2007; Reid, 2016a). A secondary trauma resulted from the gang rape; Gabrielle became pregnant and suffered a miscarriage. Gabrielle believed that her drug use and other activities while living on the streets and spending days at a trap house[6] during the pregnancy caused the miscarriage. She felt extremely guilty about the miscarriage, stating, "I killed my baby."

Following the established and standardized EMDR protocol for each disturbing memory (i.e., gang rape and miscarriage), Gabrielle identified an image, belief, affect, and bodily sensation associated with each trauma. For each trauma, Gabrielle described the image and identified a negative cognition, which was phrased in the present tense (e.g., "I am going to die") to emphasize the incongruity (i.e., although she is not in current danger, she feels she is going to die *now*). Gabrielle also identified a preferred, more adaptive, positive cognition (e.g., "I survived and I am safe"), and her level of belief in the positive cognition was measured by the Validity of Cognition (VOC) Scale (Shapiro, 2001). On this scale, a score of 7 indicates that the cognition feels completely true, whereas a score of 1 means that the cognition feels completely false. The affect associated with each event was also identified (e.g., fear, shame, sadness), and the level of disturbance was measured using the Subjective Units of Distress/Disturbance Scale (SUDS) (Kim, Bae, & Park, 2008; Wolpe, 1958), with a score of 10 indicating the highest level of disturbance imaginable and 0 representing no disturbance or neutral. The bodily sensations associated with the disturbance were also identified by Gabrielle.

Related to the gang rape, Gabrielle recalled her assault, witnessing the rape of another girl, and the gun used to threaten her. As she recalled these events, Gabrielle experienced feelings of anxiety and intense fear accompanied by rapid breathing and a tightening in her chest. Her negative cognition was, "I am going to die." After reprocessing this experience, Gabrielle's SUD level decreased from a 10 to a 0, and her reported VOC increased to 7, as she fully believed that she was now safe (her preferred positive cognition). This event was related to safety issues. In retrospect, Gabrielle's aggressive reactions to facility staff and peers appear to have been driven by hypersensitivity to threats. Prior research has found that victims of interpersonal conflicts can become aggressive due to hypersensitivity to threats and misperceptions of hostility, with even minor slights interpreted as hostile threats (Worthington, 2012).

Related to her miscarriage, Gabrielle recalled memories of being at the hospital, experiencing the miscarriage, and being told that the miscarriage was her fault. These memories elicited feelings of sadness, guilt, and fear, along with an associated discomfort in her stomach. She believed that she was "a bad person/mother." Reprocessing these memories resulted in a considerable decrease in her emotional distress based on a reduced SUD level and allowed Gabrielle to believe that she was kind and caring with an increased VOC score. This event was related to Gabrielle's depression and sadness.

Case #1 Closure and Summary

After reprocessing these two traumatic events, Gabrielle's overall functioning, as manifestly observed and measured by her number of incidents involving aggression toward others, improved remarkably. During the next four months (from the time of the two EMDR sessions until her release from the juvenile justice facility), Gabrielle was involved in only one incident that required physical intervention by facility staff and temporary placement in isolation in a confinement room. This singular incident did not involve aggression toward a particular staff or peer but rather was due to Gabrielle's intense disappointment when her mother did not visit for the Christmas holidays.

A strong indication that EMDR therapy was a significant factor in the restoration of Gabrielle's emotional equilibrium was the abrupt cessation of outbursts and aggressive behavior toward staff or other youth. Numerous staff who worked with Gabrielle in various settings reported that she had become a very composed, responsible, and productive youth in the facility. For example, she was able to complete all of her community service hours (a requirement for successful completion of sanctions) by working in the facility kitchen. Few youth are able to complete community service hours while residents in the facility. The positive shift in self-confidence and composure, as reported by both Gabrielle and facility staff, points to the potential for pervasive recovery from trauma for youth with ID. After only two EMDR sessions, Gabrielle was able to focus on the successful completion of her treatment plan, and in a relatively short period of time she was released from the residential facility.

CASE #2: Using Trauma-Focused Cognitive-Behavioral Therapy to Address CSE-Linked Trauma to Resolve Symptoms of Anxiety, Depression, and Self-Blame

Case #2 Presentation

Jessica[2] was a seventeen-year-old Caucasian girl who was being asked by the FBI to assist with the prosecution of her abuser for trafficking and attempted sexual assault of two of her friends. The FBI caseworker assigned to her reported that Jessica was transported by her trafficker to various mobile homes in the community and sold to adult males for sexual activities ranging from oral sex to anal and vaginal intercourse for $50 each. Per the FBI's recommendation, Jessica began participating in weekly counseling sessions at an outpatient counseling center that primarily utilized TF-CBT and specialized in trauma-informed care. At the time, she was residing with her mother and requested that her mother be present for all of her sessions. Her therapist agreed to help her feel less anxious.

During the intake conducted by one of the authors of this chapter, Jessica demonstrated significant intellectual and functioning difficulties, including impaired long-term memory, poor comprehension of assessment questions, poor boundaries, limited insight into her current situation, and difficulty reading and writing. She was attending exceptional student education (ESE) classes in the eleventh grade and had been doing well, but her grades recently dropped because she was skipping classes frequently to be with her alleged abuser. Jessica said she met him through a friend but could not recall exactly when they met. She thought it was when she was approximately sixteen and he was twenty-one years old. She introduced him to her mother, and her mother gave permission for him to move into Jessica's bedroom shortly thereafter.

Jessica's mother also had learning difficulties. She only completed eight years of school, was unable to read much without assistance, had very limited math skills, and had an impaired memory. She could not recall the ages of her children and had difficulty counting coin currency. She relied on Jessica's father to send money from out of state, where he was staying temporarily for work. Jessica's mother noted that he was supposed to come back to Florida weeks ago but had not yet returned and had only been making minimal contact with them by phone. He had left home for long periods of time, often working as a migrant farm laborer, but this time she feared he was trying to permanently leave the family.

When asked in the first session why she and Jessica were at the counseling center, Jessica's mother was unclear, responding that she had been getting letters in the mail that she did not understand about Jessica's "boyfriend" being in trouble with the law. Jessica reported that she understood that she was there to talk about her "boyfriend" and that he could not see her anymore, but she said she did not want to talk about this situation because it made her sad. Jessica frequently presented as numb in session but was tearful as she said she missed her father and wondered if he would ever come back. Jessica's father was living with them during the time period that the trafficking occurred and the abuser was living in their home. Her parents knew that the abuser was giving the family money, but it was unclear how much Jessica's parents knew of his illegal activities with her. At first, Jessica denied ever having sex with anyone other than her abuser. She defiantly described how her abuser was like her husband, so she contributed to his family in any way that she could, and he contributed to hers.

At intake, Jessica completed a trauma symptom checklist to assess her level of trauma symptoms. However, Jessica's score on one of the validity scales contained in the assessment designed to detect underreporting of trauma symptoms was not within the limits recommended for considering the assessment results valid (Briere, 2011). It is unclear whether Jessica underreported on the assessment because of her reluctance to disclose information or because of some other cause, such as poor understanding of the assessment items. Nevertheless, Jessica demonstrated symptoms consistent with PTSD according to the diagnostic criteria outlined in the DSM-V (American Psychiatric Association [APA], 2013), including anxiety, depression, anger, irritability, labile affect, dissociation, low self-esteem, and avoidance of abuse reminders (APA, 2013). She was also having difficulty concentrating and sleeping since the arrest of her abuser. Jessica's anger was aimed at herself for "getting him in trouble," and at her friends for "betraying" her by telling their parents about the abuse. She noted that she worried about her abuser's safety and whether he was mad at her for trusting these friends. She had no prior history of mental health issues or treatment. Primary treatment goals for Jessica were to educate her about the dynamics of sexual abuse, increase personal boundaries and self-esteem, and reduce anxiety and depression.

Case #2 Cognitive-Behavioral Treatment and Assessment of Progress

Besides strong empirical support for TF-CBT, the counseling center where Jessica received counseling selected TF-CBT because it provides specific treatment guidelines, easily available training for therapists, and can be delivered by mental health professionals who have received a reasonable level of training and supervision. The goal of TF-CBT is to provide psychoeducation to the client and the caregiver and to assist them in identifying and coping with related feelings, cognitions, and behaviors. According to Cohen, Mannarino, and Knudsen (2005), it can be effectively used as part of a larger treatment plan for youth with other challenges as well. The TF-CBT model includes individual sessions for both the client and the parents, as well as parent-child joint sessions.

Both of Jessica's therapists completed TF-CBT training given directly by one of the creators of the model, Judith Cohen, in addition to a weekly online training for certification (requiring completion of forty training hours). In sessions with Jessica, the therapist followed the empirically supported CBT treatment protocol. The protocol typically takes twelve to sixteen sessions to complete. The phases of treatment are (1) psychoeducation and parenting skills, (2) relaxation, (3) feelings expression and regulation, (4) cognitive coping, (5) trauma narrative development and processing, (6) in vivo gradual exposure, (7) conjoint parent-child sessions, and (8) enhancing safety and future development (Cohen, Mannarino, & Deblinger, 2006). Jessica attended eight sessions total, but two of these were intake sessions during which a biopsychosocial history and assessment of current support systems were completed.

TF-CBT is designed to take place in the specific order dictated by the TF-CBT protocol, but Jessica's intellectual difficulties and anxiety symptoms did not lend themselves to completion in this exact order, so the therapist made a clinical judgment to address these areas in a slightly different order in order to provide maximum benefit to the client. In addition, the conjoint parent-child therapy sessions were initiated at the start of treatment rather than later in the process as dictated by TF-CBT protocols. Additionally, the trauma narrative and in vivo gradual exposure cannot be completed prior to the client perceiving emotional safety while disclosing the abuse or engaging in imaginal exposure to reminders of the abuse. This adaptation of the TF-CBT protocols limited treatment fidelity to the TF-CBT model but had a positive impact on Jessica's progress.

Enhancing Safety and Future Development

Jessica needed to gain a sense of emotional safety before being comfortable to meet with her therapist independently, so treatment to establish safety was completed from the beginning of therapy rather than waiting until the last step. With repetition of simple risk reduction and safety tools like following her instincts, saying "no" in an assertive way, and learning whom she could talk to in potentially dangerous situations, Jessica became more comfortable acknowledging that her instincts had told her something was wrong, and she learned that she could trust herself more in the future.

Psychoeducation and Parenting Skills

Even though Jessica was initially anxious about participating in treatment and was likely concerned that what was shared in session might be used against her offender later, she presented as cooperative. She was motivated to feel better and glad to have some support outside of her family, noting that she did not have any friends she could trust and needed help to be able to get a good job. After receiving concrete information from her therapist about what abuse is, how victims are often groomed into abusive acts, and how many others have experienced similar trauma, she became more expressive. After two sessions with one therapist, she had to switch to another provider but was able to feel emotionally safe enough to interact and share progressively more with her second therapist.

Jessica had her mother attend four sessions before she felt safe enough to participate in treatment individually. In these sessions, her mother was provided with information about how to support Jessica, including education about keeping her safe from contact with potential offenders. However, her mother did not make notable progress in this area, as evidenced by repeatedly answering the cell phone in the middle of session and saying she wanted to answer in case the call was from the alleged offender. Even though she knew he had done something "bad," she thought it would make Jessica feel better to hear from him. Her progress could have been limited by factors like poor insight, fear of losing the offender's financial support, or confusion about her role in the therapy process. Even with verbal praise and encouragement from the therapist, her participation in sessions remained minimal and consisted primarily of nodding her head or waiting for Jessica to respond for her. Jessica's mother's own intellectual disability and related factors appeared to be too substantial to overcome within this particular therapeutic context.

Relaxation

In the fourth treatment session, the therapeutic focus was on increasing Jessica's use of relaxation skills like deep breathing, and grounding techniques like counting, when feeling scared or overwhelmed emotionally. She practiced these relaxation skills in session, and she said she planned to use them while applying for jobs this week, because meeting new people usually made her nervous.

Trauma Narrative Development and Processing

It was not until Jessica understood in the fifth session that what she experienced with her trafficker was wrong that she was able to get in touch with and express feelings related to the abuse. She did not share more specifics of the trauma and said she still did not want to talk to the FBI more about it, but Jessica expressed that it felt good to not keep the secret.

Feelings Expression/Regulation and Cognitive Coping

At the end of treatment, Jessica acknowledged that she was told to participate in sexual activities by her "boyfriend" and that it was his idea to "earn money" this way. She cried, saying that she did not want to engage in these activities, but she wanted him to like her and knew that her family needed the money. When Jessica talked about how her trafficker insisted on being in charge of how much money was distributed to her and her family, the therapist gently initiated exploration of her cognitive distortion that she was to blame. In addition, he asked her to invite her friends over to the house, allegedly in hopes of recruiting them into sex trafficking too.

Jessica expressed that she still felt angry with her friends (who reported Jessica's abuse) and was not sure if she could ever learn to trust again. She also admitted that she was not sure if she could trust herself to not get in a fight with them if she saw them at school, but she knew that she had a choice to stop and think instead of acting out physically in anger. She was also able to talk more about feeling like she was "used." When her therapist encouraged her to look at her strengths and what made her a kind person with a bright future, she expressed feeling proud of herself for completing a job application (which was completed with the assistance of her therapist during session at Jessica's request) even though it took hours to finish. Before leaving, she smiled and said that she did look forward to a better future.

Case #2 Closure and Summary

After eight sessions, including two sessions for completion of Jessica's assessment, the FBI case worker informed Jessica's therapist that Jessica would not be able to continue counseling because of a lack of resources to transport her to the counseling center. During this relatively short time period, psychoeducational strategies were successful in normalizing Jessica's exposure to trauma and in reducing self-blame. Treatment strategies that involved teaching Jessica self-soothing skills imparted to her skills that she could use in varied environments to manage her anxiety and fear. Because she was given a safe place to revisit her trauma-related memories, she was able to identify inaccurate, self-blaming beliefs about her sexual exploitation. She was able to acknowledge her exploitation and experienced relief from the internal pressure to protect her abuser. Unfortunately, Jessica's mother was not able to fully engage in therapy, perhaps because of her own limited cognitive functioning.

Discussion

This chapter details what we know about symptomology and treatment options for girls with ID who have experienced sexual trauma involving CSE. Overall, this review of research illustrates that the treatment of sexually exploited girls with ID should focus on emotion regulation and challenging behaviors, especially self-injurious and aggressive behaviors. Adapted versions of empirically supported therapy modalities, such as CBT, DBT, and EMDR, are most commonly recommended for treating trauma symptoms in those with ID. Additionally, the therapy used should also be adapted to ensure that it is appropriate for the individual's verbal and cognitive capacities. The examination of prior research, which is limited to case study research, indicates that there is a clear need for further research into the efficacy of specific treatment modalities with individuals with ID.

The descriptions of clinical cases highlight the range of treatment needs of girls with ID who have experienced CSE and support the notion that a typology of sexually exploited youth exists with varied psychological symptomology (Reid, 2012). This chapter provides a description of one case that involved a client with severe symptomology that was significantly interfering with her functioning. The second case involved a client with ID who presented with moderate trauma symptoms, including anxiety, depression, and self-blame, as well as significant confusion about her experiences, relationships, and involvement with the prosecution of her abuser.

In the first case, CBT had been ineffective, and the client did not make progress in CBT treatment, as the client had no insight into the connection between her traumatic experiences and her disruptive behavior. With regard to EMDR treatment efficacy, the decrease of trauma symptoms in the first case following only two EMDR sessions conforms to findings of previous research describing EMDR case reports of trauma treatment for individuals with ID that also involved a relatively small number of sessions (Mevissen, Lievegoed, & De Jongh, 2011). Treatment effects of the two EMDR sessions were maintained for the entire remaining follow-up period of the client's detention in residential care, with a significant decrease in disruptive behavior, resolution in client's previous depression symptoms of sadness and guilt, and concrete evidence of improved social and adaptive skills. Currently, several treatment modalities (e.g., traumatic incident reduction, accelerated resolution therapy) have been developed that are similar to EMDR in that they focus on the resolution of traumatic memories using adaptive information processing to address dysfunctional cognitive, emotional, and somatic responses to trauma (SAMHSA's National Registry, 2016). However, we have focused on EMDR because, as shown in our research review previously discussed, its effectiveness with individuals with ID and with complex PTSD has been demonstrated in more than a few empirical studies.

In the second case, TF-CBT was effective in partially resolving the client's cognitive distortions regarding her experiences, resulting in decreased emotional distress and reduction in the client's confusion and self-blame for her abuse. Confusion and cognitive distortions regarding self-blame and self-responsibility for CSE are commonly reported as a significant problem impeding protection, intervention, and prevention of revictimization among survivors of CSE (Reid, 2010; Reid et al., 2013). The observation that TF-CBT positively impacted these common emotional and cognitive barriers to a client's acknowledgment and understanding of exploitation has important implications for this population and should be evaluated in future research.

These two clinical cases featuring EMDR and TF-CBT show positive results; nevertheless, the application of evidence-based treatment procedures for the resolution of trauma symptoms related to CSE, such as EMDR and TF-CBT, in the treatment of individuals with ID requires additional and more rigorous investigation. Research combining these two approaches is recommended to establish the most efficient treatment regime, whether EMDR, TF-CBT, or a combination of the two therapies. For example, investigating the integration of EMDR during the trauma narrative development and processing phase of TF-CBT or integrating EMDR resource development and installation (Korn & Leeds, 2002) during the enhancing safety and future development phase of TF-CBT may be beneficial.

Chapter Highlights

1. Presentation of Trauma
    a. Trauma symptom presentation may be atypical in exploited girls with intellectual disability.
    b. Trauma symptoms may be underreported and/or misperceived as developmental and/or behavioral difficulties.
    c. Aggression, agitated behavior, and avoidance of certain people, places, or activities may reflect trauma symptoms rather than noncompliance.
2. Empirically Supported Trauma Psychotherapy
    a. Trauma-focused cognitive-behavioral therapy (TF-CBT) and EMDR are most commonly recommended for treating trauma symptoms in those with intellectual disability.
    b. Therapy protocols may need to be individualized to ensure they are suited to the client's verbal and cognitive capacities.

Notes

1. One measure of intellectual functioning is based on an Intelligence Quotient (IQ) test score, with an IQ test score of around 70 or as high as 75 indicating a limitation in intellectual functioning (Schalock et al., 2010). Estimates indicate that somewhere between 1 and 3 percent of U.S. nationals have ID (Schalock et al., 2010).
2. Names of clients have been changed to protect client confidentiality.
3. Takedowns are techniques used by facility staff to redirect a youth to the ground in a controlled manner in order to limit the youth's physical resistance and to facilitate the application of a restraint device, if needed.
4. A security room used for the temporary isolation of youth from the general population. The confinement room at the facility was a small room that was locked from the outside with a metal door with a shatter-resistant observation window that allowed for observation. According to facility standards, maximum placement time for a youth in controlled observation was not to exceed 24 hours.
5. At the time of Gabrielle's detention, no youth screening for CSE or human trafficking was mandated at juvenile justice facilities.
6. A private house or an apartment, commonly in public housing projects, where drug dealers sell drugs. Also, known as a place where sex trafficking of teens occurs (Cunningham, 2015).

References

American Psychiatric Association. (2013). *Diagnostic and statistical manual of mental disorders* (5th ed.). Washington, DC: Author.

Barol, B. I., & Seubert, A. (2010). Stepping stones: EMDR treatment of individuals with intellectual and developmental disabilities and challenging behavior. *Journal of EMDR Practice and Research, 4*(4), 156–169. doi:10.1891/1933-3196.4.4.156

Briere, J. (2011). *Trauma Symptom Inventory-2: Professional manual.* Lutz, FL: PAR, Inc.

Brown, J. F., Brown, M., & Dibiasio, P. (2013). Treating individuals with intellectual disabilities and challenging behaviors with adapted dialectical behavior therapy. *Journal of Mental Health Research in Intellectual Disabilities, 6*(4), 280–303. doi:10.1080/19315864.2012.700684

Brown, S., & Shapiro, F. (2006). EMDR in the treatment of borderline personality disorder. *Clinical Case Studies, 5*(5), 403–420. doi:10.1177/1534650104271773

Cantor, C., & Price, J. (2007). Traumatic entrapment, appeasement and complex post-traumatic stress disorder: Evolutionary perspectives of hostage reactions, domestic abuse and the Stockholm syndrome. *Australian and New Zealand Journal of Psychiatry, 41*(5), 377–384. doi:10.1080/00048670701261178

Charlton, M., & Dykstra, E. (2011). Dialectical behaviour therapy for special populations: Treatment with adolescents and their caregivers. *Advances in Mental Health and Intellectual Disabilities, 5*(5), 6–14.

Choi, H., Klein, C., Shin, M., & Lee, H. (2009). Posttraumatic stress disorder (PTSD) and disorders of extreme stress (DESNOS) symptoms following prostitution and childhood abuse. *Violence Against Women, 15*(8), 933–951. doi:10.1177/1077801209335493

Clawson, H. J., Dutch, N., Solomon, A., & Grace, G. L. (2009). *Human trafficking into and within the United States: A review of the literature. Washington, DC: Office of the Assistant*

Secretary for Planning and Evaluation, U.S. Department of Health and Human Services.
Retrieved from https://aspe.hhs.gov/report/human-trafficking-and-within-united-states
-review-literature

Cohen, J. A., Mannarino, A., Berliner, L., & Deblinger, E. (2000). Trauma-focused cognitive behavioral therapy for children and adolescents: An empirical update. *Journal of Interpersonal Violence, 15*(11), 1202–1223. doi:10.1177/088626000015011007

Cohen, J. A., Mannarino, A., & Deblinger, E. 2006. *Treating trauma and traumatic grief in children and adolescents.* New York, NY: Guilford Press.

Cohen, J. A., Mannarino, A., & Knudsen, K. (2005). Treating sexually abused children: 1 year follow-up of a randomized controlled trial. *Child Abuse & Neglect, 29*(2), 135–145. doi:http://dx.doi.org/10.1016/j.chiabu.2004.12.005

Cunningham, A. (2015, September 14). *Oregon's teen trap houses offer drugs, but no exit.* WOMENSENEWS. Retrieved from http://womensenews.org/2015/09/oregons-teen-trap-houses-offer-drugs-but-no-exit/#

de Arellano, M., Lyman, D., Jobe-Shields, L., George, P., Dougherty, R., Daniels, A., . . . Delphin-Rittmon, M. (2014). Trauma-focused cognitive-behavioral therapy for children and adolescents: Assessing the evidence. *Psychiatric Services, 65*(5), 591–602. doi:10.1176/appi.ps.201300255

Estes, J. R., & Weiner, N. A. (2005). The commercial sexual exploitation of children in the United States. In S. W. Cooper, J. R. Estes, A. P. Giardino, N. D. Kellogg, & V. I. Vieth (Eds.), *Medical, legal & social science aspects of child sexual exploitation: A comprehensive review of child pornography, child prostitution, and internet crimes against children* (pp. 95–128). St. Louis, MO: GW Medical.

Frank, M. J., & Terwilliger, G. Z. (2015). Gang-controlled sex trafficking. *Virginia Journal of Criminal Law, 3,* 342–384.

Gilroy, K. A. (2015). Adapted dialectical behavior therapy skills group for adults with intellectual and developmental disabilities: A quasi-experimental trial. *Dissertation Abstracts International.* Order No. 3635742 American University, 2014. Ann Arbor: ProQuest. Web. 30 Oct. 2017.

Groce, N. E. (2004). *Global survey on HIV/AIDS and disability.* Washington, DC: World Bank.

Gust, D. A., Wang, S., Grot, J., Ransom, R., & Levine, W. (2003). National survey of sexual behavior and sexual behavior policies in facilities for individuals with mental retardation/developmental disabilities. *Mental Retardation, 41*(5), 365–373. doi:10.1352/0047-6765(2003)41<365:NSOSBA>2.0.CO;2

EMDR Institute. (2016). *US basic training overview.* Retrieved from http://www.emdr.com/us-basic-training-overview/

Farley, M., Cotton, A., Lynne, J., Zumbeck, S., Spiwak, F., Reyes, M., . . . Sezgin, U. (2004). Prostitution and trafficking in nine countries. *Journal of Trauma Practice, 2,* 33–74. doi:10.1300/J189v02n03_03

Fletcher, R., Loschen, E., Stavrakaki, C., & First, M. (2007). *DM-ID: Diagnostic manual-intellectual disability: A textbook of diagnosis of mental disorders in persons with intellectual disability.* Kingston, NY: National Association for the Dually Diagnosed (NADD) Press.

Future of Sex Education Initiative. (2012). National sexuality education standards: Core content and skills, K-12. Retrieved from http://www.futureofsexed.org/documents/josh-fose-standards-web.pdf

Herman, J. L. (1992). Complex PTSD: A syndrome in survivors of prolonged and repeated trauma. *Journal of Traumatic Stress, 3,* 377–391. doi:10.1002/jts.2490050305

Ijadi-Maghsoodi, R., Cook, M., Barnert, E., Gaboian, S., & Bath, E. (2016). Understanding and responding to the needs of commercially sexually exploited youth: Recommendations for the mental health provider. *Child & Adolescent Psychiatric Clinics of North America, 25*(1), 107–122. doi:http://dx.doi.org/10.1016/j.chc.2015.08.007

Isler, A., Tas, F., Beytut, D., & Conk, Z. (2009). Sexuality in adolescents with intellectual disabilities. *Sexuality and Disability, 27*(1), 27–34. doi:10.1007/s11195-009-9107-2

Keilty, J., & Connelly, G. (2001). Making a statement: An exploratory study of barriers facing women with an intellectual disability when making a statement about sexual assault to police. *Disability & Society, 16*(2), 273–291. doi:10.1080/09687590120035843

Kennedy, M. A., Klein, C., Bristowe, J., Cooper, B., & Yuille, J. (2007). Routes of recruitment: Pimps' techniques and other circumstances that lead to street prostitution. *Journal of Aggression, Maltreatment & Trauma, 15*(2), 1–19.

Kim, D., Bae, H., & Park, Y. C. (2008). Validity of the subjective units of disturbance scale in EMDR. *Journal of EMDR Practice and Research, 2*(1), 57–62. doi:10.1891/1933-3196.2.1.57

Korn, D. L. (2009). EMDR and the treatment of complex PTSD: A review. *Journal of EMDR Practice and Research, 3*(4), 264–278. doi:10.1891/1933-3196.3.4.264

Korn, D. L., & Leeds, A. (2002). Preliminary evidence of efficacy for EMDR resource development and installation in the stabilization phase of treatment of complex posttraumatic stress disorder. *Journal of Clinical Psychology, 58*(12), 1465–1487. doi:10.1002/jclp.10099

Linehan, M., & Wilks, C. (2015). The course and evolution of dialectical behavior therapy. *American Journal of Psychotherapy, 69*(2), 97–110.

Mansell, S., Sobsey, D., & Calder, P. (1992). Sexual abuse treatment for persons with developmental disabilities. *Professional Psychology: Research and Practice, 23*(5), 404–409. doi:10.1037/0735-7028.23.5.404

Mevissen, L., & de Jongh, A. (2010). PTSD and its treatment in people with intellectual disabilities: A review of the literature. *Clinical Psychology Review, 30*(3), 308–316. doi:http://dx.doi.org/10.1016/j.cpr.2009.12.005

Mevissen, L., Lievegoed, R., & De Jongh, A. (2011). EMDR treatment in people with mild ID and PTSD: 4 cases. *Psychiatric Quarterly, 82*(1), 43–57. doi:10.1007/s11126-010-9147-x

Mevissen, L., Lievegoed, R., Seubert, A., & de Jongh, A. (2011). Do persons with intellectual disability and limited verbal capacities respond to trauma treatment? *Journal of Intellectual and Developmental Disability, 36*(4), 278–283. doi:10.3109/13668250.2011.621415

Phasha, T. N., & Myaka, L. D. (2014). Sexuality and sexual abuse involving teenagers with intellectual disability: Community conceptions in a rural village of KwaZulu-Natal, South Africa. *Sexuality and Disability, 32*(2), 153–165. doi:10.1007/s11195-014-9344-x

Reid, J. A. (2010). Doors wide shut: Barriers to the successful delivery of victim services for domestically trafficked minors in a southern U.S. metropolitan area. *Women & Criminal Justice, 20*(1–2), 147–166. doi:10.1080/08974451003641206

——. (2012). *Evidence of a typology of trafficked girls: Submissives, sex slaves, and daredevils.* Paper presented at the annual meeting of the ASC Annual Meeting, Palmer House Hilton, Chicago, IL. Retrieved from http://citation.allacademic.com/meta/p585771_index.html

——. (2016a). Entrapment and enmeshment schemes used by sex traffickers. *Sexual Abuse: A Journal of Research and Treatment, 28*(6), 491–511. doi:10.1177/1079063214544334

——. (2016b). Sex trafficking of girls with intellectual disabilities: An exploratory mixed methods study. *Sexual Abuse: A Journal of Research and Treatment.* doi:10.1177/1079063216630981

Reid, J. A., Haskell, R., Dillahunt-Aspillaga, C., & Thor, J. A. (2013). Contemporary review of empirical and clinical studies of trauma bonding in violent or exploitative relationships. *International Journal of Psychology Research, 8*(1), 37–73.

Reid, J. A., Huard, J., & Haskell, R. (2015). Family-facilitated juvenile sex trafficking. *Journal of Crime and Justice, 38*(3), 361–376. doi:10.1080/0735648X.2014.967965

Rodenburg, R., Benjamin, A., de Roos, C., Meijer, A., & Stams, G. J. (2009). Efficacy of EMDR in children: A meta-analysis. *Clinical Psychology Review, 29*(7), 599–606. doi:http://dx.doi.org/10.1016/j.cpr.2009.06.008

Rodenburg, R., Benjamin, A., Meijer, A., & Jongeneel, R. (2009). Eye movement desensitization and reprocessing in an adolescent with epilepsy and mild intellectual disability. *Epilepsy & Behavior, 16*(1), 175–180. doi:http://dx.doi.org/10.1016/j.yebeh.2009.07.015

SAMHSA's National Registry of Evidence-Based Programs and Practices. (2016). Retrieved from http://nrepp.samhsa.gov/01_landing.aspx

Schalock, R. L., Borthwick-Duffy, S., Bradley, V., Buntinx, W., Coulter, D., . . . Yeager, M. (2010). *Intellectual disability: Definition, classification, and systems of supports* (11th ed.). Washington, DC: American Association on Intellectual and Developmental Disabilities.

Shapiro, F. (2001). *Eye movement desensitization and reprocessing: Basic principles, protocols, and procedures* (2nd ed.). New York, NY: Guilford Press.

Sobsey, R. (1992). *Violence and abuse in the lives of people with disabilities: The end of silent acceptance?* Baltimore, MD: Paul H. Brookes.

Solomon, E. P., & Heide, K. (2005). The biology of trauma: Implications for treatment. *Journal of Interpersonal Violence, 20*(1), 51–60. doi:10.1177/0886260504268119

Soylu, N., Alpaslan, A., Ayaz, M., Esenyel, S., & Oruç, M. (2013). Psychiatric disorders and characteristics of abuse in sexually abused children and adolescents with and without intellectual disabilities. *Research in Developmental Disabilities, 34*(12), 4334–4342. doi:http://dx.doi.org/10.1016/j.ridd.2013.09.010

Tharner, G. (2006). About the application of EMDR in the treatment of people with mild intellectual disabilities. In R. Didden (Ed.), *In Perspectief: Gedragsproblemen, psychiatrische stoornissen en lichte verstandelijke beperking (In perspective: Behavior problems, psychiatric disorders and mild mental disorders)* (pp. 145–168). Houten, Netherlands: Bohn Stafleu van Loghum.

Tomasulo, D. J., & Razza, N. J. (2007). Post-traumatic stress disorder. In R. Fletcher, E. Loschen, C. Stavrakaki, & M. First (Eds.), *Diagnostic manual—intellectual disability (DM-ID): A textbook of diagnosis of mental disorders in persons with intellectual disability* (pp. 365–378). Kingston, NY: NADD Press.

U.S. Department of State (2012). *Trafficking in persons report 2012.* Retrieved from http://www.state.gov/j/tip/rls/tiprpt/2012/

van der Kolk, B., McFarlane, A., & Weisaeth, L. (2007). *Traumatic stress: The effects of overwhelming experience on mind, body, and society.* New York, NY: Guilford Press.

Wechsler, D. (2003). *Wechsler intelligence scale for children* (4th ed.). San Antonio, TX: The Psychological Corporation.

Wissink, I. B., van Vugt, E., Moonen, X., Stams, G., & Hendriks, J. (2015). Sexual abuse involving children with an intellectual disability (ID): A narrative review. *Research in Developmental Disabilities, 36*, 20–35. doi:http://dx.doi.org/10.1016/j.ridd.2014.09.007

Wolpe, J. (1958). *Psychotherapy by reciprocal inhibition.* Stanford, CA: Stanford University Press.

World Health Organization. (2013). *Assessment and management of conditions specifically related to stress: mhGAP intervention guide module* (version 1.0). Geneva: World Health Organization. Retrieved from http://apps.who.int/iris/bitstream/10665/85623/1/9789241505932_eng.pdf?ua=1

Worthington, R. (2012). Dealing with trauma as an intervention for aggression: A review of approaches and the value of reprocessing. *Journal of Aggression, Conflict and Peace Research, 4*(2), 108–118. doi:10.1108/17596591211208319

PART III

PROGRAMMATIC DESIGN

Part III focuses on programmatic design, specifically on organizational models and policies that could be adopted by various organizations serving trafficked and exploited people. This set of chapters opens with chapter 12, which offers a description of the Sanctuary Model, an evidence-supported, trauma-informed, and trauma-responsive organizational culture approach to addressing the needs of children, adolescents, adults, and families who have been exposed to repeated and sustained violence and abuse. The author maintains that victims of commercial exploitation, abuse, and trafficking have experienced physical and psychological injuries but also suffer from moral injury, defined as a betrayal of what is right and a related denial of agency. The Sanctuary Model is a trauma-informed and trauma-responsive whole-organization model that works to establish an organizational cultural approach to enable a program, a system, or even an entire community to organize itself around a shared vision, a knowledge foundation, and a set of values, language, and practices to counter the complex effects of trauma. This model can provide the foundation for any program working with trafficked and exploited people.

Chapter 13 follows three individual case examples from practice experiences that highlight extensive challenges within multiple areas of service provision and law enforcement. Written from the dual perspectives of a mental health practitioner with a street-outreach program and a researcher, this chapter describes three individuals in St. Louis, Missouri, who experienced sexual exploitation and were particularly vulnerable to existing gaps in services. This chapter highlights the barriers and supports that practitioners experience in meeting the needs of each individual with available resources, in addition to the strengths and challenges of providing time-intensive, long-term, and client-centered support with sexually exploited individuals. The authors close by discussing the ability of current, available resources and evidence-based practices to meet the needs of individuals in a practice environment, as well as the service and research gaps to be addressed in the future.

Chapter 14 documents the challenges to programmatic design in child welfare systems and gives recommendations for change. The author notes that sex traffickers often seek out those with vulnerability and employ manipulative tactics to create opportunity for exploitation. A review of 93 cases of sexually exploited girls and interviews with their case managers revealed that in approximately half of these cases exploitation in sex trafficking occurred after the girls had contact with child welfare and/or had been placed in state care. This chapter examines the links between the schemes and strategies of sex traffickers and various factors such as victim and situational characteristics observed in cases involving girls in foster care. The unique design of the child welfare system made girls in state care more susceptible to exploitation—such as placing previously trafficked girls in homes without providing appropriate protection for other girls, allowing girls placed in foster care to keep cell phones provided by traffickers, and locating group homes within high-crime areas, thus furnishing sex traffickers with easy access to runaway girls. Complex youth distress—such as frequent running away, extensive maltreatment histories, and heightened reactivity to stress—made protection efforts by child welfare very difficult. It is crucial to implement and evaluate program designs that consider these factors.

Chapter 15 focuses specifically on commercially sexually exploited (CSE) survivors of human trafficking, highlighting the strengths of social work models and theories that assist CSE survivors and the professionals that serve them. The chapter describes the utility of the single-point-of-contact social worker model, which provides coordinated and streamlined services, including the immediate, short-, and long-term services necessary to rebuild the lives of people exploited through trafficking. Safety from their traffickers, housing, medical treatment, and other basic human needs, as well as trauma-informed services, are needed during the period of immediate stabilization; this period is followed by an intermediate period in which survivors may need assistance with employment and permanent housing, and for foreign-born victims, legal assistance for family reunification and adjustment of legal immigration status. Social workers are at the center of providing immediate and stabilizing support.

CHAPTER 12

THE SANCTUARY MODEL AND SEX TRAFFICKING

Creating Moral Systems to Counteract Exploitation and Dehumanization

SANDRA BLOOM, MD, DREXEL UNIVERSITY

Given the many psychological devices for disengaging moral control, societies cannot rely entirely on individuals, however righteous their moral standards, to provide safeguards against human cruelty. Civilized life requires, in addition to humane personal codes, social systems that uphold compassionate behavior and renounce cruelty. (Bandura, 2002, p. 116)

The Sanctuary Model is an evidence-supported, trauma-informed, and trauma-responsive organizational culture approach to addressing the needs of children, adolescents, adults, and families who have been exposed to overwhelming and usually repeated and sustained maltreatment, violence, and systematic dehumanization. We will describe the application of the Sanctuary Model to the treatment of trafficking victims from the lens of one young survivor, Maria.

Maria and the Nightmare of a Trafficked Childhood[1]

When Maria was three years old, her mother abandoned her for reasons that are unclear, leaving her in the care of her maternal grandmother. Given the behavior of the grandmother, we certainly can speculate as to what was behind that maternal abandonment. Whatever the case, after a few years, the grandmother brought Maria from Puerto Rico to the United States. The grandmother was Maria's first trafficker, selling the child for sex in the back room of their home when she was only eleven years old. When Maria protested, her grandmother beat her and threatened to abandon her in Philadelphia and return to Puerto Rico. By adolescence, Maria's development was entirely skewed around disrupted attachment experiences, maltreatment, a lack of love, and utter perplexity about meaning and purpose other than basic survival.

When Maria turned fifteen, she fled from her grandmother's home, believing that she would be better off on her own. On the streets of Philadelphia, she met another girl her age. The two quickly bonded, and her new friend offered to introduce Maria to her boyfriend, Mario, who had a place where the two girls could stay. Maria agreed, relieved to find a home, and unknowingly moved in with the predator who would become her second trafficker.

Initially, the girls had a great time with Mario. He paid to have their hair and nails done and took them out to clubs, buying the girls drinks and food without question. For girls who have known hunger and deprivation, these actions served to bond them ever more closely to their captor. Soon things changed. One evening Mario brought the girls to a hotel for a party. When they got inside the hotel room, Mario put a gun to her head and told Maria to strip. Both girls were raped repeatedly that night. In the days that followed, the girls were held in the hotel and told they needed to perform sex acts with men or they would be killed. Food was brought in only when the girls stopped fighting and complied. Mario provided the girls with alcohol, marijuana, and cocaine but kept them in captivity for weeks. Soon life in the hotel became routine, the men continued to come, and Mario would beat the girls if they protested. Following each beating Mario would apologize and talk about how they were a "family," each needing to do their part. The idea of family as defined by Mario would not have been a difficult concept for Maria to accept. She had always been abused in her family, so Mario's behavior was normative, not exceptional. At the same time, for such a child, the need to attach to a family would have been too intense to ignore, and even if she could have found a way to escape, where would she go?

A year had passed since Maria had left her grandmother's home. Mario recruited several more girls but was most attentive to Maria. It was not long before Maria was pregnant with his child. While he initially beat her for becoming pregnant, he required less work from her as long as she kept his other girls in line, behavior that then coerced Maria into becoming a persecutor of her friends, transforming her into a cotrafficker. Following the birth of her child, Mario took the baby to be raised by his mother, allowing Maria visits only when he felt she "deserved" to see her child, that is, when she had been most compliant to his wishes. She let the baby go without much protest, never having the chance to properly bond with the child and never grieving the child's loss. Let's pause at this point in Maria's story and explore what we can surmise about

Maria's development, as well as review some of the literature published about this critical issue.

Victims of commercial exploitation, abuse, and enslavement like Maria have experienced profound physical and psychological injuries. Many of them suffer from what has been described as "Complex PTSD" so that they have significant difficulties with regulation of emotions while experiencing challenges in maintaining attention and may chronically dissociate into altered states of awareness (Herman, 1992). Their self-perception is largely determined by the extreme exposure to continual helplessness and an inability to exert mastery in their environment because of enslavement. Likewise, they will perceive their perpetrators as all-powerful, even when they are no longer actually present in their lives, conferring on them the magical powers of a god to whom they owe total obedience. This willingness to obey would have been prepared for by abandonment and maltreatment in earlier childhood, laying the groundwork for a "normal" experience of human attachment.

Called "Stockholm Syndrome," "capture bonding," or "trauma bonding," the phenomenon of developing strong and often impermeable bonds to those who are abusive is well documented among prisoners of war, victims of domestic violence, child abuse survivors, cult members, and hostages (Dutton & Painter, 1981; Herman, 1992; Lifton, 1963; Strenz, 1982). The human need to attach to other humans in order to survive is so powerful that it strengthens even as the attachment figures are the very ones who are threatening survival.

For victims of trafficking, all other relationships are likely to be strongly influenced by their previous relational experiences, which are likely to be compulsively reenacted within every new relationship. Maria has already played out the three key roles of traumatic reenactment, also known as the Drama Triangle: Victim, Persecutor, Rescuer (Bloom & Farragher, 2010). She has clearly been victimized repeatedly in every relationship, so Maria falls readily into the Victim role in this nightmarish relationship dynamic. In her imagination, and to the extent he fed and clothed her, Mario began as her Rescuer and then quickly became her Persecutor. Then by coercing her into controlling the other captive girls, he placed her squarely in the role of Persecutor while another girl became Victim, and sometimes this situation also gives Maria the opportunity to play out the role of Rescuer as she defends or protects one of the other girls. In fact, Maria knows very little about playing any *other* roles. She has never been able to be a loved child, a mother, a friend, or a student or have any normal and healthy relationships. Traumatic reenactment is her normative experience.

And even her body is not her own. Trafficking victims like Maria are exposed to constant physical brutality so that over time they develop chronic injuries. Compounding the injuries is the ever-present threat of violence, and such chronic stress may exacerbate the medical problems, as will the body memories typically associated with PTSD secondary to captivity and serious bodily harm.

Maria's Moral Development

Given the enormity of these problems, it is easy to overlook another component of complex PTSD: "alterations in systems of meaning." Victims of trafficking have not only suffered physical, sexual, and psychological injury but have also experienced profound "moral injury," defined as "betrayal of what's right in a high-stakes situation by someone who holds power" (Shay, 2003, p. 240). How do you maintain any sense of right and wrong when other human beings, often your own family members, systematically corrupt everything that gives life purpose and meaning and no one else in the culture protects you? The resultant loss of moral agency—the loss of the power to refrain from behaving inhumanely as well as the power to actively behave humanely—requires repair, and this repair must be a fundamental component of healing (Bandura, 2002; Doron, Sar-El, Mikulincer, & Kyrios, 2012).

At the point where we interrupt her story, Maria has transited through childhood and adolescence, and her developmental trajectory—physically, psychologically, socially, and morally—has been profoundly affected by the systematic dehumanization and brutalization that she has been exposed to throughout her young life. Normally, during adolescence a growing sense of agency and moral identity, or "thinking about the sort of person I want to be, and how I make the choices that fulfill and embody my moral identity," are consolidating, grounded in previous attachment relationships (Adshead, 2013, p. 341).

A growing body of research has demonstrated that human morality is constrained by the evolutionary and biological forces that have determined human survival (Johnson, 1993). We have evolved as a social primate species with a hierarchy of needs that begin as individual survival needs but then extend to family, extended family, community, and the entire species and biosphere (Shermer, 2004). It has been theorized that humans evolved a moral instinct that serves these fundamental group needs, a capacity that naturally grows within each child, designed to generate rapid judgments about what is morally right or wrong based on an unconscious grammar of action (Hauser, 2007).

According to theorists who have been studying the role of moral development in the human species, morality serves to bind the individual to his or her social group, culture, or "moral system." Moral systems can be viewed as "interlocking sets of values, virtues, norms, practices, identities, institutions, technologies, and evolved psychological mechanisms that work together to suppress or regulate selfishness and make coordinated social life possible" (Graham & Haidt, 2012, p. 14).

However, it is becoming clear that the further we move away from our biological and evolutionary roots, now driven by our cultural evolution, the more problematic our adaptation to our environment becomes. That people can be viewed as property and enslaved to serve the need for material wealth and sexual insatiability is but one of many examples (van Schaik & Michel, 2016).

Because moral development extends throughout childhood, the earlier that children are exposed to abusive and unjust experiences, the more likely they are to have their moral development negatively impacted and to suffer the damaging biological, psychological, and social impacts that we know exist. As one key author points out, "Everything that psychologists know from the study of children's moral development indicates that moral identity—the key source of moral commitment throughout life—is fostered by multiple social influences that guide a child in the same general direction" (Damon, 1999, p. 77). These social influences begin at birth and continue throughout our lives, and because of the lengthy and complicated nature of human development, relational problems can throw a wrench into the process of healthy moral development that supports individuals being able to define and function within the complex balancing act of satisfying individual needs and the needs of the group (National Scientific Council on the Developing Child, 2004).

Maria's moral system thus far is purely focused on survival and exploitation. She has been consistently lied to and betrayed by other human beings, and it is from other human beings that we develop a shared sense of our moral universe. Her internal moral compass has not developed beyond the early stages that focus more on the exigencies of basic survival and obedience to authority, regardless of how brutal. She has known nothing else. The world of trafficking is the normal world for Maria.

Can anything be done for Maria? Let's look at what she will need from what we know so far. We know that Maria's attachments to other human beings are based on exploitation and traumatic reenactment, so she will need an entire context of consistent, reliable, safe, and trustworthy relationships so that she can experience human beings in relationship in an entirely different way. For quite some time she is unlikely to trust the quality and nature of those relationships, so she will be constantly testing the boundaries and limits with other people in a wide variety of ways—physically, sexually, and psychologically. This means that she will learn by trial and error, so there will be mistakes. She is likely to flee many times, perhaps psychologically or perhaps physically, before she trusts a new normative environment. It is very difficult for humans to change norms, and she will be readily seduced back into her former life if the predators she knows gain access to her. She will look closely for any moral inconsistencies in a new environment, using those inconsistencies as a way of confirming an internal and unstated belief that "they" (other people) are all alike. There is comfort in this notion because hopelessness about ever having meaningful relationships will successfully keep her away from the enormity of loss that she will inevitably experience if she confronts the horror of her past. She is likely to suffer from symptoms of dissociation, a survival skill for living with chronic abuse.

The chronic hyperarousal, so typical of those exposed to systematic violence, will also be obvious. Thus at some point she is going to need trauma-specific treatment to help alleviate those symptoms. A new environment must be enriched by options for further development that Maria has never had—academic development, artistic and creative outlets, and relationship opportunities. She will need help defining for the first time, with no role models of her own, what it means to be a parent if she is going to have any future relationship with the child she has already birthed as well as other children she may have in the years to come. Given this level of complexity, what do we already know about addressing the needs of trafficking victims? For that we turn to a review of the literature.

Literature Review

Ideally, Maria would have access to a residential setting where the complexity of her needs could be systematically assessed and delivered. Although the body of literature related to sex trafficking is growing rapidly, we still do not have an extensive body of knowledge about treatment, particularly treatment in a residential setting (Clawson & Grace, 2007; Williamson, Dutch, & Clawson, 2010). In 2013 a national survey of residential programs aimed at victims of sex trafficking was released (Reichert & Sylwestrzak, 2013). The survey found that there were 33 residential programs nationally with 682 beds in sixteen states and the District of Columbia. Twenty-eight states had no residential programs specifically for victims of sex trafficking and at the time had no plans to open any. Only 36 percent were exclusive to victims of domestic sex trafficking, and most available beds were designated for minor victims. There were fewer than 28 beds for male victims of sex trafficking.

It is well established that many of the young girls and women who come into residential settings have already experienced abuse at the hands of family members and have run away from home to escape this maltreatment, only to be exploited by professional traffickers (Estes & Weiner, 2001). It is clear that female victims of sex trafficking develop symptoms very similar to those of girls and women who have experienced high levels of adverse childhood experiences, including childhood sexual abuse trauma, as well as those experiencing domestic violence or political torture. For example, according to one study, 82 percent of trafficked victims had experienced sexual abuse before being trafficked (Farley, Lynne, & Cotton, 2005). Another study of residents in a program demonstrated that over half had been victims of physical abuse by a household member (Thomson, Hirshberg, Corbett, Valila, & Howley, 2011). In a study comparing youth who had been commercially sexually abused with other sexually abused comparison youth, those who had been prostituted had a significantly higher array of emotional and behavioral symptoms (Cole, Sprang, Lee, & Cohen, 2016).

To complicate matters further, victims of trafficking are often labeled as criminals who are willingly engaged in prostitution (Mitchell, Finkelhor, & Wolak, 2010). As a consequence, engagement in any kind of therapeutic process has often been negatively affected by the girls' or young women's previous experience in other settings, such as juvenile justice, homeless shelters, child welfare, and foster care (Ward & Patel, 2006), as well as by a lack of specialized services for this population (Clawson & Grace, 2007; Fong & Berger Cardoso, 2010; Murrell, 2016). The emphasis in child welfare on family preservation and least restrictive environments, beside the constant demand for lowering costs, contradicts what is known about an approach to trafficking victims, which often requires restrictive, well-prepared, and specialized approaches to people who have no available family (Murrell, 2016).

In one descriptive study of a group home program for adolescent girls who had been engaged in prostitution and were sent to the facility through juvenile court, these girls had had considerable exposure to violence and abuse throughout their lives and had high rates of mental disorders, including PTSD, as well as low IQs. The recidivism for the program was 50 percent (Twill, Green, & Traylor, 2010). In another study, adopting a specialized approach significantly improved recidivism rates in a residential program. The authors suggested that for better treatment outcomes, youth admitted for residential treatment for sexual exploitation should display three key characteristics: (1) willingness to acknowledge sexual exploitation and/or at-risk behaviors; (2) ability to commit to living safely in a group home, and (3) desire to transform their lives. This particular program used a "Stages of Change" approach that helped the young people be more receptive to treatment and that assessed progress. Having survivor mentors as part of the program was seen to be an important component of care. The authors also emphasized that the living environment should balance freedom with clear structure and boundaries, accompanied by life skills education and family therapy in a culturally competent context (Thomson et al., 2011).

Research and experience have shown that victims of sex trafficking are likely to need intensive residential treatment to address the complex problems related to a lifetime of abuse. It is within such a structured and safe environment that active treatment can be implemented. Cognitive therapy, cognitive-behavioral therapy, stress inoculation, exposure therapy, psychoeducational approaches, and EMDR have all shown evidence of positive results in some complex cases (Kotrla, 2010; Williamson et al., 2010). Coordinating service delivery is a critical component of improvement, and these young people often have extremely complicated case management issues relating to court cases, other legal matters, medical complications, educational and financial needs, and family concerns. Experts agree that residential placement should be part of a continuum of care but should last at least eighteen months (Clawson & Grace, 2007). Richard Estes, a social policy professor at the University of Pennsylvania and an expert on child sexual exploitation, has said that the "best fighting chance for victims is 24/7 residential care for a long period of time. This is not a quick fix situation. It really is a rebuilding and remolding of personality and character" (Markman, 2009, p. 1). Given this shortage of residential settings, it is unlikely that Maria will find that level of intervention.

Most victims of international and domestic sex trafficking do not receive adequate services because of multiple barriers, including (1) an inadequate understanding of sex trafficking on the part of providers; (2) an emphasis throughout the U.S. healthcare system on minimizing residential services and costs as well as the time people spend in any protective setting, including shelters; (3) serious security concerns, given that most residential types of placement are geographically known by traffickers and the women that are getting services in the program may become trafficking recruiters within the program itself; and (4) the enormous complexity of the problems associated with chronic abuse and degradation, including the formation of trauma bonds also known as the "Stockholm Syndrome." In a recent doctoral dissertation, the author illustrates many of the significant barriers to achieving more long-lasting change in residential settings, while at the same time emphasizing previous research on the importance of organizational culture in positively influencing the staff (Murrell, 2016).

Maria Finally Gets Help

Maria's life began to change when she was arrested during a police sting operation in a local hotel where she was engaged in sex work. She became violent with the police officers and was subsequently taken into custody. While she was being charged with assault and possession, she was identified by the juvenile court system as a trafficking victim. Her case was transferred to a special court for juvenile trafficking victims. Maria was referred to New Day, a Salvation Army outpatient program, for case management services. Over a decade ago, leaders in the Philadelphia arm of the Salvation Army had been trained in the Sanctuary Model. The Salvation Army has a long history and mission of fighting the dehumanizing horrors of human trafficking both internationally and domestically. It was natural, then, when developing a program for trafficking victims, that the program would be grounded in the Sanctuary Model.

What Is the Sanctuary Model?

The Sanctuary Model is a trauma-informed and trauma-responsive methodology for creating a moral system that supports recovery from trauma and the restoration of moral agency; when appropriate, it includes trauma-specific therapy that can be coherently offered (Bloom, 2016). An organizational culture approach enables a program, a system, or even an entire community to organize itself around a shared vision, a knowledge foundation, values, language, and practice to create a total service delivery environment to counter the complex effects of traumatic exposure. The overarching intent of the model is to enable groups of people to consciously and deliberately create a moral climate that can be sustained by new generations of administrators, staff, and clients. The model is based on a structured process that enables the staff and clients within organizations to shift their mental models, the very basic assumptions that exist far below conscious awareness and everyday function and yet guide and determine what we can and cannot think about and act upon (Senge, 1994). In Maria's case, changing mental models requires that staff, law enforcement, and courts thoroughly understand the dynamics of trafficking and respond in a therapeutic, not punitive, way.

The origins of the Sanctuary Model date back to the mid-1980s, when my colleagues and I created a short-term, voluntary psychiatric inpatient unit for adults who had been maltreated as children. We called that program "The Sanctuary," building on the idea that many youth had experienced the "sanctuary trauma" of expecting a protective environment and finding only more trauma (Silver, 1986). From 1991 to 2001, when we closed the program because the mental health system was unwilling to pay for specialty care, we treated thousands of trauma survivors, most of whom had endured a wide variety of adverse childhood experiences and then more trauma as adults. During that period of ever-increasing systemic stress on the human service delivery system—a situation that continues to this day—we began to develop a methodology for quickly and efficiently getting everyone in the environment "on the same page." Later, that evolved into the evidence-supported methodology now known as the Sanctuary Model.[2] Over time and in collaboration with many colleagues in a variety of settings, including an NIMH study that began to supply an evidence base, this original learning evolved into an organizational culture approach that has now influenced service delivery in hundreds of settings, including residential programs for children and adults, substance abuse facilities, juvenile justice programs, inpatient and outpatient psychiatric settings, shelters, and schools (Abramovitz & Bloom, 2003; Bloom, 2012, 2013; Bloom & Farragher, 2010, 2013; Esaki et al., 2013; Rivard, 2004; Rivard et al., 2003; Rivard et al., 2004).

It is the goal of the Sanctuary Model to reduce sanctuary trauma, vicarious trauma, burnout, and treatment failure. We organize the Sanctuary Model into four main categories that we call "pillars": Trauma Theory, the Sanctuary Commitments, SELF, and the Sanctuary Toolkit. The overriding purpose is to help organizations to create and maintain physical, psychological, social, and moral safety within their environment and to confront and eliminate systemic violence in all its forms, while counteracting the destructive parallel processes that so typically characterize human service delivery organizations (Bloom & Farragher, 2013).

The Sanctuary Model and a New Day

The Salvation Army New Day Drop-In Center is the centerpiece of the effort to address human trafficking in Philadelphia. The center is a safe, trauma-informed, welcoming, and nonjudgmental space for women suffering from sex trafficking and commercial sexual exploitation in the Kensington neighborhood of Philadelphia. It is strategically located in the heart of the neighborhood; a simple sign on the door reading, "women only drop-in: food, clothing, toiletries" identifies the center, which is open during the day and two late nights per week when other service agencies are not available. Many of the women seen are suffering from the "force, fraud and coercive" tactics of sex trafficking and are seeking safety. Staff members work to build rapport with individuals who have had their trust violated and are trained to look for human-trafficking red flags; they are also trained to address the women's specialized psychological, social, emotional, and physical needs. In addition to the physical drop-in center space, the Salvation Army provides an array of case management services. Staff, interns, and volunteers are also trained in trauma-informed care and are a consistent presence in the community. The center incorporates the Sanctuary Model, which includes teaching the staff about trauma theory with a specific emphasis on trafficking, using the Sanctuary Commitments as anchoring values, and running weekly SELF (safety, emotions, loss, and future) groups.

Pillar One: Trauma Theory

When the police brought Maria to New Day, she encountered a staff who were already well versed in Trauma Theory, the first pillar of the Sanctuary Model. Trauma theory represents an extensive knowledge base that includes what we now know about the impact of trauma and adversity; child development; developmental, social, and spiritual neuroscience; and group dynamics.

Implementing the Sanctuary Model begins with a process of education (see the box titled Universal Training in the Sanctuary Model). The knowledge base that now exists around trauma and adversity is extensive. To adequately embrace an organizational culture approach, everyone in the system must be on the same page. Staff members must be equipped to teach women like Maria about a new understanding of what has happened to her and how the maltreatment continues to affect her decisions, behaviors, thoughts, and feelings. The main premise of systems theory is that every individual component of any system influences and is influenced by every other component (Napier & Gershenfeld, 2004). The education process, therefore, needs to extend from the Board of Directors, regulatory agencies, and management staff to the clinicians, care staff, food service workers, maintenance people, finance and administrative staff, clients, and, as much as possible, their families. Regular trainings occur for new staff, done by a long-term manager in the Salvation Army who has been instrumental in maintaining the Sanctuary Model over the last decade.

SELF Group Psychoeducation

Educating the clients about the effects of trauma and adversity is critically important as an early part of the treatment process, and it is more effective when peers can be learning together. The group dynamics theorist Kurt Lewin believed that the primary task of psychoeducation was to promote a change in the person's self-perception. He found that the change in the perception of oneself preceded changes in knowledge, values, and beliefs, and only when this change occurred would there be a lasting change in behavior (Coghlan & Jacobs, 2005).

Psychoeducation has always been an indispensable part of the Sanctuary Model. As a result of their experiences in the world, including previous experiences with the mental health and social service systems, many trafficking victims enter environments that are supposed to be therapeutic with very negative perceptions of themselves and the world around them. Psychoeducation about the impact of psychological injuries can change those beliefs. By understanding how they came to be injured, people begin to develop hope that recovery from those injuries is possible. When the staff see what the clients do with this information and how readily they understand and relate to the material, the staff realize that they are now much better aligned with the clients, at least on a cognitive level, and then treatment planning becomes more coherent for both staff and clients. Instead of drawing on their own folk psychology, which may or may not be helpful, all staff members can draw on a scientific knowledge base for why we do what we do and feel what we feel under conditions of extreme stress.

We have created a number of psychoeducational curricula that are organized around SELF, the fundamental parts of recovery—safety, emotional management, loss, and future—that help clients shift their understanding of what has happened to them, how they have responded to those events, and the role they must play in their own recovery (see the box titled SELF: A Trauma-Informed Group Psychoeducational Curriculum).

In the fast-paced human service world that most of us function in today, if a curriculum is going to be useful and if it going to create an interactive group process, it has to be simple enough to be delivered by staff members who have a minimum of training while still being applicable when used by more experienced professionals. In many cases, one cannot expect that every client will have the time to experience the entire curriculum. Many treatment experiences, like those at New Day, are so brief that a curriculum that builds on previous lessons, as is typical in an educational setting, is simply not appropriate. Therefore, each lesson must embody at least part of the whole curriculum, and the entire curriculum must be flexible enough so that each lesson can stand on its own. To be maximally useful in a short-term treatment or shelter setting, it must be possible for a staff member to decide that "Today, we need to focus on loss" or "We are confronting some safety issues in the community, and I am going to do the lesson on social safety today" and not have to use the material in a set sequence. At New Day, the staff focus mostly on safety and emotional management, largely because the women they see there are still "in the life," and it is critical to help them develop concepts for safety, learn how to achieve safety, and learn how to manage overwhelming emotions. New Day uses a "Stages of Change" model; most of the women they see are in "precontemplation," and they hope to move them toward "contemplation" and some toward "action" (Levesque, Prochaska, & Prochaska, 1999).

Pillar Two: The Sanctuary Commitments—a Moral System

To create deep and long-term organizational change, we need just the right number of values that are based on principles that guide short-term, everyday conduct as well as long-term strategy. If there are too many rules, the system becomes rigid, inflexible, and even paralyzed, as witnessed by morally absolutist, dictatorial systems. If there are too few, it becomes purely individualistic and chaotic. The Sanctuary Commitments require organizational members to remember the multiple ways in which we demonstrate our moral principles through what we say, what we do, and how we do it.

The Sanctuary Commitments represent ancient wisdom. We have taken the tenets of this ancient wisdom and compiled them, articulated them into a cohesive whole, and developed a methodology to organize disparate groups around them. They cannot be "cherry-picked"; all seven Sanctuary Commitments are interactive and interdependent. They become the norms that change the habits of thought and behavior that structure the organizational culture and make it easier for organizational leaders to consciously and deliberately apply Sanctuary principles to whatever they do. They help everyone in a system to become morally aligned with one another. These principles are especially important when the organization is under stress. Under conditions of chronic stress, group processes that lead to moral disengagement are more likely to occur (Bandura, 2002).

When Maria entered New Day for the first time, what she first saw was the Sanctuary Commitments painted on the walls of the facility. These remind the women served, the volunteers, and the staff of the organization's values and expectations. All staff and volunteers are trained in the Sanctuary Model and support the Sanctuary Commitments. The model emphasizes establishing healthy group environments that are values-based and anchored by all seven Sanctuary Commitments, and this emphasis encourages everyone to take moral action whenever there is a perceived violation of basic principles. This is critically important for survivors like Maria, who have never been in an environment utilizing any kind of moral principles and who therefore have never had the opportunity to develop a coherent moral identity.

In the Sanctuary Model, prevention and early intervention are key to developing and sustaining a healthy environment. Participants are guided toward an understanding of collective dynamics, learn about the development and resolution of "collective disturbances," and learn how to manage and redirect traumatic reenactment (Bloom & Farragher, 2013).

For the organizational moral climate to be ethically consistent, the Sanctuary Commitments need to be embraced by the Board of Directors and senior leadership and then conveyed throughout the organization: through middle management, to the direct care and support staff, and ultimately to the clients. When organizational leaders hear the Seven Commitments, they often believe that these commitments already constitute the organizational culture. But when these leaders engage in a different kind of dialogue with other members of their community, they find that people's views vary on what these commitments mean and how to make them real in everyday interactions. Experience has taught that moral leadership is critical to system change, and without it, substantial change is unlikely to occur (Bloom, 2013; Bloom & Farragher, 2010, 2013). In the following pages we will expand on what the seven Sanctuary Commitments mean in a Sanctuary framework.

Commitment to Nonviolence

Because victims of sex trafficking often engage in a wide variety of unsafe behaviors, helping them redefine safety within a group context is vital to recovery.

At New Day, physical safety is paramount because the center is in a neighborhood known for high crime, easy access to heroin, and vulnerability to sex traffickers. Not only do new women enter weekly, but most of the women seen in the center manage to survive in the community every day, and the program needs a structure to keep the drama of the streets outside of the center. Maria has a long history of exposure to violence and of being violent herself, so making a commitment to giving up violence, even when threatened, is a major step for Maria and important in her development of an adult identity as a moral individual.

The Commitment to Nonviolence refers to the active creation of nonviolent environments for everyone. Our caregiving environments have often become dangerous and unsafe for the people who work in them as well as for the people who seek help. We must learn—as a whole species—how to practice nonviolence in our daily lives, everywhere, all of the time. Institutions—hospitals, mental health programs, group homes, prisons, shelters, schools—then become laboratories for what is required if life is to survive. Such commitment would constitute a social revolution. Working and living nonviolently takes tremendous discipline, self-reflection, and group support. Many of the components of the Sanctuary Toolkit, like Community Meetings, Safety Plans, and Self-Care Plans, are designed to facilitate nonviolent action.

Commitment to Emotional Intelligence

Emotional dysregulation is a primary problem for trauma survivors and manifests in many different behaviors that are problematic. For someone like Maria, who has had such abusive experience with caretakers from the beginning of her life, a compromised ability to manage distress is typical and may show up in problematic behaviors such as self-harm, fighting, running away, substance abuse, compulsive sexuality, and compulsive criminal acting-out. The development of emotional intelligence is therefore a primary aim of intervention. But that means that emotional regulation will need to be modeled for Maria by the staff members she interacts with. It means the staff must have or develop a high level of emotional intelligence.

"Emotional intelligence" refers to the ability to identify, understand, and put into words one's own feelings, to accurately read and comprehend emotional states in others, to manage strong emotions and to express them in a constructive manner, to regulate one's own behavior, to develop empathy for others, and to establish and sustain relationships (Goleman, 1995; Mayer & Salovey, 1997). Since this is a fundamental problem in all of our helping institutions, the development of emotional management skills is a critical function. To do that, organizations must build respect for the tough emotional labor that all staff members engage in, minimize the paralyzing effects of fear, and expand awareness of problematic cognitive-behavior patterns and of how to change them—in everyone (Ashforth & Humphrey, 1993).

Simple measures such as Safety Plans, a part of the Sanctuary Toolkit, can help everyone in a system develop heightened levels of emotional intelligence, while the SELF framework grounds problem solving and decision making in a coherent way that helps people manage chaotic situations more effectively.

It is critical that Maria understands the way she becomes trapped and thereby traps others in the Reenactment or Drama Triangle as a result of her own abusive experiences with others (Bloom & Farragher, 2010; Harrison & Yanosy, 2010). But that means that the staff must be able to recognize reenactment behavior and understand how to exchange those dramatic roles for new, healthier roles. In this way, Maria can come to understand the repetitious and destructive roles we play in each other's lives as a prelude to changing those roles.

Commitment to Social Learning

Healing and recovery necessitate that victims recognize their own self-destructive patterns of thought, feeling, and behavior. Maria has to learn a whole new way of being in the world. To do so, ideally she must be immersed in environments where constant learning is expected and rewarded. The Commitment to Social Learning is a whole organizational culture vow to create a "living-learning" environment for clients, their families, and everyone who works in that setting (Jones, 1968). An underlying assumption is that our organization is working for positive change, that if people are exactly the same (or worse) after leaving our care, then we have done a terrible job.

The Sanctuary Model is not about stabilization. We believe that everybody can change, even if only a little bit. But change that is self-determined has to come about by learning something. We learn things in the context of relationship. So we believe that the Sanctuary Model has to guide our organization in creating an environment where all clients have multiple opportunities to learn, grow, adapt, and change in a way that benefits them, their community, and their society. That means we must all unlearn some things, learn some new things, remember useful information from the past, and let go of things from the past that are no longer useful. It requires us to develop better decision-making and problem-solving capacities, part of which is learning to honor dissent. There are so many thoughts, feelings, and behaviors that Maria must unlearn that, to the outside world, such demands may be incomprehensible and impossible to meet. But within a structured setting where such unlearning and then new learning are encouraged and socially approved, change can often be quite rapid.

Learning experiences occur regularly when people call a "Red Flag Review," a component of the Sanctuary Toolkit that is used to mobilize a collective response to any kind of conflict or problem, and when they regularly use SELF as an organizing framework. Learning should be ongoing in regular SELF Service Delivery Planning and SELF Team Meetings. All of this can be best implemented in a residential setting, but New Day adapts these principles to keep the staff on the same page and to provide a different kind of normative experience for trafficking victims. Because staff members are attending to women who are still actively involved in "the life," most of their activity centers on safety. As Maria's life is illustrating, this in no way means that the women at New Day will not make change. We learned that even though the women had ever-decreasing lengths of stay in our original hospital unit, even a brief exposure to the possibility of a different normative environment could profoundly and positively affect a traumatized person.

Commitment to Open Communication

Victims of sex trafficking have usually experienced massive exposure to violence and degradation, all typically associated with fragmentation and dissociation. The pathways of communication between the various components of the self are broken and blocked. To heal from trauma, people must put the pieces back together. In an organization, the communication network is analogous to the vascular system of our bodies. Any breakdown in that system causes dysfunction and potentially death. The goal of this commitment is to help organizational members overcome barriers to healthy communication.

Maria has lived a life characterized by the manipulation of others for nefarious purposes. It is likely that her styles of communication are indirect and that her nonverbal communication contradicts what she says. For women like Maria, lying and manipulation are often deeply entrenched survival skills, not easily unlearned. She and the staff who work with her will need to directly confront these difficulties and help her develop more open, clear, and honest communication. Without that, her future relationships are likely to repeat the errors of the past. But if Maria is to learn all this, then open, clear, and honest communication must be modeled in the organizational context that she sees.

Today's overuse of electronic communication creates barriers to productive meetings and meaningful dialogue. To overcome these barriers, people will have to dare to discuss the "undiscussables," the important things that are talked about only in the meetings-after-the-meetings, and then unearth the skeletons in the organizational closet and give them proper burial (Hammond & Mayfield, 2004). Only by doing so can they overcome the organizational alexithymia—the inability to put into words the most disturbing aspects of organizational function.

This means increasing transparency, developing better conflict management skills, and establishing or reinforcing healthy boundaries. The Sanctuary Organizational Assessment process and then the maintenance of a Sanctuary Communication Plan, regular staff meetings using SELF as a framework, Community Meetings, SELF Service Delivery Planning, and SELF Team Meetings are all part of the Sanctuary Toolkit that help to promote improved organizational communication.

Commitment to Democracy

Maria's entire life has been characterized by a lack of agency in the context of systematic abuse. She will enter any treatment setting expecting more abuse and authoritarian control, and yet to become a productive member of society, she must learn how to participate with others. She must learn the skills of bargaining, negotiating, exercising power constructively, and speaking up against oppression and coercion while still being diplomatic. She must learn respect for others and expect that others will give her the same respect. These are all complex social skills that are vastly eroded, if they have developed at all, by exposure to maltreatment and captivity. Exposure to repetitive trauma generates both helplessness and hopelessness that often lead to disengagement and a lack of participation.

We define a democracy as a cohesive community of people living and working together and finding fair, nonviolent ways to reconcile conflicts (Gastil, 1993, p. 5). Helping demoralized people to reengage is one purpose of the Commitment to Democracy. Another is defining how we deal with the issue of power and its abuse in our organizations, which becomes a vital learning experience for victims of trafficking, who have been so exposed to and shaped by the abusive use of power. Through this commitment, we recognize that the problems we face are collective and that the only good solutions will also be collective. Whether we are talking about a child in residential care, a woman involved in sex trafficking, or the state of our global climate, we are talking about the need for emergent solutions, and those have to *emerge* from the brains of people who know how to get along together, how to civilly disagree with each other, and how to compromise, bargain, negotiate, synthesize, and manage power. In many ways, the skills required for democratic participation are antidotes to the experience of trauma and the deficits that trauma can promote. Along with the Commitment to Nonviolence, creating participatory environments is fundamental to any real and lasting change within our human service delivery environments.

Commitment to Social Responsibility

Social responsibility is a notion that has become almost passé in our fiercely competitive, market-driven, consumer culture, and yet for victims of familial and social abuse, neglect, and maltreatment like Maria, the sense of balance between one's own self-interest and that of the common good will be completely distorted when she first enters a therapeutic environment of any kind. Restoring that balance and a sense of justice and meaning is a critical component of recovery. We are deeply and genetically programmed for justice for ourselves and social justice for each other. In the Sanctuary Model, this commitment urges us to harness the energy of reciprocity and a yearning for justice by rebuilding restorative social connection skills, establishing healthy and fair attachment relationships, and transforming the desire for revenge into a driving need for social justice and concern for the common good.

Commitment to Growth and Change

This final commitment focuses on two significant domains: loss and change. People like Maria who have been systematically maltreated have lost many options in their lives, and when engaged in criminal enterprise, they are likely to have lost any moral purpose they may have developed, along with many people, places, and things. When this begins in childhood, it can become difficult and painful to imagine any alternative to abuse, and thus the imaginative sphere that contains the energy and motivation for change often becomes stagnant and unavailable. An unavoidable fact of life is that all growth, all change, necessitates loss. In fact, we usually have to give something up before we get the rewards of something new. Maria's entire existence has been characterized by unrelenting experiences of loss and betrayal. Our experience tells us that the fundamental sign in individuals and in groups of a failure to finish the grieving process is repeating the past or traumatic reenactment. Maria and other women with similar experiences will inevitably come into a therapeutic environment and automatically reenact the key roles of Victim, Rescuer, and Persecutor with staff members, and in that way—entirely outside of conscious awareness—they compulsively reenact their previous life experiences. Helping the women to understand the Reenactment Triangle and using it as a way of deliberately and consciously altering their interactions with others is profoundly meaningful and may be enough to launch a trafficking victim onto an entire new path.

   That means that an organization that hopes to be productive, useful, and healthy for all organizational members must face the fundamental reality of the human tendency to repeat the past; the members must then cease repeating irrelevant or destructive past patterns of thought, feeling, and behavior. Human beings avoid pain, and we will not let go of old habits—which are comforting because they are predictable—unless we have a vision of a possible future that we want to get to, a future that is worth the risk of letting go to see what happens next. Using SELF regularly as a problem-solving tool helps us integrate loss and future into daily life. Working with the Reenactment Triangle helps everyone understand the dynamics of repetition and how to bring about worthwhile and meaningful change.

When therapeutic engagement begins, it may be quite difficult for both clients and staff to imagine a road to true recovery. When applied to problems that have moral implications, this particular human faculty has been called "moral imagination." Although this term goes back at least as far as Adam Smith, moral imagination has been more recently defined as "an ability to imaginatively discern various possibilities for acting in a given situation and to envision the potential help and harm that are likely to result from a given action" (Johnson, 1993, p. 202).

When the moral decisions that need to be made are being made not by a single individual but by a group of individuals, each of whom is adapting to change in his, her, or their situation over time, a set system of rules becomes staggeringly complex. In organizational settings, moral imagination has been defined as "a reasoning process thought to counter the organizational factors that corrupt ethical judgment" (Moberg & Seabright, 2000, p. 845). Nowhere is this more important than in circumstances where human life and well-being are at stake and where the moral development of people like Maria has been so compromised.

The use of moral imagination becomes critically important when we are confronting violence and, most particularly, the violence already done to others. As one commentator has pointed out, "Transcending violence is forged by the capacity to generate, mobilize, and build the moral imagination" (Lederach, 2010). But to use our imaginative capacities requires mobilizing mental capacities that may not be well exercised within most organizational settings and has not had any opportunity to develop in the life of someone like Maria, whose very existence depended exclusively on the struggle for moment-to-moment survival. It requires us to transcend the false dichotomies that are so typical in human discourse about who is right and who is wrong, who is good or who is bad, and to instead become fiercely curious and willing to embrace complex ideas.

To do so, however, requires individuals and groups to step out of their usual comfort zones into an area of uncertainty and, therefore, some risk. Typically, in our organizational and cultural settings, everyone knows the landscape of violence but is much less familiar with the landscape of nonviolence and social learning. This is what makes the Sanctuary Commitments such a valuable asset in the process of organizational change. These trauma-informed, values-based, whole culture commitments become the anchors for shared assessment, planning, and intervention. Less moral distress is generated because the people who are involved are on the same page, know what and why they are doing what they are doing, and are able to consistently articulate the purpose and meaning of their strategies to each other, to the clients, and to regulators.

How does moral imagination function? Organizational development theorists have outlined some of the dimensions, all of which are consistent with Sanctuary Implementation. Being morally imaginative requires all members of a group to be self-reflective and to know themselves well enough to recognize their own limitations and their role in the particular decisions that are being made. In every conversation she has with New Day staff, Maria is challenged to use her moral imagination to think of what could lie ahead for her that is different from her past. She has been asked to imagine being the parent she never had and imagine having friendships and love relationships that do not depend on exploitation. This requires understanding the mental models or scripts that dominate the current situation and being willing to look at the underlying moral conflicts or moral disagreements that might arise in evaluating possible decisions. Being around people who recognize, understand, and show compassion toward those past dilemmas helps Maria to imagine better alternatives. Moral imagination requires a willingness to imagine new possibilities, to think individually and collectively "outside the box," and to be willing to tolerate the uncertainty that inevitably accompanies not having a fixed set of behavioral routines for each situation (P. Werhane, 2002; P. H. Werhane, 1998).

Pillar Three: SELF: A Trauma-Informed Moral Compass

Families as well as communities must share a language so they can communicate about the most vital aspects of their shared lives and organize an overwhelming amount of data into a more coherent and manageable framework. For that, the Sanctuary program uses SELF, an acronym standing for safety, emotions, loss, and future.

Moral alignment is critical to creating a morally safe workplace environment. But individuals bring to the workplace their own set of values from their own upbringing and/or religious beliefs. Until we actually get to know each other and work with each other, we have no way of knowing whether there is alignment between the values of the individual and those that the organization endorses. And in our current environments, very little time is spent ensuring alignment between members of staff and management. Creating moral alignment in an organization takes ongoing communication, learning, and growth. For most organizations this requires a developmental process over the course of years, not days. We thus require brief and immediately useful strategic devices that help us to manage the enormous complexity of the problems encountered by clients, staff, management, and the organizational as a whole.

SELF helps us to manage that complexity and organize chaos. In its day-to-day and moment-to-moment use, it becomes a compass for moral alignment. In the Sanctuary Model we use SELF for assessing, planning, solving problems, measuring change, and guiding interventions. Solving problems then becomes easier (see "SELF Problem-Solving Outline"). SELF doesn't automatically solve the problem, but it shows us what direction to go in.

Thursday at the New Day Drop-In is group day. The SELF group is first on the agenda. New Day staff facilitate SELF groups, working through one lesson each week. Some women attend weekly, some women come when they can, and some simply find themselves at the center on group day. A whiteboard is used as a visual tool. With the group's permission, notes and drawings from the group remain on the board throughout the week to share the lesson with the rest of the community. Because of the transient nature of the women who frequent the Drop-In Center, staff bring closure to each session.

Maria attends a SELF group weekly with three other women; they have formed a core group. They like that they can speak freely about being "in the life" and support one another regardless of their activities outside the center. One day's focus was on loss, and it was their second session on loss. Maria expressed great sadness at the loss of her mother. She wondered why she was abandoned and questioned what her life would be like if her mother had never left. She questioned her ability to be a loving parent. Margaret, another core group member, lost custody of two children because she could not care for them while in her addiction and under control of her trafficker. As the group was working on how to reconcile such losses, Margaret reached out to Maria directly. She told Maria how proud she was of the woman and mother she had fought to be. She spoke about having to give up her children because she could not care for them herself and how she loved them too much to expose them to the way she was living. Maria had never framed the loss of her mother in this way. She had often talked about seeking love from her trafficker as if it was all she deserved. After some consideration, Maria thanked Margaret and acknowledged how hard that must have been for her. In their efforts to reconcile these losses, these two women found a way to affirm one another and reframe their losses. These are the kinds of encounters that occur every day at New Day that support the healing, recovery, and growth of very traumatized and vulnerable clients.

Pillar Four: Sanctuary Toolkit

The Sanctuary Toolkit includes practical skills that everyone within an organization adopts to more effectively deal with challenging situations, build community, develop a deeper understanding of the effects of adversity and trauma, and share a common language. Community Meetings, Safety Plans, SELF Groups, and Self-Care Plans are all a part of the toolkit.

Outcomes of the Sanctuary Model

Organizations that use the Sanctuary Model should be able to observe and measure the program's outcomes, often by paying special attention to things that are already being measured in the organization. Every organization that chooses to adopt the Sanctuary Model must decide for itself what key outcomes they expect to achieve. Some examples of expected outcomes are more engagement in recovery processes; less physical, verbal, and emotional violence, including but not limited to reduced coercive measures; system-wide understanding of the complex biopsychosocial and developmental impact of trauma and abuse and what that means for the service environment; decreased staff turnover; less victim blaming; fewer punitive and judgmental responses; clearer and more consistent boundaries on the part of staff, as well as higher expectations and better linkage between rights and responsibilities; earlier identification of and confrontation with the abusive use of power in all its forms; improved ability to articulate goals and create strategies for change; expanded understanding and awareness of reenactment behavior and resistance to change and of how to achieve different and better outcomes; a more participatory environment at all levels; more diversified leadership and embedding of leadership skills in all staff; and most importantly, better outcomes for children, staff, and the organization.

Conclusion

Although caregivers are often powerless to change adverse political and social climates, the Sanctuary Model demonstrates that there is much we can do, even within those constraints, to make life better for ourselves and each other. We know that there is little protection against the impact of repetitive and overwhelming trauma except for social support and social acknowledgment. Social acknowledgment occurs when victims of trauma perceive that individuals or societal systems react positively to them and appreciate their traumatic experiences and current difficult situations. It is the opposite of societal disapproval, criticism, or rejection, which create social conditions that cause trauma survivors to feel unsupported, misunderstood, or otherwise alienated from others (Mueller, Moergeli, & Maercker, 2008). We contend that the moral alignment of everyone in a group is another vitally important source of protection. For trafficking victims, the experience of moral clarity, along with the social acknowledgment of their profound moral injuries, is likely to be vitally important.

The Sanctuary Model represents a moral system that situates itself in the middle space between the two extreme positions of moral absolutism and moral relativity. The model therefore constitutes a more modern and scientifically complex view of morality consistent with the notion of "moral pluralism." Moral absolutism proposes that there are absolute laws against which all moral questions may be judged. Based on these rules, actions can be considered right or wrong, regardless of the circumstances within which those actions are taken. Western ideas about morality have been grounded in this idea of finite and definable universal moral laws, and correct moral reasoning based on these laws supposedly permits us to apply these laws to all concrete situations in daily life. The decisions that Maria and many trafficking victims have had to face, such as whether to save themselves or betray another, illustrate the absurdity of moral absolutes.

Moral relativism, on the other hand, reflects a belief that there are not and cannot be any objective or universal moral truths; instead, all moral decisions and actions must be understood as being relative to social, cultural, historical, or personal circumstances. The notion that everything is relative to situational factors contradicts what we have learned about human evolution and human development. In fact, although we now know that human moral development is far more complex than moral absolutism would have us believe, we also have come to recognize that there do seem to be very real constraints that prohibit the more extreme perspectives of moral relativism.

In Maria's case, part of her recovery will depend on the fundamental decisions she makes going forward. As we leave her story, her child has been removed from the trafficker and is in the custody of child welfare. Maria is working on a reunification plan with her child. But once reunified, what kind of mother is Maria going to be? She will be drawn—as are all human beings—to reenact what has been a normal experience in her own past, but one that would be disastrous for her child. She will need to learn how to parent and how to parent well. She is currently living in permanent supportive housing, but soon she will need to find some way to earn a living that does not depend on abuse and exploitation. She is in weekly outpatient therapy and visits the New Day Drop-In Center during the week when she has free time in part because idle time is a trigger for her. In the setting of supportive living, a therapy relationship, and New Day, Maria has the opportunity to try on and rehearse new relational skills that will help her break the grip of traumatic reenactment. For Maria, already an adult, it is necessary to revisit all the steps of child and adolescent development as quickly as possible, only this time within the context of healthy relationships. Will she have the time? Will her society provide the options she needs to recover? Those are not just practical questions for Maria; they are also moral questions for the larger society.

Moral pluralism is the view that moral beliefs, though not wrong, are limited, partial, and incomplete and that human evolutionary biology constrains and helps to define moral positions (Stevens, 1997). The real life decisions that trafficking victims have had to confront and the current decisions that caregivers will have to face within constricted systems of care require an attitude of moral pluralism. Such an attitude keeps in mind the ideal while dealing with the very real.

Understanding the complexity of morality in human experience is vital because of what emerges out of our broadening understanding of how the human mind actually works, particularly of what has been missing when people have considered creating environments that promote human health and recovery. Human beings have proven to be almost infinitely adaptable in their ability to deal with situations and circumstances that are far more equivocal, confusing, and complex than a morally absolute universe would necessitate. Although still evolving, it is human imagination that functions as a moral agent within a morally pluralistic system. It is imagination that we tap into whenever we use SELF as a problem-solving tool because we continually need to refer to a future that may seem unreachable. This is especially important to victims of trafficking, who are likely to suffer from complex post-traumatic stress disorders.

The Sanctuary Model is explicitly designed to promote the use of a moral imagination within an organizational or community context. When faced with the complex problems of trauma survivors, particularly those who, like victims of sex trafficking, have been exposed to moral degradation, one must be willing to confront evil, transcend trauma, and transform suffering. One must confront and work through the moral challenges associated with the causes of survivors' trauma, the resultant damage from those experiences, and the difficulties inherent in recovery. To discover the optimal moral action, then, requires an explorative and dialogical process of using and integrating reflection, emotions, cultural awareness, situational factors, and moral imagination, all of which are at the heart of the Sanctuary Model (Bloom, in press).

Maria is one client who is moving through the stages of change and is now taking action to improve her life. Maria has participated in many activities at New Day, and she has begun using SELF as a way of organizing the complex problems confronting her. Her moral identity is growing and developing, and it is entirely possible that with sufficient help and social acknowledgment, Maria will heal and become a proud parent, a loving friend, and a positive contributor to her society. Maria must do her own work to move through the stages of change. The rest is up to us and the decisions we must make as a society to prevent the systematic abuse and exploitation of people like Maria.

Universal Training in the Sanctuary Model

Development of the Sanctuary Model

- Moral treatment
- Social psychiatry
- Systems theory
- Psychodynamic theory
- Democratic therapeutic community
- Original Sanctuary programs
- History of traumatic stress studies
  - History of child maltreatment and response

Shared Knowledge: Trauma Theory

Knowledge About People

- Evolutionary biology
- How we think and mental models
- The role of emotions
- Attachment and our social nature
- The role of loss
- Habits and repetition
- Moral development

Knowledge About People Under Stress

- Kinds of stress
- Adverse childhood experiences
- Disrupted attachment
- Betrayal trauma
- Trauma bonding
  - Psychobiology of trauma
  - Dissociation
- Reenactment
- Intergenerational transmission
- Complex responses to toxic events
- Vicarious trauma
- Healing and recovery in people
- Stages of change

- Barriers to recovery
- Process of healing
- Trauma-specific treatment

Knowledge About Groups

- Group dynamics
- Group consciousness
- Organizations as machines vs.
- Organizations as living systems

Knowledge About Groups Under Stress

- Stressed staff
- Traumatized staff
- Stressed organizations
- Traumatized organizations
- Parallel process
- Collective disturbance

Knowledge About Healing and Recovery

- Establishing safety
- Managing emotions
- Rescripting reenactment and loss
- Envisioning a different future

Shared Values: The Sanctuary Commitments

- Nonviolence
- Emotional Intelligence
- Social Learning
- Open Communication
- Democracy
- Social Responsibility
- Growth and Change

Shared Language: SELF
- Safety
  - Physical

- ○ Psychological
- ○ Social
- ○ Moral
- Emotions
- Loss
- Future

Shared Practice: Sanctuary Toolkit

- Community Meeting
- Safety Plans
- SELF Psychoeducation
- Red Flag Reviews
- Reenactment Triangle
- SELF Service Planning
- SELF Team Meetings
- Self-Care Strategies
- Sanctuary Communication Plan
- Sanctuary Supervision
- Sanctuary Leadership Development

SELF: A Trauma-Informed Group Psychoeducational Curriculum

List of Lessons

SELF: Introduction

- Introductory Materials
- What Does SELF Mean?
- Who Are You? A SELF Self-Assessment
- Putting the Pieces Together: What Trauma Does to the SELF

Safety

- It's All About Survival: Fight-Flight-Freeze
- SELF Begins with Safety

- What Does It Mean to Be Physically Safe?
- What Does It Mean to Be Psychologically Safe?
- What Does It Mean to Be Socially Safe?
- What Does It Mean to Be Morally Safe?
- The First Language of Safety: Yes, No, Uh-oh, Ouch
- What Does It Mean to Trust? Social Safety
- Fences Make Good Neighbors: What Is a Boundary?
- Living Without the Terrorist Within

Emotion

- Volume Control
- Introduction to the World—and the Words—of Emotion
- Problem Solving
- To Connect or Disconnect: That Is the Question
- How to Stay Grounded
- SELF-Soothing and Stress Management
- Hurt People Hurt People
- Addictions, Safety, and Self-Soothing
- Resolving Conflict

Loss

- What Do We Mean by Loss?
- Using SELF to Work Through Loss
- Never Having to Say Goodbye—Reenactment
- Learning to Let Go
- How to Lose Your SELF: Turning People into Chameleons
- Habits and Resisting Change
- What We Resist Persists

Future

- One Step at a Time—Is That All You Need to Know?
- How Does Change Happen?
- Empowerment
- How to Influence the Future: Self-Fulfilling Prophecies
- Relapse Prevention
- Moving On and Giving Back
- Imagining a Better Future

SELF Problem-Solving Outline

1. Establish time for the meeting, outline agenda.
2. Define the problem from different points of view—limit time of discussion in beginning and follow agreed-upon time limits.
3. Then, break key points into four domains:

- S = What are the safety issues?
  - Physical safety
  - Psychological safety
  - Social safety
  - Moral safety

FIGURE 12.1

How can we address them?

- E = What are the emotions involved? How can we effectively manage them?
- L = What have we lost or are likely to lose? What will we have to give up in order to change?
- F = Why change? Where do we want to end up?

4. Derive conclusions, action steps, and an evaluative mechanism from the outcome of this conversation.
5. Plan follow-up.

Notes

1. Thanks to Susan Brotherton, director of Philadelphia Social Service Ministries, Salvation Army Greater Philadelphia, for her assistance with this chapter.
2. Extended descriptions and articles can be found at www.sanctuaryweb.com.

References

Abramovitz, R., & Bloom, S. L. (2003). Creating sanctuary in a residential treatment setting for troubled children and adolescents. *Psychiatric Quarterly, 74*(2), 119–135.

Adshead, G. (2013). Psychopaths and moral identity. *Philosophy, Psychiatry & Psychology: PPP, 20*(4), 339–343, 381.

Ashforth, B. E., & Humphrey, R. H. (1993). Emotional labor in service roles: The influence of identity. *Academy of Management Review, 18*(1), 88–115.

Bandura, A. (2002). Selective moral disengagement in the exercise of moral agency. *Journal of Moral Education, 31*(2), 101–119.

Bloom, S. L. (2012). Building resilient workers and organisations: The Sanctuary Model of organizational change. In N. Tehrani (Ed.), *Workplace bullying: Symptoms and solutions* (pp. 260–277). London, UK: Routledge.

——. (2013). *Creating sanctuary: Toward the evolution of sane societies* (2nd ed.). New York, NY: Routledge.

——. (2016). Advancing a national cradle-to-grave-to-cradle public health agenda. *Journal of Trauma & Dissociation, 17*(4), 383–396. doi:10.1080/15299732.2016.1164025

——. (in press). The Sanctuary Model: Through the lens of moral safety. In J. Cook, C. J. Dalenberg, & S. Gold (Eds.), *Handbook of trauma psychology*. Washington, DC: American Psychological Association.

Bloom, S. L., & Farragher, B. (2010). *Destroying sanctuary: The crisis in human service delivery systems*. New York, NY: Oxford University Press.

——. (2013). *Restoring sanctuary: A new operating system for organizations*. New York, NY: Oxford University Press.

Clawson, H., & Grace, L. G. (2007). *Finding a path to recovery: Residential facilities for minor victims of domestic sex trafficking*. Washington, DC: U.S. Department of Health and Human Services. Retrieved from https://aspe.hhs.gov/basic-report/finding-path-recovery-residential-facilities-minor-victims-domestic-sex-trafficking

Coghlan, D., & Jacobs, C. (2005). Kurt Lewin on reeducation: Foundations for action research. *The Journal of Applied Behavioral Science, 41*(4), 444–457.

Cole, J., Sprang, G., Lee, R., & Cohen, J. (2016). The trauma of commercial sexual exploitation of youth: A comparison of CSE victims to sexual abuse victims in a clinical sample. *Journal of Interpersonal Violence, 31*(1), 122–146. doi:10.1177/0886260514555133

Damon, W. (1999). The moral development of children. *Scientific American, 281*(2), 72.

Doron, G., Sar-El, D., Mikulincer, M., & Kyrios, M. (2012). When moral concerns become a psychological disorder: The case of obsessive-compulsive disorder. In M. Mikulincer & P. R. Shaver (Eds.), *The social psychology of morality: Exploring the causes of good and evil* (pp. 293–310). Washington, DC: American Psychological Association.

Dutton, D., & Painter, S. (1981). Traumatic bonding: The development of emotional attachments in battered women and other relationships of intermittent abuse. *Victimology: An International Journal, 6*, 139–155.

Esaki, N., Benamati, J., Yanosy, S., Middleton, J., Hopson, L., Hummer, V., & Bloom, S. L. (2013). The Sanctuary Model: Theoretical framework. *Families in Society, 94*(2), 29–35.

Estes, R. J., & Weiner, N. A. (2001). *The commercial sexual exploitation of children in the U.S., Canada and Mexico.* Philadelphia, PA: University of Pennsylvania. Retrieved from http://www.gems-girls.org/Estes%20Wiener%202001.pdf

Farley, M., Lynne, J., & Cotton, A. J. (2005). Prostitution in Vancouver: Violence and the colonization of First Nations women. *Transcultural Psychiatry, 42*(2), 242–271. doi:10.1177/1363461505052667

Fong, R., & Berger Cardoso, J. (2010). Child human trafficking victims: Challenges for the child welfare system. *Evaluation and Program Planning, 33*(3), 311–316. doi:10.1016/j.evalprogplan.2009.06.018

Gastil, J. (1993). *Democracy in small groups: Participation, decision making, and communication.* Philadelphia, PA: New Society Publishers.

Goleman, D. (1995). *Emotional intelligence: Why it can matter more than IQ.* New York, NY: Bantam Books.

Graham, J., & Haidt, J. (2012). Sacred values and evil adversaries: A moral foundations approach. In M. Mikulincer & P. R. Shaver (Eds.), *The social psychology of morality: Exploring the causes of good and evil* (pp. 11–31). Washington, DC: American Psychological Association.

Hammond, S. A., & Mayfield, A. B. (2004). *The thin book of naming elephants: How to surface undiscussables for greater organizational success.* Bend, OR: Thin Book Publishing.

Harrison, L. A., & Yanosy, S. M. (2010). Traumatic reenactment: How this triangle can sabotage intervention and treatment. In *SPECIAL REPORT: Summary of selected papers from ISPCAN's XVIIIth International Congress and Youth Empowerment Forum, 1,* 3–4. Retrieved from http://www.academia.edu/15143891/Traumatic_Reenactment_How_This_Triangle _can_Sabotage_Intervention_and_Treatment

Hauser, M. D. (2007). *Moral minds: How nature designed our universal sense of right and wrong.* New York, NY: HarperCollins.

Herman, J. (1992). *Trauma and recovery.* New York, NY: Basic Books.

Johnson, M. (1993). *Moral imagination: Implications of cognitive science in ethics.* Chicago, IL: University of Chicago Press.

Jones, M. (1968). *Beyond the therapeutic community: Social learning and social psychiatry.* New Haven, CT: Yale University Press.

Kotrla, K. (2010). Domestic minor sex trafficking in the United States. *Social Work, 55*(2), 181–187.

Lederach, J. P. (2010). *The moral imagination: The art and soul of building peace.* New York, NY: Oxford University Press.

Levesque, D. A., Prochaska, J. M., & Prochaska, J. O. (1999). Stages of Change and integrated service delivery. *Consulting Psychology Journal: Practice and Research, 51*(4), 226–241.

Lifton, R. J. (1963). *Thought reform and the psychology of totalism: A study of brainwashing in China.* New York: W. W. Norton.

Markman, J. (2009, December 8). Rescued child prostitutes not receiving help. *Los Angeles Times.* Retrieved from http://www.newdayforchildren.com/uploads/4/5/7/8/45780549 /__la_times_dec_8_2009.350171032.pdf

Mayer, J. D., & Salovey, P. (1997). What is emotional intelligence? In P. Salovey & D. J. Sluyter (Eds.), *Emotional development and emotional intelligence: Educational implications* (pp. 3–31). New York, NY: Basic Books.

Mitchell, K. J., Finkelhor, D., & Wolak, J. (2010). Conceptualizing juvenile prostitution as child maltreatment: Findings from the National Juvenile Prostitution Study. *Child Maltreatment, 15*(1), 18–36. doi:10.1177/1077559509349443

Moberg, D. J., & Seabright, M. A. (2000). The development of moral imagination. *Business Ethics Quarterly, 10*(4), 845–884.

Mueller, J. P., Moergeli, H. P., & Maercker, A. M. D. P. (2008). Disclosure and social acknowledgement as predictors of recovery from posttraumatic stress: A longitudinal study in crime victims. *Canadian Journal of Psychiatry, 53*(3), 160–168.

Murrell, R. G. (2016). *Impact of sex-trafficking directives on Maryland youth residential facilities: A multi-site case study* Capella University, ProQuest Dissertations Publishing, 2016. 10006977.

Napier, R. W., & Gershenfeld, M. K. (2004). *Groups: Theory and experience* (7th ed.). Boston, MA: Houghton Mifflin.

National Scientific Council on the Developing Child. (2004). *Young children develop in an environment of relationships: Working paper no. 1.* Retrieved from www.developingchild. harvard.edu

Reichert, J., & Sylwestrzak, A. (2013). *National survey of residential programs for victims of sex trafficking.* Retrieved from Chicago, IL: The Illinois Criminal Justice Information Authority, https://traffickingresourcecenter.org/resources/national-survey-residential -programs-victims-sex-traficking

Rivard, J. C. (2004). Initial findings of an evaluation of a trauma recovery framework in residential treatment. *Residential Group Care Quarterly, 5*(1), 3–5.

Rivard, J. C., Bloom, S. L., Abramovitz, R. A., Pasquale, L., Duncan, M., McCorkle, D., & Fedel, S. (2003). Assessing the implementation and effects of a trauma-focused intervention for youths in residential treatment. *Psychiatric Quarterly, 74*(2), 137–154.

Rivard, J. C., McCorkle, D., Duncan, M. E., Pasquale, L. E., Bloom, S. L., & Abramovitz, R. (2004). Implementing a trauma recovery framework for youths in residential treatment. *Child and Adolescent Social Work Journal, 21*(5), 529–550.

Senge, P. (1994). *The fifth discipline: The art and practice of the learning organization.* New York, NY: Doubleday.

Shay, J. (2003). *Odysseus in America: Combat trauma and the trials of homecoming.* New York, NY: Scribner.

Shermer, M. (2004). *The science of good & evil: Why people cheat, gossip, care, share and follow the golden rule.* New York, NY: Henry Holt.

Silver, S. (1986). An inpatient program for post-traumatic stress disorder: Context as treatment. In C. Figley (Ed.), *Trauma and its wake, Volume II: Post-traumatic stress disorder: Theory, research and treatment.* New York, NY: Brunner/Mazel.

Stevens, E. (1997). *Developing moral imagination: Case studies in practical morality.* Kansas City, MO: Sheed & Ward.

Strenz, T. (1982). The Stockholm Syndrome. In F. Ochberg & D. Soskis (Eds.), *Victims of terrorism* (pp. 149–164). Boulder, CO: Westview.

Thomson, S., Hirshberg, D., Corbett, A., Valila, N., & Howley, D. (2011). Residential treatment for sexually exploited adolescent girls: Acknowledge, Commit, Transform (ACT). *Children and Youth Services Review, 33*(11), 2290–2296. doi:10.1016/j.childyouth.2011.07.017

Twill, S. E., Green, D. M., & Traylor, A. (2010). A descriptive study on sexually exploited children in residential treatment. *Child & Youth Care Forum, 39*(3), 187–199. doi:10.1007 /s10566-010-9098-2

van Schaik, C., & Michel, K. (2016). *The good book of human nature: An evolutionary reading of the Bible.* New York, NY: Basic Books.

Ward, J., & Patel, N. (2006). Broadening the discussion on "sexual exploitation": Ethnicity, sexual exploitation and young people. *Child Abuse Review, 15*(5), 341–350. doi:10.1002 /car.953

Werhane, P. H. (1998). Moral imagination and the search for ethical decision-making in management. *Business Ethics Quarterly, 1,* 75–98.

——. (2002). Moral imagination and systems thinking. *Journal of Business Ethics, 38*(1–2), 33–42. doi:10.1023/A:1015737431300

Williamson, E., Dutch, N. M., & Clawson, H. (2010). *Evidence-based mental health treatment for victims of human trafficking.* Washington, DC: U.S. Department of Health and Human Services. Retrieved from https://aspe.hhs.gov/pdf-report/evidence-based-mental-health-treatment-victims-human-trafficking

CHAPTER 13

HOW DO WE HELP?

A Clinical and Empirical Review of Challenges to Service
Provision for Sexually Exploited Clients

LARA GERASSI, PhD, MSW, LCSW, UNIVERSITY
OF WISCONSIN MADISON

ABBY HOWARD, MSW, LCSW, UNIVERSITY OF DENVER

Providing services to sexually exploited and trafficked individuals comes with a host of challenges. Practitioners are tasked with understanding the known risk factors, consequences, and available services from the literature. However, the literature alone cannot fully prepare practitioners for the numerous challenges they will experience in the field as they seek to meet the needs of survivors with limited agency resources and funding. Therefore, it is important for practitioners to provide their colleagues with examples of their challenges navigating services with clients, so that providers may learn which strategies were most and least effective. This is of particular importance when seeking to understand the experiences of those individuals who are unable to access or cannot engage with services because they do not fit within the rules or policies of those systems.

This chapter seeks to do the following: (1) review the current state of evidence on the available interventions for sexually exploited and trafficked individuals; (2) present vignettes of a practitioner's experiences with sexually exploited individuals and review the challenges these clients and their practitioner faced in navigating available services; and (3) discuss how research and practice can further connect with one another to improve currently available services for all trafficked and exploited individuals. This chapter gives voice to three clients whose circumstances and identities did not fit neatly into the currently available landscape of services. It also analyzes how the literature corresponds to these identified gaps and provides suggestions for how to respond if practitioners find themselves in similar situations.

Literature Review

Much of the literature on sex trafficking and commercial sexual exploitation remains descriptive. Since sexually exploited individuals are most often identified through law enforcement or social service organizations (Newton, Mulcahy, & Martin, 2008), adequate service referral and provision can be effective but sometimes challenging. Sexually exploited individuals are more likely to disclose their legal and abuse histories to mental health and addiction service providers than to legal providers (Sloss & Harper, 2010), a situation that presents distinct opportunities for social service providers to address the many challenges such individuals face. Generally, sexually exploited individuals require legal assistance, intensive case management, medical care, substance abuse treatment/counseling, mental health counseling, life skills training, education, and job training/employment (Clawson, Dutch, Solomon, & Grace, 2009; Cohan et al., 2006; Gibbs, Hardison, Lutnick, Miller, & Kluckman, 2015; Kalergis, 2009; Raphael & Shapiro, 2002). Unfortunately, there are not many evaluations of interventions for this population, and the existing literature has methodological problems.

Trauma-Informed Care

The need for trauma-informed care (TIC) is imperative for populations at high risk of experiencing complex trauma, such as sexually exploited and trafficked individuals (Hom, 2013, Leidholdt, 2004; Logan, Walker, & Hunt, 2009; Wilson & Butler, 2013). Principles of trauma-informed practice include recognizing the impact of violence and victimization on coping strategies and setting primary goals to recover from trauma, utilizing an empowerment model, maximizing choices and control over recovery in collaboration with providers, highlighting strengths and resiliency over pathology, and reducing possibilities of retraumatization in a culturally competent way (Elliott, Bjelajac, Fallot, Markoff, & Reed, 2005). Because sexually exploited individuals have mental health issues such as PTSD and depression (Arnold, 2000; Farley, 2004a, 2004b; Hossain, Zimmerman, Abas, Light, & Watts, 2010; Twill, Green, & Traylor, 2010) and are also substance users (Clatts, Goldsamt, Yi, & Gwadz, 2005; El-Bassel, Witte, Wada, Gilbert, & Wallace, 2001; Miller et al., 2011; Syvertsen et al., 2013; Valera, Sawyer, & Schiraldi, 2001), they require comprehensive TIC.

Given the state of knowledge regarding trauma and substance use among sexually exploited individuals, existing interventions addressing trauma and substance use together may provide appropriate and urgently needed treatments for this population. Multiple systematic reviews compared psychotherapeutic integrated treatments (that address both substance abuse and trauma) with nonintegrated treatments (that address substance abuse only) and found that despite methodological issues, integrated treatments effectively reduced substance use and trauma symptoms better than nonintegrated treatments (Cocozza et al., 2005; Torchalla, Nosen, Rostam, & Allen, 2012; Van Dam, Vedel, Ehring, & Emmelkamp, 2012). As discussed in Part I of this book, cognitive processing therapy, prolonged exposure, and eye movement desensitization and reprocessing are considered evidence-based treatments for survivors of sexual violence and should be considered potential treatments for trafficked and exploited individuals with PTSD and depression. Complex trauma coupled with sexually exploited individuals' short and long-term needs (Kurtz, Surratt, Kiley, & Inciardi, 2005) requires long-term care across multiple types of organizations and interventions, including street outreach services, residential housing, and mental health counseling. Longer-term care may help sexually exploited individuals heal and thrive rather than simply survive and stabilize (Gibbs et al., 2015).

Street Outreach Services

One method of meeting sexually exploited individuals where they are employs a street outreach approach to access high-risk potential clients. Outreach involves meeting persons (often youths) in their environment, forming a relationship with them, and then providing services and information before connecting them to other services (Connolly & Joly, 2012). Since people who trade sex are not a homogenous group and represent varied races, genders, and sexualities (Nichols, 2016), meeting individuals where they are across multiple settings may be helpful. Because of the extreme isolation of sexually exploited populations, particularly those who are also abusing substances, traditional street outreach efforts during the day may be ineffective and therefore must be adapted to evening hours. In addition, it is helpful to address basic needs by providing things like fresh water and access to showers (Kurtz et al., 2005). Conducting outreach on streets may access at-risk youth through multiple avenues.

Evidence suggests that outreach advocates must deliver on promises made to individuals and form relationships with their clients in subtle ways that may not be necessary with other stationary models of service (Saldanha & Parenteau, 2013). For example, sexually exploited youth participating in a study conducted in Minneapolis and St. Paul reported that they needed outreach workers to (1) use "soft words," meaning gentler terms for sexual exploitation than the clinical terms used by professionals in law enforcement, medical, and social service fields, and to (2) bring hygiene and safe sex supplies with them throughout their outreach to build relationships (Holger-Ambrose, Langmade, Edinburgh, & Saewyc, 2013). Being attentive to language choices and using subtlety in their approach may help outreach workers or other advocates provide appropriate services and connect exploited individuals to those services.

General street outreach practices have been found to be efficacious with youth at large across the United States. In a meta-analysis of outreach with street-involved youth, Connolly and Joly (2012) determined that 63 percent of youth contacted through outreach later participated in an offered service; they also found that outreach conducted by workers with strong bonds to youth can be an effective strategy for involving youth in agency services. Very few studies have examined outreach practices with sexually exploited individuals, and most have focused their outcome measures on drug use reduction only (Bowser, Ryan, Smith, & Lockett, 2008). This is an area of great potential, as individuals engaged in prostitution and commercial sexual exploitation are most frequently identified through street outreach efforts (Holger-Ambrose et al., 2013; Raphael & Shapiro, 2002; Yahne, Miller, Irvin-Vitela, & Tonigan, 2002), and there has been consistent evidence that this intervention approach increases positive outcomes.

Residential Services

Residential programs continue to be a high priority for sexually trafficked and exploited individuals, especially for emerging youth who may have aged out of child protective services (CPS) and other systems geared to assist minors with housing options. The most recent national survey of residential programs for victims of sex trafficking found a total of thirty-three currently operational residential programs with a total of 682 beds in Alabama, Arizona, California, Florida, Georgia, Illinois, Massachusetts, Minnesota, Missouri, New York, North Carolina, Ohio, Oklahoma, Oregon, Pennsylvania, Texas, and Washington (Reichert & Sylwestrzak, 2013). At the time of the report, twenty-seven programs offering an additional 354 beds planned to open. Respondents from this national survey indicated that the majority of referrals came from law enforcement, the court system, social workers/service providers, street outreach, and hotline calls. However, Reichert and Sylwestrzak (2013) did not seek to measure the quality of the services, and no literature is yet available on the effectiveness of these programs.

Generally speaking, how individuals are screened for admission to housing programs remains unknown, with few exceptions, such as the Acknowledge, Commit, Transform (ACT) program, which provides an individual case study and evaluation of a model for sexually exploited adolescent girls (Thomson, Hirshberg, Corbett, Valila, & Howley, 2011). ACT admits only adolescent girls who are at least in the contemplating stage of the five Stages of Change.[1] ACT is based in Massachusetts and provides group programs focusing on healthy sexuality, life skills, family therapy (if the family is available), and a psychoeducational group called My Life My Choice. ACT only accepts individuals who have been assessed for their readiness to acknowledge sexual exploitation and/or at-risk behaviors. Existing evidence indicates that all individuals from the first year finished the program, and 85 percent were living safely with their families after planned discharges. No other evidence in the literature could be found regarding this program. Given the screening procedures, this model may show some promise for a particular subpopulation of girls who are ready and wanting to change their sexual risk behaviors.

Federally funded housing services targeting runaway and homeless youth, a population at well-documented high risk of sexual exploitation (Estes & Weiner, 2001; Reid, 2011; Tyler, Hoyt, Whitbeck, & Cauce, 2001), were instituted long before the development of sex-trafficking legislation and grant-funded residential programs. Last amended as the Reconnecting Homeless Youth Act of 2008, the Runaway and Homeless Youth Act of 1974 federally funded shelters targeting a population of youth that remains at high risk for multiple problems (Micetic, 2016). One study in Oregon, however, found that federally funded housing services only suffice for 18.5 percent of the runaway youth sample, as the larger sample required more comprehensive services to address a host of other issues, including addiction, behavior management, and clinical issues not funded by this act (Coward Bucher, 2008).

Since the passage of the Runaway and Homeless Youth Act, the evidence for effective housing interventions for runaway youth is rather limited and often lacking methodological rigor. For example, one study found that 42 percent of young women involved in a residential treatment program were successful in that they lived independently or in stable situations, attended school and/or were employed, and had not engaged in prostitution or substance abuse (Schram & Giovengo, 1991). However, the authors disclose that their original evaluation plan was too ambitious and the successes noted were only for "a small number of clients" (p. 569) who received a full evaluation follow-up. Evidence has not strengthened greatly since that time, as a 2013 systematic review of interventions reducing harmful behavior in street-connected youth found that there were no consistent results on outcomes, including psychosocial health, substance misuse, and sexual risky behaviors, among drop-in and shelter-based samples (Coren et al., 2013).

Shelter housing continues to be a central challenge in serving youth, as one study indicated that the lack of coordination between housing systems and other services may raise questions about the efficacy of this shelter system in its current form (Staller, 2004). Staller suggests that if homeless youth only lived on the streets or in shelters, shelter services might be effective despite the lack of coordination. However, the current reality of youths' involvement with child welfare systems and youths living with friends and extended relatives is not conducive to the linear model of providing housing only to homeless youth on the streets. Additionally, Staller maintains that a twenty-one-day stay in a shelter, as stated in the current policy, is insufficient to produce effective change.

Intimate Partner and Sexual Violence Services

Given the overlapping similarities between intimate partner violence (IPV), sexual violence (SV), and sex trafficking, as well as the experience and understanding of IPV/SV service providers, some experts have stated that domestic and sexual violence service staff may be best equipped to serve this vulnerable population (Busch, Fong, & Williamson, 2004). Increasing evidence suggests that pimps or exploiters will force or coerce their "girlfriends" or "boyfriends" into selling or trading sex; survivors of such exploitation and abuse may consequently come into contact with IPV services (Anderson, Coyle, Johnson, & Denner, 2014; Holger-Ambrose, Langmade, Edinburgh, & Saewyc, 2013; Raphael, Reichert, & Powers, 2010). Similarly, exploited victims experience sexual trauma and may also come in contact with rape crisis centers (Gragg et al., 2007; Macy & Graham, 2012; Stark & Hodgson, 2003). State domestic and sexual violence coalitions have begun to recognize this intersection and have issued guidelines to help their organizations assess and provide services to trafficking victims (Clawson et al., 2009).

Sex-trafficking victims require extensive safety planning and the development of rapport with their advocates (Briere & Jordan, 2004), techniques that are well suited to IPV and SV programs and individual advocacy services generally. Although case management and individual advocacy services have not been tested for their efficacy with victims of sexual exploitation, they have been studied for IPV services. In fact, a systematic review of the impact of case management among IPV services (Ramsay et al., 2009) found that brief advocacy services (less than twelve hours' duration) may increase safety behaviors for up to twenty-four months. Such advocacy services and techniques may be essential to sex-trafficking victims' overall safety.

LGBTQ+ Services

One particular population that has increased barriers to services includes members of the lesbian, gay, bisexual, transgender, queer (LGBTQ+) community. Biases of service providers and law enforcement against members of this community may contribute to missed identification of these individuals and fewer services provided to individuals who identify as LGBTQ+ (U.S. Department of State, 2014). LGBTQ+ sex-trafficking cases are rarely reported by local and national government, further stigmatizing this vulnerable population (Martinez & Kelle, 2013). Individuals who identify as LGBTQ+ are also overrepresented among homeless youth populations and therefore remain at increased risk for trafficking (Clatts et al., 2005; Walls & Bell, 2011). Therefore, organizations that serve LGBTQ+ individuals, including homeless services, HIV/STI testing sites, and youth outreach services, may be essential to connecting LGBTQ+ individuals with critically important mental health, housing, and other services.

Child Protective Services and Foster Care

Systems addressing the needs of children, such as Child Protective Services (CPS) and foster care, serve as key interventions that can potentially identify sexually exploited youth and minors (Clawson et al., 2009; Reid, 2010). According to a National Colloquium hosted by John Hopkins University in conjunction with End Child Prostitution and Trafficking (ECPAT), Shared Hope International, and the Protection Project, 88 percent of direct service practitioners received referrals for domestic minor sex trafficking from child protective services (2013). Many exploited youth report involvement in child protective services or foster care prior to or at some point during their sexual exploitation (Halter, 2010; Holger-Ambrose et al., 2013). Service providers are legally obligated to report to child protective services when a minor victim is identified (Macy & Graham, 2012), which has created a helpful avenue for connecting victims to resources. As the support for emerging youth is usually disengaged around ages eighteen to twenty-one, depending on the state, CPS may offer a helpful avenue for minors but may be less effective for those aging out of the system and/or for those who do not view themselves as victims of sexual exploitation (Pearce, 2006).

Although there are recommendations for and existing collaborations between CPS, antitrafficking coalitions, and law enforcement (Boxill & Richardson, 2007; Clawson et al., 2009), there is scant literature on whether support given through CPS or foster care services is effective with this population. For example, the California Child Welfare Council (2013) established a multisystem model to provide collaborative interventions and policy recommendations. This report emphasized the child welfare system's unique position in providing early-stage interventions, such as assessment for trafficking, care plans, and referrals. Because this initiative and others are new and require implementation within a large system, no evaluations of these programs have been found in peer-reviewed literature.

Aging Out of Services

The fact that youths aging out of foster care have significant associations with transactional sex suggests that specialized services are needed for these individuals (Ahrens, Katon, McCarty, Richardson, & Courtney, 2012). However, services for "aging out" youth are limited (Osgood, Foster, & Courtney, 2014). Emerging adults (ages eighteen to twenty-five) often age out of services offered by child protective services and foster care, thus remaining at increased risk for commercial sexual exploitation. For example, youth exiting foster care who have a history of sexual abuse continue to be more likely to have transactional sex (Ahrens et al., 2012) and remain at increased risk for prostitution. Another study of forty-seven women in prostitution showed that 64 percent had been involved in the child welfare system and 78 percent of those had lived in foster care or group homes (Nixon, Tutty, Downe, Gorkoff, & Ursel, 2002). Many child victims often present without parental or legal guardianship and therefore also experience contact with the foster care system (Fong & Berger Cardoso, 2010) but are soon no longer eligible for services. However, there is still much to be learned about effective practices for this population.

Connecting Research to Practice: Case Examples from the Field

There appears to be limited evidence of effective programs and services specifically for victims of sexual exploitation, despite the increased recognition of domestic sexual exploitation and calls for services that include case management, housing, and mental health treatment (Clawson et al., 2009; Macy & Graham, 2012; Wilson, Critelli, & Rittner, 2015). This is evidently a critical area requiring further development, especially as victim identification and referral to needed services increase. In order to connect some of the systemic challenges in the literature to practice settings, three vignettes of cases were chosen that illustrate some of the challenges and struggles one practitioner faced in providing appropriate referrals and resources for this vulnerable population.

The following vignettes are based on three individuals seen by the second author, a licensed clinical social worker (LCSW) and practitioner, through a street outreach program in a midwestern city. The names of the clients and demographic details have been changed to protect their identity and confidentiality. The information in these vignettes is provided firsthand by the practitioner based on her perspective and knowledge of the clients' situations during their time on her caseload. The practitioner will be referred to as Amber throughout this chapter.

Angelica

Angelica identified, at the time of initial service, as a nineteen-year-old, cisgender, white female who was adopted from the [Country] by a family in [State] when she was approximately eight years old. Angelica's initial contact with Amber came through a referral made to a youth hotline by a local faith-based leader who found Angelica sleeping behind a bush on church property. Amber and an additional street outreach worker were dispatched to respond to Angelica's situation and met with the youth within an hour after the call was placed.

After the practitioner built some rapport with Angelica, Angelica reported that she was homeless and would occasionally live with her boyfriend and his father. She stated that she was being forced to have sex with the father in exchange for a place to sleep, unbeknownst to her boyfriend. Angelica stated that when she refused to have sex with the boyfriend's father, he would force her to sleep outside and sometimes refused to let her stay on the property at all. Angelica also reported an extensive history of sexual, physical, and emotional violence at the hand of her boyfriend. In the initial meeting and the meetings that followed, Angelica repeatedly appeared undernourished and showed signs of bruising and scratching or cuts on her arms, legs, and neck from the intimate partner violence.

Angelica refused to report the abuse to the police and denied wanting to go into care at a shelter. The Street Outreach Team continued to follow up with Angelica, provide case management, and build rapport, and within a week Angelica agreed to stay at a local youth shelter. However, within less than seventy-two hours Angelica was reported as AWOL by shelter staff. Angelica did make contact with Amber, stating she had decided to return to her boyfriend's house because he threated to kill her if she continued to stay at the shelter. Because the youth shelter was not held at a confidential location, Angelica's boyfriend was able to locate where she was and picked her up near where the shelter was located.

Angelica continued to contemplate leaving her boyfriend and experienced the cycle of violence for over two years until the boyfriend was suddenly killed in a car accident. In addition to homelessness and victimization via both intimate partner violence and coerced sex acts, Angelica reported that she had engaged in sexual acts with several other men in exchange for basic needs such as food and shelter. Angelica also reported multiple sexual abuse encounters at the hands of various men and caregivers dating back to before she left her home country, including her birth father, boyfriend, boyfriend's father, and multiple others. Angelica also reported frequent drug and alcohol use, including marijuana, cocaine, and opioids. Angelica stated that she was aware that the drug and alcohol use was harmful to her health and sometimes put her at greater risk for victimization. Angelica denied wanting any type of treatment for her drug and alcohol use, and Amber assessed that Angelica was in a precontemplative stage of change.

Amber continued to maintain contact with Angelica to the extent that was possible, as the youth was consistently changing phone numbers and living in different locations. She reported on more than one occasion being "taken in" by men she met at the mall or in gas stations. These men often bought her new makeup, underwear, clothing, jewelry, and phones in addition to providing for her basic needs and paying for hotel rooms. Angelica stated that in return she simply had to "be nice to them" and occasionally sleep with them. Angelica reported that these men were protective and territorial with her and would occasionally become physically abusive as well. Angelica attempted several times to hold down a job, but because of her highly transient nature was unable to successfully maintain employment.

Although Angelica had experienced serious and extensive sexual, physical, and emotional violence, only one adult domestic violence shelter in the area agreed to allow Angelica to come into its care. Other shelters that excluded her from services indicated that Angelica did not meet the traditional definition of "domestic" or "intimate partner violence" because she was not living with a domestic partner consistently but rather was technically considered homeless and living on and off the streets. Angelica aged out of youth services at the age of twenty-one and was not provided the same amount of protection and anonymity as a domestic violence shelter would have given. Therefore, she remained exposed to more threats and violence at the hands of people who preyed on her vulnerabilities.

Chase

Chase identified, at the time of initial service, as a nineteen-year-old Black, gender-queer, male-bodied, gay person who primarily preferred that Amber use male pronouns when addressing him. Chase had been involved with the Street Outreach Program prior to Amber's hire and had recently returned to [City] from [State], where he had been living with a man he met through an online dating site. Prior to working with Amber, Chase had been in and out of various shelters for over a year. Chase was only allowed to stay in certain shelters because of his zip code, which determined certain funding sources and limited his access to several shelters. In the shelters the youth was allowed to enter, he would typically stay the maximum number of days and then leave and either be on the streets or stay with a "friend," which was code for someone who required sex in exchange for shelter. Chase also reported that he did not feel safe or welcome in several shelters because of his gender and sexual identity and reported that staff had made negative comments about his engagement in sex in exchange for basic needs. He also reported that several youth in the shelters used pejorative terms toward him and often perceived there to be few consequences for their behaviors. Eventually, Chase would be allowed back into one of the few shelters he could stay at and repeated the pattern again and again.

Chase reported that the man he had met online had paid for his plane ticket to go to another state and provided his basic needs, including food, clothing, and shelter. Chase stated that upon arriving in the state, the man, whom Chase referred to as his ex-boyfriend, required him to engage in various sexual acts in exchange for payment of the plane ticket and housing. Chase reported that this was not an unusual occurrence for him and that he would frequently exchange sex for basic needs; however, Chase said that he no longer wanted to do this and knew that he was risking both his physical and sexual safety every time that he engaged in this type of sex act. Because of his homelessness and serious mental health symptoms, Chase struggled to maintain employment and stated that he thought that exchanging sex was one of the only ways he could take care of himself.

Chase had been diagnosed as bipolar and schizophrenic prior to working with Amber and was resistant to taking medications or working with a psychiatrist for treatment of his mental health symptoms. Amber utilized motivational interviewing techniques and rapport building, and Chase eventually agreed to meet with a psychiatrist to engage in mental health treatment and work toward accessing additional services for his symptoms. At the time, Chase was eligible for free psychiatric services through a program that had a three-month waiting list; however, Amber was able to advocate on Chase's behalf and arrange an appointment within two weeks. Amber and the director of the psychiatric program had a previous professional relationship from doing community organizing work together, and Amber was able to contact the director directly to advocate for her client. Chase attended the initial appointment but did not attend any follow-up appointments and did not adhere to his treatment.

In addition to working with Chase on mental health treatment, Amber advocated for him to have safe housing through a local youth shelter. Chase spent less than one month in a youth shelter before he was referred to a transitional living program. The agency providing the transitional living services was resistant to take the youth because he did not have a GED or employment, at least one of which was required to be eligible for placement. However, Amber and other agency staff advocated on the youth's behalf, stating that there was an increased likelihood of his victimization in adult shelters because of the youth's gender-queer and gay identities. The lack of shelter services for adult men proved to be a serious barrier to helping Chase adhere to mental health treatment and obtain employment. Chase reported after being accepted into the transitional living program that he did not feel accepted there and that he was "moving to another state to live with a family member." The staff working with Chase suspected that the person he was living with in the other state was not a family member but another person that he met online.

Jessica

Jessica identified, at the time of initial service, as a Black seventeen-year-old cisgender female who would turn eighteen years old the week following initial assessment. Jessica had contacted a youth hotline about being "kicked out" of her mother's house, and Amber and a street outreach worker were dispatched to meet with the youth for housing referrals. The youth was staying in a hotel that had the reputation for holding prostitution rings. When Amber made contact with Jessica, she stated she was staying with her boyfriend at the hotel and disclosed that she identified as a prostitute. Jessica reported that her basic needs were often provided for by men with whom she performed oral sex. She also reported that her mother was engaged in the same behaviors.

Jessica and Amber attempted to contact Jessica's mother, but her mother refused to talk to anyone. Amber contacted the Child Abuse and Neglect Hotline (CANH) to report that a minor had been kicked out of the home and was staying in a hotel known for prostitution rings. By the time the CANH workers investigated the situation, Jessica had returned home to her mother, and no further action was taken by CANH. A report was also made to the police regarding the possible prostitution ring, but Amber is not aware of any follow-up from the investigation.

Jessica disappeared shortly after the initial assessment, and Amber could not make contact with the Jessica for months. Eventually another call was placed through the hotline, and Amber learned that Jessica's mother had again refused to allow her to stay home and Jessica was attempting to find a job so she could "get her own place." After multiple failed meeting attempts on Amber's part, she finally met with Jessica. At this meeting, Jessica disclosed that her boyfriend had been incarcerated for prostitution and drug charges but stated that she had to "remain true to him while he was in prison" because if he found out she was cheating "he would have her killed." Jessica's affect appeared flat while stating these facts, and she reported that she was using several "hard drugs" such as cocaine and heroin as well. Amber attempted to work with the youth on housing options, substance abuse treatment, and other referrals, but Jessica denied assistance and stated that she could do it on her own. Shortly after this meeting, Amber continued to attempt building a relationship with Jessica through phone calls and social media; however, no further contact was made.

Practice Implications: Connecting Practice to Research

There is no doubt that direct practice is difficult with a population as challenging as sexually exploited individuals, who often have experienced complex trauma, homelessness, poverty, and/or a plethora of other challenging health and mental health situations (Clawson et al., 2009; Macy & Graham, 2012). As previously mentioned, the evidence suggests that advocates, particularly outreach workers, must follow through on promises made to sexually exploited individuals in order to be effective (Saldanha & Parenteau, 2013). In practice, however, following through on referral connections and other matters can be challenging when particular services remain closed off to clients, as seen in the case vignettes. Similarly, such challenges can be exacerbated when individuals often do not see themselves as victims, as demonstrated in the three case examples. Consequently, they may not feel that particular services directed toward survivors of trafficking specifically or victims generally apply to them. For these reasons, there are several important considerations when connecting these practice examples to knowledge in research.

The Need for Long-Term, Trauma-Informed Care (TIC)

Victim- or client-centered approaches are usually recommended when working with sexually exploited individuals and must be given time and funding to be most effective (Wilson et al., 2015). The case vignettes provide just a few examples of multiple individuals from Amber's caseload who did not experience TIC across the various services they accessed. Accessing TIC is difficult when access to a shelter is based on zip code rather than need, there is no access to confidential locations for youth shelters, shelter staff have not been trained in TIC techniques, staff utilize punitive measures for punishments instead of trauma-informed consequences, and youth and young adults engaged in commercial sex are stigmatized. Any organizational staff members (practitioners, intake counselors, etc.) who may come into contact with sexually exploited individuals through homeless shelters, IPV organizations, outreach services, schools, and addiction treatments must be trained in TIC interventions and language.

While there are multiple ways to access such training, an organization may begin this process at little to no cost. Organizations may access organizational assessment tools such as the Trauma-Informed Organizational Toolkit for Homeless Services (Guarino, Soares, Konnath, Clervil, & Bassuk, 2009), a free resource designed to begin the conversation of assessing for and implementing TIC. Such tools can help organizations assess TIC and develop a strategic plan to implement trauma-informed changes. The tool assesses for TIC at both practitioner and supervisory levels, which are both imperative to providing TIC because supervisors are essential in helping practitioners process some of the challenging situations they encounter. Furthermore, trainings that focus on providing TIC should be accessed on a continuous basis. Training and information can often be found through universities, as well as in the Runaway and Homeless Youth Training and Technical Assistance Center (RHYTTAC, n.d.). Information is also available through the U.S. Department of Health and Human Services, and in the *Trauma-Informed Approaches and Trauma-Specific Interventions* provided by the Substance Abuse and Mental Health Services Administration (SAMHSA, n.d.). In addition to implementing trauma-informed changes as necessary, there are a few other important challenges that were described in the vignettes and are important to address.

Inclusion Criteria

IPV Services

In the second author's practice experience, organizations' inclusion criteria were often an issue when serving sexually exploited individuals. According to the Centers for Disease Control and Prevention, IPV is defined as "physical, sexual, or psychological harm by a current or former partner or spouse" and can include current or former "spouses, boyfriends/girlfriends, dating partners, ongoing sexual partners" (Breiding, Basile, Smith, Black, & Mehendra, 2015, p. 11). Angelica considered the person who was exploiting her to be her "boyfriend," which should be included in the definition of IPV. Yet, when Amber assisted Angelica in seeking IPV housing services, she was denied because she did not meet inclusion criteria. Despite increasing recognition of the intersection between trafficking/exploitation and intimate partner violence in the literature (Busch et al., 2004), this intersection appears to remain a challenge within the field. It is essential for IPV services to provide care for any individual who indicates that his or her partner, according to the client, is abusive. Organizations should structure their services accordingly and continually provide internal trainings to ensure that no individuals are excluded from services if they indicate that the person abusing or victimizing them is a partner, as defined by the Centers for Disease Control and Prevention.

Age

At the time of the vignette, Jessica was seventeen and identified herself as a prostitute. Under the federal statute, sex trafficking occurs when "a commercial sex act is induced by force, fraud, or coercion, or . . . the person *induced to perform such an act has not attained 18 years of age*" (22 U.S.C. § 7102). As such, the client would legally be considered a victim until her next birthday, when she would be viewed as a criminal. Amber had a limited time period in which to access services targeted toward child/youth victims. While the literature review did address the many challenges of individuals aging out of foster care and youth services, in practice this remains an extraordinary challenge. Legally, Angelica and Chase could be criminals, whereas Jessica should be considered a victim until her next birthday.

Adding further complexity to terminology and law, age of consent varies at the federal and state levels. While federal law mandates a legal age of eighteen for sexual consent, this only applies to federal crimes or sexual acts that occur across state lines or on federal property (Gerassi & Nichols, 2017). Accordingly, the most common age of consent at the state level is sixteen, which encompasses 30 of the 50 states. Nine states mandate the age of consent to be seventeen, while an additional 11 states match federal law with an age of consent of eighteen. Furthermore, 23 states also have a close-in-age-exemption to their age of consent legislation, protecting people close in age who engage in consensual sexual acts from prosecution. Each state has the option to adopt the federal or state age of consent for the prosecution of sex-trafficking crimes. For example, the age of consent in Missouri is seventeen; however, Missouri adopted the federal statute for sex-trafficking crimes (MO 566.223), thereby raising the age of consent to eighteen for all sex-trafficking crimes. This creates additional confusion in prosecuting sex-trafficking crimes at the state level, and practitioners working with this population are likely to face additional challenges when working with individuals as they approach or pass their eighteenth birthdays. Therefore, community-based responses must ensure that emerging adults, defined as ages eighteen to twenty-five (Gerassi & Nichols, 2017), are adequately provided for in services. This may involve extending an organization's youth services to include individuals up to age twenty-five or providing new specific services to this population. Outreach services may be particularly useful when designing services to reach this population (Holger-Ambrose et al., 2013). To effectively serve all victims, it is essential that this age group be prioritized when addressing issues of commercial sexual exploitation.

LGBTQ+- and Gender-Specific Resources

Queer youth and young adults (including lesbian, gay, bisexual, transgender, and genderqueer individuals) who are sexually exploited remain at increased risk for marginalization. When the second author of the paper sought shelter services for Chase, a male survivor of sexual exploitation, there were no options specific for this population, and she was limited to general youth or adult shelters. It is likely that practitioners working with boys or young men will face additional challenges in obtaining housing for them, as many of the shelters for survivors of intimate partner violence or trafficking are designated for women and girls (Baker, 2015; Reichert & Sylwestrzak, 2013). Additionally, most of the intervention studies for sexually exploited individuals, such as those relating to addiction treatments and housing programs, involve women or girls (Begun & Hammond, 2012; Saewyc & Edinburgh, 2010; Sherman, German, Cheng, Marks, & Bailey-Kloche, 2006; Thomson et al., 2011; Yahne et al., 2002). Furthermore, education and awareness initiatives often focus on preventing men from becoming perpetrators of sexual exploitation, which can be helpful, but often without acknowledging that males can also experience sexual exploitation. Thus, there is an extensive gap in the literature and a need for increased services provided to individuals who identify as men or males.

It is essential to work with service providers of existing shelters and related housing services to understand the needs of LGBTQ+ individuals. Increased training and implementation of safety measures within organizations are essential. One possible intervention includes Safe Zone programs, which are designed to develop, enhance, and maintain environments that are culturally competent and supportive to LGBTQ+ individuals (The Safe Zone Project, n.d.). Additionally, steps should be taken to ensure that women's shelters are inclusive of transwomen and IPV services of individuals with same-sex partners. While new organizations dedicated to individuals who identify as LGBTQ+ are important, housing resources must work toward being inclusive of all populations of exploited people. Task forces or committee groups among any coalitions or community-based groups addressing sexual exploitation and trafficking may also be helpful in working with service providers to better serve this population. Continued attention must be paid to populations that do not fit into many of the inclusion requirements of housing and other programs so as to provide access to equal care for all sexually exploited individuals, regardless of sex, gender, or sexual orientation.

Conclusion

Without question, resources serving survivors of sex trafficking and exploitation are scarce, and even more so for particular subgroups of the population. Advocates in this field require a steadfast amount of persistence and dedication to conduct this work and navigate the many challenges that arise in the process. Although there are advancements in the understanding of this population and the need for services, this chapter has highlighted some of the gaps that still exist between practice and research, as well as between the documented need and available services. Practitioners' experiences with clients are invaluable, particularly as both practitioners and researchers must work together to reduce the disconnection between their respective areas of expertise. Task forces and coalitions may help to facilitate difficult conversations about lack of resources and provide an avenue for problem solving in practice and with research. Too often, practitioners will face challenges for which the classroom alone cannot fully prepare them. It is the authors' hope that these examples of individuals who were not able to access and experience TIC will encourage service providers to strengthen their own organizations' training in trauma-informed practice and ultimately better serve *all* sexually exploited and trafficked individuals.

Note

1. The precontemplative stage is one of the early stages within the Stages of Change model. The Stages of Change model was originally designed help physicians facilitate change in patients with addictions and has been applied to address multiple types of behaviors, including within child maltreatment and IPV contexts (Brown, Melchior, Panter, Slaughter, & Huba, 2000; Frasier, Slatt, Kowlowitz, & Glowa, 2001; Littell & Girvin, 2004).

References

Ahrens, K. R., Katon, W., McCarty, C., Richardson, L. P., & Courtney, M. E. (2012). Association between childhood sexual abuse and transactional sex in youth aging out of foster care. *Child Abuse & Neglect, 36*(1), 75–80. doi:10.1016/j.chiabu.2011.07.009

Anderson, P. M., Coyle, K. K., Johnson, A., & Denner, J. (2014). An exploratory study of adolescent pimping relationships. *The Journal of Primary Prevention, 35*(2), 113–117. doi:10.1007/s10935-014-0338-3

Arnold, E. M. (2000). The psychosocial treatment needs of street-walking prostitutes: Perspectives from a case management program. *Journal of Offender Rehabilitation, 30*, 117–132.

Baker, C. K. (2015). A descriptive analysis of transitional housing programs for survivors of intimate partner violence in the United States. *Violence Against Women, 4*, 460–481.

Begun, A. L., & Hammond, G. C. (2012). CATCH Court: A novel approach to "Treatment as Alternative to Incarceration" for women engaged in prostitution and substance abuse. *Journal of Social Work Practice in the Addictions, 12*(3), 328–331. doi:10.1080/1533256X.2012.703920

Bowser, B. P., Ryan, L., Smith, C. D., & Lockett, G. (2008). Outreach-based drug treatment for sex trading women: The Cal-Pep risk-reduction demonstration project. *The International Journal on Drug Policy, 19*(6), 492–495. doi:10.1016/j.drugpo.2007.07.007

Boxill, N. A., & Richardson, D. J. (2007). Ending sex trafficking of children in Atlanta. *Affilia, 22*(2), 138–149.

Breiding, M. J., Basile, K. C., Smith, S. G., Black, M. C., & Mehendra, R. (2015). *Intimate partner violence surveillance: Uniform definitions and recommended data elements.* National Center for Injury Prevention and Control, Centers for Disease Control and Prevention. Retrieved from https://www.cdc.gov/violenceprevention/pdf/intimatepartner violence.pdf

Briere, J., & Jordan, C. E. (2004). Violence against women: Outcome complexity and implications for assessment and treatment. *Journal of Interpersonal Violence, 19*(11), 1252–1276. doi:10.1177/0886260504269682

Brown, V. B., Melchior, L. A., Panter, A. T., Slaughter, R., & Huba, G. J. (2000). Women's steps of change and entry into drug abuse treatment: A multidimensional stages of change model. *Journal of Substance Abuse Treatment, 18*(3), 231–240.

Busch, N. B., Fong, R., & Williamson, J. (2004). Human trafficking and domestic violence: Comparisons in research methodology needs and strategies. *Social Work Research, 5*(2), 137–147.

California Child Welfare Council. (2013). *Ending the commercial sexual exploitation of children: A call for multi-system collaboration in California.* Retrieved from http://www.chhs .ca.gov/Child%20Welfare/Ending%20CSEC%20-%20A%20Call%20for%20Multi -System%20Collaboration%20in%20CA%20-%20February%202013.pdf

Clatts, M. C., Goldsamt, L., Yi, H., & Gwadz, M. V. (2005). Homelessness and drug abuse among young men who have sex with men in New York city: A preliminary epidemiological trajectory. *Journal of Adolescence, 28*(2), 201–214. doi:10.1016/j.adolescence .2005.02.003

Clawson, H., Dutch, N., Solomon, A., & Grace, L. G. (2009). *Human trafficking into and within the United States: A review of the literature.* U.S. Department of Health and Human Services. Retrieved from https://aspe.hhs.gov/report/human-trafficking-and-within-united -states-review-literature

Cocozza, J. J., Jackson, E. W., Hennigan, K., Morrissey, J. P., Reed, B. G., Fallot, R., & Banks, S. (2005). Outcomes for women with co-occurring disorders and trauma: Program-level effects. *Journal of Substance Abuse Treatment, 28*(2), 109–119. doi:10.1016/j. jsat.2004.08.010

Cohan, D., Lutnick, A., Davidson, P., Cloniger, C., Herlyn, A., Breyer, J., . . . Klausner, J. (2006). Sex worker health: San Francisco style. *Sexually Transmitted Infections, 82*(5), 418–422. doi:10.1136/sti.2006.020628

Connolly, J. A., & Joly, L. E. (2012). Outreach with street-involved youth: A quantitative and qualitative review of the literature. *Clinical Psychology Review, 32*(6), 524–534. doi:10.1016/j.cpr.2012.05.006

Coren, E., Hossain, R., Pardo, J., Veras, M., Chakraborty, K., Harris, H., & Martin, A. (2013). Interventions for promoting reintegration and reducing harmful behaviour and lifestyles in street-connected children and young people: A systematic review. *Campbell Systematic Reviews, 6*, 1–171. doi:10.4073/csr.2013.6

Coward Bucher, C. E. (2008). Toward a needs-based typology of homeless youth. *The Journal of Adolescent Health: Official Publication of the Society for Adolescent Medicine, 42*(6), 549–554. doi:10.1016/j.jadohealth.2007.11.150

ECPATUSA, Shared Hope International, The Protection Project, & John Hopkins University. (2013). *National Colloquium 2012 final report: An inventory and evaluation of the current shelter and services response to domestic minor sex trafficking.* Retrieved from http://sharedhope.org/wp-content/uploads/2013/05/National-Colloquium-2012 -Report-B.pdf

El-Bassel, N., Witte, S. S., Wada, T., Gilbert, L., & Wallace, J. (2001). Correlates of partner violence among female street-based sex workers: Substance abuse, history of childhood abuse, and HIV risks. *AIDS Patient Care and STDs, 15*(1), 41–51. doi:10.1089/108729101460092

Elliott, D. E., Bjelajac, P., Fallot, R. D., Markoff, L. S., & Reed, B. G. (2005). Trauma-informed or trauma-denied: Principles and implementation of trauma-informed services for women. *Journal of Community Psychology, 33*(4), 461–477. doi:10.1002/jcop.20063

Estes, R. J., & Weiner, N. A. (2001). *The commercial sexual exploitation of children in the U.S., Canada and Mexico.* Retrieved from https://www.thenightministry.org/070_facts _figures/030_research_links/060_homeless_youth/CommercialSexualExploitationof Children.pdf

Farley, M. (2004a). "Bad for the body, bad for the heart": Prostitution harms women even if legalized or decriminalized. *Violence Against Women, 10*(10), 1087–1125. doi:10.1177 /1077801204268607

——. (2004b). Prostitution, trafficking, and traumatic stress. *Journal of Trauma Practice, 2*(3–4), 37–41. Retrieved from https://digitalbookocean.com/product/prostitution -trafficking-and-traumatic-stress-journal-of-trauma-practice-ebook-only/

Fong, R., & Berger Cardoso, J. (2010). Child human trafficking victims: Challenges for the child welfare system. *Evaluation and Program Planning, 33*(3), 311–316. doi:10.1016/j. evalprogplan.2009.06.018

Frasier, P. Y., Slatt, L., Kowlowitz, V., & Glowa, P. T. (2001). Using the stages of change model to counsel victims of intimate partner violence. *Patient Education and Counseling, 43*(2), 211–217. Retrieved from http://www.pec-journal.com/article/S0738-3991(00)00152-X/fulltext

Gerassi, L.B. & Nichols, A.J. (2017). *Sex trafficking and commercial sexual exploitation: Prevention, advocacy and trauma informed practice.* New York, NY: Springer Publishing Company.

Gibbs, D., Hardison Walters, J., Lutnick, A., Miller, S., & Kluckman, M. (2015). Services to domestic minor victims of sex trafficking: Opportunities for engagement and support. *Children and Youth Services Review, 54*, 1–7.

Gragg, F., Petta, I., Bernstein, H., Eisen, K., & Quinn, L. (2007). New York prevalence study of commercially sexually exploited children: Final report. New York: New York State Office of Children and Family Services. Guarino, K., Soares, P., Konnath, K., Clervil, R., & Bassuk, E. (2009). *Trauma-informed organizational toolkit for homeless services.* Rockville, MD: Center for Mental Health Services, Substance Abuse and Mental Health Services Administration, and the Daniels Fund, the National Child Traumatic Stress Network, and the W. K. Kellogg Foundation. Retrieved from http://www.performwell.org/index.php/component /mtree/trauma-informed-organizational-toolkit/print?tmpl=component&Itemid=

Halter, S. (2010). Factors that influence police conceptualizations of girls involved in prostitution in six U.S. cities: Child sexual exploitation victims or delinquents? *Child Maltreatment, 15*(2), 152–160. doi:10.1177/1077559509355315

Holger-Ambrose, B., Langmade, C., Edinburgh, L. D., & Saewyc, E. (2013). The illusions and juxtapositions of commercial sexual exploitation among youth: Identifying effective street-outreach strategies. *Journal of Child Sexual Abuse, 22*(3), 326–340. doi:10.1080/105 38712.2013.737443

Hom, K. (2013). Trauma and its aftermath for commercially sexually exploited women as told by front-line service providers. *Issues in Mental Health Nursing, 34*(2), 75–81.

Hossain, M., Zimmerman, C., Abas, M., Light, M., & Watts, C. (2010). The relationship of trauma to mental disorders among trafficked and sexually exploited girls and women. *American Journal of Public Health, 100*(12), 2442–2449. doi:10.2105/AJPH.2009.173229

Kalergis, K. I. (2009). A passionate practice: Addressing the needs of commercially sexually exploited teenagers. *Journal of Women and Social Work, 24*(3), 315–324.

Kurtz, S. P., Surratt, H. L., Kiley, M. C., & Inciardi, J. A. (2005). Barriers to health and social services for street-based sex workers. *Journal of Health Care for the Poor and Underserved, 16*(2), 345–361. doi:10.1353/hpu.2005.0038

Leidholdt, D. A. (2004). Prostitution and trafficking in women: An intimate relationship. *Journal of Trauma Practice, 2*(3–4), 167–183. Retrieved from http://www.nycourts.gov/ip/womeninthe courts/pdfs/PROSTITUTION_TRAFFICKING_TRAUMATIC%20STRESS_4_d_1.pdf

Littell, J. H., & Girvin, H. (2004). Ready or not: Uses of the stages of change model in child welfare. *Child Welfare League of America, 83*(4), 341–366.

Logan, T. K., Walker, R., & Hunt, G. (2009). Understanding human trafficking in the United States. *Trauma, Violence, & Abuse, 10*(1), 3–30. doi:10.1177/1524838008327262

Macy, R. J., & Graham, L. M. (2012). Identifying domestic and international sex-trafficking victims during human service provision. *Trauma, Violence, & Abuse, 13*(2), 59–76. doi:10.1177/1524838012440340

Martinez, O., & Kelle, G. (2013). Sex trafficking of LGBT Individuals: A call for service provision, research, and action. *International Law News, 42*(4), 1–6.

Micetic, S. (2016). Reducing risk of domestic minor sex trafficking among runaway and homeless youth. In E. C. Heil & A. J. Nichols (Eds.), *Broadening the scope of human trafficking research*. Durham, NC: Carolina Academic Press.

Miller, C. L., Fielden, S. J., Tyndall, M. W., Zhang, R., Gibson, K., & Shannon, K. (2011). Individual and structural vulnerability among female youth who exchange sex for survival. *The Journal of Adolescent Health, 49*(1), 36–41. doi:10.1016/j.jadohealth.2010.10.003

Newton, P. J., Mulcahy, T. M., & Martin, E. (2008). Finding victims of human trafficking. U.S. Department of Justice. Retrieved from https://www.ncjrs.gov/pdffiles1/nij/grants/224393.pdf

Nichols, A.J. (2016). *Sex trafficking in the United States: Theory, research, policy and practice*. New York, NY: Columbia University Press.

Nixon, K., Tutty, L., Downe, P., Gorkoff, K., & Ursel, J. (2002). The everyday occurrence: Violence in the lives of girls exploited through prostitution. *Violence Against Women, 8*(9), 1016–1043. doi:10.1177/107780120200800902

Osgood, D. W., Foster, E. M., & Courtney, M. E. (2014). Vulnerable populations and the transition to adulthood. *The Future of Children, 20*(1), 209–229.

Pearce, J. (2006). Who needs to be involved in safeguarding sexually exploited young people? *Child Abuse Review, 15*(5), 326–340. doi:10.1002/car.954

Ramsay, J., Carter, Y., Davidson, L., Dunne, D., Eldridge, S., Hegarty, K., . . . Feder, G. (2009). *Advocacy interventions to reduce or eliminate violence and promote the physical and psychosocial well-being of women who experience intimate partner abuse* (Review). . doi:10.1002/14651858.CD005043.pub3

Raphael, J., Reichert, J. A., & Powers, M. (2010). Pimp control and violence: Domestic sex trafficking of Chicago women and girls. *Women & Criminal Justice, 20*(1–2), 89–104. doi:10.1080/08974451003641065

Raphael, J., & Shapiro, D. L. (2002). Sisters speak out: The lives and needs of prostituted women in Chicago. *Center for Impact Research*. Retrieved from https://www.issuelab.org/resource/sisters-speak-out-the-lives-and-needs-of-prostituted-women-in-chicago-a-research-study.html

Reichert, J., & Sylwestrzak, A. (2013). *National survey of residential programs for victims of sex trafficking*. Chicago, IL: The Illinois Criminal Justice Information Authority. Retrieved from http://www.icjia.state.il.us/assets/pdf/ResearchReports/NSRHVST_101813.pdf

Reid, J. A. (2010). Doors wide shut: Barriers to the successful delivery of victim services for domestically trafficked minors in a southern U.S. metropolitan area. *Women & Criminal Justice, 20*(1–2), 147–166. doi:10.1080/08974451003641206

——. (2011). An exploratory model of girls' vulnerability to commercial sexual exploitation in prostitution. *Child Maltreatment, 16*(2), 146–157. doi:10.1177/1077559511404700

RHYTTAC. (n.d.) *Runaway and homeless youth training and technical assistance center*. Retrieved from https://www.rhyttac.net/

The Safe Zone Project. (n.d.) Retrieved from http://thesafezoneproject.com/

Saewyc, E. M., & Edinburgh, L. D. (2010). Restoring healthy developmental trajectories for sexually exploited young runaway girls: Fostering protective factors and reducing risk behaviors. *The Journal of Adolescent Health, 46*(2), 180–188. doi:10.1016/j.jadohealth .2009.06.010

Saldanha, K., & Parenteau, D. (2013). "Well, if you can't smile you should go home!" Experiences and reflective insights on providing outreach to young sex trade workers. *Children and Youth Services Review, 35*(8), 1276–1283. doi:10.1016/j.childyouth.2013.04.015

SAMHSA. (n.d.) *Trauma-Informed Approach and Trauma-Specific Interventions.* Retrieved from https://www.samhsa.gov/nctic/trauma-interventions

Schram, D. D., & Giovengo, M. (1991). Evaluation of threshold: An independent living program for homeless adolescents. *Journal of Adolescent Health, 12*, 576–572.

Sherman, S. G., German, D., Cheng, Y., Marks, M., & Bailey-Kloche, M. (2006). The evaluation of the JEWEL project: An innovative economic enhancement and HIV prevention intervention study targeting drug using women involved in prostitution. *AIDS Care, 18*(1), 1–11. doi:10.1080/09540120500101625

Sloss, C. M., & Harper, G. W. (2010). Legal service needs and utilization of women who trade sex. *Sexuality Research and Social Policy, 7*(3), 229–241. doi:10.1007/s13178-010 -0025-y

Staller, K. M. (2004). Runaway youth system dynamics: A theoretical framework for analyzing runaway and homeless youth policy. *Families in Society, 85*(3), 379–390. doi:10.1606 /1044-3894.1499

Stark, C., & Hodgson, C. (2003). Sister oppressions: A comparison of wife battering and prostitution. *Journal of Trauma Practice, 2*(3–4), 17–32.

Syvertsen, J. L., Robertson, A. M., Rolón, M. L., Palinkas, L. A., Martinez, G., Rangel, M. G., & Strathdee, S. A. (2013). *"Eyes that don't see, heart that doesn't feel"*: Coping with sex work in intimate relationships and its implications for HIV/STI prevention. *Social Science & Medicine, 87*, 1–8. doi:10.1016/j.socscimed.2013.03.010

Thomson, S., Hirshberg, D., Corbett, A., Valila, N., & Howley, D. (2011). Residential treatment for sexually exploited adolescent girls: Acknowledge, Commit, Transform (ACT). *Children and Youth Services Review, 33*(11), 2290–2296. doi:10.1016/j.childyouth .2011.07.017

Torchalla, I., Nosen, L., Rostam, H., & Allen, P. (2012). Integrated treatment programs for individuals with concurrent substance use disorders and trauma experiences: A systematic review and meta-analysis. *Journal of Substance Abuse Treatment, 42*(1), 65–77. doi:10.1016/j.jsat.2011.09.001

Twill, S. E., Green, D. M., & Traylor, A. (2010). A descriptive study on sexually exploited children in residential treatment. *Child & Youth Care Forum, 39*(3), 187–199. doi:10.1007/ s10566-010-9098-2

Tyler, K. A., Hoyt, D. R., Whitbeck, L. B., & Cauce, A. M. (2001). The effects of a high-risk environment on the sexual victimization of homeless and runaway youth. *Violence and Victims, 16*(4), 441–455. Retrieved from http://www.ncbi.nlm.nih.gov/pubmed/11506452

U.S. Department of State. (2014). *Trafficking in persons report 2014.* Retrieved from https:// www.state.gov/j/tip/rls/tiprpt/2014/

Valera, R. J., Sawyer, R. G., & Schiraldi, G. R. (2001). Perceived health needs of inner-city street prostitutes: A preliminary study. *American Journal of Health Behavior, 25*(1), 50–59. Retrieved from http://www.ncbi.nlm.nih.gov/pubmed/11289729

Van Dam, D., Vedel, E., Ehring, T., & Emmelkamp, P. M. G. (2012). Psychological treatments for concurrent posttraumatic stress disorder and substance use disorder: A systematic review. *Clinical Psychology Review, 32*(3), 202–214. doi:10.1016/j.cpr.2012.01.004

Walls, N. E., & Bell, S. (2011). Correlates of engaging in survival sex among homeless youth and young adults. *Journal of Sex Research, 48*(5), 423–436. doi:10.1080/00224499.2010.50 1916

Wilson, B., & Butler, L. D. (2013). Running a gauntlet: A review of victimization and violence in the pre-entry, post-entry, and peri-/post-exit periods of commercial sexual exploitation. *Psychological Trauma: Theory, Research, Practice, and Policy.* doi:10.1037/a0032977

Wilson, B., Critelli, F. M., & Rittner, B. A. (2015). Transnational responses to commercial sexual exploitation: A comprehensive review of interventions. *Women's Studies International Forum, 48*, 71–80. doi:10.1016/j.wsif.2014.10.005

Yahne, C. E., Miller, W. R., Irvin-Vitela, L., & Tonigan, J. S. (2002). Magdalena pilot project: Motivational outreach to substance abusing women street sex workers. *Journal of Substance Abuse Treatment, 23*, 49–53.

CHAPTER 14

SYSTEM FAILURE!

Is the Department of Children and Families Facilitating
Sex Trafficking of Foster Girls?[1]

JOAN A. REID, PhD, LMHC UNIVERSITY OF SOUTH FLORIDA
ST. PETERSBURG

P rotecting children and adolescents from exploitation in sex trafficking is an emerging and urgent concern of child protective
and child welfare workers. Disconcertingly, numerous governmental reports have documented that a high proportion of detected cases of
sex trafficking involve girls in foster care (for a review, see Lillie, 2013). Sex
trafficking of girls in state care is of particular concern because of the obvious
mandate given to child welfare systems to provide safe and secure shelter for
youth removed from their homes and placed in state care. The detrimental
and potential lifelong psychological and health consequences suffered by girls
exploited in sex trafficking make it critically important to have comprehensive
protection of children and adolescents, particularly those in state care. In light
of these priorities, this chapter will highlight child welfare system vulnerabilities that facilitate sex trafficking of girls in foster care. An examination of
the particular circumstances linked to sexual exploitation of girls in foster
care will enable service providers to develop and implement more effective
prevention strategies.

Elevated Vulnerability to Victimization
Among Foster Care Youth

The child welfare system encompasses both private and governmental service
agencies mandated to provide social services to children and families. Child

welfare procedures vary from state to state (for a state-by-state review, see Foundation for Government Accountability, 2012). In all states the primary purpose of the child welfare system is to provide child protective services to maltreated children. Children are commonly placed in state care because of caregiver drug and/or alcohol abuse, neglect, physical abuse, or sexual abuse (U.S. Department of Health and Human Services et al., 2016). The key functions of the child welfare system are to (1) manage investigations of all reports of alleged child maltreatment; (2) provide services for families who are considered unsafe or unable to protect and care for their children; (3) place children with foster families if they must be removed from an unsafe home environment; and (4) seek permanent adoptive families for children leaving foster care. Foster care, or what is often labeled "out of home" care, is a service overseen by child welfare that provides shelter to children who have been removed from the care of their parents or legal guardians or who have been relinquished to the state by their parents. Children in foster care are placed in homes of relatives, nonrelatives, or group homes. Foster parents or group homes are provided with a stipend from the state in exchange for their care. Group homes are licensed by the state and may be run by house parents who live with the children 24/7 or by shift staff who transfer in and out during a twenty-four-hour period. Reports show that approximately four hundred thousand U.S. children were in foster care during 2014 (U.S. Department of Health and Human Services, 2015). These figures indicate that approximately one out of every two hundred children (or 0.5 percent of children) in the United States is in foster care during any given year.

Victimization of Foster Girls

Child maltreatment is an almost certain precondition to placement in foster care. Therefore, children and adolescents in foster care share certain factors that put them at higher risk for psychosocial difficulties and at heightened peril for other forms of victimizations. Traumatic experiences, such as child maltreatment, are considered more detrimental if they occur during childhood or adolescence (Macmillan, 2001; Putnam, 2003). Child maltreatment decreases the expectancy of finding safety in the world, shatters optimistic beliefs about self-efficacy, and diminishes the capability to form intimate attachments (Herman, 1997; Macmillan, 2001). Moreover, when the perpetrator of abuse or neglect is a caregiver, the effects are exceedingly harmful because the perpetrator is both the originator of danger and the primary basis of the child's sense of safety and social attachment (Finkelhor & Browne, 1985; Herman, 1997; Putnam, 2003).

Survivors of child maltreatment often experience profound deficiencies in their ability to self-protect, leaving them highly vulnerable to revictimization

(Herman, 1997). Studies have confirmed that diminished familial closeness and acceptance are strong predictors of later violent victimization (Schreck & Fisher, 2004). The detrimental and lasting effects of repeated victimizations, coupled with a severe lack of family attachment or nurturance, lead multiply victimized children or adolescents to actually constitute their own crime "hot spot" and continue to experience multiple types of victimization (Pease & Laycock, 1996; Reid & Sullivan, 2009). For foster children, victimization may resemble an enduring, chronic condition rather than a one-time or occasional incident (Finkelhor, Ormrod, Turner, & Hamby, 2005; Reid & Sullivan, 2009).

Sex Trafficking and Foster Care

Poor parent-child bonding, emotional neglect, and lack of caregiver protection heighten the likelihood that children will seek affection and support outside their family, thereby escalating their susceptibility to other types of victimization (Benedict & Zautra, 1993). According to research on the victim selection patterns of sex offenders by Beauregard, Rossmo, and Proulx (2007), sex offenders will seek out "a child with family problems, without supervision, always on the street and in need of help" (p. 455). In a similar way, several studies have included accounts of sex traffickers recruiting victims from youth homeless shelters and foster care group homes (Lillie, 2013; Reid, 2010). Sex traffickers often target vulnerable and maltreated teens, who, in comparison to adults, are easy to manipulate and who are not likely to expose traffickers' illegal activities (Brayley, Cockbain, & Laycock, 2011; Reid, 2010, 2014a; Reid & Jones, 2011).

Beyond vulnerabilities created by childhood maltreatment, limitations or deficiencies in the child welfare system may also increase youth susceptibility to exploitation in sex trafficking. Running away from placements in foster homes or foster group homes is a relatively common occurrence; one-third to one-half of older teens in foster care report running away, and most report running away more than once (Pergamit & Ernst, 2011). Significantly, running away and being homeless are documented risk factors for exploitation by sex traffickers (Reid, 2011, 2012). In addition, staff employed at foster group homes or runaway shelters are not always trained or skilled at responding to youth with extensive trauma histories (Clawson & Grace, 2007; U.S. Department of Health and Human Services et al., 2016).

In summary, girls in foster care make up a disproportionately high percentage of detected cases of domestic minor sex trafficking in more than a few U.S. states (Lillie, 2013), and the link between foster care and sex trafficking is a recurring research finding (Estes & Weiner, 2005; Reid, 2011, 2012). However, less is known about the percentage of trafficked girls in foster care who have experienced exploitation in sex trafficking *prior to* placement and the percentage who were exploited *after placement* in foster care. Although the previously noted psychosocial risk factors common among girls in foster care may provide a partial explanation of their increased susceptibility to exploitation in sex trafficking, it is vitally important to understand the child welfare system environments, procedures, or practices that are also contributing to foster girls' disproportionate risk for sex trafficking.

Risk factor studies and governmental reports indicate that being in foster care is, in itself, a risk factor or trigger for sex trafficking. An alternative explanation of this association is that children and adolescents placed in foster care were maltreated prior to placement and are more vulnerable regardless of foster care placement, with some even being exploited in sex trafficking prior to placement. To provide a better understanding of the risk of exploitation in sex trafficking faced by girls in foster care, the authors conducted a study that (1) examined the percentage of foster girls within an overall sample of girls exploited in sex trafficking; (2) used available case records with detailed childhood histories to determine whether these foster girls were placed in state care prior to or after exploitation in sex trafficking; and (3) identified youth- and system-based vulnerabilities that facilitated their initial exploitation in sex trafficking after placement in foster care.

Study Setting: Privatization of Child Welfare System in Florida

As the data for this study were collected from a sample of trafficked girls, many of whom had received child welfare services in Florida, a brief overview of the privatization of the child welfare system in Florida is outlined here to provide context for the study. Beginning a multiyear process initiated in 1999, all child welfare services in Florida, except for child investigation units, have been gradually outsourced to local service agencies. Referred to as Community Based Care (CBC), this complete redesign of the child welfare system has resulted in increased local community responsibility for and ownership of child welfare services delivery and design (Foundation for Government Accountability, 2013). Within the redesigned CBC system, services for abused and neglected children and their families are provided by local community-based agencies that are governed by boards of directors in each county composed of local community members. The lead agency in each county, in cooperation with many local community agencies, provides a continuum of services for children in state care.

Child welfare services were transferred from governmental agencies to private providers because the Department of Children and Families (DCF) in Florida was coming under heavy criticism. One of the most publicized cases involved the disappearance of a five-year-old girl from Miami who disappeared while in foster care (Canedy, 2002). Her case manager continued to submit written reports updating her care and housing after she was missing, clearly falsifying the reports to avoid performing the required site evaluations. The ensuing investigation found that caseloads of one hundred to two hundred children per case manager were not uncommon, and substantial falsification of records by case managers was occurring.

Since the redesign and privatization of the child welfare system in Florida, numerous successful accomplishments have been reported. In 2012, an independent study of child welfare services in the United States ranked Florida as the fourth best in the country. Florida scored high on reducing the overall foster care population, reducing abuse in foster care, responding rapidly to child abuse inquiries, and finding permanent homes for children (Foundation for Government Accountability, 2012). However, there have been allegations that the child welfare system is persistently resistant to outside scrutiny and criticism. Recently, allegations were raised that Florida's DCF orchestrated a cover-up of an investigation into the failure to report thirty child deaths in the Miami area; the investigation yielded no documents, making it impossible to review the findings (Miller, 2014). Privatization and the redesigned CBC child welfare system allowed Florida's DCF to shirk responsibility for trafficking of foster children out of group homes in Florida. The spokesman for Florida DCF responded to the news that sex traffickers were recruiting girls in group homes by noting that "group homes are subcontractors that don't report directly to DCF. There is not a department employee specifically involved in these children's lives. We contract the care of foster children in the state to community groups who then often subcontract that work out too" (Menzel, 2012).

The information provided in this chapter is based on de-identified data drawn from a sample of 93 case records from girls exploited in juvenile sex trafficking (JST)—defined as exploitation in sex trafficking prior to turning eighteen years old. The case records comprised all cases of trafficked girls served by four social service agencies between 2007 and 2014. These girls received services such as intensive case management and mental health counseling in major metropolitan areas in southern and central Florida.

The case records included three categories of de-identified information. First, the case files outlined the biographical information of each girl, including demographics, family characteristics, reported history of maltreatment, and/or prior involvement in foster care or with child protective services. Second, the case files contained results of psychological evaluations and/or assessments of the girls. Lastly, case files provided detailed information on the circumstances leading to sex trafficking based on youths' self-reports, caregivers' reports, official reports by law enforcement, and/or records provided by child protective services. Information was reported regarding the circumstances surrounding the initiation and involvement in commercial sexual exploitation, such as details about pimp/traffickers and their relationship with the victim, the initiation or recruitment process, the length and extent of sexual exploitation, and how the youth was eventually identified or escaped. Access to these original reports mitigated retrospective bias, which is common in case file research that is largely based on summary reports of a subject's life written after the effects of particular importance have already taken place (in the case of this study, after the onset of sex trafficking). In this study, not only did external reports included in the case files originate from various individuals or agencies, but these reports also were collected and described the survivor and her life circumstances occurring at different times in the girl's life. In most cases, records from child services were available that predated initial exploitation in sex trafficking.

Additionally, to ensure accuracy and gain further insight into the data drawn from the case files, service providers with in-depth knowledge of the documented cases were interviewed regarding the entrapment strategies employed by sex traffickers and sex traffickers' tactics and specific circumstances facilitating exploitation. All mental health counselors and case managers who were interviewed for this study had extensive and direct experience in counseling or assisting trafficked girls. The semistructured interviews with service providers were completed in approximately one hour (for more information of the interview questions, see Reid, 2014a). The case file review and interviews with service providers were conducted between July 2012 and March 2014.

Notably, the use of data available in case records of trafficked girls satisfied several ethical considerations of human-subjects research involving children and vulnerable populations. By reviewing and analyzing previously collected and de-identified information available in the case records and interviewing social service providers engaged in assisting these girls, this study was conducted without exposing these girls to any potential risk arising from direct contact with researchers.

Sample Demographics and Subsample Comparisons

From the sample of 93 case records, the race/ethnic distribution was 46 percent African American ($n = 42$), 29 percent Hispanic ($n = 27$), 13 percent Caucasian ($n = 12$), 9 percent Haitian ($n = 8$), and 3 percent other races/ethnicities ($n = 3$). Initial JST occurred when the girls were between the ages of four and seventeen ($M = 14.02$; $SD = 2.71$), and 58 girls (62 percent) had histories involving placement in state care. The gender of the traffickers was 67 percent male ($n = 44$) and 33 percent female ($n = 22$). The types of trafficker-victim relationships were 31 percent relative ($n = 19$), 29 percent stranger ($n = 18$), 26 percent boyfriend ($n = 16$), 10 percent girlfriend ($n = 6$), and 4 percent other type of relationship ($n = 3$).

Youth Vulnerabilities

Girls with and without histories of foster care had comparable levels of vulnerabilities or behaviors likely to heighten susceptibility to exploitation in JST (i.e., mental health diagnosis, intellectual disability, running away, drug/alcohol use) (table 14.1). They also had very similar routes of victim identification or intervention by law enforcement or service providers (i.e., arrest for prostitution, pregnancy, sexual assault). However, as would be expected, girls in foster care experienced all forms of child maltreatment at a greater rate than trafficked girls not in foster care (table 14.1).

TABLE 14.1 Descriptive Statistics of Subsamples

	Girls with History of Foster Care (*n* = 58) *M* (*SD*)/%	Girls Without History of Foster Care (*n* = 35) *M* (*SD*)/%
Age at initial JST	13.98 (2.93)	14.06 (2.38)
Running away	93%	81%
Drug/alcohol use	83%	71%
Mental health diagnosis (yes/no)^	100%	94%
Intellectual disability	30%	29%
Sexual assault (other than JST)	78%	65%
Pregnancy	33%	30%
Arrested for prostitution	26%	29%
Witnessed domestic violence**	52%	14%
Child sexual abuse**	63%	29%
Child physical abuse***	65%	20%
Child neglect/abandonment***	76%	23%

Note: Chi-square test significant at *p* < .05, ** *p* < .01, *** *p* < .001. ^Not confirmed as preexisting prior to JST.

Pathways Between Foster Care and Juvenile Sex Trafficking

Twenty-six percent of the girls ($n = 15$) were exploited in JST before placement in foster care, with approximately half of these cases involving foreign-born girls (7 girls of Hispanic ethnicity and 1 Haitian girl) who were trafficked into the United States or exploited after they arrived in the United States by sex traffickers identified as citizens of other countries. Sample case file notations included "[name] was held captive for 2 months by Mexican human traffickers"; "mother [living in another country] sold child to uncle for sex . . . escaped from trafficking by uncle . . . uncle forced her to do agricultural work and to provide sex to his friends and acquaintances"; and "arrived in the U.S. about 2 years ago . . . brought by 27-year-old boyfriend who forced her into prostitution for 2 months." Girls exploited prior to placement were also more likely to have been exploited in JST by a relative compared to girls exploited after placement (60 percent vs. 14 percent). More specifically, 9 out of the 15 cases involving girls who were exploited prior to placement in foster care had been trafficked at a young age by family members, most prominently by mothers who were addicted to drugs. Notes from case records provide compelling examples: "sexually exploited by mother when 4 years old"; "pimped by biological mother to support drug habit when she was very young"; "exposed to pornography, witnessed her mother engaging in prostitution . . . sexually exploited by mother at the age of 6 [years]"; "her mother sold her or let men rape her in exchange for drugs"; started prostitution when she was 12 years old . . . mother had a pimp and taught her 'the rules' of 'the game.' "

Notably, 74 percent ($n = 43$) of JST trafficking victims with histories of placement in state care were exploited in JST after placement in state care. One girl explicitly stated, "Going to group homes has 'turned me out' . . . I didn't do this until I got there." The race/ethnic distribution of this subsample of girls was 56 percent African American ($n = 24$), 16 percent Caucasian ($n = 7$), 14 percent Hispanic ($n = 6$), 12 percent Haitian ($n = 5$), and 2 percent other races/ethnicities ($n = 1$). Only two endangering circumstances were significantly more common among girls exploited after placement in foster care: they were more likely to have run away (100 percent vs. 71 percent) and more likely to use drugs or alcohol (90 percent vs. 64 percent).

The most commonly noted circumstance related to initial exploitation in JST was running away. Case notes regarding running away described the connection between running away and JST: "during her most recent runaway episode she was a victim of sexual exploitation/prostitution and became pregnant"; "met pimp during her first or second runaway episode"; "ran away because she did not like how she was being treated . . . while on elopement stayed with a friend from school who recruited her . . . school friend's cousin was a pimp";

"ran away from group home when 12 years old and met a pimp who introduced her to prostitution . . . from age of 12 to 17 had 'hundreds' of perpetrators
[pimps and buyers] in various cities throughout the United States"; "ran away
from group home and was picked up by a pimp when she was 13 years old."

As noted, all of the girls who were exploited in JST after receiving child
welfare services reported running away. Many of these girls were described
as chronic or habitual runaways, with girls and/or their case managers stating
they were triggered to run when upsetting situations or news involving family
members was discussed. Length of time on the run ranged from a few hours to
many years. In some of the cases, the girls walked around in the neighborhood
surrounding their group homes. The girls did not view these incidences as
running away; rather, they went outside "for some fresh air," "out of boredom,"
or because they "couldn't sleep" and had no plans to run away or stay away for
an extended time. These incidences of walking out of the group homes for a
short time were linked to sexual assaults and JST: "on route back to the house,
a guy pulled up and told her to get in the car . . . she was gang raped . . . forced
to give oral sex to many different boys"; "pimp found her walking near the
group home."

Recruitment

The second most common circumstance linked to exploitation in JST of girls
after placement in foster care was recruitment by another girl while in foster
care: "trafficking ring used foster girl as a recruiter of numerous girls in group
home"; "placed in home with girls with known involvement in human trafficking. Ran away together to pimp, prostituted at local bar"; "reported that
another girl who resided at the same foster home approached her and asked her
if she wanted friends and wanted to make money. She did not know what she
was getting herself into and gradually adapted to the environment." Additional
system-related vulnerabilities included recruitment in JST by the foster family.
For instance, in one case the survivor "had pimp/sex trafficker in previous
foster home . . . foster parent's adult son." Another way that traffickers accessed
girls in foster care was through online chatrooms: "goes on chatline to meet
men and has them calling the house."

Several girls were recruited by peers from school: "she was recruited by
another girl in her school"; "the longest time she's spent out of her foster home
is two weeks . . . she stayed at her 'best friend's daddy's house' who gave her
money . . . friend is possible recruiter."

Sadly, some of the girls were recruited and trafficked by their noncustodial
(biological) mothers: "[Name] has been in foster care since age 3 . . . biological mother actively involved in prostitution and girl running away to biological

mother repeatedly"; "Mother was in prison. . . . after release prostituted herself and prostituted child"; "mother (noncustodial parent) encourages child to run away and prostitute and gives her a place to stay."

Location and Supervision of Group Homes

The most commonly noted facility- or system-related vulnerability was the location of group homes in high-crime areas. Case files noted: "pimp found her walking near the group home"; "left house because couldn't sleep, seen one of her 'homeboys' . . . guy pulled up in car and took her to a house . . . gang raped . . . went on for days." Providing external confirmation of this problem, numerous news reports in Florida have highlighted the placement of vulnerable girls in group homes located in high-crime areas. For instance, one news article expressed concern over the fact that young teenage mothers and their babies had found "safe haven" in a high-crime area located just a few feet away from a residence where a SWAT police unit had recently broken down a door and arrested drug dealers (Michael, 2016).

Compounding endangerment due to the location of group homes was evidence that the girls were inadequately supervised while in group homes: "no/little supervision, youth come and go as they please"; "men came into the group home . . . caught in room with young man"; "young men seen jumping the fence of the group home"; "prostitution and drug dealing occur regularly in previous group home." Nonprotective agency policies were also noted in the case files: "girls are out after curfew . . . and per policy staff delayed reporting child missing to police until morning."

Cell Phones

One ongoing, intense debate within social service agencies was related to the role of cell phones in facilitating JST of youth placed in group homes. Some social service providers considered cell phones "as the girls' last lifeline to them" and one way girls could call for help if they were in danger. On the other hand, the case files provided substantial evidence that possessing a cell phone while in foster care facilitated recruitment of new victims: "[Name] refused to stay at group home without cell phone. Within 24 hours the cell phone used to call trafficker to arrange ride for self and 3 other girls who ran away with her to her pimp." Cell phones also provided a way for traffickers to arrange meetings between girls and buyers of sex: "since coming to group home, client ran twice and grown men are calling her at all times of day and night"; "members of the sex trafficking ring called girls in group home on cell phones supplied by the men and arrange for them to have sex at a building used as a kind of brothel"; "text messages on girl's phone recovered by police included several messages from pimp involving johns, including a message that 'somebody wanna pay u to [have sex].'"

Common Youth Vulnerabilities

Sexual Assault/Abuse

There were no statistically significant differences in the age of onset of exploitation in JST for girls in foster care or not in foster care. On average, initial exploitation in JST occurred when the girls were fourteen or fifteen years old. Importantly, both foster (78 percent) and nonfoster girls (65 percent) experienced high rates of sexual assault (beyond exploitation in JST). Numerous case files contained descriptions of ongoing sexual abuse during childhood and early adolescence: "[Name] was raped by biological father for several years starting when 11 years old." As evidenced by these case details, some of the sexual victimization occurred in the girls' foster care placements: "[Name] was raped by foster brother at age 11 for 8 months"; [Name] was raped at age 11 raped by family friend . . . [subsequently] removed from mother's care and molested by foster parents"; "recruiter for pimp had been previously sexually victimized by foster care case manager." Others were sexually assaulted when they encountered strangers/sex offenders when running away or via the Internet: "raped by man she met on the Internet at age 15." These cases support a substantial body of research that has consistently linked JST to sexual assault or abuse during childhood or adolescence (e.g., Reid, 2011; Tyler, Hoyt, Whitbeck, & Cauce, 2001; Widom & Kuhns, 1996; Wilson & Widom, 2008, 2010). Compared to children and adults, adolescent girls face the highest risk for sexual victimization; during adolescence girls are at risk for sexual assault by caregivers, acquaintances, or boyfriends (Snyder, 2000). Despite the high risk for sexual assault during adolescence, research on adolescent sexual victimization lags behind research on childhood sexual abuse (Howard & Wang, 2005). However, numerous studies have documented a link between experiencing forced intercourse during adolescence and subsequent risky sexual behavior (Howard & Wang, 2005), with findings from a relatively recent study indicating that poor decision making and poor social skills enhanced this association (Marchand & Smolkowski, 2013).

Mental Health

A high proportion of both foster (100 percent) and nonfoster girls (93 percent) in this sample of trafficked girls had been diagnosed with a mental health disorder. The majority (62 percent) had been diagnosed with more than one mental health disorder. The most commonly noted mental health disorders included post-traumatic stress disorder (PTSD), conduct disorder, attention deficit hyperactivity disorder (ADHD), and depression. In addition, approximately 30 percent of girls in this sample, both foster girls and girls without a history of placement in foster care, had an intellectual disability. Intellectual and psychological or emotional disabilities impact youth decision making and social skills, reduce awareness of sexual exploitation and its endangerments, and increase susceptibility to trafficker entrapment strategies and manipulation (Hershkowitz, Lamb, & Horowitz, 2007; Reid, 2016; Turner, Vanderminden, Finkelhor, Hamby, & Shattuck, 2011; Wissink, van Vugt, Moonen, Stams, & Hendriks, 2015).

Implications for Providers

Although this sample is not nationally or regionally representative, when taking into account that approximately twenty thousand children are in foster care in Florida out of four million children residing in the state (Children's Defense Fund, 2011), the high percentage of trafficked girls in foster care within the study sample suggests that girls in foster care face a disproportionately high risk of exploitation in JST. This finding corresponds to prior studies that have documented high rates of JST among girls in foster care (Lillie, 2013). When examining the timing of initial exploitation in JST, in approximately half of the cases ($n = 43$) exploitation in sex trafficking occurred after the girls had contact with child welfare and/or had been placed in state care. Running away, which appeared to be a symptom of heightened reactivity to stress, had an endangering effect and was frequently linked to initial exploitation. The location of group homes in high-crime areas magnified the dangers of running away. Previously exploited girls also played a key role in exploitation of new victims by taking other foster girls with them when they ran away or by recruiting new girls for their trafficker. Other girls were recruited into sex trafficking after placement in foster care by their noncustodial, biological mothers. Cell phones and social media facilitated communication between traffickers and victims.

Running Away and JST

The most commonly reported risk-inflating behavioral response in this sample of trafficked girls was running away. Running away was reported by 100 percent of girls who were exploited in JST after placement in foster care, and in many cases running away was explicitly linked to initial exploitation in JST. Prior research has found that, in general, youth run from neglectful and abusive circumstances, holding on to the belief that a better life exists and that even life on the streets will be better than what they are experiencing (Baron, 2003;

Estes & Weiner, 2005). Interestingly, Pergamit and Ernst (2011) found that girls in foster care were more likely to run away than boys and that foster girls in group homes were more likely to run away than those in foster homes or those placed with relatives.

In this current study, information in several case files indicated that girls ran away after being triggered by conflicts with staff or caregivers or because of family problems. This aligns with a prior study of foster girls (Pergamit & Ernst, 2011) that reported that girls ran away from group homes because they felt cooped up or bored, were angered by all the drama in the house, were frustrated with the rules, or felt desperate because of unreasonable restrictions for getting passes to visit family. Additionally, in the prior study by Pergamit and Ernst, two-thirds of the foster girls reported that they decided to run away on the spur of the moment with no prior planning. The high percentage of girls who reported running away without any prior planning demonstrates that adolescents are strongly swayed by short-term outcomes and discount possible long-term consequences, tendencies that amplify their immaturity in judgment and poor decisions (Reid & Jones, 2011; Romer, 2010; Steinberg, 2008; Steinberg & Scott, 2003). When strain or stress triggers an inherent motivation to escape, adolescents lack the necessary knowledge, psychological maturity, or resources available to most adults in similar circumstances (Romer, 2010). This natural and inherent aversion to and desire to escape stress, combined with the inexperience of youth, increase the likelihood that adolescents will choose risky escape routes such as running away or select unreliable rescuers such as sex traffickers masquerading as boyfriends (Reid, 2014a). Moreover, without any opportunity for legitimate employment or any financial resources, runaway girls are highly vulnerable to exploitation in JST (Clawson, Dutch, Solomon, & Grace, 2009; Estes & Weiner, 2005; Wilson & Widom, 2010).

These findings can be used to inform JST prevention efforts and safety strategies for foster girls. In this study sample, running away facilitated offender access and exposed girls to exploitation by sex traffickers. As most girls run away from foster care without any prior planning (Pergamit & Ernst, 2011), it seems vital to incorporate personally tailored safety plans for all girls, particularly those placed in group homes, as part of the intake process at each new placement. Youth-crafted safety plans, which include whom to call in an emergency and where to go to find safety should they run away, could reduce the likelihood that youth would run away at all and also ensure that they know where they can go and whom to contact if they run away.

Second, based on evidence from the case files and other research studies, foster girls often run away as a way of coping with uncomfortable or intolerable negative emotions. Therefore, teaching (and allowing) youth to engage in healthier and safer self-soothing skills as part of trauma-informed care may reduce the number of runaway episodes. Too often group homes are operating on inadequate budgets and cannot provide youth with opportunities to try out new self-soothing coping strategies that can be learned through participation in yoga or fitness classes, sport competitions, animal therapy, or music and art therapy. Similarly, strong school ties and participation in after-school activities (e.g., museums, lessons, classes, and cultural events) have also been recommended to reduce runaway episodes from foster care (N.C. Division of Social Services, 2012). Furthermore, school success is important in lowering the risk of long-term exploitation in sex trafficking (Reid, 2014b).

System-Related Risk Factors

Several types of system-related deficiencies present in the child welfare system emerged from the study data. The first limitation involved the placement of girls in group homes or shelters in high-crime areas. As mentioned earlier, prior research has shown that girls placed in group homes are more likely to run away than boys or girls placed in any other type of placement (Pergamit & Ernst, 2011). Based on prior research, it should be assumed that most girls will run at some point if placed in a group home. Additionally, numerous reports in the past decade have noted that sex traffickers loiter around group homes for the purpose of recruiting new victims (Little, 2013; Reid, 2008). In light of this sex trafficker strategy, the location of group homes is critically important to victims' safety. Each group home goes through an approval process and must be licensed by the state. The neighborhood crime rate should be included in the approval process. Additionally, no state funding should be granted to group homes located in high-crime areas. Placement of girls in group homes should be used sparingly and only as a temporary placement, not as a permanent placement. Research has shown that therapeutic foster homes, in which foster families provide a structured, nurturing, therapeutic environment to youth with mental, emotional, and behavioral health challenges, are more beneficial for troubled youth and more cost effective than therapeutic group homes (for a review of research, see Wisconsin Partnership Program, 2013).

Peer-to-peer recruitment is commonly used by traffickers to entrap new victims (Reid, 2010, 2014a). This sex-trafficking strategy is effective because most adolescents are more heavily influenced by peers than by caregivers or other adults (Gardner & Steinberg, 2005). Recruitment into sex trafficking within foster group homes could be thwarted in several ways. First, creating and maintaining a database of all suspected and verified child or adolescent victims of human trafficking would allow case managers and group home directors to identify girls in foster care who may attempt to recruit others into JST. For example, in Florida the child abuse hotline accepts and keeps records of suspected cases of human trafficking involving minors. These child abuse reports could be used to create a database of suspected and verified victims. This proposed database, if made available to child welfare and juvenile justice case managers and facility intake supervisors, could reduce the likelihood of placement of potential recruiters in the same facility with potential victims. Facility supervisors should not accept new youth without being provided information regarding any prior youth involvement in human trafficking. Youth with histories of exploitation in JST need specialized care and are best served by placement in therapeutic foster homes or therapeutic group homes with a small number of youth (Hahn et al., 2005; Wisconsin Partnership Program, 2013). Additionally, currently most JST prevention programs focus on educating adults about JST. However, peer-to-peer prevention strategies have been successful in preventing other types of adolescent victimizations (Allnock, 2015) and may be more effective in preventing JST by thwarting sex traffickers' attempts to use peer-to-peer recruiting.

Lastly, another system-related vulnerability that emerged from the case files was related to poor supervision of girls while in group homes. Beyond supplying an additional incentive to reduce the number of girls placed in group homes, this finding points to the need to provide sufficient resources and training to group home staff and supervisors to ensure that the primary caregivers for this vulnerable population are adequately equipped for the task they have been given (Clawson & Grace, 2007; U.S. Department of Health and Human Services et al., 2016).

An issue connected to inadequate supervision of foster girls is cell phone use; cell phones (some provided by traffickers) and youth Internet access were also mentioned as electronic facilitators of JST. Unsupervised Internet use by girls gave traffickers easy ways to groom and manipulate vulnerable teens (Kloess, Beech, & Harkins, 2014; Wolak, Finkelhor, & Mitchell, 2004). Trafficking cases of girls have been initiated by the offender contacting the potential victims on social networking sites (Latonero, 2011). Smart or web-enabled cell phones have aided traffickers by allowing them to reach a larger consumer base and schedule more sexually exploitive occurrences per child per day (Latonero, 2011). The examples of traffickers' use of cell phones to communicate and facilitate JST in this study demonstrate that advances in technology have made committing this crime easier for sex traffickers. Trafficker use of cell phones, particularly pay-as-you-go cell phones, to communicate with victims and consumers also hinders law enforcement investigations (Latonero, 2011).

Conclusion

Drawing from the implications listed here, an optimal treatment plan for foster care youth who are suspected or confirmed victims of JST would include

Triage at Emergency Foster Home	Therapeutic Foster Home (TFH)	TFH Pods	Intensive Outpatient Treatment	Independent Oversight of TFHs for Trafficked Youth
Emergency Trafficking Triage Foster Homes – emergency drop-offs with length of stay of 24–72 hours and limit of 1 child/home	Therapeutic foster homes must have sufficient outside support: A) specialized case manager and therapist, B) other TFH in close proximity C) community support – supported by church, university, or civic group before placing child in TFH	Pods to be comprised of 4–6 TFHs located in low crime areas with limit of 1 child/home. Homes in each Pod work together to provide foster parent support and child support with specialized on-call case manager and therapist providing 24-hour support assigned to each TFH Pod.	Biweekly individual sessions and biweekly support group for youth and foster parents led by case managers and therapists (2X week individual session for youth, 2X week group session for youth and for foster parents)	Independent oversight by committee appointed by and reporting directly to Statewide Council on Human Trafficking or Statewide Child Advocacy Program

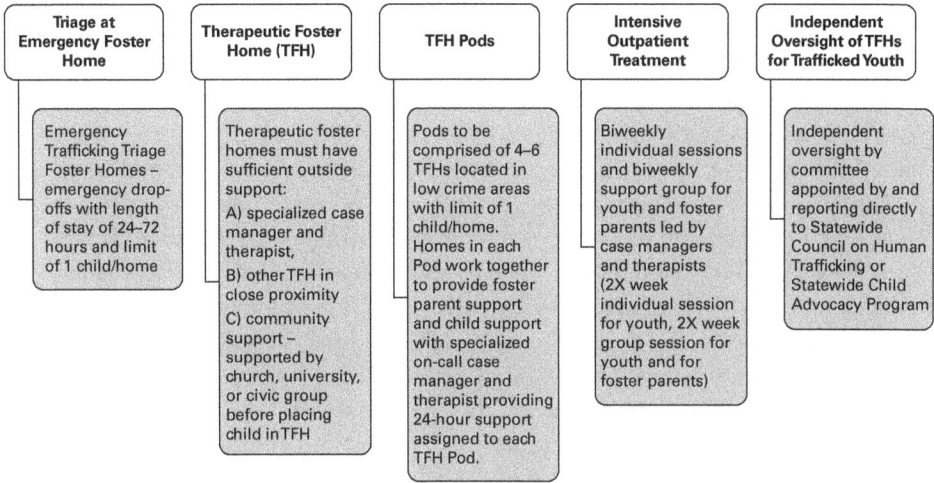

FIGURE 14.1 Optimal Structure for Response and Treatment of Trafficked Youth in Foster Care

(1) emergency triage at a specialized emergency foster care home and (2) place-ment in a therapeutic foster home (TFH) situated within a TFH pod that is run by specialized case managers and therapists and that receives substantial community support. TFHs designated for trafficked youth should have inde-pendent oversight to ensure protection of youth from further victimization (see figure 14.1). Although this structure may seem to be cost-prohibitive, research indicates that TFHs are cost-effective in comparison to therapeutic group homes (Wisconsin Partnership Program, 2013). The proposed structure would facilitate critical elements of care, including close collaboration of treat-ment providers and foster parents, separation from other potential victims, maximum support for foster parents, and individualized monitoring and men-toring for each youth.

Although the study described in this chapter offers useful information regarding the vulnerabilities and circumstances that facilitate exploitation of girls in foster care, the study has several limitations, most of which are related to the size and characteristics of the study sample. First, the study sample is not nationally representative, and the case files all contained data regarding female victims of sex trafficking, restricting the generalizability of the study findings. The investigation of sex trafficking involving male youth, both those in and out of foster care, is also needed and should be a focus of future studies (Reid & Piquero, 2016). Additionally, the sample of cases utilized for the study was composed of sex-trafficking cases that had been discovered or detected by law enforcement or social service providers. Given the hidden nature of JST, the characteristics and dynamics of undetected JST cases may differ in some ways from the sample of cases available for this study. Although the study sample does not reflect a comprehensive or all-inclusive sample of trafficked youth, quantitative and qualitative data on JST victims are not commonly available, and the study findings could be useful in informing prevention strategies and protecting girls in foster care.

In closing, preventing JST is among the most important tasks currently facing the child welfare community. Like other types of sex offenders, sex traffickers often prey on vulnerability and employ manipulative tactics to create opportunities for exploitation. Millions of dollars have been invested to combat this problem; yet, in spite of these extensive efforts, JST of youth in foster care continues to occur. In this study, over two-thirds of the trafficking victims with histories of placement in state care were exploited after placement. This chapter highlighted youth vulnerabilities and child welfare system limitations that must be addressed to prevent the continued recruitment and entrapment of girls in sex trafficking. Implementation of system-based changes drawn from the study findings described in this chapter will strengthen efforts to protect children in state care from exploitation in sex trafficking.

Note

1. This research project was supported by the American Psychology–Law Society Early Career Professional Grant.

References

Allnock, D. (2015). Child maltreatment: How can friends contribute to safety? *Safer Communities, 14*(1), 27–36. doi:doi:10.1108/SC-02-2015-0005

Baron, S. W. (2003). Street youth violence and victimization. *Trauma, Violence, & Abuse, 4*(1), 22–44. doi:10.1177/1524838002238944

Beauregard, E. D., Rossmo, K., & Proulx, J. (2007). A descriptive model of the hunting process of serial sex offenders: A rational choice perspective. *Journal of Family Violence, 22*(6), 449–463. doi:10.1007/s10896-007-9101-3

Benedict, L. W., & Zautra, A. (1993). Family environmental characteristics as risk factors for childhood sexual abuse. *Journal of Clinical Child Psychology, 22*(3), 365–374. doi:10.1207/s15374424jccp2203_7

Brayley, H., Cockbain, E., & Laycock, G. (2011). The value of crime scripting: Deconstructing internal child sex trafficking. *Policing, 5*(2), 132–143. doi:10.1093/police/par024

Canedy, D. (2002, May 1). Miami 5-year-old missing for year before fact noted. *New York Times.* Retrieved from http://www.nytimes.com/2002/05/01/us/miami-5-year-old-missing-for-year-before-fact-noted.html

Children's Defense Fund. (2011). *Children in Florida.* Retrieved from http://www.childrensdefense.org/library/data/state-data-repository/cits/2011/children-in-the-states-2011-florida.pdf

Clawson, H. J., Dutch, N., Solomon, A., & Grace, L. G. (2009). *Human trafficking into and within the United States: A review of the literature.* Washington, DC: Office of the Assistant Secretary for Planning and Evaluation, U.S. Department of Health and Human Services. Retrieved from https://aspe.hhs.gov/basic-report/human-trafficking-and-within-united-states-review-literature

Clawson, H. J, & Grace, L. G. (2007). *Finding a path to recovery: Residential facilities for minor victims of domestic sex trafficking.* Washington, DC: Office of the Assistant Secretary for Planning and Evaluation, U.S. Department of Health and Human Services. Retrieved from https://aspe.hhs.gov/basic-report/finding-path-recovery-residential-facilities-minor-victims-domestic-sex-trafficking

Estes, J. R., & Weiner, N. A. (2005). The commercial sexual exploitation of children in the United States. In S. W. Cooper, J. R. Estes, A. P. Giardino, N. D. Kellogg, & V. I. Vieth (Eds.), *Medical, legal & social science aspects of child sexual exploitation: A comprehensive review of child pornography, child prostitution, and internet crimes against children* (pp. 95–128). St. Louis, MO: GW Medical.

Finkelhor, D., & Browne, A. (1985). The traumatic impact of child sexual abuse: A conceptualization. *American Journal of Orthopsychiatry, 55*(4), 530–541. doi:10.1111/j.1939-0025.1985.tb02703.x

Finkelhor, D., Ormrod, R., Turner, H., & Hamby, S. (2005). The victimization of children and youth: A comprehensive, national survey. *Child Maltreatment, 10*(1), 5–25. doi:10.1177/1077559504271287

Foundation for Government Accountability. (2012). *Right for kids ranking.* Retrieved from https://www.childnetswfl.org/press/Right%20for%20Kids%20BookletFINALDRAFT.pdf

——. (2013). *Florida's right for kids reform.* Retrieved from https://thefga.org/news/floridas-right-for-kids-foster-care-turnaround-explored-in-new-foundation-report/Gardner, M., & Steinberg, L. (2005). Peer influence on risk taking, risk preference, and risky decision making in adolescence and adulthood: An experimental study. *Developmental Psychology, 41*(4), 625–635. doi:10.1037/0012-1649.41.4.625

Hahn, R. A., Bilukha, O., Lowy, J., Crosby, A., Fullilove, M., Liberman, A., . . . Schofield, A. (2005). The effectiveness of therapeutic foster care for the prevention of violence. *American Journal of Preventive Medicine, 28*(2), 72–90. doi:10.1016/j.amepre.2004.10.007

Herman, J. L. (1997). *Trauma and recovery.* New York, NY: Basic Books.

Hershkowitz, I., Lamb, M., & Horowitz, D. (2007). Victimization of children with disabilities. *American Journal of Orthopsychiatry, 77*(4), 629–635. doi:10.1037/0002-9432.77.4.629

Howard, D. E., & Wang, M. Q. (2005). Psychosocial correlates of U.S. adolescents who report a history of forced sexual intercourse. *Journal of Adolescent Health, 36*(5), 372–379. doi:http://dx.doi.org/10.1016/j.jadohealth.2004.07.007

Kloess, J. A., Beech, A., & Harkins, L. (2014). Online child sexual exploitation: Prevalence, process, and offender characteristics. *Trauma, Violence, & Abuse, 15*(2), 126–139. doi:10.1177/1524838013511543

Latonero, M. (2011). *Human trafficking online: The role of social networking sites and online classifieds.* Los Angeles, CA: The USC Annenberg Center on Communication Leadership & Policy.

Lillie, M. (2013). *An unholy alliance: The connection between foster care and human trafficking.* Paper of the OLP Foundation and the human trafficking search. Retrieved from http://digitalcommons.unl.edu/humtrafcon5/4/

Macmillan, R. (2001). Violence and the life course: The consequences of victimization for personal and social development. *Annual Review of Sociology, 27*(1), 1–22. doi:doi:10.1146/annurev.soc.27.1.1

Marchand, E., & Smolkowski, K. (2013). Forced intercourse, individual and family context, and risky sexual behavior among adolescent girls. *Journal of Adolescent Health, 52*(1), 89–95. doi:http://dx.doi.org/10.1016/j.jadohealth.2012.04.011

Menzel, M. (2012, July 6). DCF examining group homes after sex trafficking. *The Daily Record.* Retrieved from https://www.jaxdailyrecord.com/showstory.php?Story_id=536922

Michael, M. (2016, March 1). St. Pete home for human trafficking victims receives amazing gift. *WFLA.* Retrieved from http://wfla.com/2016/03/01/st-pete-home-for-human-trafficking-victims-receives-amazing-gift/

Miller, C. M. (2014, June 23). Sweeping child-welfare changes signed by Florida Gov. Rick Scott. *Miami Herald.* Retrieved from http://www.miamiherald.com/news/state/florida/article1967744.html

N.C. Division of Social Services and the Family and Children's Resource Program. (2012). Preventing and responding to runaways from foster care. *Children's Services Practice Notes, 17*(3). Retrieved from http://www.practicenotes.org/v17n3/runaway.htm

Pease, K., & Laycock, G. (1996). *Revictimization: Reducing the heat on hot victims.* Washington, DC: National Institute of Justice. Retrieved from https://www.ncjrs.gov/pdffiles/revictim.pdf

Pergamit, M. R., & Ernst, M. (2011). *Running away from foster care: Youths' knowledge and access of services.* Chicago, IL: The University of Chicago—NORC, The Urban Institute, Chapin Hall. Retrieved from http://www.1800runaway.org/wp-content/uploads/2015/05/Part-C-Youth-in-Foster-Care.pdf

Putnam, F. W. (2003). Ten-year research update review: Child sexual abuse. *Journal of the American Academy of Child & Adolescent Psychiatry, 42*(3), 269–278. doi:http://dx.doi.org/10.1097/00004583-200303000-00006

Reid, J. A. (2008). *Rapid assessment of domestic minor sex trafficking in the Clearwater/Tampa Bay Area.* Arlington, VA: Shared Hope International. Retrieved from http://works.bepress.com/joan_reid/2

——. (2010). Doors wide shut: Barriers to the successful delivery of victim services for domestically trafficked minors in a southern U.S. metropolitan area. *Women & Criminal Justice, 20*(1–2), 147–166. doi:10.1080/08974451003641206

——. (2011). An exploratory model of girl's vulnerability to commercial sexual exploitation in prostitution. *Child Maltreatment, 16*(2), 146–157. doi:10.1177/1077559511404700

——. (2012). Exploratory review of route-specific, gendered, and age-graded dynamics of exploitation: Applying life course theory to victimization in sex trafficking in North America. *Aggression and Violent Behavior, 17*(3), 257–271. doi:http://dx.doi.org/10.1016/j.avb.2012.02.005

——. (2014a). Entrapment and enmeshment schemes used by sex traffickers. *Sexual Abuse: A Journal of Research and Treatment, 28*(6), 491–511. doi:10.1177/1079063214544334

——. (2014b). Risk and resiliency factors influencing onset and adolescence-limited commercial sexual exploitation of disadvantaged girls. *Criminal Behaviour and Mental Health, 24*(5), 332–344. doi:10.1002/cbm.1903

——. (2016). Sex trafficking of girls with intellectual disabilities: An exploratory mixed methods study. *Sexual Abuse: A Journal of Research and Treatment.* doi:10.1177/1079063216630981

Reid, J. A., & Jones, S. (2011). Exploited vulnerability: Legal and psychological perspectives on child sex trafficking victims. *Victims & Offenders, 6*(2), 207–231. doi:10.1080/15564886.2011.557327

Reid, J. A., & Piquero, A. (2016). Applying general strain theory to youth commercial sexual exploitation. *Crime & Delinquency, 62*(3), 341–367. doi:10.1177/0011128713498213

Reid, J. A., & Sullivan, C. (2009). A latent class typology of juvenile victims and exploration of risk factors and outcomes of victimization. *Criminal Justice and Behavior, 36*(10), 1001–1024. doi:10.1177/0093854809340621

Romer, D. (2010). Adolescent risk taking, impulsivity, and brain development: Implications for prevention. *Developmental Psychobiology, 52*(3), 263–276. doi:10.1002/dev.20442

Schreck, C. J., & Fisher, B. (2004). Specifying the influence of family and peers on violent victimization: Extending routine activities and lifestyles theories. *Journal of Interpersonal Violence, 19*(9), 1021–1041. doi:10.1177/0886260504268002

Snyder, H. N. (2000). *Sexual assault of young children as reported to law enforcement: Victim, incident, and offender characteristics* (Bureau of Justice Statistics Bulletin NCJ 182990). Washington, DC: Government Printing Office. Retrieved from http://www.bjs.gov/content/pub/pdf/saycrle.pdf

Steinberg, L. (2008). A social neuroscience perspective on adolescent risk-taking. *Developmental Review, 28*(1), 78–106. doi:http://dx.doi.org/10.1016/j.dr.2007.08.002

Steinberg, L., & Scott, E. (2003). Less guilty by reason of adolescence: Developmental immaturity, diminished responsibility, and the juvenile death penalty. *American Psychologist, 58*(12), 1009–1018. doi:10.1037/0003-066X.58.12.1009

Turner, H. A., Vanderminden, J., Finkelhor, D., Hamby, S., & Shattuck, A. (2011). Disability and victimization in a national sample of children and youth. *Child Maltreatment, 16*(4), 275–286. doi:10.1177/1077559511427178

Tyler, K. A., Hoyt, D., Whitbeck, L., & Cauce, A. (2001). The impact of childhood sexual abuse on later sexual victimization among runaway youth. *Journal of Research on Adolescence, 11*(2), 151–176. doi:10.1111/1532-7795.00008

U.S. Department of Health and Human Services. (2015). *The AFCARS report*. Retrieved from http://www.acf.hhs.gov/sites/default/files/cb/afcarsreport22.pdf

U.S. Department of Health and Human Services, Administration for Children and Families, Administration on Children, Youth and Families, Children's Bureau. (2016). *Child maltreatment 2014.* Retrieved from http://www.acf.hhs.gov/programs/cb/research-data-technology/statistics-research/child-maltreatment

Widom, C. S., & Kuhns, J. (1996). Childhood victimization and subsequent risk for promiscuity, prostitution, and teenage pregnancy: A prospective study. *American Journal of Public Health, 86*(11), 1607–1612. doi:10.2105/AJPH.86.11.1607

Wilson, H. W., & Widom, C. S. (2008). An examination of risky sexual behavior and HIV in victims of child abuse and neglect: A 30-year follow-up. *Health Psychology, 27*(2), 149–158. Retrieved from https://www.ncbi.nlm.nih.gov/pubmed/18377133

——. (2010). The role of youth problem behaviors in the path from child abuse and neglect to prostitution: A prospective examination. *Journal of Research on Adolescence, 20*(1), 210–236. doi:10.1111/j.1532-7795.2009.00624.x

Wisconsin Partnership Program. (2013). *What works for health: Treatment foster care.* Madison, WI: University of Wisconsin School of Medicine and Public Health. Retrieved from http://whatworksforhealth.wisc.edu/program.php?t1=20&t2=113&t3=103&id=485

Wissink, I. B., van Vugt, E., Moonen, X., Stams, G. J., & Hendriks, J. (2015). Sexual abuse involving children with an intellectual disability (ID): A narrative review. *Research in Developmental Disabilities, 36*, 20–35. doi:http://dx.doi.org/10.1016/j.ridd.2014.09.007

Wolak, J., Finkelhor, D., & Mitchell, K. (2004). Internet-initiated sex crimes against minors: Implications for prevention based on findings from a national study. *Journal of Adolescent Health, 35*(5), 411–424. doi:http://dx.doi.org/10.1016/j.jadohealth.2004.05.006

CHAPTER 15

SUPPORTING SEX-TRAFFICKING SURVIVORS THROUGH A COLLABORATIVE SINGLE-POINT-OF-CONTACT MODEL

Mezzo and Micro Considerations

MAURA NSONWU, PhD, MSW, LCSW, NORTH CAROLINA
AGRICULTURAL AND TECHNICAL STATE UNIVERSITY

LAURIE COOK HEFFRON, PhD, LMSW,
ST. EDWARD'S UNIVERSITY

CHIQUITIA WELCH-BREWER, PhD, NORTH CAROLINA
AGRICULTURAL AND TECHNICAL STATE UNIVERSITY

NOËL BRIDGET BUSCH-ARMENDARIZ, PhD, LMSW, MPA

This chapter focuses specifically on commercially sexually exploited survivors of human trafficking, although throughout the chapter it will become apparent that there are many demoralizing and complex ways that children, youth, and adults are exploited in both sex and labor industries (Busch-Armendariz, Nsonwu, & Cook Heffron, in press). The chapter emphasizes the ability of social work models and theories to assist commercially sexually exploited (CSE) survivors and the professionals that serve them. It presents a single-point-of-contact social work perspective as the overarching framework and argues that this framework can coordinate and streamline the services for human-trafficking survivors.

Busch-Armendariz, Nsonwu, and Cook Heffron (2011) found that survivors of human trafficking need immediate, short- and long-term services to rebuild their lives. Immediate needs include safety from their traffickers, housing, medical treatment, and other basic human needs (Busch-Armendariz et al., 2011; Clawson & Dutch, 2008). Trauma-informed services are needed during the period of immediate stabilization (Domoney, Howard, Abas, Broadbent, & Oram, 2015); in the following intermediate period, survivors often need assistance with employment, permanent housing, and, for foreign-born victims, legal assistance for family reunification and adjustment of legal immigration status (Busch-Armendariz et al., 2011). Social workers are at the center of providing all of this immediate and stabilizing support. Nsonwu and colleagues (2015) write that "increasingly human trafficking victims are coming into contact with social service, criminal justice, educational, and health care system service providers; therefore it is incumbent upon social work educators and curricula developers to ensure that prospective and current social workers are trained to advocate for and provide the most appropriate, high quality and effective services to victims of human trafficking" (p. 10).

To support this premise, this chapter discusses two major and familiar social work components of the ecological model. The first part explores the strengths of the mezzo-level components, and the second explores the micro components for working with this vulnerable population. Although macro issues are an important aspect of an ecological model, they are not presented in this chapter (see Orme & Ross-Sheriff, 2015, for a discussion of social work macro issues; see also chapter 17).

Situated in a Mezzo Framework

The mezzo system, the principal framework for this section, situates social workers' philosophy and critical thinking about this vulnerable population in a broader context in which direct and indirect services are coordinated. The section covers four broad areas: the single-point-of-contact social work model, a social work perspective, professional self-care, and ethical conundrums. Discussions are situated in the mezzo-level system of practice so that as communities develop and refine services for commercially sexually exploited survivors, informed decisions about those services can be based on current empirical evidence and practice-informed projects.

Rationale for a Single-Point-of-Contact Social Work Model and Its Definition

The single-point-of-contact model utilizes the expert knowledge and empathy of a key professional, many times a social worker, to assist the client(s) in navigating an often complex service delivery system. This model has been a useful paradigm in the fields of domestic violence, child welfare, criminal justice, and healthcare (Mills, 1998) and with identifying children at risk for harm

(Stein, 2009). Social work clinicians use the single-point-of-contact model in therapeutic interventions and referrals when working with children and families (Spray & Jowett, 2011). In the United Kingdom, this framework is often referred to as the "key worker" model of service delivery in the healthcare system and is recognized as working "not only within the health care system but across systems" (Drennan, Wagner, & Rosenbaum, 2005, p. 1). The single-point-of-contact model emphasizes trust building between the client and the professional team, effective advocacy, and empowerment strategies that value the voice of the client.

While this is not a new model for social work, Busch-Armendariz, Nsonwu, and Cook Heffron (2014) explored its use and success specifically in the delivery of services for human-trafficking survivors. They suggest that over the past decade communities have turned to social work professionals to work directly with survivors of human trafficking. In many communities, social workers are the human service professionals who possess the most comprehensive knowledge and understanding of human trafficking and the short-term and long-term services that survivors require. The single-point-of-contact model ensures that services will be coordinated to deliver competent support.

In contrast to former case management models, in the single-point-of-contact model the social worker is "privy to guarded and confidential law enforcement operations and other policy decisions. This insight allows the social worker to be proactive and initiate innovative strategies and new developments" (Busch-Armendariz et al., 2014, p. 13). For example, social workers can work on the legal case against the traffickers or on immigration issues for the client and possible family reunification. This synchronization of care has been a groundbreaking example of *best practice* in the delivery of services to survivors of human trafficking and has replaced former models that lacked continuity of care or led to poor communication among professionals (Busch-Armendariz et al., 2014). With the single-point-of-contact model, the social worker serves as the case manager for survivors and organizes the work of an interdisciplinary team that often includes legal advocates, law enforcement, health and mental health providers, and many other social service providers, such as those from child welfare, domestic violence, or sexual assault organizations that often serve on the human-trafficking task force, as well as other supportive community groups.

Complementary Models: Historical and Contemporary

Coordinated, collaborative, crisis response teams have long been used in responses to both domestic violence and sexual assault (Danis, 2006; Greeson & Campbell, 2013; Whetstone, 2001). While these models have not been

explicitly applied to human trafficking, they merit attention as relevant complements to a single-point-of-contact model. Coordinated community responses,
strategic alliances, and interorganizational task forces in the domestic violence
field are born out of the recognition that, given the complexity of the crime
and its repercussions, no one entity can tackle it alone (Danis, 2006). Collaborative models that integrate social services personnel and law enforcement are
thought to improve the quality of investigation and prosecution of domestic
violence cases as well as the quality of life for survivors (Whetstone, 2001).
Those working to respond to and prevent sexual assault have developed similar
models. Sexual assault response teams, often referred to as SARTs, grew out of
the understanding that responses to sexual assault from medical, mental health,
and legal systems were often inadequate and disjointed (Greeson & Campbell,
2013). SARTs aim to be coordinated, multidisciplinary, and survivor-centered
and typically engage in regular collaborative meetings, strategic problem solving, cross-training, and outreach. Utilized in communities across the United
States, SARTs have generally shown positive impacts: they have improved multidisciplinary relationships and decision making; increased participation in the
legal system; improved outcomes of the legal system; enhanced referrals for
survivors; and decreased secondary trauma among survivors interacting with
the criminal justice system (Greeson & Campbell, 2013).

Today single-point-of-contact and coordinated response team models are
being implemented on college campuses in response to mandated reporting
policies under Title IX. Many universities are now using a single-point-of-
contact model, often the Title IX coordinator, to report forms of violence z
under federal Title IX that include sexual harassment, dating violence, stalking, and sexual violence. One university is piloting an interesting model that
blends the coordinated team approach with the single-point-of-contact model.
In this model, a social work faculty member serves as a proxy to the single
point of contact to better facilitate decision making about these complex forms
of violence; this faculty member reports to a university system and serves as an
additional resource. This model recognizes the strengths of the single-point-of-
contact model, as described in this chapter, while also recognizing the difficulties that professionals and nonprofessionals may have in addressing the
complex issues of sexual violence or human-trafficking crimes, which may
include the fact that reporting is limited to a single person.

Mezzo-Level Strengths of the Single-Point-of-Contact Model

The single-point-of-contact model offers three specific mezzo-level strengths:
a continuum of services, building of trust, and collaborative case management
(Busch-Armendariz et al., 2014). The first element of the best practice model is

a holistic continuum of care (Busch-Armendariz et al., 2014; Busch-Armendariz et al., in press). This means that the multidisciplinary team is coordinated by a single-point-of-contact social worker and that trust is a fundamental tenet of this relationship (Busch-Armendariz et al., in press). The coordinated effort can expand over time as a variety of partnering professionals join the interdisciplinary team. It is crucial that there is an ongoing link, the single-point-of-contact social worker, who connects the collaborative team and their affiliated agency/profession, with the client and is able to assist in moving the case forward. Survivors especially benefit from a consistent relationship with this social worker over the trajectory of their recovery as it facilitates feelings of safety, trust, and reliability. CSE/human-trafficking survivors need a dependable support system, as their confidence in themselves and others has often been violated by the trafficker(s) and their diminished feelings of security can magnify their trauma. Additionally, client needs evolve over the long duration of the criminal justice and immigration processes of CSE/human-trafficking cases, and it is imperative that the unique needs of the client are anticipated and addressed by the single-point-of-contact professional.

Second, the single-point-of-contact social worker helps to establish, negotiate, and maintain strong trust relationships between and among survivors and the many professionals involved in the interdisciplinary team, as well as with the multiple systems that will engage with them. The social worker also reduces survivors' apprehension about professionals, the challenges within various systems that may arise, and discussions on victimization and trauma (Brennan, 2005; Busch-Armendariz et al., in press; Roby, Turley, & Cloward, 2008). Traffickers control CSE/human-trafficking victims by instilling fear that law enforcement will arrest them and that they could be prosecuted or imprisoned for their actions. Moreover, CSE/human-trafficking survivors may have limited and/or negative past interactions with the professionals in the collaborative team, and therefore the single-point-of-contact professional may have to make a concerted effort to address their hesitation or trepidation in receiving services. Sigmon (2008) suggests that foreign-born victims may lack an understanding of current culture and laws, so the single point of contact social worker's interventions in immigrant communities are particularly valuable. Immigrants and other marginalized groups within the United States often come from communities that distrust law enforcement. Moreover, immigrant CSE/human-trafficking survivors often come from countries where they do not trust law enforcement to maintain the best interests of the community and where the local police, the controlling political parties, or paramilitary groups exert control through violence, intimidation, and bribery. Additionally, if foreign-born victims are undocumented, they fear that they will be deported and/or that their traffickers will terrorize them or the family members residing in their native country. A single-point-of-contact professional can also facilitate and negotiate linguistic barriers and provide access to legal immigration remedies such as the T or U visa.

Finally, the single-point-of-contact social worker supports collaborative case management by using transparent communication, respecting the various roles of interdisciplinary team members, and having confidence in the collective process. In this framework, the needs of CSE survivors are identified, together with survivors, carefully coordinated, and met to reduce secondary trauma (Busch-Armendariz et al., in press). The goal is to avoid disrupting the relationships between CSE survivors and service providers and to improve the connections between services without placing the burden of that networking solely on the shoulders of the clients (Domoney et al., 2015). The single-point-of-contact social work model recognizes that continuous, successful, and thorough engagement with an individual human-trafficking case has positive results for the case itself and for the collective antitrafficking work of a community.

Professional coalitions often include representatives from local, state, and government agencies (e.g., law enforcement, medical and mental health providers, legal aid providers, and social services), as well as from nonprofit organizations that serve vulnerable and high-risk groups (e.g., the homeless, juveniles, refugees, and victims of domestic violence and sexual assault) (Busch, Fong, Heffron, Faulkner, & Mahapatra, 2007; Office for Victims of Crime, 2012). Interdisciplinary teams also review the service delivery process, evaluate feedback from survivors and professionals to enhance service provision, and minimize future obstacles to continuity of support. A collaborative case management design has been recognized as a best practice model by the President's Interagency Task Force and the Federal Strategic Action Plan on Services for Victims of Human Trafficking because it efficiently utilizes limited resources while maintaining a survivor-centered and trauma-informed approach to interdisciplinary partnership (President's Interagency Task Force, 2017).

Rationale for the Social Work Approach

There are a number of reasons that social work is a strong practice approach with survivors of CSE. Social work is rooted in a number of strong and relevant conceptual models and theories, including Bronfenbrenner's Ecological Systems Theory (1979), the Person-in-Environment (PIE) perspective, and the Eco-Systems Theory. All these theories embrace the philosophy that individuals cannot and should not be viewed as singular entities, but rather as connected to various intertwining systems (micro, mezzo, and macro) (Martin, 2016). These theories and perspectives help the social worker examine the multiple, interacting factors that are constantly present in the lives of individuals, especially when working with survivors of CSE and coordinating services among numerous interdisciplinary professionals and the agencies they represent (Busch-Armendariz et al., 2014). Social workers also incorporate a working knowledge of Maslow's Theory of Human Motivation/Hierarchy of Needs, the understanding that an individual's basic needs (physiological and safety) must be met before higher needs (self-esteem and self-actualization) can be addressed (Maslow, 1970). This knowledge relates to the social work principle of "meeting clients where they are."

Social workers are trained to *meet clients where they are*, to *affirm each person's individuality and right to self-determination*, and to *have respect for diversity*. Social workers who work with survivors meet clients where they are, affirm each person's individuality and right to self-determination, and respect diversity by "acknowledging that no two situations are the same . . . each individual [has] her own history, resilience, personality, tolerance for risk, family makeup, and ties to the trafficker and other survivors" (DeBoise, 2014, p. 229). Drawing upon these principles, social workers work collaboratively with survivors to identify fundamental short-term and long-term objectives that support their self-sufficiency and self-worth. The social worker is able to uphold the essential needs and goals of the client while simultaneously preserving the integrity of a complex and diverse interdisciplinary team whose members often have competing professional lenses, aims, and objectives. In the human-trafficking context, single-point-of-contact social workers must negotiate complex and often thorny conversations. They must affirm the client's right to self-determination when working with collaborative team members who hold differing perspectives on decision making, and they must engage in challenging discussions on how to proceed on the best course of action. The stakes are high, so the social worker must be able to understand and apply clear and respectful communication and effective leadership. "Social workers bring communication skills, to engage and create rapport, give professional empathy, [and] develop relationships built on trust" (Romeo, 2015, p. 206); they facilitate dialogue that leads to consensus about agreed-upon goals and expectations.

Professional Self-Awareness

Many helping professionals who work to combat human trafficking are drawn to their profession as a "calling"; social workers say they chose their profession "because of their love and desire to help others, their strong commitment to social change, and a dedication to work for disenfranchised individuals and communities" (Nsonwu, Casey, Cook, & Busch-Armendariz, 2013, p. 5). Although this commitment to assist others and act as a social change agent is a strength, social workers must also have insight into their own personal and professional knowledge, attitudes, and perceptions of the human-trafficking problem and exercise responsibility by ensuring continued self-awareness and self-care as a part of ethical practice (Nsonwu et al., 2015). Self-awareness, self-introspection, and "meeting clients where they are" are essential for social workers to combat their "own stereotypes, narratives, and, most importantly, agendas in order to effectively join with the client at their personal stage of readiness for change" (DeBoise, 2014, p. 229).

Indeed, the work of antitrafficking coalition members, including the single-point-of-contact social worker, is often taxing and can contribute to physical, emotional, and spiritual exhaustion. Salston and Figley (2003) contend that such work settings are "an occupational hazard of caring service providers" (p. 173). In the field of social work, this phenomenon is often called burnout, compassion fatigue, vicarious trauma, secondary traumatic stress disorder, or trauma exposure. Lipsky and Burk (2009) assert in *Trauma Stewardship: An Everyday Guide to Caring for Self While Caring for Others* that trauma exposure relates to "anyone who interacts with the suffering, pain, and crisis of others" (p. 11), while Figley (1995) defines secondary traumatic stress disorder as "the natural consequent behaviors or emotions resulting from knowing about a traumatizing event experienced by a significant other—the stress resulting from helping or wanting to help a traumatized or suffering person" (p. 7). Although there are some subtleties in definitions among each of these terms, the overarching premise is that value-laden, antitrafficking work involves hearing and witnessing stories of trauma and that this experience can have tangible repercussions for antitrafficking task force coalitions, first-responders, and ongoing support systems of CSE survivors (Busch-Armendariz et al., in press). The single-point-of-contact social worker is especially vulnerable to secondary trauma because of the length of time that he or she works with the CSE/human-trafficking survivor.

From an organizational perspective, it is crucial that social work professionals receive training modules on human trafficking (Nsonwu et al., 2015) and are taught a self-care model, such as trauma stewardship, to prepare and sustain them for this demanding work environment (Lipsky & Burke, 2009). To build principled organizations, community coalitions should share elements of their mission, values, ethics, and policies that frame their work with CSE survivors. Organizations should also assess how they may positively or negatively address the stress of the social problems that they are charged to ameliorate. Through education and self-awareness there is often a realization that first-responders and long-term, single-point-of-contact providers need to avoid "saving" survivors and instead accept clients, value clients' self-determination, and empower them to make decisions that support their own self-sufficiency. Rachel Lloyd "talk[s] about it in terms of empowerment versus rescuing. If you frame it as 'rescuing' them from trafficking, it's sensational, but 'empowering' them is better in terms of helping them heal" (Kalergis, 2009, p. 319). Organizations should support positive self-care strategies for the single-point-of-contact worker and create an environment in which asking for support and assistance to deal with issues of trauma is viewed as a strength.

Social Work's Ability to Identify and Manage Ethical Conundrums

Social workers experience ethical conundrums regularly in the human-trafficking field. This may seem surprising given that most people would agree that human trafficking is wrong; however, the field is complex and nuanced because of the nature of the missions and strategies for prevention and intervention. Social workers are trained to sort through complexities for individuals and program development. As a professional discipline, social work provides value-based training in making decisions about ethical conundrums in which principled professionals might disagree about next steps (Wolfer, 2006). Historically, there have been situations where social work has blamed individuals and families for their circumstances, such as poverty, mental health, or addictions, to name a few. However, as more evidence has emerged, social work explanations, theories, and perspectives have improved (although many social workers may argue that improvements are too slow for our social justice roots). At the same time, social workers have also been credited with leading the charge and challenging harmful and demoralizing practices against vulnerable groups (Wahab & Panichelli, 2013).

Understanding individual and collective social justice has been a function of social workers in the antitrafficking field across the country and globally. For example, until recently and perhaps currently in some jurisdictions, children and youth who are being exploited in sex industries may be referred to as "child prostitutes" (Mitchell, Finkelhor, & Wolak, 2010). This "blaming the victim" approach needed to be replaced with the recognition that children cannot consent to commercial sex. Social work researcher Kotrla (2010) indicted society when she discussed the "culture of tolerance, fueled by the glamorization of pimping, [that] is embodied in multiple venues of daily life, including clothing, songs, television, video games, and other forms of entertainment" (p. 183). Regulations enacted to protect minors, such as safe harbor laws, have made headway over time; according to the Polaris Project (2014), "only 15 states have full 'safe harbor' laws that protect child victims of sexual exploitation, and another 7 have passed partial versions of the law" (p. 1); this situation improved as of the fall of 2015, when 34 states had safe harbor laws, "many of which vary significantly" (Polaris, 2015, p. 1). However, further action is needed; the lack of comprehensive legislation further victimizes CSE youth, as they are often arrested and charged with juvenile prostitution.

Social workers have also made contributions in the antitrafficking field by advising emerging organizations that are developing programs and services for survivors. Recently, social work researcher Wachter and colleagues (2016) explored principle-based practices for organizations serving survivors of sex trafficking with the major aim to shape ethical practices by learning from veteran organizations. The five principle-based practices that emerged include the following: nurture the humanity and dignity of clients; contextualize survivor needs within a social justice framework; prioritize the immediate and practical needs of clients; support the dynamic nature of survivors' healing; and help identify and engage essential community and professional partners (Wachter et al., 2016). This last principle is indeed reflective of the strength of a single-point-of-contact social work model in building multidisciplinary collaborative responses to sex trafficking.

Addressing Micro Issues

Social workers have continued to play a major role in meeting the direct needs of survivors of CSE in the United States and globally. This section focuses on social workers' micro-level practice in three broad areas: social workers' ability to increase identification of victims, social workers' ability to listen to and learn from clients' perspectives, and social workers' ability to meet the unique needs of survivors.

Social Workers' Ability to Increase Identification

Because traffickers isolate victims, screening and identification in nontraditional settings are major goals of many antitrafficking task forces throughout the nation (Busch-Armendariz et al., in press; Goździak, 2010; Okech, Morreau, & Benson, 2012; Sigmon, 2008). Risk factors for domestic and international victimization include poverty, gender, gender identity, age, sexual orientation, and history of homelessness (Bales, 2007; Busch-Armendariz, Nsonwu, Heffron, Garza, & Hernandez, 2009; Busch-Armendariz et al., 2014; Gozdziak, Bump, Duncan, MacDonnell, & Loiselle, 2006; Kristof & WuDunn, 2009; Macy & Johns, 2011); acknowledging these risk factors, anti–human trafficking task forces have created public awareness programs and trained law enforcement and other professionals working in all types of sectors, such as health, education, social services, housing, and other essential needs, to screen for victims. Law enforcement and human service professionals often have the first opportunity to identify victims (Kappelhoff, 2008; Okech et al., 2012).[1] As the single point of contact, social workers have played major roles in creating awareness campaigns and training these relevant stakeholders. Additionally, because they are networkers, collaborators, and client brokers, social workers are well positioned to serve as the point of contact in those settings where universal screening for victimization may be advantageous (e.g., schools, public health departments, homeless shelters, domestic violence and sexual assault advocacy organizations, child welfare organizations, and others).

Social Workers' Ability to Learn from Clients' Perspectives

Social work initially developed a strengths-based approach, which contrasted with the medical or deficit-based model that focused on challenges, short-falls, and disorders (Rawana & Brownlee, 2009). With a deficit-based model, the provider/professional takes the lead in a crisis, directs the identification of problems, develops goals, and may have a pessimistic outlook about recovery because positive assets are not acknowledged. In contrast, a strength-based approach rejects the idea that "all people who face trauma and pain in their lives inevitably are wounded or incapacitated or become less than they might be" (Saleebey, 1996, p. 298). A strength-based model embraces the premise that healing is possible and must be led by the client, as self-determination is a valued concept. The professional's role is to serve as an agent in the recovery process; "in doing so, this approach requires that those working with survi-vors of human trafficking meet on an even playing field, in a spirit of equality, and pay attention to addressing power differentials between survivor and pro-vider" (Busch-Armendariz et al., in press). This perspective supports a holistic approach in which clients are viewed in relation to their environment and there is a belief in resilience and transformation. The social worker often initially serves as a model for other professionals (law enforcement, medical providers, etc.) in helping team members work collaboratively with one another and with the survivor of CSE or human trafficking.

Building trust and maintaining confidentiality are critical factors in deter-mining the comfort level of the client; clients who have confidence in the system/process and believe in the professionals who assist them are able to create an open dialogue and share important information to move their case forward and address their own needs and goals. Confidence and assurance among coalition or taskforce professionals also facilitate team members' trust in one another despite differences in their professional fields. Many disciplines (e.g., nursing, law, education, law enforcement, etc.) are governed by a code of ethics that guides their professional behavior and conduct. According to the social work code of ethics, trust and confidentiality are at the heart of any professional relationship, and the social worker's unique capacity to build trust by learning from a survivor's perspective is characteristic of social workers' professional training (NASW, 2008). This professional philosophy is the bedrock of the single-point-of-contact model, as the social worker strives to develop trust, rapport, and mutual respect with clients and the interdisciplinary team.

The Substance Abuse and Mental Health Services Administration [SAMHSA] (2014) defines trauma as resulting from "an event, series of events, or set of circumstances that is experienced by an individual as physically or emotionally harmful or life threatening and that has lasting adverse effects on the individual's functioning and mental, physical, social, emotional, or spiritual well-being" (p. 7). Social workers and the professionals that they partner with in serving CSE survivors have begun to utilize a trauma-informed theoretical framework. This model recognizes the multiple physical and psychological effects of trauma, such as victimization from human trafficking, in shaping the perspective of the survivor and the process of healing. As a result of trauma, survivors may put up protective barriers as learned coping mechanisms to protect from continued harm or to prevent further abuse. This self-defensive behavior may be viewed by others as being noncompliant, sabotaging, or being obstinate or angry because the CSE survivor displays a lack of trust in the system/professionals. Fostering this distrust in the victim is a calculated move by traffickers, as their intent is to manipulate and coerce their subject. Deliberate physical and psychological abuse help traffickers maintain control over their victim. Traffickers and their victims also may have deeply engrained psychological bonds similar to victims of intimate partner violence (IPV), who, like victims of sex trafficking/CSE, frequently experience coercion and physical, emotional, and psychological violence at the hands of their abusers but remain emotionally tied to them. Stockholm Syndrome, a phenomenon in which survivors begin to emotionally connect to and protect their abuser, may be an outcome of the trafficker's influence. Thus survivors of human trafficking, whether they have been trafficked for sex or labor (or both), often have a persistent distrust of others due to a fundamental lack of safety and security and a concerted effort by their perpetrator to create mistrust and lack of self-confidence.

For all these reasons, learning to trust professionals is often a key element of the case management and recovery process. Providers in turn must operate with an understanding that regaining trust is often an arduous and long-term task for survivors. Professionals can facilitate the trust-building process by acknowledging that survivors are "the experts of their own experience" (Hom & Woods, 2013, p. 78). Professionals working with survivors of CSE must understand the complex experience of trauma in order to provide best practices and prevent revictimization (SAMHSA, 2014). Social workers' comprehension of the various effects of trauma will help them educate their client(s) as well as the team about the unique manifestations of trauma resulting from sex trafficking/CSE. They will also be able to address the process of healing and recovery.

The accrediting agency for social work education, the Council on Social Work Education (CSWE), and its professional association dedicated to advocacy, the National Association of Social Workers (NASW), both regard cultural competency as a core value and skill of the social work profession. Social workers are charged with examining their own culture to cultivate a personal awareness of their life experience and epistemology. They are also expected to develop and sustain a working knowledge of their diverse clienteles' culture in order to respond appropriately, without bias and prejudice. Collaboration with survivors of sex trafficking requires that social workers are introspective, nonjudgmental, and open to understanding new paradigms so they can promote trust with their client and advance culturally relevant interventions. For example, Busch and colleagues (2014) emphasize that social workers must educate themselves on the criminality of human trafficking to understand the legal and policy implications, as well as the traumatic impact for their clients.

Meeting the Unique Needs of Survivors

Busch-Armendariz et al. (2014) and Cecchet and Thoburn (2014) apply the quintessential social work ecological approach. Busch-Armendariz et al. (2014) state that "the social worker's attention to coordination of services (affirmative ecological approach in social work), understanding of trust building (affirmative strengths-based perspective in social work), and cultural competency (affirmation of survivor-centered focus) provide for a thoughtful and thorough catalyst towards survivor restoration" (p. 13). Culturally grounded services ensure that trained interpreters and translators are provided for clients so that their voice is adequately understood and appreciated; this model aligns with a survivor-centered approach. Busch-Armendariz and colleagues also suggest that "to be effective, specialized intervention strategies need to be culturally grounded and consider age and developmental stage, type and length of exploitation, relationship with traffickers, nationality, previous history of victimization, and many other factors" (2014, p.17). The single-point-of-contact approach means that services are developed around the specific needs of the individual client and reflect culturally developed services. This approach allows social workers to effectively address the unique needs of their client while facilitating agreed-upon goals among the interdisciplinary team (Busch-Armendariz et al., 2014).

In addition to providing direct services to CSE survivors, social workers have played a major part in helping average citizens understand the warning signs about human trafficking and make informed connections about gender disparities, supply chains, and how to access human-trafficking resources when they recognize a situation of concern (Busch-Armendariz et al., in press). Moreover, social workers understand that these goals are complicated by traffickers' strategies to create isolation and the physical and psychological tactics used against their victims (Busch-Armendariz et al., in press; Clawson & Dutch, 2008; Faulkner, Mahapatra, Heffron, Nsonwu, & Busch-Armendariz, 2013). Social workers also understand that CSE survivors, including those that are undocumented, may have similar responses to formal and informal reporting as survivors of intimate and interpersonal violence, for whom danger, fear, and confusion may prevail and for whom reporting, receiving help, and leaving are processes, not events. Social workers learn to support survivors and the people around them, who often have steep learning curves for understanding the complexities of the impact of trauma, the neurobiology of trauma, the impacts of trauma on memory and interactions with the criminal justice system, empowerment and self-determination, and other challenges faced by survivors of interpersonal violence.

Conclusion

In sum, social work theory, skills, and training provide the essential foundation of a single-point-of-contact model. This model represents the scaffolding with which to support CSE survivors and the professionals and systems that serve them. Such a platform helps social workers incorporate systems theory, a strength-based approach, and trauma- and survivor-informed practices to facilitate both micro-level and mezzo-level components of this work. From this strategic and comprehensive vantage point, social workers are better able to increase identification, negotiate survivors' perspectives and needs, develop trust with survivors and among multiple entities, address continuum of care and collaborative case management, identify ethical conundrums, and influence the development of principle-based services and programs. In the face of the overwhelming suffering of exploitation, the single-point-of-contact model has almost unlimited ability to bring survivors and providers together toward action, change, and restoration.

Resources

National Human Trafficking Resource Center: https://traffickingresourcecenter .org/audience/service-providers

Trafficking Victim Identification Tool: https://www.vera.org/publications/out -of-the-shadows-identification-of-victims-of-human-trafficking

Note

1. People buying or selling sex may also be a first point of contact, although it is more complicated for either of those groups to access resources and to receive training to identify sex trafficking.

References

Bales, K. (2007). What predicts human trafficking? *International Journal of Comparative and Applied Criminal Justice, 31*(2), 269–279. doi:10.1080/01924036.2007.9678771

Brennan, D. (2005). Methodological challenges in research with trafficked persons: Tales from the field. *International Migration, 43*(1–2), 35–54. doi:10.1111/j.0020-7985.2005.00311.x

Bronfenbrenner, U. (1979). *The ecology of human development: Experiments by nature and design.* Cambridge, MA: Harvard University Press.

Busch, N. B., Fong, R., Heffron, L. C., Faulkner, M., & Mahapatra, N. (2007). *Assessing the needs of human trafficking victims: An evaluation of the Central Texas Coalition Against Human Trafficking.* Retrieved from https://utexas.app.box.com/s/npw97jmur5nojwjl1butdwny8obt2k9r

Busch-Armendariz, N. B., Nsonwu, M. B., & Cook Heffron, L. (2011). Human trafficking victims and their children: Assessing needs, vulnerabilities, strengths, and survivorship. *Journal of Applied Research on Children: Informing Policy for Children at Risk, 2*(1), Article 3. Retrieved from http://digitalcommons.library.tmc.edu/childrenatrisk/vol2/iss1/3

——. (2014). A kaleidoscope: The role of the social work practitioner and the strength of social work theories and practice in meeting the complex needs of people trafficked and the professionals that work with them. *International Social Work, 57*(1), 7–18. doi:10.1177/0020872813505630

——. (in press). *Human trafficking: Applying research, theory, and case studies.* Thousand Oaks, CA: Sage.

Busch-Armendariz, N., Nsonwu, M., Heffron, L. C., Garza, J., & Hernandez, M. (2009). *Understanding human trafficking: Development of typologies of traffickers.* Retrieved from https://utexas.app.box.com/v/Human-Trafficking-Phase2

Cecchet, S. J., & Thoburn, J. (2014). The psychological experience of child and adolescent sex trafficking in the United States: Trauma and resilience in survivors. *Psychological Trauma: Theory, Research, Practice, and Policy, 6*(5), 482.

Clawson, H., & Dutch, N. (2008). *Identifying victims of human trafficking: Inherent challenges and promising strategies from the field.* Washington, DC: Office of the Assistant Secretary for Planning and Evaluation (ASPE). Retrieved from https://aspe.hhs.gov/report/identifying-victims-human-trafficking-inherent-challenges-and-promising-strategies-field

Danis, F. (2006). In search of safe campus communities. *Journal of Community Practice, 14*(3), 29–46.

DeBoise, C. (2014). Human trafficking and sex work: Foundational social-work principles. *Meridians: Feminism, Race, Transnationalism, 12*(1), 227–233.

Domoney, J., Howard, L. M., Abas, M., Broadbent, M., & Oram, S. (2015). Mental health service responses to human trafficking: A qualitative study of professionals' experiences of providing care. *BMC Psychiatry, 15*(1), 1.

Drennan, A., Wagner, T., & Rosenbaum, P. (2005). The 'Key Worker' Model of Service Delivery. . Keeping Current #1-2005. Hamilton, Ontario: CanChild Centre for Disability Research. http://bluewirecs.tzo.com/canchild/kc/KC2005-1.pdf

Faulkner, M., Mahapatra, N., Heffron, L. C., Nsonwu, M. B., & Busch-Armendariz, N. (2013). Moving past victimization and trauma toward restoration: Mother survivors of sex trafficking share their inspiration. *International Perspectives in Victimology*, 7(2), 46–55.

Figley, C. R. (1995). *Compassion fatigue: Coping with secondary traumatic stress disorder in those who treat the traumatized*. New York, NY: Brunner/Mazel.

Goździak, E. M. (2010). Identifying child victims of trafficking. *Criminology & Public Policy*, 9(2), 245–255. doi:10.1111/j.1745-9133.2010.00623.x

Gozdziak, E., Bump, M., Duncan, J., MacDonnell, M., & Loiselle, M. B. (2006). The trafficked child: Trauma and resilience. *Forced Migration Review*, 25, 14–15.

Greeson, M. & Campbell, R. (2013). Sexual assault response teams (SARTs): An empirical review of their effectiveness and challenges to successful implementation. *Trauma, Violence, & Abuse*, 14(2), 83–95.

Hom, K. A., & Woods, S. J. (2013). Trauma and its aftermath for commercially sexually exploited women as told by front-line service providers. *Issues in Mental Health Nursing*, 34(2), 75–81. doi:10.3109/01612840.2012.723300

Kalergis, K. I. (2009). A passionate practice: Addressing the needs of commercially sexually exploited teenagers. *Affilia*, 24(3), 315–324. doi:10.1177/0886109909337706

Kappelhoff, M. J. (2008). Federal prosecutions of human trafficking cases: Striking a blow against modern day slavery. *University of St. Thomas Law Journal*, 6(1), 9–20.

Kotrla, K. (2010). Domestic minor sex trafficking in the United States. *Social Work*, 55(2), 181–187. doi:10.1093/sw/55.2.181

Kristof, N., & WuDunn, S. (2009). *Half the sky: Turning oppression into opportunity for women worldwide*. New York, NY: Random House.

Lipsky, L. v. D., & Burk, C. (2009). *Trauma stewardship: An everyday guide to caring for self while caring for others*. San Francisco, CA: Berrett-Koehler.

Macy, R. J., & Johns, N. (2011). Aftercare services for international sex trafficking survivors: Informing U.S. service and program development in an emerging practice area. *Trauma, Violence, & Abuse*, 12(2), 87–98. doi:10.1177/1524838010390709

Martin, M. E. (2016). *Introduction to social work: Through the eyes of practice settings*. Boston, MA: Pearson.

Maslow, A. H. (1970). *Motivation and personality* (2nd ed.). New York, NY: Harper & Row.

Mills, L. G. (1998). *The heart of intimate abuse: New interventions in child welfare, criminal justice, and health settings*. New York, NY: Springer.

Mitchell, K. J., Finkelhor, D., & Wolak, J. (2010). Conceptualizing juvenile prostitution as child maltreatment: Findings from the National Juvenile Prostitution Study. *Child Maltreatment*, 15(1), 18–36. doi:10.1177/1077559509349443

NASW. (2008). Code of Ethics. Retrieved from https://www.socialworkers.org/LinkClick.aspx?fileticket=KZmmbz15evc%3D&portalid=0

Nsonwu, M. B., Casey, K., Cook, S. W., & Busch-Armendariz, N. (2013). Embodying social work as a profession: A pedagogy for practice. *SAGE Open*, 3(3).

Nsonwu, M. B., Welch-Brewer, C., Heffron, L. C., Lemke, M. A., Busch-Armendariz, N., Sulley, C., . . . Li, J. (2015). Development and validation of an instrument to assess social work students' perceptions, knowledge, and attitudes about human trafficking questionnaire (PKA-HTQ): An exploratory study. *Research on Social Work Practice*, 27(5), 561–571.

Office for Victims of Crime. (2012, September). *Human trafficking* (NCJ 240570). Retrieved from http://www.ncdsv.org/images/OVCTTAC_HumanTraffickingResourcePaper_2012.pdf

Okech, D., Morreau, W., & Benson, K. (2012). Human trafficking: Improving victim identification and service provision. *International Social Work*, 55(4), 488–503. doi:10.1177/0020872811425805

Orme, J., & Ross-Sheriff, F. (2015). Sex trafficking: Policies, programs, and services. *Social Work, 60*(4), 287–294.

Polaris. (2014). State ratings reveal progress in human trafficking laws, more needed to assist victims (Press release). Retrieved from http://polarisproject.org/news/press-releases/state -ratings-reveal-progress-human-trafficking-laws-more-needed-assist-victims

———. (2015). *Human trafficking issue brief: Safe harbor* (Issue Brief Fall 2015). Retrieved from https://polarisproject.org/sites/default/files/2015%20Safe%20Harbor%20Issue%20Brief .pdf

President's Interagency Task Force. (2017). *Federal human trafficking strategic plan*. Retrieved from https://www.ovc.gov/pubs/FederalHumanTraffickingStrategicPlan.pdf

Rawana, E., & Brownlee, K. (2009). Making the possible probable: A strength-based assessment and intervention framework for clinical work with parents, children and adolescents. *Families in Society: The Journal of Contemporary Social Services, 90*(3), 255–260.

Roby, J. L., Turley, J., & Cloward, J. G. (2008). U.S. response to human trafficking: Is it enough? *Journal of Immigrant & Refugee Studies, 6*(4), 508–525. doi:10.1080/15362940802480241

Romeo, L. (2015). Social work and safeguarding adults. *The Journal of Adult Protection, 17*(3), 205–207.

Saleebey, D. (1996). The strengths perspective in social work practice: Extensions and cautions. *Social Work, 41*(3), 296–305.

Salston, M. D., & Figley, C. R. (2003). Secondary traumatic stress effects of working with survivors of criminal victimization. *Journal of Traumatic Stress, 16*(2), 167–174. doi:10.1023/A:1022899207206

Sigmon, J. N. (2008). Combating modern-day slavery: Issues in identifying and assisting victims of human trafficking worldwide. *Victims & Offenders, 3*(2–3), 245–257. doi:10.1080/15564880801938508

Spray, C., & Jowett, B. (2011). *Social work practice with children and families*. Thousand Oaks, CA: Sage. Retrieved from http://public.eblib.com/choice/publicfullrecord.aspx?p=820073

Stein, M. (2009). *Quality matters in children's services: Messages from research*. Retrieved from https://www.rip.org.uk/~ftp_user/quality_matters_in_childrens_services/files/assets /common/downloads/quality_matters_in_childrens_services.pdf

Substance Abuse and Mental Health Services Administration [SAMHSA]. (2014). *SAMHSA's concept of trauma and guidance for a trauma-informed approach*. Retrieved from http:// www.scattergoodfoundation.org/sites/default/files/SAMHSA_Concept_of_Trauma _and_Guidance.pdf

Wachter, K., Cook Heffron, L., Busch-Armendariz, N., Nsonwu, M. B., Kerwick, M., Kellison, B., . . . Sanders, G. M. (2016). Responding to domestic minors sex trafficking (DMST): Developing principle-based practices. *Journal of Human Trafficking, 2*(4). doi:10.1080/23 322705.2016.1145489

Wahab, S., & Panichelli, M. (2013). Ethical and human rights issues in coercive interventions with sex workers. *Affilia: Journal of Women and Social Work, 28(4)*, 344–349. doi:10.1177/0886109913505043

Whetstone, T. (2001). Measuring the impact of a domestic violence coordinated response team. *Policing: An International Journal, 24*(3), 371–398.

Wolfer, T. A. (2006). An introduction to decision cases and case method learning. In T. A. Wolfer & T. L. Scales (Eds.), *Decision cases for advanced social work practice: Thinking like a social worker* (pp. 3–14). Belmont, CA: Thomson Brooks/Cole.

PART IV

PREVENTION AND OUTREACH

P art IV examines prevention and outreach efforts. First, chapter 16 examines the salient risk factors of commercial sexual exploitation and discusses these as key considerations in developing a prevention approach to the commercial sexual exploitation of children (CSEC). The My Life My Choice Exploitation Prevention program is offered as a model for decreasing risk and is part of a larger, one-of-a-kind, nationally recognized program that uses a survivor-led approach to empower and inform adolescent girls about the realities of commercial sexual exploitation. The prevention education programming has been used in schools and community organizations across the nation and shows positive outcomes.

Chapter 17 posits that weak social institutions combined with weak social safety nets create an environment conducive to trafficking and exploitation. Situating known risk factors of sexual exploitation in an ecological model, the chapter recommends engaging in prevention efforts that target weaknesses in economic, education, family, healthcare, criminal justice, and legislative systems, while simultaneously building the social safety nets that are intended to address such systemic weaknesses. Identity-based oppression is also a key focal point, as those experiencing oppression based on race, ethnicity, sexual orientation, sex, gender identity, or other identities are disproportionately exposed to weak social institutions and social safety nets. Prevention and outreach efforts to address these factors through macro practice, as well as targeted initiatives in the highest-risk communities, are recommended.

The book closes with chapter 18, which critically analyzes imagery commonly used in antitrafficking efforts. The chapter critiques images that mischaracterize the issue of sex trafficking, providing only a very narrow picture of trafficking and exploitation. The chapter also suggests that such imagery is not trauma informed and can serve as a trauma trigger or as a way to reexploit survivors of sex trafficking and commercial sexual exploitation. In addition, the imagery often does not include diverse images or any accompanying wording related to race, gender identity, sex/gender, and sexual orientation. The chapter offers recommendations for imagery used in organizational materials and other forms of media.

CHAPTER 16

PREVENTING THE COMMERCIAL SEXUAL EXPLOITATION OF CHILDREN

The My Life My Choice Model

LISA GOLDBLATT GRACE, LICSW, MPH, COFOUNDER
AND EXECUTIVE DIRECTOR

KATHERINE BRIGHT, MA, RESEARCH ASSISTANT

AMY CORBETT, LMHC, DIRECTOR OF PREVENTION

AUDREY MORRISSEY, ASSOCIATE DIRECTOR

In 2001, a young girl from Boston named Latasha was brutally murdered while being commercially sexually exploited. She was seventeen years old and living in a child welfare–funded group home. Unbeknownst to any of the caring adults in her life (her family, her Department of Children and Family Services [DCFS] worker, the group home staff), she was being controlled by a third party and exploited through prostitution.

For social workers, it can be far too easy to see the commercial sexual exploitation of girls[1] as an inevitable and egregious form of child abuse, sewn deep into the fabric of our society. It is not. Young victims of commercial sexual exploitation are hidden in plain sight—in our schools, group homes, juvenile justice facilities, and probation departments. As a result of familial abuse (Farley, 2003), they are often seen as victims in the child protective services system and later as delinquents in the juvenile justice system, criminalized for the exploitation they have suffered. Trauma and abandonment are central to the narratives of adolescent girls in the commercial sex industry. Girls recount a profound sense of being alone, without resources, and are taught by exploiters, pimps, and traffickers that they have "chosen" this life, that no one will believe them and that there is no way out (Lloyd, 2012). While there are multiple ways to ensure a safer, healthier upbringing for all girls, targeted strategies can be implemented to decrease the likelihood that commercial sexual exploitation and the trauma and degradation associated with it will be part of a young girl's trajectory.

Out of Latasha's death, My Life My Choice (MLMC) was born and the My Life My Choice Exploitation Prevention Curriculum ("the curriculum") was created. This chapter will examine some tangible correlates to commercial sexual exploitation and discuss key considerations in developing a prevention approach to the commercial sexual exploitation of children (CSEC). The My Life My Choice Exploitation Prevention program is offered as a model for decreasing risk and is part of a larger, one-of-a-kind, nationally recognized program that uses a survivor-led approach to empower and inform adolescent girls about the realities of commercial sexual exploitation.[2] As of January 2016, My Life My Choice has successfully trained over 8,000 youth providers throughout Massachusetts and the United States and has provided prevention groups to more than 1,900 girls. In addition, survivor mentors at MLMC have individually mentored over 350 girls in the Greater Boston area. In 2006, My Life My Choice was recognized by the United States Department of Justice as a national model for sex-trafficking prevention.

What Is CSEC, and What Is Preventable?

Young people are deceived, manipulated, or coerced into prostitution every day. Nationally, it is reported that the most frequent age of entry into prostitution is twelve to fifteen years (Estes & Weiner, 2001; Lloyd, 2005; Nixon, Tutty, Downe, Gorkoff, & Ursel, 2002). For program clients at My Life My Choice, the average age of entry has held steady at fourteen years old over the past three years. In 2015, a full 84 percent of MLMC youth had been commercially sexually exploited between the ages of twelve and fifteen. "Pimps" (in this article referred to as "traffickers" and "exploiters" to avoid glamorization and the minimization associated with the mainstream word *pimp/s*) systematically target vulnerable girls by frequenting locations where they congregate: malls, schools, bus and train stations, group homes, and, in the past decade, social networking sites and Internet chatrooms (Piening & Cross, 2012). The picture of commercial sexual exploitation has changed dramatically since the explosion of the Internet. Whereas most of the prostitution of juveniles formerly occurred on public streets in plain sight of law enforcement and the community, today the exploitation of minors has gone indoors.

Though all young women are at risk of recruitment solely because of their age, a subpopulation of adolescent girls are the most vulnerable—those who have been sexually abused (Murphy, 1993; Nixon et al., 2002; Piening & Cross, 2012). At some point in their lives, children who experience sexual abuse are twenty-eight times more likely to be arrested for prostitution than children who do not (Sherman & Grace, 2011). Girls and staff at MLMC report that for girls who have been sexually exploited, being raped at home by a family member or acquaintance and then being raped outside the home by buyers can feel like an inevitable pattern. Girls who experience sexual abuse are taught very clear messages about the world, their bodies, and their value: that they are valued only for sex; sex, love, and violence are all connected; no one can protect them from harm; and if they do tell someone, no one will believe them. Exploiters actively seek girls with a history of abuse, believing it renders them an easier target, and teach girls these very same messages to ensure they are "willing" participants in their exploitation.

In addition to child sexual abuse, the risk of exploitation is heightened for girls who are exposed to active addiction by a parent or caregiver in the home, witness domestic violence, experience the death of or abandonment by a parent, run away or are kicked out of their homes, or have learning disabilities and/or cognitive limitations (Estes & Weiner, 2001). At some point during their formative years, children exposed to this level of violence and abuse frequently enter the child welfare system, living within foster homes, group homes, or residential treatment facilities. It follows that a disproportionate number of CSEC victims have a history of child welfare involvement (Nixon et al., 2002). The National Center for Missing and Exploited Children reports that 86 percent of children missing were in the care of social services of foster care when reported missing(National Center for Missing and Exploited Children [NCMEC], 2014), and in 2015, a full 80 percent of girls served by MLMC for intervention services were also involved with the child welfare system. After interviewing a young victim of CSEC, one reporter described the child welfare system as a potential facilitator of trafficking: "Foster care was training ground for being trafficked. She understood that she was attached to a check. And what she points out is that at least the pimp told her he loved her, and she never heard that in any of her foster care placements" (NPR 2013). After a combined twenty-plus years in the field and after working with hundreds of clients on the ground, the authors can attest to the fact that exploiters know where every regularly used foster home, group home, or residential treatment center is and that programs in every type of community report that exploiters troll around, looking for vulnerable residents. One MLMC prevention group participant stated, "No one knows what it's like to be in the system and be faced with this [sex trafficking] every time I'm on the run. And this is only one of the issues I have to deal with."

While the correlation between child welfare involvement and recruitment into the sex industry is easy to understand, it is important to note that it is not only girls in the system who are vulnerable. The developmental tasks of adolescence renders all girls vulnerable simply by being teenage girls. It is both normal and appropriate for girls to feel misunderstood by adults, to argue with their parents, to want to fall in love, and to want to take risks (Lloyd, 2012). Exploiters can take advantage of the need for love, belonging, and acceptance, as well as the low self-esteem that is a typical part of adolescence. In a 2007 Health and Human Services study of services to trafficking victims across the United States, researchers found that the tactics used by exploiters to recruit, lure, coerce, and force girls into working for them were extraordinarily similar (Clawson, Dutch, Salamon, & Goldblatt Grace, 2009). This picture of normal developmental vulnerability, circumstance-specific vulnerability, and systemic targeting by exploiters must be foremost in the mind of anyone thinking about preventing the commercial sexual exploitation of young girls. A comprehensive prevention strategy must include multiple levels of care: primary (reaching girls whose only risk factor is the fact that they are teenage girls), secondary (reaching girls with a disproportionate number of risk factors, such as a history of child sexual abuse and child welfare involvement), and tertiary (reaching girls who have already been exploited and with whom you hope to prevent revictimization). Furthermore, it is important to note that the authors assume a victim-centered approach to prevention and do not hold young girls responsible for preventing their own victimization. Instead, we propose that girls have a right to receive the information and skills necessary to decrease the risk of recruitment and potential exploitation.

Prevention and Commercial Sexual Exploitation of Children

Since the passage of the Trafficking Victims Protection Act in 2000, the United States has focused antitrafficking efforts on prevention, protection, and prosecution (the "three Ps"). The increase in public and political attention has led to significant advancements in the response to human trafficking. However, worldwide and within the United States, prevention efforts have been slower to gain traction and have typically received less funding, public recognition, and government attention (Duger, 2015; Todres 2010). Scholars have pointed to a long list of risk factors that increase vulnerability for youth in the United States, including housing instability, abuse, low socioeconomic status, lack of viable employment opportunities, low self-esteem, family discord, substance abuse, and external community factors (Duger, 2015; Estes & Weiner, 2001; Lloyd, 2012). To address the complicated set of circumstances that at-risk girls face in the United States, a few NGOs have incorporated psychoeducational prevention groups into their model of care, combining various strategies to help youth learn how to self-advocate, develop life skills, build self-esteem, and gain knowledge about the realities of commercial sexual exploitation.

According to Hickle and Roe-Sepowitz (2014), group work can "break silence on taboo subjects, adapt to various learning styles, and allow the presence of witnesses (Drumm, 2006, p.7); that is, group members who wrestle with difficulty and promote growth alongside one another." Their 2014 evaluation of a twelve-week pilot curriculum designed for adolescents who had experienced sexual exploitation suggests that groups should be limited to those who meet the criteria of at-risk or confirmed exploitation (in order to create a safe space for children and reduce stigmatization) and should include a survivor cofacilitator as a way to provide youth with a relatable and positive role model.

A 2014 study of twenty-three runaway and homeless youth involved in or at risk for abusive/exploitative relationships found that as a result of the psychoeducational group, 24 percent of participants reported they no longer engaged in survival sex, and 71 percent reported feeling less likely to engage in sex trafficking. This group program was ten sessions in length, spanning a three-month period, and covered topics such as healthy versus unhealthy relationships, ways in which abusive partners manipulate to gain power, how to develop a positive sense of self, and ways to engage in intimacy that are healthy and respectful (Countryman-Roswurm & Bolin, 2014).

Additionally, scholars have begun to explore more intensive treatment programs that include a psychoeducational group component into their model of care. For example, a 2011 case study of thirteen high-risk or exploited girls residing in a residential program recommends that CSEC treatment should include educational groups that help youth understand exploitation and begin to build a resistance to vulnerability, as well as survivor mentoring, culturally competent treatment, homelike environments, and an admission process that requires youth to recognize risky behavior and show a willingness to change (Thomson, Hirshberg, Corbett, Valila, & Howley, 2011). Similarly, Twill, Green, and Traylor (2010) evaluated a ninety-day residential treatment center for young girls who were involved in the court for prostitution charges. The twenty-two participants were twelve to sixteen years old, had an average of three prior offenses, had experienced poverty during their childhood, and were all African American. The treatment facility provided group work on relationships, gender roles, life skills, and entertaining activities designed to increase self-esteem and help youth socialize. In addition, youth received case management, treatment planning, and other more intensive supports. None of the participants were charged with prostitution offenses following completion of the program, although 50 percent were charged with status offenses that could have been connected to prostitution (i.e., running away). In another study of sixty-eight sexually assaulted or sexually exploited runaway youth, Saewyc and Edinburgh (2010) found that participants who faced the highest rates of risk (distress, low levels of support, low self-esteem) benefited the most from an intervention model that included case management, home visiting, health education/access to healthcare, and an optional empowerment group. Overall, at six months participants reported positive changes in their interpersonal relationships, such as being able to talk to a parent or family and being engaged in school. In addition, self-esteem improved at both the six-month and one-year time points.

While research on CSEC-specific, psychoeducational prevention models is limited, similar and connected fields, such as teen dating violence, child sex abuse, HIV prevention, and teen pregnancy prevention, have provided a foundation for best practices in educating and supporting at-risk youth. Elements of these more established fields, as well the Health Belief Model, Relational Theory, and Positive Youth Development methodology, were employed in partnership with survivor leadership to create the MLMC curriculum.

History of the My Life My Choice Exploitation Prevention Curriculum

With a desire to reduce risk for the girls at greatest risk of exploitation, the curriculum was written by merging survivor experiential wisdom with an evidence-based understanding of effective prevention rooted in both public health and social work. Central to the writing of the curriculum was input from multiple exploited or formerly exploited women and girls who answered key questions about the realities of the commercial sex industry and what might have prevented exploitation from occurring. These themes became key facets of each session of the curriculum. Some of these primary ideas included the fact that the girls did not know they were being recruited into the sex industry when it was happening. As one adult survivor explained:

> [My best friend and I] decided that night to go to the arcade . . . There I met this really cute guy who invited us to ride around with him and get something to eat. We hung out all that evening and he told me he was a businessman who had lots of money and he could take care of me. He talked to me a lot about my family life and said he understood and my parents didn't. He said he used to feel the same way.

They believed they were falling in love or being taken care of. They were unaware that they were being groomed—or "seasoned" as it is called in the sex industry—and that the tactics used against them had been used on countless other girls as well. Many believed that knowing these tactics might have helped them spot an exploiter earlier and could have saved them from the significant pain and trauma they experienced in their childhood.

Even after getting out of the sex industry, many adult women remained unaware that these methods were, in fact, well-prescribed tactics. Many still believed that they had been involved with a "boyfriend" (as opposed to a trafficker) and that they were "stupid," had "acted too grown," or were simply "bad kids." Because the narratives of their exploitation were never rewritten so that they understood their victimization, they were vulnerable to revictimization.

In addition, they reported feeling trapped and defeated. The sense of being stuck was not something that came with being in "the Life" for years—it may have happened after only a few days or weeks with a skilled trafficker. Exploiters brainwashed them into believing they had "chosen" this life, that the people in their old life wouldn't take them back, and that the only way out would be "in a coffin."

Before getting into "the Life," the girls and women we worked with believed that "prostitutes" could make a lot of money and that it could be a glamorous lifestyle. As one adult survivor explained, "They were all very pretty and wore mink jackets and diamond bracelets, rings and watches. He told me that I could have all this. He said that I could be his special girl because guys were always looking for young looking pretty blondes." Conversely, they believed "prostitutes" got what they deserved. Any derision was directed toward the "hos" because they did not have the context to direct anger at the true perpetrators in this industry: the traffickers and the buyers who derived money and pleasure at the girls' expense. Before they were exploited, girls believed that they could be "safe" in the sex industry and decide who, what, and where they were sold. Although this feeling of agency was in contrast to what they had experienced throughout their childhood, they quickly learned that this sense of safety and control was false.

By recognizing the multiple points at which exploitation might have been prevented and by honing in on what kinds of attitudes, knowledge, or skills would have been necessary to reduce those risks, the authors of the curriculum began to craft a curriculum and a process that might bolster girls and reduce victimization. It was clear that a prevention curriculum could not rewrite some of the most profound vulnerabilities—most notably, a history of child sexual abuse. However, the sequelae of these histories could in fact be mitigated by a targeted, gender-specific prevention program. Prevention is less painful then intervention. As stated by one group participant, "It's not easy changing your life, especially getting away from a pimp. It's better if you can recognize one ahead of time." In addition, the authors understood that a ten-session curriculum could not, on its own, prevent the commercial sexual exploitation of children. That must be accomplished in collaboration with demand reduction strategies (i.e., targeting high school-age boys to reduce the likelihood they will become men who buy sex) and strategies that prevent individuals (most notably boys) from growing up to become traffickers.

In addition to synthesizing these powerful stories, the curriculum authors sought to examine the prevailing public health prevention practice wisdom in both the nascent field of CSEC and the more established fields of violence, teen pregnancy, and HIV prevention. Through this research, the Health Belief Model emerged as an evidence-based framework (Janz & Becker, 1984; Jones, Smith, & Llewellyn, 2014; Laraque, Mclean, Brown-Peterside, Ashton, & Diamond, 1997; Wright, Randall, & Hayes, 2012) that could be useful in seeking to prevent CSEC. The Health Belief Model posits that the motivation for behavior change depends on the presence of a sufficient degree of perceived risk in combination with self-efficacy. Further, to retool their trajectory, individuals must shift their attitude, knowledge, and skills. Specifically, as the curriculum evolved, the targeted goals, grounded in the Health Belief Model, were as follows:

- To change attitudes: To decrease teens' perception of the commercial sex industry as innocuous or glamorous; to increase teens' perception of the commercial sex industry as dangerous and debilitating
- To change knowledge: To improve teens' understanding of commercial sexual exploitation: the realities of the Life, recruitment, the demand, the media, etc.
- To change skills: To increase teens' ability to reduce the risk of exploitation (through assertiveness, negotiation skills, etc.) and increase the likelihood that teens can find the path and resources to exit if they become exploited

The curriculum further sought to maintain a level of political action and outrage. While CSEC is clearly an issue of trauma and clinical response, it is first and foremost a human rights issue. This level of anger and confrontation is central to moving toward an end of CSEC. Therefore, the curriculum reflects the intensity of CSEC as a human rights issue.

Beyond ensuring that the content was designed to lead to behavior change, the curriculum authors looked to both Relational Theory and Positive Youth Development methodology. With these frameworks, it was clear that a prevention group program must include a relational component in which young girls built meaningful connections with both safe and healthy empowered adult women and with each other. Girls most vulnerable to exploitation include those without a strong relationship to a healthy mother. This protective and guiding force is most frequently absent in the lives of exploited girls or, at best, complicated. Further, girls at greatest risk are also girls who are likely to state, "I don't hang with other females." They don't have strong, healthy relationships with other girls who "have their back." They are steeped in competition and have found their most salient relationships to be with boys and men. A prevention program must both seek to decrease the risk factors previously described and aim to boost protective factors.

The My Life My Choice Exploitation Prevention Program

As outlined in following text, multiple factors make the MLMC Curriculum so effective. Girls who have participated in groups have reported that they "like this group more than most I've been in because you keep it real" (Maria,[3] age sixteen, 2014).

Overview

The curriculum is broken out into ten sessions and uses a psycho-education group model. Groups are facilitated by a clinically trained group leader and a survivor of exploitation. Prevention group work focuses on understanding and avoiding the recruitment tactics of exploiters as well as developing a critical lens to understand the violence, degradation, and oppression inherent in the commercial sex industry. The curriculum helps young girls figure out whom to trust and how to navigate community resources, examines common vulnerabilities, builds self-esteem, addresses the link between substance abuse and exploitation, targets sexual and emotional health, and helps girls learn ways to remain safe. The first group session includes establishing guiding principles— guidelines—so that all members of the group feel safe and comfortable enough to participate. In congregate care settings, all of the girls live together and therefore spend a lot of time together; in other settings, such as in a public school, often the girls are unfamiliar with one another.

The curriculum includes a session that provides girls with a panel of survivor speakers to help participants further understand the process by which a woman could become commercially sexually exploited and to provide specific strategies to exit the commercial sex industry. Similarly, it is also beneficial to invite other service providers who have specific areas of expertise to share personal experiences. For example, inviting someone from law enforcement or someone in recovery from substance abuse not only ensures the accuracy of the information but can also give participants an opportunity to hear from a number of different adults and provide avenues for exploring community resources. Finally, each ten-week group cycle wraps up with a celebration and farewell to give participants the opportunity to reflect on their personal growth over the course of the ten sessions.

The curriculum is structured to include a variety of activities and approaches to meet the needs of various learning styles. Each session begins with an icebreaker and check-in to settle the group and allow for cohesion. Facilitators then move the group into a discussion about one of the weekly topics mentioned previously. Generally, each session includes a number of different modalities, including lecture, discussion, and experiential activities, and each session concludes with hearing a written survivor story and then journal writing to allow time for the girls to process the session. It is recognized that many group participants may not feel comfortable speaking up in group or sharing personal experiences. Journal writing is a powerful tool that is utilized over the course of the ten sessions and is intended to be an ongoing dialogue between the group facilitators and each individual participant. It is critical that the facilitators read the journals each week, with the participants' knowledge, and respond directly.

It is also necessary that participants are clear about the terms of confidentiality related to journaling.

The order of the curriculum sessions was created thoughtfully to provide girls with critical information about commercial sexual exploitation throughout the initial sessions and to create a bond and develop group attachment and safety. The curriculum then moves toward more difficult topics that allow for some self-reflection and critical analysis of how CSEC may permeate their lives. Regardless of the session, all of the material in the curriculum has the potential to trigger memories, discomfort, and sadness for the participants, so it critical to plan for keeping participants physically and emotionally safe (further discussed in following text).

Chapters of the curriculum are intentionally designed to reach girls on each of the three prevention levels. For instance, the session on self-esteem provides education on what self-esteem is, explores the media's influence on a young person's identity, and helps the group to recognize their own individual uniqueness. While this content might help those who are at lower risk gain a better sense of themselves, the section's deeper context about the link between self-esteem and commercial sexual exploitation may help a young person who is at greater risk gain insight into how she may be vulnerable to exploitation, explore ways to combat the messages she receives from the media, and also take care of herself.

It is possible to provide an abridged version of the My Life My Choice group curriculum in short-term settings where girls may not remain for a full ten weeks (for example, a forty-five-day assessment program or a Division of Youth Services [DYS] lock-up facility). My Life My Choice has developed a condensed version of four sessions that focuses on providing concrete information and explaining realities about commercial sexual exploitation. In order to incorporate the survivor's voice into an abbreviated group cycle, My Life My Choice includes content from and facilitation of curriculum by women who have experienced sexual exploitation. See the text box for additional information on curriculum content.

Targeted Population

As previously noted, the girls at greatest risk of exploitation are those with experience of childhood trauma and system involvement. They are seen by multiple providers and systems but are rarely identified in terms of this significant risk. In other words, they are hidden in plain sight. Intentionally meeting young women where they're at is key to targeted secondary and tertiary prevention efforts, as many do not possess the means or support to participate independently. To reach young women at greatest risk of exploitation, the My Life My Choice Prevention groups are facilitated in middle and high school settings, group home and residential treatment facilities, and juvenile justice programs.

Introduction and Welcome*

Introduces participants to the content and structure of the group as well as the style of the facilitators. Participants complete a prequestionnaire that covers their attitudes and knowledge of CSEC.

Understanding Predators and Recruitment*

Increases participants' awareness of the presence of pimps in their communities and online. Explores ways in which pimps try to recruit girls and provides an overview of the language and structure of "the Life," including specific vulnerabilities that put girls at greatest risk for exploitation.

Figuring Out Whom You Can Trust

Increases participants' understanding of healthy versus exploitive relationships. Defines trust and discusses the continuum of exploitation.

Reducing Your Risk of Exploitation

Allows participants to increase their ability to reduce their risk of exploitation. Participants will discuss the risks to physical safety inherent in the Life and examine the different communication styles to see where they fall on the continuum. Participants will also think critically about the demand for exploited girls.

Substance Abuse and Exploitation

This session exposes participants to the links between substance use and CSEC. Participants discuss the most commonly used drugs and their impact on physical and emotional health. Participants will explore how to recognize signs of addiction, learn about the impact of addiction, and learn about resources for help. Participants will also be challenged to look at their own substance use and examine their own vulnerabilities.

Developing Self-Esteem

This session affords participants the opportunity to think critically about their self-esteem and discusses the links between low self-esteem and CSEC. Participants examine how the media influence how they see themselves and work on deconstructing these messages. Participants also explore how to handle difficulties in their lives and identify ways to take care of themselves.

My Body, My Health

This session increases participants' awareness of the risk to their sexual health associated with CSEC. Participants analyze their own values around sex and sexuality. Participants also develop an understanding of the absence of control over their sexual health that is associated with being in the commercial sex industry.

Stories from the Life*

This session gives participants the chance to hear firsthand from women who have been victims of CSEC. This is an opportunity to further bring the information from the previous sessions to life.

Finding Help and Finding Safety*

Participants have the opportunity to explore the wealth of resources available to keep them from becoming victims of CSEC and to help them if they ever find themselves being exploited. Participants will practice synthesizing what they have learned in previous sessions in order to avoid or escape involvement in the commercial sex industry. Participants will also think critically about supports in their life that they can trust in a crisis situation.

Celebration and Farewell*

This session gives participants the opportunity to reflect on their personal growth over the 10 sessions. Participants complete the same questionnaire that they did in the first session and compare their answers over time to assess what they have learned.

(Copywritten 2003; 2008; 2011)
*Indicates sessions that should be used if a shorter-term group is necessary.

In Boston, groups are also facilitated in child welfare offices, community-based programs, and housing developments. The groups present a unique opportunity to reach as many vulnerable youth as possible, so creativity is encouraged when considering settings where groups can be facilitated.[4]

Facilitation Model

What makes the My Life My Choice Prevention Groups so unique and influential is the fact that that they are survivor informed and survivor led. The model of facilitation includes pairing a licensed clinician or clinically trained service provider with a trained survivor of exploitation, as girls benefit from hearing the survivors' personal stories and the expertise of two trained professionals who understand how to create a safe place for girls to share with one another. Unlike in traditional education experiences, discussing sexual behavior can be difficult for both youth and the adult facilitators responsible for curriculum implementation. As in the teen pregnancy/STI prevention field, where peer facilitators are trained to address and mollify socially taboo subjects, creating space where youth feel comfortable engaging in CSEC-specific conversation requires a dedicated strategy. While research on peer-led facilitation is mixed in terms of increased knowledge and reduction of risk behavior (Causey, Zuniga, Bailer, Ring, & Gil-Trejo, 2012; Kim & Free, 2008), some scholars have pointed to the benefits of this peer-led model, indicating that when young people feel that facilitators are not so far removed from their world and they do not feel judged, they are more likely to engage in the program (Ferguson, 1998; Harper, Dolcini, Benhorin, Watson, & Boyer, 2014; Layzer, Rosapep, & Barr, 2014; Pinkleton, Austin, Cohen, Chen, & Fitzgerald, 2008;). Including survivors in the model helps to make the group more authentic and gives survivors the opportunity to dispel myths and the potential glamorization of exploitation. Trained survivor facilitators are able to respond to youth from personal experience and help girls come to terms with the fact that exploitation is not a choice, but instead a form of victimization. The impact is clear and immediate, as evidenced by these journal entry quotes from group participants:

> "Your story really moved me. I'm so sorry that happened to you . . . But! I want to learn from it; your story, that is. Maybe I'll be able to. I don't know, actually learn a lesson?" (Sydni, age sixteen, 2015)
>
> "I almost cried but I held it in. I've actually been through a lot being exposed to that. There's so many things I would like to learn and so many things to tell you about my life." (Beth, age fourteen, 2014)
>
> "Wow . . . her story was sooo inspiring, now I really want to do better in life. I really want better for myself. I felt her, well I felt like I was with her. She really opened my eyes." (Keisha, age fifteen, 2014)

"You are a very strong woman. I want to be that strong & beautiful. You inspire me as a Black beautiful young woman. I'm glad you shared your story." (Erika, age fifteen, 2015)

As previously mentioned, it is well documented that children who experience commercial sexual exploitation have often also experienced childhood sex abuse (Murphy, 1993; Roe-Sepowitz 2012) and experience similar feelings of shame as a result of their victimization. Additionally, the fear of stigmatization can prevent victims of exploitation from disclosing abuse. In line with the literature on the prevention of childhood sex abuse, a benefit of the survivor-led model is that when young women hear survivors speak openly about their experience, without shame, the women often feel that "this is a safe space, and it is ok for me to share this information." In this way, prevention groups can do more than provide direct deterrence; they can also build a community of people who are able to better respond to children who are sexually abused, reducing feelings of self-blame and increasing disclosure (Finkelhor, 2009). For example, Gibson and Leitenberg (2000) showed that although rates of disclosure did not significantly change between participants who had received prevention education and those who did not, participants who had received prevention education disclosed abuse roughly a year earlier than those who had not, and the length of abuse was roughly five months shorter for those who had received prevention education. Many young women who attend a My Life My Choice Prevention Group have never disclosed personal experiences of exploitation or other forms of sexual violence because of worry about feeling judged, unsupported, or ashamed.

Additionally, girls who become exploited quickly feel trapped and cannot imagine a road to safety. Meeting a healthy, strong, adult survivor who describes her path out of the Life can seed this information in a group, and girls are empowered to share this information with their sisters, cousins, and best friends. For girls who experience commercial sexual exploitation, the survivor model brings a concrete sense of hope, showing them that there are other women who have survived this particular form of violence and are successful today. One final note is that, out of respect for the group and the survivor, it is important not to further exploit the survivor facilitator by having others come into the group when she shares her personal experience.

Training and Support

The My Life My Choice Prevention Group model is different from that of other therapeutic groups. Most clinicians are trained to have prescribed boundaries that prohibit them from sharing personal information. Given this, even if the clinician is in fact a survivor of exploitation, she is unable to share this part of herself with youth. Having the voice of a survivor in the group helps youth feel that they are in a less clinical, less treatment-like setting, which in turn seems to make it easier for them to engage. Cofacilitators should approach groups as a team; the social worker provides clinical support while allowing the survivor facilitator to provide real-life experience. Other key aspects to consider when identifying appropriate facilitators for a group include training and support. All group facilitators are required to be trained in understanding and responding to victims of CSEC; they must also attend a full day of training by My Life My Choice on using the curriculum. Facilitators must have prior training in mental health and trauma-informed care. My Life My Choice also believes that it is best practice for groups to be facilitated by women. There is a clear role for non-exploitive men in the care of traumatized girls—however, this group is effective partly because it creates a space for women and girls only. Furthermore, wherever a group is taking place (school, group home, etc.), at least a few additional staff on site must be trained in understanding and responding to victims of CSEC so that they have the correct language and information to support girls on a day-to-day basis and to reinforce the work being done in group. It is also necessary that a protocol is in place to follow up on disclosures that are made and to support girls who are at risk of exploitation or who are being exploited (see section "Handling Disclosures" later in this chapter).

When a My Life My Choice group is taking place, clinical, milieu, academic, and other appropriate personnel must be notified so that all parties are aware and can potentially support girls who are a part of the group. The only adults in the group should be the two facilitators. Additional, nontrained staff should not be present in the group. Instead, if there are concerns that a group member might have a difficult time in group, an identified staff person should wait outside the group location to offer support during or after the group. In residential settings, the girls' individual clinicians should be made aware of the content of each week's group so that they can weave that content into individual therapy. For example, a clinician might say, "I know that in this week's group, the facilitators talked about pimps and recruitment. What did that bring up for you?"

Place

The location of the group is critical, as group participants need to feel a sense of physical safety. Groups should be held in a private, confidential location that is free of interruptions. Whatever setting a group is being facilitated in, it is critical that there is a point of contact at the site who can help navigate the system, ensure there is a good understanding about which girls to consider referring for the group, discuss what is needed by the group facilitators, be someone to speak with if any issues arise in group, and establish how to develop the most positive partnership so that the group best serves the girls. For example, at one high school in Boston, the social worker and group facilitators check in before group so that facilitators can be made aware of any dynamics that may impact the upcoming group (conflict between specific girls, incidents at school that might impact the group). After each group ends, the group facilitators check back in with the social worker to let her know if any girls were absent or if there were any issues that could impact the rest of the school day.

Timing

While things like timing may seem inconsequential, it is actually quite important to be thoughtful about the time of day and day of the week that a prevention group is taking place. It is ideal to facilitate this type of group in the earlier part of the day so that the girls have time to access supports and have other, less triggering activities to engage them. Additionally, group is best held during the middle of the week (Tuesday, Wednesday). While facilitating a group on a Friday is not impossible, it is not ideal because girls might be left with fewer supports over the weekend. Facilitating this type of group during the evening hours may be triggering and make rest challenging for participants. Each group session is written to be seventy-five minutes long; however, at certain sites (such as a school), this time has to be condensed. It is important that group facilitators have at least one hour to lead an effective group session.

Size: Who to Refer and How to Refer

The ideal group size is eight to twelve young women, though in most cases twelve to fifteen girls should be initially referred because all will likely not remain in the group for the full ten sessions (they might not feel ready to be a part of this group, they may be moved to a new placement, etc.). When working with service providers, it is important to keep in mind that just by virtue of being an adolescent girl, all young women would benefit from being part of a prevention program at some point in their life (primary level of prevention); however, girls who are referred to this group are traditionally those who are disproportionately at higher risk for exploitation (secondary level of prevention). Screening in child welfare–funded group homes, residential treatment facilities, and juvenile justice facilities is a primary way to ensure that the groups reach those who are most vulnerable. In schools and community-based settings, referral sources may need guidance on red flags or warning signs to look for so that they are able to correctly consider what factors place youth at higher risk than others. As previously noted, the group is also effective with girls with a known history of exploitation (tertiary level of prevention). Group facilitators comment that it is quite productive to have groups include girls from all levels of care so that peer experience can help the group process.

High-risk girls who are referred to a My Life My Choice Prevention group should be met with prior to the start of group and informed of the content of the group. It is valuable to frame the group as an empowering, leadership opportunity where girls can learn information to help their sisters, friends, cousins, and so on. Young women who are referred to group should not be told that they need to be in the group because they are believed to be at high risk of exploitation, as this only leaves them feeling judged, misunderstood, ashamed, and without a choice. Some young women may not be ready to attend a group like this, but they should be encouraged to attend the first session to gain a better understanding of the group. Participants have reported, "I want to learn how you guys got out of exploitation so I can tell other people how to get out of it if they are in that situation" and "I have a younger sister. I hope she is never exploited. So to prevent this, I will pass on this knowledge to her as she gets older." The groups may be challenging for girls who have family members who are currently being exploited— "Maybe this is not a group for me . . . The topic is something I don't want to talk about. Because I just found out that my mother is out there. So it is a lot for me right now." Girls in this type of situation may need additional outreach to understand how useful the experience of group may be for them.

Ensuring Safety

Many girls who participate in the My Life My Choice Prevention groups are coping with a variety of experiences; sometimes the group facilitators know about these experiences, but often they do not. In our secondary prevention groups, the majority of the girls have not actually been exploited, but many have similar experiences to the survivor cofacilitator, such as being a victim of bullying, having a history of physical and/or sexual abuse, suffering home removal, engaging in substance use, and being involved with child welfare. The My Life My Choice Prevention Curriculum covers many issues to which girls can relate. Regardless of where the group is taking place, it is critical to ensure not only physical safety but also emotional well-being. Many girls worry that if they share their experiences in group this information will be shared with others. While it is the group facilitator's job to create a safe environment, there are instances when the group may not feel emotionally safe for girls. We have addressed this in a number of ways, including meeting with the girls outside of group to mediate the situation and engaging a clinician from the program or school to help support the interaction.

Much of the material covered in the group may trigger memories, uncomfortable feelings, or sadness, so it is critical that the facilitators have a plan to keep all group participants physically and emotionally safe. It is important to check in with participants one-on-one if necessary, to follow up with appropriate providers or offer referral sources, and to also allow a participant to pass if she is not comfortable or ready to share.

When discussing commercial sexual exploitation, peer recruitment is often a reality and a challenge that facilitators will likely face. The safety of the group and of the girls participating is of utmost importance, but it is important to recognize that a young woman may be recruiting others because she is threatened or coerced by her exploiter. Facilitators must take recruitment seriously and handle it immediately by meeting with the young woman outside of group and determining whether she is ready to be in group at the current time. Any girl found to be recruiting is not allowed to participate in group.

Handling Disclosures

Before a My Life My Choice group begins, there must be a protocol established to handle any disclosures that are made by the girls in the group. In addition, many girls tend to share personal experiences through journaling and not in the larger group setting. If there is a disclosure of exploitation or of past or current abuse, or if a participant reports that she has a desire to harm herself or someone else, the facilitators must respond to this immediately as mandated reporters. Facilitators simply state within the groups that they are mandated reporters. Girls who have been involved in systems of care (child welfare, juvenile justice)—which most highly vulnerable girls have been—know the constraints of mandated reporting. It has not been an issue in terms of relationship building.

If a disclosure of CSEC is made or there is a suspicion of CSEC, the facilitators, as mandated reporters, must file a report of suspected child abuse with child protective services and notify appropriate personnel (such as a supervisor) immediately. When gathering information about the disclosure and filing a report of suspected child abuse, it is helpful to learn the location(s) of possible exploitation, the time frame of exploitation, and any identifying information pertaining to the alleged offender(s). If there is an immediate threat to safety, 911 should be called.

Group facilitators should never take action or share information that a youth discloses without first discussing with the youth their responsibility as a facilitator. As a group facilitator and clinician, it is helpful to provide information to the young woman so that she understands why you are filing the report and you can support her through the next steps. Being open and forthcoming will likely help to maintain your relationship with her. It is also helpful to reiterate to the young women that group facilitators are only in their lives for a short time and part of their job is to connect them with positive supports who will remain in their lives on an ongoing basis. In addition, it is best if the girls can then share whatever information they disclosed to their therapist or their guardian, with the support of the group facilitator. Once a report is filed, the group facilitator must work with the organization where the group was conducted and young woman to establish a safety plan and make any necessary referrals.

Consent

All participants who are under eighteen must have consent and approval from their guardian to participate in a My Life My Choice Prevention group.

Outcomes

Historically MLMC has used pre and post surveys that are included in the curriculum to evaluate group participants' progress over the course of ten sessions. These surveys assess the curriculum's relevance and effectiveness in changing girls' attitudes and knowledge of the commercial sex industry and in developing skills to avoid being recruited. Quotes from participant journals reveal that the program has directly addressed vulnerabilities and made a significant impact on the attitudes, knowledge, and skills of participants. For example:

"Today I realized the many dangers of pimps. I knew that there were many girls out there being sexually exploited but I didn't know that they were hanging out in public places that normal people hang out in like the mall, programs, parks, maybe even your school. It's so crazy." (Kara, age fifteen, 2014)

"I learned that pimps come in all shapes and sizes and it can be a regular person, male or female, but on the other side it can be a normal person/ student." (Nicole, age fourteen, 2015)

"The topic is important because young girls lives are put on the line because of pimps or men that want a business for themselves or over control." (Liz, age thirteen, 2014)

"What might make me vulnerable is that I used to think I was ugly so I loved hearing I was pretty, beautiful, cute, etc. but now nothing would make me vulnerable." (Alexa, age sixteen)

In addition to conducting internal pre and post surveys, MLMC has partnered with outside researchers to ensure program effectiveness. In 2014, researchers from Boston University School of Public Health and Northeastern

University received a National Institute of Justice grant to evaluate the effectiveness and impact of the My Life My Choice Prevention Curriculum (as well as the My Life My Choice Survivor Mentoring model). Although this comprehensive research is in the early stages, researchers will follow participants for three months after the completion of the group and will evaluate participant knowledge of CSEC and engagement in risky behavior. Similarly, in 2015, Rutgers University School of Public Health (Chin, 2014) released a 2015 evaluation of the My Life My Choice Prevention Curriculum. Researchers analyzed a total of 235 girls who were included in the study, with a 66 percent completion rate for pre and post surveys (155 participants). Results revealed significant increases in knowledge, attitudes, and self-esteem after participating in the MLMC group. For example, after completion of the MLMC prevention curriculum, there was an 81 percent increase in participants' ability to correctly identify three pimp tactics (up from 68 percent in the pretest). However, advancing skills (utilizing resources should they ever become involved in CSEC) did not increase significantly.

Outcome measurements can indicate which parts of the curriculum are working well for youth and which need to be adapted or improved upon to increase prevention efforts. While funding can be hard to secure, agencies looking to run CSEC prevention curricula should seek out evidence-based models before implementation and consider partnering with external evaluators to ensure continued effectiveness. Evidence-based feedback is critical in continuing to ensure that youth receive the best prevention curriculum possible.

Lessons Learned from My Life My Choice Curriculum

CSEC Is Preventable

Social workers are key change makers in the movement to end commercial sexual exploitation of children. It is imperative that social workers initiate prevention efforts of this egregious human rights abuse. The My Life My Choice Curriculum model offers insight into key elements of any robust prevention program. Rather than simply think about the service provision, social workers must retain a sense of outrage in regard to the issue of commercial sexual exploitation and work on strengthening vulnerable girls to fight back.

Prevention and Awareness Curricula Are Not Synonymous

Since 2010, the number of "human trafficking prevention" curricula has skyrocketed, although the vast majority of these curricula are awareness curricula rather than robust prevention programs. An awareness program seeks to ensure that all young people know that trafficking is real and exists within the United States. While this is billed as primary prevention, the authors would argue that it is not. It does increase knowledge, and this knowledge makes for more empathetic, committed citizens. However, this is not the same as helping to create a safer, healthier path for our youth. While not detrimental, using an awareness curriculum should not allow our schools or community programs to feel that they checked a proverbial box showing that they prevented CSEC.

Instead, a robust primary prevention program should include student-run and student-initiated efforts to shift school norms around misogyny and rape culture and push back against the glorification of pimping among the student body. When led by young people, this kind of systemic cultural shift can have a lasting impact on a school or community program. An example of one such program is the Students Against Human Trafficking Club at Brookline High School in Massachusetts. Among other initiatives, this student-run club leads an annual full day of education, discussion, and norm shifting in which the bulk of the student body learns about the issue and is pushed toward change around the intersections of race, class, and gender through student-led discussions.

Who Delivers the Prevention Message Matters

Survivors of CSEC are in a unique position to communicate understanding, build skills, and impart hope. This leadership must be part and parcel of a well-crafted prevention initiative.

Notes

1. Please note that girls, boys, and transgender youth are all at risk of commercial sexual exploitation. Many of their vulnerabilities are similar, while others remain unique. Because of their unique circumstances and needs and because their pathways into the sex industry often follow a similar pattern, this chapter will focus on biological girls. This by no means implies a lack of interest in the prevention needs of boys and transgender youth. However, these require greater study and specialization and will not be covered here.
2. The curriculum is not appropriate for boys. The experiences of girls in the commercial sex industry are different from those of boys (most notably, in the ubiquitous nature of pimp control for girls and the frequent absence for boys), and the curriculum is gender specific. We have had transgender females in the group, as well as transgender boys if their experience of being exploited was as a female-bodied person and therefore in line with the curriculum. There are other curricula specifically designed for boys (recommended: Empowering Young Men by CAASE). MLMC does offer a one-session curriculum specifically designed for LGBTQ youth communities.

3. Names have been changed to protect youths' identities.
4. The curriculum does include scenarios in which the perpetrator is female, and this possibility is reinforced throughout. It is also discussed in the curriculum that boys can be victims.

References

Causey, K., Zuniga, M., Bailer, B., Ring, L., & Gil-Trejo, L. (2012). Using theater arts to engage Latino families in dialogue about adolescent sexual health: The PATH-AT Program. *Journal of Health Care for the Poor and Underserved, 23*(1), 347–357. doi:10.1353/hpu.2012.0036

Chin, S. (2014). *Prevent child abuse: New Jersey's 'My Life, My Choice' program data analysis: Assessing the knowledge, attitudes, and skills of youth with increased risk of domestic minor sex trafficking in New Jersey.* Rutgers University School of Public Health.

Clawson, H. J., Dutch, N., Salamon, A., & Goldblatt Grace, L. (2009). *Study of HHS programs serving human trafficking victims: Final report.* U.S. Department of Health and Human Services, Office of the Assistant Secretary for Planning and Evaluation.

Countryman-Roswurm, K., & Bolin, B. (2014). Domestic minor sex trafficking: Assessing and reducing risk. *Child and Adolescent Social Work Journal, 31*(6), 521–538. doi:10.1007/s10560-014-0336-6

Drumm, K. (2006). The essential power of group work. *Social Work with Groups, 29*(2–3), 17–31. doi:10.1300/j009v29n02_02

Duger, A. (2015). Focusing on prevention: The social and economic rights of children vulnerable to sex trafficking. *Health and Human Rights, 17*(1), 114–123. doi:10.2307/healhumarigh.17.1.114

Estes, R., & Weiner, N. (2001). *The commercial sexual exploitation of children in the US, Canada and Mexico.* Philadelphia, PA: University of Pennsylvania, School of Social Work, Center for the Study of Youth Policy.

Farley, M. (2003). *Prostitution, trafficking and traumatic stress.* Binghamton, NY: Haworth Maltreatment & Trauma Press.

Ferguson, S. L. (1998). Peer counseling in a culturally specific adolescent pregnancy prevention program. *Journal of Health Care for the Poor and Underserved, 9*(3), 322–340. doi:10.1353/hpu.2010.0291

Finkelhor, D. (2009). The prevention of childhood sexual abuse. *The Future of Children, 19*(2), 169–194. doi:10.1353/foc.0.0035

Gibson, L. E., & Leitenberg, H. (2000). Child sexual abuse prevention programs: Do they decrease the occurrence of child sexual abuse? *Child Abuse & Neglect, 24*(9), 1115–1125.

Harper, G. W., Dolcini, M., Benhorin, S., Watson, S., & Boyer, C. (2014). The benefits of a friendship-based HIV/STI prevention intervention for African American youth. *Youth & Society, 46*(5), 591–622. doi:10.1177/0044118x12444210

Hickle, K. E., & Roe-Sepowitz, D. (2014). Putting the pieces back together: A group intervention for sexually exploited adolescent girls. *Social Work with Groups, 37*(2), 99–113. doi:10.1080/01609513.2013.823838

Janz, N. K., & Becker, M. H. (1984). The health belief model: A decade later. *Health Education & Behavior, 11*(1), 1–47. doi:10.1177/109019818401100101

Jones, C. J., Smith, H., & Llewellyn, C. (2014). Evaluating the effectiveness of health belief model interventions in improving adherence: A systematic review. *Health Psychology Review, 8*(3), 253–269. doi:10.1080/17437199.2013.802623

Kim, C. R., & Free, C. (2008). Recent evaluations of the peer-led approach in adolescent sexual health education: A systematic review. *Perspectives on Sexual and Reproductive Health, 40*(3), 144–151. doi:10.1363/4014408

Laraque, D., Mclean, D., Brown-Peterside, P., Ashton, D., & Diamond, B. (1997). Predictors of reported condom use in central Harlem youth as conceptualized by the health belief model. *Journal of Adolescent Health, 21*(5), 318–327.

Layzer, C., Rosapep, L., & Barr, S. (2014). A peer education program: Delivering highly reliable sexual health promotion messages in schools. *Journal of Adolescent Health, 54*(3).

Lloyd, R. (2005). Acceptable victims? Sexually exploited youth in the U.S. *Encounter: Education for Meaning and Social Justice, 18*(3), 6–18.

——. (2012). *Girls like us: Fighting for a world where girls are not for sale.* New York, NY: HarperCollins.

Murphy, P. A. (1993). *Making the connections: Women, work, and abuse.* Orlando, FL: PMD Press.

NCMEC. (2014).*Child Sex Trafficking.* Retrieved from http://www.missingkids.org/1in6

NPR. (2013). *Finding and stopping child sex trafficking.* Retrieved from http://www.npr.org /templates/story/story.php?storyId=207901614

Nixon, K., Tutty, L., Downe, P., Gorkoff, K., & Ursel, J. (2002). The everyday occurrence: Violence in the lives of girls exploited through prostitution. *Violence Against Women, 8*(9), 1016–1043. doi:10.1177/107780120200800902

Piening, S., & Cross, T. (2012). *From "The Life" to my life: Sexually exploited children reclaiming their futures: Suffolk County Massachusetts' response to commercial sexual exploitation of children (CSEC).* Boston, MA: Children's Advocacy Center of Suffolk County.

Pinkleton, B. E., Austin, E., Cohen, M., Chen, Y., & Fitzgerald, E. (2008). Effects of a peer-led media literacy curriculum on adolescents' knowledge and attitudes toward sexual behavior and media portrayals of sex. *Health Communication, 23*(5), 462–472. doi: 10.1080/10410230802342135

Roe-Sepowitz, D. E. (2012). Juvenile entry into prostitution: The role of emotional abuse. *Violence Against Women, 18*(5), 562–579.

Saewyc, E. M., & Edinburgh, L. (2010). Restoring healthy developmental trajectories for sexually exploited young runaway girls: Fostering protective factors and reducing risk behaviors. *Journal of Adolescent Health, 46*(2), 180–188. doi:10.1016/j.jadohealth .2009.06.010

Sherman, F. T., & Grace, L. G. (2011). The system response to the commercial sexual exploitation of girls. In F. T. Sherman & F. H. Jacobs (Eds.), *Juvenile justice: Advancing research, policy, and practice* (pp. 331–351). Hoboken, NJ: John Wiley. doi:10.1002/9781118093375.ch16

Thomson, S., Hirshberg, D., Corbett, A., Valila, N., & Howley, D. (2011). Residential treatment for sexually exploited adolescent girls: Acknowledge, Commit, Transform (ACT). *Children and Youth Services Review, 3*(11), 2290–2296. doi:10.1016/j.childyouth.2011.07.017

Todres, J. (2010). Taking prevention seriously: Developing a comprehensive response to child trafficking and sexual exploitation. *Vanderbilt Journal of Transnational Law, 43*(1), 1–56.

Twill, S. E., Green, D., & Traylor, A. (2010). A descriptive study on sexually exploited children in residential treatment. *Child Youth Care Forum, 39*(3), 187–199. doi:10.1007/ s10566-010-9098-2

Wright, P. J., Randall, A., & Hayes, J. G. (2012). Predicting the condom assertiveness of collegiate females in the United States from the expanded health belief model. *International Journal of Sexual Health, 24*(2).

CHAPTER 17

PREVENTION AND OUTREACH TO AT-RISK GROUPS

ANDREA J. NICHOLS, PhD,
WASHINGTON UNIVERSITY IN ST. LOUIS

O utreach and prevention efforts are embedded within many of the agencies serving survivors of sex trafficking and commercial sexual exploitation (CSE).[1] Such efforts may involve providing related education or prevention curricula in schools or community groups, posting information in public spaces about available services as a form of outreach, or engaging in street outreach. Yet lack of funding and resources makes it impossible to provide such initiatives evenly and consistently across the United States. Furthermore, it may not make sense to do so, as this chapter argues that based on known risk factors, trafficking and exploitation are likely to occur in varying frequencies in different locations. The "everyone is at equal risk" model has been debunked, as research clearly shows that some groups are at higher risk than others (Dank et al., 2015; Egyes, 2016; Gonzalez, 2016; Heil, 2016; Martin et al., 2014; Micetic, 2016; Nichols, 2016; Polaris Project, 2014; 2015a; Raphael & Myers-Powell, 2010; Reid, 2011; Schwarz et al., 2016). The chapter first highlights known risk factors of sex trafficking/CSE and then relates them to structural and demographic risk factors. It focuses on the weak social institutions, weak social safety nets, and interrelated dynamics of identity-based oppression that create heightened risk, indicating patterns that can be used for targeted prevention and outreach. The chapter concludes by calling for social change activism within organizations and among individual service providers as a means of establishing structural change to address and prevent some of the root causes of sex trafficking and exploitation.

Prevention

Prevention can be viewed as preventing trafficking/CSE from initially occurring or preventing further trafficking of an already trafficked person. Preventing trafficking/CSE from initially occurring includes endeavors such as providing education to guide individual decision making and addressing structural and socio-environmental issues to prevent risk in a "big picture" approach. Present initiatives to prevent initial trafficking/CSE involve education in schools for children, which may include providing information about healthy relationships, setting boundaries, the techniques of pimps/traffickers, empowerment, and sex/gender inequality and/or sexual objectification. Current initiatives to prevent further trafficking/CSE rely heavily on identification and referral to appropriate services. Individuals who are likely to come into contact with trafficked and exploited people are trained to recognize the warning signs and to appropriately screen for trafficking in healthcare, social services, and law enforcement settings (see chapter 2). Prevention of further trafficking/CSE involves street outreach efforts by social workers, who work to build trust and transformational relationships, provide information about available services, offer harm-reduction techniques (see chapter 6), and post posters or other materials with contact information for local resources or the national trafficking hotline or text line. "Big picture" approaches to prevent initial and further trafficking/CSE are not generally a visible part of antitrafficking initiatives, yet it is imperative to examine macro-structural components of risk to address the root sources of the problem (Martin et al, 2014; Nichols, 2016). This chapter indicates that new or already existing outreach and prevention efforts can be adapted to prioritize high-risk areas, and it also calls for social change activism to address the known structural weaknesses that are associated with risk factors.

Identifying Risk Factors to Guide Targeted Prevention

Risk factors disproportionately appear in the backgrounds of trafficked and exploited people (Curtis, Terry, Dank, Dombrowski, & Khan, 2008; Dank et al., 2015; Egyes, 2016; Gonzalez, 2016; Heil, 2016; Heil & Nichols, 2015; Kyckelhahn, Beck, & Cohen, 2009; Martin, Pierce, Peyton, Gabilondo, & Tulpule, 2014; Micetic, 2016; Nichols, 2016; Raphael & Myers-Powell, 2010; Raphael, Reichert, & Powers, 2010; Reid, 2014; Reid & Jones, 2011; Reid & Piquero, 2013; Schwarz et al., 2016). Known risk factors include, but are not limited to:

- High truancy, school mobility, and high dropout rates or low graduation rates
- Low socioeconomic status and poverty

- Limited access to housing
- Limited access to employment
- Homelessness
- Runaway status
- Domestic/intimate partner violence in the home
- Child abuse, child sexual abuse, neglect
- Involvement in foster care/child welfare systems
- Substance abuse

Many of these risk factors are intertwined with systemic problems embedded in weak social institutions. This "big picture," or sociostructural theoretical approach, indicates that addressing these risk factors on a structural level and working to ameliorate their effects will reduce the risk to vulnerable populations.

The Weak Social Institutions Perspective

The weak social institutions theoretical approach holds that weak social institutions, combined with weak social safety nets, create an environment conducive to sex trafficking/CSE vulnerability (Nichols, 2016). Social institutions are widely understood to include the family, education systems, economic systems, healthcare systems, the criminal justice system, and governmental systems. Social safety nets include *supports for accessing healthcare*, including substance abuse rehabilitation and mental healthcare; *social services*, including various forms of shelter, job skills training, services related to intimate partner violence (IPV), crisis intervention, and more; and *supports to attain basic needs*, such as a living wage as a minimum wage, unemployment benefits, Temporary Assistance for Needy Families (TANF), subsidized housing, subsidized daycare, and other social supports. Any weaknesses in social institutions or social safety nets create heightened risk. Moreover, those who are disproportionately exposed to weak social institutions, typically those experiencing identity-based oppression, are at heightened risk. Identity-based oppression is the systematic oppression of any structurally disadvantaged or culturally marginalized population. This includes those experiencing marginalization or oppression that targets race, class, sex, gender identity or expression, sexual orientation, ethnicity, and/or undocumented citizenship status (see figure 17.1).

It has been well documented that Black women and girls, Native women and girls, Latinx, and LGBTQ+ people are at heightened risk (Dank et al., 2015; Egyes, 2016; Gonzales, 2016; Heil & Nichols, 2015; Martin et al., 2014; Kyckelhahn, Beck, & Cohen, 2009). Identities intersect and interact, impacting one's

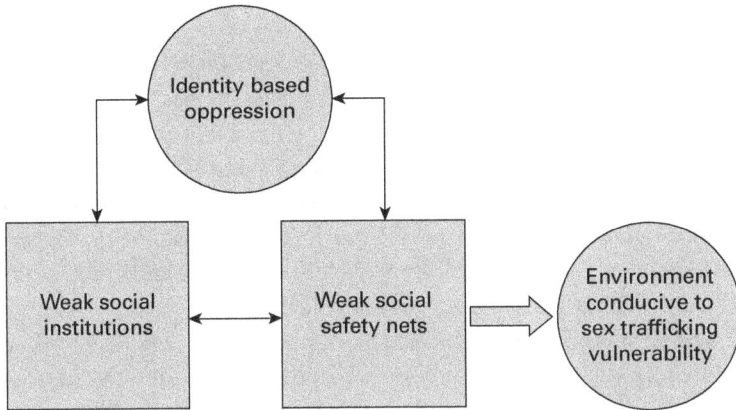

FIGURE 17.1 Conceptual Model of Risk Factors: The Weak Social Institutions Perspective

experiences with oppression and marginalization. "It is the increased presence of multiple risk factors that push[es] people towards exploitation and trafficking. When people are disenfranchised along multiple axes—where many structural inequalities converge—their risk of trafficking increases" (Schwarz et al., 2016). Moreover, vulnerabilities do not exist in a vacuum; micro, mezzo, and macro interactions can increase or decrease risk. For example, LGBTQ+ kids with a supportive loving parent(s) are at significantly lower risk, as the increased risk to this population is heavily intertwined with parents' negative reactions to their children's gender identity or sexual orientation. Similarly, African American children who are of middle- or upper-class backgrounds and who attend good schools are at much lower risk than those who are in low-income areas with poor-quality education systems. Women and girls are more likely to experience sexual objectification and heightened sex trafficking/CSE than cisgender heterosexual boys[2]; yet surrounding environmental factors work to instigate or mitigate risk. While anyone is at risk, risk is increased for some groups compared to others. The following subsections provide more details about the relationship between weak social institutions and the ways that known risk factors for sex trafficking are embedded within them; they also discuss the role of weak social safety nets and identity-based oppression and review implications for social workers who wish to engage in targeted prevention and outreach efforts.

Education Systems

Some related risk factors for sex trafficking—truancy, high dropout rates, and low graduation rates—are entrenched within weak education systems

(Heil & Nichols, 2015; Oselin, 2014; Raphael & Reichert, 2008; Schwarz et al., 2016). Inequality exists in the U.S. K-12 education system: lower-income areas have reduced school funding (due to lower property tax revenues), resulting in larger class sizes, less qualified teachers, out-of-date books, books that cannot be taken home to do homework, not enough books to go around, lack of technology in the classroom, and a focus on social control rather than education (Ferguson, 2001; Kozol, 2012). In low-income areas, adequate yearly progress (AYP) and standardized test scores are much more likely to be lower; truancy, dropout, and student mobility rates are likely to be higher; and graduation rates are likely to be lower partly because of these factors.

For adults, it is apparent that unequal opportunity in education influences life chances. In their adulthood, those who drop out or do not graduate from high school have fewer occupational opportunities and are much more likely to hold low-wage employment. Raphael and Reichert (2008) found lower educational attainment (those who dropped out or did not graduate) among those who experienced commercial sexual exploitation. Even for those who do graduate, because of the disproportionate likelihood of lower standardized test scores, there is reduced likelihood of getting into a college or university, and acceptance of lower-wage labor is much more likely. It is generally well known that a minimum wage in the United States does not provide a living wage (Ehrenreich, 2011; Klein, 2008).

Research bears out that youth and adults may enter into commercial sex markets in order to supplement their wages or as a constrained choice to access basic needs for themselves or their families (Curtis et al., 2008; Dank et al., 2015; Heil & Nichols, 2015; Raphael & Reichert, 2008). For minors this action, often referred to as survival sex, equates to sex trafficking. Exploiting the vulnerability of adults in such circumstances may be viewed as commercial sexual exploitation; adult involvement in commercial sex may also be seen as a constrained choice due partly to the inequity in existing education systems. Low-income individuals are at increased risk of exploitation by a buyer, pimp, or trafficker or may seek out sex trade opportunities on their own (Lutnick, 2016). Coercion and violence in such circumstances tend to escalate over time. Studies document that what begins as an arrangement with a pimp can become violent, coercive, and exploitive (Raphael & Reichert, 2008).

For those still of school age, research shows that truancy and dropout status increase the likelihood of exposure to a pimp/trafficker (Curtis et al., 2008; Dank et al., 2015; Heil & Nichols, 2015; Nichols, 2016; Polaris Project, 2014; Raphael & Myers-Powell, 2010; Raphael & Riechart, 2008; Reid, 2010, 2011, 2014). For example, Heil and Nichols (2015) found that adolescents interacting with the family courts in St. Louis had backgrounds of chronic truancy, which increased their exposure to pimps and resulted in heightened likelihood of sex trafficking. When kids are not in school, they are susceptible to getting recruited by a pimp/trafficker. Traffickers are actively seeking out teens who seem rebellious (such as those who skip school or drop out) or are otherwise in need of a friend, boyfriend, or father-figure (Polaris Project, 2014, 2015a; Smith, Vardaman, & Snow, 2009). Pimps are also recruiting outside of courthouses and in juvenile facilities (through other girls), and status offenders are likely to interact with them in these places (a status offense is anything that would not be considered an offense if an adult did it, such as truancy).

School mobility rates may also pose a less direct risk factor. *School mobility* refers to student turnover, a measure of students moving in and out of school districts. School mobility is likely to occur when a parent cannot afford to pay rent and then moves on to the next low-rent property, often in a different school district. While certainly schools cannot control the mobility of the families they serve, there is an effect on the students and the schools (Heil & Nichols, 2015). When students are moving in and out of school districts, they have a reduced connection to the school, their teachers, and their peers. This increases likelihood of truancy, as well as disengagement from healthy social relationships (pimps are looking for such disengagement). They also are more likely to fall behind academically—it is well documented that student mobility correlates with AYP. School mobility is also impacted by lost accreditation.

In St. Louis, Missouri, thirty-six schools had mobility rates higher than 50 percent in the St. Louis public school system between 2011 and 2012 (Missouri Department of Elementary and Secondary Education, n.d). The graduation rate in the St. Louis public school district overall was only 68 percent in the 2014 school year, with a dropout rate of nearly 18 percent (Missouri Department of Elementary and Secondary Education, n.d). Another school district in the St. Louis metro area that showed heightened risk included Normandy, which had a 13 percent dropout rate and a 53 percent graduation rate. For perspective, the average state dropout rate was 1.5 percent and the average graduation rate for the state of Missouri in 2014 was 92 percent. Using the state of Illinois as another example, whose average dropout rate was 2.2 percent and graduation rate was 86 percent in 2014, school districts that stand out in southern Illinois are East St. Louis, with a nearly 8 percent dropout rate and 69 percent graduation rate, and Cahokia at 4.4 percent dropout rate and 69 percent graduation rate (Illinois State Board of Education, n.d.). Accordingly, these would be considered areas with heightened education-based risk factors and therefore sites for targeted prevention and outreach. In its study of homeless youth in Philadelphia, Washington, D.C., and Phoenix, the Covenant House (2017) reported that "education also appears to have a protective factor. Of those who reported being sex trafficked, only

22 percent had a high school diploma and 11 percent had attended some college. A full 67 percent had not graduated from high school."

Schools at highest risk are more likely to be in low-income areas. Similarly, lower socioeconomic status (SES) intersects with race and ethnicity, as Black Americans, Native people, and Hispanic/Latinx Americans disproportionately live in low-income areas due to structural racism and generational educational inequality (going to a low-performing school, getting lower standardized test scores, not getting into a college or university, having fewer job opportunities; the cycle of inequality repeats itself) and are consequently disproportionately exposed to unequal opportunity in education. The role of identity-based oppression and LGBTQ+ status in education systems is addressed in chapter 10.

To address weaknesses in education systems associated with heightened risk, social workers can engage in the following actions. Data on graduation rates, dropout rates, mobility rates, truancy or attendance rates, and AYP can be obtained from state departments of education. At times, they are readily available online; at other times, they are available upon request. The recommendation is to get at least two years of data to get a more accurate measure and then to analyze these data and create a prioritized list based on education-based risk factors. By examining these education-based risk factors, social workers can identify high-priority areas that have schools with heightened risk.

This identification can inform targeted prevention and outreach, such as described in chapter 16. Prevention curricula could easily be added to health or other related courses. Furthermore, high-risk schools and areas with high education-based risk factors can be targeted for posting outreach materials, conducting street outreach, or providing outreach within schools. Working with lists of truant and dropout students for outreach and prevention is also recommended. Social workers, or school psychologists or counselors, working in outreach or in schools can make the initial contact. This initial contact should not be based on the assumption that trafficking is occurring; rather, the focus should be on building a trusting relationship and focusing on needs, acknowledging that the potential for trafficking may be present. This form of outreach can be intertwined with a prevention initiative taken by an individual organization in community partnership with high-risk school districts, and perhaps with juvenile justice or family courts working with truant youth. It is important to develop partnerships with schools (and school social workers, counselors, or psychologists, if present) to increase identification and provide appropriate services. This would mean educating teachers, staff, and social workers in high-risk schools about risk factors and red flag signs of sex trafficking (see chapter 2). Finally, social workers can work at a community and policy level to advocate for increased funding for and improvement of high-risk schools.

Family Systems

Weaknesses in family systems are associated with risk of trafficking/CSE, such as backgrounds of IPV, child abuse, child sexual abuse, child neglect, and family conflict in the home, which can result in runaway or throwaway status and/or homelessness. Research indicates that trafficked and exploited youth disproportionately have backgrounds of child abuse, neglect, and intimate partner violence within the home (Cole, Sprang, Lee, & Cohen, 2016; Oselin, 2014; Raphael, Reichert, & Powers, 2010; Schwarz et al., 2016). The intimate partner violence typically involves a father or boyfriend abusing a child's mother (Heil & Nichols, 2015; Raphael & Myers-Powell, 2010). At times, children will also experience abuse, including physical, psychological, or sexual abuse by their mothers, fathers, or mother's boyfriends. In addition, as a form of familial trafficking, cases have been documented in which one or both parents have a substance abuse issue and their adolescent girl is used to "trade" or appease a drug dealer for nonpayment (Heil & Nichols, 2015). In terms of neglect, which is important but less commonly discussed in the sex-trafficking literature, kids who don't have enough food to eat and whose homes do not consistently have heat, water, or electricity may look for better options outside the home (Heil & Nichols, 2015; Lutnick, 2016; Oselin, 2014; Raphael & Myers-Powell, 2010). Abuse and neglect can render home life unbearable for some children, who run away from home to avoid the conflict or abuse or are looking for a better option.

Runaway minors have limited employment options, and minors are quickly recruited into commercial sex markets by pimps, other kids living on the streets, or buyers who are actively seeking them out (Curtis et al., 2008; Dank et al., 2015; Nichols & Heil, 2015; Smith et al., 2009;). Housing and shelter options are also limited for runaway or otherwise homeless youth. Youth employment and housing options often require a documented history of years of homelessness, or of a mental health disorder, to meet eligibility requirements. As Lutnick describes it (2016), the young person's situation has to inevitably get worse before it gets better under this model. Furthermore, youth want to avoid child welfare, so it can be difficult for them to find housing. "Because these youth are younger than 18, want to avoid child . . . they have limited to no housing options available to them" (Lutnick, 2016, p. 99).

Sex-trafficked minors are also disproportionately represented in foster care placement (Cole et al., 2016; Reid & Piquero, 2013). This is likely a reflection of chronic runaway status or of social workers deeming the parents unfit and the child being unable to return home (Lloyd, 2012; Oselin, 2014; Polaris Project, 2014; Raphael & Myers-Powell, 2010; Reid, 2010, Reid & Piquero, 2013. Trafficked children frequently run away from foster homes, perhaps due to unaddressed trauma resulting from the initial problematic home life and the resulting "fight or flight" tendencies. Runaways are highly vulnerable, as traffickers and buyers are looking for kids in the street who are easy to recruit— they have limited means for survival and they don't want to be found.

In terms of identity-based oppression, LGBTQ+ youth show heightened runaway risk. It is estimated that LGBTQ+ youth compose nearly 40 percent of the homeless youth population (Ray, 2006). Many are homeless because of a problematic family life. Their parents may not accept their sexual orientation or gender identity, and the parents then either ask them to leave the family home or make the home life so conflict ridden that kids choose to run away (Curtis et al., 2008; Dank et al., 2015).

To prevent runaway risk, as well as the factors that precede it, social workers can use various approaches. First, the National Runaway Safeline data can be used to find areas of heightened risk in a state. Simply identifying areas with higher numbers of runaways is useful. The data are limited, because they are only represented by area code, but dividing the number of calls by the population the area covers can provide some insight into risk per population. Population size based on area code can be found by typing "area code [insert area code]" "census data" into an Internet search. The National Runaway Safeline data by state can be accessed at http://www.1800runaway.org /runaway-statistics/crisis-hotline-online-services-statistics/. The organization also provides a free runaway prevention education curriculum, which can be accessed at http://www.1800runaway.org/providers-educators/. Preventing initial runaway behaviors can reduce risk of sex trafficking and can be viewed as a preventative measure.

Once high-risk areas for runaway youth are uncovered, outreach to homeless youth populations to prevent initial and further trafficking is called for, as well as prevention education in schools in these areas. Outreach can include street outreach, or posting of trafficking resources and referrals in areas where runaway or homeless youth are more likely to congregate—youth-serving agencies, bus stops, train stations, public libraries, and 24-hour coffee shops (see chapter 10). It is important that outreach contains relatable language and imagery (see chapter 18), as most people who are experiencing trafficking and exploitation will not identify with the language of trafficking, modern-day slavery, or commercial sexual exploitation. Mirroring the language that runaway youth use (see chapter 3), and acknowledging that leaving the sex trade may not be their first priority, are important. At the same time, one should offer resources for assistance. Survivor-centered practice and a harm-reduction approach are key to successful outreach efforts (see chapter 6). Disclosing to clients about mandated reporting is also necessary.

Taking a different approach, the "big picture approach" would involve preventing initial trafficking by providing more resources to address

"Family System" risk factors, such as domestic/intimate partner violence, child abuse, and neglect, thereby building stronger social safety nets such as expanded shelter provisions, teaching about healthy relationships in schools, and expanded funding to address such issues seen within families. Increased training for identification in related organizations, such as child welfare/ children's services is also called for. Working to reduce parental rejection of their LGBTQ+ children is also called for. This could involve social change action efforts at a higher level, or it could involve individual education initiatives for parents provided through schools or community programs (see chapter 10).

Weak Economic Systems

Poverty and low socioeconomic status are intertwined with many of the factors listed thus far, such as weaknesses in education systems and the resulting low-wage labor, and are a source of education inequality. Poverty is a fact of life for homeless and runaway minors who may not be of age to gain legitimate employment, and those who are of age will be confined to low-wage labor. Low socioeconomic status is linked to housing instability; Lutnick (2016) found that housing was a salient need among CSE-involved people in four cities. In fact, access to housing is frequently cited as one of the most common needs among people involved in commercial sex, including sexually exploited youth (Curtis et al., 2008; Dank et al., 2015; Macy & Johns, 2011).

Low economic status is intertwined with lack of access to mental healthcare and substance abuse rehabilitation (discussed in following text), which are also found as needs among sex-trafficked/CSE people (Heil & Nichols, 2015; Macy & Johns, 2011).

The United States is a high-income country, regarded as the wealthiest in the world. At the same time, it is also characterized by income inequality and rising gaps between the wealthy and the poor. At first glance, one might be hard pressed to describe the U.S. economy as weak, yet social stratification is a systemic weakness, and there is a lack of social safety nets to assist low-income people. The United States has more children in poverty and holds more working poor than any other high-income nation. Accordingly, the disenfranchised are susceptible to alternate means of survival and are especially vulnerable to buyers, pimps, and traffickers. They may also seek out sex work on their own, as they can make more money trading sex than working in low-wage labor (Lutnick, 2016). Further, minors who do not want to be found, whether they are avoiding conflict-ridden homes, child welfare systems, or juvenile justice systems, may find the sex trade their only available choice or the best available choice.

In terms of identity-based oppression, women, gay, transgender, and queer people are more likely to face workplace discrimination in hiring, promotion, and wages. Transgender individuals experience particular discrimination and are more likely to be overlooked in hiring practices. Moreover, there is a lack of state protection against hiring discrimination and termination of employment due to gender identity. The feminization of poverty is well documented; women compose 51 percent of the population, yet 65 percent of the poor. The feminization of poverty is heightened by marginalization based on race, ethnicity, gender identity, and sexual orientation. Similarly, wage, hiring, and promotion discrimination is heightened for women of color, undocumented people, and people of color more broadly.

Social workers have two calls to action. First, social workers can pinpoint economically disenfranchised areas within their service region through census data for prevention and outreach. Social workers can readily access information about poverty, unemployment, and household income in individual cities within their service area at http://factfinder.census.gov/faces /nav/jsf/pages/index.xhtml. Second, social workers can address such issues at a state level by lobbying for a higher minimum wage and expanded unemployment benefits, becoming active in TANF-related legislation, and working in other areas that impact socioeconomic status. In addition, social workers should advocate for state protections that address workplace discrimination directed toward transgenderpeople, as well as workplace discrimination and wage inequality more broadly and with an intersectional perspective.

The following subsections—on weak healthcare, criminal justice, and governmental systems—do not focus on targeted geographical regions and their resulting prevention and outreach efforts. Rather, they focus on weaknesses within these systems, calling on social workers to engage in structural-level activism to address the risk factors embedded within these systems.

Weak Healthcare Systems

The United States has issues with its healthcare system similar to the weaknesses in its economic system. While the country has top medical schools and doctors, health stratification is prevalent. The uninsured and underinsured have difficulty accessing mental healthcare and substance abuse rehabilitation. Those experiencing sex trafficking/CSE victimization, especially those in street-based work in which a pimp or trafficker is taking the bulk of their money, as well as those engaged in survival sex, may similarly have difficulty accessing substance abuse rehabilitation or mental healthcare. Problems include lengthy wait-times, lack of available services, and barriers to accessing services (personal communication with Celeste Souza, Director, Magdalene St. Louis).

First, timing may be an issue. In facilities that receive state funding to treat uninsured or underinsured people for substance abuse issues, waiting lists tend to be longer, typically between two weeks and one month. With time-sensitive health issues like addiction and mental health, waiting for two weeks to get an appointment is problematic, as individuals might change their mind or might not remember their appointment. Moreover, those who need assistance must engage in intensive follow-up. They are required to continue to call to ensure their appointment. For those who are insured, they may not be able to afford their co-pay or may not have transportation to get to their appointment (personal communication with Celeste Souza, Director, Magdalene St. Louis).

Another issue relates to eye care and dental care, as eye doctors and dentists are less likely to accept Medicaid patients because they get less reimbursement. In some states, Medicaid does not cover adults' dental or eye care (Medicaid. gov, 2016). The stigma of missing or broken teeth and of broken or old glasses is a barrier to getting legitimate jobs (personal communication with Celeste Souza, Director, Magdalene St. Louis). The uninsured would not have access to such care. While such barriers are disproportionately experienced by low-income people more broadly, people involved in sex trafficking/CSE, specifically those engaging in street-based work or survival sex, are disproportionately low income. Macy and Johns (2011) report that people who are experiencing trafficking express that they need access to health and dental care. "For example, survivors often have suffered broken teeth or jaws as well as poor oral health stemming from neglect, poor diet, and poor physical health. Similar to other health needs, survivors' dental needs should be addressed as quickly as possible" (p. 94).

It is also difficult to gain access to sex trafficking–specific services, such as residential care with experts working exclusively with trafficked or exploited people. Insurance companies may not cover this care, individuals or families may not have the ability to privately pay for services, or such services may not be available in their area, have long waiting lists, or have stringent entrance requirements. Many residential sex-trafficking organizations rely on private donations to be able to accept clients into care when clients cannot pay for services themselves or insurance will not cover it. "Some 57 percent of our clients last year were private, meaning they had no daily billing source. We could sometimes get individual or group therapy covered, but [for] their day to day rate we had to provide everything" (personal Communication with Anonymous, Director of Operations, Safe Harbour House). Moreover, the issue is problematized when minors working to access residential care cross state lines, which is common due to the shortage of such services (38 across the country). "One of our biggest problems is with kids from out of state. There is an extensive system to get kids on Medicaid from state to state some-times taking months. We also struggle because you can only bill for so many sessions. One girl they only allowed 10 sessions and then refused to pay further. Also, if they are already in another facility, we have to offer our services gratis because they've already billed" (ibid.).

States with limited social supports or limited Medicaid are sites of social action for social workers. Becoming involved in existing efforts to expand Medicaid in one's state can help one's clients access much-needed treatments, such as mental health and substance abuse treatments. Social workers can access information on contacting state representatives and senators at www.common cause.org/take-action/find-elected-officials/. There are also national movements to address Medicaid expansion, such as Families USA: The Voice for Health Care Consumers (http://familiesusa.org/product/momentum-medicaid-expansion), as well as state-based movements, such as the Save Our Selves (SOS) Medicaid expansion movement in Alabama.

Weak Criminal Justice Systems[3]

As stated in the beginning of this chapter, prevention efforts include a focus on preventing further trafficking of an already trafficked person through identification and referral to appropriate resources. As first-responders, police are in a prime position to identify victims and may interact with individuals engaged in commercial sex markets, sex workers who have experienced rape and sexual assault, or those experiencing intimate partner violence— all circumstances associated with sex trafficking/CSE. However, weaknesses within individual police departments, or among individual officers' practices, may stymie identification and prevention of further trafficking. For example, in a focus group of service providers and law enforcement, Nichols and Heil (2015) found that police did not typically investigate incidents of rape, sexual assault, or intimate partner violence experienced by those involved in commercial sex for their possible links to trafficking; they thereby missed potential cases, failed to identify and refer to appropriate services, and failed to prevent further trafficking. In a review of police incidence reports of prostitution, Farrell et al. (2012) discovered that signs of trafficking were apparent in 10 percent of them, yet the cases were not further investigated. Researchers have also found that in general police officers lack understanding of trafficking (Farrell et al., 2012; Wilson & Dalton, 2008; Wilson, Walsh, & Klueber, 2006).

Another weakness identified within the criminal justice system is lack of identification based on undocumented status and transgender identities. For example, Egyes (2016) noted that some police officers did not take seriously the claims of immigrant and transgender clients who had been trafficked. Police did not acknowledge that Egyes's clients were trafficking victims and would not take action, despite evidence of trafficking. Gonzalez (2016) similarly noted that some police officers are more likely to see Black women and girls as prostitutes and criminals than as victims. Among arrestees for juvenile prostitution (which is sex trafficking based on most state laws and federal laws), nearly 60 percent are Black, a disproportionately high number, as Black juveniles constitute about 13 percent of the general youth population (Snyder & Mulako-Wangota, 2015). Thus, there is failure to recognize such juveniles as trafficking victims; instead they are revictimized through criminalization and arrest. Similarly, researchers have found that when undocumented immigrants are trafficked, at times Homeland Security simply deports them or their traffickers rather than referring them to legal and social services, thereby missing an important opportunity to identify trafficking and provide social services to prevent further trafficking (Hepburn & Simon, 2010; Nichols & Heil, 2015). There is also criminalization and overreach in policing of transgender people and racial minorities as a result of identity-based oppression (Koyama, 2011). Researchers report increased police scrutiny, harassment, and abuses of transgender people, regardless of whether they are working or not (described as "walking while trans") (Dank et al., 2015 Lutnick, 2016) (see also chapter 10). Increased distrust of police creates dangerous environments where racial minorities and transgender people lack recourse for victimization and serves as a barrier to seeking help. A general distrust of authority figures may impact trust of social service providers as well (Koyama, 2013).

To address such issues with appropriate identification and responses, social workers can use already existing coalitions or task forces in their communities to engage in cross-training or, if none exist, to develop relationships with local police departments to provide education about human trafficking, red flag signs, and appropriate responses to guide prevention of further trafficking. This would need to include a discussion of the disproportionate risk based on race/ethnicity and LGBTQ+ identities. For example, Egyes (2016) documented issues with some officers who dismissed reports of her sex-trafficked transgender clients. She began working with local officials to train and educate law enforcement in this area, and she described the development of collaborative relationships and improved responses for her clients as a result of this action. Ideally, it would be useful to form a partnership or crisis response team, similar to those used to address intimate partner violence as well as rape and sexual assault. Trafficked and exploited individuals would be identified and referred to appropriate services with an advocate on call to prevent further trafficking/CSE from occurring. Particularly in populations with heightened distrust of police, such as in African American, immigrant, and transgender communities, having an advocate on site who is educated in cultural competency may mitigate this distrust.

Weak Governmental Systems

Weaknesses within governmental systems include inadequate legislation and revictimizing legislation, which social workers can work to address through activism and political involvement. As previously mentioned, social workers can lobby state legislatures to expand Medicaid under the Affordable Care Act, expand the provisions of the Violence Against Women Act (VAWA), advocate for improved and targeted state funding for education and for increasing the minimum wage, or lobby on a federal level for easing the immigration process.[4] This is by no means outside the scope of a typical service provider's activities. For example, it has been reasonably well documented that advocates in the battered women's movement worked to improve justice system responses to intimate partner violence (see Goodman & Epstein [2008] for an overview). Advocates' activism resulted in the Violence Against Women Act, the establishment of a national hotline, hundreds of shelters, and national and state coalitions against domestic and sexual violence. Activism in other areas of social work have resulted in dramatic change, and this can be done with antitrafficking/CSE activism as well.

On a political level, researchers and practitioners indicate that consistency between state and federal trafficking laws, as well as consistency between states, is important to treat survivors with dignity and respect, to avoid revictimization through criminalization, and to get people the services they need. For social workers to advocate for their clients on a policy level, activism can take the following forms. First, social workers can check to see if their city or state has an active antitrafficking coalition or task force and consider using this existing framework to uncover the unmet needs in their area or state. They can check with their state coalition against domestic violence and sexual assault as well, as some of the state coalitions include a focus on sex trafficking/CSE. Next, they can lobby their state representatives and governors, as a coalition, an organization, or as an individual, clearly explaining what type of legislation is needed.

In addition, state report cards are developed by the Polaris Project, as well as by Shared Hope International (2016). This information may be useful when recommending that state legislators draft legislation. The state report cards developed by Shared Hope International (2016) can be accessed at https://sharedhope.org/what-we-do/bring-justice/reportcards/#reportcards, and the state ratings provided by the Polaris Project can be accessed at https://polarisproject.org/sites/default/files/2014-State-Ratings.pdf. The recommendations from these sources should be discussed and vetted through organizations whose service populations are affected, such as organizations that assist people in leaving prostitution, those that work with people actively engaged in commercial sex markets, and organizations that provide shelter, therapy, or other services to trafficked and exploited people. Survivors should also be consulted, such as through the National Survivor Network. At times, there are negative latent consequences of the best-intended legislation—these groups can help mitigate such mistakes. Importantly, social workers should note that these state report cards do not emphasize legislation regarding homelessness, runaway youth, inequality in education and wages, IPV, and the other interrelated social problems discussed throughout this chapter. Thus, it is imperative to look beyond the scope of the state report cards to investigate weak social safety nets and politically engage in areas that will improve the lives of trafficked and exploited people and reduce the risk of initial and further trafficking. Social workers' role in working with clients to gain federal benefits, as well as benefits offered in some states, such as vacating/expunging convictions and benefits surrounding T and U visas, can be found in chapter 7.

Conclusion

Heightened education-based risk factors, such as truancy, low graduation rates, and high dropout rates, can be targeted for outreach and prevention efforts. Moreover, areas with higher numbers of runaways can also be identified to guide prioritized outreach and prevention efforts. Economically disenfranchised locations are also at heightened risk and should be considered priority target areas for prevention and outreach.

Targeted prevention and outreach are useful, but they should be combined with social change activism. There is a legacy of social change activism by social workers and advocates. This is apparent in the violence against women's movement, children's rights movement, and trans rights movement, among others. Social work departments across the United States commonly include courses examining social justice, inequality, cultural competency, and related dynamics, as such phenomena are often intertwined with practice. This chapter calls for activism among social workers at a systems level to address issues of sex trafficking and commercial sexual exploitation. It is important for new generations of social workers to become activists and advocate for their clients on a macro-structural level, and for already established social workers to facilitate mentalities of social change activism within their organizations. To target the root causes of sex trafficking, it is imperative to address identity-based oppression (such as sexism, racism, xenophobia, transphobia, homophobia) and systemic weaknesses in social institutions and social safety nets.

Summary of Recommendations

Risk Factors

Education-Based (truancy, low graduation rates, high student mobility, high dropout rates)

- Identify school districts with heightened risk through data from their State Department of Education.
- Prioritize these areas for outreach and prevention efforts, such as by including an education curriculum in a health course, posting outreach materials, and conducting street outreach.
- Work with lists of truant youth for outreach efforts to channel youth into appropriate services. This may be done in partnership with the local juvenile division of the family courts and schools.
- Develop partnerships with schools to increase identification and provide appropriate services.
- Become politically involved to improve education systems and to support increased funding to poorly funded schools.

Family-Based (intimate partner violence, child abuse, child sexual abuse, neglect in the home leading to runaway and homeless youth)

- Identify areas with larger numbers of runaways from the National Runaway Safeline.
- Prioritize those areas for outreach and prevention efforts, such as by engaging in street outreach, placing posters in hot spots to provide information about accessing services, and developing runaway prevention education curricula in schools.
- Become politically involved to support increased funding to address issues of violence and abuse in the home.
- Provide community education to parents to reduce their rejection of LGBTQ+ youth.

Economic-Based (poverty, low SES)

- Identify areas with higher rates of poverty and low SES.
- Prioritize those areas for outreach and prevention efforts.

- Become politically involved to support economic safety nets, such as by increasing the minimum wage and expanding TANF and unemployment benefits.
- Engage in political activism to address identity-based oppression in hiring and wage discrimination.

Healthcare-Based (inaccessibility to mental healthcare, substance abuse rehabilitation, and sex-trafficking/exploitation services)

- Become politically involved to expand Medicaid in your state, particularly if your state is one that did not accept federal dollars under the Affordable Care Act for that purpose.
- Lobby for expanded funding for mental health and substance abuse services.

Criminal Justice System–Based (failure to identify victims; revictimization of LGBTQ+ individuals, black Americans, Native Americans, undocumented people, and people "in the life")

- Partner with your local police departments to provide education about sex trafficking and red flag signs.
- Develop a crisis response team model, partnering relevant local social service organizations with the local police department or FBI.
- Provide education that is culturally competent and inclusive of races, ethnicities, LGBTQ+ individuals, and undocumented immigrants.

Government-Based (inadequate or revictimizing legislation)

- Examine your state report cards; see Polaris Project and Shared Hope International.
- Examine and discuss these ratings and categories with local organizations serving affected populations. Be sure to include survivors and those in "the life."
- Be sure to include "big picture" risk factors, such as those described in previous sections.
- Lobby your state legislature to change existing legislation or to add new legislation.

Notes

1. This chapter focuses primarily on those who experience trafficking or exploitation. Trafficking is defined using the legal definition, including commercial sex involvement by force, fraud, coercion, or involvement of minors. Exploitation is defined as commercial sex involvement as a constrained choice (e.g., the absence of alternatives, or exploitation of a vulnerability such as addiction, poverty, mental illness, or homelessness by traffickers, pimps, or buyers). Sex work as a constrained choice is both similar to and different from working at low-wage jobs (such as in fast food or at Walmart). It is similar in that this labor may be exploited by others, who profit from the worker's labor and do not provide a sufficient share of that profit; the author views low-wage labor as exploitative as well. It is different in two primary ways: sex work has heightened risks for victimization, especially for those at the "lower" ends of the hierarchal sex trade (for example, fast food workers are not singled out for violence because they are fast food workers, whereas sex workers are); and those in the commercial sex industry face intense stigma, especially those engaged in street-based prostitution. Individuals are more liable to engage in sex work in situations of homelessness, poverty, and low socioeconomic status than in situations in which they are better positioned to protect themselves and control their labor. The context in which such commercial sex operates cannot be ignored, including the ways in which it is distinct from how other low-wage/exploitative jobs operate because of the cultural load borne by "sex" as it intersects with gender, race, class, LGBTQ (lesbian, gay, bisexual, transgender, queer) identities, and additional social identities. The author thanks Dr. Jody Miller for her assistance in addressing this argument.

2. Research using street-based snowball sampling methods or respondent-driven sampling to study homeless or transient youth finds nearly equal rates of trafficking among male and female youth (Curtis et al., 2008). Research using samples drawn from the justice system and social service organizations (excepting youth-serving agencies and homeless organizations) shows significantly higher rates of sex trafficking among women and girls. While various studies are limited by their methodologies, they make it clear that LGBTQ people and women and girls are at heightened risk (see Nichols, 2016, for an overview). More recently, a 10-city study of homeless youth found that 20 percent of female youth who were not LGBTQ experienced sex trafficking, and 24 percent of LGBTQ youth experienced sex trafficking compared to 11 percent of young men who were not LGBTQ.

3. Some would attribute problems in the criminal justice system to the system's undue strength. While certainly this is the case, the author labels abuses of power or unchecked power as weaknesses, or weaknesses within the system. Similarly, the power of the for-profit healthcare industry could be viewed as unchecked power and strength or could be labeled as a weak and problematic system. Both frameworks are accurate.

4. In states where cutting rather than expanding seems likely, this is a governmental weakness that negatively impacts trafficked and exploited people. Similarly, should cutting rather than expanding be adopted at a federal level, the consequences would also be detrimental to trafficked and exploited people and would further increase risk.

References

Cole, J., Sprang, G., Lee, R., & Cohen, J. (2016). The trauma of commercial sexual exploitation of youth: A comparison of CSE victims to sexual abuse victims in a clinical sample. *Journal of Interpersonal Violence, 31*(1), 122–146.

Covenant House, Loyola University (New Orleans), and University of Pennsylvania. (2017). *Labor and sex trafficking among homeless youth.* Retrieved from http://covenanthousestudy .org/docs/Loyola-Research-Results.pdf

Curtis, R., Terry, K., Dank, M., Dombrowski, K., & Khan, B. (2008, September). *Commercial sexual exploitation of children in New York City, volume one: The CSEC population in New York City: size, characteristics, and needs. U.S. Department of Justice.* Retrieved from https://www.ncjrs.gov/pdffiles1/nij/grants/225083.pdf

Dank, M., Yahner, J., Madden, K., Bañuelos, I., Yu, L., Ritchie, A., . . . Conner, B. (2015). *Surviving the streets of New York: Experiences of LGBTQ youth, YMSM, and YWSW engaged in survival sex. Urban Institute.* Retrieved from http://www.urban.org/research /publication/surviving-streets-new-york-experiences-lgbtq-youth-ymsm-and-ywsw -engaged-survival-sex

Egyes, L. (2016). Borders and intersections: The unique vulnerabilities of LGBTQ immigrants to trafficking. In E. Heil & A. J. Nichols (Eds.), *Broadening the scope of human trafficking research: A reader.* Durham, NC: Carolina Academic Press.

Ehrenreich, B. (2011). *Nickel and dimed: On (not) getting by in America.* New York, NY: Picador.

Farrell, A., McDevitt, J., Pfeffer, R., Fahy, S., Owens, C., Dank, M., & Adams, W. (2012). *Identifying challenges to improve the investigation and prosecution of state and local human trafficking cases.* Washington, DC: National Institute of Justice.

Ferguson, A. A. (2001). *Bad boys: Public schools in the making of black masculinity.* Ann Arbor, MI: Michigan University Press.

Goodman, L.A., & Epstein, D. (2008). *Listening to battered women: A survivor-centered approach to advocacy, mental health, and justice.* Washington D.C.: American Psychological Association.

Gonzalez, C. (2016). On the fringes: Black women and domestic human trafficking. In E. Heil & A. J. Nichols (Eds.), *Broadening the scope of human trafficking research: A reader.* Durham, NC: Carolina Academic Press.

Heil, E. C. (2016). Sex trafficking in Indian Country: An analysis of anti-trafficking tribal codes, multi-jurisdiction, and unprotected communities. In E. Heil & A. J. Nichols (Eds.), *Broadening the scope of human trafficking research: A reader.* Durham, NC: Carolina Academic Press.

Heil, E. C., & Nichols, A. J. (2015). *Human trafficking in the Midwest: A case study of St. Louis and the bi-state area.* Durham, NC: Carolina Academic Press.

Hepburn, S., & Simon, R. (2010). Hidden in plain sight: Human trafficking in the United States. *Gender Issues, 27*(1–2), 1–26. doi:10.1007/s12147-010-9087-7

Illinois State Board of Education. (n.d.) *Public school district lookup.* Retrieved from https:// www.isbe.net/Pages/PublicSchoolDistrictLookup.aspx

Klein, N. (2008). *The shock doctrine: The rise of disaster capitalism.* New York, NY: Picador.

Koyama, E. (2011, October 8). *Understanding the complexities of sex trafficking and sex work/trade: Ten observations from a sex worker activist/survivor/feminist [Web log post].* Retrieved from http://eminism.org/blog/entry/268

——. (2013, September 20). *Rescue is for kittens: Ten things everyone needs to know about "rescues" of youth in the sex trade [Web log post].* Retrieved from http://eminism.org/blog/entry/400

Kozol, J. (2012). *Savage inequalities: Children in America's schools.* New York, NY: Random House.

Kyckelhahn, T., Beck, A. J., & Cohen, T. H. (2009). *Characteristics of suspected human trafficking incidents, 2007–08.* Bureau of Justice Statistics Special Report. Retrieved from http://bjs.ojp.usdoj.gov/content/pub/pdf/cshti08.pdf

Lloyd, R. (2012). *Girls like us: Fighting for a world where girls are not for sale: A memoir.* New York, NY: Harper Perennial.

Lutnick, A. (2016). *Domestic minor sex trafficking: Beyond victims and villains.* New York, NY: Columbia University Press.

Macy, R. J., & Johns, N. (2011). Aftercare services for international sex trafficking survivors: Informing U.S. service and program development in an emerging practice area. *Trauma, Violence & Abuse, 12*(2), 87–98.

Martin, L., Pierce, A., Peyton, S., Gabilondo, A. I., & Tulpule, G. (2014). *Mapping the market for sex with trafficked minor girls in Minneapolis: Structures, functions, and patterns.* Full Report: Preliminary Findings. Retrieved from https://uroc.umn.edu/sites/uroc.umn.edu/files/MTM_SexTraf_Summ.pdf

Medicaid.gov. (2016). *Dental care.* Retrieved from https://www.insurekidsnow.gov/coverage/index.html

Micetic, S. (2016). Reducing risk of domestic minor sex trafficking among runaway and homeless youth. In E. Heil & A. J. Nichols (Eds.), *Broadening the scope of human trafficking research: A reader.* Durham, NC: Carolina Academic Press.

Missouri Department of Elementary and Secondary Education. (n.d.). *School data.* Retrieved 2014 from http://dese.mo.gov/school-data

Nichols, A. J. (2016). *Sex trafficking in the United States: Theory, research, policy, and practice.* New York, NY: Columbia University Press.

Nichols, A. J., & Heil, E. C. (2015). Challenges to identifying and prosecuting sex trafficking cases in the Midwest United States. *Feminist Criminology, 10(1), 7–35.* doi:10.1177/1557085113519490

Oselin, S. (2014). *Leaving prostitution: Getting out and staying out of sex work.* New York, NY: New York University Press.

Polaris Project. (2014). *Sex trafficking.* Retrieved from http://www.polarisproject.org/human-trafficking/sex-trafficking-in-the-us

——. (2015). *Sex trafficking in the U.S.—A closer look at U.S. citizen victims.* Retrieved from http://www.polarisproject.org/human-trafficking/sex-trafficking-in-the-us/us-citizen-sex-trafficking-closer-look

Raphael, J., & Myers-Powell, B. (2010). *From victims to victimizers: Interviews with 25 ex-pimps in Chicago.* DePaul University College of Law. Retrieved from http://media.virbcdn.com/files/cc/FileItem-149884-depaul25_Pimp_Research_Final_Aug2010.pdf

Raphael, J., Reichert, J., & Powers, M. (2010). Pimp control and violence: Domestic sex trafficking of Chicago women and girls. *Women & Criminal Justice, 20,* 89–104.

Ray, N. (2006). *Lesbian, gay, bisexual and transgender youth: An epidemic of homelessness. New York: National Gay and Lesbian Task Force Policy Institute and the National Coalition for the Homeless.* Retrieved from http://www.thetaskforce.org/downloads/HomelessYouth.pdf

Reid, J. (2010). Doors wide shut: Barriers to the successful delivery of victim services for domestically trafficked minors in a southern U.S. metropolitan area. *Women & Criminal Justice, 20*(1–2), 147–166.

———. (2011). An exploratory model of girl's vulnerability to commercial sexual exploitation in prostitution. *Child Maltreatment, 16*(2), 146–157. doi:10.1177/1077559511404700

Reid, J. (2014). Risk and resiliency factors influencing onset and adolescence-limited commercial sexual exploitation of disadvantaged girls. *Criminal Behavior and Mental Health, 24*(5), 332–344.

Reid, J., & Piquero, A. (2013). Age-graded risks for commercial sexual exploitation of male and female youth. *Journal of Interpersonal Violence, 29*(9), 1747–1777.

Schwarz, C., Unruh, E., Cronin, K., Evans-Simpson, S., Britton, H., & Ramaswamy, M. (2016). Human trafficking identification and service provision in the medical and social service sectors. *Health and Human Rights Journal, 18*, 12–21.

Shared Hope International. (2016). *State report cards*. Retrieved from https://sharedhope.org /what-we-do/bring-justice/reportcards/#reportcardsSmith, L., Vardaman, S. H., & Snow, M. (2009). *The national report on DMST*. Vancouver, WA: Shared Hope International.

Snyder, H., & Mulako-Wangota, J. (2015, May 18). *Arrest data analysis tool*. Washington, DC: Bureau of Justice Statistics. Retrieved from http://www.bjs.gov.

Wilson, D. G., Walsh, W. F., & Klueber, S. (2006). Trafficking in human beings: Training and services among US law enforcement agencies. *Police Practice and Research, 7*, 149–160.

Wilson, J. M., & Dalton, E. (2008). Human trafficking in the Heartland: Variation in law enforcement awareness and response. *Journal of Contemporary Criminal Justice, 2*(3), 296–313.

CHAPTER 18

_____

CHALLENGES TO SENSATIONAL IMAGERY USED IN THE ANTITRAFFICKING MOVEMENT AND IMPLICATIONS FOR PRACTICE

LAUREN S. PEFFLEY, MSW, EDEN'S GLORY

ANDREA J. NICHOLS, PhD,
WASHINGTON UNIVERSITY IN ST. LOUIS

T his chapter includes images and a discussion of sensational imagery used in the antitrafficking movement that may be triggering to survivors of trafficking, sexual assault, or intimate partner violence. Simply entering the words "sex trafficking" into a Google image search yields a host of pictures. The first photos that populate the page display women and girls branded, in chains, shackles, and handcuffs, and bound in ropes or duct tape. One image includes bloody handprints, and another includes lash marks, as if from a whip, on a naked chained woman's back. Still another photo shows a woman with a noose around her neck. Images of hands over women's and girls' mouths are also common. Yet another image shows a woman being choked; a man's hands are squeezing her throat while she appears to be struggling for breath. There is even an image that shows young distressed girls stuck inside pickle jars on a grocery store shelf, who, according to the wording accompanying the image, are from countries outside the United States. The top of the picture says: "Human Trafficking: It's Happening Here, It's Happening Now." The bottom of the picture says: "Every year over 50,000 women and children are brought to the United States to work as slaves." These are just some of many similar images that have been used by countless individuals in anti–human trafficking trainings, community awareness events, and antitrafficking conferences. This chapter will examine the ways such images and media tactics are problematic to antitrafficking work. The chapter makes four assertions:

1. This imagery mischaracterizes sex trafficking by poorly telling the stories of survivors; providing misleading, atypical, or incomplete information about

trafficking; and failing to provide the context for trafficking or describe its complexities.

2. The imagery and wording exclude diverse survivor identities, rarely depicting African American women and girls, Native women and girls, men and boys of all races and ethnicities, and LGBTQ+ identities.

3. This kind of shock-provoking imagery fuels skepticism about the existence of sex trafficking and validates criticisms by authors who refer to the antitrafficking movement as a "moral crusade" with a propensity toward telling "horror stories" (Weitzer, 2010) and who fault the movement for its "ideological capture" (Chuang, 2010), which results in backlash.

4. Finally, this brand of storytelling and imagery is potentially revictimizing to survivors and survivor activists. Such imagery could be triggering for those experiencing or who have experienced sex trafficking, commercial sexual exploitation, or sexual violence and intimate partner violence more broadly.

The following subsections examine these assertions and their related challenges in depth; they also discuss implications for social work practice and provide recommendations for imagery to be used in antitrafficking efforts.

Poorly Telling Survivor Stories

At first glance, the pickle jar picture might appear to be an outlier. Yet upon closer consideration, this photo is not an aberration. In fact, another photo uncovered through a simple Google image search of "sex trafficking" shows a photo of young white women packaged like chicken meat. On the cellophane of this package is a sticker with the words *FRESH MEAT*. The intent of the images is clear—such images are critiquing the commodification and dehumanization of women and girls. Yet, while these images are intended to draw attention to the issue, they may be counterproductive. An image can never tell a full story, but if viewers were to guess what human trafficking is based on the images commonly used in antitrafficking awareness campaigns, here are some assumptions they might make.

Trafficking Only Affects Female-Identified Individuals— Mostly Young Girls

Girls who appear to be between the ages of eight and fourteen are commonly depicted in antitrafficking imagery. The reality is that cisgender men and boys are also victims and survivors of sex trafficking and commercial sexual exploitation, as well as transgender and genderqueer people, particularly among the homeless youth population (Curtis, Terry, Dank, Dombrowski, & Khan, 2008; Dank et al., 2015; Egyes, 2016; Heil & Nichols, 2015; Nichols, 2016).[1] LGBTQ-inclusive imagery and outreach materials are discussed later in this chapter (also see chapter 10).

Moreover, adults are as affected or slightly more likely to experience trafficking and/or exploitation than are minors. Several studies show that the average age of entry into commercial sex among youth populations is between fifteen and nineteen (Covenant House, 2017; Curtis et al., 2008; Dank et al., 2015; Martin et al., 2014; Reid & Piquero, 2013). Early research indicated that twelve to fourteen was the most typical age of entry; however, more recently researchers report that this prior work only examined domestic minor sex trafficking, thereby skewing the age grouping (Lutnick, 2016; Nichols, 2016; Polaris Project, 2014). The Polaris Project (2014), for example, finds an average age of entry as nineteen, and it includes populations of adults and minors in its research sample. Imagery should include a variety of different age groups and should not highlight disproportionately the least common cases involving very young children. Although trafficking of preadolescent children occurs, it is comparatively rare.

Women and Girls Affected by Trafficking Are All White or from Another Country

The pimps/traffickers are usually depicted as men of color in images, as evidenced by a particularly problematic and commonly used photo of a young white girl whose mouth is being covered by a black man's large hand (see figure 18.1). This is currently (09/02/2016) the first photo that pops up from a Google image search for "sex trafficking." The image has appeared on billboards, on social media, and in antitrafficking education and awareness events across the country.

FIGURE 18.1 Taken from a Google image search for "sex trafficking"

(accessed 09/02/2016 from www.theheartsofhope.org)

Research indicates that a majority of trafficking is intraracial; individuals who experience trafficking are more likely to be trafficked by someone of their own race or ethnicity (Estes & Wiener, 2001; Lloyd, 2012). Certainly interracial trafficking occurs, yet when images like this become commonplace, they yield a limited view of trafficking and distort the racial dynamics of trafficking. They also reinforce the historical legacy of the portrayal of black men as perpetrators of sexual violence against white women, as well as antimiscegenation and segregationist ideologies (Gonzalez, 2016; Lutnick, 2016). Particularly in light of racial tensions within the United States, images like this proliferating in the antitrafficking movement is problematic. Moreover, Black women and girls show heightened risk compared to white women and girls (see chapter 9). Native and Latinx people also show heightened risk. Yet these groups, particularly those who are Black, are virtually invisible in the antitrafficking movement (Heil & Nichols, 2015; Nichols, 2016). Women and girls who are White or who are trafficked internationally are overrepresented in antitrafficking imagery. Race and ethnicity and their relative depictions in imagery are discussed later in this chapter.

Trafficking Is About Movement Across Borders

This can be illustrated in a variety of luggage-related imagery. For example, one image depicts a white woman packed into a suitcase, appearing like a mannequin, with eyes wide open. Another image focuses on a luggage tag typical at airports, accompanied by antitrafficking language. The reality is that 80 to 85 percent of those experiencing sex trafficking in the United States are domestic (i.e., U.S. citizens) (Farrell et al., 2012; Polaris Project, 2014). While certainly social workers should include diverse images of individuals of various ethnicities, including those from other countries, images implying travel, movement, and borders can mischaracterize the issue, resulting in lack of attention to domestic trafficking. In fact, research indicates that police officers, who are in a prime position to identify sex trafficking, are often unfamiliar with their own state laws as well as federal laws, erroneously believing that sex trafficking only involves crossing borders (Farrell et al., 2012; Wilson et al., 2006; Wilson & Dalton, 2008). Accordingly, imagery indicative of crossing borders should be accompanied by imagery and wording emphasizing both international and domestic trafficking.

Trafficking Involves Physical Entrapment, Physical Restraint, Being "Held" by Someone Else, and Complete Containment

This assumption can be seen in images of women in various forms of packaging and with various types of physical restraints and wounds, such as wrists bound in rope, shackles, or chains, as seen in figure 18.2.

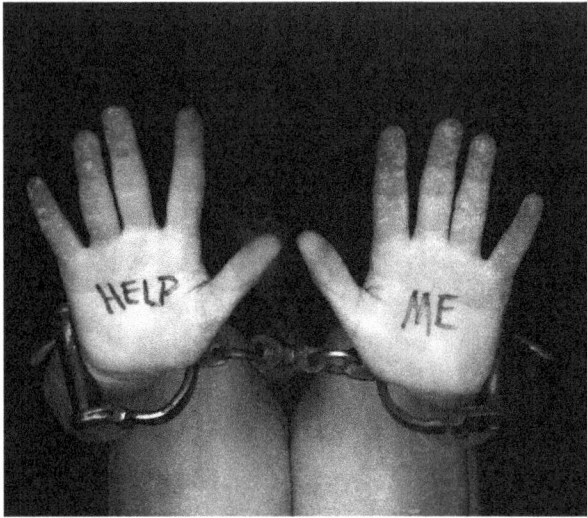

FIGURE 18.2A Taken from a Google image search for "sex trafficking"

(accessed 09/02/2016 from listdose.com)

FIGURE 18.2B Taken a Google image search for "sex trafficking"

(accessed 09/02/2016 from religionnerd.com)

This "hands in chains" photo is one that is commonly used in presentations, lectures, trainings, and websites—sometimes featured as a large image on a website or a small icon at the bottom of a PowerPoint. The authors have seen this image as a giant cardboard placard or banner in multiple human-trafficking community awareness events. This is not to say that there are not survivors who have been trapped, tied up, and tortured. That storyline is a painful reality for some survivors. However, this narrative is atypical;

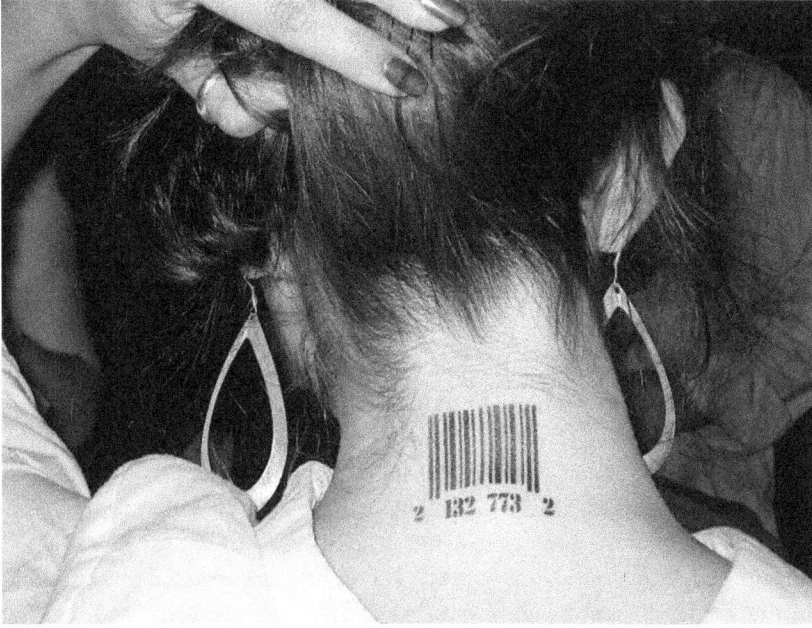

FIGURE 18.3 Taken from Google image search for "sex trafficking"

(photo credit: rejuvenatingwomen.com)

many more survivors are not physically trapped by their pimps/traffickers, and they typically have some mobility (Heil, 2012; Heil & Nichols, 2015; Lloyd, 2012). Some trafficking survivors even return to their homes each night or go to school each day. Similarly, while many survivors report having tattoos of barcodes or their pimps' names, many survivors have no physical evidence of their trafficking whatsoever—despite the misleadingly high number of barcode images used in antitrafficking awareness materials.[2] See figure 18.3. Emphasizing force and captivity dangerously reinforces who is deserving of services and who is not.

Media Representation

The media also play a role in both sensationalistic imagery and in reporting, often perpetuating the assumptions previously illustrated and poorly telling survivors' stories. Logan, Walker, and Hunt (2009) point out that "counter to many media reports" of violence, being "held" or physically restrained, and physical evidence of abuse, "physical violence is *only one of many tactics that are used*" against survivors (p. 14—italicization added). None of the commonly used images allude to any kind of romantic relationship between a pimp and a survivor, but that is actually an incredibly common theme in the realm of sexual exploitation. Survivors, researchers, and advocates alike have concurred that sex trafficking is quite commonly an extension of intimate partner violence. Moreover, another incredibly common form of sex trafficking that is erased by these images involves minors who independently sell sex to meet basic needs (i.e., those engaged in survival sex) (Lutnick, 2016). In their study on sex trafficking in the Midwest, Heil and Nichols (2015) assert that the most common forms of sex trafficking included survival sex of minors, as well as pimp-controlled prostitution in which the pimp poses as a "boyfriend." Therefore, survivors' entrapment typically has much more to do with emotional manipulation, histories of abuse, and economic need than it has to do with pickle jars, barcodes, cellophane, and chains.

Johnston, Friedman, and Shafer (2014) conducted a yearlong, quantitative study on news media coverage of sex trafficking. They opened their article with an explanation of "media framing," saying that frames have four basic functions: "defining the problem, identifying causes, conveying a moral judgment, and suggesting remedies" (p. 422). These authors assert that frames influence the way audience members process the information given to them. In their analysis, they found that most articles on sex trafficking did not focus on underlying themes or causes, nor did the majority of them offer any remedies. They found a glaring "absence of explanations of why trafficking exists and who are its victims" and found that "certain aspects of sex trafficking were featured and emphasized over others" (pp. 420, 432). Gulati (2011), in examining articles about human trafficking in the *New York Times* and the *Washington Post* from 1980 to 2006, similarly found that the stories rarely discussed causes and were framed in a way that mirrored the dominant antitrafficking discourse. Given the results of a simple Google image search, a few of the aspects featured and emphasized in this dominant discourse include kidnapping, chains, barcodes, mouths covered, and innocence lost. Upon seeing an abundance of images of "little girls crying, some in pigtails and some holding teddy bears with slogans touting lost innocence," author and survivor Holly Austin Smith (2014) reacted by saying: "*This was not me. By eighth grade I was angry, undisciplined, and sexually active. Did this make me less of a victim?*" (p. 36). She went on to say that while still in the life, "if someone offering street outreach showed me pictures of kids in chains, I would have told them they were talking to the wrong person" (pp. 98–99). Both the findings of Johnston and colleagues (2014) and Holly Austin Smith's reaction to this kind of framing support the assertion presented in this section—namely, that inappropriately or simplistically framed news stories and misguided imagery poorly tell the stories of survivors.

In order to stifle the stereotypes and start telling accurate stories—those more holistically depicting the variety of survivor experiences—it is important that news outlets "engage with a wider constituency to offer a wider range of news frames and sources" (Johnston et al., 2014, p. 432). Gulati (2011) also believes that there are plenty of opportunities to make space for differing experiences and voices in the conversation about sex trafficking. Also of import is the suggestion that journalists and all members of the antitrafficking movement should start talking to advocacy organizations that are directly connected to, informed by, or run by survivors before publishing stories or circulating images regarding sex trafficking (Johnston et al., 2014). If a survivor does not support the way a story is written, perhaps it should not be published; if a survivor does not approve of a public service announcement, then it should remain unaired; if a survivor does not promote a particular image, then it should not be placed in any presentation or pamphlet.

Author and activist Emi Koyama (2013) makes the claim that sensationalism, along with the obsessive focus on the trafficking of very young people, "is harmful because it misdirects necessary policy responses." More specifically, it misdirects the way issues are prioritized and resources are allocated (Barnett, 2016; Gulati, 2011; Johnston et al., 2014; Koyama, 2013; Small, 2012; Uy, 2011). Jamie Small (2012) reviewed three films that highlight human trafficking and found that none of them critically examined the historical conditions and present vulnerabilities that lead to trafficking. Small (2012) believes that turning sex trafficking into a simplistic "spectacle" can lead to a host of "challenges and contradictions" in discussing this issue and seeking solutions (p. 418). Barbara Barnett (2016) analyzed magazines covering the topic of sex trafficking from 2000 to 2010, and her findings mirrored those of Small, Gulati, and Johnston et al. She found that the current conversation around trafficking has reinforced hierarchies and created three unfortunate divides: between men and women (in that men and boys are rarely, if ever, discussed in these stories), between women who help (such as anti-trafficking advocates) and women who are helped, and between women—namely, between "the 'good' victims who were forced into prostitution and the 'bad sluts' who *chose* prostitution" (Barnett, 2016, p. 216).

These problematic divides can be seen in the images displayed in this chapter. The innocent and helpless young girls, the glaring lack of male or trans survivors, and the absence of any sense of agency in these images serve as a reminder that our current conversation is incomplete. In another article, Koyama (2011) makes a statement that seems obvious, but it is rarely—if ever—addressed in mainstream antitrafficking conversations; she posits that stories from the sex industry are "diverse and complicated" (Koyama, 2011). Survivor voices—especially those with stories that do not fit within the narrow narrative of the current antitrafficking discourse—appear to be getting "lost in the channels of corporate media" (Small, 2012, p. 419). Diverse and complicated stories are not being told very often, and if they are, the survivor is not usually the one telling the story. Beyond corporate media, antitrafficking organizations themselves participate in this myopic depiction of sex trafficking.

Johnston et al. (2014) concurred with Koyama's assertions. They discovered that "survivors of trafficking and their advocates were the least heard-from sources" throughout news media articles on sex trafficking (p. 419). Gulati's (2011) study revealed that survivors were only cited as sources in 15 percent of the articles about trafficking published during a 26-year time span (p. 371). In the absence of survivor voices, other voices can overtake these stories and fill in the gaps. Johnston et al. (2014) acknowledge that the absence of survivor voices could be due, at least in part, to the difficulty of safely finding and interviewing survivors; however, they posit that it could also be due in part to the fact that many media outlets believe that law enforcement and legislative voices are more important than survivor voices. Gulati's (2011) findings showed that policymakers were the most often cited sources in the articles on trafficking in the *New York Times* and *Washington Post*. The second most commonly cited sources were representatives from various nonprofit and non-governmental organizations. The third and fourth most commonly cited sources were law enforcement officials and UN representatives (Gulati, 2011, pp. 370–371). This growing body of work finds that misguided sourcing and media sensationalism—especially the obsession with the dichotomy of perfect victim versus the evil perpetrator—prevent individuals from grasping the complexity of sex trafficking and generating possible remedies.

As a result of this misguided imagery and co-opting of survivors' journey, survivors' stories are being told for the sake of shock value and awareness-raising efforts. However, one could argue that this kind of awareness raising leaves people quite ignorant because it fails to tell the nuanced, complicated, and extensive stories of survival. Nichols (2016) posits that this kind of imagery not only hinders efforts to identify trafficking but also creates barriers to survivors' ability to access services. These images and news stories speak of problems without any context, discuss issues without discussing interventions, and display faces without fully acknowledging their humanity. Johnston et al. (2014) label these as "reductive stories" and point out that they do little to help audiences understand that survivors are a part of a larger community, a larger context, and a larger "ongoing story" (p. 431) and that survivors are not a monolithic group (see chapter 1).

Accordingly, images that are not sensational and that relate to people experiencing sex trafficking/exploitation should be used to better characterize sex trafficking. Images should be more relatable to survivors, particularly in outreach efforts. An example is shown in figure 18.4, which is used by the National Human Trafficking Resource Center, the Polaris Project, and CAST (which sponsors the National Survivor Network).

FIGURE 18.4 Taken from a Google image search for "sex trafficking"

(accessed 09/02/2016 from the www.traffickingresourcecenter.org)

The National Survivor Network has a board of survivors who provide feedback in a variety of different areas. This would be one group that images could be vetted through. Further, several organizations offer guides to media news outlets that describe the ways they portray trafficking incidents in reporting the news. For example, a task force in San Francisco notes that media coverage is important to draw attention to the issue and recommends that information provided to and reported on by the media should include "myths and facts regarding human trafficking; state and federal laws; how people can report crimes of trafficking; community and system-based resources for victim assistance; [and] best practices on messaging around human trafficking" (Murase & Lee, 2015). The task force highlights the importance of confidentiality and informed consent to avoid reexploitation of survivors. In addition, the task force suggests that news outlets should not be present in trafficking-related raids or investigations. To have news media present is unethical, violates the privacy of survivors, and can also interfere with investigations. The recommendations can be accessed at http://sfgov.org/dosw /sites/default/files/Recommendations%20for%20City%20Departments %20on%20Media%20Access%20to%20Human%20Trafficking%20Survivors. pdf. The same group offers background information that can be used for reporting purposes; this information can be found on the Mayor's Task Force on Anti-Human Trafficking website: http://sfgov.org/dosw/sites/default/files /Recommendations%20for%20City%20Departments%20on%20Media %20Access%20to%20Human%20Trafficking%20Survivors.pdf. Like the San Francisco task force, The Wichita State Center for Combating Human Trafficking also offers an excellent guide that offers tips to survivors, service providers, coalitions, and the media about reporting on survivors' stories; the

guide can be accessed at http://combatinghumantrafficking.org/Document
/CCHT_Public_Awareness_and_Media_Guide_06052014.pdf.

Excluding and Ignoring Diverse Survivor Identities

Various authors have critiqued the antitrafficking movement for being exclusionary and color-blind. Gonzalez (2016) maintains that Black women and girls
experience heightened victimization in sex trafficking (see also chapter 9) and
increased criminalization for adult prostitution and so-called juvenile prostitution (which is sex trafficking by federal and most state laws), yet they are
largely excluded from images in the antitrafficking movement, with the exception of some organizations who work directly with survivors. Similarly, Nichols
(2016) maintains that imagery used in antitrafficking outreach posters and in
the antitrafficking movement in the United States rarely depicts Black women
or girls, or people of color more broadly. Research also indicates a disproportionate victimization of Latinx people, as well as heightened risk for Native
women and girls (Curtis et al., 2008; Dank et al., 2015; Egyes, 2016; Heil, 2016),
who are also often marginalized in antitrafficking efforts. Native people are
rarely a focus at all, and Latinx people are disproportionately represented in
labor-trafficking imagery.

Further, various researchers uncover disproportionate victimization of
LGBTQ people in sex trafficking and commercial sexual exploitation (Curtis
et al., 2008; Dank et al., 2015; Egyes, 2016; Heil & Nichols, 2015; Schwarz
& Britton, 2015), yet such groups are generally excluded from antitrafficking organizations' outreach, education, and awareness imagery (Nichols,
2016). While the majority of research shows that sex-trafficking survivors are
women and girls, research specifically examining homeless or transient youth
populations shows male, female, trans, and genderqueer people experiencing
sexual exploitation or trafficking at similar or heightened rates, showing a
population in need of related services (Curtis et al., 2008; Dank et al., 2015;
Lutnick, 2016).

This exclusion is problematic on different levels. First, as already briefly
described, it shapes the public perception of survivors as only white, female,
cisgender, and heterosexual. If community education and awareness initiatives aim to increase identification by ordinary citizens, and the community is looking for twelve- to fourteen-year-old white suburban girls who
have experienced kidnapping or abduction, then such initiatives will uncover
only a fraction of cases. Second, outreach materials and other organizational materials should include relatable images that welcome individuals
from diverse racial and ethnic backgrounds, genders, and sexual orientations,

as a form of cultural competency/humility. Displaying cultural humility in designing organizational materials—whether brochures, outreach posters, or signage—tells individuals that they are included and wanted. Lack of cultural competency has shown to be a barrier to accessing services. Accordingly, while images of young white women are important to maintain, inclusivity is extremely important to better reflect disproportionate victimization; this inclusivity may help those who are seeking help, as well as improve the perceptions of those who are in positions to identify such cases in law enforcement, social services, and healthcare settings and among ordinary citizens (Nichols, 2016).

Keeping racial and ethnic diversity in mind, social workers should consider including diverse images in their outreach, awareness, and other organizational materials. Groups like MISSEY, CAST, and the National Human Trafficking Resource Center, operated by the Polaris Project, offer examples of outreach and awareness materials that depict individuals from a variety of racial and ethnic groups. Depending on the region, it might also make sense to have outreach materials in various languages.

Indicating if an organization is a Safe Zone partner in outreach materials also may create a sense of belonging and inclusivity. The authors were unable to locate outreach materials specifically regarding sex trafficking/exploitation and LGBTQ people; however, we recommend imagery using rainbow colors as representative of the LGBTQ pride flag, culturally competent language reflecting these populations, and relatable imagery and wording. For example, it may be useful to present a simple picture of an individual with wording such as "queer and looking for a way out" followed by an organization's information about related resources. This model, accompanied by wording in rainbow coloring, and/or with a Safe Zone designation, is recommended (if the organization is indeed a Safe Zone organization; we recommend all organizations receive Safe Zone or similar training; see chapter 10). Organizations serving diverse populations could also make visible an inclusive mission statement on outreach and other organizational materials. For example, the mission statement of the organization Youth in Need in St. Louis, Missouri (http://www .youthinneed.org), states,

> Believing in the power of potential, DIVERSITY is intentionally embracing and valuing the differences and similarities, both visible and invisible, that make us who we are—ONE COMMUNITY. Together our attitudes, actions, policies and physical environment are vital to ensure that all feel comfortable, respected, and included regardless of race, sex, gender identity or expression, age, income, faith, ability, political affiliation, sexual orientation, or cultural background.

Fueling Skepticism and Validating Criticism of the Antitrafficking Movement

Sensationalistic imagery also fuels skepticism and validates criticism of antitrafficking work. For example, Ronald Weitzer (2010) levels a series of criticisms against the neo-abolition movement. He refers to this movement as a "robust moral crusade" and defines a moral crusader as a person on a mission "to combat a particular condition or activity that is defined as an unqualified evil" (pp. 62–63). Weitzer (2010) accuses crusaders of inflating the magnitude of the problem of trafficking, describing worst-case scenarios of trafficking—"horror stories"—as typical, and refusing to recognize any shades of gray within the commercial sex industry (p. 63). He asserts that "the grand claims made by abolitionist groups . . . are entirely unsubstantiated, but quite strategic" (p. 65). He goes on to say that "the size of a social problem matters in attracting media coverage, donor funding, and attention from policy makers" (p. 65). Therefore, according to Weitzer (2010), moral crusaders have a "vested interest in inflating the magnitude of the problem" (p. 65). In all of these statements, Weitzer suggests that antitrafficking advocates are quite cunning and manipulate followers by using faulty figures and shocking imagery.

Those engaged in antitrafficking work may accuse Weitzer of ignoring the realities of trafficking/CSE and failing to adequately address the often violent, misogynistic nature of the sex industry. However, some of the criticisms Weitzer levels against the antitrafficking movement are accurate, particularly if one's only exposure to it is reflected in the images and corresponding content commonly shown in antitrafficking initiatives at church conferences, in student group presentations, and/or in the content of well-meaning community awareness events, even those run by established antitrafficking organizations.

Weitzer is not the only author to critique this aspect of the neo-abolition movement. Janie Chuang (2010) described the "ideological capture" of the antitrafficking movement by the media. Chuang (2010) discusses the obsessive media coverage and antitrafficking movement focus on sex trafficking and the complete dismissal of labor trafficking from current conversations about trafficking. She attributes this disparity to "the 'mediagenic' nature of sex-trafficking" and "the fact that 'sex sells' " (Chuang, 2010, p. 1698). Robert Uy (2011) also discusses this disparity and the disservice it does to labor-trafficking survivors, saying that the myopic media focus on sex trafficking has prevented survivors of labor trafficking from gaining access to resources. Chuang (2010) goes on to critique "the reductive narrative" of women and girls forced into prostitution, which can be identified in many of the images examined in this chapter.

Chuang (2010) believes these narratives resonate with audiences because of their "simple narrative structure, with a bad guy (evil trafficker or deviant, sex-crazed male) doing bad things (sexual violence or enslavement) to an innocent, ignorant, impoverished victim (trafficked woman or child, sex slave, or prostitute)" (p. 1698). Johnston et al. (2014) concur with this analysis, saying that mass media draw on "melodramatic narratives," thus reinforcing notions of "female passiveness . . . and male aggression" (p. 421).

This narrative description definitely rings true in the majority of the images popularized in antitrafficking campaigns, as do the critiques that labor trafficking and male survivors are almost completely ignored (Chuang, 2010; Uy, 2011). Chuang (2010) suggests that the "male farm worker is not nearly so compelling an object of pity or compassion as a brothel captive" (p. 1698),[3] Perhaps that is why there are so few images of male-identified individuals and/or people forced into industries other than the sex industry. Regardless of the reasoning behind the gender-lopsided imagery and narrow narratives, Chuang (2010) and Uy (2011) are justified in their critiques of the neo-abolition movement based on the images presented thus far.

The neo-abolition movement is not the only entity generating problematic imagery and narrowly focused stories; news media outlets have joined ranks with antitrafficking groups in publishing statistics without direct sources and telling stories without including survivor voices. In many ways, the neo-abolition movement has been increasingly fueled by news coverage, and news outlets have increased readership by covering stories on sex trafficking. If the news is horrifyingly outrageous, then it will ostensibly be better for ratings. Johnston et al. (2014) argue that despite the vast complexities of sexual exploitation, U.S. news media have kept "a fairly provincial and monolithic perspective" on this issue (p. 432). In their yearlong study, they discovered certain "lapses" in coverage that contributed to "audience misunderstanding or apathy toward the crime of sex trafficking" (p. 420). If audiences cannot comprehend the issue or understand how to get involved, they can feel helpless and apathetic.

Thus, this sensationalistic imagery is problematic because it fuels skepticism about sex trafficking and validates some of the critiques leveled against the antitrafficking movement. It justifies Chuang's (2010) assertion that the movement has been ideologically captured and misdirected. All the while, some members of the general public get shocked into action, despite the fact that they are uninformed about the complexities of the issue and have no idea how to get engaged in a way that is useful to people who have been trafficked and exploited. Still another swath of the population sees this outrageous imagery and ignores the problem altogether. Amidst these black-and-white conversations, survivor stories and survivor voices may be lost.

Revictimizing Survivors

Sensationalistic imagery may also result in the unintended reexploitation and revictimization of survivors of sex trafficking and other survivors of violence. Amidst all of these misdirected arguments and this misguided imagery, survivors are potentially revictimized and dehumanized. Some images depicting extreme violence may act as a trauma trigger, such as those described in the opening to this chapter; see figure 18.5 for an example.

If we are to truly improve the imagery or deepen the discourse within the antitrafficking movement, taking a trauma-informed approach could prove very helpful. Heffernan and Blythe (2014) offer insightful advice on developing a trauma-informed approach to working with survivors of trafficking. Although their work deals primarily with providing trauma-informed care and case management in an aftercare setting, this basic principle could prove useful in informing the imagery and language used by the antitrafficking community. Heffernan and Blythe (2014) provide the following definition of trauma-informed care: "a philosophy or cultural point of view integrating awareness and understanding of trauma" and its impact on affected individuals (p. 2). If someone has experienced the trauma of sex trafficking involving physical restraints or barcodes, and then sees images of ropes, barcode tattoos, and chains, it could cause a great deal of painful memories to resurface and/or cause other trauma triggers. In contrast, survivors who do not have these experiences may feel marginalized by these images that do not represent their experience, and triggered by such marginalization (Sanders, 2015). Being trauma-informed means taking this into account and avoiding the use of potentially traumatic

FIGURE 18.5 Taken from a Google image search for "sex trafficking"

(accessed 09/02/2016 from lbinternationalconsulting.com)

imagery; it also means being open to critical conversation, listening empath-ically, and being willing to change if survivors inform an individual, organi-zation, coalition, or other group that something displayed or said was painful for them.

Rachel Lloyd is the founder and president of Girls Education and Mentoring Services, one of the best known anti-trafficking organizations in the country. She is an activist, author, CEO, educator, mentor, and amazing public speaker. She is also a survivor of sex trafficking. On more than one occasion, antitrafficking advocates have focused solely on the exploitation she survived, as opposed to all of her incredible accomplishments afterwards. She reported that after her speech at a particular event, her cofacilitator retold graphic details from Lloyd's own story while she was still standing on the stage. She recalls feeling completely "dismissed" and "humiliated" in front of a room filled with over one hundred people (Lloyd, 2013). Unfortunately, this is not an isolated event that can be attributed to one misguided ally. Lloyd (2013) states that this is a relatively regular experience for herself and other survivor leaders, saying that they continually show up to various events "only to discover that the only interest people have in them is for their 'story' and ideally the more sensational, the more graphic the better." Survivor and social worker Savannah Sanders (2015) similarly highlights tokenism, paternalism, and exploitation of survivors.

Lloyd (2013) calls this "salacious" storytelling and says that this represen-tation is "at best questionable and at worst voyeuristic." Small's (2012) analy-sis of several films about sex trafficking also calls into question this kind of storytelling and accuses these films of being overly sexualized for the sake of raising awareness, without taking into account the potential cost to survivors. Lloyd (2013) points out that even under the guise of good intentions and awareness raising, this voyeuristic approach can be hurtful and humiliating to survivors (Lloyd, 2013). Johnston et al. (2014) identify this kind of inap-propriate response in their study and attribute it to a narrow-minded focus on the "wretched victim and heroic rescuers" narrative (p. 421). Logan et al. (2009) assert that if this sort of stereotyping from the media and the move-ment is not addressed, survivors will remain "unidentified, revictimized, and silenced" (p. 22).

Survivors will remain *unidentified* because these images do not help us identify the most prevalent forms of trafficking. Sexual exploitation and traf-ficking often involve elements of intimate partner violence, such as manip-ulation and coercion, that are not easily or accurately depicted in any single image. Other common elements of trafficking that cannot be comprehen-sively shown in image form include histories of abuse and instability within a survivor's household of origin, past/present poverty and identity-based oppression, and the all-too-often gray area between sex trafficking and sex work. Survivors may be *revictimized* by these images because many of them are degrading and dehumanizing or potential trauma triggers. They will remain *silenced* because survivor voices are often being drowned out by advocacy and awareness-raising efforts.

All of the problematic images presented in this chapter do the same thing to survivors that pimps/traffickers do: they silence, victimize, and dehumanize. Johnston et al. (2014) support this claim, saying that this type of storytelling further reinforces "the commodification of women's bodies and loss of agency" (p. 420). Uy (2011) criticizes the "perfect victim" narrative, calling it racist and sometimes imperialistic—especially as it relates to the othering and fetishizing of the "disheveled, non-English speaking, helpless Asian woman" (p. 210). He posits that the obsession with this image is "an extension of continued hegemonic oppression" (p. 210). Not only are these images demeaning, but they are drastically different from the imagery used on survivor-run organizations' websites. The massive divide between those images used so frequently by certain members of the antitrafficking community and the pictures used on survivor-informed websites suggests that the images are not even remotely survivor-informed. Johnston et al. (2014) believe that when survivors are a part of telling their own story, they will be depicted as "someone with agency and power" (p. 431). They will be seen as humans who have survived a great deal of tragedy, but also as humans who are more than just the tragedy they have survived.

When searching for imagery for presentations or news stories, social workers and organizations should instead conduct a search on survivor-run organizations. Veronica's Voice in Kansas City (Kansas), GEMS in New York (New York), and Breaking Free in St. Paul (Minnesota) will all appear among that list of organizations. Bright colors such as purple, green, and pink are splashed across their website homepages, in stark contrast to the dull black-and-white images discussed earlier. Hopeful images and humanity can be seen in each of their website pages that describe their various missions, visions, and services, as opposed to the destructive and depressing imagery in mainstream media. Even in the various organizational logos, one can see vast representational differences. On survivor-led organizational websites, images depict strength, poise, and the declaration that individuals are "more than survivors" and "more than their stories," and have images representing positivity, hope, strong support networks, and more (see www.gems-girls.org, http://misssey .org/ and https://www.veronicasvoice.org/ for examples) See figure 18.6.

These organizations do not typically choose to display chains, wounds, barcodes, brokenness, or captivity, even though some survivors have faced all of the above. The fact that survivor-informed imagery is bright and hopeful should be taken seriously by all advocates and abolitionists. If we claim to represent and

FIGURE 18.6 Veronica's Voice Logo, Survivor-Run Organization in Kansas City, Kansas

(image taken from the Veronica's Voice website: http://www.veronicasvoice.org/)

respect survivors, perhaps we should actually listen to them, follow their example, and use their imagery.

Heffernan and Blythe (2014) also discuss a strengths-based approach to working with survivors that could serve as a great guide when selecting images to insert into presentations and pamphlets. They define being strengths-based as viewing "persons via their 'capacities, talents, competencies, possibilities, vision, values, and hopes' " (Heffernan & Blythe, 2014, p. 3; Saleebey, 1996, p. 297). This approach also includes the following themes: empowerment, the potential for growth and development, and the idea that people can identify their own needs, use their voice, and journey towards healing (ibid.). If antitrafficking advocates were to keep this approach in mind while developing presentations and organizational materials, the language and the imagery within the antitrafficking movement would improve greatly. After examining the representation of sex trafficking in magazines over a 10-year time span, Barnett (2016, p. 212) asks readers a poignant and necessary question: would stories, images, or presentations be less accurate if they included information about how individuals "found the strength to withstand and resist harm, not just information about the harm itself?" This is a question that all advocates and practitioners should ponder on a regular basis.

In response to the misuse of stories within the movement, the criticism from outside of the movement, and the dehumanizing revictimization on all sides, Holly Austin Smith, Savannah Sanders, Rachel Lloyd and other survivor activists have asked everyone to stop and think for a moment. Lloyd (2013) problematizes the fact that "people aren't willing to take a breath, to pause and think through how this approach might affect survivors." In light of this critique, all individuals who have ever sensationalized, misidentified, or misrepresented the stories of survivors should stop and ask themselves: "How would I feel if someone co-opted my story and ONLY talked about the worst parts of my life—about pain, loss, tragedy, and betrayal? What if someone painted a picture of the most heartbreaking day of my life and plastered it on billboards across the country to prove a point?" Further still, "How would I feel if that same person stealing my story and blasting my sadness was leading a movement that claimed to 'save' me?"[4] Heil and Nichols (2015) assure their readers that "survivors are real, not just a representation of media sensationalism" (p. 197). The people whose stories are being stolen and rewritten deserve more respect, more dignity, and more humanity than what can be seen in these images.

Conclusion

The imagery used in antitrafficking education, awareness, and advocacy has been critiqued in this chapter for poorly telling the stories of survivors by providing incomplete information about trafficking, for mischaracterizing the issue, and for excluding diverse survivor identities. This imagery also fuels skepticism about the existence of sex trafficking, validates criticism against the antitrafficking movement, and revictimizes survivors and survivor activists. The critiques laid out in this chapter beg for serious attention and consideration by advocates and allies. After recounting several painful incidents of having her story co-opted by fellow antitrafficking advocates, Rachel Lloyd (2013) calls attention to the "constant level of damage done by those who are within the movement, those who are our allies, those who are apparently on our side." Survivors, practitioners, social workers, and/or allies have the ability to reshape such imagery and the related discourse used in the antitrafficking movement. Rather than rely on shock and awe to get the attention of community members, they should tell stories and show images of strength and survival. Perhaps this approach will raise more holistic awareness of sexual exploitation, include more diverse survivor identities, quell criticisms and skepticism directed at the antitrafficking movement, and—most importantly— give survivors and survivor activists the dignity they deserve.

Assertions and Practitioner Recommendations

- This imagery sometimes mischaracterizes sex trafficking by poorly telling the stories of survivors and providing misleading or incomplete information about trafficking.
  - Don't use any of the images critiqued in this chapter or images that express the same ideas (i.e., avoid images of chains, barcodes, ropes, cages, nooses, etc.).
  - Do look at the websites of the following survivor-led agencies: GEMS, Breaking Free, Veronica's Voice, Healing Action, Rahab's Hideaway, EVE, MISSSEY, Courtney's House, and National Survivor Network (CAST). Use their imagery and give credit to them in your presentation or your materials.
  - Do use imagery similar to the imagery you see presented by survivor-led, survivor-informed organizations.
- It excludes diverse survivor identities.
  - Don't use images that only represent one monolithic group of survivors (i.e., do not use images that only depict females, white people, young children, etc.).
  - Do use imagery that reflects a diverse population of survivors: include images of people of color, of adults, of boys and men, and of individuals from the LGBTQ community (relevant accompanying wording is important here, as gender identity and sexual orientation are not captured in an image), as well as those who are traditionally depicted.
  - Do conduct further research on how sex trafficking affects diverse populations/identities and include this information in your presentations/materials.
  - Do make sure that your outreach materials and efforts use inclusive imagery and language that adhere to principles of cultural competency.
- Shock-provoking imagery fuels skepticism about the existence of sex trafficking and validates criticism against the antitrafficking movement.
  - Don't use imagery that is bloody or gruesome or that depicts some of the tropes discussed in this chapter (barcodes, chains, ropes, etc.).
  - Don't use facts or figures that you cannot cite or have not researched.

- ○ Do your research! Go into your presentations and make your materials having done thorough research on this issue. This textbook is a GREAT resource and has a host of helpful references. Check them out and use them!
- ○ Do make sure that the statistics you use in your presentations and outreach materials come from reliable sources and have all of the qualifying information alongside them. Also, make sure that you understand them and can properly explain them to an audience.
- This brand of storytelling and imagery is revictimizing to survivors and survivor activists.
  - ○ Don't use images that could serve as trauma triggers.
  - ○ Don't talk over survivors or tell their story in community events without their express permission. If they are in a space to speak about other accomplishments or efforts, do not call attention to their identity as a survivor unless they wish it. Simply ask their preference of how they wish to be identified. o Don't violate survivors' confidentiality and privacy.
  - ○ Do use imagery and language that you see/hear from survivor-led agencies and in survivor presentations or publications. (Examples of agencies listed above). Draw from material written by survivors in their own words to amplify their voices.
  - ○ Using the best practices detailed throughout this textbook and this chapter specifically, do use your artistic abilities or issue a call to local artists to create dignified imagery that raises awareness about human trafficking without dehumanizing those affected by it. If that is a possibility, consider creating an event or a gallery around these dignifying and empowering images to raise real awareness and funds for agencies doing this work in your community (See GEMS More than a Survivor Campaign).
  - ○ Do use the guides recommended in this chapter by the San Francisco Mayor's Task Force on Anti-Human Trafficking and the Wichita State Center for Combating Human Trafficking.
  - ○ Do share this information with your fellow antitrafficking advocates!

Notes

1. Studies of homeless or transient youth populations find nearly equal proportions of males and females involved in commercial sex (e.g., Curtis et al., 2008). Studies drawn from the justice system, social services, and independent research largely find that women and girls overwhelmingly compose the majority of sex-trafficked/exploited people. These discrepancies are likely due to sampling methods, all of which present with limitations (see Nichols, 2016, for an overview).
2. Also of import is the fact that even for survivors who have barcode tattoos, seeing images that serve as reminders of that can be very triggering. In a conversation with one survivor who was given a barcode tattoo by a former pimp, she discussed some very painful experiences with seeing that kind of imagery in antitrafficking campaign materials. This suggests that barcodes could either misrepresent survivor stories OR serve as a painful trigger. It is imperative for antitrafficking agencies to keep this information in mind.
3. After serving a year with International Justice Mission doing anti–bonded labor casework, I can attest to the tragedy of forced labor, and it saddens me that a large segment of the antitrafficking movement has all but forgotten these faces.
4. It must be noted here that many of the people who should ask themselves these questions are often quite privileged. I (Lauren Peffley) am one of those individuals who used to use shock tactics, sensational imagery, and woefully inaccurate statistics in my own presentations. I am ashamed to admit that I used to consider it a successful lecture if I could make at least one person cry. It was in asking myself these questions that I realized the error of my ways—even though the worst day of my life is in no way comparable to sexual exploitation, violence, and/or manipulation.

References

Barnett, B. (2016). Dividing women: The framing of trafficking for sexual exploitation in magazines. *Feminist Media Studies, 16*(2), 205–222. doi:10.1080/14680777.2015.1052004

Chuang, J. (2010). Rescuing trafficking from ideological capture: Prostitution reform and antitrafficking law and policy. *University of Pennsylvania Law Review, 158*(6), 1655–1728.

Covenant House, Loyola University (New Orleans), and University of Pennsylvania. (2017). *Labor and sex trafficking among homeless youth.* Retrieved from http://covenanthouse study.org/docs/Loyola-Research-Results.pdf

Curtis, R., Terry, K., Dank, M., Dombrowski, K., & Khan, B. (2008). *Commercial sexual exploitation of children in New York City, volume one: The CSEC population in New York City: Size, characteristics, and needs.* U.S. Department of Justice. Retrieved from https://www.ncjrs.gov/pdffiles1/nij/grants/225083.pdf

Dank, M., Yahner, J., Madden, K., Banuelos, I., Yu, L., Ritchie, A.,...Conner, B. (2015). *Surviving the streets of New York: Experiences of LGBTQ youth, YMSM, and YWSW engaged in survival sex.* Urban Institute. Retrieved from http://www.urban.org/research/publication/surviving -streets-new-york-experiences-lgbtq-youth-ymsm-and-ywsw-engaged-survival-sex /view/full_report

Egyes, L. (2016). Borders and intersections: The unique vulnerabilities of LGBTQ immigrants to trafficking. In E. Heil & A. Nichols (Eds.), *Broadening the scope of human trafficking research: A reader* (pp. 107–123). Durham, NC: Carolina Academic Press.

Estes, R., & Weiner, N. (2001). The commercial sexual exploitation of children in the U. S., Canada and Mexico. The National Institute of Justice of the U. S. Department of Justice.

Farrell, A., McDevitt, J., Pfeffer, R., Fahy, S., Owens, C., Dank, M., & Adams, W. (2012). Identifying challenges to improve the investigation and prosecution of state and local human trafficking cases. Washington, DC: National Institute of Justice.

Gonzalez, C. (2016). On the fringes: Black women and domestic human trafficking. In E. Heil & A. J. Nichols (Eds.), *Broadening the scope of human trafficking research: A reader.* Durham, NC: Carolina Academic Press.

Gulati, G. (2011). News frames and story triggers in the media's coverage of human trafficking. *Human Rights Review, 12*(3), 363–379. doi:10.1007/s12142-010-0184-5

Heffernan, K., & Blythe, B. (2014). Evidence-based practice: Developing a trauma-informed lens to case management for victims of human trafficking. *Global Social Welfare, 1*(4), 169–177. doi:10.1007/s40609-014-0007-8.

Heil, E. C. (2012). Sex slaves and serfs: The dynamics of human trafficking in a small Florida town. Boulder: First Forum Press.

Heil, E. (2016). Sex trafficking in Indian Country: An analysis of anti-trafficking tribal codes, multi-jurisdiction, and unprotected communities. In E. Heil & A. J. Nichols (Eds.), *Broadening the scope of human trafficking.* Durham, NC: Carolina Academic Press.

Heil, E., & Nichols, A. (2015). *Human trafficking in the Midwest: A case study of St. Louis and the bi-state area.* Durham, NC: Carolina Academic Press.

Johnston, A., Friedman, B., & Shafer, A. (2014). Framing the problem of sex trafficking. *Feminist Media Studies, 14*(3), 419–436. doi:10.1080/14680777.2012.740492

Koyama, E. (2011, October 8). Understanding the complexities of sex trafficking and sex work/trade: Ten observations from a sex worker activist/survivor/feminist [Web log post]. Retrieved from http://eminism.org/blog/entry/268

——. (2013, September 20). Rescue is for kittens: Ten things everyone needs to know about "rescues" of youth in the sex trade [Web log post]. Retrieved from http://eminism.org/blog/entry/400

Lloyd, R. (2012). *Girls like us: Fighting for a world where girls are not for sale: A memoir.* New York, NY: Harper Perennial.

——. (2013, December 4). *At what cost: The road to anti-trafficking is paved with good intentions.* GEMS. Retrieved from http://www.gems-girls.org/shifting-perspective/at-what-cost-the-road-to-anti-trafficking-is-paved-with-good-intentions

Logan, T. K., Walker, R., & Hunt, G. (2009). Understanding human trafficking in the United States. *Trauma, Violence, & Abuse, 10*(3), 3–30. doi:10.1177/1524838008327262

Lutnick, A. (2016). *Domestic minor sex trafficking: Beyond victims and villains.* New York, NY: Columbia University Press.

Martin, L., Pierce, A., Peyton, S., Gabilondo, A.I., & Tulpule, G. (2014). Mapping the market for sex with trafficked minor girls in Minneapolis: Structures, functions, and patterns. Full report: Preliminary Findings. Retrieved from http://uroc.umn.edu/sextrafficking

Murase, E., & Lee, E. (2015). *Recommendations for city departments on media access to human trafficking survivors.* Retrieved from http://sfgov.org/dosw/sites/default/files/Recommendations%20for%20City%20Departments%20on%20Media%20Access%20to%20Human%20Trafficking%20Survivors.pdf

Nichols, A. J. (2016). *Sex trafficking in the United States: Theory, research, policy, and practice.* New York, NY: Columbia University Press.

Polaris Project. (2014). Sex Trafficking in the U.S. Retrieved from http://www.polarisproject.org/human-trafficking/sex-trafficking-in-the-us

Reid, J.A., & Piquero, A.R. (2013). Age-Graded risks for commercial sexual exploitation of male and female youth. Journal of Interpersonal Violence. doi: 10.1177/0886260513511535.

Saleebey, D. (1996). The strengths perspective in social work practice: Extensions and cautions. *Social Work, 41*(3), 296–305.

Sanders, S. (2015). *Sex trafficking prevention*. Scottsdale, AZ: Unhooked Books.

Schwarz, C., & Britton, H. E. (2015). Queering the support for trafficked persons: LGBTQ communities and human trafficking in the Heartland. *Social Inclusion, 3*(1).

Small, J. L. (2012). Trafficking in truth: Media, sexuality, and human rights evidence. *Feminist Studies, 38*(2), 415–443.

Smith, H. A. (2014). *Walking prey: How America's youth are vulnerable to sex slavery.* New York, NY: Palgrave Macmillan.

Uy, R. (2011). Blinded by red lights: Why trafficking discourse should shift away from sex and the "perfect victim" paradigm. *Berkeley Journal of Gender, Law & Justice, 26*, 204–219.

Weitzer, R. (2010). The movement to criminalize sex work in the United States. *Journal of Law and Society, 37*(1), 61–84.

Wilson, D.G., Walsh, W.F., & Klueber, S. (2006). Trafficking in human beings: Training and services among US Law enforcement agencies. *Police Practice and Research, 7*, 149–160.

Wilson, J.M., & Dalton, E. (2008). Human trafficking in the Heartland: Variation in law enforcement awareness and response. *Journal of Contemporary Criminal Justice, 2*(3), 296–313.

CONCLUSION

ANDREA J. NICHOLS, PhD, WASHINGTON UNIVERSITY
IN ST. LOUIS

T he aim of this edited volume is to provide a guide to social workers, therapists, practitioners, and staff working in organizations
serving those experiencing sex trafficking or commercial sexual
exploitation (CSE). The editors acknowledge that many individuals involved in
interventions with trafficked and exploited people do not have a background
in social work or related fields. For example, the faith-based community has
formed a strong base for activism in this area and is founding and leading
organizations that provide community awareness, direct services, and housing;
the staff of these organizations may not have expertise as survivor-leaders or as
social workers or practitioners. Thus, it is our goal that this guide be accessible
to a broad array of individuals doing work with survivors, including those
unfamiliar with practice techniques more broadly, students who are preparing
to work in the field, and those who are well versed in practice techniques and
programmatic design and are looking for a guide specifically for working with
survivors of sex trafficking/CSE. However, this manual is not a substitute for
professional staff. Ongoing education and training is key.

Aside from this book, there are multiple organizations and sites offering
training and resources in key areas, including those offered by contributors to
this volume. For example, GEMS regularly offers on-site trainings and webinars
on programmatic design, practice, collaboration, and more (see http://www.
gems-girls.org/get-trained). GEMS offers the Victim-Survivor-Leader curriculum, which fosters leadership among survivors. It also offers the More than a
Survivor campaign, showing through photographic art that healing is possible

and that survivors are more than their experience in commercial sex. The My Life My Choice curriculum is also available at http://www.fightingexploitation .org/. Similarly, more about the Sanctuary Model and trauma-informed organizational models can be gleaned from http://sanctuaryweb.com/. Andrea J. Nichols offers free educational PowerPoints and teaching resources at www. sextraffickingintheunitedstates.com. In addition, multiple resource links are offered throughout this book, including for online education in practice techniques, recommendations for media reporting, identification and screening tools, and more.

The practice techniques detailed in Part I highlight the importance of harm-reduction, survivor-centered, evidence-based practice and practice-based evidence. The role of the social worker in safety planning, identification, and legal advocacy is also detailed. As stated in chapters 3 and 4, practice techniques with the population experiencing trafficking and exploitation remain underresearched and underevaluated. More evaluation work is needed in these areas to increase our understanding of trafficking and to improve interventions utilized by survivors. More qualitative work is also needed to provide important context and to highlight survivors' voices and experiences with such interventions.

Part II delineates practice recommendations with specific populations, including black or African American people, LGBTQ+ (lesbian, gay, bisexual, transgender, queer) individuals, immigrants, and those with an intellectual disability. Research examining the experiences of these and other groups, such as Native people and cisgender heterosexual men and boys, is also needed. There is a small but growing body of work examining the role of identity-based oppression and risk of trafficking, as well as useful interventions with these populations. Continued and increased momentum in such efforts is necessary.

This book primarily focuses on experiences within the United States. Accordingly, the unique locally grounded contextual dynamics present in all societies must be accounted for when considering interventions. For example, safety planning in conflict zones may look different than safety planning in the United States. Similarly, political activism and macro practice will vary according to the society it is embedded within.

Part III emphasizes programmatic design, showing how a trauma-informed program can be beneficial to trafficked and exploited people. Incorporating central tenets of social work and highlighting the importance of a single-point-of-contact social worker may also benefit response models. Acknowledging barriers and challenges within programs is also central to building knowledge and making organizational shifts in programming to best meet the needs of trafficked and exploited people. Further work in this area is needed, such as in juvenile justice, healthcare, domestic violence, and sexual assault organizations, to better understand the barriers and challenges within systems responding to trafficking and exploitation.

Lastly, prevention is important in responding to trafficking and exploitation, yet the form prevention typically takes is prosecution and a law-and-order response. This is not enough. Those in the antitrafficking movement need to focus on the root sources of trafficking—those macro-structural risk factors that simultaneously produce traffickers and vulnerability to trafficking. Efforts to combat racism, transphobia, homophobia, sexism, xenophobia, and more are needed to create cultural and structural shifts in society. It is also necessary to expand resources and social services related to healthcare, substance abuse treatment, mental health, poverty, homelessness, and domestic abuse and neglect, as these are identified risk factors. Identification and screening in related services is also called for. Prevention education in high-risk areas is also called for, such as the My Life My Choice model described in Part IV.

At the same time, prevention must be culturally competent and nonexploitive of survivors. Ignoring structural sources of oppression, focusing only on law-and-order responses, disregarding the voices of survivors, sensationalizing, and misrepresenting and homogenizing survivors will allow for and perpetuate continued oppression of trafficked and exploited people. Listening to and respecting survivors, and drawing from the expertise of survivor-leaders and the practitioners who work with them, as well as drawing from the evidence-based work in trauma treatment, are key to the success of the antitrafficking movement.

BIOGRAPHIES OF EDITORS
AND CONTRIBUTORS

Editor Biographies

Andrea J. Nichols, PhD, is Lecturer for the Women Gender and Sexuality Studies Department and Brown School of Social Work at Washington University in St. Louis, as well as Professor of Sociology at Forest Park College. Andrea received her PhD in Criminology from the University of Missouri–St. Louis in 2011. Andrea holds an interdisciplinary teaching and research background in the areas of Sociology, Social Work, Women Gender and Sexuality Studies, and Criminology. Her teaching and research interests broadly include sex trafficking/CSE/sex work and intimate partner violence. Her practitioner-centered research examines victim advocacy and community-based responses, as well as social work practice with survivors. Andrea teaches the course Sex Trafficking to both undergraduate and graduate students. She is also the Anti-Trafficking Initiative Coordinator for the Brown School of Social Work at Washington University in St. Louis. She is author of the book *Sex Trafficking in the United States: Theory, Research, Policy, and Practice*, as well as of *Feminist Advocacy*, and is coauthor of the books *Human Trafficking in the Midwest: A Case Study of St. Louis and the Bi-State Area* and *Broadening the Scope of Human Trafficking Research*. Andrea has also published multiple articles in *The Journal of Interpersonal Violence, Feminist Criminology, Sexualities, Action Research, Contemporary Justice Review*, and *Criminal Justice Review*. She won the New Scholar Award from the American Society of Criminology's Division on Women and Crime in 2015. She is a Carnegie Award–winning Professor and *Feminist Criminology*'s 2013 Best Article of the Year Award winner.

Dr. Tonya Edmond, PhD, MSW, is a Faculty Fellow in the Office of the Provost, the Associate Dean for Diversity, and an Associate Professor at the George Warren Brown School of Social Work at Washington University in St. Louis. Prior to coming into academia, she practiced as a social worker for fifteen years in both clinical and administrative roles in domestic violence and rape crisis centers. She is committed to strengthening services for survivors through her research and teaching to advance the development of trauma-informed systems of care and the implementation of evidence-based trauma treatments. Dr. Edmond, a faculty affiliate with the Center for Violence and Injury Prevention, focuses her research on violence against women with a specific interest in testing trauma-focused interventions for survivors of childhood sexual abuse, sexual assault, and intimate partner violence. She is the co-investigator of a CDC-funded study investigating the effectiveness of a trauma-focused, cognitive-behavioral group intervention with adolescent girls who have experienced maltreatment. She conducted a national survey of the theoretical and practice preferences of domestic violence and sexual assault service providers to assess the extent to which evidence-based trauma treatments appear to be in use in this service sector. She most recently conducted a statewide study of rape crisis centers in Texas to assess practitioner receptivity to evidence-based treatments and to identify the clinician and organizational characteristics that could inhibit or facilitate their adoption. In addition, she conducted a study to further our understanding of the trauma treatment needs of justice-involved women. Dr. Edmond received her MSW and PhD from the University of Texas at Austin and joined the George Warren Brown School of Social Work in 1999. She has been advancing the importance of evidence-based practice in the field of social work through publications and her leadership in the development of a model comprehensive evidence-based MSW curriculum. She has authored more than thirty publications. She currently serves on the Task Force on Advanced Social Work Practice in Trauma for the National Center for Social Work Trauma Education & Workforce Development. She teaches Intervention Approaches with Women, Core Concepts in Trauma Treatment with Children & Adolescents, and Social Work Practice with Individuals, Families & Groups. She is also a recipient of the Brown School Excellence in Teaching Award and the Alumni Association Distinguished Faculty Award.

Erin C. Heil, PhD, is an Associate Professor of Criminal Justice Studies at Southern Illinois University Edwardsville. She received her PhD in Criminal Justice from the University of Illinois at Chicago in 2008. Her teaching and research interests deliberate upon labor trafficking, immigration issues, criminal law, and law enforcement. Erin has also focused her research on exploitation of vulnerable populations, and relevant intersections of the law, in the context of the landless movement in Brazil, illegal international adoption, and sex trafficking of Native people. Erin has published in *Critical Criminology*, *Feminist Criminology, Advances in Sociology Research*, and *Contemporary Justice Review*. Her expertise in human trafficking is regularly requested at congressional summits, human-trafficking conferences, public forums, and training events. She is the author of *Sex Slaves and Serfs* (2012), coauthor of *Human Trafficking in the Midwest: A Case Study of St. Louis and the Bi-State Area* (2015), and coauthor of *Broadening the Scope of Human Trafficking Research* (2016).

Contributor Biographies

Sandra Bloom, MD, is a board-certified psychiatrist and graduate of Temple University School of Medicine; she was awarded the Temple University School of Medicine Alumni Achievement Award. Dr. Bloom currently serves as Associate Professor of Health Management and Policy at the Dornsife School of Public Health at Drexel University and in 2016 received the Public Health Practice Award from her school. She is President of CommunityWorks, an organizational consulting firm committed to the development of nonviolent environments. Dr. Bloom is a Past-President of the International Society for Traumatic Stress Studies and presently cochairs the ACEs Task Force for Philadelphia as well as the Campaign for Trauma-Informed Policy and Practice, based in Washington, D.C. From 1980 to 2001, Dr. Bloom served as Founder and Executive Director of the Sanctuary programs, inpatient psychiatric programs for the treatment of trauma-related emotional disorders. Over 350 programs have been trained in the Sanctuary Model. The Sanctuary Model is now being applied in residential and multiservice treatment programs for children, inpatient mental health programs, schools, domestic violence shelters, group homes, and homeless shelters. Dr. Bloom is author or coauthor of a series of books on trauma-informed care. Her first book, *Creating Sanctuary: Toward the Evolution of Sane Societies*, now in a second edition, tells the story of the journey she and her colleagues began in the 1980s in understanding the connections between a wide variety of emotional disturbances and the legacy of child abuse and other forms of traumatic exposure. Her second, coauthored book, *Bearing Witness: Violence and Collective Responsibility*, published in 1998, was the first book devoted to looking at the deep and wide connections between trauma and public health. Her third and fourth books, also coauthored, were published by Oxford University Press in 2010 and 2013 and focus on the evolution and development of the Sanctuary Model. One deals with the effects of organizational stress on our helping systems, titled *Destroying Sanctuary: The Crisis in Human Service Delivery Systems*, and the other is titled *Restoring Sanctuary: A New Operating System for Organizations*. She has also published a number of articles and chapters available on her website, www.sanctuaryweb.com.

Katherine Bright, MA, is a Research Associate at the Institute on Race and Justice at Northeastern University. Her primary research interests include human trafficking, particularly the commercial sexual exploitation of domestic minors and expectant and parenting youth, and youth partnership models as a successful intervention tool. Her recent research has focused on labor trafficking within the United States, police responses to human trafficking, evaluation of the methodologies used in human trafficking research, and the intersection of teen pregnancy, homelessness, and commercial sexual exploitation in Massachusetts.

Noël Bridget Busch-Armendariz, PhD, LMSW, MPA, is the School of Social Work's Presidential University Professor, the Associate Vice President for Research at the University of Texas at Austin, and the director of the Institute on Domestic Violence and Sexual Assault (IDVSA), a collaboration of the Schools of Social Work, Nursing, and Law and the Bureau for Business Research with more than 150 affiliate community organizations. Noël's areas of specialization are human trafficking, domestic violence, sexual assault and campus sexual assault, refugees, asylees, and international social work. She is regularly called as an expert witness in criminal trials that include the prosecution of human-trafficking, civil, and federal cases and directs statewide and national trainings on the topic. Noël serves as editor-in-chief of *Affilia: Journal of Women and Social Work*. She is a coauthor of a forthcoming textbook on human trafficking, *Human Trafficking: Applied Research, Theory, and Case Studies*.

Laurie Cook Heffron, PhD, LMSW, is an Assistant Professor in the School of Behavioral and Social Sciences at St. Edward's University in Austin, Texas. She has interest and expertise in the areas of forced migration, domestic and sexual violence, and human trafficking, and her research explores the experiences of, and relationships between, violence against women and migration, particularly among Central American migrant women in the United States. Laurie also draws from direct social work practice experience with a variety of communities, including refugees, asylum seekers, trafficked persons, and other immigrants. Laurie studied linguistics at Georgetown University and earned a Master of Social Work (MSW) and Doctorate in Social Work from the University of Texas at Austin.

Amy Corbett, LMHC, is the Director of Prevention at My Life My Choice. Ms. Corbett joined My Life My Choice in 2013 to support curriculum development, provider trainings, and prevention programming for youth who are at risk of commercial sexual exploitation. Her professional experience includes over fifteen years of providing services to vulnerable girls and their families, including providing therapeutic services on an inpatient eating disorders program, facilitating rapid response to victims of sexual assault, overseeing clinical programming for a short-term assessment program for adolescent girls, running a group home for adolescent girls who are victims of commercial exploitation, and providing clinical supervision to clinicians pursuing licensure. Ms. Corbett also provides community outreach around preventing exploitation and has presented trainings on youth risk and development. Ms. Corbett obtained her MA in Counseling Psychology from Boston College and is a Licensed Mental Health Clinician.

Lynly S. Egyes, Esq., is the Legal Director at the Sex Workers Project (SWP) at the Urban Justice Center. Prior to becoming legal director, Ms. Egyes managed SWP's criminal immigration program, which provides legal advocacy, advice, and information to sex workers and survivors of human trafficking on a variety of issues, including immigration, criminal law, victim's rights, and family reunification. Ms. Egyes launched the LGBT Anti-Trafficking Program and has served hundreds of clients in applications for Special Immigrant Juvenile Status, permanent residency, asylum, U visas, and T visas, as well as clients in deportation proceedings. Ms. Egyes is a trained facilitator with ten years of experience conducting trainings throughout the United States and Mexico on topics such as Immigration Relief for Trafficking Victims, Screening and Interviewing Trafficking Victims, Trafficking Victims' Rights, Understanding Differences of Sex Work and Human Trafficking, LGBTQ Trafficking Victims, and Working with LGBTQ and Homeless Youth. Ms. Egyes's acknowledgments include an award from Make the Road New York for her work with the LGBTQ community, an honor from New York City Council Member Daniel Dromm, and AILA's Michael Maggio Pro Bono Award. She also authored a chapter in the book *Broadening the Scope of Human Trafficking Research* and coauthored the report *Immigration on ICE: A Report on Immigration Home Raids Operations*.

Lara B. Gerassi, PhD, LCSW, is an Assistant Professor at the School of Social Work and an affiliate of the Department of Gender and Women's Studies at the University of Wisconsin–Madison. She earned her PhD from the Brown School of Social Work at Washington University in St. Louis, where she was a National Institute on Drug Abuse (NIDA) TranSTAR T32 predoctoral fellow. She is the author of numerous publications and other works focusing on sex trafficking and commercial sexual exploitation and has presented her work at national conferences for the Society for Social Work Research and the Council on Social Work Education.

Lisa Goldblatt Grace, LICSW, MPH, is the Cofounder and Director of My Life My Choice (MLMC), a program of Justice Resource Institute. Begun in 2002, My Life My Choice is a groundbreaking, nationally recognized initiative designed to stem the tide of the commercial sexual exploitation of adolescents. My Life My Choice offers a unique continuum of survivor-led services spanning provider training, exploitation prevention groups for vulnerable adolescent girls, survivor mentoring to young victims of commercial sexual exploitation, and advocacy and leadership development. Ms. Goldblatt Grace has been working with vulnerable young people in a variety of capacities for over twenty-five years. Her professional experience includes running a long-term shelter for homeless teen parents, developing a diversion program for violent youth offenders, and working in outpatient mental health, health promotion, and residential treatment settings. Ms. Goldblatt Grace has served as a consultant to the Massachusetts Administrative Office of the Trial Court's "Redesigning the Court's Response to Prostitution" project and as a primary researcher on the 2007 U.S. Department of Health and Human Services study of programs serving human-trafficking victims. She has served as the Cochair of the Training and Education Committee and as Chair of the Implementation Subcommittee of the Massachusetts Attorney General's appointed Task Force on Human Trafficking. She is a Licensed Independent Clinical Social Worker and holds master's degrees in both social work and public health.

Rachael A. Haskell earned her PhD in Social Work from the University of South Florida and is a Licensed Clinical Social Worker with over fifteen years of experience as a therapist and educator. She has taught graduate and undergraduate courses in social work at Saint Leo University, University of South Florida, Rhode Island College, and the Community College of Rhode Island. She provides professional training on trauma-informed care while treating survivors of sex trafficking, domestic violence, and other forms of abuse in private practice. Her research interests include evidence-based treatment of trauma survivors, disability awareness and cultural competence, and human trafficking.

Abby Howard, holds a Master of Social Work from Washington University in St. Louis and is a Licensed Clinical Social Worker. She has over seven years of experience providing training and technical assistance to nonprofits on trauma-informed care, best behavioral health practices, and domestic human trafficking. Upon graduating with her MSW, she led the Rescue & Restore Coalition for the Eastern District of Missouri, training first-responders on how to identify and refer potential clients of human trafficking. She also served as the lead therapist for a street outreach program working with homeless adolescents, many of whom had experienced commercial sexual exploitation. Abby currently owns her own business; she provides individualized coaching and psychotherapy to adults in helping professions to improve their well-being as well as consultation and training services to nonprofits seeking to improve their behavioral health practices. She also teaches at the Graduate School of Social Work at Denver University.

Rachel Lloyd, MA, is a Survivor and President and Founder of Girls Education and Mentoring Services (GEMS). Rachel founded GEMS in 1998, it has grown to be a nationally recognized and acclaimed organization and now is one of the largest providers of services to commercially sexually exploited and domestically trafficked youth in the US. GEMS advocates at the local, state, and national level to promote policies that support young women who have been commercially sexually exploited and domestically trafficked. GEMS offers the Survivor Leadership Institute, More than a Survivor Campaign, and numerous trainings, workshops, and webinars. Rachel Lloyd and GEMS have received multiple awards and honors for their work. Rachel is the author of numerous books and articles, including *Girls Like Us: Fighting for a World Where Girls are not for Sale*, and is a co-author of *The Survivor's Guide to Leaving*.

Rebecca J. Macy, PhD, ACSW, LCSW, is the L. Richardson Preyer Distinguished Chair for Strengthening Families at the University of North Carolina (UNC) at Chapel Hill School of Social Work, where she teaches courses in mental health, trauma and violence, social work practice, and statistics. She joined the UNC faculty in 2002, after receiving her doctoral degree in social welfare from the University of Washington in Seattle. She has fourteen years' experience conducting community-based studies that focus on intimate partner violence, sexual violence, and human trafficking. She has dedicated her research efforts to violence prevention and to improving services for violence survivors. To find the most effective and feasible strategies, she has conducted investigations in various community settings in collaboration with survivors, service providers, and policymakers. She has received funding for her research from foundations, federal agencies, and state governments. She has also published more than sixty peer-reviewed articles, book chapters, and invited commentaries on these topics and given more than one hundred peer-reviewed and invited research presentations at national and international venues. The rigor of her research and its benefit to practice have been recognized with awards from both the Office of the University of North Carolina-CH Provost and the Orange County Rape Crisis Center.

Audrey Morrissey is the Associate Director of My Life My Choice. Ms. Morrissey has been an integral part of My Life My Choice since 2003 and was the first survivor in Massachusetts to mentor commercially sexually exploited girls. Drawing from her personal experience in "the Life," Ms. Morrissey has helped develop and lead survivor-led programs that aim to prevent the exploitation or revictimization of vulnerable girls aged twelve to eighteen, reaching more than two hundred girls annually. Her expertise has also informed My Life My Choice's nationally recognized exploitation prevention curriculum, which she coauthored and which is currently used in twenty-seven states. Ms. Morrissey currently leads educational, training, and public awareness initiatives at My Life My Choice. She has served as a consultant to the Administrative Office of the Trial Court's "Redesigning the Court's Response to Prostitution" project, as well as the Vice Chair of the Survivor Services Task Force as part of the Massachusetts Human Trafficking Task Force chaired by Attorney General Martha Coakley. Audrey is a 2008 recipient of the prestigious Petra Foundation Fellowship and a 2012 Boston Neighborhood Fellow.

Maura Nsonwu, PhD, MSW, LCSW, is an Associate Professor and Interim Bachelor of Social Work Program Director in the Department of Social Work and Sociology at North Carolina Agricultural & Technical State University. Maura has practiced as a clinician, educator, and researcher in the areas of refugee resettlement, human trafficking, healthcare, child welfare, and social work education for thirty years.

Lauren S. Peffley earned a Master of Social Work and Certificate for Violence & Injury Prevention from the Brown School of Social Work at Washington University in St. Louis. Before pursuing her MSW, she spent a year doing anti-exploitation work in southern India with the International Justice Mission and then served two years on the public speaker's bureau and the executive board of Not For Sale–Minnesota. During her time at the Brown School and shortly thereafter, Lauren worked with Healing Action as a practicum student and then as Program Coordinator. She completed several research projects to learn more about local anti-exploitation work being done and certain barriers that create challenges in this field, conducted case management, and created trauma-informed curricula. Lauren completed training with the YWCA's Sexual Assault Response Team (SART) and currently serves as a SART advocate, providing hospital advocacy and support to survivors of sexual assault. Lauren is also Interim Program Director at Eden's Glory. She has been passionate about anti-exploitation work for over a decade, taking every opportunity to learn about it, write about it, speak about it, and volunteer with organizations doing something about it.

Kathleen M. Preble, PhD, MSW, served in the Peace Corps; after deciding she wanted to continue the work she had started during this experience, Dr. Preble began her social work career resettling refugees in the Fort Worth, Texas, area and assisting human-trafficking victims obtain needed services through case management. She moved on to become the program coordinator of a governmental program designed to support law enforcement efforts to identify trafficking victims, arrest traffickers, and promote public awareness of human trafficking throughout north Texas. Currently, she is an Assistant Professor of Social Work at the University of Missouri, Columbia, where she studies human-trafficking populations and their perceptions of traffickers' coercive power throughout the trafficking experience to better understand how to improve prevention, intervention, and aftercare services for survivors. Dr. Preble is passionate about developing and improving evidenced-based practices for trafficked populations as well as about developing a deeper understanding of perceptions of coercion among this and similar populations such as sex workers.

Joan A. Reid earned her PhD in Criminology and her MA in Rehabilitation and Mental Health Counseling from the University of South Florida. She is an Assistant Professor at the University of South Florida St. Petersburg, where she teaches courses on victimology and human trafficking. She is a Licensed Mental Health Counselor in the state of Florida with over ten years of practitioner experience providing mental health counseling to survivors of rape, childhood sexual abuse, and sex trafficking. She has published numerous scholarly articles focused on sex trafficking and other forms of sexual victimization. Her research has appeared in *Sexual Abuse: A Journal of Research and Treatment*, *Child Maltreatment*, and *Criminal Behaviour and Mental Health*.

Julia Strauss earned her BA in Psychology from the University of South Florida St. Petersburg, where she was awarded the 2016 Outstanding Graduate Award. Currently, she is a graduate student in the MEd program in Special Education at Vanderbilt University and a Registered Behavior Technician. Her research focus is on human trafficking, autism spectrum disorder, and parent training.

Amber Sutton is the Prevention Education Coordinator for Safehouse of Shelby County. She holds a Bachelor's Degree in Social Work from the University of Montevallo and a Master's Degree in Social Work from Washington University in St. Louis. She has worked with survivors of intimate partner violence and their families for the past five years in a multitude of settings, including residential services, prevention education, and the criminal justice system. She spent two years in St. Louis, where she managed the domestic violence felony caseload at the Circuit Attorney's office, and was an intervention advocate with YWCA Woman's Place, where she handled high-risk cases as well as facilitated support groups for survivors. She is now expanding prevention efforts and training individuals on how to best support and respond to those harmed by intimate partner violence in Shelby, Clay, Coosa, and Chilton Counties. She lives in Birmingham with her partner Jeff and their dog Ollie.

Dr. Valandra is an Assistant Professor in the School of Social Work and Department of African and African American Studies in Fulbright College of Arts and Sciences at the University of Arkansas. She has post-MSW direct social work practice experience with survivors of trauma in the fields of child welfare, sex trafficking, and interpersonal violence. Her research and published work focus on oppression-sensitive research methods, intergenerational Afrocentric approaches to social work practice and policy, and African American parenting and family resilience, risks, and protective factors in navigating the intersections of poverty, prostitution, and gender-based community, interpersonal, and sexual violence.

Melanie Weaver earned her MFA in Sculpture from the University of North Texas and was an art professor for twelve years. She is a thirty-eight-year survivor of commercial sexual exploitation of children (CSEC) and has created art work about the psychological impact of sex trafficking. She is currently a Justice Studies PhD student at Arizona State University. Her research focus is on the issues survivors face in the decades after exiting the commercial sex industry. Her PhD work seeks to raise awareness of the need for long-term support systems for survivors and to provide space for survivors of ten or more years to share their lived experiences.

Chiquitia Welch-Brewer, PhD, is an Assistant Professor of Social Work in the Department of Sociology and Social Work at North Carolina Agricultural and Technical State University. Her areas of teaching and research interests include juvenile delinquency, human behavior in the social environment, girls and risk behaviors, and social work practice skills with vulnerable populations. She has practice experience in child welfare and school settings and seeks to conduct research that ultimately aids practitioners in service delivery to girls with multiple risks and needs and their families.

INDEX